Concurrent and
Real-time Systems

WORLDWIDE
SERIES IN
COMPUTER
SCIENCE

Series Editors   Professor David Barron, Southampton University, UK
Professor Peter Wegner, Brown University, USA

The Worldwide Series in Computer Science has been created to publish textbooks which both address and anticipate the needs of an ever evolving curriculum thereby shaping its future. It is designed for undergraduates majoring in Computer Science and practitioners who need to reskill. Its philosophy derives from the conviction that the discipline of computing needs to produce technically skilled engineers who will inevitably face, and possible invent, radically new technologies throughout their future careers. New media will be used innovatively to support high quality texts written by leaders in the field.

Books in series   Ammeraal, *Computer Graphics for Java Programmers*
Ben-Ari, *Ada for Software Engineers*
Gollmann, *Computer Security*
Goodrich & Tamassia, *Data Structures and Algorithms in Java*
Kotonya & Sommerville, *Requirements Engineering: Processes and Techniques*
Lowe & Hall, *Hypermedia & the Web: An Engineering Approach*
Magee & Kramer, *Concurrency: State Models and Java Programs*
Peters, *Software Engineering: An Engineering Approach*
Preiss, *Data Structures and Algorithms with Object-Oriented Design Patterns in C++*
Preiss, *Data Structures and Algorithms with Object-Oriented Design Patterns in Java*
Reiss, *A Practical Introduction to Software Design with C++*
Winder & Roberts, *Developing Java Software*

Concurrent and Real-time Systems

The CSP approach

Steve Schneider

Department of Computer Science
Royal Holloway, University of London

JOHN WILEY & SONS, LTD
Chichester / New York / Weinheim / Brisbane / Singapore / Toronto

Other Wiley Editorial Offices

New York · Weinheim · Brisbane · Singapore · Toronto

British Library Cataloguing in Publication Data

ISBN 0-471-62373-3
Produced from author's PostScript files
Printed and bound in Great Britain by Bookcraft (Bath) Ltd, Midsomer Norton, Somerset.
This book is printed on acid-free paper responsibly manufactured from sustainable forestry, in which at least two trees are planted for each one used for paper production.

Contents

Preface

By relieving the brain of all unnecessary work, a good notation sets it free to concentrate on more advanced problems.

Alfred North Whitehead

This book provides an introduction to Communicating Sequential Processes (CSP) and its use as a formal method for concurrency. The CSP approach has been widely used in the specification, analysis, and verification of concurrent and real-time systems, and for understanding the particular issues that can arise when concurrency is present. It provides a good notation which enables specifications and designs to be clearly expressed and understood, together with a supporting theory which allows them to be analysed and shown to be correct.

Concurrent systems are complicated: they consist of many components which may execute in parallel, and the complexity arises from the combinations of ways in which their parts can interact. The design of such systems requires ways of keeping these interactions under control. Concurrency by its very nature introduces phenomena not present in sequential systems, such as deadlock and livelock. Deadlock can arise when a number of components are each awaiting an interaction from some other component before they can themselves continue. Livelock arises when components descend into an endless sequence of interaction among themselves, excluding any other components and the outside world. These properties arise not from individual components but from the way they are combined. Nondeterminism can also arise naturally in parallel compositions, for example when race conditions arise. The presence of time adds another dimension to the complexity. A theory of concurrency such as CSP provides a way of understanding and thereby controlling such phenomena.

The language of CSP is appropriate for capturing system descriptions at different stages in the development process:

- **Specifications** describe the required or expected behaviour of a system or component. These may be captured within the language of CSP.

- **Design** decisions are concerned with how components might be combined to provide a system meeting a particular specification.

- **Implementation** descriptions contain only those aspects of the language of CSP that can be directly converted into program code.

These levels are not rigid. It may be difficult to tell whether a CSP description is a specification or an abstract design, or to distinguish a more detailed design from an implementation. This allows a stepwise development from specification to implementation, since all intermediate stages may be considered as designs which progressively fill in more detail. One benefit of using a single language is that different levels of description can be compared and related within a single framework.

Even individual features of the language may be used at a number of different levels. Parallel combination may be used at the level of specification to denote conjunction, at the level of design to describe a concurrent architecture, and at the level of implementation to describe how processes must synchronize. Internal choice likewise is appropriate in specifications to denote a disjunction of possibilities, at the level of design to indicate that a number of approaches may be appropriate to provide some service, and at the level of implementation when run-time nondeterminism is present. Other operators of the language are appropriate only at some stages of the development process. Event abstraction is not appropriate in specifications, since it is concerned with internalizing events—and internal events should not appear in specifications. It is used in design, when describing the structure of complex systems which have some internal detail.

The language has been evolving since its inception, even recently as application of the model-checking tool FDR[1] to real problems shows which operators are useful in practice, and motivates new operators and alterations to existing ones.

Organization

This book is organized into four parts. Parts I and II are concerned with the untimed language and theory of CSP, and Parts III and IV are concerned with the introduction of time into the language and underlying theory. Part I introduces the core language of CSP, explaining in operational terms how CSP processes might execute. Chapter 1 discusses the central notion of processes, introduces the labelled transition system approach to operational semantics, and covers the sequential part of the language: the performance of events, input and output, and

---

[1] 'Failures Divergences Refinement'; developed and marketed by Formal Systems Europe Ltd.

the various forms of choice. Chapter 2 provides the ways in which processes can be combined in parallel and introduces the various forms of concurrency into the language. Chapter 3 completes the discussion of the language, introducing the various abstraction mechanisms provided by CSP, and the ways in which flow of control can be described.

Part II introduces the semantic models which provide ways of understanding the language in terms of how processes can behave, and which provide foundations for specification and verification techniques. Chapter 4 provides the simplest model, using *traces* as observations, and illustrates the denotational approach, particularly the way recursion is treated. Chapter 5 introduces the approach taken to specification of processes, and provides a compositional proof system based upon the traces model for verification of safety properties. These two chapters between them exemplify the approach taken throughout the book to providing a denotational semantics for CSP, and for specifying and verifying processes. Chapter 6 introduces a more detailed kind of observation, the *stable failure*, which allows analysis of phenomena such as nondeterminism and deadlock. The stable failures model is closely related to the classical *failures-divergences* model—they are identical for divergence-free processes—and provides a cleaner introduction to the notion of failures. Chapter 7 covers the additional specifications that this model permits; and provides a proof system for their verification. Finally, Chapter 8 introduces the *failures-divergences-infinite traces* model which allows questions of liveness and arbitrary nondeterminism to be properly addressed. This model is an extension of the traditional failures-divergences model to handle unbounded nondeterminism, and relates more crisply to the timed models introduced later in the book.

In Part III, time is introduced into the CSP language. Chapter 9 presents new language constructs to describe timeouts, delays, and timed interrupts, and provides a timed operational semantics for the enhanced language which describes how processes are to be executed with respect to the explicit passage of time. Chapter 10 considers in greater depth the nature and character of the timed labelled transition systems used to provide CSP with a timed operational semantics.

Part IV provides an understanding of the language in terms of timed observations. Chapter 11 introduces timed observations in terms of *timed failures*, and presents the corresponding semantic model, together with the timed failures denotational semantics for CSP. Chapter 12 discusses the use of timed failures as a basis for specification of real-time requirements, and covers a specification macro language for expressing common timed specification idioms. It also provides a compositional proof system for verification of time-sensitive systems with respect to such specifications. Finally, Chapter 13 draws together the untimed and timed approaches to CSP through the theory of *timewise refinement*, and shows how to exploit the links between the various models in order to combine analyses at different levels of abstraction.

Notes on work related to CSP and to timed CSP appear at the end of Parts I and III respectively, and notes on the development of the theory appear at the end of Parts II and IV. Exercises on the material appear at the end of each chapter.

The book has an associated web site

```
http://www.cs.rhbnc.ac.uk/books/concurrency
```

on which answers to many of the exercises can be found (some with restricted access), as well as a variety of other course material related to this book.

Course suggestions

This book is intended primarily as a textbook, aimed at final year undergraduates and post-graduates. As such, it can support a variety of courses on CSP.

Traditional CSP: The first two parts of the book are self-contained, and provide an introduction to the language and theory of untimed CSP. These two parts (leaving out the difficult material of Chapter 8) can form the basis of a one-semester postgraduate or advanced undergraduate course on concurrency. The tool support provided by ProBe (Process Behaviour Explorer) and FDR will enhance any such course significantly. If used, emphasis should be placed on process-oriented specification at the expense of property-oriented specification, and the main models to cover will be the traces model and the stable failures model. There may even be some time at the end of the course to cover an introduction to timed CSP.

Concurrent and real-time systems: A less formal course covering issues in concurrency can instead concentrate on the language of timed and untimed CSP and ignore the semantic models. Parts I and III of the book between them introduce and explain the full CSP language, and are self-contained. This course would still benefit from introducing traces as a basis for verification (and traces refinement in FDR), and a discussion of deadlock and divergence, though failures and divergences semantics would most likely be beyond its scope.

Real-time concurrency: The third and fourth parts of the book comprise a one-semester course on timed CSP, or the basis for a course on design of real-time systems. Parts III and IV rest to some extent on previous exposure to CSP, and ideally this course would follow a course based on the first half of the book. However, the required CSP can be obtained as the course progresses by dipping into the earlier parts as and when necessary, at the cost of a slower pace. These two parts are self-contained and mostly independent of the first half (apart from Chapter 13, which covers the relationship between untimed and timed CSP).

Semantic approaches

In this book the CSP language is introduced operationally: CSP programs are defined in terms of how they are to be executed. This is for purely the purposes of explanation—experience has shown the author that CSP operators are easier to understand initially when explained through operational semantics. However, the CSP approach is denotational in nature, the design of the language is driven by denotational considerations, and reasoning and analysis should be carried out at the level of the appropriate denotational model. The operational presentation is essentially for elucidation of the language. Different semantic approaches have relative strengths and weaknesses, and there are benefits to be gained from combining them, as elucidated in Hoare and He's programme to unify theories of programming [48].

The denotational semantics will associate a CSP program with a set of *observations* that may be made of it while it is executing. The denotational observations relate to executions given by the operational semantics and may be extracted directly. However, the benefits of the denotational approach derive from its *compositional* nature: the observations of a program may also be deduced from the observations of its components, without any need to refer to the operational semantics directly.

Different kinds of observation give rise to different semantic models. The four models introduced in this book—the traces model, the stable failures model, the failures-divergences-infinite traces model, and the timed failures model—all arise from progressively more detailed observations of processes, but all models have the same underlying philosophy: a process is determined by what may be observed of it. A program P is always associated with the set

$$\{obs : OBS \mid P \text{ `exhibits' } obs\}$$

where the type of observation OBS determines the model.

An important theme running through this book concerns the relationship between the untimed and the timed versions of CSP. The untimed language particularly is introduced in such a way as to make its relationship with the timed language plain. This book takes the view that analysis of system behaviour is appropriate at a number of levels of abstraction, and provides a unified framework for the results to be combined. Timed systems have a number of functional or logical properties which are independent of time considerations, and these are best treated within the more abstract untimed models without carrying the unnecessary additional baggage of timing information where it is not needed. Timed properties which rely on the timed behaviour must necessarily be verified in the less abstract timed world, but the relationships between the different levels of abstraction allow results to be carried from one level to another.

There are a number of reasons for taking this approach. The untimed theory is more abstract, enabling simpler proofs. It is also more mature, so there is more experience within the CSP community in analysing and verifying untimed CSP descriptions, and there are more case studies. A third reason concerns computer aided verification, which is presently available for untimed CSP in the form of the Failures Divergences Refinement checker FDR but which is not yet available for timed CSP.

The models presented in this book are those that best support the theory of timewise refinement. In particular, the inclusion of infinite behaviours supports a much cleaner link between the untimed and the timed levels of abstraction, and enables that link to be exploited in the design and development of concurrent real-time systems.

Steve Schneider
Royal Holloway

Acknowledgements

I first became involved in CSP on the Oxford MSc in Computation a decade ago. The Programming Research Group under Tony Hoare's leadership provided an inspiring and stimulating research environment, and I was fortunate to become a doctoral student at an exciting time in the development of timed CSP. I enjoyed working closely with Jim Davies, Dave Jackson, Mike Reed, and Bill Roscoe, and I am grateful to them for their friendship and advice over the years. I have also benefited from working with other researchers including Jeremy Bryans, Tony Hoare, Alan Jeffrey, Guy Leduc, Luc Léonard, Mike Mislove, and members of the Oxford Programming Research Group and the ESPRIT SPEC and CONCUR projects.

Thanks are also due to Paul Baker, Phil Brooke, Jeremy Bryans, John Derrick, Simon Gay, Gavin Lowe, Joel Ouaknine, Bill Roscoe, Peter Ryan, Bryan Scattergood, Andrew Simpson, Dyke Stiles, Helen Treharne, and Lok Yeung, for their careful reading of various drafts of this book, and for their comments, insights and valuable suggestions.

Finally, my special thanks go to my family: Elizabeth, Katherine, and Eleanor, for their unfailing encouragement, support, and sense of perspective, and for providing me with a reason to finish.

SAS

Part I

The language of CSP

1

Sequential processes

1.1 EVENTS AND PROCESSES

Any approach to describing the world must concentrate on features of interest. Architects, engineers, economists, cartographers, biologists, physicists, and computer scientists all categorize and describe the world from their own particular point of view, appropriate to the phenomena they are trying to understand and control. They will focus on those aspects of the world relevant to their study.

This book is concerned with the description and analysis of systems which consist of interacting components. In such systems it is the myriad possibilities for interaction between components that are difficult to understand. Since we are interested not only in understanding such systems, but also in designing them, the description language used will influence how we think about systems, and will dictate the way in which these systems will be designed.

The language of Communicating Sequential Processes (CSP) was designed for describing systems of interacting components, and it is supported by an underlying theory for reasoning about them. The conceptual framework taken by CSP is to consider components, or *processes*, as independent self-contained entities with particular interfaces through which they interact with their environment. This viewpoint is compositional, in the sense that if two processes are combined to form a larger system, that system is again a self-contained entity with a particular interface—a (larger) process. This is the framework provided by CSP for analysing the world.

Example 1.1.1 The kitchen of a fast-food outlet might be considered as a process. Its interface will include the door through which the ingredients come in, the counter where the cooked food is passed to the till staff, and the tannoy on which orders come in.

Another process within the fast-food outlet is the customer serving area. The interface here will include the tills, the till counter where the customer's food is placed, the tannoy for relaying orders to the kitchen, the food counter for picking up food placed there by the kitchen.

The kitchen and the customer serving area may be considered as distinct processes, and this separation may be appropriate from the management and company organization point of view. Furthermore, their combination will also be a process, whose interface will include the tills, the till counter, and the door through which ingredients come into the kitchen.

The kitchen itself need not be considered as an atomic process, and may instead be viewed as a combination of more primitive processes, such as a grill process, a deep-fry process, a microwave process, and an ingredients-sort-and-distribute process. ■

Since a process interacts with other processes only through its interface, the important information in the description of a process concerns its behaviour on that interface. In describing systems made up of interacting components and analysing the effects of their interaction, the appropriate level will abstract away the internal workings of the process and will focus on its activity at the interface: its external activity.

The interface of a process will be described as a set of *events*. An event describes a particular kind of atomic indivisible action that can be performed or suffered by the process. In describing a process, the first issue to be decided must be the set of events which the process can perform. This set provides the framework for the description of the process.

Example 1.1.2 A printer can accept jobs, and it can print them. Its interface may be given as the set $\{accept, print\}$. ■

Example 1.1.3 A telephone has 12 buttons, a handset, and a bell. The handset may be lifted or replaced. The telephone's interface might be given as the set

$$\{1, 2, 3, 4, 5, 6, 7, 8, 9, 0, \#, *, handset.lift, handset.replace, ring\}$$

This set is precisely the ways in which the telephone can interact with its environment. ■

Example 1.1.4 A lift system which serves floors 0 to 3 has an *up* button on each floor (apart from the top), a *down* button on each floor (apart from the bottom) and a *goto.i* button for each floor, within the lift. It also has doors at each floor which can open and close. Finally, it has an emergency *halt* button within the lift. Its interface will be described by the following:

$$\{up.0, up.1, up.2, down.1, down.2, down.3,$$
$$goto.0, goto.1, goto.2, goto.3,$$
$$open.0, close.0, open.1, close.1, open.2, close.2, open.3, close.3,$$
$$halt\}$$

All interaction with the lift is via this set of events. ■

Fig. 1.1   A machine with buttons

Fig. 1.2   A black box with wires

Processes may be thought of in a number of ways: a machine with a collection of buttons corresponding to the events in its interface, as in Figure 1.1; or alternatively as a black box with a collection of wires corresponding to the events in its interface, as illustrated by Figure 1.2.

The interface given for a process can be considered as its static specification. Its dynamic specification describes how it will actually behave at its interface. A process will be willing to engage in interface events only at particular times. More generally, there will be constraints on the sequences of events that it can engage in. For example, the lift in Example 1.1.4 would be required to alternate on the opening and closing of doors. The dynamic part of the process description will describe its permissible patterns of events.

Transitions

An operational semantics provides a way of interpreting a language—of stepping through executions of programs written in that language. It describes an operational understanding of the language. CSP is concerned with the performance of events, so the operational semantics will describe at what stages events may occur.

The operational semantics in fact defines how a CSP interpreter should execute. It provides the first possible execution steps (if any) for any CSP process, together with an expression of the subsequent behaviour in the form of another CSP process. An execution step will be described in terms of *labelled transitions* of the form $P_1 \xrightarrow{\mu} P_2$, where P_1 and P_2 are both processes. This describes a *transition* from P_1 to P_2, or equivalently a change in state. The label μ describes the action which accompanies this transition. It can be either an external event (from P_1's interface), a termination event $\checkmark$ (introduced on page 13), or an internal action τ which indicates that no interface event accompanied the change of state. The set of all possible external events is denoted Σ, so μ will range over $\Sigma \cup \{\checkmark, \tau\}$, which is written $\Sigma^{\checkmark,\tau}$. Variables a, b, c, will be used for events that must be external: they range over $\Sigma \cup \{\checkmark\}$, which is abbreviated $\Sigma^{\checkmark}$.

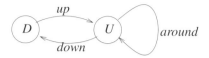

Fig. 1.3   The finite state machine for D **and** U

The labelled transition $P_1 \xrightarrow{\mu} P_2$ asserts that there is an execution of P_1 which begins with the occurrence of the event μ, and its subsequent behaviour is that of process P_2. The operational semantics offers a way of stepping through executions one step at a time. Since any execution unfolds one step at a time, this operational semantics provides all the information necessary to step through an execution. At every stage, the rules will describe the next possible steps (if any) for the execution.

Example 1.1.5 The following system has two states, D and U, and three transitions between them:

- $D \xrightarrow{up} U$

- $U \xrightarrow{around} U$

- $U \xrightarrow{down} D$

This describes the finite state machine of Figure 1.3.   ∎

Event names will be written in lower case, and process names in upper case.

Inference rules

An *inference rule* allows the *deduction* of a predicate from a collection of other predicates. It will be of the following general form:

antecedent 1

$\vdots$

antecedent n
_____   [side condition]
conclusion

This rule allows the conclusion to be deduced if all of the antecedents are true, and the side condition is also true. In the special case where there are no antecedents and no side condition, then the conclusion may be immediately deduced.

A number of conclusions which may all be drawn from the same set of antecedents may be listed as conclusions one after the other beneath the line. This provides an alternative to writing a separate rule with the same antecedents and side condition for each conclusion.

Inference rules will be used in two ways in this book. Firstly, rules may be given to formalize inferences concerning particular kinds of predicate. These rules can be independently checked by considering the meaning of the predicate. For example, the rule *modus ponens* can be given in this way:

$$\frac{p \qquad p \Rightarrow q}{q}$$

If p and q are both logical statements, then *modus ponens* allows q to be deduced from the pair of statements p and $p \Rightarrow q$. The proof rule can be checked for soundness by considering the possible meanings of p and q: when both antecedents are true, then so too must be the conclusion.

The law of the excluded middle is an example of a rule with no antecedents:

$$\frac{}{p \lor \neg p}$$

The inference rules given in the later chapters concerning **sat** specifications are of this kind: an independent definition of the **sat** relation is given, and the rules are sound with respect to this definition, and provide ways of reasoning about it.

Rules may also be used *axiomatically* to *define* predicates. For example, if the relation 'is a parent of' is already known, then a pair of rules can be used to define the relation 'is an ancestor of':

$$\frac{p \text{ is an ancestor of } q \qquad q \text{ is a parent of } r}{p \text{ is an ancestor of } r}$$

$$\frac{}{p \text{ is an ancestor of } p}$$

The relation 'is an ancestor of' is defined to hold between two people precisely when the rules can be used to deduce this. Technically, it is the smallest relation closed under these inference rules.

Structured operational semantics are conventionally defined in this way, and this will be the approach taken in this book. The ternary relation $P_1 \xrightarrow{\mu} P_2$ between P_1, P_2, and μ, asserts that there is a transition labelled μ between P_1 and P_2. The relation $\longrightarrow$ will be defined axiomatically through inference rules. A process P_1 can perform a μ transition to P_2 precisely when the relation $P_1 \xrightarrow{\mu} P_2$ can be deduced from the rules.

The operational semantics is just this relation between terms of the language and event labels.

1.2 PERFORMING EVENTS

The simplest process of all is *STOP*. This process is never prepared to engage in any of its interface events. It might be used to describe the fast-food outlet after it has closed down, or a broken printer that cannot accept or print jobs.

The operational semantics for *STOP* are extremely simple. It has no event transitions. Any execution of *STOP* will be unable to make any progress, and will remain in the same state for ever. An explicit description of its interface will describe precisely what it is unable to perform.

Event prefix

If P is a CSP process, and $a \in \Sigma$ is an event in the interface of P, then the following new process may be constructed:

$$a \rightarrow P$$

It is pronounced 'a then P'. This process is initially able to perform only a, and after performing a it behaves as P. The labelled transition semantics captures this understanding:

$$\frac{}{(a \rightarrow P) \xrightarrow{\ a\ } P}$$

There are no antecedents and no side condition to this rule. It is always the case that $a \rightarrow P$ may perform an a transition and subsequently behave as P.

Example 1.2.1 A one-shot printer is described by the process

$$PRINTER0 \ = \ accept \rightarrow print \rightarrow STOP$$

Initially it is able only to *accept* a job, after which it will behave as *print* $\rightarrow$ *STOP*. This subsequent process is able to *print* a job, after which no further action is possible. Its complete maximal execution is described as

$$
\begin{aligned}
&accept \rightarrow print \rightarrow STOP \\
&\quad \downarrow accept \\
&print \rightarrow STOP \\
&\quad \downarrow print \\
&STOP
\end{aligned}
$$

The corresponding finite state machine is given in Figure 1.4. ∎

Fig. 1.4   The finite state machine for *PRINTER*0

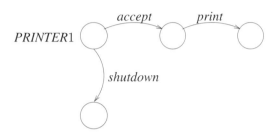

Fig. 1.5   The finite state machine for *PRINTER*1

Choosing between events

If $A \subseteq \Sigma$ is a set of events, and for each a in A the process $P(a)$ is defined, then a new process can be defined:

$$x : A \to P(x)$$

This is called a menu choice, or prefix choice, since a menu of events A is offered as a prefix to the subsequent behaviour. It is pronounced 'x from A then $P(x)$'. This process is prepared initially to engage in any of the events in the set A. After an event a is chosen, the subsequent behaviour is that of the process $P(a)$ corresponding to the event a.

Example 1.2.2 A printer which initially has a *shutdown* option as well as an *accept* option can be described using this form of choice. The initial choice is between *accept* and *shutdown*. The process following *accept* is to be *print* $\to$ *STOP*, and the behaviour subsequent to *shutdown* is simply *STOP*. This situation may be described as follows:

$$
\begin{aligned}
PRINTER1 \quad &= \quad x : \{accept, shutdown\} \to P(x) \\
\text{where} \quad & \\
P(accept) \quad &= \quad print \to STOP \\
P(shutdown) \quad &= \quad STOP
\end{aligned}
$$

The corresponding finite state machine is given in Figure 1.5.   ∎

Prefix choice allows a notation for conditional choices to be introduced to CSP. In a choice $x : A \to P(x)$, the definition of $P(x)$ might involve a conditional. For example, the printer of the example above might have P defined by

$$P(x) \quad = \quad \begin{array}{ll} print \to STOP & \text{if } x = accept \\ STOP & \text{otherwise} \end{array}$$

or even by

> **if** $x = accept$
> **then** $print \to STOP$
> **else** $STOP$

Neither of these is strictly within the language of CSP. Rather, they are constructions used in the definition of a parameterized process $P(x)$. However, they are conventionally used within CSP descriptions, resulting for example in a description of *PRINTER*1 as follows:

$$PRINTER1 \quad = \quad x : \{accept, shutdown\} \to \quad \begin{array}{l} \textbf{if } x = accept \\ \textbf{then } print \to STOP \\ \textbf{else } STOP \end{array}$$

In the case where the choice set A is finite, of the form $\{a_1, a_2 \ldots a_n\}$, the branches of the choice may be listed explicitly as follows:

$$\begin{array}{l} a_1 \to P(a_1) \\ \mid a_2 \to P(a_2) \\ \vdots \\ \mid a_n \to P(a_n) \end{array}$$

Example 1.2.3 The printer above can be written as follows:

$$PRINTER1 \quad = \quad \begin{array}{l} accept \to print \to STOP \\ \mid shutdown \to STOP \end{array}$$

The events offered by the choice are listed explicitly. ∎

Example 1.2.4 A printer which begins with a *startup* event:

$$PRINTER2 \quad = \quad startup \to \quad \begin{array}{l} (accept \to print \to STOP \\ \mid shutdown \to STOP) \end{array}$$

The choice is offered after the first event. ∎

In the case where the set A is empty, the choice is equivalent to *STOP*. No initial events are possible, so there can be no subsequent behaviour.

The transitions for $x : A \to P(x)$ are given by the following rule:

$$\frac{\rule{6cm}{0.4pt}}{(x : A \to P(x)) \xrightarrow{a} P(a)} \quad [\, a \in A \,]$$

For each $a \in A$ there is a corresponding transition. There are no other transitions.

Compound events

Events are considered to be atomic and indivisible in their occurrence. However, a single event may still contain various pieces of information, so events can have some structure. An example of this has already been given in Example 1.1.4, where events are structured by the kind of event they are, together with the floor they are concerned with. Another instance of a structured event is given by a communication channel which carries messages. In order to model values v being communicated along channel c, each possible communication is described as a separate possible event $c.v$ in the interface of the process. If a process P has an input channel *in* that carries 0s and 1s, then both $in.0$ and $in.1$ will appear in the interface set of P. The event $in.0$ describes the appearance of value 0 on channel *in*. Events $in.0$ and $in.1$ are distinct events, though the intention is to consider them both as inputs of particular values along channel *in*.

If c is a particular channel name, and T is the *type* of the channel—the set of values that may be passed along it—then the set $\{c.t \mid t \in T\}$ will be the set of events associated with c. For convenience this will be denoted $c.T$. More generally, it is often useful to allow a Cartesian generalization of the 'dot' separator to sets. For example, $c.d.S.T = \{c.d.s.t \mid s \in S \wedge t \in T\}$.

Example 1.2.5 The alphabet of the kitchen given in Example 1.1.1 might be given by

$$door.I \cup counter.F \cup tannoy.O$$

where I is the set of all possible ingredients, F is the set of food dishes, and O is the set of possible orders. ∎

Input and output

If c is a channel name of type T, and v is a particular value of type T, then the CSP expression

$$c!v \to P$$

describes a process which is initially willing to output v along channel c, and subsequently behave as P. This means that the only event it is initially willing to perform is $c.v$, and its transition semantics is

$$\frac{\rule{3cm}{0.4pt}}{(c!v \to P) \stackrel{c.v}{\longrightarrow} P}$$

This process has the same behaviour as $c.v \to P$, but the intention of the designer in considering it as output is made explicit. It is simply a convenient syntactic distinction.

If processes $P(x)$ are defined for each $x \in T$ then the CSP input expression

$$c?x : T \to P(x)$$

describes a process which is initially ready to accept any value x of type T along channel c. Its subsequent behaviour, described by $P(x)$, is determined by the value v that it receives as input.

$$\frac{\rule{5cm}{0.4pt}}{(c?x : T \to P(x)) \stackrel{c.v}{\longrightarrow} P(v)} \quad [\, v \in T \,]$$

Example 1.2.6 A 'squaring' server could be described by

$$in?x : \mathbb{N} \to out!(x^2) \to STOP$$

The output value is the square of the input.   ■

Example 1.2.7 If *JOBS* is the set of all possible print jobs that can be accepted by a printer, then a more detailed description of a one-shot printer would be

$$PRINTER3 \quad = \quad accept?j : JOBS \to print!j \to STOP$$

■

Example 1.2.8 A multiplication server could be described by

$$in?m : \mathbb{N} \to in?n : \mathbb{N} \to out!(m * n) \to STOP$$

or alternatively by

$$in?(m, n) : (\mathbb{N} \times \mathbb{N}) \to out!(m * n) \to STOP$$

The first process takes in one input followed by another, and then produces an output. The second process requires the pair of numbers to be submitted as a single input.   ■

Successful termination

Successful termination is the point that a process reaches when its execution has completed. The process representing this state is

SKIP

which can do nothing except indicate that it has reached termination. It achieves this by performing the special termination event $\checkmark$. It does nothing else.

$$SKIP \xrightarrow{\checkmark} STOP$$

The event $\checkmark$ is a special event used purely to denote termination, so it is not a member of the universal set of events Σ. It therefore cannot appear as an event prefix $a \rightarrow P$, or as one of the choices in a menu choice: such processes describe behaviour subsequent to their events, and this is inappropriate for termination.

1.3 RECURSION

The process constructors introduced thus far allow the construction only of finite processes, which execute for a finite number of steps before stopping. In order to describe infinitely executing processes, a *recursion* construct is introduced. This allows looping executions to be defined. For example, the process $LIGHT = on \rightarrow off \rightarrow LIGHT$, illustrated in Figure 1.6, allows the alternation of the events *on* and *off* indefinitely.

A process *name N* may be used as a component process in a process definition. It is bound by the definition

$N = P$

where P is an arbitrary CSP expression which may include process name N. The process expression P is the *body* of the recursive definition.

The rule for unwinding a process name N recursively bound to a process definition P is as follows:

$$\frac{P \xrightarrow{\mu} P'}{N \xrightarrow{\mu} P'} \quad [\, N = P \,]$$

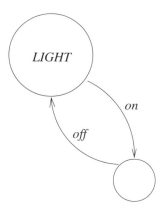

Fig. 1.6   The finite state machine for LIGHT

This rule states that any execution of P will be an execution of N.

Another way to consider P is as a process dependent on N. To make this relationship explicit, P may also be written as $F(N)$.

The notation $P_1[P_2/N]$ is used to denote the substitution meta-operation, where all (free) instances of the process name N appearing in P_1 are replaced by the process expression P_2. For example

$$(on \rightarrow off \rightarrow LIGHT)[on \rightarrow STOP/LIGHT] \;=\; on \rightarrow off \rightarrow on \rightarrow STOP$$
$$(on \rightarrow off \rightarrow LIGHT)[Y/LIGHT] \;=\; on \rightarrow off \rightarrow Y$$

If $N = P$ is a recursive definition, then $F(Y) = P[Y/N]$ is the function (in Y) corresponding to the body of the definition.

Example 1.3.1 The process *LIGHT* is recursively defined as follows:

$$LIGHT \;=\; on \rightarrow off \rightarrow LIGHT$$

Equivalently, $LIGHT = F(LIGHT)$, where $F(Y) = on \rightarrow off \rightarrow Y$.

The execution of *LIGHT* unfolds as follows:

$$LIGHT$$
$$\downarrow on$$
$$off \rightarrow LIGHT$$
$$\downarrow off$$
$$LIGHT$$
$$\downarrow on$$
$$off \rightarrow LIGHT$$
$$\vdots$$

It may alternate between the states *LIGHT* and *off* $\rightarrow$ *LIGHT* for ever.   ∎

Example 1.3.2 The one-place buffer *COPY* is initially ready to accept any message of type *T* as input, and will then hold it until it is output.

$$COPY \quad = \quad in?x : T \rightarrow out!x \rightarrow COPY$$

After output, it returns to its initial state.   ∎

Example 1.3.3 A specification of a railway crossing describes the required interactions between the raising and lowering of the gate, and the arrival and departure of a train.

$$CROSS \quad = \quad train.approach \rightarrow train.enter \rightarrow train.leave \rightarrow CROSS$$
$$\mid gate.raise \rightarrow train.approach \rightarrow gate.down \rightarrow$$
$$train.enter \rightarrow train.leave \rightarrow CROSS$$

The initial state has the gate lowered, blocking road vehicles from crossing the rails. Either the gate is raised, or else a train approaches the crossing. If the gate is raised then it must be lowered on the approach of a train. If the train enters the crossing then it must leave before the gate may be raised. The transition graph for *CROSS* is given in Figure 1.7. Compound events are used here simply to associate each event with either the train or the gate.   ∎

Mutual recursion

A collection of recursive definitions will bind a number of process names to process definitions. It is often useful to allow the process definitions to contain a number of the names being defined, so that in fact the various processes are defined in terms of each other. This construction is known as *mutual recursion*.

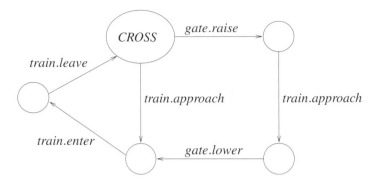

Fig. 1.7   Transition graph for CROSS

Example 1.3.4 The process *LIGHT* may be defined in terms of a process *ON*, which is itself defined in terms of *LIGHT*:

$$
\begin{aligned}
LIGHT &= on \rightarrow ON \\
ON &= off \rightarrow LIGHT
\end{aligned}
$$

These recursive definitions define two processes, each in terms of the other.   ∎

In order for a set of recursive definitions to be a mutual recursion, each name appearing in any of the process bodies must be bound in one of the recursive definitions. The single definition *LIGHT* = *on* → *ON* by itself is not suitable as a recursive definition: the process name *ON* must also be bound.

The transition rule for unwinding a recursive definition is exactly the same as that given for a single recursion. The transitions that can be made for a process name N_i in the context of a collection of bindings which binds N_i to P_i are precisely the transitions of P_i.

$$
\frac{P_i \overset{\mu}{\rightarrow} P'}{N_i \overset{\mu}{\rightarrow} P'} \quad [\, N_i = P_i \,]
$$

The process *CROSS* defined in Example 1.3.3 might also have been given using a mutual recursion:

$$
\begin{aligned}
CROSS &= gate.raise \rightarrow train.approach \rightarrow gate.lower \rightarrow ENT \\
&\quad \mid train.approach \rightarrow ENT \\
ENT &= train.enter \rightarrow train.leave \rightarrow CROSS
\end{aligned}
$$

The behaviour of this version of *CROSS* is indistinguishable from the single recursive process given earlier.

One execution of *CROSS* is as follows:

CROSS
    ↓ *gate.raise*
(*train.approach* → *gate.lower* → *ENT*)
    ↓ *train.approach*
(*gate.lower* → *ENT*)
    ↓ *gate.lower*
ENT
    ↓ *train.enter*
(*train.leave* → *CROSS*)
    ⋮

This is one of the paths through the transition graph shown in Figure 1.7. The names of the recursive processes used in the definition of *CROSS* have been chosen to reflect the important states of the system: *ENT* is the point at which the train will enter the crossing.

This convention may be used more generally with a family of process names $N(i)$ parameterized by $i \in I$. A mutual recursion will bind them to a family of processes containing these names. Alternatively, they will be bound to a family of functions $F(i)$ where each is a function of the family of names $N(i)$.

Example 1.3.5 A heater has four power settings, which can be changed by the events *up* and *down*. We use the four process names $HEATER(0)$, $HEATER(1)$, $HEATER(2)$, and $HEATER(3)$ to describe the four possible states. Their interrelationships are described by mutual recursion:

$$
\begin{aligned}
HEATER(0) &= up \rightarrow HEATER(1) \\
HEATER(1) &= up \rightarrow HEATER(2) \mid down \rightarrow HEATER(0) \\
HEATER(2) &= up \rightarrow HEATER(3) \mid down \rightarrow HEATER(1) \\
HEATER(3) &= down \rightarrow HEATER(2)
\end{aligned}
$$

At any point in the execution, the process will be at one of the $HEATER(i)$ nodes. The value of i might be thought of as the state of the heater, corresponding to the setting on a dial. ∎

It is appropriate to keep track only of those aspects of internal state that have an impact on the external behaviour patterns of the process. The CSP notation is intended primarily to support description and analysis of processes in terms of their interactions. However, the interactions possible for a process might depend on the value of some internal state variable, and so it is necessary in such situations to keep track of the relevant information, but only in so far as it affects the process's external behaviour. In the *HEATER* example above, the value of the state determines how many *up* and *down* events are possible. The heater might also contain a thermostat, but if its setting does not have any effect on the behaviour under consideration, then its value is superfluous to the description of the process, and should not be included.

Example 1.3.6 A counter can be *incremented* or *decremented* at any point, provided the total number of *decrement* events does not exceed the number of *increment* events. The family of process names $COUNT(i)$ will be used to define $COUNTER$, where i will track the difference between the number of *increment* events and the number of *decrement* events.

$$
\begin{aligned}
COUNT(0) &= increment \to COUNT(1) \\
COUNT(i) &= increment \to COUNT(i+1) \qquad \text{if } i > 0 \\
&\quad \mid decrement \to COUNT(i-1)
\end{aligned}
$$

The counter begins at 0:

$$
COUNTER = COUNT(0)
$$

If there could be any number of *increment* and *decrement* events, in any order, then it would be unnecessary to keep track of the difference between them, and the process description

$$
C = increment \to C \mid decrement \to C
$$

would be sufficient. State information should be carried only where it affects the possible executions of the process. ∎

Example 1.3.7 An $ACCUMULATOR$ is used to keep track of running totals of sequences of numbers. It has a *reset* event, a *query* channel on which the current total can be output, and an *add* channel where it is possible to add another number. The family of process names $TOT(i)$ will be used to define this process, where i represents the running total.

$$
\begin{aligned}
TOT(i) &= reset \to TOT(0) \\
&\quad \mid query!i \to TOT(i) \\
&\quad \mid add?x : \mathbb{N} \to TOT(i+x)
\end{aligned}
$$

$ACCUMULATOR$ can now be defined:

$$
ACCUMULATOR = TOT(0)
$$

Its initial state will be 0. ∎

Indices for recursive process names need not be restricted to numbers: more generally, any kind of index may be used. This allows processes to be parameterized by more abstract values such as sets or strings. They do not need to be directly representable within a computer.

Example 1.3.8 A process which models a set of elements of type T allows elements to be added, and provides information about whether a particular element is in the set. It will be parameterized by S, the current set of elements:

$$SET = SET(\{\})$$

$$SET(S) = add?x : T \rightarrow SET(S \cup \{x\})$$

$$| \ query?y : T \rightarrow \left\{ \begin{array}{ll} answer!yes \rightarrow SET(S) & \text{if } y \in S \\ answer!no \rightarrow SET(S) & \text{otherwise} \end{array} \right.$$

The response depends both on the parameter S and the input y.   ■

Example 1.3.9 A buffer of infinite capacity is always prepared to input a fresh message, and when it is non-empty it is prepared to output the message at the head of the queue. It may be parameterised by the sequence s of messages currently in the buffer.

$$BUFFER(\langle\rangle) = in?x : M \rightarrow BUFFER(\langle x \rangle)$$

$$BUFFER(\langle y \rangle \frown s) = in?x : M \rightarrow BUFFER(\langle y \rangle \frown s \frown \langle x \rangle)$$

$$| \ out!y \rightarrow BUFFER(s)$$

x and y range over M, and s ranges over M^*, the (finite) strings of elements of M. The notation $\langle m \rangle$ represents a singleton sequence containing just m, and '$\frown$' is sequence concatenation, discussed in more detail in Section 4.1.

An initially empty buffer is described by

$$BUFFER = BUFFER(\langle\rangle)$$

One execution of *BUFFER* is

$$BUFFER$$
$$\downarrow in.3$$
$$BUFFER(\langle 3 \rangle)$$
$$\downarrow in.8$$
$$BUFFER(\langle 3, 8 \rangle)$$
$$\downarrow out!3$$
$$BUFFER(\langle 8 \rangle)$$
$$\vdots$$

The parameter consists of the items still in the buffer.   ■

Example 1.3.10 The description of a stack is very similar to that of the buffer:

$$
\begin{aligned}
STACK(\langle\rangle) &= push?x : M \to STACK(\langle x \rangle) \\
STACK(\langle y \rangle \frown s) &= push?x : M \to STACK(\langle x \rangle \frown \langle y \rangle \frown s) \\
&\quad | \; pop!y \to STACK(s)
\end{aligned}
$$

The only difference is that input messages are placed at the beginning of the string rather than at the end. ∎

1.4 CHOICE

Prefix choice has already introduced the possibility of process executions having a number of possible courses of action. Whereas that operator offers a choice between events, this section will introduce choices between processes.

In concurrent systems it is useful to distinguish between the cases where control over resolution of choice resides within a process itself, and where control is outside it. For example, a car showroom advertising cars in any colour might allow either the customer or the manufacturer Henry Ford [1] to make the choice; and these two possibilities are different. The distinction is important in concurrent systems, since problems may arise if two processes have both been given control over a particular choice. If both Henry Ford and the customer are considered to have control over the choice of colour then problems arise if they do not agree. It is therefore important to distinguish between *external choice*, where control over the choice is external to a process, and *internal choice*, where the environment of the process has no such control.

External choice

An external choice between two processes is initially ready to perform the events that either process can engage in. The choice is resolved by the performance of the first event, in favour of the process that performs it. This choice is written

$$P_1 \; \square \; P_2$$

and is pronounced 'P_1 external choice P_2'.

---

[1]Ford offered the purchasers of his cars the choice of 'any colour as long as it's black'.

Example 1.4.1 A particular bus journey is covered by two bus routes: the 37 and the 111. The service offered for that journey is then described as the choice between these two bus services.

$$SERVICE \quad = \quad BUS\_37 \sqcap BUS\_111$$

This choice can be described even before the initial events of the *BUS* processes are known.

The bus services are used to travel from the bus station at *A* to a destination at *B*. The pertinent events for this journey in the description of a *BUS* process are *board*, *alight*, and *pay*.

$$BUS\_37 \quad = \quad board.37.A \rightarrow (pay.90 \rightarrow alight.37.B \rightarrow STOP$$
$$| \; alight.37.A \rightarrow STOP)$$

On boarding the bus at *A*, a passenger must either pay the fare and then travel to *B*, or alight again at *A* without travelling.

The rival bus route charges a lower fare.

$$BUS\_111 \quad = \quad board.111.A \rightarrow (pay.70 \rightarrow alight.111.B \rightarrow STOP$$
$$| \; alight.111.A \rightarrow STOP)$$

The description *SERVICE* describes the situation in the bus station. There is a choice of two buses, and the choice between them is resolved when the first one is boarded.   ■

The transition rules for external choice reflect the fact that the first external event resolves the choice in favour of the process performing the event, and that the choice is not resolved on the occurrence of internal events.

$$
\begin{array}{|ll|}
\hline
& \\
\dfrac{P_1 \xrightarrow{a} P_1'}{\begin{array}{l} P_1 \square P_2 \xrightarrow{a} P_1' \\ P_2 \square P_1 \xrightarrow{a} P_1' \end{array}} & \qquad \dfrac{P_1 \xrightarrow{\tau} P_1'}{\begin{array}{l} P_1 \square P_2 \xrightarrow{\tau} P_1' \square P_2 \\ P_2 \square P_1 \xrightarrow{\tau} P_2 \square P_1' \end{array}} \\
& \\
\hline
\end{array}
$$

Control over resolution of the choice is external because the events of both choices are initially available. Considering processes as machines with buttons, the buttons that are initially enabled are those enabled by either of the choice processes. The choice is made externally because the choice of which button to press is not restricted by the process. The choice of buses is not made by the process *SERVICE*, but this choice is instead offered to the customer.

However, if the same event is offered by both of the choice processes, then an external agent will not have control over which process is chosen. An external agent has control only over the choice of initial event, not over the possible subsequent behaviours in the case where both processes offer the chosen initial event.

Example 1.4.2 The previous description of the bus service provided at the bus station was appropriate in the case where the passenger looks at the number on the front of the bus and so can distinguish the events *board*.37.*A* and *board*.111.*A*.

The buses available to a passenger who cannot read the bus number are better described simply as two buses *BUS_1* and *BUS_2*.

$$
\begin{aligned}
BUS\_1 \;=\; & board.A \rightarrow (pay.90 \rightarrow alight.B \rightarrow STOP \\
& \;\;|\; alight.A \rightarrow STOP) \\
BUS\_2 \;=\; & board.A \rightarrow (pay.70 \rightarrow alight.B \rightarrow STOP \\
& \;\;|\; alight.A \rightarrow STOP)
\end{aligned}
$$

The choice $BUS\_1 \;\Box\; BUS\_2$ still offers the option of boarding either bus, but since the two *board* events are not distinguished, the passenger has no control over which bus is boarded. Ignoring the number on the front of the bus results in the inability to distinguish routes. The passenger becomes unable to choose which fare to pay, since no further control over the choice is possible. In the previous case, the passenger could control the fare by ensuring the appropriate bus was boarded. ∎

Indexed external choice

The binary form of external choice can be generalized to an external choice between any finite number of processes. If I is a finite indexing set (which can be empty) such that P_i is defined for each $i \in I$, then it may be given an operational semantics as follows:

$$
\frac{P_j \xrightarrow{a} P'}{\Box_{i \in I} P_i \xrightarrow{a} P'} \; [\, j \in I \,] \qquad\qquad \frac{P_j \xrightarrow{\tau} P'_j}{\Box_{i \in I} P_i \xrightarrow{\tau} \Box_{i \in I} P'_i} \; [\, j \in I \,]
$$

where $P'_i = P_i$ for $i \neq j$.

In fact, the relationship between indexed external choice and binary external choice is captured by the following alternative definition of indexed external choice in terms of the binary operator.

$$
\begin{aligned}
\Box_{j \in \{i\}} P_j \;&=\; P_i \\
\Box_{j \in I \cup \{i\}} P_j \;&=\; (\Box_{j \in I} P_j) \;\Box\; P_i
\end{aligned}
$$

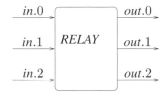

Fig. 1.8 The RELAY process

The external choice operator is associative, in the sense that $P_1 \square (P_2 \square P_3)$ and $(P_1 \square P_2) \square P_3$ have the same execution possibilities[2]. It is also commutative: $P_1 \square P_2$ and $P_2 \square P_1$ also have the same possible execution patterns. These two properties ensure that the order in which components are added to an indexed choice is irrelevant to the resulting behaviour of the choice. The only information required is the identity of the actual processes to be combined.

Example 1.4.3

$$RELAY \quad = \quad \square_{i \in I} \; in.i?x : T \to out.i!x \to RELAY$$

This process describes a relay service between a number of channels of the form $in.i$ and $out.i$ where i is in some (finite) indexing set I. It is prepared to input a message x along any of the $in.i$ channels, and then output it along the corresponding output channel $out.i$.

Observe that this description has exactly the same transitions as the alternative description

$$RELAY2 \quad = \quad in?i?x : I \times T \to out!i!x \to RELAY2$$

The difference is in the intention of the designer. In the first case, the model is of a process with a number of channels of the form $in.i$ and $out.i$, each of type T. The picture of this process is given in Figure 1.8.

In the second case, the model is of a process with a single input channel and a single output channel of type $I \times T$. This is pictured in Figure 1.9.

An event of the form $in.2.7$ can be considered either as the message '7' on the channel $in.2$, or as the message '2.7' on channel in. The transition system treats these both as the same single event.

---

[2]Technically, they are *strongly bisimilar* (see [77])—any internal or visible transition that one process can perform can be matched by the other. This is what is meant in this chapter by two processes having the same execution possibilities.

Fig. 1.9   The *RELAY2* **process**

Observe, however, that *RELAY2* is well-defined even in the case where I is infinite, whereas *RELAY* is not well-defined in this case. This is because external choices $\square_{i \in I} P_i$ are not permitted over infinite sets I.   ■

Example 1.4.4 A mail system connects a set of nodes *NODE*. It may accept an input at any node l consisting of a destination and message $(d.m)$. This is captured as an input $in_l?(d.m)$. When there are such pairs $(d.m)$ in the system, then it may also perform $out_d!m$ corresponding to outputting message m at the destination node d.

This specification of a mail system may be described using indexed external choice within a mutually recursive definition. The *MAIL* processes are indexed by multi-sets (or bags), which maintain the number of copies of each element. A fresh copy is added each time a message is input, and one copy is removed when output occurs.

$$
\begin{aligned}
MAIL &= MAIL_{\{\}} \\
MAIL_{\{\}} &= \square_{l \in NODE} \, in_l?(d.m) \rightarrow MAIL_{\{(d.m)\}} \\
MAIL_B &= \square_{l \in NODE} \, in_l?(d.m) \rightarrow MAIL_{B \uplus \{(d.m)\}} \\
&\quad \square \square_{(d.m) \in B} \, out_d!m \rightarrow MAIL_{B \setminus \{(d.m)\}}
\end{aligned}
$$

where B ranges over non-empty bags, $\uplus$ is bag union, and $\setminus$ is bag subtraction.   ■

Internal choice

A process considered as a specification describes a contract between the customer and the system designer. It encapsulates the behaviour of the system that is acceptable to the customer, and gives the designer the requirements that must be met.

The internal choice operator is commonly used as a specification construct. It is a choice over which the user has no control, and for this reason it is often called nondeterministic choice. The process

$$P_1 \sqcap P_2$$

pronounced 'P_1 internal choice P_2', describes a choice between P_1 and P_2, and the choice is resolved by the process itself, without any influence from its environment.

Transition rules given for a specification construct cannot completely characterize the nature of this construct, since they provide a particular approach to implementation. One way of implementing the choice construct is to resolve the choice immediately. This is accompanied by a silent transition, due to the state change from $P_1 \sqcap P_2$ to one of its components. Either of the choices is possible:

$$\frac{}{(P_1 \sqcap P_2) \stackrel{\tau}{\to} P_1}$$
$$(P_1 \sqcap P_2) \stackrel{\tau}{\to} P_2$$

These rules describe an operational understanding of one way this choice could be implemented, though its use is more often as a specification construct. The process $P_1 \sqcap P_2$ is a process which is guaranteed to behave on any particular execution either as P_1 or as P_2. As a specification, if $P_1 \sqcap P_2$ describes the customer requirement then the implementer is free to provide either P_1 or P_2 for any execution and the customer will find either acceptable.

There are a number of ways a system designer might choose to provide a system which meets the specification $P_1 \sqcap P_2$:

- P_1 and P_2 could both be developed, and whenever the process is run then a coin is tossed to decide which one to provide.

- P_1 and P_2 could both be constructed, and whenever the process is run then resource considerations determine which one is provided.

- P_1 alone is provided.

- P_2 alone is provided.

These possibilities are illustrated in Figure 1.10. In each case a black box labelled with $P_1 \sqcap P_2$ is provided, but the implementations inside the boxes are different.

Example 1.4.5 A mail router program might offer one of two routes: $ROUTER = VIA\_A \sqcap VIA\_B$. Whenever this program is invoked, the choice is resolved at run-time internally by considering the network traffic. The user is not concerned with the route, but simply in the correct delivery of the message, and is therefore happy to devolve responsibility for making the choice to the $ROUTER$ program. ∎

Example 1.4.6 A bus company guarantees to provide buses between A and B, but does not guarantee any particular route. There are two routes, the 37 and the 111. The passenger is happy to accept either, so the service offered by $BUS\_37 \sqcap BUS\_111$ is acceptable. The bus

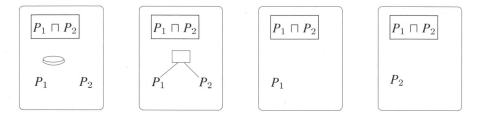

Fig. 1.10 *Implementing* $P_1 \sqcap P_2$

company decides to scrap the 37 bus service and run only the 111. This is indistinguishable to the customer from the situation where the decision to run the 111 in preference to the 37 is in fact made every morning. ∎

Example 1.4.7 A customer who will accept a car of any colour must necessarily find a black car acceptable. A manufacturer who guarantees to provide a car meeting the specification $CAR_{black} \sqcap CAR_{coloured}$ may decide always to provide CAR_{black}. ∎

Indexed internal choice

Since the internal choice operator corresponds to the disjunction operator as used in specification, it is natural to generalize it. If J is a set of indices (which may be finite or infinite[3], but must be non-empty) and P_i is defined for each $i \in J$, then the process

$$\bigsqcap_{i \in J} P_i$$

is a process which can behave as any of the P_i. As a specification this process describes the requirement that any execution should be appropriate to at least one of the P_i.

Operationally the indexed internal choice operator resolves immediately to one of its arguments:

$$\frac{}{(\bigsqcap_{i \in J} P_i) \xrightarrow{\tau} P_j} \quad [j \in J]$$

Example 1.4.8 The range of possibilities for a random number generator might be described by the infinite choice

$$\bigsqcap_{n \in \mathbb{N}} out!n \rightarrow STOP$$

---

[3]Technically, there is a given universal set of indices which contains J.

Any positive integer might be output. CSP does not express the probabilities of the numbers, it simply records the fact that they are possible. ■

Example 1.4.9 A process which can perform some event from the set of events A, but where its environment has no control over which, could be described as follows:

$$\bigsqcap_{a \in A} a \to STOP$$

A process D which can repeatedly perform some event from the set A could be defined recursively as follows:

$$D = \bigsqcap_{a \in A} a \to D$$

The choice can be resolved differently each time round the recursive loop. ■

Exercises

Exercise 1.1 Give suitable interface sets for the following. In each case you should decide the events that would be required in a description of how the process behaves.

1. A video recorder

2. A vending machine

3. An automated teller machine

4. A personal computer

5. A computer chip

6. A telephone answering machine

7. A multiplexor

8. An analogue to digital converter

Exercise 1.2 Write a CSP description of a square-root server with channels *in* and *out*.

Exercise 1.3 Write a CSP description of a multiplication component which has three input channels in_1, in_2, and in_3, and one output channel *out*. It reads in one number from each input channel (in any order) and outputs their product.

Exercise 1.4 Write a CSP description of a small fast-food outlet which serves only two items: burgers at 75p, and chicken at 95p. The sequence of interactions involves placing an order for one of the items, paying for the order, and receiving the order. Only one customer at a time can be handled.

Exercise 1.5 Give the transition graph for process *PRINTER*2 of Example 1.2.4.

Exercise 1.6 Give the transition graph for the process *HEATER* of Example 1.3.5.

Exercise 1.7 Give the transition graph for the process *COPY* of Example 1.3.2.

Exercise 1.8 What are the possible executions for $X = X$?

Exercise 1.9 Define a variant of the *COPY* process which accepts a value on its input channel, and stops if that value is 0, otherwise it outputs it and begins again.

Exercise 1.10 Define a process with an interface consisting of the events *press* and *finish*.$\mathbb{Z}$. It accepts a number of *press* events, and then outputs along the channel *finish* the number of *press* events that have occurred, after which it stops.

Exercise 1.11 Are the choices in the following processes internal or external?

1. A shop which offers discounts of 10%, 30% or 50% on sale items.

2. A cafe which offers *tea* or *coffee*.

3. A mail-order book company which offers the choice between sending back the form within two weeks, or receiving the book-of-the-month.

4. A lottery 'lucky dip' machine which gives any 6 numbers of 49 possibilities.

Exercise 1.12 Write a process which offers a choice between three bus routes.

Exercise 1.13 Write a CSP process which describes the choices presented by a sweet trolley containing two pieces of cheese cake, one piece of apple pie and one piece of chocolate cake.

Exercise 1.14 Write a process which describes the pattern of choices presented by the maze in Figure 1.11

1. if the alphabet is $\{east, west, north, south, in, out\}$;

2. if the alphabet is $\{left, right, forward, back, in, out\}$, where for example *right* means 'turn right and then move'.

Exercise 1.15 Give the transition graph of the process *SERVICE* of Example 1.4.1.

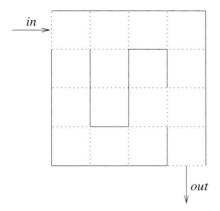

Fig. 1.11   A maze offering choices

2

Concurrency

When two processes are executed concurrently, they constitute a parallel combination. Each process executes independently, in accordance with its prescribed patterns of behaviour, but its range of possibilities will be influenced by the other process.

The way parallel CSP processes interact is intimately bound up with the view of events as synchronizations. Any event which appears in the interface of both processes must involve both processes whenever it occurs. This is the mechanism by which parallel processes interact—by *synchronizing* on events in the interface between them. Synchronization is symmetric and instantaneous, and occurs only when both participants engage in it simultaneously, much like a handshake. For this reason it is often known as *handshake synchronization*. A single event occurs—the handshake—with a number of participants. Examples of handshake synchronizations include: the passing of a baton in a relay race; the delivery of a registered letter; the closure of a contract; becoming married; inserting a coin in a vending machine; starting a phone conversation; sending an email message; adding a job to a printer queue.

2.1 ALPHABETIZED PARALLEL

A process description includes a dynamic part, captured using the process description language of CSP, which describes the possible patterns of events or synchronizations. When processes are put together in parallel, it is also necessary to specify how they will interact. One way of achieving this is by providing an explicit description of the interface or alphabet of each process: its static specification.

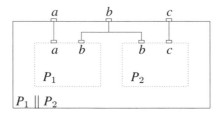

Fig. 2.1 Synchronization with buttons

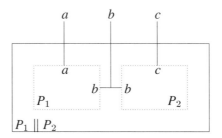

Fig. 2.2 Synchronization with wires

The interface of a process is the set of all the events that the process has the potential to engage in. If a process is considered as a black box, the interface consists of the names of all its buttons. If the process is viewed as a component with wires, then the interface provides a list of all the wires. In either case, it describes all of the events that the process is potentially able to perform. Since all external events are synchronizations between processes and their environment, the interface is the point at which a process and its environment influence each other.

A parallel combination of two processes P_1 and P_2 whose interfaces are given as $A \subseteq \Sigma$ and $B \subseteq \Sigma$ respectively is described as

$$P_1 \ {}_A\|_B \ P_2$$

(pronounced 'P_1 parallel on A, B P_2'). In this combination P_1 can perform only events in A, P_2 can perform only events in B, and they must simultaneously engage in events in the intersection of A and B. This is illustrated by Figures 2.1 and 2.2. It is conventional for the interface A of process P_1 to contain at least all of the events used in the definition of P_1. Similarly, B should contain all of the events appearing in P_2.

Parallel components of the combination $P_1 \ {}_A\|_B \ P_2$ must also agree on termination, even though the $\checkmark$ event does not appear explicitly in the interface sets A and B. This means that a parallel combination does not terminate until all of its components are terminated.

There are two rules that define the possible transitions of a parallel combination. One rule describes the independent execution of each of the components, and the other describes the performance of a joint step. The set $A^\checkmark$ is defined to be $A \cup \{\checkmark\}$.

$$\frac{P_1 \xrightarrow{\mu} P_1'}{\begin{array}{c} P_1 \ {}_A\|_B\ P_2 \xrightarrow{\mu} P_1' \ {}_A\|_B\ P_2 \\ P_2 \ {}_B\|_A\ P_1 \xrightarrow{\mu} P_2 \ {}_B\|_A\ P_1' \end{array}} \quad [\,\mu \in (A \cup \{\tau\} \setminus B)\,]$$

$$\frac{\begin{array}{c} P_1 \xrightarrow{a} P_1' \\ P_2 \xrightarrow{a} P_2' \end{array}}{P_1 \ {}_A\|_B\ P_2 \xrightarrow{a} P_1' \ {}_A\|_B\ P_2'} \quad [\,a \in A^\checkmark \cap B^\checkmark\,]$$

The first transition rule states that each side can execute independently through performing events which are not in the common interface. The second transition rule states that if both components can perform an event a which appears in each of their interfaces, then the parallel combination can also perform it.

These rules also capture the fact that the interfaces of the components do not change as the processes execute: they remain fixed throughout the life of the parallel combination.

Example 2.1.1 The parallel combination

$$(a \to P_1) \ {}_{\{a\}}\|_{\{a,b\}}\ (a \to P_2 \mid b \to P_3)$$

can perform an a transition initially, and reach $P_1 \ {}_{\{a\}}\|_{\{a,b\}}\ P_2$, or else it can perform a b transition initially to reach $(a \to P_1) \ {}_{\{a\}}\|_{\{a,b\}}\ P_3$.

However, the same processes combined in a different way

$$(a \to P_1) \ {}_{\{a,b\}}\|_{\{a,b\}}\ (a \to P_2 \mid b \to P_3)$$

can perform only a initially, since the presence of b in both interfaces means that both components are required to co-operate on its occurrence; and the left-hand process is not able initially to perform b. ∎

Example 2.1.2 A race between two competitors should have a single *start* event which both of the participants synchronize on. However, each competitor will independently finish, so two events *finish*$_1$ and *finish*$_2$ are used to describe these separate events. Participant 1 will be described as $start \rightarrow finish_1 \rightarrow STOP$, and participant 2 similarly. The race can then be described as

$$RACE =$$
$$start \rightarrow finish_1 \rightarrow STOP \, {}_{\{start,finish_1\}}\|_{\{start,finish_2\}} \, start \rightarrow finish_2 \rightarrow STOP$$

The fact that each *finish* event occurs in only one interface set captures the fact that the competitors can finish independently of each other. ∎

Example 2.1.3 On entering a restaurant, the cloakroom attendant might help the customer off or on with her coat, as captured by the events *coat.off* and *coat.on* respectively, storing and retrieving coats as appropriate. This activity might be described by the following process description:

$$
\begin{aligned}
ATT \quad &= \quad coat.off \rightarrow store \rightarrow ATT \\
&\qquad \square \\
&\quad retrieve \rightarrow coat.on \rightarrow ATT
\end{aligned}
$$

with an interface described as

$$\alpha_{ATT} \quad = \quad \{coat.off, coat.on, store, retrieve\}$$

The dining behaviour of the customer is as follows:

$$
\begin{aligned}
CUST \quad &= \quad enter \rightarrow coat.off \rightarrow eat \rightarrow coat.on \rightarrow CUST \\
\alpha_{CUST} \quad &= \quad \{coat.off, coat.on, enter, eat\}
\end{aligned}
$$

In the parallel combination

$$ATT \, {}_{\alpha_{ATT}}\|_{\alpha_{CUST}} \, CUST$$

the events *enter* and *eat* are performed solely by *CUST*; the events *coat.on* and *coat.off* are synchronizations between *CUST* and *ATT*; and the events *store* and *retrieve* are entirely under the control of *ATT*—the attendant is left to deal with the coat appropriately. ∎

Example 2.1.4 A pay and display parking permit machine accepts cash, and issues tickets and change. A designer might decide to implement these functions using two separate processes:

$$
\begin{aligned}
TICKET \quad &= \quad cash \rightarrow ticket \rightarrow TICKET \\
CHANGE \quad &= \quad cash \rightarrow change \rightarrow CHANGE
\end{aligned}
$$

The machine is then captured as the parallel combination of these two components:

$$MACHINE \quad = \quad TICKET \, {}_{\{cash,ticket\}}\|_{\{cash,change\}} \, CHANGE$$

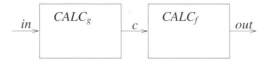

Fig. 2.3 A pipeline of two calculations

The two components both participate in the *cash* event, but they exercise independent control over the *ticket* and *change* events. ∎

Example 2.1.5 A process to calculate and output $f(g(x))$ from input x may be constructed from two processes which calculate f and g.

$$
\begin{aligned}
CALC_g &= in?x : \mathbb{Z} \to c!g(x) \to CALC_g \\
CALC_f &= c?y : \mathbb{Z} \to out!f(y) \to CALC_f
\end{aligned}
$$

The composition of f and g may be calculated by the parallel combination of $CALC_g$ and $CALC_f$. The output of $CALC_g$ is connected to the input of $CALC_f$, resulting in a pipeline of two processes which together compute $f(g(x))$ from input x. This is described by

$$
CALC_g \;_{in.\mathbb{Z} \cup c.\mathbb{Z}}\|_{c.\mathbb{Z} \cup out.\mathbb{Z}} \; CALC_f
$$

which is illustrated in Figure 2.3. ∎

A parallel combination of processes is itself a process, with an alphabet and a range of possible executions. Synchronization on an event a by two concurrent components results in a single occurrence of that event, and there can be no information contained in the occurrence of a as to the number of participants. A further process may be run in parallel with the existing combination, also synchronizing on a. This approach to parallel composition results in a mechanism for multi-way synchronization. No matter how many parallel components a system contains, all those with an event a in their alphabet are required to participate in every occurrence of it.

Example 2.1.6 A team of furniture removers contains a number of people with responsibilities for moving different kinds of furniture. Pianos require several people to lift them, so the event *lift_piano* will be in the alphabet of several members of the team, and they must all synchronize on this event for it to occur. The event *lift_piano* will occur only once, no matter how many participants it has. This event is a multi-way synchronization—it can occur only when all its participants are ready. There is also the possibility of adding further participants by extending the system: if a new person is added to the team with piano-lifting among their responsibilities, then they will also participate in the event *lift_piano*. ∎

A parallel component of a system constrains the occurrence of all events in its alphabet, since the co-operation of that component is required for the performance of such events. The event *lift_piano* can be prevented from occurring by any team member who is not ready to perform it. This means that any constraint on the occurrence of events can be introduced through the addition of a parallel component which enforces that constraint. Introduction of constraints may be carried out at the specification level, where different facets of desired behaviour are captured by different process descriptions which are then combined in parallel. It may also be carried out at the design level, where responsibility for enforcing different constraints is assigned to different processes.

Example 2.1.7 A number of shopping opportunities are described by the process *SHOPPING*. An item may be selected by the customer; the customer might pay; or the customer might leave, in which case the other possibilities are lost until the shop is re-entered.

$$
\begin{aligned}
SHOPPING \quad = \quad & select \rightarrow SHOPPING \\
& \square\, pay \rightarrow SHOPPING \\
& \square\, leave \rightarrow enter \rightarrow SHOPPING
\end{aligned}
$$

There are a number of restrictions that the shop places on the free performance of events as described by *SHOPPING*. One is concerned with ensuring that goods are paid for; and another requires goods to be selected before payment.

Security ensures that selected goods are paid for by the time the customer leaves the shop:

$$
\begin{aligned}
SECURITY \quad = \quad & select \rightarrow WATCH \\
& \square\, pay \rightarrow SECURITY \\
& \square\, leave \rightarrow SECURITY \\[1em]
WATCH \quad = \quad & select \rightarrow WATCH \\
& \square\, pay \rightarrow SECURITY
\end{aligned}
$$

This process is concerned with tracking the occurrence of events *select* and *pay* and restricting the possibility of the event *leave* under the appropriate circumstances. The event *enter* is not part of its alphabet.

The shop operating under this constraint is described by

$$
\begin{aligned}
SECURE\_SHOP = \\
(enter \rightarrow SHOPPING)\; {}_{\{enter,leave,select,pay\}}\|_{\{leave,select,pay\}}\; SECURITY
\end{aligned}
$$

The cash tills impose another constraint: that payment is possible only after some item has been selected. The initial situation is captured by *BROWSING*, whose alphabet is {*pay*, *select*}. Before any item has been selected, payment is not possible. Once an item has been selected, then payment is possible, though further items may also be selected.

$$BROWSING \quad = \quad select \to TILL$$

$$TILL \quad = \quad select \to TILL$$
$$\square \; pay \to BROWSING$$

The alphabet of this process does not contain either *enter* or *leave*, since it is concerned only with the relationship between the events *select* and *pay*.

The shop as a whole, integrating this last constraint, is described by

$$SHOP \quad = \quad SECURE\_SHOP \; {}_{\{enter,leave,select,pay\}} \| {}_{\{select,pay\}} \; BROWSING$$

Each parallel component restricts the behaviour of the whole to some degree. The process *enter* $\to$ *SHOPPING* restricts all occurrences of *select* and *pay* to between *enter* and *leave*; the process *SECURITY* restricts occurrences of *leave*; and the process *BROWSING* restricts occurrences of *pay*. All three processes are concerned with the events *pay* and *select*, and so all three processes participate in those events—each occurrence is a multi-way synchronization. Since these events are all part of the alphabet of *SHOP*, and hence available for further synchronization, they may be further constrained by additional parallel components. ■

The default interface for a process P is its alphabet $\alpha(P)$: those events mentioned in the process description. If the required interface in a process description is precisely this set, then it need not be mentioned explicitly. In the case of $P_1 \; {}_{\alpha(P_1)}\|_{\alpha(P_2)} \; P_2$ the alphabets may be dropped and $P_1 \| P_2$ written instead. The process *SHOP* described above could be rewritten as

$$SHOP \quad = \quad ((enter \to SHOPPING) \| SECURITY) \| BROWSING$$

since the interface sets given for each component process are precisely their alphabets. The definition of the alphabet operator $\alpha(P)$ is given in Figures 3.7 and 3.8 on pages 76 and 77.

Deadlock

The introduction of concurrency brings with it the possibility of deadlock, which is not possible for purely sequential programs. In a concurrent system the execution of one process might inhibit or temporarily suspend the execution of another. There are a number of situations in which this might arise, such as resource sharing, or awaiting communication. It is thus possible that every process in a concurrent system is waiting for some other process. Since no process is actively executing, each process will remain blocked, for ever waiting for some other process to make progress. This unfortunate phenomenon is called *deadlock*: each process individually would be able to continue execution if it were in a different environment, but all are prevented from doing so. Incompatible states between parallel components often arise as a result of unforeseen and unexpected sequences of interactions.

The combined state of all the deadlocked components is known as the *deadlock state*. From the point of view of an execution, a sequence of transitions has resulted in a deadlocked process if the final process description of the sequence has no possible transitions. In this sense, the process *STOP* can be considered as a deadlocked process: no further progress can be made, although the execution has not completed normally.

Example 2.1.8 Two children share a paint box and an easel. Whenever they wish to paint, they first search for the easel and the box until both are found. After they have finished painting, they drop the box and then the easel.

$$
\begin{aligned}
ISABELLA \quad = \quad & isabella.get.box \rightarrow isabella.get.easel \rightarrow isabella.paint \rightarrow \\
& \quad isabella.drop.box \rightarrow isabella.drop.easel \rightarrow ISABELLA \\
& \square \; isabella.get.easel \rightarrow isabella.get.box \rightarrow isabella.paint \rightarrow \\
& \quad isabella.drop.box \rightarrow isabella.drop.easel \rightarrow ISABELLA
\end{aligned}
$$

$$
\begin{aligned}
KATE \quad = \quad & kate.get.box \rightarrow kate.get.easel \rightarrow kate.paint \rightarrow \\
& \quad kate.drop.box \rightarrow kate.drop.easel \rightarrow KATE \\
& \square \; kate.get.easel \rightarrow kate.get.box \rightarrow kate.paint \rightarrow \\
& \quad kate.drop.box \rightarrow kate.drop.easel \rightarrow KATE
\end{aligned}
$$

The easel and the box can each be held only by one child at a time:

$$
\begin{aligned}
EASEL \quad = \quad & isabella.get.easel \rightarrow isabella.drop.easel \rightarrow EASEL \\
& \square \\
& kate.get.easel \rightarrow kate.drop.easel \rightarrow EASEL
\end{aligned}
$$

$$
\begin{aligned}
BOX \quad = \quad & isabella.get.box \rightarrow isabella.drop.box \rightarrow BOX \\
& \square \\
& kate.get.box \rightarrow kate.drop.box \rightarrow BOX
\end{aligned}
$$

The combination of the children and the painting equipment is described as

$$
PAINTING \quad = \quad ISABELLA \parallel KATE \parallel BOX \parallel EASEL
$$

The arrangement works well on the whole, but occasionally both children decide at about the same time to paint. If this happens, then there is a danger that one of them will find the easel, and the other will find the box, after which neither of them can make any further progress (see Exercise 2.3). The two items could be released, but their owners are not ready to release them:

they are each waiting for the other item to become available first, a classic deadlock situation. In this case the system could be made deadlock-free by insisting that the items are acquired in a particular order: the box first, and then the easel. Restricting the possibilities on the children, to only the first branch of the choice in each case, results in an overall improvement to the system.   ■

Example 2.1.9 A team of two furniture removers is required to move a number of pianos and tables, and each piece of furniture requires two people to lift it. Each remover independently makes his own decision as to which piece of furniture to lift first—this is an internal choice, since in each case it is a decision made by the furniture remover.

$$
\begin{aligned}
PETE \;\; &= \;\; lift\_piano \to PETE \\
&\qquad \sqcap lift\_table \to PETE
\end{aligned}
$$

$$
\begin{aligned}
DAVE \;\; &= \;\; lift\_piano \to DAVE \\
&\qquad \sqcap lift\_table \to DAVE
\end{aligned}
$$

$$
TEAM \;\; = \;\; DAVE \parallel PETE
$$

If each remover makes the same choice, then they are able to co-operate and synchronize on lifting the item. However, if their choices differ, then the result is deadlock.

DAVE comprises part of *PETE*'s environment, and so both *PETE* and his environment have control over the way the choice is resolved. Since it is not possible for two independent parties both to exercise complete and independent control over resolution of a choice, the result might be deadlock.

If *PETE* instead offered an external choice

$$
\begin{aligned}
PETE' \;\; &= \;\; lift\_piano \to PETE' \\
&\qquad \Box \; lift\_table \to PETE'
\end{aligned}
$$

then he gives up control over the choice and instead is prepared to go along with the decision of the environment. Since there is now only one agent making the choice, the resulting team *PETE'* $\parallel$ *DAVE* will no longer deadlock.   ■

Indexed alphabetized parallel

The binary parallel composition operator may be generalized to model situations where there are a number of concurrent interacting components. If I is a finite set of indices such that P_i and A_i are defined for each $i \in I$, then the following system may be defined:

$$
\Big\|_{A_i}^{i \in I} P_i
$$

This describes a combination of components where each P_i has interface $A_i \subseteq \Sigma$. Any event a must be performed in a multi-way synchronization by all those processes P_i which have $a \in A_i$: all parties interested in a particular event must be involved in all of its occurrences.

The indexed parallel composition may be defined using successive applications of the binary parallel operator. If I contains only two indices i_1 and i_2, then the indexed parallel is equivalent to the binary form:

$$\Big\|_{A_i}^{i \in \{i_1, i_2\}} P_i = P_{i_1} {}_{A_{i_1}}\big\|_{A_{i_2}} P_{i_2}$$

An inductive definition is provided for the case where the set I has more than two elements, defining the case with $n + 1$ elements in terms of the definition for n elements. The interface of $\big\|_{A_i}^{i \in I} P_i$ is the union of all the individual interfaces: $\bigcup_{i \in I} A_i$. The addition of one more component P_j ($j \notin I$) with interface A_j results in the parallel composition $\big\|_{A_i}^{i \in I \cup \{j\}} P_i$.

$$\Big\|_{A_i}^{i \in I \cup \{j\}} P_i = \big(\Big\|_{A_i}^{i \in I} P_i \big) {}_{\cup_{i \in I} A_i}\big\|_{A_j} P_j$$

It transpires that the binary parallel operator is associative, in the sense that the combination $P_1 {}_A\|_{B \cup C} (P_2 {}_B\|_C P_3)$ has the same executions as $(P_1 {}_A\|_B P_2) {}_{A \cup B}\|_C P_3$, and commutative: $P_1 {}_A\|_B P_2$ has the same executions as $P_2 {}_B\|_A P_1$. These two facts mean that the same process will result whichever order the processes are added to the parallel combination. As in the binary case, the interface sets A_i may be dropped from the process description, in which case the alphabet of each process is taken as its default interface. The resulting combination is written $\big\|^{i \in I} P_i$.

Example 2.1.10 A group of people are all required to be present for a meeting to be quorate. If *NAMES* is the set of all the people's names, then the alphabet and behaviour of a particular person may be described as follows:

$$A_n = \{enter.n, leave.n, meeting\}$$

$$PERSON_n = enter.n \to PRESENT_n$$

$$PRESENT_n = leave.n \to PERSON_n$$
$$\square \ meeting \to PRESENT_n$$

The situation is then described as

$$GROUP = \Big\|_{A_n}^{n \in NAMES} PERSON_n$$

The event *meeting* is in the alphabet of all the components, so it can occur when they are all able to perform it. This can only be when *enter.n* has occurred for all $n \in NAMES$ without a

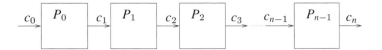

Fig 2.4 A chain of buffers

subsequent *leave.n*. All the events of the form *enter.n* and *leave.n* appear in the alphabet of only one process, $PERSON_n$, so their occurrence is entirely under the control of that process. ∎

Example 2.1.11 A chain of processes which act simply as buffers, passing on an item of data, is given in Figure 2.4. There are n such components, indexed by the set $\{0, \ldots, n-1\}$.

For every i between 0 and $n-1$, the buffer P_i and its interface A_i are given by the following definition:

$$A_i = c_i.\mathbb{Z} \cup c_{i+1}.\mathbb{Z}$$
$$P_i = c_i?x : \mathbb{Z} \rightarrow c_{i+1}!x \rightarrow P_i$$

The chain of buffers is then defined as

$$CHAIN = \left\|\begin{matrix} i \in \{0\ldots n-1\} \\ A_i \end{matrix}\right. P_i$$

Each occurrence $c_i.m$ of a message passing along the chain involves exactly two participants, P_{i-1} and P_i, apart from the two end channels c_0 and c_n which in each case involve only one component. ∎

Example 2.1.12 A network which sorts a set of $n+1$ numbers into ascending order may be constructed from cells each of which sort two numbers at a time, as in Figure 2.5. Here the set of numbers is input along $v_{0,0}$ and the $h_{0,i}$ for $0 \leqslant i < n$. The numbers appear in ascending order along the $v_{j,n+1} (0 \leqslant j \leqslant n)$.

Each cell $C_{i,j}$ inputs a number on its left and a number from above, outputs the smaller of these below, and the larger to its right. For internal cells, these are inputs to neighbouring cells; and for the cells in the bottom row, they are the outputs of the array.

For $i < j$ the $C_{i,j}$ are defined as follows:

$$C_{i,j} = h_{i,j}?x \rightarrow v_{i,j}?y \rightarrow v_{i,j+1}!\min\{x,y\} \rightarrow h_{i+1,j}!\max\{x,y\} \rightarrow C_{i,j}$$

Cells on the diagonal of the array are defined slightly differently, reflecting their different connections:

$$C_{i,i} = h_{i,i}?x \rightarrow v_{i,i}?y \rightarrow v_{i,i+1}!\min\{x,y\} \rightarrow v_{i+1,i+1}!\max\{x,y\} \rightarrow C_{i,i}$$

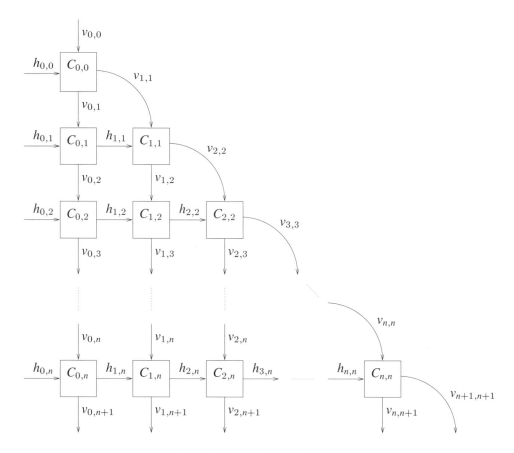

Fig. 2.5 An array for sorting

The network for sorting may then be defined using indexed parallel composition:

$$SORTER \quad = \quad \Big\|^{0 \leqslant i \leqslant j \leqslant n} C_{i,j}$$

The indexing set is given implicitly: the predicate $0 \leqslant i \leqslant j \leqslant n$ is shorthand for $(i,j) \in \{(k,l) \mid 0 \leqslant k \leqslant l \leqslant n\}$. ∎

Example 2.1.13 A collection of 2^n nodes in a network can be efficiently connected for the purposes of routing messages by assigning each node to the corner of a hypercube. Its coordinates will be an n-tuple, with each value of the tuple either 0 or 1. The set of possible coordinates is given by $COORD = \{0, 1\}^n$.

To specify the connections between nodes, it is necessary to decide which pairs of nodes should be adjacent. These will be those pairs whose coordinates differ in exactly one place.

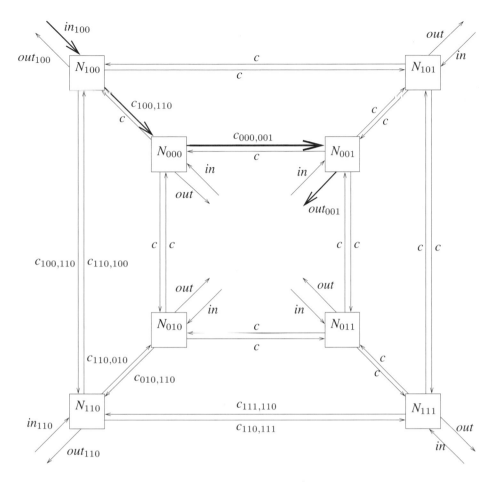

Fig. 2.6 *Message routing through a hypercube of* 2^3 *nodes;* 100 *to* 001 *emphasized*

The set of coordinates adjacent to l is given by $adj(l)$:

$$adj(l) \quad = \quad \{k : COORD \mid \exists\, i \bullet (k(i) \neq l(i) \wedge \forall j \neq i \bullet k(j) = l(j))\}$$

This network is pictured in Figure 2.6. The notation $l(i)$ denotes the ith bit of coordinate l. For example, if $l = 001$ then $l(0) = 0$, $l(1) = 0$, and $l(2) = 1$.

In order to route messages, it is sensible to send a message to a node closer to its destination.

$$next(l, d)$$
$$= \quad \{k : COORD \mid \exists\, i \bullet (k(i) \neq l(i) \wedge k(i) = d(i) \wedge \forall j \neq i \bullet k(j) = l(j))\}$$

The set $next(l, d)$ is the set of those coordinates which are adjacent to l and which differ from d on fewer bits than l does: the neighbours of l which are closer to the destination d.

A node N_l will have channels to and from all of its neighbours: for each k, l, the channel $c_{k,l}$ carries messages from N_k to N_l. It also has channels in_l and out_l for input and output outside the network. The interface of N_l will be

$$A_l \quad = \quad \{in_l, out_l\} \cup \{c_{k,l} \mid k \in adj(l)\} \cup \{c_{l,k} \mid k \in adj(l)\}$$

The cell N_l itself is always prepared to accept messages (unless it is waiting to output), and it maintains a list of all the messages it has outstanding. When this list is non-empty, N_l is also ready to send the oldest message to the next node in the network.

$$N_l(\langle\rangle) \quad = \quad \Box_{k \in adj(l)} \; c_{k,l}?(d.m) \rightarrow N_l(\langle(d, m)\rangle)$$
$$= \quad \Box \; in_l?(d.m) \rightarrow N_l(\langle(d, m)\rangle)$$

$$
\begin{aligned}
N_l(\langle(d, m)\rangle \frown s) \quad = \quad & out_l!m \rightarrow N_l(s) & \text{if } d = l \\
& (\Box_{k \in next(l,d)} \; c_{l,k}!(d.m) \rightarrow N_l(s)) & \text{otherwise} \\
& \Box \\
& \Box_{k \in adj(l)} \quad c_{k,l}?(d'.m') \rightarrow \\
& \qquad \qquad N_l(\langle(d, m)\rangle \frown s \frown \langle(d', m')\rangle)
\end{aligned}
$$

Finally, the network may be described using indexed parallel composition:

$$MAILER \quad = \quad \|_{A_l}^{l \in COORD} N_l(\langle\rangle)$$

Each node is initially empty. ∎

2.2 INTERLEAVING

Synchronization on common events provides one form of parallel execution of processes. Concurrent execution of processes P_1 and P_2 where no such synchronization is required is described by the combination

$$P_1 \; ||| \; P_2$$

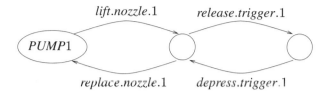

lift.nozzle.1   *release.trigger*.1

replace.nozzle.1   *depress.trigger*.1

Fig. 2.7 **Transitions for** *PUMP*1

pronounced 'P_1 interleave P_2'. In this process, the components P_1 and P_2 execute completely independently of each other, and do not interact on any events apart from termination. Each event is performed by exactly one process. The operational semantics rules are straightforward:

$$\frac{P_1 \overset{\mu}{\to} P_1'}{\begin{array}{c} P_1 \mid\mid\mid P_2 \overset{\mu}{\to} P_1' \mid\mid\mid P_2 \\ P_2 \mid\mid\mid P_1 \overset{\mu}{\to} P_2 \mid\mid\mid P_1' \end{array}} \quad [\,\mu \neq \checkmark\,] \qquad \frac{P_1 \overset{\checkmark}{\to} P_1' \quad P_2 \overset{\checkmark}{\to} P_2'}{P_1 \mid\mid\mid P_2 \overset{\checkmark}{\to} P_1' \mid\mid\mid P_2'}$$

Unlike synchronous parallel, there is no event that both P_1 and P_2 engage in simultaneously (except termination).

Example 2.2.1 A garage has two petrol pumps: *PUMP*1 and *PUMP*2. The petrol supply service offered by the garage is described as

$$FORECOURT \quad = \quad PUMP1 \mid\mid\mid PUMP2$$

A customer will always interact with only one pump on any transaction; and the pumps operate independently. The description of *PUMP*1 is a sequential process, defined by a mutual recursion:

$$
\begin{aligned}
PUMP1 \quad &= \quad lift.nozzle.1 \to READY1 \\
READY1 \quad &= \quad replace.nozzle.1 \to PUMP1 \\
&\qquad \Box \\
&\quad depress.trigger.1 \to release.trigger.1 \to READY1
\end{aligned}
$$

The state graph corresponding to *PUMP*1 is given in Figure 2.7.

The description of *PUMP*2 is entirely similar:

$$
\begin{aligned}
PUMP2 \quad &= \quad lift.nozzle.2 \to READY2 \\
READY2 \quad &= \quad replace.nozzle.2 \to PUMP2 \\
&\qquad \Box \\
&\quad depress.trigger.2 \to release.trigger.2 \to READY2
\end{aligned}
$$

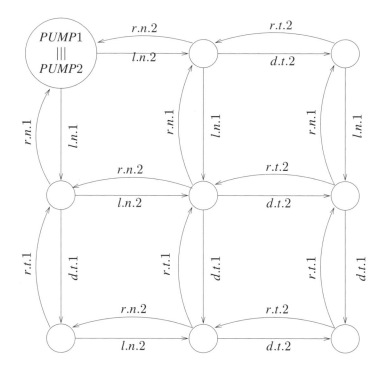

Fig. 2.8   Transitions for *PUMP*1 ||| *PUMP*2

The executions of the two pumps are unrelated. The process *PUMP*1 will remain ready to engage in the event *lift.nozzle*.1 until it occurs, independently of the progress that *PUMP*2 makes. The state transitions for the combination of processes are given in Figure 2.8.   ■

When two processes P_1 and P_2 have alphabets $\alpha(P_1)$ and $\alpha(P_2)$ that do not intersect, then their parallel combination $P_1\ _{\alpha(P_1)}\|_{\alpha(P_2)}\ P_2$ will behave the same as their interleaved combination $P_1\ |||\ P_2$. Since they do not have any events in common to interact on, execution of each component process will be independent in both cases. Given the definitions of *PUMP*1 and *PUMP*2, an alternative definition of *FORECOURT* would be *PUMP*1 || *PUMP*2. However, for the purposes of design, use of the ||| operator describes the design decision to provide the *FORECOURT* service as an interleaving of two processes, before those processes are described any further.

Interleaved processes do not synchronize on events even when their alphabets do overlap. In the case where both components are able to perform the same event, only one of the processes will actually engage in any particular occurrence of that event. In such a case, the environment which is interacting with the interleaved combination has no control or influence over which of the two processes actually performs it.

Example 2.2.2 A company that offers a telephone ordering service will operate a number of phone lines.

$$LINE_n \quad = \quad ring \rightarrow connect.n \rightarrow order \rightarrow disconnect \rightarrow LINE_n$$

A line operated by person n will repeatedly take calls as follows: the phone will firstly ring, then a connection will be made to n, then the order takes place, and finally the call is disconnected, and n is ready to receive the next order.

The service employs Chris and Sandy to run one line each, both connected to the same phone number, modelled by the fact that they each have the same event *ring* in their alphabet. The service is described by

$$SERVICE \quad = \quad LINE_{chris} \; ||| \; LINE_{sandy}$$

In this situation, only one of the phones will ring when a customer dials in. The customer has no control over which, and hence has no control over whether the next event in the call will be *connect.chris* or *connect.sandy*. A customer who wishes to talk only to Sandy may be disappointed.

There is an internal choice between the two components over which of them performs the event *ring*. The choice of which of the *LINE* processes takes the call is made internally by *SERVICE*. It cannot be made externally, by the customer, since initially there is only *ring* on offer; a choice cannot be resolved externally if there is only one event to choose. ■

The interleaving operator is appropriate for describing a number of identical resources which are all available for use.

Example 2.2.3 A fax machine may be described as

$$FAX \quad = \quad accept?d : DOCUMENT \rightarrow print!d \rightarrow FAX$$

The machine is initially ready to accept any document. After accepting a document d, it prints d and reverts to its initial state.

A collection of four fax machines may be connected to the same phone number (with four lines): any of them is suitable for processing incoming faxes.

$$FAXES \quad = \quad (FAX \; ||| \; FAX) \; ||| \; (FAX \; ||| \; FAX)$$

This system provides the facility for processing up to four incoming faxes at the same time. It can accept up to four faxes before printing. An incoming fax has no influence over which machine is actually chosen to process it, but in this case this makes no difference since all choices have exactly the same behaviour. ■

Dynamic process creation

Dynamic process creation can be modelled by use of an interleaving construction within a recursive loop. In general, a fresh copy of the entire process description is generated every time a recursive invocation occurs. Dynamic process creation occurs when such invocations take place while the parent process continues to execute. This may be set up in a recursive definition which contains a number of paths, some of which concern execution of the parent process, and where others contain recursive calls.

Example 2.2.4 A mail forwarder receives messages on channel *in* and forwards them along channel *out* at some later stage. It should always be willing to accept messages.

One approach to designing such a process would be to allow it to accept a message, and then create two processes: one to take responsibility for sending the message on, and the other to be a fresh copy of the original. This approach is described in CSP as follows:

$$NODE \quad = \quad in?x \rightarrow (NODE \,|||\, OUT(x))$$

The process $OUT(x)$ describes the part of the process which deals with sending x along channel *out*.

There are two views with respect to dynamic process creation. The parent process might be considered as the process $N = in?x \rightarrow N$ which is responsible for accepting inputs; and a child output process is generated every time an input occurs. Alternatively, the parent process might be considered as $in?x \rightarrow OUT(x)$, where a fresh version of the entire process, ready to handle the next input, is generated every time an input occurs. Both of these viewpoints is consistent with the description above.

This structure is given before the process $OUT(x)$ is defined, and there are different possibilities for this process definition.

The expectation may be that the thread described by $OUT(x)$ should finish after x has been output. This would be described by

$$OUT(x) \quad = \quad out!x \rightarrow SKIP$$

After the output has occurred, this thread of execution will finish—there is nothing further that it is required to do. All further activity of the process will come from other parallel components. Observe that any process $P \,|||\, SKIP$ has the same executions as P, so a garbage collector could remove component processes that have finished without affecting the execution.

An alternative approach to defining the spawned thread might allow it to continue with a fresh version of *NODE* after its initial output. This possibility is described by

$$OUT(x) \quad = \quad out!x \rightarrow NODE$$

so that after one input and its corresponding output the result is two interleaved versions of *NODE*. The number of active threads of control in this process will grow without limit, with a fresh thread generated on every input, and no thread ever finishing. Despite this proliferation, this implementation has no more executions than the previous tidier definition.

A different requirement might be that x should be logged as well as output. This could be achieved sequentially as $out!x \rightarrow log!x \rightarrow SKIP$, or alternatively by two interleaved threads $out!x \rightarrow SKIP \;|||\; log!x \rightarrow SKIP$. ∎

Example 2.2.5 A bookshop operates a system whereby customers pay for books at a cashier's counter and collect them at a different counter where they had previously been lodged. The operation of the book counter may be described as follows:

$$BOOK \;\; = \;\; lodge \rightarrow issue\_chit \rightarrow BOOK$$
$$\Box$$
$$receive\_receipt \rightarrow claim \rightarrow BOOK$$

A customer may *lodge* a chosen book with the counter, and have a chit issued in return. In order to *claim* the book to take away, a receipt must be provided. This may be obtained from the cashier, described as follows:

$$CASHIER \;\; = \;\; receive\_chit \rightarrow payment \rightarrow issue\_receipt \rightarrow CASHIER$$

Book chits must be issued by the book counter before they can be received by the cashier:

$$CHIT \;\; = \;\; issue\_chit \rightarrow (CHIT \;|||\; receive\_chit \rightarrow SKIP)$$

Similarly, receipts must be issued before they can be exchanged for books:

$$RECEIPT \;\; = \;\; issue\_receipt \rightarrow (RECEIPT \;|||\; receive\_receipt \rightarrow SKIP)$$

Each of these components imposes some constraint on the customer; and they are all in place together. The complete payment system which the customer must navigate is captured as the parallel combination

$$CASHIER \;\|\; BOOK \;\|\; CHIT \;\|\; RECEIPT$$

The first two processes represent the parts of the system which the customer interacts with. The other two processes describe the relevant properties of the objects used by the customer and by the bookshop: that chits and receipts can be created only by the book counter and the cashier respectively. The bookshop's payment system relies on the fact that chits and receipts cannot be forged. ∎

Indexed interleaving

The interleaving parallel operator is associative, in the sense that $P_1 \mathbin{|||} (P_2 \mathbin{|||} P_3)$ has exactly the same execution possibilities as $(P_1 \mathbin{|||} P_2) \mathbin{|||} P_3$; and commutative, in the sense that $P_1 \mathbin{|||} P_2$ and $P_2 \mathbin{|||} P_1$ have the same execution possibilities. It can therefore be generalized to finite combinations of processes. The generalization takes the form

$$\mathbin{|||}_{i \in I} P_i$$

where I is a finite set of indices, and P_i is defined for each $i \in I$. An alternative way of writing an indexed interleaving in the special case where the indexing set is an interval of integers $\{ i \mid m \leqslant i \leqslant n \}$ is

$$\mathbin{|||}_{i=m}^{n} P_i$$

Example 2.2.6 A node similar to the *NODE* process of Example 2.2.4, but which can hold a maximum of n messages, could be described as an interleaved combination of n versions of *COPY*:

$$n\_NODE \quad = \quad \mathbin{|||}_{0 \leqslant i < n} C(i)$$

where each $C(i)$ is defined to be *COPY*, for $0 \leqslant i < n$. To describe an interleaved combination of n copies of the same process P there is a convenient shorthand

$$\mathbin{|||}_{0 \leqslant i < n} P$$

so an alternative description of n_NODE would be given by

$$n\_NODE \quad = \quad \mathbin{|||}_{0 \leqslant i < n} COPY$$

∎

2.3 INTERFACE PARALLEL

Synchronizing parallel and interleaving parallel can be blended into a hybrid form of parallel combination, which requires synchronization only on those events appearing in a common interface $A \subseteq \Sigma$ (as well as termination). This is described as

$$P_1 \underset{A}{\|} P_2$$

The operational semantics is straightforward:

$$
\frac{\begin{array}{c} P_1 \xrightarrow{a} P_1' \\ P_2 \xrightarrow{a} P_2' \end{array}}{P_1 \underset{A}{\|} P_2 \xrightarrow{a} P_1' \underset{A}{\|} P_2'} \quad [\, a \in A^{\checkmark} \,]
$$

$$
\frac{P_1 \xrightarrow{\mu} P_1'}{\begin{array}{c} P_1 \underset{A}{\|} P_2 \xrightarrow{\mu} P_1' \underset{A}{\|} P_2 \\ P_2 \underset{A}{\|} P_1 \xrightarrow{\mu} P_2 \underset{A}{\|} P_1' \end{array}} \quad [\, \mu \notin A^{\checkmark} \,]
$$

P_1 and P_2 co-operate on any event drawn from A, and interleave on events not in A.

Example 2.3.1 A runner in a race engages in two events, *start* and *finish*:

$$RUNNER \;=\; start \rightarrow finish \rightarrow STOP$$

Two runners should synchronize on the *start* event, but they *finish* independently.

$$RACE \;=\; RUNNER \underset{\{start\}}{\|} RUNNER$$

■

Indexed interface parallel

This parallel operator is associative provided the same interface set is used throughout: $P_1 \underset{A}{\|}$ $(P_2 \underset{A}{\|} P_3)$ has the same executions as $(P_1 \underset{A}{\|} P_2) \underset{A}{\|} P_3$. It is also commutative. This allows the operator to be generalized as follows:

$$\underset{A}{\|}_{i \in I} P_i$$

where I is a finite indexing set, and P_i is defined for each $i \in I$. It describes the process where any occurrence of an event from A must involve all of the P_i. An occurrence of any event not in A involves exactly one of those processes.

Example 2.3.2 A marathon involving 30,000 runners could be described as

$$MARATHON \quad = \quad \underset{\{start\}_{i=1}}{\|} {}^{30,000} \ RUNNER$$

All runners start at the same time, but each of them finishes independently.   ■

Example 2.3.3 A function applied to a particular argument can be computed in two ways: using algorithm g and using algorithm h. These two functions should agree on the value they compute for any particular input x, so the intention is that $g(x) = h(x)$ for any input x.

A module is written for each algorithm. The communication pattern of the modules is written as

$$G \quad = \quad in?x : T \rightarrow out!g(x) \rightarrow SKIP$$
$$H \quad = \quad in?x : T \rightarrow out!h(x) \rightarrow SKIP$$

These modules can be run concurrently, but there are a number of ways in which this may be accomplished.

1. A fault-tolerant approach would run G and H in parallel, synchronizing on input and output. The combination $G \parallel H$ accepts one input which is received by both G and H, and also synchronizes on output. This means that an output can occur only if both modules agree on its value. If the modules disagree, then a deadlock occurs and successful termination cannot occur.

2. To receive the result of the fastest calculation, an independent approach could be adopted, interleaving G and H. The combination $G \parallel\parallel H$ has to accept the input twice, since each module accepts its input independently of the other. If only one input is provided, then only one of the modules is executed, though the user has no control over which. Furthermore, the combination does not ensure that the same input is provided to each module.

3. The combination $G \underset{in.T}{\parallel} H$ allows a single input to be received by both modules, but allows for independent output, so a result can be obtained after the first module has completed its calculation. It cannot terminate until both outputs have occurred.

Different flavours of concurrency are appropriate for different requirements.   ■

Exercises

Exercise 2.1 Give the transition graph for *MACHINE* of Example 2.1.4.

Exercise 2.2 Give the transition graph for *CUST* || *ATT* of Example 2.1.3. What behaviour does this parallel combination exhibit that you would not expect to find in a real cloakroom system? Amend the descriptions of the interacting parties *CUST* and *ATT* appropriately to remove this possibility.

Exercise 2.3 Give the transition graph for *PAINTING* of Example 2.1.8, and use it to identify all the ways in which deadlocks can occur.

Exercise 2.4 The bookshop of Example 2.2.5 does not contain sufficient detail to prevent fraud: it allows any book to be claimed with any receipt. Adapt the description to keep track of the identity of the book that has been lodged throughout the payment procedure, so that customers can only take the books that have been paid for.

Exercise 2.5 A dishonest shopper will select an item, and will then either leave without paying, or else will pay if the circumstances in the shop make the first course of action infeasible. This can be described by the following process:

$$DCUSTOMER \quad = \quad enter \to select \to (\ pay \to leave \to DCUSTOMER$$
$$\square \ leave \to DCUSTOMER)$$

What is the expected behaviour of this customer in parallel with the *SHOP* process of Example 2.1.7? What difference does it make to the expected behaviour if the external choice is replaced with an internal one?

Exercise 2.6 Draw the hypercube in the case where $n = 4$. How many ways are there for a message to get from $(1, 0, 0, 1)$ to $(0, 0, 1, 0)$ using the message routing algorithm?

Exercise 2.7 Consider the hypercube network of Example 2.1.13.

1. Not all of the channel names in Figure 2.6 have been given their subscripts. Give the subscripts for the remaining channels.

2. Is *MAILER* deadlock-free?

3. Is it deadlock-free if the next destination for a message is chosen internally by nodes, rather than by an external choice, as follows:

$$N_l(\langle\rangle) \quad = \quad \square_{k \in adj(l)} \ c_{k,l}?(d.m) \to N_l(\langle(d,m)\rangle)$$
$$\square \ in_l?(d.m) \to N_l(\langle(d,m)\rangle)$$

$$N_l(\langle(d,m)\rangle \frown s)$$
$$= \quad out_l!m \to N_l(s) \qquad\qquad\qquad\qquad \text{if } d = l$$
$$(\sqcap_{k \in next(l,d)} \ c_{l,k}!(d.m) \to N_l(s)) \qquad\qquad \text{otherwise}$$
$$\square$$
$$\square_{k \in adj(l)} \ c_{k,l}?(d'.m') \to$$
$$N_l(\langle(d,m)\rangle \frown s \frown \langle(d',m')\rangle))$$

4. Is it deadlock-free if nodes can hold at most one message, i.e. they block input when they hold a message (rather than being able to hold arbitrarily many), as follows:

$$N_l(\langle\rangle) = \square_{k \in adj(l)} c_{k,l}?(d.m) \rightarrow N_l(\langle(d,m)\rangle)$$

$$= \square \ in_l?(d.m) \rightarrow N_l(\langle(d,m)\rangle)$$

$$
N_l(\langle(d,m)\rangle) = \begin{array}{ll}
out_l!m \rightarrow N_l(\langle\rangle) & \text{if } d = l \\
(\square_{k \in next(l,d)} c_{l,k}!(d.m) \rightarrow N_l(\langle\rangle)) & \text{otherwise}
\end{array}
$$

5. What is the maximum number of nodes a message will pass through in a network of 2^n nodes?

Exercise 2.8 Consider the array *SORTER* of Example 2.1.12:

1. Is it deadlock-free?

2. Is it deadlock-free if the order of each cell's output is reversed (so output occurs on the h channel before the v channel) as follows:

$$C_{i,j} = h_{i,j}?x \rightarrow v_{i,j}?y \rightarrow h_{i+1,j}! \max\{x,y\} \rightarrow v_{i,j+1}! \min\{x,y\} \rightarrow C_{i,j}$$

3. Is it deadlock-free if the order of both inputs and outputs for a cell is reversed as follows:

$$C_{i,j} = v_{i,j}?y \rightarrow h_{i,j}?x \rightarrow h_{i+1,j}! \max\{x,y\} \rightarrow v_{i,j+1}! \min\{x,y\} \rightarrow C_{i,j}$$

Which other orders of inputs and outputs avoid deadlock?

Exercise 2.9 Show that interface parallel is not associative in general when the event sets are different, by finding processes P_1, P_2, and P_3 and sets A and B such that $P_1 \parallel_A (P_2 \parallel_B P_3)$ is different from $(P_1 \parallel_A P_2) \parallel_B P_3$.

3

Abstraction and control flow

3.1 HIDING

When a collection of processes has been combined into a system, there will often be communications between the components which should be internal. Such events are inappropriate to include at the system interface, which should contain only those events through which the system interacts with its environment.

When processes are placed in parallel, the events on which they synchronize remain in the interface of the combination. This is the mechanism which supports multi-way synchronization. It also means that even when all the intended participants in an event have been described and composed in parallel, the event is still in the interface of the combination. A new CSP operator, *event hiding*, is required to encapsulate the event within the process, and to remove it from the interface.

A set of events A may be encapsulated within a process P using the notation

$P \setminus A$

(pronounced 'P hide A'). This operation describes the case where all participants of all events in A are already known and described in P. All these events are removed from the interface of the process, since no other processes are required to engage in them. These events become *internal* to the process *P*. The operational rules reflect this:

$$\frac{P \stackrel{a}{\rightarrow} P'}{P \setminus A \stackrel{\tau}{\rightarrow} P' \setminus A} \quad [\, a \in A \,]$$

$$\frac{P \stackrel{\mu}{\rightarrow} P'}{P \setminus A \stackrel{\mu}{\rightarrow} P' \setminus A} \quad [\, \mu \notin A \,]$$

The process $P \setminus A$ may make the same transitions as P, but all the events in A are renamed to the internal event τ. Termination cannot be hidden, so the event $\checkmark$ must not appear in the set A.

This operator is used in design and in implementation. It explains a process in terms of internal activity, so it is used in a description of how a particular end is accomplished. It is not appropriate at the level of specification, since at that level internal events should not even be mentioned: specifications of processes should be concerned purely with the behaviour on their external events.

Example 3.1.1 A spy listens out for particular pieces of information (of type *T*), and then relays them to a master spy who logs them. In order for the spy to be effective, it is important that the relaying of information is kept hidden from its environment.

$$\begin{aligned} SPY &= listen?x : T \rightarrow relay!x \rightarrow SPY \\ MASTER &= relay?y : T \rightarrow log!y \rightarrow MASTER \end{aligned}$$

The combination of the master and the spy is described by

$$(SPY \parallel MASTER) \setminus relay.T$$

The only visible activity the spy is involved in is listening. ∎

Example 3.1.2 A stop-and-wait protocol implements a one-place buffer. It consists of two halves, *S* and *R*: a message is input to *S*, passed to *R*, and finally output from *R*.

$$\begin{aligned} S &= in?x : T \rightarrow mid!x \rightarrow ack \rightarrow S \\ R &= mid?y : T \rightarrow out!y \rightarrow ack \rightarrow R \end{aligned}$$

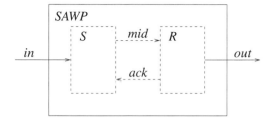

Fig. 3.1   A stop-and-wait protocol

Having accepted a message, the sender S passes the message to R along channel *mid*, and then waits for an acknowledgement before accepting the next message. The receiver R accepts messages along *mid*, and sends an acknowledgement once a message has been output.

The two halves of the protocol are designed to combine in parallel. The channel *mid* and the acknowledgement event *ack* are private connections and should have no participants other than S and R. The protocol is then described as

$$SAWP \;\; = \;\; (S \parallel R) \setminus (mid.T \cup \{ack\})$$

This is pictured in Figure 3.1.   ■

Example 3.1.3 Each cell N_l in the network of cells connected as vertices of a hypercube, described in Example 2.1.13 as *MAILER*, has interface

$$A_l \;\; = \;\; \{in_l, out_l\} \cup \{c_{k,l} \mid k \in adj(l)\} \cup \{c_{l,k} \mid k \in adj(l)\}$$

The in_l and out_l channels are intended for communication with the users of the network, and the c channels are used for the cells to pass messages between each other. The intention is that no external parties are involved in the communications on the c channels. The only processes involved in communications on any particular channel $c_{k,l}$ are the cells N_k and N_l. In order to encapsulate the c channels within the process *MAILER* the hiding operator is used:

$$MAIL\_SERVICE \;\; = \;\; MAILER \setminus \{c_{i,j} \mid i,j \in COORD \wedge j \in adj(i)\}$$

The only external events that *MAIL_SERVICE* can perform are communications along the channels in_l and out_l for each l; only through these events can it interact with its environment.   ■

A process exercises complete control over its internal events. With this control over when internal events are performed comes the responsibility to perform them: internal events should not be delayed indefinitely once they are enabled, since otherwise progress could not be expected. In the stop-and-wait protocol in Example 3.1.2 the environment can expect a

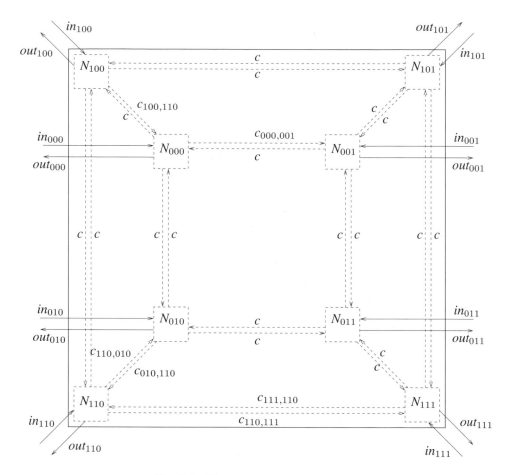

Fig. 3.2   The process *MAIL_SERVICE*

message to be offered as output after it has been input. The message must be passed internally along *mid* after it has been received on the *in* channel, and *SAWP* cannot refuse to perform a *mid* event, or indeed an *ack* event, once it is enabled.

When the events offered by an external choice are hidden, the environment no longer has any control over how the choice is resolved: it is resolved internally.

Example 3.1.4 A fax is to be sent to someone who has two fax machines. A secretary is given the fax to send (modelled by the event *in.x*). It can be sent to the first, modelled by the channel *send*.1, or it can be sent to the second, modelled by channel *send*.2. The secretary is prepared to send it to either number, and offers the choice to her boss, modelled as an external choice. Sometime later a receipt is obtained indicating successful transmission to the corresponding machine. This situation is described by *SEC*.

$$SEC \quad = \quad in?x \to (send.1!x \to received.1 \to STOP$$
$$\square \; send.2!x \to received.2 \to STOP)$$

If the boss does not wish to be involved in the choice between different fax numbers, she delegates the choice by hiding the channels *send*.1 and *send*.2, giving complete control over them to the secretary.

$$SEC \setminus (send.1.T \cup send.2.T)$$

The hiding of these events removes them from those communications on which the boss and the secretary have to agree. They are encapsulated within the process *SEC*, indicating that all participants (in this case just one) have been identified. Although the secretary has complete control over which one to perform, she is still obliged to perform one of them: the boss can expect a receipt. From the point of view of the boss, this choice will now be resolved internally. After giving a fax to the secretary she has no control over which of the two machines will receive the fax, and will only find out which it was once the receipt is obtained. Observe that if the receipts were indistinguishable (both modelled by the single event *receipt*) then the boss would have no way of determining which way the choice was made. ∎

Example 3.1.5 In Example 2.1.13, when a cell C_l is waiting to send a message to an adjacent cell, it offers an external choice of all the possibilities. It is willing to send its message to any cell that is ready to receive it, and its environment—the rest of the network and the rest of the world—will determine how the choice is made. Since all cells are always ready to receive messages, the choice is available externally. When the rest of the world is excluded by hiding the communication channels between cells to obtain *MAIL_SERVICE* (pictured in Figure 3.2), the choice must be made internally within the process *MAIL_SERVICE* itself. The environment is not concerned with the routes that messages travel, only with the assurance that they will arrive. ∎

When only one event of a binary external choice is made internal, the process is required to make a choice between performing the internal one autonomously, or waiting for a synchronization on the external one. If its environment is not prepared to engage in the external event, then its responsibility to perform the internal event means that it cannot wait indefinitely for the external one, since this would involve indefinitely delaying the internal event. On the other hand, if the environment is prepared to engage in the external event, then one of two things could happen: either the choice has not yet been made, and the external event can occur and resolve the choice in its favour; or the internal event has already occurred, since the environment cannot prevent it from occurring, and the external event is no longer available.

Example 3.1.6 A printer queue which can hold one message at a time is described as follows:

$$PRINTQ \quad = \quad in?x : JOB \to (print!x \to out!x \to PRINTQ$$
$$\square \; dequeue \to PRINTQ)$$

When a job is queued, either it will be sent to the printer and received as output, or else it could be removed from the queue. The user is not normally involved in the communications between the queue and the printer, so the communications along the *print* channel will be internal. The process which the user interacts with is

$$PRINTQ \setminus print.JOB$$

The user has no control over when the job will be sent to the printer. After inputting a job, it may be possible to dequeue it if it has not yet reached the printer, but the other possibility, entirely outside the control of the user, is that it may already have been sent to the printer and the option of dequeuing has been withdrawn.   ■

Example 3.1.7 A course of action might be made available for a particular interval, but is then timed out if it has not yet been chosen. Although timed CSP will enable a more precise description of this kind of behaviour, it is possible to analyse it in terms of a timeout event. In this case a choice is offered between the initial event and the timeout event. For example, a special offer is available only for a limited period, after which the offer lapses and purchase must then be at the standard rate:

$$OFFER \quad = \quad ((cheap \to STOP) \;\square\; (lapse \to standard \to STOP)) \setminus \{lapse\}$$

The user has no control or influence over when the cheap offer will end, so the timeout event *lapse* is made internal. It is possible to buy at the cheap price if the offer has not yet lapsed, but it is also possible that the cheap price has been retracted at the point the purchaser is ready to buy, and that only the standard price is available.   ■

Example 3.1.8 A stop-and-wait protocol which permits its input to be overwritten once if it has not already passed along the *mid* channel, might be described as follows:

$$
\begin{aligned}
S2 &= in?x \to (S2 \;\square\; (mid!x \to ack \to S2)) \\
R2 &= mid?y \to out!y \to ack \to R2
\end{aligned}
$$

After an input, the sender $S2$ is prepared either to pass the input along *mid*, or to accept another input which displaces the previous one. The receiver $R2$ is exactly the same as the original receiver R of Example 3.1.2. The two halves of the protocol are combined as $S2 \parallel R2$, and the internal channels are hidden:

$$SAWP2 \quad = \quad (S2 \parallel R2) \setminus mid.T \cup \{ack\}$$

After its first input *in.x*, the process $SAWP2$ is in the position where a choice is to be made between an external event *in.w* and an internal event *mid.x*. If at this point the environment simply waits for output to be offered, and offers no further input, then the internal event must occur, and output is indeed offered. If instead the environment offers a second input, then there are two possibilities: the internal event has not yet occurred, and the second input is accepted; or the choice has already been made in favour of the internal communication, in which case the second input will be refused. The environment is unable to prevent this second possibility.   ■

The internalization of events may introduce the possibility of internal events occurring indefinitely. Since the environment has no control over the internal events of a process, this means that the process is free to execute these internal events for ever and consequently avoid any further interaction with its environment. This possibility is called *divergence*. When applying the hiding operator, care should be taken to avoid divergence, since progress cannot be guaranteed for any divergent process—it may consume computing resources for ever without any assurance that it will ever again respond to its environment.

Example 3.1.9 A parity server offers alternating bits on its output channel:

$$PARITY \quad = \quad out!0 \to out!1 \to PARITY$$

If its output channel is hidden, then it simply repeats *out*.0 and *out*.1 internally for ever. The process $PARITY \setminus out.\{0,1\}$ behaves as an internal loop, unable to interact with its environment, but consuming computing resources and thereby possibly preventing other processes from executing. In this respect it is worse than a deadlocked process, which is also unable to interact with its environment but at least is not consuming resources.   ■

Example 3.1.10 A process reads data from two input channels, and outputs on a single channel. It is able to be ready only on one input channel at a time, but it may switch between them by means of an event *switch*. At any point where it is waiting for input, it offers a choice between accepting input on that channel and switching to wait on the other channel.

$$POLL \quad = \quad in.1?x \to out!x \to POLL$$
$$\square \; switch \to (in.2?x \to out!x \to POLL$$
$$\square \; switch \to POLL)$$

If the *switch* event is hidden, to enable the polling process to switch channels independently of its environment, then the process $POLL \setminus \{switch\}$ is obtained. Unfortunately, this process may spend its entire time switching between channels in preference to ever accepting any message on either of them. At any stage, there is a choice between an external communication or an internal *switch*. Although the external communication is possible, so is the internal event. Both are of equal priority, but the internal event is entirely under the control of *POLL* and cannot be prevented from occurring. Since this is true at every stage of an execution, it is possible that *POLL* simply resolves the choice in favour of *switch* every time, resulting in an execution consisting entirely of internal events. This is possible even if its environment is offering input on both *in*.1 and *in*.2—there is no guarantee that either input will ever be accepted.   ■

3.2 EVENT RENAMING

When a process's pattern of communication has been described in terms of particular events, it is possible to obtain a new process by renaming those events. Its executions are essentially those of the original process but where the events are renamed. This allows the reuse of particular descriptions of process behaviour without the need to rewrite the process in full and replacing all the original event names with the new ones.

A total function on events $f : \Sigma^{\checkmark} \to \Sigma^{\checkmark}$ is used to describe the required change of event names. For any such function, there are two ways a process can have its events renamed: by applying the function f to each event, or by applying its inverse f^{-1} to each event. The interface through which the process interacts with its environment is transformed by f and f^{-1} respectively. The function f must map external events to external ones—it cannot be used to make events internal. Termination cannot be renamed, so $f(a) = \checkmark \Leftrightarrow a = \checkmark$ for any event renaming function.

Forward renaming

The process $f(P)$ is able to perform an event $f(a)$ precisely when the process P could perform the corresponding event a. Furthermore, $f(P)$ can perform internal events whenever P can. This behaviour is captured by the following transition rules:

$$\frac{P \overset{a}{\to} P'}{f(P) \overset{f(a)}{\longrightarrow} f(P')}$$

$$\frac{P \overset{\tau}{\to} P'}{f(P) \overset{\tau}{\to} f(P')}$$

If the function f is one-one, then the process P might be thought of as capturing a generic behaviour pattern, with $f(P)$ a particular instance of it. Whenever $f(P)$ offers or performs some event b, then that corresponds to P offering or performing $f^{-1}(b)$. Choices offered by P become choices offered by $f(P)$.

Example 3.2.1 The children of Example 2.1.8 have similar patterns of behaviour. The behaviour of Isabella was described by

$$
\begin{aligned}
ISABELLA \quad = \quad & isabella.get.box \to isabella.get.easel \to isabella.paint \to \\
& isabella.drop.box \to isabella.drop.easel \to ISABELLA \\
& \Box\ isabella.get.easel \to isabella.get.box \to isabella.paint \to \\
& isabella.drop.box \to isabella.drop.easel \to ISABELLA
\end{aligned}
$$

and the behaviour of Kate was obtained by taking the description *ISABELLA* and replacing all occurrences of the name *isabella* with the name *kate*. Instead of doing this explicitly, this may be accomplished by means of event renaming. Let the function $f : \Sigma^\checkmark \rightarrow \Sigma^\checkmark$ be defined by

$$
\begin{aligned}
f(isabella.x) &= kate.x \\
f(y) &= y \qquad \text{if } y \text{ is not of the form } isabella.x
\end{aligned}
$$

We will adopt the convention in function definition that the function is defined to be the identity on events which are not explicitly covered by the definition. Hence the above function could have been defined simply by the clause $f(isabella.x) = (kate.x)$. In either case,

$$
KATE = f(ISABELLA)
$$

gives an alternative definition for *KATE*.   ■

Example 3.2.2 The process *CHAIN* in Example 2.1.11 is made up of a number of individual one-place buffers. Each of those buffers behaves in essentially the same way, but on different channels. The behaviour pattern can be captured as the generic one-place buffer *COPY* of type $\mathbb{Z}$, defined first in Example 1.3.2:

$$
COPY = in?x : \mathbb{Z} \rightarrow out!x \rightarrow COPY
$$

This process has $in.\mathbb{Z} \cup out.\mathbb{Z}$ as its interface.

Each process P_i in the chain was defined explicitly as

$$
P_i = c_i?x : \mathbb{Z} \rightarrow c_{i+1}!x \rightarrow P_i
$$

Each one could instead be defined using a corresponding event renaming function f_i defined by

$$
\begin{aligned}
f_i(in.m) &= c_i.m \\
f_i(out.m) &= c_{i+1}.m
\end{aligned}
$$

The processes P_i could instead have been defined as

$$
P_i = f_i(COPY)
$$

The interface of each P_i will be the interface of *COPY* transformed by f_i, which is $c_i.\mathbb{Z} \cup c_{i+1}.\mathbb{Z}$.   ■

One special form of one-one event renaming attaches a particular label to all events in a process description. If the label is l, then the function f_l to be applied is given by

$$
f_l(x) = l.x
$$

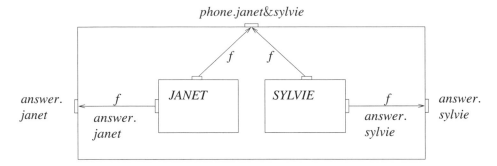

Fig. 3.3 *The interface of the process* $f(OFFICE)$

for all $x \in \Sigma$, and $f_l(\checkmark) = \checkmark$. Then the process $f_l(P)$ performs events $l.a$ whenever P would have performed a. There is a special form for this kind of event renaming. The process construction $l : P$ is shorthand for $f_l(P)$ where f_l is as defined above.

Example 3.2.3 In Example 2.1.8, the generic behaviour pattern of a child painting is captured as the process *PAINT*:

$$
\begin{aligned}
PAINT \\
= \quad &get.box \rightarrow get.easel \rightarrow paint \rightarrow drop.box \rightarrow drop.easel \rightarrow PAINT \\
&\square \; get.easel \rightarrow get.box \rightarrow paint \rightarrow drop.box \rightarrow drop.easel \rightarrow PAINT
\end{aligned}
$$

Then *KATE* and *ISABELLA* can be described as particular instances of this process, as *kate : PAINT* and *isabella : PAINT* respectively. ∎

All aspects of process behaviour are transformed directly when a process is renamed under a one-one function. A function which maps a number of different events to the same single event can alter some features of the process's behaviour, particularly with regard to choice. If two events of a choice are mapped to the same event, then the environment is no longer able to choose between these two branches of the choice, since they are now both triggered by the same event: if the environment chooses that event, then either branch could be chosen, and no further control over which one is actually chosen is available externally. Hence many-one event renaming may affect the nature of particular choices and may introduce some internal choices where there were previously external ones.

Example 3.2.4 Janet and Sylvie share an office which contains two phones. To converse with either of them it is sufficient to dial their phone number. The possibilities for phoning and answering are described as follows:

$$
\begin{aligned}
OFFICE \; &= \; JANET \; ||| \; SYLVIE \\
JANET \; &= \; phone.janet \rightarrow answer.janet \rightarrow JANET \\
SYLVIE \; &= \; phone.sylvie \rightarrow answer.sylvie \rightarrow SYLVIE
\end{aligned}
$$

The two phones are given the same number, required to serve both Janet and Sylvie. The effect of this is to map both *phone.janet* and *phone.sylvie* to a single event *phone.janet&sylvie*. The effect on *OFFICE* is to transform it through the event mapping f given by

$$
\begin{aligned}
f(phone.janet) &= phone.janet\&sylvie \\
f(phone.sylvie) &= phone.janet\&sylvie
\end{aligned}
$$

The process $f(OFFICE)$, pictured in Figure 3.3, initially offers the event *phone.janet&sylvie*. The next event could be either *answer.janet* or *answer.sylvie*, and the caller no longer has any control over which of these will occur. The event renaming has altered the nature of the choice available to the caller. ∎

Backward renaming

A process may also have its interface changed through renaming under f^{-1} where f is again a total function on $\Sigma^{\checkmark}$. The intention here is that the process $f^{-1}(P)$ can perform a whenever P can perform $f(a)$. Internal events are again unchanged by this form of renaming. Its effect is described by the following transition rules:

$$
\frac{P \xrightarrow{f(a)} P'}{f^{-1}(P) \xrightarrow{a} f^{-1}(P')}
$$

$$
\frac{P \xrightarrow{\tau} P'}{f^{-1}(P) \xrightarrow{\tau} f^{-1}(P')}
$$

In the case where f is bijective then f^{-1} is also a bijection and the process $f^{-1}(P)$ can also be treated as a forward renamed process (renamed by the function f^{-1}).

When f is many-one, then backward renaming is different from any form of forward renaming. In this case, whenever P is able to perform an event a, the process $f^{-1}(P)$ is able to perform any of the events that map onto the event a. This allows a single event in the description of a process's behaviour pattern to correspond to a choice of alternatives at its interface: all the events that map onto a are available to the environment of $f^{-1}(P)$, and any of them can be chosen. This form of renaming represents interface expansion, where single events in the behaviour pattern can be triggered by a number of different possibilities at its interface.

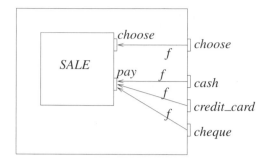

Fig. 3.4   Interface expansion of *SALE* **through backward renaming**

Example 3.2.5 The generic pattern of behaviour when a shop makes a sale is that items are chosen, and then paid for. This simple pattern may be described by the process

$$SALE \quad = \quad choose \rightarrow pay \rightarrow SALE$$

The shop offers a number of alternative payment methods: cash, credit card, or cheque. Rather than redefine the process *SALE* it is possible to describe these alternatives by use of the event renaming function

$$
\begin{aligned}
f(cash) &= pay \\
f(credit\_card) &= pay \\
f(cheque) &= pay
\end{aligned}
$$

Then whenever the process *SALE* is ready to accept *pay*, the process $f^{-1}(SALE)$ is prepared to engage in any of those events that map onto *pay*: it offers a choice to the customer between the events *cash*, *credit_card*, and *cheque*, as illustrated in Figure 3.4. ■

Chaining

Using event renaming, any event in the interface of one process can be connected to any event from a second process's interface so the two processes must synchronize on their performance of these events. The two events are each renamed to the same new event, and then the processes are composed in parallel. Their interfaces are effectively reconfigured so that they must now co-operate on these events.

A special form of this interface reconfiguration is useful for pipe processes, which have exactly two channels: *in* and *out*. When two such processes are connected together, the intention is that the output of the first is connected to the input of the second. This is accomplished by renaming each of these channels to *mid*, composing the resulting processes

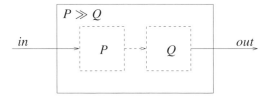

Fig. 3.5   A chain of two pipe processes

in parallel, and finally hiding the *mid* channel. The renaming functions required are particular instances of $swap_{c,d}$ for channel names c and d, defined as follows:

$$swap_{c,d}(c.x) = d.x$$
$$swap_{c,d}(d.x) = c.x$$
$$swap_{c,d}(y) = y \qquad \text{if } y \neq c.x \text{ and } y \neq d.x$$

The *chaining* operator on pipe processes may then be defined in terms of renaming, parallel composition, and hiding:

$$P_1 \gg P_2 \equiv (swap_{out,mid}(P_1) \parallel swap_{in,mid}(P_2)) \setminus mid$$

The resulting process is again a pipe: the only two channels it has are *in* and *out*. The operator is illustrated in Figure 3.5.

Example 3.2.6 Two instances of the *COPY* process chained together produce a pipe which is a buffer of capacity two:

$$2COPY = COPY \gg COPY$$

This process is initially ready for input. After the first data item is input, the left-hand *COPY* passes it along the internal channel *mid* to the right-hand *COPY*, which makes it available for output. At this point the left-hand *COPY* is empty, and is ready to accept a second input, which would lead to the buffer becoming full. Alternatively the right-hand *COPY* is ready to output, which would lead to 2*COPY* returning to its original empty state.   ∎

The chaining operator is associative: $P_1 \gg (P_2 \gg P_3)$ has the same executions as $(P_1 \gg P_2) \gg P_3$. This allows a generalized form on sequences of processes. If P_i are processes for i between 1 and n, then $\gg_{i=1}^{n} P_i$ is the chaining together of all of those n processes in order:

$$\gg_{i=1}^{n} P_i \equiv P_1 \gg P_2 \gg \ldots \gg P_n$$

If each P_i is actually a copy of the same process P, then it is conventional to write $\gg_{i=1}^{n} P$ for the sequence of n copies of P chained together.

Example 3.2.7 Newton's method for approximating square roots of a positive number n states that if a_i is an approximation to $\sqrt{n}$, then $a_{i+1} = \frac{1}{2}(a_i + \frac{n}{a_i})$ is a better approximation. Successive values of a_i are calculated, and the final one in the sequence is taken to be the best approximation.

A pipe which calculates one step of the sequence is defined as follows:

$$NEWTON \quad = \quad in?(n,a) : \mathbb{N} \times \mathbb{R} \to out!(n, (a + \frac{n}{a})/2) \to NEWTON$$

If n successive approximations are required, then n copies of *NEWTON* should be chained together. The first copy requires the first approximation as input: this can be provided by a *HEAD* process. The last copy outputs both the original number and the square-root approximation: a *FOOT* process can extract the information required—the final approximation. These bracketing processes are defined as follows:

$$HEAD \quad = \quad in?n : \mathbb{N} \to out!(n,1) \to HEAD$$
$$FOOT \quad = \quad in?(n,a) : \mathbb{N} \times \mathbb{R} \to out!a \to FOOT$$

The entire square-root extracting process consists of all of these components chained together into one pipe:

$$SQRT \quad = \quad HEAD \gg (\gg_{i=1}^{n} NEWTON) \gg FOOT$$

The initial approximation to the square-root is 1. ∎

Renaming recursive calls

Applying an event renaming function to recursive calls allows fresh invocations of the process to offer different events. This allows for the event possibilities to change dynamically as the execution unwinds. In the case where a process is spawned, and the fresh invocation of the process runs in parallel with the original one, it allows different channels on the fresh process to connect to existing channels on the original: altering the interface of a process alters the way in which it synchronizes with other processes.

Example 3.2.8 The hour changer on a 24 hour clock cycles repeatedly through the hours from 0 to 23, outputting the value on the channel *hour*, with *hour*.0 as its first output. This may be described using an event renaming function *inc* that increments the hour value by 1, modulo 24:

$$inc(hour.n) \quad = \quad hour.((n+1) \bmod 24)$$

The hour changer is then defined as follows:

$$HOUR \quad = \quad hour!0 \rightarrow inc(HOUR)$$

Each time an hour value h is output, the process is recursively invoked under the *inc* function.

∎

Example 3.2.9 A process which models a set with two operations, *add* and *query*, can be described using new invocations of the process in parallel with existing ones. The operation *add* allows the addition of an element to the set; and the operation *query* permits an enquiry as to whether a particular element is in the set or not. The answer, drawn from $ANS = \{yes, no\}$, is passed on channel *answer*.

The empty set can be defined as follows:

$$
\begin{aligned}
SET \quad = \quad & query?x : T \rightarrow answer!no \rightarrow SET \\
& \Box \ add?x : T \rightarrow (NODE(x) \underset{INT}{\parallel} i : SET) \setminus INT
\end{aligned}
$$

$$
\begin{aligned}
NODE(x) \quad = \quad & query?y : T \rightarrow \quad answer!yes \rightarrow NODE(x) \qquad\quad \text{if } y = x \\
& \qquad\qquad\qquad i.query!y \rightarrow i.answer?z : ANS \rightarrow \quad \text{if } y \neq x \\
& \qquad\qquad\qquad\qquad answer!z \rightarrow NODE(x) \\
& \Box \ add?x : T \rightarrow i.add!x : T \rightarrow NODE(x)
\end{aligned}
$$

When an element x is added to the empty set, it is stored in $NODE(x)$, with a fresh copy of the empty set subordinated, labelled with i and hidden. The internal channels are given by

$$INT \quad = \quad i.add.T \cup i.query.T \cup i.answer.ANS$$

The process $NODE(x)$ communicates with the fresh empty set using the internal channels *i.query*, *i.answer*, and *i.add*. When a query is input, if $NODE(x)$ cannot answer it then it passes the query on to the rest of the set and passes the answer on to the user. When a fresh item is to be added to the set, $NODE(x)$ passes it on to the rest of the set. The state after two items have been added to the set is pictured in Figure 3.6.

This process provides an implementation of the process specified in Example 1.3.8.

∎

3.3 SEQUENTIAL COMPOSITION

Processes execute when they are invoked, and it is possible that they continue to execute indefinitely, retaining control over execution throughout. It is also possible that control may

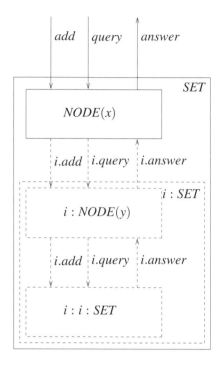

Fig. 3.6 The process *SET* **after** *x* **and** *y* **have been added**

pass to a second process, either because the first process reaches a particular point in its execution where it is ready to pass control, or because the second process demands it.

The mechanism for transferring control from a terminated process to another process is sequential composition. The process

$$P_1; P_2$$

executes component P_1 until it terminates, as indicated by its performance of a $\checkmark$ event, and then executes component P_2. The operational understanding is captured as follows:

$$\frac{P_1 \xrightarrow{\mu} P_1'}{P_1; P_2 \xrightarrow{\mu} P_1'; P_2} \quad [\, \mu \neq \checkmark \,]$$

$$\frac{P_1 \xrightarrow{\checkmark} P_1'}{P_1; P_2 \xrightarrow{\tau} P_2}$$

The sequential composition $P_1; P_2$ initially executes as P_1. When P_1 terminates, its $\checkmark$ event becomes internal to the composition, since $P_1; P_2$ should not indicate that it has finished until P_2 finally terminates.

Process descriptions may be structured using sequential composition, where processes describe the different phases of the overall process. Specifications and system descriptions may thus be provided in a top-down fashion, firstly identifying the phases that the process will pass through, and later providing the detailed description of the behaviour in the individual phases.

Example 3.3.1 A different view of the purchasing process is provided by the description

$$PURCHASE \quad = \quad CHOOSE; PAY$$

Each of the components represents a stage of the purchase process. These must be elaborated in order to complete the definition of $PURCHASE$, but its high-level structure is already clear. We may model $CHOOSE$ and PAY in a number of alternative ways, without affecting the structure. Here we elect to use $CHOOSE$ to describe a process where a shopper cannot rest until a suitable item has been found. The process PAY describes a variety of payment possibilities.

$$
\begin{aligned}
CHOOSE \quad = \quad & select \rightarrow (keep \rightarrow SKIP \\
& \qquad\qquad \Box \ return \rightarrow CHOOSE)
\end{aligned}
$$

$$
\begin{aligned}
PAY \quad = \quad & cash \rightarrow receipt \rightarrow SKIP \\
& \Box \ cheque \rightarrow receipt \rightarrow SKIP \\
& \Box \ card \rightarrow swipe \rightarrow (sign \rightarrow receipt \rightarrow SKIP \\
& \qquad\qquad\qquad\qquad \Box \ reject \rightarrow PAY)
\end{aligned}
$$

Repeated execution of the same component or sequence of components can be described by means of a recursive loop. The recursion

$$SPENDING \quad = \quad PURCHASE; SPENDING$$

describes recurrent spending. ∎

Example 3.3.2 A one-time stack accepts data along channel in. It continues to do this until the command $produce$ occurs, after which all the data are output in reverse order. This can be described by use of a recursive call inside a sequential composition:

$$
\begin{aligned}
STORE \quad = \quad & in?x : T \rightarrow (STORE; out!x \rightarrow SKIP) \\
& \Box \ produce \rightarrow SKIP
\end{aligned}
$$

Each time a recursive call occurs, the message that was last input is stored up awaiting output. For example, after the three inputs $in.5$, $in.3$, $in.8$, the resulting process is

$$STORE; (out!8 \rightarrow SKIP); (out!3 \rightarrow SKIP); (out!5 \rightarrow SKIP)$$

While *STORE* continues to input data, the list of outputs can continue to grow. Once the event *produce* occurs then the potential for any further recursive calls is lost, and the sequence is output in the order of last-in-first-out. ■

3.4 INTERRUPT

Control can also pass from one process P_1 to another process P_2 by means of an interrupt construction

$$P_1 \triangle P_2$$

This allows a process P_1 to have control removed from it at an arbitrary point of an execution. Unlike sequential composition, the process P_1 relinquishing control has no influence over when this occurs. The interrupting process P_2 may begin execution at any point throughout the execution of P_1: the performance of P_2's first external event is the point at which control passes, and P_1 is discarded. The operational rules are as follows:

$$\frac{P_1 \xrightarrow{\mu} P_1'}{P_1 \triangle P_2 \xrightarrow{\mu} P_1' \triangle P_2} \quad [\, \mu \neq \checkmark \,]$$

$$\frac{P_1 \xrightarrow{\checkmark} P_1'}{P_1 \triangle P_2 \xrightarrow{\checkmark} P_1'}$$

$$\frac{P_2 \xrightarrow{\tau} P_2'}{P_1 \triangle P_2 \xrightarrow{\tau} P_1 \triangle P_2'}$$

$$\frac{P_2 \xrightarrow{a} P_2'}{P_1 \triangle P_2 \xrightarrow{a} P_2'}$$

The process is able to perform any execution of P_1. Throughout P_1's execution the interrupting process P_2 is also ready to begin, and the interruption occurs on its first external event. If P_1 terminates while it is executing then the entire construct is terminated and P_2 is discarded.

Nondeterminism could arise if P_1 and P_2 are both able to perform the same event at any stage, since if that event occurs then the result could be either that the interrupt has occurred, or that it has not. It is pragmatic to ensure where possible that P_2 cannot have as its first event any event which P_1 can perform.

Example 3.4.1 The process *KATE* of Example 2.1.8 can be interrupted at any point by *bath* in the following description:

$$KATE \, \triangle \, bath \rightarrow bed \rightarrow SKIP$$

■

Example 3.4.2 A process which models a variable of type T allows values to be written to it along channel *write*, and the current value it is holding can be read by means of the channel *read*. This may be described as follows:

$$
\begin{aligned}
VAR &= write?x : T \rightarrow (VAR(x) \, \triangle \, VAR) \\
VAR(x) &= read!x \rightarrow VAR(x)
\end{aligned}
$$

The process inputs a value and is then prepared to output it repeatedly until interrupted by the next *write*. ■

The particular form $P_1 \, \triangle \, e \rightarrow P_2$ has a single interrupt event e, and identifies it explicitly. This may also be written $P_1 \, \triangle_e \, P_2$. The situation where there is a set A of interrupt events available, and each event $a \in A$ is associated with a particular interrupt handler $P(a)$, can be described as follows:

$$P \, \triangle \, (x : A \rightarrow P(x))$$

Example 3.4.3 The main tasks of an office junior are to make tea, to do photocopying, and to do filing. This activity may be temporarily interrupted by the phone ringing, which requires a message to be taken, or by the boss arriving, where help must be provided with the removal and hanging up of a coat. When the task invoked by the interruption has completed, the main tasks are to be resumed. This structure is captured by the description *JUNIOR*.

$$JUNIOR \; = \; TASKS \, \triangle \, x : \{ring, boss\} \rightarrow P(x)$$

The component processes might be defined as follows:

$$
\begin{aligned}
TASKS \;=\; & tea \rightarrow TASKS \\
& \square \; photocopying \rightarrow TASKS \\
& \square \; filing \rightarrow TASKS
\end{aligned}
$$

$$
\begin{aligned}
P(ring) \;&=\; message \rightarrow JUNIOR \\
P(boss) \;&=\; remove\_coat \rightarrow hang\_coat \; \rangle \; JUNIOR
\end{aligned}
$$

■

Example 3.4.4 The office junior has a higher level interrupt of the fire alarm sounding. If it is due to a real fire then work ceases for the day and the junior returns home. Otherwise, it is announced that it is a drill, in which case it is necessary to return to work. The *fire* event interrupts all other activity, even the interrupt handlers $P(ring)$ and $P(boss)$ if they are executing. The complete behaviour is described by $JUNIOR2$:

$$JUNIOR2 \;=\; JUNIOR \;\triangle\; fire \to (\; real \to home \to SKIP$$
$$\Box\; drill \to JUNIOR2)$$

The event *fire* even interrupts the tasks the junior is performing for the boss.   ■

3.5   NOTES

Bibliographic notes

Tony Hoare's original proposal for the language of Communicating Sequential Processes appeared in [45], though that language is quite different to the current version of CSP, presented in this book. In the original language, systems have a specific architecture, consisting of a parallel combination of sequential processes which have their own (private) state variables and which communicate via synchronous channels. The language may be considered as the precursor to the OCCAM programming language [51, 62]. Theoretical work on the language in the early 1980s by Brookes, Hoare, and Roscoe [100, 12, 13, 14] led to the abstraction and generalization of the language to the current form of CSP, which was presented in Hoare's book [47]. Roscoe introduced a way of handling unbounded nondeterminism [101], subsequently refined by Barrett [6]. Tool support for analysis and verification of CSP processes has been provided in the form of animation [34], model-checking [33] (discussed in Appendix B), and embedding within a proof tool [17, 29, 116].

The CSP language is one of a family of process algebras—languages which focus on the communication patterns between processes, and abstract away from their internal computations. These languages all use synchronization on an atomic event as the foundation for process interaction, and all provide some way of expressing event occurrence, choice, parallel composition, abstraction, and recursion. Other languages for concurrency which developed around the same time as CSP and had an influence on its development include Milner's influential Calculus of Communicating Systems (CCS) [76, 77], and Bergstra and Klop's Algebra of Communicating Processes (ACP) [7, 5], which introduced the term *process algebra*. The ISO standard Language Of Temporal Ordering Specifications (LOTOS) [10, 52, 53] combines elements of CCS and CSP together with a language for data-types. The interface parallel originally appeared in the LOTOS language, as a hybrid of CSP's alphabetized parallel and interleaving operators. More recently the Pi-calculus [78] has been introduced. This is a process algebra in the CCS tradition based around the new concept of mobility. Many of these languages are supported by tools; see for example [19, 31, 35, 119], and the TACAS (Tools and Algorithms for the Construction and Analysis of Systems) and CAV (Computer Aided Verification) conference series.

The approach to presenting operational semantics in terms of inference rules was first introduced by Plotkin [91], and has been used extensively within the CCS tradition for language definition. An operational semantics in this form was presented for CSP in [15]. In this chapter the operational semantics has been used primarily for presentational purposes, to introduce the operators of the CSP language and give an understanding of how they behave. Other approaches use the operational rules as the basis for semantic characterizations. One such approach is that of *bisimulation* [89, 77], which considers processes to be equivalent whenever they can match the states reached by each other's transitions. The other main approach is given by *testing* [28, 42], which considers processes to be equivalent if they give the same result in any testing context; this will be discussed in subsequent chapters. It is a significant result that the denotational models discussed throughout this book yield the same equivalences as the testing approach, and can thus be thought of as characterizing testing equivalence.

Other dialects of CSP

As well as defining recursive processes equationally in the style of this book, Hoare's [47] and Roscoe's [103] treatment of recursion make use of the CSP fixpoint operator μ, so that $\mu X \bullet F(X)$ is the least fixed point of the function $F(X)$. This approach has the same expressive power as the use of recursive equations to define processes, since

$$\mu X \bullet F(X) \quad = \quad F(\mu X \bullet F(X))$$

or equivalently

$$\mu X \bullet P \quad = \quad P[\mu X \bullet P/X]$$

The μ operator allows recursive processes to be defined without the need to name them, so the process *LIGHT* of Example 1.3.1 can be defined simply as $\mu X \bullet on \to off \to X$. It also allows nested recursive definitions, such as

$$\mu X \bullet (a \to (\mu Y \bullet a \to X \mid b \to Y))$$

Roscoe uses a more general form of alphabet renaming of processes, by using relations between events rather than functions. If R is a relation on events, then $P[\![R]\!]$ can perform an event b whenever P can perform some event a for which aRb. This single operator encompasses both event renaming and inverse event renaming simply by providing the function f, or its inverse, as the relation R. The relational approach and the functional approaches are equally expressive.

$$
\begin{aligned}
\alpha(STOP) &= \{\} \\
\alpha(a \to P) &= \alpha(P) \cup \{a\} \\
\alpha(x : A \to P(x)) &= \bigcup_{a \in A} \alpha(P(a)) \cup A \\
\alpha(c!v \to P) &= \alpha(P) \cup c.T \\
\alpha(c?x : T \to P(x)) &= \bigcup_{x \in T} \alpha(P(x)) \cup c.T \\
\alpha(SKIP) &= \{\} \\
\alpha(P_1 \,\Box\, P_2) &= \alpha(P_1) \cup \alpha(P_2) \\
\alpha(\textstyle\Box_{i \in I} P_i) &= \bigcup_{i \in I} \alpha(P_i) \\
\alpha(P_1 \,\sqcap\, P_2) &= \alpha(P_1) \cup \alpha(P_2) \\
\alpha(\textstyle\sqcap_{i \in J} P_i) &= \bigcup_{i \in J} \alpha(P_i)
\end{aligned}
$$

Fig. 3.7   Default alphabets for sequential processes

The treatment of termination in this book is marginally different to that presented in [47] and in [103]. The use of the $\checkmark$ event requires certain restrictions on its occurrence to ensure that it models termination suitably. For example, parallel combinations are always required to synchronize on $\checkmark$. Roscoe's treatment ensures that if a process can possibly terminate, then the process itself can choose to terminate and refuse all other interaction: essentially, termination is under the control of the process and cannot be prevented by its environment simply withholding $\checkmark$. Hoare's treatment achieves the same result by imposing a restriction, requiring that $\checkmark$ should never be offered as an alternative in a choice. The treatment in this book differs from each of these, in that $\checkmark$ may be offered as an alternative of a choice, and termination requires the co-operation of the environment. This allows a cleaner relationship between the untimed and the timed languages, while making little difference in practice.

A note on alphabets

Hoare's presentation of CSP in [47] required every process definition to be associated explicitly with an alphabet, which might be thought of as its type. A process definition P is not complete until its alphabet αP had been given. This approach makes an alphabetized parallel operator unnecessary, since in a parallel combination the interfaces are already associated with the component processes, and there is no need for the operator also to supply them.

More recent presentations of CSP have relaxed the requirement to provide alphabets with process definitions, and instead include the interface information with the parallel operator whenever it is used. The two approaches are equally expressive. In this book, the alphabet αP of a process P is used in a less formal way, to mean the interface consisting of all of the events mentioned in the definition of the process P. The alphabet operator is defined in Figures 3.7 and 3.8.

Since chaining is a derived operator, its alphabet can be deduced in the general case from its definition. However, it is good practice to ensure that only processes with alphabets

$$
\begin{aligned}
\alpha(P_1 {}_A\|_B P_2) &= A \cup B \\
\alpha(P_1 \| P_2) &= \alpha(P_1) \cup \alpha(P_2) \\
\alpha(\|_{A_i}^{i \in I} P_i) &= \bigcup_{i \in I} A_i \\
\alpha(\|^{i \in I} P_i) &= \bigcup_{i \in I} \alpha(P_i) \\
\alpha(P_1 \,\|\|\, P_2) &= \alpha(P_1) \cup \alpha(P_2) \\
\alpha(\|\|_{i \in I} P_i) &= \bigcup_{i \in I} \alpha(P_i) \\
\alpha(P_1 \underset{A}{\|} P_2) &= \alpha(P_1) \cup \alpha(P_2) \\
\alpha(P \setminus A) &= \alpha(P) \setminus A \\
\alpha(f(P)) &= f(\alpha(P)) \\
\alpha(l : P) &= f_l(\alpha(P)) \\
\alpha(f^{-1}(P)) &= f^{-1}(\alpha(P)) \\
\alpha(P_1 ; P_2) &= \alpha(P_1) \cup \alpha(P_2) \\
\alpha(P_1 \triangle P_2) &= \alpha(P_1) \cup \alpha(P_2)
\end{aligned}
$$

Fig. 3.8   Further default alphabets

$in.T \cup out.T$ are chained together; if this is indeed both αP_1 and αP_2, then it is also $\alpha(P_1 \gg P_2)$. Similarly, if it is the alphabet of all of the P_i, then it will also be the alphabet of the indexed chain of processes $\gg_{i-1}^{n} P_i$.

In a recursive definition $N = P$, the alphabet $\alpha(N)$ is defined to be the smallest set which makes the equation $\alpha(N) = \alpha(P)$ true.

Exercises

Exercise 3.1 Give the transition graphs of the following processes

1. The process $2COPY$ of Example 3.2.6

2. The process $f(OFFICE)$ of Example 3.2.4

3. The process $f^{-1}(SALE)$ of Example 3.2.5

Exercise 3.2 Give a process which captures the generic behaviour of each cell $C_{i,j}$ in the systolic array *SORTER*, given in Example 2.1.12. What are the appropriate event renaming functions for instantiating the generic process to each cell? Give an alternative definition of *SORTER* as a parallel combination of these renamed components.

Exercise 3.3 If $A \cap B = \{\}$, then does

$$
(((P_1 \underset{A}{\|} P_2) \setminus A) \underset{B}{\|} P_3) \setminus B = ((P_1 \underset{A}{\|} P_2) \underset{B}{\|} P_3) \setminus (A \cup B)
$$

How about if $A \cap B \neq \{\}$?

Exercise 3.4 If P can never reach a deadlock state, does it follow that $P \setminus A$ can never reach one?

Exercise 3.5 A stack with operations *push* and *pop* can be defined in the style of the process *SET* of Example 3.2.9, so that

$$STACK \quad = \quad push?x : T \rightarrow (NODE(x) \parallel i : STACK) \setminus (i.push.T \cup i.pop.T)$$
$$\Box \; pop!empty \rightarrow STACK$$

Give a suitable definition of process $NODE(x)$.

Exercise 3.6 Give the transition graph of the process *PURCHASE* of Example 3.3.1.

Exercise 3.7 Give the transition graph of the process *JUNIOR* of Example 3.4.3.

Exercise 3.8 Does $P_1 \bigtriangleup (P_2 \bigtriangleup P_3)$ have the same behaviour as $(P_1 \bigtriangleup P_2) \bigtriangleup P_3$ (i.e. is the interrupt operator associative)?

Exercise 3.9 A library allows readers to register, and then repeatedly to borrow and return books until deregistration is requested.

$$
\begin{aligned}
NONREADER \quad &= \quad register \rightarrow READER \\
READER \quad &= \quad borrow \rightarrow READER \\
&\qquad \Box \; return \rightarrow READER \\
&\qquad \Box \; deregister \rightarrow STOP
\end{aligned}
$$

Introduce the following constraints, in each case by means of a fresh parallel component:

1. Readers cannot return more books than they have borrowed.

2. Readers are not permitted to deregister if there are any book loans outstanding.

3. Readers can borrow a maximum of three books.

4. Readers cannot deregister.

5. Readers can borrow books only when the library is open. Introduce a new component with extra events *open* and *close*.

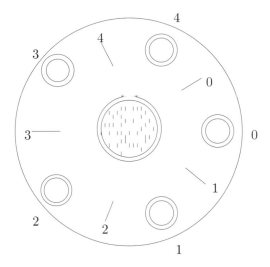

Fig. 3.9   The dining philosophers

Exercise 3.10 This exercise is concerned with the well-known 'dining philosophers' example.

A college consists of five philosophers who think and eat. They eat at a circular dining table. When they need to eat, they enter the dining hall, pick up the chopsticks on either side of their plate, eat, replace the chopsticks, and then leave.

For convenience, the philosophers are labelled 0 to 4. Each philosopher picks up two chopsticks, also labelled 0 to 4. Their relative positions are illustrated in Figure 3.9. The process describing the behaviour of philosopher i has the following interface of events:

{*enter.i*	Philosopher i enters the dining room
eat.i	Philosopher i eats
leave.i	Philosopher i leaves the dining room
pick.i.i	Philosopher i picks up right-hand chopstick
pick.i.$(i + 1 \bmod 5)$	Philosopher i picks up left-hand chopstick
put.i.i	Philosopher i replaces right-hand chopstick
put.i.$(i + 1 \bmod 5)$}	Philosopher i replaces left-hand chopstick

The possible events for $PHIL_i$ are described in the following recursive definition:

$$
\begin{aligned}
PHIL_i \quad = \quad & enter.i \rightarrow \\
& \quad ((pick.i.i \rightarrow pick.i.((i + 1) \bmod 5) \rightarrow eat.i \\
& \quad\quad \rightarrow put.i.i \rightarrow put.i.((i + 1) \bmod 5) \rightarrow leave.i \rightarrow PHIL_i) \\
& \quad \square \\
& \quad (pick.i.((i + 1) \bmod 5) \rightarrow pick.i.i \rightarrow eat.i \\
& \quad\quad \rightarrow put.i.((i + 1) \bmod 5) \rightarrow put.i.i \rightarrow leave.i \rightarrow PHIL_i))
\end{aligned}
$$

The philosophers do not synchronize on any events. Their combination can therefore be described as

$$PHILS \quad = \quad \big|\big|\big|_{i=0}^{4} PHIL_i$$

Each chopstick can be obtained by either of its neighbouring philosophers. The interface of a chopstick j is

$$\{pick.i.j \mid 0 \leqslant i \leqslant 4\} \cup \{put.i.j \mid 0 \leqslant i \leqslant 4\}$$

Its description is given by the following recursive definition:

$$CHOP_j \quad = \quad pick.j.j \rightarrow put.j.j \rightarrow CHOP_j$$
$$\square \ pick.((j-1) \bmod 5).j \rightarrow put.((j-1) \bmod 5).j \rightarrow CHOP_j$$

The chopsticks do not synchronize on any event, so their combination can be described as

$$CHOPSTICKS \quad = \quad \big|\big|\big|_{j=0}^{4} CHOP_j$$

The combination of all the components is then described by the process *COLLEGE*:

$$COLLEGE \quad = \quad PHILS \ \| \ CHOPSTICKS$$

1. Possession of a chopstick by a philosopher blocks a neighbouring philosopher from acquiring that chopstick—this provides a potential for philosophers to block other philosophers by denying them chopsticks. How can the combination *COLLEGE* reach a deadlocked state?

2. Which of the following alterations to *COLLEGE* remove the possibility of deadlock? In each case, describe the amended system in CSP.

   (a) Requiring all philosophers to lift their left chopstick first.
   (b) Requiring at least one philosopher to lift his or her right chopstick first and at least one to lift his or her left chopstick first.
   (c) Introducing a footman who allows only one philosopher to be seated at any time.
   (d) Introducing a butler who prevents all from being seated simultaneously.
   (e) Allowing philosophers to release the chopstick if they hold only one.

3. Which of these guarantee that any philosopher who sits down will eventually receive something to eat?

4. Which of these guarantee that at least one seated philosopher will eventually receive something to eat?

Fig. 3.10   Signals in a pair of segments

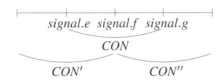

Fig. 3.11   Three pairs of adjacent segments

Exercise 3.11 A railway network imposes the safety constraint that no two trains should ever be on adjacent segments of track. A train moves from one segment of track to the next by passing through a signal. The constraint is imposed by controlling the signals so that they allow trains to pass only when it is safe to do so. An event *signal.i* will be used to describe the event of a train moving past the particular signal *i*.

For each pair of adjacent segments the signals are controlled so that trains may only enter the first segment when both segments are empty. A pair of segments will have three signals: *e* corresponding to a train entering the first segment, *f* corresponding to the train moving from the first to the second, and *g* corresponding to the train leaving the second. This is pictured in Figure 3.10.

If both segments are empty, then a train is allowed to enter the first segment, modelled by the possibility of the event *signal.e*. If the first segment is occupied, then *signal.e* is blocked, but *signal.f* can occur. If the second segment is occupied, then *signal.e* is again blocked, but *signal.g* can occur. These states are interrelated as follows:

$$
\begin{aligned}
EMPTY &= signal.e \rightarrow FIRST \\
FIRST &= signal.f \rightarrow SECOND \\
SECOND &= signal.g \rightarrow EMPTY
\end{aligned}
$$

The safety constraint is imposed by the process *CON* which participates in the control of these three signals by moving between these three states. If the segments are initially empty, then the signal controller *CON* is defined by *CON = EMPTY*. If there is a train initially on the first segment, then *CON = FIRST*. If there is a train initially on the second segment, then *CON = SECOND*. The process *CON* follows the same cycle in all cases, but the point where it starts depends on the presence or otherwise of a train.

A pair of segments is part of a larger system in which each segment is half of another pair, as illustrated in Figure 3.11. The safety property must also hold for these pairs, and will be imposed for them by their own controller processes. Each of them is also involved in

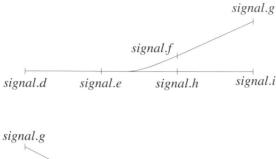

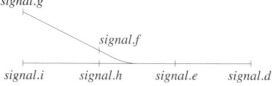

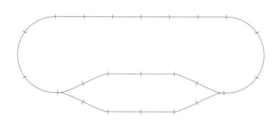

Fig. 3.12   Points sections of track

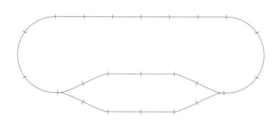

Fig. 3.13   A circuit with junctions

the event *signal.f*, since it corresponds to a train leaving the left-hand pair, and entering the right-hand pair. The event *signal.f* therefore requires the participation of three processes.

1. The constraints on the track may be described as a parallel combination of renamed copies of the generic process *CON*. Describe the conjunction of all the constraints on a circular track of 100 segments, with signals numbered from 0 to 99, and 10 trains initially spaced evenly around the track (travelling in the same direction).

2. Is the system you have described free from any potential deadlock?

3. What is the maximum number of trains for which the system is deadlock-free?

4. How does the CSP system behave if two trains are initially on adjacent segments? Can you improve on the description of *CON* so that it handles this case more satisfactorily?

5. Describe the constraints required to deal with points segments of the form pictured in Figure 3.12.

6. Describe the network pictured in Figure 3.13. Is it deadlock-free if two trains run on it?

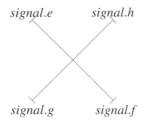

Fig. 3.14   A crossover segment

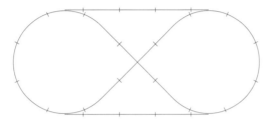

Fig. 3.15   A bi-directional track, with junctions and a crossover

7. Describe the constraints required to deal with crossover segments of Figure 3.14.

8. Alter the description of constraints to deal with (single track) bi-directional segments which trains can traverse in either direction (though trains cannot reverse their direction of travel). Also do this for points and crossover segments.

9. Describe the network (with bi-directional segments) pictured in Figure 3.15, with the trains initially moving in the same direction. Is it deadlock-free if two trains run on it?

Part II

Analysing processes

4

Traces

4.1 SEQUENCES

At the level of abstraction provided by CSP, processes interact with their environment through the performance of events in their interface. Their environment, whether it is another process, a user, or a combination of these, has no direct access to the internal state of the process or to the internal events that it performs. Two processes which are indistinguishable at their interfaces should be equally appropriate for any particular purpose; the way they are implemented cannot have any influence on their respective suitability.

There are a number of ways in which interface behaviour can be analysed, but they all concentrate exclusively on the external activity of the process. One important aspect of process behaviour concerns the occurrence of events in the right order, and that events do not occur at inappropriate points. The kind of sequence which is acceptable will be given by the requirements on the system. Such requirements will describe constraints on when particular events can occur. The environment of the process cannot know precisely which internal state the process has reached at any particular point, since it has access only to the projection of the execution onto the interface.

Example 4.1.1 A safety requirement on the railway crossing controller in Example 1.3.3 might specify that the gate should not rise between the train entering the crossing, and the train leaving the crossing. This can be expressed in terms of the events in the interface: if *train.enter* is the most recently observed of the two events *train.enter* and *train.leave*, then the event *gate.raise* should not occur. Its occurrence at any such point is undesirable in any execution. ∎

To analyse processes with respect to these requirements, it is necessary to consider those sequences of events that can be observed at the interface of the process. These observations are called *traces*, and the set of all possible traces of a process P is denoted 'traces(P)'.

Trace information is concerned with those events that could possibly occur in a process execution. One might imagine an observer watching a process execute, and recording all events in sequence as they are observed. A trace is simply a record of events in the order they occur. The set of traces of a process is the set of all sequences that might possibly be recorded.

To be sure that a process does not violate a trace specification, it is necessary to examine all of its traces and check that each is acceptable.

Notation for sequences

Sequences may be described explicitly, by listing their elements in order between angled brackets. The empty sequence is thus denoted $\langle\rangle$. If A is a set, then A^* is the set of all finite sequences of elements of A. For example, $\langle a, b, a \rangle \in \{a, b, c\}^*$.

If seq_1 and seq_2 are both sequences, then their *concatenation* described by $seq_1 \frown seq_2$ is the sequence of elements in seq_1 followed by those in seq_2. The concatenation operation is associative. The notation seq^n describes n copies of the finite sequence seq concatenated together, and so seq^0 is always the empty sequence $\langle\rangle$.

If seq is a non-empty sequence, then it may be written $\langle a \rangle \frown seq'$ where a is the first element of seq, and seq' is the remainder of the sequence. In this case, two functions on seq are defined: $head(seq) = a$ and $tail(seq) = seq'$. Similarly, if seq is non-empty and finite, then it may also be written as $seq'' \frown \langle b \rangle$, where b is the final element of the sequence seq and seq'' is the sequence of all the elements before it. Two further functions are defined: $foot(seq) = b$ and $init(seq) = seq''$.

The length $\#seq$ of a sequence is the number of elements it contains. For example, $\#\langle a, b, a \rangle = 3$.

The notation a **in** seq means that the element a appears in the sequence seq, and $\sigma(seq)$ is the set of all elements that appear in seq.

Relationships between sequences are easily expressed. If there is some sequence seq_2 such that $seq \frown seq_2 = seq_1$, then seq is a prefix of seq_1, written $seq \leqslant seq_1$. Furthermore, $seq \leqslant_n seq_1$ means that $seq \leqslant seq_1$ and their lengths differ by no more than n. If $seq \neq seq_1$ then seq is a strict prefix of seq_1, written $seq < seq_1$. The notation $seq \preccurlyeq seq_1$ means that seq is a (not necessarily contiguous) subsequence of seq_1.

For example,

$$
\begin{aligned}
\langle a, b, d \rangle &\preccurlyeq \langle a, c, b, a, d \rangle \\
\langle b, c, d \rangle &\npreccurlyeq \langle a, c, b, a, d \rangle \\
\langle a, c, b, a \rangle &\leqslant \langle a, c, b, a, d \rangle
\end{aligned}
$$

The projection of a sequence *seq* onto elements of a set A is written *seq* $\upharpoonright$ A: it is the subsequence of all elements of *seq* that are in the set A. Conversely, the notation *seq* $\setminus$ A is the subsequence of *seq* whose elements are not in A. For example, $\langle a, b, c, a \rangle \upharpoonright \{a, b\} = \langle a, b, a \rangle$, and $\langle a, b, c, a \rangle \setminus \{a, b\} = \langle c \rangle$. If f is a mapping on elements, then $f(seq)$ is the sequence obtained by applying f to each element of *seq* in turn.

These functions can be used to extract information from sequences. For instance, the value of $\#(seq \upharpoonright A)$ gives the number of occurrences of events from A in *seq*. This will be abbreviated *seq* $\downarrow$ A. In the case where A is a singleton set $\{a\}$, the set brackets will be elided and *seq* $\downarrow$ a will abbreviate *seq* $\downarrow$ $\{a\}$. Similarly, *seq* $\upharpoonright$ a will abbreviate *seq* $\upharpoonright$ $\{a\}$.

Notation for traces

Traces are simply a particular class of finite sequences of events drawn from $\Sigma^{\checkmark}$ which represent executions. Since events in a process's execution cannot occur after termination, any termination event $\checkmark$ occurring in a trace must appear at the end. The set of all such traces is defined as *TRACE*.

$$TRACE \quad = \quad \{tr \mid \ \sigma(tr) \subseteq \Sigma^{\checkmark} \wedge \#tr \in \mathbb{N} \wedge \checkmark \notin \sigma(init(tr))\}$$

The sequence $\langle a, c, b, a, d \rangle$ is a record of an execution where the events a, c, b, a, d occurred in that order. The empty sequence $\langle \rangle$ corresponds to an execution in which no events were observed.

Since all traces are sequences, they inherit all of the sequence operators. These all yield a trace when applied to traces, apart from sequence concatenation (and hence repeated concatenation) and mapping through a function.

However, sequence concatenation does map traces tr_1 and tr_2 to a trace $tr_1 \frown tr_2$ provided $\checkmark \notin \sigma(tr_1)$. Thus tr^n will be a trace if $\checkmark \notin \sigma(tr)$.

Furthermore, if a function f maps Σ into Σ and $f(\checkmark) = \checkmark$, then $f(tr)$ will always be a trace.

Events appearing in traces will often be of the form $c.v$, corresponding to a communication of a value v along channel c. In this case the following projections may be defined, where c is not of the form $x.y$ for any x and y:

$$
\begin{aligned}
\mathsf{channel}(c.v) &= c \\
\mathsf{value}(c.v) &= v
\end{aligned}
$$

The channels appearing in a trace tr can then be extracted:

$$\mathsf{channels}(tr) \quad = \quad \{\mathsf{channel}(x) \mid x \ \mathbf{in} \ tr\}$$

The sequence of values appearing on a channel c in a trace tr can also be extracted:

$$tr \Downarrow c = \langle \mathsf{value}(x) \mid x \leftarrow tr, \mathsf{channel}(x) = c \rangle$$

This sequence comprehension describes the sequence of values of items appearing on channel c. It also generalizes to sets of channels C:

$$tr \Downarrow C = \langle \mathsf{value}(x) \mid x \leftarrow tr, \mathsf{channel}(x) \in C \rangle$$

For example, if $tr = \langle in.3, in.6, out.3, in.7, in.9, out.6 \rangle$ then $tr \Downarrow in = \langle 3, 6, 7, 9 \rangle$, and $\mathsf{channels}(tr) = \{in, out\}$.

Traces and executions

The transition rules for CSP define those executions that are possible for processes. Trace information can be extracted from these executions by ignoring the intermediate states and internal transitions, and considering only the visible transitions. A trace is a record of the visible events of an execution.

The notation $P \overset{tr}{\Longrightarrow} P'$ means that there is a sequence of transitions whose initial process is P and whose final process is P', and whose visible transitions constitute the sequence tr. Since termination can occur only at the end of an execution, if $\checkmark$ occurs in tr then it must be at the end. In this case, P' will have no transitions.

The final process may be dropped in cases where it is not required: the notation $P \overset{tr}{\Longrightarrow}$ is used as shorthand for $\exists P' \bullet P \overset{tr}{\Longrightarrow} P'$.

The *traces* of a process may then be defined in terms of the sequences of events that may be exhibited by that process:

$$\mathsf{traces}(P) = \{ tr \mid P \overset{tr}{\Longrightarrow} \}$$

Example 4.1.2 The process $a \rightarrow ((b \rightarrow STOP) \sqcap (c \rightarrow d \rightarrow STOP))$ has the trace $\langle a, c \rangle$ as one of its traces. This may be extracted from the following execution:

$$a \rightarrow ((b \rightarrow STOP) \sqcap (c \rightarrow d \rightarrow STOP))$$
$$\downarrow a$$
$$((b \rightarrow STOP) \sqcap (c \rightarrow d \rightarrow STOP))$$
$$\downarrow \tau$$
$$(c \rightarrow d \rightarrow STOP)$$
$$\downarrow c$$
$$d \rightarrow STOP$$

■

Example 4.1.3 The process *STOP* has no transitions, and hence only one execution, in which it for ever remains in the same state. The trace corresponding to this trace will be the empty trace.

■

4.2 TRACE SEMANTICS

The extraction of trace information from the process transition rules provides an explanation of the relationship between the executions of a process and its traces. However, the operational characterization is too low level for reasoning about processes, since the level of abstraction remains that of process executions, with the set of traces supervenient. The *traces model* for CSP considers processes directly in terms of their traces, and lifts the entire analysis of CSP processes to this more abstract level. All of the operators of the language can be understood at this level: the traces of a composite process are dependent only on the traces of its components. This allows a *compositional* semantic model, where all processes are considered only in terms of their sets of traces, and at no stage do the underlying executions need to be considered explicitly.

In the traces model, each CSP process is associated with a set of traces—the set of all possible sequences of events that may be observed of some execution. Processes will be *trace equivalent* when they have exactly the same set of possible traces. This particular form of equality will be denoted $=_T$, and its definition is that

$$P_1 =_T P_2 \quad = \quad \mathsf{traces}(P_1) = \mathsf{traces}(P_2)$$

In the traces model, processes are equal when they have exactly the same traces. Traces equality gives rise to algebraic laws for individual operators, and also concerning the relationships between various operators. These laws allow manipulation of CSP process descriptions from one form to another while keeping the associated set of traces unchanged. Many laws are concerned with general algebraic properties such as associativity and commutativity of operators (which allow components to be composed in any order), idempotence, and the identification of units and zeros for particular operators (which may allow process descriptions to be simplified). Other laws are concerned with the relationships between different operators, which allow for example the expansion of a parallel combination into a prefix choice process.

In Chapters 6, 8 and 11 more detailed views of process executions will be used to characterize processes in different ways. Some process laws may be concerned only with traces, but others may be true in any of these models. If a law holds in any of these models, as in fact most of those given in this chapter will, then the subscript will be dropped from the equality. Hence $P_1 = P_2$ means not only that $P_1 =_T P_2$, but also that $P_1 =_{SF} P_2$, $P_1 =_{FDI} P_2$ and $P_1 =_{TF} P_2$, corresponding to the equalities that will be defined later, under the more detailed views (stable failures, failures/divergences/infinite traces and timed failures) given in Chapters 6, 8 and 11 respectively. If a law is valid in all of the untimed models, then the equality symbol will be subscripted with a U. For example, the associativity of external choice is true in all models, since the executions of $P_1 \,\Box\, (P_2 \,\Box\, P_3)$ match those of $(P_1 \,\Box\, P_2) \,\Box\, P_3$, so all views of executions of these processes, no matter how detailed, will not distinguish them. The fact that it will be true in any of these models is indicated by the lack of a subscript on the equality symbol.

$$P_1 \,\Box\, (P_2 \,\Box\, P_3) \quad - \quad (P_1 \,\Box\, P_2) \,\Box\, P_3$$

On the other hand, although the traces of $P_1 \square P_2$ and $P_1 \sqcap P_2$ will be the same, a more sophisticated view of process executions will distinguish them. This law will be written as

$$P_1 \square P_2 \quad =_T \quad P_1 \sqcap P_2$$

since it is true only in the traces model.

Any set of traces S associated with some process must contain the empty trace: any process can be observed to do nothing. It will also be prefix closed: if a process can perform a sequence of events, then it can also be observed to perform any prefix of that sequence. These properties are formalized as $T1$ and $T2$ on set S:

$T1 \qquad \langle\rangle \in S$

$T2 \qquad \forall tr_1, tr_2 : TRACE \bullet (tr_1 \leqslant tr_2 \wedge tr_2 \in S \Rightarrow tr_1 \in S)$

STOP

There is only one trace associated with the process *STOP*, and that is the empty trace. The semantics of *STOP* is given directly as

$$\mathsf{traces}(STOP) \quad = \quad \{\langle\rangle\}$$

Prefixing

In an observation of the process $a \to P$, there are two possibilities: either the event a has not occurred, in which case the observation must be $\langle\rangle$, or else the event a has occurred and the rest of the trace derives from process P.

$$\mathsf{traces}(a \to P) \quad = \quad \{\langle\rangle\}$$
$$\cup$$
$$\{\langle a\rangle \frown tr \mid tr \in \mathsf{traces}(P)\}$$

Prefix choice

An observation of the process $x : A \to P(x)$ is again one of two possibilities. Either no event has yet occurred, or else an event a in A has occurred, and the subsequent behaviour is that of the corresponding process $P(a)$.

$$\mathsf{traces}(x : A \to P(x)) \quad = \quad \{\langle\rangle\}$$
$$\cup$$
$$\{\langle a\rangle \frown tr \mid a \in A \wedge tr \in \mathsf{traces}(P(a))\}$$

$$x : \{\} \to P(x) = STOP \qquad\qquad \langle STOP\text{-step}\rangle$$
$$x : \{b\} \to P(x) = b \to P(b) \qquad\qquad \langle\text{prefix}\rangle$$

Fig. 4.1 *Laws for prefix choice*

Example 4.2.1 The process BUS_1 of Example 1.4.1 is described as follows:

$$BUS\_1 \;=\; \begin{array}{l} board.A \to (pay.90 \to alight.B \to STOP \\ \mid alight.A \to STOP) \end{array}$$

This process has the following traces:

$$\mathsf{traces}(BUS\_1) \;=\; \{\langle\rangle,$$
$$\langle board.A\rangle,$$
$$\langle board.A, pay.90\rangle,$$
$$\langle board.A, pay.90, alight.B\rangle,$$
$$\langle board.A, alight.A\rangle\}$$

It initially allows *board.A*, after which either the fare is paid and the journey made, or else the journey is not made and the passenger alights again. ∎

The definition of $\mathsf{traces}(x : A \to P(x))$ has two special cases: where A contains no elements ($A = \{\}$) and where A contains but a single element ($A = \{b\}$).

In the case where $A = \{\}$, the second clause of the definition cannot be met, since there is no event a for which $a \in A$. The semantics is thus equal to $\{\langle\rangle\}$, which is the semantics of *STOP*. In the case where $A = \{b\}$, the second clause of the definition is equivalent to

$$\{\langle b\rangle \frown tr \mid tr \in \mathsf{traces}(P(b))\}$$

which is the second clause of the event prefix definition for $b \to P(b)$. These observations support two *laws* concerning equality of process expressions, given in Figure 4.1.

Output and input

The output and input constructors are special cases of the prefix and prefix choice operators. The definition of their trace semantics follows the same pattern.

$$\mathsf{traces}(c!v \to P) \;=\; \{\langle\rangle\}$$
$$\cup \{\langle c.v\rangle \frown tr \mid tr \in \mathsf{traces}(P)\}$$

$$\text{traces}(c?m : T \to P(m)) \quad = \quad \{\langle\rangle\}$$
$$\cup \{\langle c.v \rangle \frown tr \mid v \in T \land tr \in \text{traces}(P(v))\}$$

Example 4.2.2 The traces of the process $in?x : \mathbb{Z} \to out!x \to STOP$ are given as follows:

$$\text{traces}(in?x : \mathbb{Z} \to out!x \to STOP) \quad = \quad \{\langle\rangle\}$$
$$\cup \{\langle in.v \rangle \mid v \in \mathbb{Z}\}$$
$$\cup \{\langle in.v, out.v \rangle \mid v \in \mathbb{Z}\}$$

An observation of this process might contain no events, or a single input, or an input of a particular value followed by output of that same value. ■

SKIP

The atomic process *SKIP* is used to denote successful termination, and it signals this by means of the termination event $\checkmark$, the only event it can perform. The only traces it exhibits are the empty trace and the singleton trace containing $\checkmark$.

$$\text{traces}(SKIP) \quad = \quad \{\langle\rangle, \langle\checkmark\rangle\}$$

RUN

The CSP operators describing choice and concurrency exhibit a number of useful laws on processes. A particular process which interacts well with them is the process *RUN*, defined to be the process which can do any sequence of events. It may be defined directly in the traces model as follows:

$$\text{traces}(RUN) \quad = \quad \{tr \mid tr \in TRACE\}$$

The semantics of this process consists of all possible traces. It is the most obliging process, always willing to perform any event. It may also be recursively defined using the existing operators of the language, as follows:

$$RUN \quad = \quad (x : \Sigma \to RUN) \,\square\, SKIP$$

This process may also be defined with a particular interface $A \subseteq \Sigma$. The process RUN_A is defined to be the process with interface A that can always perform any event in its interface. Its trace set is given as follows:

$$\text{traces}(RUN_A) \quad = \quad \{tr \mid tr \in TRACE \land \sigma(tr) \subseteq A\}$$

$$P \square P = P \qquad\qquad \langle \square\text{-idem} \rangle$$
$$P_1 \square (P_2 \square P_3) = (P_1 \square P_2) \square P_3 \qquad\qquad \langle \square\text{-assoc} \rangle$$
$$P_1 \square P_2 = P_2 \square P_1 \qquad\qquad \langle \square\text{-sym} \rangle$$
$$P \square STOP = P \qquad\qquad \langle \square\text{-unit} \rangle$$
$$P \square RUN =_T RUN \qquad\qquad \langle \square\text{-zero}_T \rangle$$
$$x : A \to P_1(x) \square y : B \to P_2(y) \qquad\qquad \langle \square\text{-step} \rangle$$
$$= z : A \cup B \to R(z) \text{where}$$
$$\begin{aligned} R(c) &= P_1(c) && \text{if } c \in A \setminus B \\ &= P_2(c) && \text{if } c \in B \setminus A \\ &= P_1(c) \sqcap P_2(c) && \text{if } c \in A \cap B \end{aligned}$$

Fig. 4.2   Laws for external choice

or it might alternatively be defined recursively using choice constructs:

$$RUN_A \quad = \quad x : A \to RUN_A$$

$RUN_{A\checkmark}$ behaves as RUN_A but it can also terminate:

$$RUN_{A\checkmark} \quad = \quad (x : A \to RUN_A) \square SKIP$$

The process RUN defined above is equivalent to $RUN_{\Sigma\checkmark}$.

External choice

An observer of the choice construct $P_1 \square P_2$ might observe an execution of P_1, or of P_2; there are no other possibilities. The possible traces of the choice consist of the union of the two sets of traces:

$$\text{traces}(P_1 \square P_2) \quad = \quad \text{traces}(P_1) \cup \text{traces}(P_2)$$

The treatment of external choice as the union of trace sets means that the operator inherits the properties of the union operator, in particular idempotence, associativity, and commutativity, as given in the first three laws of Figure 4.2.

The first of these laws, $\square$-idem, states that offering a choice between two copies of the same process is not actually offering a choice at all. The second and third laws allow larger sets of choices to be rearranged without altering the trace possibilities. These are the laws that guarantee that the definition of the indexed choice operator is well-defined. They allow a choice of processes to be defined purely in terms of the set of choices.

Law □-unit states that external choice gives any process *P* precedence over *STOP*, which can never resolve a choice in its favour. Law □-zero*ₜ* states that external choice allows any process *P* to be masked by *RUN*: in a choice with *RUN*, if the choice does happen to be resolved in favour of *P*, then any trace corresponding to such an execution of *P* is also possible for *RUN*. Thus every trace of *P* □ *RUN* is a trace of *RUN*, and the presence of *RUN* as an alternative masks the executions of *P*. In algebraic terms, *STOP* is a unit of external choice, and *RUN* is a zero.

Finally, an external choice of two menu choices may be rewritten as a single menu choice. Law □-step gives the correspondence. The events that are on offer in the menu choice must consist of all events that are on offer in one or other of the two component menu choices. If an event is chosen which was offered only by one component, then the subsequent behaviour must be determined by that component. If the chosen event was actually offered by both components, then the choice as to which one is subsequently executed is made internally—the environment could choose the event, but cannot choose which subsequent behaviour will arise.

Example 4.2.3 The choice between the two buses given in Example 1.4.1 is the choice *BUS_1* □ *BUS_2* where

$$BUS\_1 \quad = \quad board.A \rightarrow (pay.90 \rightarrow alight.B \rightarrow STOP$$
$$| \ alight.A \rightarrow STOP)$$

$$BUS\_2 \quad = \quad board.A \rightarrow (pay.70 \rightarrow alight.B \rightarrow STOP$$
$$| \ alight.A \rightarrow STOP)$$

Law □-step can be applied to this choice of processes. Since both components have the same single first event, the choice reduces as follows:

$$BUS\_1 \ \square \ BUS\_2 \quad =_T \quad board.A \rightarrow ((pay.90 \rightarrow alight.B \rightarrow STOP$$
$$| \ alight.A \rightarrow STOP)$$
$$\sqcap$$
$$(pay.70 \rightarrow alight.B \rightarrow STOP$$
$$| \ alight.A \rightarrow STOP))$$

This equivalence reflects the fact that the environment has no control over which of two copies of the same event is actually chosen; the choice is instead resolved internally when the event is selected. ∎

Example 4.2.4 Process P_1 offers a choice between events *a* and *b*, and P_2 offers a choice between *b* and *c*, as follows:

$$P_1 \quad = \quad a \rightarrow d \rightarrow STOP$$
$$| \ b \rightarrow e \rightarrow STOP$$

$$P_2 \quad = \quad b \rightarrow f \rightarrow STOP$$
$$| \ c \rightarrow g \rightarrow STOP$$

$$\Box_{i\in\{\}} P_i = STOP \qquad\qquad \langle\Box\text{-unit}\rangle$$

$$\sqcap_{i\in I}(x : A_i \to P_i(x)) = x : (\bigcup_{i\in I} A_i) \to \sqcap_{\{i|x\in A_i\}} P_i(x) \qquad \langle\Box\text{-step}\rangle$$

Fig. 4.3   Laws for indexed external choice

The external choice $P_1 \Box P_2$ between P_1 and P_2 offers a choice between the events a, b, and c. The environment may choose between these events, but this is the extent of its control over subsequent behaviour.

$$
\begin{aligned}
P_1 \Box P_2 \quad =_T \quad & a \to d \to STOP \\
& | \; b \to (e \to STOP \\
& \qquad\qquad \sqcap f \to STOP) \\
& | \; c \to g \to STOP
\end{aligned}
$$

If b is chosen, then the next event could be either e or f, and the choice between them will be made internally by the process $P_1 \Box P_2$.   ∎

The executions of the indexed external choice $\Box_{i\in I} P_i$ are the executions of all of its components. Its traces are given as follows:

$$\mathsf{traces}(\Box_{i\in I} P_i) \quad = \quad \bigcup_{i\in I} \mathsf{traces}(P_i) \cup \{\langle\rangle\}$$

The explicit inclusion of the empty trace $\langle\rangle$ is required in the case when I is the empty set. When the set I is non-empty, then inclusion of $\langle\rangle$ is redundant since it will be included in any of the trace sets $\mathsf{traces}(P_i)$.

There are two laws particular to indexed external choice. They are given in Figure 4.3. The first law states that an empty indexed choice is a process that can do nothing. The second law is a generalization of Law $\Box$-**step**. It states that a indexed external choice of prefix choices is equivalent to a single prefix choice over all the possible first events (i.e. the union of all the component choice sets). The process subsequent to a given x is any of the corresponding processes $P_i(x)$ from one of the prefix choices which offered x (i.e. for which $x \in A_i$).

Internal choice

The internal choice $P_1 \sqcap P_2$ behaves either as P_1 or as P_2, and its environment exercises no control over which. A recorder of traces is concerned only with the executions that are possible, and these are the executions of P_1 and of P_2. The traces of $P_1 \sqcap P_2$ are therefore

$$\mathsf{traces}(P_1 \sqcap P_2) \quad = \quad \mathsf{traces}(P_1) \cup \mathsf{traces}(P_2)$$

$$P \sqcap P = P \qquad\qquad\qquad \langle\sqcap\text{-idem}\rangle$$

$$P_1 \sqcap (P_2 \sqcap P_3) = (P_1 \sqcap P_2) \sqcap P_3 \qquad\qquad \langle\sqcap\text{-assoc}\rangle$$

$$P_1 \sqcap P_2 = P_2 \sqcap P_1 \qquad\qquad\qquad \langle\sqcap\text{-sym}\rangle$$

$$P_1 \sqcap P_2 =_T P_1 \;\square\; P_2 \qquad\qquad\qquad \langle\text{choice-equiv}_T\rangle$$

Fig. 4.4   Laws for internal choice

This form of choice has different executions to the external choice $P_1 \;\square\; P_2$, since the choice is first resolved by an internal τ transition before the appropriate choice begins execution. However, this internal transition is not recorded in any trace, and a trace observer is not concerned with identifying where responsibility lies for particular choices, but only with the possible sequences of events. Under these circumstances, the internal and external choice constructs are not distinguished. Both exhibit precisely the same possible sequences of visible events, and their trace semantics are identical. Examination of a process's set of traces is not adequate for detecting the presence or absence of nondeterminism. More detailed observations are required to distinguish internal from external choice, and these will be introduced in Chapter 6.

Since they are currently treated the same way, the internal choice operator satisfies the same laws as the external choice operator, though only in the traces model. The useful laws are given in Figure 4.4.

The indexed internal choice $\bigsqcap_{i \in J} P_i$ (where the indexing set J must be non-empty) is able to behave as any of its component processes. Its traces will therefore be the indexed union of the traces of all of its constituents:

$$\text{traces}(\textstyle\bigsqcap_{i \in J} P_i) \;=\; \bigcup_{i \in J} \text{traces}(P_i)$$

Alphabetized parallel

A parallel combination $P_1 \;_A\|_B\; P_2$ consists of P_1 performing events in A, and P_2 performing events in B. Processes P_1 and P_2 synchronize on events in $A \cap B$, and perform their other events independently.

Since P_1 is involved in the performance of all events from A, any execution of the parallel combination projected onto A must be an execution of P_1. Similarly, any execution projected onto B must be an execution of P_2. The traces of $P_1 \;_A\|_B\; P_2$ are those sequences of events which are consistent with both P_1 and P_2. Only events in A or B, or termination, can be performed, so the set of events in the trace must be contained in $(A \cup B)^{\checkmark}$:

$$
\begin{aligned}
\text{traces}(P_1 \; {}_A\|_B \; P_2) \;\; = \;\; \{ tr \in TRACE \mid \;\; & tr \upharpoonright A^{\checkmark} \in \text{traces}(P_1) \\
& \wedge \; tr \upharpoonright B^{\checkmark} \in \text{traces}(P_2) \\
& \wedge \; \sigma(tr) \subseteq (A \cup B)^{\checkmark} \}
\end{aligned}
$$

Example 4.2.5 The traces of $P_1 = a \to STOP$ are given by $\text{traces}(P_1) = \{\langle\rangle, \langle a\rangle\}$. Similarly, the traces of $P_2 = b \to STOP$ are given by $\text{traces}(P_2) = \{\langle\rangle, \langle b\rangle\}$. A trace of $P_1 \; {}_{\{a\}}\|_{\{b\}} \; P_2$ must be a sequence of events from $\{a, b, \checkmark\}$ whose projection to $\{a, \checkmark\}$ is either $\langle\rangle$ or $\langle a\rangle$, and whose projection to $\{b, \checkmark\}$ is either $\langle\rangle$ or $\langle b\rangle$. There are five such traces:

$$\{\langle\rangle, \langle a\rangle, \langle b\rangle, \langle a, b\rangle, \langle b, a\rangle\}$$

and so this set is $\text{traces}(P_1 \; {}_{\{a\}}\|_{\{b\}} \; P_2)$. ■

Example 4.2.6 The traces of the process $P_1 = a \to b \to STOP$ are given as $\text{traces}(P_1) = \{\langle\rangle, \langle a\rangle, \langle a, b\rangle\}$. Similarly, the traces of $P_2 = b \to c \to STOP$ are given by $\text{traces}(P_2) = \{\langle\rangle, \langle b\rangle, \langle b, c\rangle\}$. A trace of $P_1 \; {}_{\{a,b\}}\|_{\{b,c\}} \; P_2$ must be a sequence of events from $\{a, b, c, \checkmark\}$ whose projection to $\{a, b, \checkmark\}$ is either $\langle\rangle$, $\langle a\rangle$, or $\langle a, b\rangle$, and whose projection to $\{b, c, \checkmark\}$ is either $\langle\rangle$, $\langle b\rangle$, or $\langle b, c\rangle$. The existence of the event b in the interfaces of both P_1 and P_2 means that both processes have control over its occurrence, and its appearance in any trace must be consistent with both components. The process P_1 forces event b to occur after the event a, and P_2 forces b to occur before c. The set of traces consistent with both processes is therefore

$$\{\langle\rangle, \langle a\rangle, \langle a, b\rangle, \langle a, b, c\rangle\}$$

and so this set is $\text{traces}(P_1 \; {}_{\{a,b\}}\|_{\{b,c\}} \; P_2)$. ■

There are a number of trace laws concerning the parallel operator. These are listed in Figure 4.5.

Law $\|$-idem$_T$ is a form of idempotence: if the interface A provided for P allows all of its possible events—$\alpha(P) \subseteq A$—then the traces of P are the same as the traces of two copies of P running together. Any execution of P can be performed by both copies of P executing together synchronizing on every event. Laws $\|$-assoc and $\|$-sym are the associativity and commutativity laws for the parallel operator. The intermediate interfaces in Law $\|$-assoc depend on the order in which components are composed together, but the resulting process is the same in each case. Law $\|$-unit$_U$ provides a unit for the parallel operator: the process $RUN_{(A\cap B)^{\checkmark}}$, which is always prepared to perform any event in the common interface, and hence places no restriction on P's performance of those events. The construction of the interfaces means that the process P is not prevented from performing events in $A \setminus B$ either, so P in $P \; {}_A\|_B \; RUN_{(A\cap B)^{\checkmark}}$ is able to perform any of its executions, and the resulting process behaves exactly as P.

$$P \,_A\|_A\, P =_T P \quad \text{if } \alpha(P) \subseteq A \qquad\qquad \langle\|\text{-idem}_T\rangle$$

$$P_1 \,_A\|_B\, P_2 = P_2 \,_B\|_A\, P_1 \qquad\qquad \langle\|\text{-sym}\rangle$$

$$P_1 \,_A\|_{B \cup C}\, (P_2 \,_B\|_C\, P_3) = (P_1 \,_A\|_B\, P_2) \,_{A \cup B}\|_C\, P_3 \qquad\qquad \langle\|\text{-assoc}\rangle$$

$$P \,_A\|_B\, RUN_{(A \cap B)^\checkmark} =_U P \quad \text{if } \alpha(P) \subseteq A \qquad\qquad \langle\|\text{-unit}_U\rangle$$

$$C \subseteq A \wedge D \subseteq B \Rightarrow \qquad\qquad \langle\|\text{-step}\rangle$$

$$(x : C \to P_1(x)) \,_A\|_B\, (y : D \to P_2(y))$$

$$= z : ((C \setminus B) \cup (D \setminus A) \cup (C \cap D)) \to R(z)$$

where

$$\begin{aligned}
R(c) &= P_1(c) \,_A\|_B\, (y : D \to P_2(y)) &&\text{if } c \in C \setminus B \\
&= (x : C \to P_1(x)) \,_A\|_B\, P_2(c) &&\text{if } c \in D \setminus A \\
&= P_1(c) \,_A\|_B\, P_2(c) &&\text{if } c \in C \cap D
\end{aligned}$$

$$SKIP \,_A\|_B\, SKIP = SKIP \qquad\qquad \langle\|\text{-term 1}\rangle$$

$$(x : C \to P(x)) \,_A\|_B\, SKIP = x : C \cap (A \setminus B) \to (P(x) \,_A\|_B\, SKIP) \qquad\qquad \langle\|\text{-term 2}\rangle$$

Fig. 4.5   Laws for alphabetized parallel

Law $\|$-step shows how to reduce a parallel combination of prefix choices to a single prefix choice. The events that are initially possible are those that either side can perform without the co-operation of the other, together with those that both are initially ready to perform. The events that are blocked are those that only one side is ready to perform but where the co-operation of both is required. Figure 4.6 illustrates the situation, where process P_1 with interface A is initially able to perform events in C, and P_2 with interface B is initially able to perform events in D: the events that can initially be performed are those in the shaded regions.

Laws $\|$-term 1 and $\|$-term 2 are concerned with termination of a parallel combination. If both components are ready to terminate, then termination occurs. If only one component is ready for termination, then only the possibilities of the other side are initially available.

Example 4.2.7 The parallel combination

$$\begin{array}{l}
(a \to STOP \\
\mid c \to STOP)
\end{array} \,_{\{a,b,c\}}\|_{\{b,c,d,e\}}\, \begin{array}{l}
(b \to STOP \\
\mid c \to STOP \\
\mid d \to STOP)
\end{array}$$

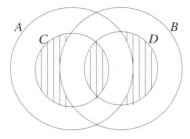

Fig. 4.6   Initial offers of a parallel combination

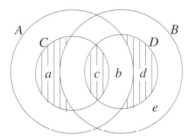

Fig. 4.7   Initial offers of the parallel combination of Example 4.2.7

can be reduced to a single prefix choice using Law $\|$-**step**. The interface sets are $A = \{a, b, c\}$ and $B = \{b, c, d, e\}$, and the initial choice sets are $C = \{a, c\}$ and $D = \{b, c, d\}$. In all cases, the subsequent processes $P_1(x)$ and $P_2(y)$ are *STOP*.

The initial choice is given by $(C \setminus B) \cup (D \setminus A) \cup (B \cap C)$. The set $C \setminus B = \{a\}$ is the set of events that can be performed initially by the left-hand process independently of the right-hand one. The set $D \setminus A = \{d\}$ is the set of events that can be performed initially be the right-hand process independently of the left. Finally, the set $B \cap C = \{c\}$ is the set of events that both processes can initially synchronize on. The combined set of events that are initially on offer is the union of these possibilities: the set $\{a, c, d\}$. Event b is blocked by the left-hand side, and event e is not offered by the right-hand side. This situation is illustrated in Figure 4.7.

Law $\|$-**step** also describes the processes subsequent to each of these events:

$$a \rightarrow (STOP \ _{\{a,b,c\}}\|_{\{b,c,d,e\}} \quad b \rightarrow STOP$$
$$| \ c \rightarrow STOP$$
$$| \ d \rightarrow STOP)$$
$$| \ d \rightarrow (a \rightarrow STOP \ | \ c \rightarrow STOP \ _{\{a,b,c\}}\|_{\{b,c,d,e\}} STOP)$$
$$| \ c \rightarrow (STOP \ _{\{a,b,c\}}\|_{\{b,c,d,e\}} STOP)$$

Law ||-step is applicable to each subsequent behaviour. The process following the performance of a is given by

$$STOP \; {}_{\{a,b,c\}}||_{\{b,c,d,e\}} \quad (b \to STOP$$
$$| \; c \to STOP$$
$$| \; d \to STOP)$$
$$= \quad d \to (STOP \; {}_{\{a,b,c\}}||_{\{b,c,d,e\}} \; STOP) \qquad \text{||-step}$$
$$= \quad d \to STOP \qquad\qquad\qquad\qquad STOP\text{-step}$$

The other branches of the initial choice reduce in a similar way, resulting in the following description, which is given entirely in terms of prefix and choice:

$$a \to d \to STOP$$
$$| \; d \to a \to STOP$$
$$| \; c \to STOP$$

Components either perform a and d independently, or synchronize on c. ■

Example 4.2.8 Two processes $P_1 = a \to b \to STOP$ and $P_2 = b \to c \to STOP$ are required to synchronize on a, b, and c.

$$(a \to b \to STOP) \; {}_{\{a,b,c\}}||_{\{a,b,c\}} \; (b \to c \to STOP)$$

The operational semantics for this process has no transitions, so it behaves the same way as $STOP$. The laws for parallel composition allow this conclusion to be reached by reasoning at the level of trace equivalences.

The interface sets A and B are both $\{a, b, c\}$, the initial set for P_1 is $C = \{a\}$, and the initial set for P_2 is $D = \{b\}$. The events initially on offer are given by the union of $C \setminus B$ (the events that P_1 can perform independently of P_2), $D \setminus A$ (the events that P_2 can perform independently of P_1), and $C \cap D$ (the events on which they can initially synchronize). Each of these sets is the empty set $\{\}$, so Law ||-step states that

$$P_1 \; {}_A||_B \; P_2 \quad = \quad x : \{\} \to P(x)$$
$$= \quad STOP \qquad\qquad \text{by } STOP\text{-step}$$

The parallel combination deadlocks immediately—no events can initially be performed. ■

Example 4.2.9 The parallel combination

$$a \to b \to STOP \; {}_{\{a,b\}}||_{\{b,c\}} \; b \to c \to STOP$$

can be rewritten to remove the parallel operator using the laws for parallel. The laws *STOP*-step and prefix are used implicitly to treat event prefixes and *STOP* as prefix choices.

$$
\begin{aligned}
& a \to b \to STOP \, _{\{a,b\}}\|_{\{b,c\}} \, b \to c \to STOP \\
= \ & a \to ((b \to STOP) \, _{\{a,b\}}\|_{\{b,c\}} \, b \to c \to STOP) \qquad \text{by } \|\text{-step} \\
= \ & a \to b \to (STOP \, _{\{a,b\}}\|_{\{b,c\}} \, c \to STOP) \qquad\quad \text{by } \|\text{-step} \\
= \ & a \to b \to c \to STOP \qquad\qquad\qquad\qquad\quad \text{by } \|\text{-step}
\end{aligned}
$$

At the first step the event b is blocked by the left-hand process, and only event a is possible. This is reflected in the application of the law, which does not make b available at the first step because it is not a choice offered by both sides.   ■

Example 4.2.10 Two processes

$$
\begin{aligned}
P_1 &= a \to x \to STOP \mid b \to y \to STOP \\
P_2 &= c \to x \to STOP \mid d \to y \to STOP
\end{aligned}
$$

have respective interfaces

$$
\begin{aligned}
A &= \{a, b, x, y\} \\
B &= \{c, d, x, y\}
\end{aligned}
$$

They are intended to operate independently on the events a, b, c, and d, but to synchronize on the events x and y. Their combination is described as

$$
P_1 \, _A\|_B \, P_2
$$

$$P \ _\Sigma\|_\Sigma \ RUN =_U P \qquad\qquad \langle\|\text{-unit}_U\rangle$$

$$P \ _A\|_\Sigma \ STOP =_T STOP \qquad\qquad \langle\|\text{-zero}_T\rangle$$

Fig. 4.8 Further laws for parallel

All the first events of each process are independent of the other process, and so all are initially available in the parallel combination. An application of Law ||-**step** gives

$$
\begin{aligned}
&P_1 \ _A\|_B \ P_2 \\
=\ \ &a \to ((x \to STOP) \ _A\|_B \ P_2) \qquad\qquad \text{by ||-step} \\
&\mid b \to ((y \to STOP) \ _A\|_B \ P_2) \\
&\mid c \to (P_1 \ _A\|_B \ x \to STOP) \\
&\mid d \to (P_1 \ _A\|_B \ y \to STOP) \\
=\ \ &a \to (c \to ((x \to STOP) \ _A\|_B \ x \to STOP) \qquad \text{by ||-step} \\
&\qquad\quad \mid d \to ((x \to STOP) \ _A\|_B \ y \to STOP)) \\
&\mid b \to (c \to ((y \to STOP) \ _A\|_B \ x \to STOP) \\
&\qquad\quad \mid d \to ((y \to STOP) \ _A\|_B \ y \to STOP)) \\
&\mid c \to (a \to ((x \to STOP) \ _A\|_B \ x \to STOP) \\
&\qquad\quad \mid b \to ((y \to STOP) \ _A\|_B \ x \to STOP)) \\
&\mid d \to (a \to ((x \to STOP) \ _A\|_B \ y \to STOP) \\
&\qquad\quad \mid b \to ((y \to STOP) \ _A\|_B \ y \to STOP)) \\
=\ \ &a \to (c \to x \to STOP \qquad\qquad\qquad \text{by ||-step} \\
&\qquad\quad \mid d \to STOP) \\
&\mid b \to (c \to STOP \\
&\qquad\quad \mid d \to y \to STOP) \\
&\mid c \to (a \to x \to STOP \\
&\qquad\quad \mid b \to STOP) \\
&\mid d \to (a \to STOP \\
&\qquad\quad \mid b \to y \to STOP)
\end{aligned}
$$

In order for the two components to synchronize on an x or y event, they must independently follow paths that lead to the same event. ∎

The parallel operator has process $STOP$ as a zero, and RUN as a unit, as given in Figure 4.8.

When applying the laws of parallel to expand a parallel composition $P_1 \parallel P_2$, the implicit interface sets $\alpha(P_1)$ and $\alpha(P_2)$ must first be made explicit. The process $P_1 \parallel P_2$ is an abbreviation for $P_1 \ _{\alpha(P_1)}\|_{\alpha(P_2)} \ P_2$.

Interleaving

An interleaving of two processes $P_1 \mathbin{|||} P_2$ executes each component entirely independently of the other, until termination. Traces of the combination will therefore appear as *interleavings* of traces of the two component processes.

A trace tr is an interleaving of two others tr_1 and tr_2 if each occurrence of each event from tr_1 and tr_2 appears exactly once in tr, and events from tr_1 and tr_2 occur in the same order. They must also agree on termination. This is denoted tr interleaves tr_1, tr_2. For example,

$$\langle a, c, b \rangle \text{ interleaves } \langle a, b \rangle, \langle c \rangle$$

$$\langle a, d \rangle \text{ interleaves } \langle \rangle, \langle a, d \rangle$$

This may be formally defined by a structural induction on sequences:

$$\langle \rangle \text{ interleaves } tr_1, tr_2 \quad \Leftrightarrow \quad tr_1 = tr_2 = \langle \rangle$$
$$\langle \checkmark \rangle \text{ interleaves } tr_1, tr_2 \quad \Leftrightarrow \quad tr_1 = tr_2 = \langle \checkmark \rangle$$

$$\langle a \rangle \frown tr \neq \langle \checkmark \rangle \Rightarrow$$
$$\langle a \rangle \frown tr \text{ interleaves } tr_1, tr_2 \quad \Leftrightarrow \quad head(tr_1) = a \wedge tr \text{ interleaves } tail(tr_1), tr_2$$
$$\vee \; head(tr_2) = a \wedge tr \text{ interleaves } tr_1, tail(tr_2)$$

If a trace beginning with a interleaves two others, then one of those two must begin with a, and the subsequent trace must be an interleaving of the subsequent two traces.

Any trace of the interleaved process $P_1 \mathbin{|||} P_2$ will be an interleaving of a trace from P_1 and a trace from P_2. The traces of $P_1 \mathbin{|||} P_2$ are given as follows:

$$traces\,(P_1 \mathbin{|||} P_2) \quad = \quad \{tr \in TRACE \mid \exists\, tr_1, tr_2 \bullet \; tr_1 \in traces(P_1) \wedge$$
$$tr_2 \in traces(P_2) \wedge$$
$$tr \text{ interleaves } tr_1, tr_2\}$$

Example 4.2.11 The traces of $(a \to b \to STOP) \mathbin{|||} (c \to STOP)$ are calculated from the trace sets of the two component processes:

$$traces(a \to b \to STOP) \quad = \quad \{\langle \rangle, \langle a \rangle, \langle a, b \rangle\}$$
$$traces(c \to STOP) \quad = \quad \{\langle \rangle, \langle c \rangle\}$$

The traces of the combined process is made up of all possible interleavings of pairs of traces:

$$traces((a \to b \to STOP) \mathbin{|||} (c \to STOP))$$
$$= \quad \{\langle \rangle, \langle a \rangle, \langle a, b \rangle, \langle c \rangle, \langle a, c \rangle, \langle c, a \rangle, \langle a, b, c \rangle, \langle a, c, b \rangle, \langle c, a, b \rangle\}$$

$$P_1 \mathbin{|||} P_2 = P_2 \mathbin{|||} P_1 \qquad\qquad \langle\mathbin{|||}\text{-sym}\rangle$$

$$P_1 \mathbin{|||} (P_2 \mathbin{|||} P_3) = (P_1 \mathbin{|||} P_2) \mathbin{|||} P_3 \qquad\qquad \langle\mathbin{|||}\text{-assoc}\rangle$$

$$P \mathbin{|||} SKIP = P \qquad\qquad \langle\mathbin{|||}\text{-unit}\rangle$$

$$P \mathbin{|||} RUN_\Sigma =_T RUN_\Sigma \qquad\qquad \langle\mathbin{|||}\text{-zero}_T\rangle$$

$$(x : C \to P_1(x)) \mathbin{|||} (y : D \to P_2(y)) = z : (C \cup D) \to R(z) \qquad\qquad \langle\mathbin{|||}\text{-step}\rangle$$

where

$$
\begin{aligned}
R(c) \;=\;& P_1(c) \mathbin{|||} (y : D \to P_2(y)) && \text{if } c \in C \setminus D \\
\;=\;& (x : C \to P_1(x)) \mathbin{|||} P_2(c) && \text{if } c \in D \setminus C \\
\;=\;& P_1(c) \mathbin{|||} (y : D \to P_2(y)) && \text{if } c \in C \cap D \\
& \sqcap\, (x : C \to P_1(x)) \mathbin{|||} P_2(c)
\end{aligned}
$$

$$SKIP \mathbin{|||} SKIP = SKIP \qquad\qquad \langle\mathbin{|||}\text{-term 1}\rangle$$

$$(x : C \to P(x)) \mathbin{|||} SKIP = (x : C \to (P(x) \mathbin{|||} SKIP)) \qquad\qquad \langle\mathbin{|||}\text{-term 2}\rangle$$

Fig. 4.9 Laws for interleaving

The a must occur before the b, but the c can occur anywhere with respect to these two events.

∎

There are a number of trace laws concerning interleaving. These are listed in Figure 4.9. The first two laws state simply that the interleaving operator is commutative and associative. The next two laws give a unit and a zero for the operator. The fifth law gives a way of expanding an interleaving of two choices into a single prefix choice. It states that such an interleaving offers the choice of any of the first events of either of its components.

Interleaving parallel allows its two component processes independent control over termination. The entire combination will terminate when either of its component processes does so. This is reflected in Laws $\mathbin{|||}$-term 1 and $\mathbin{|||}$-term 2. If both sides are ready to terminate, then only termination can occur. Alternatively, if one side is ready to terminate but the other side is able to progress, then progress occurs in accordance with the non-terminating component.

Example 4.2.12 The process $(a \to b \to STOP) \mathbin{|||} (c \to STOP)$ may be rewritten using Law $\mathbin{|||}$-step as follows:

$$
\begin{aligned}
& (a \to b \to STOP) \mathbin{|||} (c \to STOP) \\
=_T \;& a \to ((b \to STOP) \mathbin{|||} (c \to STOP)) \\
& \mid c \to ((a \to b \to STOP) \mathbin{|||} STOP)
\end{aligned}
$$

The left-hand component is initially able to perform a, and the right-hand component is initially able to perform c. The combination therefore offers a choice between a and c. Further applications of |||-step and |||-unit reduce the process to

$$a \to (b \to c \to STOP$$
$$\quad \mid c \to b \to STOP) \mid c \to a \to b \to STOP$$

■

Interface parallel

The process $P_1 \parallel_A P_2$ is a blend of both the parallel operator and the interleaving operator. Its traces will consist of combinations of traces of P_1 and P_2 which match on all occurrences of events in $A^\checkmark$, and which interleave on events not in $A^\checkmark$.

Traces tr_1 of P_1 and tr_2 of P_2 may combine in a number of ways in the combination $P_1 \parallel_A P_2$, provided they agree on events from A. The relation tr synch_A tr_1, tr_2 states that tr describes one way in which tr_1 and tr_2 can combine. It is defined as follows:

$$\langle\rangle \; \mathsf{synch}_A \; tr_1, tr_2 \quad \Leftrightarrow \quad tr_1 = tr_2 = \langle\rangle$$
$$\langle\checkmark\rangle \; \mathsf{synch}_A \; tr_1, tr_2 \quad \Leftrightarrow \quad tr_1 = tr_2 = \langle\checkmark\rangle$$

$$\langle a \rangle \frown tr \neq \langle\checkmark\rangle \Rightarrow$$
$$\langle a \rangle \frown tr \; \mathsf{synch}_A \; tr_1, tr_2 \quad \Leftrightarrow \quad (a \in A \wedge head(tr_1) = head(tr_2) = a$$
$$\wedge \; tr \; \mathsf{synch}_A \; tail(tr_1), tail(tr_2))$$
$$\vee \quad a \notin A \wedge$$
$$(head(tr_1) = a \wedge tr \; \mathsf{synch}_A \; tail(tr_1), tr_2$$
$$\vee \; head(tr_2) = a \wedge tr \; \mathsf{synch}_A \; tr_1, tail(tr_2))$$

The constraint that the traces must agree on A means that some traces tr_1 and tr_2 are not consistent. In this case, there will be no tr which relates to the pair of them. For example, $\langle a, b, a \rangle$ and $\langle a, c \rangle$ cannot agree on the set $\{a\}$.

Any trace of the parallel process $P_1 \parallel_A P_2$ will be a combination of a trace from P_1 and a trace from P_2. The traces of $P_1 \parallel_A P_2$ are given as follows:

$$\mathsf{traces}(P_1 \parallel_A P_2) \quad = \quad \{tr \in TRACE \mid \exists tr_1, tr_2 \bullet \; tr_1 \in \mathsf{traces}(P_1) \wedge$$
$$tr_2 \in \mathsf{traces}(P_2) \wedge$$
$$tr \; \mathsf{synch}_A \; tr_1, tr_2\}$$

Example 4.2.13

$$\mathsf{traces}\,((a \to b \to a \to STOP) \parallel_{\{a\}} (a \to c \to a \to STOP))$$
$$= \quad \{\langle\rangle, \langle a \rangle, \langle a, b \rangle, \langle a, c \rangle, \langle a, b, c \rangle, \langle a, c, b \rangle, \langle a, b, c, a \rangle, \langle a, c, b, a \rangle\}$$

$$P_1 \parallel_A P_2 = P_2 \parallel_A P_1 \qquad\qquad \langle\parallel_A\text{-sym}\rangle$$

$$P_1 \parallel_A (P_2 \parallel_A P_3) = (P_1 \parallel_A P_2) \parallel_A P_3 \qquad\qquad \langle\parallel_A\text{-assoc}\rangle$$

$$P \parallel_A RUN_{A\checkmark} =_U P \qquad\qquad \langle\parallel_A\text{-unit}_U\rangle$$

$$P \parallel_A RUN_{\Sigma\setminus A} =_T RUN_{\Sigma\setminus A} \qquad\qquad \langle\parallel_A\text{-zero}_T\rangle$$

$$(x : C \to P_1(x)) \parallel_A (y : D \to P_2(y)) \qquad\qquad \langle\parallel_A\text{-step}\rangle$$

$$= z : (((C \cup D) \setminus A) \cup (C \cap D \cap A)) \to R(z)$$

where

$$
\begin{aligned}
R(c) &= P_1(c) \parallel_A (y : D \to P_2(y)) && \text{if } c \in C \setminus (A \cup D) \\
&= (x : C \to P_1(x)) \parallel_A P_2(c) && \text{if } c \in D \setminus (A \cup C) \\
&= P_1(c) \parallel_A (y : D \to P_2(y)) && \text{if } c \in (C \cap D) \setminus A \\
&\quad \sqcap (x : C \to P_1(x)) \parallel_A P_2(c) \\
&= P_1(c) \parallel_A P_2(c)) && \text{if } c \in C \cap D \cap A
\end{aligned}
$$

$$SKIP \parallel_A SKIP = SKIP \qquad\qquad \langle\parallel_A\text{-term 1}\rangle$$

$$(x : C \to P(x)) \parallel_A SKIP \qquad\qquad \langle\parallel_A\text{-term 2}\rangle$$

$$= x : (C \setminus A) \to (P(x) \parallel_A SKIP)$$

Fig. 4.10   Laws for interface parallel

The traces of the component processes must agree on occurrences of a, but are otherwise independent. ∎

There are a number of trace laws concerning interface parallel. These are listed in Figure 4.10.

The first two laws are concerned with commutativity and associativity of the interface parallel operator. Associativity applies in the case that both instances A of the interface set are the same. Law $\parallel_A\text{-unit}_U$ gives a unit for the operator: RUN_A allows P to perform any event in A, and the common interface A means that P can independently perform events not in A; so the process $P \parallel_A RUN_{A\checkmark}$ has exactly the same traces as P. A zero which blocks all events in A and masks all other events, is given by Law $\parallel_A\text{-zero}_T$. Law $\parallel_A\text{-step}$ allows a parallel combination of choices to be expanded to a prefix choice of processes. The events offered by the prefix choice

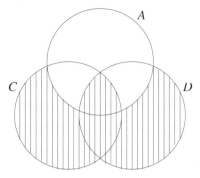

Fig. 4.11   Initial possibilities for an interface parallel combination

are those in A which are offered by both components, together with those not in A offered by either component. These possibilities are illustrated in Figure 4.11.

The behaviour of interface parallel with respect to termination is given by the last two laws. Law $\parallel_A$-term 1 states that if both components are ready to terminate then termination must occur. Law $\parallel_A$-term 2 is concerned with the case where one side is ready to terminate but the other is not; termination is not a possibility. The other process may progress on any event that it is able to perform independently—any event not in the common interface A.

The relationship between interface parallel and the other two forms of parallel is made explicit in the following two laws:

$$P_1 \ _A\|_B\ P_2 = P_1 \underset{(A \cap B)}{\parallel} P_2 \quad \text{if} \ \begin{array}{l} \alpha(P_1) \subseteq A \\ \wedge\ \alpha(P_2) \subseteq B \end{array} \qquad \langle \parallel_A\text{-equiv 1} \rangle$$

$$P_1 \ |||\ P_2 = P_1 \underset{\{\}}{\parallel} P_2 \qquad \langle \parallel_A\text{-equiv 2} \rangle$$

Law $\parallel_A$-equiv 1 covers the case where P_1 and P_2 must synchronize on all events that are in $A \cap B$, and can perform independently only those events which are in one alphabet and outside $A \cap B$. This is naturally written using the alphabetized parallel operator, but the effect is that $A \cap B$ is a common interface, and it can equally be written with the interface parallel operator.

Law $\parallel_A$-equiv 2 states simply that process interleaving is equivalent to an empty interface parallel combination.

$$(P \setminus A) \setminus B = P \setminus (A \cup B) \qquad\qquad \langle\text{hide-combine}\rangle$$

$$(a \rightarrow P) \setminus A = \begin{cases} a \rightarrow (P \setminus A) & \text{if } a \notin A \\ P \setminus A & \text{if } a \in A \end{cases} \qquad \langle\text{hide-step 1}\rangle$$

$$\left(\sqcap_{i \in I} P_i\right) \setminus A = \sqcap_{i \in I} (P_i \setminus A) \qquad\qquad \langle\sqcap\text{-dist}\rangle$$

$$STOP \setminus A = STOP \qquad\qquad \langle\text{hide-}STOP\rangle$$

$$(x : C \rightarrow P(x)) \setminus A = x : C \rightarrow (P(x) \setminus A) \quad \text{if } A \cap C = \{\} \qquad \langle\text{hide-step 2}\rangle$$

$$(x : C \rightarrow P(x)) \setminus A = \sqcap_{x \in C} (P(x) \setminus A) \quad \text{if } C \subseteq A \qquad \langle\text{hide-step 3}\rangle$$

$$SKIP \setminus A = SKIP \qquad\qquad \langle\text{hide-term}\rangle$$

Fig. 4.12 Laws for hiding

Hiding

The process $P \setminus A$ for $A \subseteq \Sigma$ has the same executions as P, except that at any point where P performs a visible event from A, the process $P \setminus A$ performs the same event internally. All events from A become internal events in $P \setminus A$, and do not appear in its traces. Any trace tr of P gives rise to a trace $tr \setminus A$ of $P \setminus A$; and conversely, any trace of $P \setminus A$ must be derived from a trace of P with the events from A made internal.

$$\text{traces}(P \setminus A) \quad = \quad \{tr \setminus A \mid tr \in \text{traces}(P)\}$$

For instance

$$\text{traces}(a \rightarrow b \rightarrow a \rightarrow STOP) \quad = \quad \{\langle\rangle, \langle a\rangle, \langle a, b\rangle, \langle a, b, a\rangle\}$$

and so

$$\text{traces}((a \rightarrow b \rightarrow a \rightarrow STOP) \setminus \{a\}) \quad = \quad \{\langle\rangle, \langle b\rangle\}$$

There are a number of laws concerning hiding. These are given in Figure 4.12. The first law states that hiding successive sets of events obtains the same process as hiding all the sets of events at once. It follows from this law that hiding is commutative: that $P \setminus A \setminus B = P \setminus B \setminus A$.

The second law is concerned with the effect of an abstraction on the occurrence of an event. If the event a does not appear in the abstracted set of events A, then it is not hidden and it appears as a prefix to the subsequent process $P \setminus A$. If a does occur in A then it is internal and so the subsequent process $P \setminus A$ is immediately reached.

The third law states that hiding distributes over indexed internal choice: abstracting events from a choice of process will yield the same traces as a single choice from a set of processes which all have their events abstracted. The fourth law is the special case in which no events are offered.

The fifth and sixth laws are special instances of hiding over a prefix choice. In the first case none of the choice events is hidden, resulting in the same choice of events being offered. In the second case all of the choice events are hidden, resulting in the choice between the subsequent processes. These two laws are often applicable when channels are hidden: if the channel c is hidden, then all events in the initial choice of the input process $c?x : T \rightarrow P(x)$ become internal in accordance with Law **hide-step 3**; if c is not hidden, then none of them become internal and the entire input choice remains, in accordance with Law **hide-step 2**. Finally, the last law states that hiding does not affect termination.

Example 4.2.14 In the case where some events of a prefix choice are hidden, but not all of them, the laws **hide-step 1** and ⊓-**dist** are used to separate out the individual branches of the choice, and then to apply the hiding operator to each one separately.

$$\left(\begin{array}{c} a \rightarrow c \rightarrow STOP \\ \Box\ b \rightarrow d \rightarrow STOP \end{array} \right) \setminus \{b\}$$

$=_T$ by ⊓-**dist** and ⊓-□-**equiv**$_T$

$$(a \rightarrow c \rightarrow STOP) \setminus \{b\} \ \Box\ (b \rightarrow d \rightarrow STOP) \setminus \{b\}$$

$=_T$ by **hide-step 1**

$$a \rightarrow (c \rightarrow STOP) \setminus \{b\}$$
$$\Box\ (d \rightarrow STOP) \setminus \{b\}$$

$=_T$ by **hide-step 1**

$$a \rightarrow c \rightarrow (STOP \setminus \{b\})$$
$$\Box\ d \rightarrow (STOP \setminus \{b\})$$

$=_T$ by **hide-step 1**

$$a \rightarrow c \rightarrow STOP$$
$$\Box\ d \rightarrow STOP$$

The b event is no longer visible in the resulting process description.   ■

Renaming

The forward renaming operator $f(P)$ behaves the same way as P but performs $f(a)$ whenever P would have performed a. Its traces are the traces of P with every event mapped through f.

The set of traces of $f(P)$ can be defined:

$$\mathsf{traces}(f(P)) \quad = \quad \{f(tr) \mid tr \in \mathsf{traces}(P)\}$$

$$f(x : C \to P(x)) = y : f(C) \to f(P(f^{-1}(y))) \quad \text{if } f \text{ is } 1-1 \qquad \langle f(.)\text{-step 1}\rangle$$

$$f(x : C \to P(x)) = y : f(C) \to \bigsqcap_{x|f(x)=y} f(P(x)) \qquad \langle f(.)\text{-step 2}\rangle$$

$$f(SKIP) = SKIP \qquad \langle f(.)\text{-term}\rangle$$

$$l : (x : C \to P(x)) = y : (l.C) \to P(f_l^{-1}(y)) \qquad \langle l :\text{-step}\rangle$$

$$\quad \text{where } l.C = \{l.c \mid c \in C\}$$

$$l : SKIP = SKIP \qquad \langle l :\text{-term}\rangle$$

$$f^{-1}(x : C \to P(x)) = y : f^{-1}(C) \to f^{-1}(P(f(y))) \qquad \langle f^{-1}(.)\text{-step}\rangle$$

$$f^{-1}(SKIP) = SKIP \qquad \langle f^{-1}(.)\text{-term}\rangle$$

Fig. 4.13   Laws for renaming

This is indeed a set of traces, since the restrictions on alphabet renaming mean that f maps Σ into Σ, and $f(\checkmark) = \checkmark$.

For instance,

$$\text{traces}(a \to b \to a \to STOP) \quad = \quad \{\langle\rangle, \langle a\rangle, \langle a, b\rangle, \langle a, b, a\rangle\}$$

and so if $f(a) = c$ and $f(b) = d$ then

$$\text{traces}(f(a \to b \to a \to STOP)) \quad = \quad \{\langle\rangle, \langle c\rangle, \langle c, d\rangle, \langle c, d, c\rangle\}$$

If $g(a) = g(b) = c$ then

$$\text{traces}(g(a \to b \to a \to STOP)) \quad = \quad \{\langle\rangle, \langle c\rangle, \langle c, c\rangle, \langle c, c, c\rangle\}$$

If the mapping f is one-one, then renaming with f has a straightforward interaction with prefix choice, as given by Law $f(.)$-step 1 in Figure 4.13. A choice of events from C becomes a choice of events from $f(C) = \{f(c) \mid c \in C\}$. The fact that f is injective means that the event y chosen corresponds to exactly one event $x(= f^{-1}(y))$ from the original choice of events from C, so the subsequent behaviour is that of $P(x)$ transformed through f.

In general, the renaming operator interacts with prefix choice as given by Law $f(.)$-step 2 in Figure 4.13. If a process P initially is prepared to perform any event from C, then the initial choice for $f(P)$ is the set of events $f(C)$. However, the result of choosing y could be any of the processes which follow an event mapping to y: if a and b both appear in C, and f maps them both to the same event c, then $f(P)$ is in effect offering c in two different ways, once resulting from a and once resulting from b. The process subsequent to c can be either $f(P(a))$ or $f(P(b))$.

All of the term laws state that the various sorts of renaming cannot affect a process's ability to terminate.

Example 4.2.15 The process P initially offers a choice from the set of three events $\{a, b, c\}$:

$$
\begin{aligned}
P \quad = \quad & a \rightarrow d \rightarrow STOP \\
& | \ b \rightarrow e \rightarrow STOP \\
& | \ c \rightarrow STOP
\end{aligned}
$$

Let the mapping f be defined by

$$
\begin{aligned}
f(a) \ &= \ k \\
f(b) \ &= \ k \\
f(c) \ &= \ l \\
f(d) \ &= \ m \\
f(e) \ &= \ n
\end{aligned}
$$

so f maps both a and b to the same event k. Then the process $f(P)$ reduces under Law $f(.)$-step 2 to

$$
\begin{aligned}
& k \rightarrow (m \rightarrow STOP \sqcap n \rightarrow STOP) \\
& \Box \ l \rightarrow STOP
\end{aligned}
$$

The process $f(P)$ only offers a choice between two events, where P offered a choice between three. The process following the choice of k can be one of two possibilities, derived from the behaviour of P following a, or following b. ∎

Process relabelling $l : P$ is a special form of forward renaming in which all events a are associated with the label l, by means of the renaming function f_l which maps a to $l.a$ for any event $a \neq \checkmark$, and $f_l(\checkmark) = \checkmark$. The set of traces is given by the trace definition of forward renaming:

$$
\mathsf{traces}(l : P) \quad = \quad \{f_l(tr) \mid tr \in \mathsf{traces}(P)\}
$$

The function f_l is one-one, so the relabelling law is a specialization of Law $f(.)$-step 1.

The backward renaming operator $f^{-1}(P)$ also behaves in a similar fashion to P, but any event a that is performed by $f^{-1}(P)$ corresponds to an event $f(a)$ performed by P. Hence a trace tr of $f^{-1}(P)$, when mapped through the function f, must yield a trace $f(tr)$ of P.

$$
\mathsf{traces}(f^{-1}(P)) \quad = \quad \{tr \mid f(tr) \in \mathsf{traces}(P)\}
$$

The interaction between backward renaming and prefix choice is straightforward, and the laws are given in Figure 4.13.

A set of events C offered as a choice by P becomes a choice over $f^{-1}(C)$ offered by $f^{-1}(P)$, since it is precisely the events in $f^{-1}(C)$ that map to an event that P can initially perform—an event in C. If a particular event a is chosen, then the subsequent behaviour is determined by the behaviour of P following $f(a)$.

Example 4.2.16 The process P' initially offers a choice from the set of two events $\{k, l\}$.

$$
\begin{aligned}
P' \quad &= \quad k \rightarrow (m \rightarrow STOP \mid n \rightarrow STOP) \\
&\quad \mid l \rightarrow STOP
\end{aligned}
$$

If the mapping f is defined as in Example 4.2.15, then the process $f^{-1}(P')$ reduces under Law f^{-1}-**step** to

$$
\begin{aligned}
&a \rightarrow (d \rightarrow STOP \mid e \rightarrow STOP) \\
\Box\ &b \rightarrow (d \rightarrow STOP \mid e \rightarrow STOP) \\
\Box\ &c \rightarrow STOP
\end{aligned}
$$

The resulting choice is between three events. In the case where a or b is chosen, the subsequent behaviour is that of $f^{-1}(P(f(a))) = f^{-1}(P(f(b))) = f^{-1}(P(k))$

The process P' is equivalent to $f(P)$ where P was defined in Example 4.2.15. However, $f^{-1}(P')$ is not equivalent to P, since there are some possibilities for $f^{-1}(P')$ which are not possible for P; one example is the performance of event e following event a. This is manifested in the sets of traces in the fact that $\langle a, e \rangle \in \mathsf{traces}(f^{-1}(P'))$ but $\langle a, e \rangle \notin \mathsf{traces}(P)$. Hence P and $f^{-1}(P') = f^{-1}(f(P))$ are not trace equivalent. ∎

Sequential composition

The sequential composition $P_1; P_2$ behaves as P_1 until P_1 terminates successfully, at which point it passes control to P_2. Since termination of P_1 does not denote termination of the entire construct, P_1's $\checkmark$ event is made internal.

The traces of $P_1; P_2$ fall into two categories: traces of P_1 before termination, and terminating traces of P_1 followed by traces of P_2.

$$
\begin{aligned}
\mathsf{traces}(P_1; P_2) \quad = \quad &\{tr \mid tr \in \mathsf{traces}(P_1) \wedge \checkmark \notin \sigma(tr)\} \\
&\cup \{tr_1 \,^\frown tr_2 \mid tr_1 \,^\frown \langle\checkmark\rangle \in \mathsf{traces}(P_1) \wedge tr_2 \in \mathsf{traces}(P_2)\}
\end{aligned}
$$

There are a number of laws appropriate to sequential composition. These are given in Figure 4.14.

Law ; -**assoc** simply states that sequential composition is associative. The **unit** laws state that $SKIP$ is a left and right unit of sequential composition: that $SKIP$ is absorbed by

$$(P_1; P_2); P_3 = P_1; (P_2; P_3) \hspace{3cm} \langle; \text{-assoc} \rangle$$

$$SKIP; P = P \hspace{5cm} \langle; \text{-unit-l} \rangle$$

$$P; SKIP =_T P \hspace{5cm} \langle; \text{-unit-r}_T \rangle$$

$$(x : C \rightarrow P(x)); P_1 = x : C \rightarrow (P(x); P_1) \hspace{2cm} \langle; \text{-step} \rangle$$

$$STOP; P = STOP \hspace{4.5cm} \langle; \text{-zero-l} \rangle$$

Fig. 4.14   *Laws for sequential composition*

sequential composition (though the right unit law holds only in the traces model). Law ; -step states that a prefix choice in a sequential composition is equivalent to a prefix choice of sequentially composed processes. Law ; -zero-l is a special case of Law ; -step, in which no events are initially offered—this yields a left zero for sequential composition.

Example 4.2.17 The process P_1 is defined as follows:

$$
\begin{aligned}
P_1 \quad &= \quad a \rightarrow SKIP \\
&\quad | \ b \rightarrow STOP
\end{aligned}
$$

If P_1 is sequentially composed with process $P_2 = c \rightarrow SKIP$ then the result is

$$
\begin{aligned}
P_1; P_2 \quad &= \quad \left(\begin{array}{l} a \rightarrow SKIP \\ \square \ b \rightarrow STOP \end{array} \right) ; c \rightarrow SKIP \\
&= \quad a \rightarrow (SKIP; c \rightarrow SKIP) \\
&\quad\ | \ b \rightarrow (STOP; c \rightarrow SKIP) \\
&= \quad a \rightarrow c \rightarrow SKIP \\
&\quad\ | \ b \rightarrow STOP
\end{aligned}
$$

The c event can follow the a but not the b.   ■

Interrupt

The process $P_1 \triangle P_2$ executes as P_1, but at any stage before termination it can begin executing as P_2. There are therefore two possibilities for any given trace: it is either a trace of P_1, or

$$(P_1 \mathbin{\triangle} P_2) \mathbin{\triangle} P_3 = P_1 \mathbin{\triangle} (P_2 \mathbin{\triangle} P_3) \qquad \langle \triangle\text{-assoc} \rangle$$

$$(x : C \rightarrow P_1(x)) \mathbin{\triangle} P_2 = P_2 \mathbin{\square} (x : C \rightarrow (P_1(x) \mathbin{\triangle} P_2)) \qquad \langle \triangle\text{-step} \rangle$$

$$STOP \mathbin{\triangle} P = P \qquad \langle \triangle\text{-unit-l} \rangle$$

$$P \mathbin{\triangle} STOP = P \qquad \langle \triangle\text{-unit-r} \rangle$$

$$SKIP \mathbin{\triangle} P = SKIP \mathbin{\square} P \qquad \langle \triangle\text{-term} \rangle$$

Fig. 4.15   Laws of interrupt

else it is a non-terminating trace of P_1 followed by a trace of P_2.

$$
\begin{aligned}
\mathsf{traces}(P_1 \mathbin{\triangle} P_2) \;=\; & \mathsf{traces}(P_1) \\
& \cup \\
& \{ tr_1 \mathbin{\frown} tr_2 \mid tr_1 \in \mathsf{traces}(P) \wedge \checkmark \notin \sigma(tr_1) \\
& \qquad\qquad \wedge\, tr_2 \in \mathsf{traces}(P_2) \}
\end{aligned}
$$

Interrupt satisfies a number of laws, given in Figure 4.15, concerning its interaction with choice and with termination. Law $\triangle$-assoc states that the interrupt operator is associative: the bracketing of different levels of interrupt is irrelevant. Law $\triangle$-step shows how a prefix choice interrupted by P_2 unwinds: either it behaves as P_2 immediately, or else one of the events of the prefix choice occurs, resulting in the subsequent process which may still be interrupted. Law $\triangle$-unit-l is a special case of $\triangle$-step in which a process that does nothing may be interrupted by P: in this case, the only possible activity is generated by P. Law $\triangle$-unit-r states that the process $STOP$ is ineffective as an interrupting process, since there are no events it can perform to interrupt another process. Finally, Law $\triangle$-term states that if termination occurs, then the interrupting process is discarded.

Distributive laws

In addition to all of the laws given above for the various CSP operators, there is also a law for each of them concerning distributivity over internal choice. All of the CSP operators (except recursion) distribute over both binary and indexed internal choice, in the traces model, and in fact in all of the models for CSP. For example, the laws for prefix will be as follows:

$$a \to (P_1 \sqcap P_2) = (a \to P_1) \sqcap (a \to P_2) \qquad\qquad \langle\text{prefix-dist}\rangle$$

$$a \to \textstyle\bigsqcap_{i \in J} P_i = \textstyle\bigsqcap_{i \in J}(a \to P_i) \qquad\qquad \langle\text{prefix-Dist}\rangle$$

These laws effectively state that no observer can distinguish the case where the internal choice is made after performance of the a from the case where it is made beforehand. In fact the second law subsumes the first.

Binary operators will also distribute over internal choice. For example,

$$P_1 \;{}_A\|_B (P_2 \sqcap P_3) = (P_1 \;{}_A\|_B P_2) \sqcap (P_1 \| P_3) \qquad\qquad \langle\|\text{-dist}\rangle$$

$$P_1 \;{}_A\|_B \textstyle\bigsqcap_{i \in J} P_i = \textstyle\bigsqcap_{i \in J}(P_1 \;{}_A\|_B P_i) \qquad\qquad \langle\|\text{-Dist}\rangle$$

Since the parallel operator is symmetric, as indicated by Law $\|$-**sym**, it follows from these laws that it will also distribute over internal choice in its left-hand argument.

For binary operators that are not symmetric, both a left-hand and a right-hand version of distributivity are given. One example is sequential composition:

$$(P_1 \sqcap P_2); P_3 = (P_1; P_3) \sqcap (P_2; P_3) \qquad\qquad \langle;\text{-dist-l}\rangle$$

$$P_1; (P_2 \sqcap P_3) = (P_1; P_2) \sqcap (P_1; P_3) \qquad\qquad \langle;\text{-dist-r}\rangle$$

$$(\textstyle\bigsqcap_{i \in J} P_i); P = \textstyle\bigsqcap_{i \in J}(P_i; P) \qquad\qquad \langle;\text{-Dist-l}\rangle$$

$$P; (\textstyle\bigsqcap_{i \in J} P_i) = \textstyle\bigsqcap_{i \in J}(P; P_i) \qquad\qquad \langle;\text{-Dist-r}\rangle$$

All CSP operators (except recursion) are distributive in all arguments over internal choice, and so there will be corresponding distributivity laws for each CSP operator. Law choice-equiv$_T$ of Figure 4.4 stating that $P_1 \sqcap P_2 =_T P_1 \,\Box\, P_2$ means that in the traces model, though not more generally, all operators also distribute over external choice.

4.3 RECURSION

The case of recursion has been left until last, since it requires a different treatment to all of the other operators. Traces of processes constructed using the other operators can be deduced from the traces of their components, but in the case of a recursively defined process $N = P$ or

$N = F(N)$ which should define the traces of N, the traces of the component P or $F(N)$ depend on the traces of N itself, resulting in a circularity. For instance, if $P = F(N) = a \rightarrow N$, then the traces of P are going to be

$$\{\langle\rangle\} \cup \{\langle a \rangle \frown tr \mid tr \in \textsf{traces}(N)\}$$

which depends on the set $\textsf{traces}(N)$.

The traces of N can be derived directly from the operational semantics by use of the characterization

$$\textsf{traces}(N) \quad = \quad \{tr \mid N \overset{tr}{\Longrightarrow} \}$$

but the intention of providing trace semantics is to remove the need to consider processes at the operational level and to support reasoning purely at the level of traces.

Recursion involves defining a process in terms of itself, $N = F(N)$, so it is not surprising that a circularity arises concerning the traces of N simultaneously determining and being determined by the traces of $F(N)$. Even before the traces of N can be determined, there is one fact that must hold:

$$\textsf{traces}(N) \quad = \quad \textsf{traces}(F(N))$$

The recursive definition defines an *equation* which must be satisfied by the set $\textsf{traces}(N)$. In fact, $\textsf{traces}(N)$ is a *fixed point* of the function on trace sets represented by the CSP expression F; when that function is applied to $\textsf{traces}(N)$ to obtain $\textsf{traces}(F(N))$, then the result is again $\textsf{traces}(N)$. This fact is extremely valuable: there are well-established techniques for finding fixed points of functions, and for reasoning about them. They will allow the traces of recursively defined processes to be identified by reasoning purely in terms of traces.

Traces are records of finite executions, so every trace of a recursive process $N = P$ may be obtained by unwinding the recursive definition a finite number of times. Every process contains the empty trace as one of its possible traces, so it follows that $\langle\rangle \in \textsf{traces}(N)$, or, equivalently,

$$\textsf{traces}(STOP) \quad \subseteq \quad \textsf{traces}(N)$$

Applying the function F to each side of the subset relationship yields that

$$\textsf{traces}(F(STOP)) \quad \subseteq \quad \textsf{traces}(F(N)) = \textsf{traces}(N)$$

which states simply that the traces obtained by unwinding the recursive function F once are all traces of N. This is justified because all of the CSP operators are *monotonic* with respect to $\subseteq$: in other words, if $\textsf{traces}(P_1) \subseteq \textsf{traces}(P_2)$, then $\textsf{traces}(F(P_1)) \subseteq \textsf{traces}(F(P_2))$ for any function F constructed out of CSP operators and terms.

It is a standard induction to show that for any n

$$\mathsf{traces}(F^n(STOP)) \quad \subseteq \quad \mathsf{traces}(F(N)) = \mathsf{traces}(N)$$

which corresponds to the fact that all of the traces obtained by unwinding the definition $N = F(N)$ n times are still traces of the recursive process N.

All of the $F^n(STOP)$ processes correspond to the finite unwindings of the recursive definition, so between them they cover all of the possible traces of $N = P$. Hence

$$\mathsf{traces}(N = F(N)) \quad = \quad \bigcup_{n \in \mathbb{N}} \mathsf{traces}(F^n(STOP))$$

This concurs with the expectation that the resulting set of traces must be a fixed point of the function corresponding to F.

Example 4.3.1 Consider the recursively defined process $LIGHT = on \rightarrow off \rightarrow LIGHT$ of Example 1.3.1. The recursive function is $F(Y) = on \rightarrow off \rightarrow Y$.

$$
\begin{aligned}
\mathsf{traces}(STOP) &= \{\langle\rangle\} \\
\mathsf{traces}(F(STOP)) &= \{\langle\rangle, \langle on \rangle, \langle on, off \rangle\} \\
\mathsf{traces}(F(F(STOP))) &= \{\langle\rangle, \langle on \rangle, \langle on, off \rangle, \langle on, off, on \rangle, \langle on, off, on, off \rangle\}
\end{aligned}
$$

It appears that

$$
\begin{aligned}
\mathsf{traces}(F^n(STOP)) \quad &= \quad \{\langle on, off \rangle^i \mid 0 \leqslant i \leqslant n\} \\
&\qquad \cup \\
&\qquad \{\langle on, off \rangle^i \,^\frown \langle on \rangle \mid 0 \leqslant i < n\}
\end{aligned}
$$

and this conjecture may be established by induction. The base case ($n = 0$) is immediate, so there is only the inductive step to consider. Assuming the result for n:

$$
\begin{aligned}
\mathsf{traces}&(F^{n+1}(STOP)) \\
&= \quad \mathsf{traces}(on \rightarrow off \rightarrow F^n(STOP)) \\
&= \quad \{\langle\rangle, \langle on \rangle\} \\
&\qquad \cup \{\langle on, off \rangle \,^\frown tr \mid tr \in F^n(STOP)\} \\
&= \quad \{\langle\rangle, \langle on \rangle\} \\
&\qquad \cup \{\langle on, off \rangle \,^\frown tr \mid tr \in \{\langle on, off \rangle^i \mid 0 \leqslant i \leqslant n\}\} \\
&\qquad \cup \{\langle on, off \rangle \,^\frown tr \mid tr \in \{\langle on, off \rangle^i \,^\frown \langle on \rangle \mid 0 \leqslant i < n\}\} \\
&= \quad \{\langle\rangle, \langle on \rangle\} \\
&\qquad \cup \{\langle on, off \rangle^i \mid 1 \leqslant i \leqslant n + 1\} \\
&\qquad \cup \{\langle on, off \rangle^i \,^\frown \langle on \rangle \mid 1 \leqslant i < n + 1\} \\
&= \quad \{\langle on, off \rangle^i \mid 0 \leqslant i \leqslant n + 1\} \\
&\qquad \cup \{\langle on, off \rangle^i \,^\frown \langle on \rangle \mid 0 \leqslant i < n + 1\}
\end{aligned}
$$

which establishes the result for $n + 1$.

The traces of *LIGHT* are given by $\bigcup_{n \in \mathbb{N}} \text{traces}(F^n(STOP))$, which is given by

$$\text{traces}(LIGHT) \quad = \quad \{\langle on, off \rangle^i \mid i \in \mathbb{N}\}$$
$$\cup \{\langle on, off \rangle^i \frown \langle on \rangle \mid i \in \mathbb{N}\}$$

All finite alternating sequences of *on* and *off* are present. ∎

The first law for recursion is straightforward:

'$N = F(N)$' $\Rightarrow$ $N = F(N)$ $\qquad\qquad\qquad$ ⟨recursion-unwinding⟩

The law simply captures the discussion above. The left-hand side is a statement about the definition of the process N: that is a process defined by a recursive definition $N = F(N)$. The right-hand side is a result (in the traces model for this chapter) about the traces of the process so defined (and there are corresponding results for the models defined in later chapters). The traces associated with N must be the same as those associated with $F(N)$, and this law states exactly this. It is generally used to 'unwind' recursive definitions, or (used from right to left) to fold them up. For instance, it may be used to show that the process $N = a \rightarrow N$ begins with the occurrence of two a events. Initially $N =_T a \rightarrow N$ follows from the definition of N, and then $a \rightarrow N =_T a \rightarrow a \rightarrow N$ may be deduced from another application of the law. This makes explicit the fact that N begins with two as, since it follows that $N =_T a \rightarrow a \rightarrow N$.

Unique fixed points

Functions used in recursive definitions have been seen to have at least one fixed point. The functions correspond to functions on sets of traces. In some cases, there may be exactly one fixed point: exactly one set of traces that the function maps to itself. For instance, in the case of the function $F(Y) = a \rightarrow Y$, the only fixed point of the function is the process identified with the set of traces

$$\{\langle a \rangle^n \mid n \in \mathbb{N}\}$$

This corresponds to the only process which satisfies the equation $N =_T a \rightarrow N$.

In other cases, there may be a multitude of fixed points. For instance, in the case of the function $F(Y) = Y \square a \rightarrow STOP$ (on sets of traces) the set of traces

$$\{\langle \rangle, \langle a \rangle\}$$

is a fixed point of the function. However, so is the set of traces

$$\{\langle \rangle, \langle a \rangle, \langle b \rangle\}$$

and indeed any set of traces which contains both $\langle\rangle$ and $\langle a\rangle$ will be a fixed point of the function.

In the case where a CSP function F has a unique fixed point, it follows that *all* CSP processes which are solutions of the equation $Y =_T F(Y)$ must have the same set of traces, since there is only one such set possible. This means that if $N = F(N)$ is a recursively defined process and F has a unique fixed point, and if it can then be shown that another process P satisfies the equation $P =_T F(P)$, then the conclusion $N =_T P$ follows.

Guardedness

This result is so useful that it is worthwhile exploring a general condition under which a CSP function will indeed have a single fixed point. This condition is *guardedness*, which is present in a function F when any execution of $F(N)$ must perform some visible event before reaching the first invocation of N. If this is the case, then every occurrence of the name N is said to be *guarded* in $F(N)$. It will be more precisely defined by the following clauses, which give rules for deducing when a process name N is guarded in a process expression which may contain a number of process names.

The hiding operator may remove guards, by internalizing guarding events. It is the only operator which has this effect: all other operators preserve guardedness when it is already present. Guards are introduced either by means of the event prefixing operators, or else through a sequential composition whose left-hand process (which is providing the guard) does not terminate immediately.

A process name N is *event guarded* in process expression P if either

1. N does not appear in P; or

2. (a) P does not contain the hiding operator; and

    (b) every occurrence of process name N is either

        i. within the scope of a prefixing operator (prefix, prefix choice, input, or output); or

        ii. contained within the second argument of a sequential composition whose first argument does not terminate immediately.

A process P terminates immediately if one of its possible traces is $\langle\checkmark\rangle$: it can terminate having performed no actions. Equivalently, if the equation $P =_T P \square SKIP$ can be established for P then P can terminate immediately. The equation provides evidence that $SKIP$ describes one of the executions already possible for P.

Example 4.3.2

- N is guarded in $a \to N \square b \to STOP$, since it is in the scope of the component process $a \to N$.

- N is guarded in $in?m : T \to N \;|||\; in?n : T \to N$.

- N is guarded in $(a \to SKIP \;\Box\; b \to SKIP); N$ because the left-hand process cannot terminate immediately.

- N is guarded in $(SKIP \;\Box\; a \to SKIP); b \to N$ because it is in the scope of $b \to N$.

- N is not guarded in $(SKIP \;\Box\; a \to SKIP); N$.

- N is not guarded in $a \to b \to (N \setminus \{a\})$ because the expression contains the hiding operator.

- N is guarded in $a \to M$ (where $M \neq N$) because it does not appear.

- N is guarded in $a \to M \setminus \{b\}$ (where $M \neq N$) because it does not appear.

■

Example 4.3.3

- The function $F(N) = on \to off \to N$ is guarded, both by the event on and by the event off.

- The function $F(N) = on \to off \to N \;\Box\; off \to on \to N$ is guarded, since each branch of the choice is guarded.

- The function $F(N) = (on \to N) \;|||\; (off \to N)$ is guarded, since each component of the interleaving composition is guarded.

- The function $F(N) = (on \to N) \;\Box\; N$ is not guarded, since one of the components of the choice is unguarded. This means that uniqueness of a fixed point is not guaranteed. In fact, in this case F has a number of distinct fixed points.

- The function $F(N) = STOP \;\|_{\Sigma}\; N$ is not guarded, since the right-hand component of the parallel composition is unguarded. However, in this particular case there is only one fixed point.

- The function $F(N) = on \to (N \setminus \{on\})$ is not guarded, because the use of the hiding operator destroys the guard. This function has a number of distinct fixed points.

■

The second law for recursion can now be given:

$$(F(Y) \text{ guarded} \wedge (F(P_1) =_T P_1) \wedge (F(P_2) =_T P_2)) \Rightarrow P_1 =_T P_2 \qquad \langle \mathsf{UFP}_T \rangle$$

The law is labelled UFP_T, for 'unique fixed point'. It states that if two processes are both fixed points of a guarded function (which must have a unique fixed point), then those two processes must be equivalent. The guardedness is sufficient to establish that the fixed point is unique, but it is not necessary—see Exercise 4.16. The law is often applied when one of the processes is defined in terms of F, for example where $P_1 = F(P_1)$; once P_2 is shown to be trace equivalent to $F(P_2)$, the equality $P_1 =_T P_2$ follows.

Example 4.3.4 Consider the recursive processes

$$N = (a \rightarrow N) \square b \rightarrow STOP$$

and

$$M = a \rightarrow M$$

where the aim is to establish that $N =_T M \triangle (b \rightarrow STOP)$.

Note first that the function $F_N(Y) = (a \rightarrow Y) \square (b \rightarrow STOP)$ used for the definition of N is guarded. This means that UFP_T is applicable, provided $N =_T F_N(N)$ and $M =_T F_N(M)$. The condition for N follows immediately by Law **recursion-unwinding**, from its recursive definition. The equivalence will follow if it can be shown that process $M \triangle (b \rightarrow STOP)$ is a fixed point of the function $F_N(Y)$:

$$
\begin{aligned}
M \triangle (b \rightarrow STOP) \quad &=_T \quad \text{by recursion-unwinding} \\
&\quad (a \rightarrow M) \triangle (b \rightarrow STOP) \\
&=_T \quad \text{by } \triangle\text{-step} \\
&\quad (a \rightarrow (M \triangle (b \rightarrow STOP))) \square b \rightarrow STOP \\
&=_T \quad \text{by definition of } F_N \\
&\quad F_N(M \triangle (b \rightarrow STOP))
\end{aligned}
$$

So the laws for trace equality show that $M \triangle (b \rightarrow STOP)$ is a fixed point of F_N, the function which defines N, and so it has the same traces as N. ∎

Example 4.3.5 The ticket and change machine of Example 2.1.4 is a parallel combination of two recursive processes:

$$MACHINE \quad = \quad TICKET \; {}_{\{cash,ticket\}}\|_{\{cash,change\}} \; CHANGE$$

where the component processes are given by the following recursive definitions:

$$
\begin{aligned}
TICKET \quad &= \quad cash \rightarrow ticket \rightarrow TICKET \\
CHANGE \quad &= \quad cash \rightarrow change \rightarrow CHANGE
\end{aligned}
$$

Their alphabets are given by $\alpha T = \alpha(TICKET)$ and $\alpha C = \alpha(CHANGE)$.

The parallel expansion law ‖-**step** may be applied to expand the parallel combination to a sequence of choices:

$TICKET\ _{\alpha T}\|_{\alpha C}\ CHANGE$

$=_T$ by recursion-unwinding

  $(cash \rightarrow ticket \rightarrow TICKET)\ _{\alpha T}\|_{\alpha C}\ (cash \rightarrow change \rightarrow CHANGE)$

$=_T$ by ‖-**step**

  $cash \rightarrow (ticket \rightarrow TICKET\ _{\alpha T}\|_{\alpha C}\ change \rightarrow CHANGE)$

$=_T$ by ‖-**step**

  $cash \rightarrow (ticket \rightarrow (TICKET\ _{\alpha T}\|_{\alpha C}\ change \rightarrow CHANGE)$
  $\qquad\qquad |\ change \rightarrow ((ticket \rightarrow TICKET)\ _{\alpha T}\|_{\alpha C}\ CHANGE))$

$=_T$ by recursion-unwinding

  $cash \rightarrow$

    $ticket \rightarrow$
      $((cash \rightarrow ticket \rightarrow TICKET)\ _{\alpha T}\|_{\alpha C}\ change \rightarrow CHANGE)$
    $|\ change \rightarrow$
      $((ticket \rightarrow TICKET)\ _{\alpha T}\|_{\alpha C}\ cash \rightarrow change \rightarrow CHANGE)$

$=_T$ by ‖-**step**

  $cash \rightarrow$

    $ticket \rightarrow$
      $change \rightarrow ((cash \rightarrow ticket \rightarrow TICKET)\ _{\alpha T}\|_{\alpha C}\ CHANGE)$
    $|\ change \rightarrow$
      $ticket \rightarrow (TICKET\ _{\alpha T}\|_{\alpha C}\ (cash \rightarrow change \rightarrow CHANGE))$

$=_T$ by recursion-unwinding

  $cash \rightarrow (ticket \rightarrow change \rightarrow (TICKET\ _{\alpha T}\|_{\alpha C}\ CHANGE)$
  $\qquad\qquad |\ change \rightarrow ticket \rightarrow (TICKET\ _{\alpha T}\|_{\alpha C}\ CHANGE))$

Observe that Law ‖-**step** applies to processes of the form $x : C \rightarrow P(x)$, which is why the recursive definitions of *TICKET* and *CHANGE* must be unfolded (by an application of recursion-unwinding) before that law can apply.

The above equivalence establishes that $TICKET\ _{\alpha T}\|_{\alpha C}\ CHANGE$ is a fixed point of the guarded function

$$F(Y)\ =\ cash \rightarrow\ \ ticket \rightarrow change \rightarrow Y$$
$$|\ change \rightarrow ticket \rightarrow Y$$

and so it is trace equivalent to the recursively defined sequential process

$$MACHINE'\ =\ cash \rightarrow\ \ ticket \rightarrow change \rightarrow MACHINE'$$
$$|\ change \rightarrow ticket \rightarrow MACHINE'$$

This provides a description of a process equivalent to *MACHINE*, but with the parallelism removed. ∎

Example 4.3.6 The stop-and-wait protocol of Example 3.1.2 is defined as

$$SAWP \quad = \quad (S \parallel R) \setminus (mid.T \cup \{ack\})$$

where the sender and receiver are defined by S and R respectively.

$$S \quad = \quad in?x : T \to mid!x \to ack \to S$$
$$R \quad = \quad mid?y : T \to out!y \to ack \to R$$

Several applications of Law $\parallel$-**step** yield that

$$S \parallel R \quad =_T \quad in?x : T \to mid!x \to out!x \to ack \to (S \parallel R)$$

Hiding the *mid* and *ack* channels has the following effect:

$(S \parallel R) \setminus (mid.T \cup \{ack\})$
$\quad =_T \quad$ by the previous equivalence
$\qquad (in?x : T \to mid!x \to out!x \to ack \to (S \parallel R)) \setminus (mid.T \cup \{ack\})$
$\quad =_T \quad$ by hide-step 2
$\qquad in?x : T \to (mid!x \to out!x \to ack \to (S \parallel R)) \setminus (mid.T \cup \{ack\})$
$\quad =_T \quad$ by hide-step 3
$\qquad in?x : T \to (out!x \to ack \to (S \parallel R)) \setminus (mid.T \cup \{ack\})$
$\quad =_T \quad$ by hide-step 2
$\qquad in?x : T \to out!x \to (ack \to (S \parallel R)) \setminus (mid.T \cup \{ack\})$
$\quad =_T \quad$ by hide-step 3
$\qquad in?x : T \to out!x \to ((S \parallel R)) \setminus (mid.T \cup \{ack\})$

Hence $(S \parallel R) \setminus (mid.T \cup \{ack\})$ is a fixed point of the guarded function $F(Y) = in?x : T \to out!x \to Y$, which is the function used to define the one-place buffer *COPY* of Example 1.3.2. It follows from UFP$_T$ that

$$(S \parallel R) \setminus (mid.T \cup \{ack\}) \quad =_T \quad COPY$$

which establishes that the stop-and-wait protocol really does implement a one-place buffer. ∎

Mutual recursion

The approach taken to mutually defined families of processes is a generalization of the approach taken above. In a mutual recursion, each of the processes is defined in terms of a number of the processes. The general case of a mutual recursion is concerned with a family, or *vector* of process names $\underline{N}$. Each member of the family is referred to with a particular index i, and the ith component of vector $\underline{N}$ is referred to as $\underline{N}_i$.

For example, three processes *HIGH*, *MID*, and *LOW* may be defined by means of a mutual recursion. This family of process names may be considered in terms of the vector $\underline{N}$, indexed by the set $\{0, 1, 2\}$, with $\underline{N}_0 = HIGH$, $\underline{N}_1 = MID$, and $\underline{N}_2 = LOW$. Another way of writing this is $\underline{N} = \langle HIGH, MID, LOW \rangle$.

The mutual recursion defining $\underline{N}$ uses a corresponding family, or vector of functions $\underline{F}$, with the same indexing set. Each element of $\underline{F}$ is a CSP function on a vector of processes which gives a CSP process as output. Hence the entire vector $\underline{F}$ is a function from vectors of processes to vectors of processes. The recursive definition then takes the form $\underline{N} = \underline{F}(\underline{N})$.

For instance, the three processes *HIGH*, *MID*, and *LOW* might be defined as follows:

$$
\begin{aligned}
HIGH \;\; &= \;\; around \rightarrow HIGH \\
&\quad \mid down \rightarrow MID \\[4pt]
MID \;\; &= \;\; up \rightarrow HIGH \\
&\quad \mid down \rightarrow LOW \\[4pt]
LOW \;\; &= \;\; jump \rightarrow HIGH \\
&\quad \mid up \rightarrow MID \\
&\quad \mid down \rightarrow up \rightarrow LOW
\end{aligned}
$$

In this case, each of *HIGH*, *MID*, and *LOW* is defined in terms of a function of the three processes, and the traces associated with each of these processes is dependent on those traces associated with the others.

All three processes are *simultaneously* defined by the recursive equations. There is a CSP function associated with each process, which in each case is a function of three arguments:

$$
\begin{aligned}
F_0(H, M, L) \;\; &= \;\; around \rightarrow H \mid down \rightarrow M \\
F_1(H, M, L) \;\; &= \;\; up \rightarrow H \mid down \rightarrow L \\
F_2(H, M, L) \;\; &= \;\; jump \rightarrow H \mid up \rightarrow M \mid down \rightarrow up \rightarrow L
\end{aligned}
$$

Observe that some functions do not mention all of the names in their definition.

The recursive definitions may then be rewritten as

$$
\begin{aligned}
HIGH \;\; &= \;\; F_0(HIGH, MID, LOW) \\
MID \;\; &= \;\; F_1(HIGH, MID, LOW) \\
LOW \;\; &= \;\; F_2(HIGH, MID, LOW)
\end{aligned}
$$

or alternatively as

$$\underline{N} = \langle F_0(\underline{N}), F_1(\underline{N}), F_2(\underline{N}) \rangle$$

or alternatively as

$$\underline{N} = \underline{F}(\underline{N})$$

To calculate the traces of each process defined by the mutual recursion, the same approach is taken as in the treatment of single recursion, taking as the starting point that the only trace known to be in each component is the empty trace $\langle \rangle$. The process *STOP* will be the first approximation to these processes, and successive unwindings of the definition provide successive approximations: the point for beginning the recursive unwinding is the vector $\underline{STOP}$, and successive unwindings are then given by $\underline{F}^n(\underline{STOP})$. This allows successive approximations to each process $\underline{N}_i$ to be built up as the ith component $\underline{F}^n(\underline{STOP})_i$ of the approximations. The traces of $\underline{N}_i$, where $\underline{N} = \underline{F}(\underline{N})$, are given by

$$\text{traces}(\underline{N}_i) = \bigcup (\text{traces}(\underline{F}^n(\underline{STOP})))_i$$

In the case of *HIGH*, *MID*, and *LOW*, the family of functions F_0, F_1, and F_2 together define a mapping from a family of three processes H, M, and L to another family of three processes $F_0(H, M, L)$, $F_1(H, M, L)$, and $F_2(H, M, L)$. To calculate the traces associated with each of the processes defined recursively as part of this family, it is necessary to begin with the family *STOP*, *STOP*, and *STOP*, similarly to the starting point for a single recursion: that $\langle \rangle$ is the only trace known to be in each process. Unwinding the recursive definitions once yields the family $H_1 = F_0(STOP, STOP, STOP)$, $M_1 = F_1(STOP, STOP, STOP)$, and $L_1 = F_2(STOP, STOP, STOP)$, which are written in full as follows:

$$
\begin{aligned}
H_1 \;=\;\; & around \to STOP \\
& |\; down \to STOP
\end{aligned}
$$

$$
\begin{aligned}
M_1 \;=\;\; & up \to STOP \\
& |\; down \to STOP
\end{aligned}
$$

$$
\begin{aligned}
L_1 \;=\;\; & jump \to STOP \\
& |\; up \to STOP \\
& |\; down \to up \to STOP
\end{aligned}
$$

and their traces are then given as follows:

$$
\begin{aligned}
\text{traces}(H_1) &= \{ \langle \rangle, \langle around \rangle, \langle down \rangle \} \\
\text{traces}(M_1) &= \{ \langle \rangle, \langle up \rangle, \langle down \rangle \} \\
\text{traces}(L_1) &= \{ \langle \rangle, \langle jump \rangle, \langle up \rangle, \langle down \rangle, \langle down, up \rangle \}
\end{aligned}
$$

The next unwinding yields the three processes:

$$
\begin{aligned}
H_2 &= F_0(H_1, M_1, L_1) \\
M_2 &= F_1(H_1, M_1, L_1) \\
L_2 &= F_2(H_1, M_1, L_1)
\end{aligned}
$$

Observe that all of the processes from the first unwinding are required in order to calculate the processes reached after the second unwinding. Each stage is calculated from the previous stage:

$$
\begin{aligned}
H_{i+1} &= F_0(H_i, M_i, L_i) \\
M_{i+1} &= F_1(H_i, M_i, L_i) \\
L_{i+1} &= F_2(H_i, M_i, L_i)
\end{aligned}
$$

The traces contained in the recursive processes are precisely those reached after some finite number of unwindings. Hence the traces of the process *HIGH* are the traces of all the H_i approximations, and the traces of *MID* and *LOW* are obtained similarly:

$$
\begin{aligned}
\text{traces}(\mathit{HIGH}) &= \bigcup_i \text{traces}(H_i) \\
\text{traces}(\mathit{MID}) &= \bigcup_i \text{traces}(M_i) \\
\text{traces}(\mathit{LOW}) &= \bigcup_i \text{traces}(L_i)
\end{aligned}
$$

Example 4.3.7 A collection of three processes $\langle C_i \mid 0 \leqslant i \leqslant 2 \rangle$ indexed by the set $\{0, 1, 2\}$ may be defined as follows:

$$
C_i = \begin{array}{ll}
\mathit{around} \to C_i & \text{if } i = 0 \\
\left(\begin{array}{l} \mathit{around} \to C_i \\ \square\, \mathit{down} \to C_{i-1} \end{array}\right) & \text{otherwise}
\end{array}
$$

The conditional statement simply allows the expression of a family of process definitions as a single parameterized definition. It is shorthand for the family of process definitions

$$
\begin{aligned}
C_0 &= \mathit{around} \to C_0 \\
C_1 &= \mathit{around} \to C_1 \,\square\, \mathit{down} \to C_0 \\
C_2 &= \mathit{around} \to C_2 \,\square\, \mathit{down} \to C_1
\end{aligned}
$$

The notation $C_{i,j}$ will refer to the jth approximation to C_i. Since the starting point for the unwindings is *STOP*, each $C_{i,0}$ must be *STOP*. The first approximations are

$$
\begin{aligned}
C_{0,1} &= \mathit{around} \to \mathit{STOP} \\
C_{1,1} &= \mathit{around} \to \mathit{STOP} \,\square\, \mathit{down} \to \mathit{STOP} \\
C_{2,1} &= \mathit{around} \to \mathit{STOP} \,\square\, \mathit{down} \to \mathit{STOP}
\end{aligned}
$$

and their traces are as follows:

$$\text{traces}(C_{0,1}) = \{\langle\rangle, \langle around\rangle\}$$
$$\text{traces}(C_{1,1}) = \{\langle\rangle, \langle around\rangle, \langle down\rangle\}$$
$$\text{traces}(C_{2,1}) = \{\langle\rangle, \langle around\rangle, \langle down\rangle\}$$

The second approximations are

$$C_{0,2} = around \rightarrow C_{0,1}$$
$$C_{1,2} = around \rightarrow C_{1,1} \,\square\, down \rightarrow C_{0,1}$$
$$C_{2,2} = around \rightarrow C_{2,1} \,\square\, down \rightarrow C_{1,1}$$

The traces of the second approximations are derived from those of the first:

$$\text{traces}(C_{0,2}) = \{\langle\rangle, \langle around\rangle, \langle around, around\rangle\}$$
$$\text{traces}(C_{1,2}) = \{\langle\rangle, \langle around\rangle, \langle down\rangle, \langle around, around\rangle,$$
$$\langle around, down\rangle, \langle down, around\rangle\}$$
$$\text{traces}(C_{2,2}) = \{\langle\rangle, \langle around\rangle, \langle down\rangle, \langle around, around\rangle,$$
$$\langle around, down\rangle, \langle down, around\rangle, \langle down, down\rangle\}$$

In general, the traces of the nth approximations will be

$$\text{traces}(C_{0,n}) = \{tr \mid tr \in \{around\}^* \wedge \#tr \leqslant n\}$$
$$\text{traces}(C_{1,n}) = \{tr \mid tr \in \{around, down\}^* \wedge \#tr \leqslant n \wedge tr \downarrow down \leqslant 1\}$$
$$\text{traces}(C_{2,n}) = \{tr \mid tr \in \{around, down\}^* \wedge \#tr \leqslant n \wedge tr \downarrow down \leqslant 2\}$$

The traces of each C_i is the union of the traces of the approximations: $\text{traces}(C_i) = \bigcup_n \text{traces}(C_{i,n})$:

$$\text{traces}(C_0) = \{tr \mid tr \in \{around\}^*\}$$
$$\text{traces}(C_1) = \{tr \mid tr \in \{around, down\}^* \wedge tr \downarrow down \leqslant 1\}$$
$$\text{traces}(C_2) = \{tr \mid tr \in \{around, down\}^* \wedge tr \downarrow down \leqslant 2\}$$

Each C_i can do a maximum of i *down* events. ∎

A mutual recursion $\underline{N} = \underline{P}$ is event guarded in $\underline{F}$ if any name N_i appearing on the right-hand side of any equation has its corresponding process P_i event guarded for each name: whenever N_i appears in any of the P_j, then P_i must be event guarded for each N_j. If a process name N_i does not appear in any of the right-hand processes P_j, then there will never be any recursive calls to the process P_i and so it need not itself be guarded—only those processes which will be recursively called need to provide guards. For example, in the recursive definition

$$
\begin{aligned}
START &= LEFT \\
LEFT &= right \to RIGHT \\
RIGHT &= left \to LEFT
\end{aligned}
$$

only process variables _LEFT_ and _RIGHT_ appear in any of the right-hand process expressions, and both processes corresponding to those variables are event guarded. It follows that the mutual recursion is event guarded. Observe that the function $F_{START}(S, L, R) = L$ is not event guarded. However, _START_ does not appear on the right-hand side of the definition, and so this family of definitions is event guarded.

An event guarded function has a unique fixed point. This is a direct generalization of the same result for the case of a single recursion. It allows two families of processes to be shown to be equal, by establishing that they are both fixed points of a function whose variables are guarded. This is expressed in the third rule we give for recursion, which is a more general form of the unique fixed point result:

$$
(\underline{F}(\underline{Y}) \text{ guarded} \wedge (\underline{F}(\underline{P_1}) =_T \underline{P_1}) \wedge (\underline{F}(\underline{P_2}) =_T \underline{P_2})) \Rightarrow \underline{P_1} =_T \underline{P_2} \qquad \langle \mathsf{UFP}_T \rangle
$$

Example 4.3.8 This rule may be used for simplifying an interleaved combination of recursive processes.

$$
\begin{aligned}
BOUNCE &= up \to down \to BOUNCE \\
WOBBLE &= left \to right \to WOBBLE
\end{aligned}
$$

The process _BOUNCE_ ||| _WOBBLE_ cannot be written as a single recursive process. Expanding the interleaving yields

$\qquad$ _BOUNCE_ ||| _WOBBLE_

$=_T$ recursion-unwinding

$\qquad (up \to down \to BOUNCE)$ ||| $(left \to right \to WOBBLE)$

$=_T$ |||-step

$\qquad up \to ((down \to BOUNCE)$ ||| $(left \to right \to WOBBLE))$

$\qquad \Box \ left \to ((up \to down \to BOUNCE)$ ||| $(right \to WOBBLE))$

$=_T$ rule recursion-unwinding

$\qquad up \to ((down \to BOUNCE)$ ||| $WOBBLE)$

$\qquad \Box \ left \to (BOUNCE$ ||| $right \to WOBBLE)$

Similarly

$(down \rightarrow BOUNCE) \;|||\; WOBBLE$

$\quad =_T \quad down \rightarrow (BOUNCE \;|||\; WOBBLE)$

$\qquad\quad \Box \; left \rightarrow ((down \rightarrow BOUNCE) \;|||\; (right \rightarrow WOBBLE))$

$(down \rightarrow BOUNCE) \;|||\; (right \rightarrow WOBBLE)$

$\quad =_T \quad down \rightarrow (BOUNCE \;|||\; (right \rightarrow WOBBLE))$

$\qquad\quad \Box \; right \rightarrow ((down \rightarrow BOUNCE) \;|||\; WOBBLE)$

$BOUNCE \;|||\; (right \rightarrow WOBBLE)$

$\quad =_T \quad up \rightarrow ((down \rightarrow BOUNCE) \;|||\; (right \rightarrow WOBBLE))$

$\qquad\quad \Box \; right \rightarrow (BOUNCE \;|||\; WOBBLE)$

The result is a vector of four parallel processes

$$\underline{BW} \;\; = \;\; \left\langle \begin{array}{l} BOUNCE \;|||\; WOBBLE \\ BOUNCE \;|||\; (right \rightarrow WOBBLE) \\ (down \rightarrow BOUNCE) \;|||\; (right \rightarrow WOBBLE) \\ (down \rightarrow BOUNCE) \;|||\; WOBBLE \end{array} \right\rangle$$

given as functions of each other. The functions, given in terms of processes $\underline{N}$ indexed from 0 to 3, may be extracted and made explicit:

$$
\begin{aligned}
F_0(\underline{N}) &= (up \rightarrow \underline{N}_1) \;\Box\; (left \rightarrow \underline{N}_3) \\
F_1(\underline{N}) &= (down \rightarrow \underline{N}_0) \;\Box\; (left \rightarrow \underline{N}_2) \\
F_2(\underline{N}) &= (down \rightarrow \underline{N}_3) \;\Box\; (right \rightarrow \underline{N}_1) \\
F_3(\underline{N}) &= (up \rightarrow \underline{N}_2) \;\Box\; (right \rightarrow \underline{N}_0)
\end{aligned}
$$

Then if $\underline{N} = \underline{F}(\underline{N})$, then UFP_T allows the deduction that $\underline{BW} =_T \underline{N}$, since they are both fixed points of $\underline{F}$. This means that $BOUNCE \;|||\; WOBBLE =_T \underline{N}_0$, so it can be rewritten as a mutual recursion to remove explicit parallelism. Its state space is illustrated in Figure 4.16. ∎

Example 4.3.9 Suppose that the counter of Example 1.3.6 is adapted so that it can only perform increments, and no longer has decrements as an option:

$$COUNTUP(n) \;\; = \;\; increment \rightarrow COUNTUP(n+1)$$

Then any of the $COUNTUP(n)$ processes can perform arbitrary sequences of *increment* events, and no other events. It appears that each process is equivalent to $N = increment \rightarrow N$. In

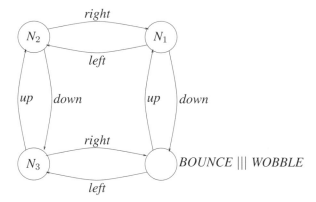

Fig. 4.16 **The transitions of** *BOUNCE ||| WOBBLE*

fact, this can be shown by setting a vector of processes $\underline{N}$ so that each $\underline{N}_i = N$ as defined by the recursion. Then

$$
\begin{aligned}
\underline{N}_n &=_T & N \\
&=_T & increment \to N \\
&=_T & increment \to \underline{N}_{n+1}
\end{aligned}
$$

so the vector $\underline{N}$ is a fixed point of the guarded function used to define $\underline{COUNTUP}$, and hence by UFP_T the two families of processes must be the same. It follows that each $COUNTUP(n)$ is trace equivalent to $N = increment \to N$. ■

Example 4.3.10 The counter of Example 1.3.6 is defined as a mutual recursion, which maintains the difference between the numbers of *increment*s and *decrement*s, and allows *decrement* provided this number is strictly positive:

$$
\begin{aligned}
COUNT(0) &= increment \to COUNT(1) \\
COUNT(n+1) &= increment \to COUNT(n+2) \\
&\qquad \Box\; decrement \to COUNT(n)
\end{aligned}
$$

The following process expression *SPAWN* describes a process with the same behaviour as $COUNT(0)$: every time *increment* is performed, a process is spawned which can independently perform *decrement* exactly once.

$$
SPAWN \;=\; increment \to (SPAWN \;|||\; decrement \to STOP)
$$

To show that $SPAWN =_T COUNT(0)$ it is sufficient to find a family of processes $\underline{S}$ which is a fixed point of the function defining $\underline{COUNT}$, and such that $\underline{S}_0 = SPAWN$.

Define

$$\underline{S}_n \quad = \quad SPAWN \; ||| \; (\big|\big|\big|_{i=1}^{n}(decrement \to STOP))$$

Observe (recalling Exercise 4.7) that

$$\big|\big|\big|_{i=1}^{n+1}(decrement \to STOP) \quad =_T \quad decrement \to (\big|\big|\big|_{i=1}^{n} decrement \to STOP)$$

Then

$$
\begin{aligned}
S_0 \quad &= \quad SPAWN \\
&=_T \quad increment \to (SPAWN \; ||| \; decrement \to STOP) \\
&=_T \quad increment \to S_1
\end{aligned}
$$

$$
\begin{aligned}
\underline{S}_{n+1} \quad &= \quad SPAWN \; ||| \; \big|\big|\big|_{i=1}^{n+1}(decrement \to STOP) \\
&=_T \quad (increment \to (SPAWN \; ||| \; decrement \to STOP)) \\
&\qquad ||| \; decrement \to \big|\big|\big|_{i=1}^{n}(decrement \to STOP) \\
&=_T \quad increment \to (SPAWN \; ||| \; decrement \to STOP \\
&\qquad\qquad\qquad ||| \; \big|\big|\big|_{i=1}^{n+1}(decrement \to STOP)) \\
&\qquad \Box \, decrement \to (SPAWN \; ||| \; \big|\big|\big|_{i=1}^{n} decrement \to STOP) \\
&=_T \quad increment \to \underline{S}_{n+2} \; \Box \; decrement \to \underline{S}_n
\end{aligned}
$$

The $\underline{S}_n$ meet the same guarded equations as the $COUNT(n)$, so they must be the same by UFP_T. This means that $\underline{S}_0 =_T SPAWN =_T COUNT(0)$. ■

4.4 TESTING

A completely different approach to understanding CSP processes can be given directly in terms of the operational semantics. Some very simple and natural notions of how processes should be distinguished and when they should be considered equivalent can be given purely in terms of the possibility of a single event's occurrence within some test. It turns out that this approach gives the same results as the denotational traces model for CSP, and this equivalence provides a better understanding of the traces model.

Processes may be analysed in terms of how they behave in particular contexts. The response of processes to particular *tests* can be used to compare different process expressions, and two processes will be considered equivalent if each of their responses to any test is the same: two processes are judged equivalent if no test can tell them apart.

Tests will themselves be constructed from the CSP language, extended with a special process $SUCCESS$ which will be used to indicate that an execution has succeeded by means of performing a special 'success' event $\omega \notin \Sigma^{\checkmark}$. The operational semantics of $SUCCESS$ is given by

$$SUCCESS \xrightarrow{\omega} STOP$$

For example, the test

$$T_0 = a \to SUCCESS$$

will reach the success state after the occurrence of an a event, and the test

$$T_1 = a \to SUCCESS \,\square\, b \to SUCCESS$$

succeeds after either an a or a b event.

A test T can be used to test a CSP process P by running P and T together in parallel, and hiding all events apart from the success event ω:

$$(P \underset{\Sigma}{\|} T) \setminus \Sigma$$

Since all events apart from ω are hidden, the only visible event that this combination might possibly perform is an ω event, which denotes a successful execution[1]. The test T_0 above will succeed if a is one of the first events that the tested process P can perform. For example, the process $a \to b \to STOP$ will have a successful execution with T_0, since $(a \to SUCCESS \underset{\Sigma}{\|} a \to b \to STOP) \setminus \Sigma$ can perform ω after the internal synchronization on a. However, $b \to a \to STOP$ has no successful execution.

The approach of *may testing* is concerned with the possibility of successful execution of a process under a test. The notation P **may** T indicates that there is some successful execution of P under test T:

$$P \text{ \bf may } T \quad = \quad ((P \underset{\Sigma}{\|} T) \setminus \Sigma) \xRightarrow{\langle \omega \rangle}$$

Two processes P_1 and P_2 will be distinguished under may testing if there is some test T which distinguishes them: in other words, either P_1 **may** T and $\neg (P_2 \text{ \bf may } T)$ or else P_2 **may** T

---

[1] Unlike other events, ω may also occur after termination to allow testing for termination. A new construct $SKIP_\omega$ which has one transition $SKIP_\omega \xrightarrow{\checkmark} SUCCESS$ may also be used in the construction of tests.

and $\neg\,(P_1\ \textbf{may}\ T)$. If there is no such test, then they will be considered equivalent under may testing:

$$P_1 \equiv_{may} P_2 \quad = \quad \forall\,T \bullet P_1\ \textbf{may}\ T \Leftrightarrow P_2\ \textbf{may}\ T$$

For example, $a \to b \to STOP$ and $b \to a \to STOP$ are distinguished by the test $a \to SUCCESS$. On the other hand, the processes $a \to STOP \sqcap b \to STOP$ and $a \to STOP \;\square\; b \to STOP$ may pass exactly the same tests, and so will be equivalent under may testing.

$$(a \to b \to STOP \quad \not\equiv_{may} \quad b \to a \to STOP)$$
$$a \to STOP \;\square\; b \to STOP \quad \equiv_{may} \quad a \to STOP \sqcap b \to STOP$$

The definition of may testing equivalence, although it provides a natural approach to process equivalence, would be cumbersome to use in practice since it requires consideration of all possible tests in order to show that two processes are equivalent. A significant result is that this form of equivalence is exactly the same as traces equivalence:

$$P_1 \equiv_{may} P_2 \quad \Leftrightarrow \quad \mathsf{traces}(P_1) = \mathsf{traces}(P_2)$$

This means that the traces model provides exactly the framework required for establishing may testing equivalence. Technically, the traces model is said to be *fully abstract* with respect to may testing. The traces model contains exactly the information required to compare and contrast processes in terms of how they might behave in a may testing context. If two processes have different trace sets, then there will be some test which can distinguish them, and conversely if they have exactly the same trace sets, then no test can distinguish them.

Testing also naturally gives rise to a refinement relation:

$$P_1 \sqsubseteq_{may} P_2 \quad = \quad \forall\,T \bullet \neg\,(P_1\ \textbf{may}\ T) \Rightarrow \neg\,(P_2\ \textbf{may}\ T)$$

This states that if a specification process P_1 is unable to pass a given test T, then this indicates a limitation on what P_1 considered as a specification allows, and so no implementation should be able to pass the test T either. Although this definition is intuitive, it would be laborious to apply directly in practice because it would involve consideration of an infinity of tests. However, it does provide an alternative understanding of refinement in the traces model (introduced in the next chapter, on page 168), since these two characterizations of refinement are equivalent:

$$P_1 \sqsubseteq_{may} P_2 \quad \Leftrightarrow \quad P_1 \sqsubseteq_T P_2$$

4.5 CONGRUENCE

May testing defines a way of identifying when two processes should be considered equivalent. All that is required for a relation to be an equivalence relation $\equiv$ on a set S is that it is reflexive, symmetric, and transitive:

reflexive: $\forall x : S \bullet x \equiv x$

symmetric: $\forall x, y : S \bullet x \equiv y \Leftrightarrow y \equiv x$

transitive: $\forall x, y, z : S \bullet x \equiv y \wedge y \equiv z \Rightarrow x \equiv z$

For example, an equivalence on the positive integers $\mathbb{N}^+$ might identify two integers if they are the same modulo 3, so 1 and 4 are considered equivalent modulo 3. This could be written as $1 \equiv_3 4$.

A *congruence* is a stronger form of equivalence, which is preserved by the operations on that set. In other words, if the same operation is carried out on two elements that are equivalent, then the two results should again be equivalent. Equivalence modulo 3 on $\mathbb{N}^+$ is a congruence when the only operations of interest are addition and multiplication. However, if exponentiation is also allowed as an operation, then it is no longer a congruence, since for example $1 \equiv 4$ but $\neg(2^1 \equiv_3 2^4)$. This operation allows a context in which some equivalent numbers can be distinguished, by giving a different result when applied to each of them. Whether or not an equivalence on S is also a congruence on S depends on the operations allowed.

Any equivalence $\equiv$ on a set S will have an associated congruence $\cong$: the weakest congruence which is stronger than it. Two conditions must hold: firstly $\cong$ is stronger than $\equiv$ if

1. $\forall x, y : S \bullet x \cong y \Rightarrow x \equiv y$

For example, equivalence modulo 6 is stronger than equivalence modulo 3—if two numbers are equivalent modulo 6, then they are equivalent modulo 3: $x \equiv_6 y \Rightarrow x \equiv_3 y$. However, equivalence modulo 2 is not stronger than equivalence modulo 3, since for example $2 \equiv_2 10$ but $\neg(2 \equiv_3 10)$.

Being the *weakest* congruence stronger than $\equiv$-equivalence means that the associated congruence should be weaker than any other congruence $\cong'$ which is stronger than $\equiv$:

2. If $\cong'$ is a congruence stronger than $\equiv$ then it is also stronger than $\cong$.

For example, under the operations of addition, multiplication, and exponentiation, equivalence modulo 6 is the weakest congruence stronger than equivalence modulo 3.

Generally in considering CSP processes, an equivalence relation itself is not so useful as its associated congruence relation. This is because processes are components of systems, and so their behaviour in a variety of contexts is more important than their behaviour in isolation. An equivalence relation allows natural distinctions between processes to be expressed, and the associated congruence establishes what else is required for equivalence to be preserved in all contexts.

A denotational model such as the traces model automatically provides a congruence for the language simply by virtue of the compositional way the language semantics is defined. Since trace equivalence is the same as may testing equivalence, this means that may testing equivalence must also be a congruence, so any two processes which cannot be distinguished by any test can replace each other within any process context without changing the overall result.

Exercises

Exercise 4.1 What are the traces associated with the following finite state machines?

Exercise 4.2 Give the traces of the following processes:

1. $a \rightarrow STOP \mid b \rightarrow c \rightarrow STOP$

2. $a \rightarrow STOP \mid b \rightarrow (c \rightarrow STOP \mid d \rightarrow STOP)$

3. $a \rightarrow STOP \;\square\; a \rightarrow b \rightarrow STOP$

4. $\bigsqcap_{n \in \mathbb{Z}} out!n \rightarrow out!(n^2) \rightarrow STOP$

5. $a \rightarrow b \rightarrow RUN_{\{a,b\}}$

6. $(a \rightarrow b \rightarrow STOP) \;\sqcap\; RUN_{\{a,c\}}$

Exercise 4.3 Why is the empty trace explicitly included in the definition of indexed external choice? Why is it not also included in the definition of indexed internal choice?

Exercise 4.4 Prove the soundness of Law $\square$-zero$_T$ from the definition given for traces$(P_1 \;\square\; P_2)$.

Exercise 4.5 Prove the soundness of Law $\square$-unit.

Exercise 4.6 Simplify each of the following where possible, where $\alpha(P) \subseteq A$:

1. $P \ _A\|_A \ RUN_A\checkmark$
2. $P \ _A\|_B \ RUN_B\checkmark$ (where $B \subseteq A$)
3. $P \ _A\|_B \ RUN_B\checkmark$ (where $B \not\subseteq A$)
4. $P \ _A\|_B \ RUN_{(B \setminus A)}\checkmark$ (where $A \subseteq B$)
5. $P \ _A\|_A \ STOP$
6. $P \ _A\|_B \ STOP$ (where $A \subseteq B$)
7. $P \ _A\|_B \ STOP$ (where $A \not\subseteq B$)

Exercise 4.7 Given that $\left|\left|\left|\right.\right._{i=1}^1 \ a \to STOP =_T a \to STOP$, prove (by induction on n) that

$$\left|\left|\left|\right.\right.\right._{i=1}^{n+1} a \to STOP \quad =_T \quad a \to \left(\left|\left|\left|\right.\right.\right._{i=1}^{n} a \to STOP\right)$$

Exercise 4.8 What are the traces of the following processes?

1. $coin \to change \to SKIP \ \Box \ coin \to ticket \to SKIP$
2. $coin \to change \to SKIP \ \| \ coin \to ticket \to SKIP$
3. $coin \to change \to SKIP \ \|\|\| \ coin \to ticket \to SKIP$
4. $coin \to change \to SKIP \ \triangle \ coin \to ticket \to SKIP$

Exercise 4.9 What are the traces of P_1, P_2, and $P_1 \ _A\|_B \ P_2$ of Example 4.2.10?

Exercise 4.10 Is $f(f^{-1}(P)) =_T P$ true for any alphabet renaming function f? How about $f^{-1}(f(P)) =_T P$? In each case give a proof or a counterexample.

Exercise 4.11 What are the traces of the recursive process *TASKS* of Example 3.4.3?

Exercise 4.12 Calculate the traces of the recursive process

$$P \ = \ up \to (P \ \Box \ SKIP); down \to SKIP$$

Exercise 4.13 Calculate the traces of the recursive process

$$P \ = \ in?x : \mathbb{N} \to ((out!x \to P) \gg COPY)$$

Exercise 4.14 Is $F(Y) = a \to Y \;\Box\; b \to Y$ guarded? What are the traces of $N = F(N)$? Are there any other fixed points?

Exercise 4.15 Is $F(Y) = a \to Y \;{}_{\{a\}}\|_{\{a\}}\; Y$ guarded? What are the traces of $N = F(N)$? Are there any other fixed points?

Exercise 4.16 Is $F(Y) = ((x : \Sigma \to Y) \;\Box\; SKIP) \;\||\;\; Y$ guarded? What are the traces of $N = F(N)$? Are there any other fixed points?

Exercise 4.17 Rewrite $ATT \;\|\; CUST$ of Example 2.1.3 as a recursion which does not contain any parallel operators.

Exercise 4.18 Show that $(SPY \;\|\; MASTER) \setminus \{relay\}$ of Example 3.1.1 is equivalent to $listen?x \to RECORD(x)$, where $RECORD$ is defined by a mutual recursion

$$
\begin{aligned}
RECORD(x) \;=\; & listen?y \to log!x \to RECORD(y) \\
& \Box\; log!x \to listen?y \to RECORD(y)
\end{aligned}
$$

Exercise 4.19 If $OUT_x = out!x \to OUT_x$, then a variable can be described recursively as $V_x = OUT_x \;\triangle\; in?y \to V_y$. It can also be defined using the equation $VAR_x = in?y \to VAR_y \;\Box\; out!x \to VAR_x$. Use the unique fixed point law to show that these define the same process.

Exercise 4.20 Find a test which distinguishes $a \to b \to STOP$ from $a \to b \to c \to STOP$ under may testing.

Exercise 4.21 Find a test that distinguishes $M = (a \to b \to M \sqcap b \to a \to M)$ from $N = (a \to N \sqcap b \to N)$ under may testing.

Exercise 4.22 Is there a test that distinguishes $a \to STOP \sqcap a \to b \to STOP$ from $a \to b \to STOP$ under may testing?

Exercise 4.23 Is there a test that distinguishes $a \to b \to STOP$ from $a \to STOP \;\||\; b \to STOP$ under may testing?

Exercise 4.24 Is there a test that distinguishes $N = a \to N$ from $\bigsqcap_{n \in \mathbb{N}} A(n)$ under may testing, where $A(0) = STOP$ and $A(n + 1) = a \to A(n)$?

Exercise 4.25 Can the processes $STOP$ and $SKIP$ be told apart without the presence of $SKIP_\omega$ in the language of tests?

Exercise 4.26 A congruence over a language is dependent on the constructs of the language. If new operators are introduced to the language, then the requirements for an equivalence to be a congruence alter, since the equivalence must also be respected by the new operators.

Suppose that a new operator $Int(P)$ is added to the language of CSP, with transitions as follows:

$$\frac{P \xrightarrow{a} P'}{Int(P) \xrightarrow{a} Int(P')} \qquad\qquad \frac{P \xrightarrow{\tau} P'}{Int(P) \xrightarrow{\tau} STOP}$$

$Int(P)$ can deadlock at any stage where internal transitions are possible for P.

1. Is may testing equivalence still a congruence in the language extended with this new operator?

2. What is the congruence associated with the equivalence relation $\equiv_{may}$ for the extended language?

3. Can a denotational definition be given for this operator in the traces model?

5

Specification and verification with traces

5.1 PROPERTY-ORIENTED SPECIFICATION

Systems are designed to satisfy particular requirements, and one of the uses of their semantics is to enable them to be judged against given specifications. In the traces model, a specification on a CSP process is given in terms of the traces it may engage in. It will characterize the traces that are acceptable and those that are not. A process meets the specification if all of its executions are acceptable: no matter which choices are taken, any execution of the process is guaranteed not to violate the specification.

If $S(tr)$ is a predicate on traces tr, then process P *meets* or *satisfies* $S(tr)$ if $S(tr)$ holds for every trace tr of P.

$$P \textbf{ sat } S(tr) \quad = \quad \forall\, tr \in \textsf{traces}(P) \bullet S(tr)$$

The specification $S(tr)$ is said to be a *property-oriented specification*, since the required property is captured directly in terms of restrictions on traces. The predicate S may be expressed in any notation, though in practice first order logic and elementary set and sequence notation are generally sufficient.

Example 5.1.1 The requirement that there should not be more *down* events than *up* events is captured as the predicate

$$S(tr) = tr \downarrow down \leqslant tr \downarrow up$$

This states that the length of the trace restricted to the *down* event (i.e. the number of occurrences of *down*) should not exceed the length of the trace restricted to the *up* event. For a process to satisfy this specification, no possible trace should have more *down* events than *up* events: at no stage must the specification be violated.

The process $up \rightarrow up \rightarrow down \rightarrow STOP$ has as its trace set

$$\text{traces}(up \rightarrow up \rightarrow down \rightarrow STOP) \quad = \quad \{ \ \langle\rangle, \langle up \rangle, \langle up, up \rangle, \langle up, up, down \rangle \ \}$$

and every trace *tr* in that set meets $S(tr)$. It follows that

$$up \rightarrow up \rightarrow down \rightarrow STOP \quad \textbf{sat} \quad tr \downarrow down \leqslant tr \downarrow up$$

■

If a process P fails to meet a specification $S(tr)$, then this must be because it has some (finite) trace for which S fails to hold: there is a point where the performance of a particular event takes the execution of P outside the specification. To meet a trace specification, it is necessary to ensure that at every stage of an execution no violating events are performed. This kind of specification is called a *safety* specification, which requires that nothing 'bad' should ever happen, and it is precisely this kind of property that is expressed as specifications on traces.

Since every process has the empty trace $\langle\rangle$ as one of its traces, any specification S which is satisfiable by some process must hold for the empty trace. If $S(\langle\rangle)$ does not hold, then this means that the specification is violated before the process even begins to execute, and so no process could meet it. The check $S(\langle\rangle)$ is a necessary condition for satisfiability.

Conversely the process *STOP* has the empty trace as its only trace. Hence any satisfiable specification will be met by *STOP*. It is certainly the safest process in the sense of trace specifications: it is always safe to do nothing, even if it is not very useful. In subsequent chapters other forms of specification will be discussed, notably *liveness* specifications, which *STOP* will not satisfy. But within the context of observations as traces, and considering only safety specifications, *STOP* is the process that meets all satisfiable specifications.

Example 5.1.2 The requirement $PR(tr)$ that some event a should always precede another event b may be expressed a number of different ways:

$$
\begin{aligned}
PR_1(tr) &= (tr = tr_0 \frown \langle b \rangle \frown tr_1) \Rightarrow tr_0 \upharpoonright a \neq \langle\rangle \\
PR_2(tr) &= (tr = tr_0 \frown \langle b \rangle \frown tr_1) \Rightarrow tr \upharpoonright a \neq \langle\rangle \\
PR_3(tr) &= tr \upharpoonright a = \langle\rangle \Rightarrow tr \upharpoonright b = \langle\rangle
\end{aligned}
$$

The first predicate, PR_1, states that if a trace may be split around the event b, then the segment before the b event should contain an a event. The second predicate, PR_2, states that if a trace contains a b event, then it should contain an a event somewhere within it. PR_2 is not equivalent to PR_1 at the level of traces, since there are some traces (the simplest being $\langle b, a \rangle$) which meet PR_2 but not PR_1. However, they are equivalent at the level of *specifications* on processes, in the sense that P **sat** $PR_1(tr) \Leftrightarrow P$ **sat** $PR_2(tr)$ for any process P. This is a result of the downward closure property $T2$. If a trace tr of P meets PR_2 and P **sat** PR_2, then any prefix of tr should also meet PR_2. In particular, if $tr_0 \frown \langle b \rangle \frown tr_1$ is such a trace, then $tr_0 \frown \langle b \rangle$ is another such trace. Since PR_2 states that a is in the latter trace, it must be in tr_0, the part of the trace that precedes b.

The predicate $PR_3(tr)$ is equivalent to $PR_2(tr)$, but expressed rather differently: it states that if a has not yet occurred, then b cannot yet have occurred. ∎

Example 5.1.3 The typical requirement on a buffer or queue process is that messages are output in the same order as, and subsequent to, their input. This is captured by the specification that at any stage, the sequence of outputs that have been observed must be a prefix of the sequence of inputs.

$$B(tr) \;=\; tr \Downarrow out \leqslant tr \Downarrow in$$

This safety specification can be violated only by a process performing the wrong output at some point. ∎

5.2 VERIFICATION

The compositional nature of the trace semantics for CSP allows a compositional proof system to be provided for trace specifications. Specifications of processes may be deduced from specifications about their components, in a way which reflects the trace semantics of the CSP operators. The proof system is given as a set of proof rules for all of the CSP operators, in each case giving as conclusion a specification which holds of a composite process, from antecedents which describe specifications which hold for the component processes. The proof rules are sound with respect to the trace semantics given for the CSP operators, and complete relative to completeness of the specification language.

There are three rules whose validity is due to the nature of **sat** specification, and which therefore hold for all CSP processes.

The first is that any process meets the vacuous specification $true(tr)$, which holds for all traces tr.

$$\frac{}{P \text{ **sat** } true(tr)}$$

The second is that any specification may be weakened:

$$\frac{P \text{ **sat** } S(tr)}{P \text{ **sat** } T(tr)} \quad [\, \forall tr : TRACE \bullet S(tr) \Rightarrow T(tr) \,]$$

The final rule states that if $S(tr)$ and $T(tr)$ have been established separately, then the specification consisting of their conjunction is also established:

$$\frac{\begin{array}{l} P \text{ sat } S(tr) \\ P \text{ sat } T(tr) \end{array}}{P \text{ sat } (S \wedge T)(tr)}$$

This last rule allows separate proofs for $S(tr)$ and $T(tr)$, and then for the results to be combined. For instance, one proof may establish that $P \text{ sat } tr \downarrow a \leqslant tr \downarrow b$, and another proof may establish that $P \text{ sat } tr \downarrow b \leqslant tr \downarrow c$. This rule allows the deduction that

$$P \text{ sat } (tr \downarrow a \leqslant tr \downarrow b \wedge tr \downarrow b \leqslant tr \downarrow c)$$

and the previous rule, which allows weakening of a specification within a **sat** specification, is used to deduce

$$P \text{ sat } (tr \downarrow a \leqslant tr \downarrow c)$$

This chain of reasoning is independent of the nature of the process P, once the initial specifications for P are established.

STOP

There is only one trace of the process *STOP*: the empty trace. The strongest specification that is met by the process *STOP* is that $tr = \langle \rangle$. This is encapsulated in the rule

$$\frac{}{STOP \text{ sat } tr = \langle \rangle}$$

The rule has no antecedents, corresponding to the fact that *STOP* has no component processes.

The weakening rule given above can be used to show that any specification which is satisfiable by any process must be satisfiable by *STOP*. If $P \text{ sat } S(tr)$ (for some process P), then S must hold of the empty trace: $S(\langle \rangle)$. This follows from the fact that $\langle \rangle$ is a trace of every process, and hence in particular of P. This means that $(tr = \langle \rangle) \Rightarrow S(tr)$, which may be used in an instance of the weakening rule:

$$\frac{STOP \text{ sat } (tr = \langle \rangle)}{STOP \text{ sat } S(tr)} \quad [\, \forall tr : TRACE \bullet (tr = \langle \rangle) \Rightarrow S(tr) \,]$$

In fact, the side condition is equivalent to the assertion $S(\langle \rangle)$.

Prefix

A trace of the process $a \rightarrow P$ is either empty, or begins with the event a followed by a trace of P. If P **sat** $S(tr)$ then the part of the trace after a (that is: $tail(tr)$) must meet the specification S. This leads to the following proof rule:

$$\frac{P \textbf{ sat } S(tr)}{a \rightarrow P \textbf{ sat } \quad tr = \langle \rangle \\ \vee \\ head(tr) = a \wedge S(tail(tr))}$$

For instance, to show that $b \rightarrow a \rightarrow STOP$ **sat** $tr \downarrow a \leqslant tr \downarrow b$, the fact that $STOP$ **sat** $tr = \langle \rangle$ may be used. The proof rule for prefix allows the deduction that

$$a \rightarrow STOP \textbf{ sat } (tr = \langle \rangle \vee (head(tr) = a \wedge (tail(tr) = \langle \rangle)))$$

which may be weakened to

$$a \rightarrow STOP \textbf{ sat } tr \downarrow a \leqslant 1$$

This intermediate weakening allows a more concise specification to be carried through the rest of the proof.

A second application of the prefix rule then yields

$$b \rightarrow a \rightarrow STOP \textbf{ sat } \quad tr = \langle \rangle \\ \vee \\ head(tr) = b \wedge tail(tr) \downarrow a \leqslant 1$$

and each disjunct in turn may be weakened to produce

$$b \rightarrow a \rightarrow STOP \textbf{ sat } \quad tr \downarrow a \leqslant tr \downarrow b \\ \vee \\ tr \downarrow b \geqslant 1 \wedge tr \downarrow a \leqslant 1$$

which weakens finally to produce

$$b \rightarrow a \rightarrow STOP \textbf{ sat } tr \downarrow a \leqslant tr \downarrow b$$

Prefix choice

The prefix choice operator generalizes the prefix operator: it contains a number of component processes, and the first event that is performed can be any one of the menu of events offered.

The antecedent to the rule assumes a family of specifications $S_a(tr)$, one for each of the components $P(a)$.

$$\frac{\forall\, a \in A \bullet P(a) \textbf{ sat } S_a(tr)}{\begin{aligned} x : A \to P(x) \textbf{ sat } \quad & tr = \langle\rangle \\ & \vee \\ & \exists\, a \in A \bullet head(tr) = a \wedge S_a(tail(tr)) \end{aligned}}$$

Output and input

The output process $c!v \to P$ is simply a particular kind of prefix process, and the proof rule reflects this:

$$\frac{P \textbf{ sat } S(tr)}{\begin{aligned} c!v \to P \textbf{ sat } \quad & tr = \langle\rangle \\ & \vee \\ & head(tr) = c.v \wedge S(tail(tr)) \end{aligned}}$$

Similarly, the input process $c?x : T \to P(x)$ is a special form of prefix choice, and so the proof rule is very similar:

$$\frac{\forall\, v \in T \bullet P(v) \textbf{ sat } S_v(tr)}{\begin{aligned} c?x : T \to P(x) \textbf{ sat } \quad & tr = \langle\rangle \\ & \vee \\ & \exists\, v \in T \bullet head(tr) = c.v \wedge S_v(tail(tr)) \end{aligned}}$$

SKIP

The process *SKIP* does nothing except terminate successfully. It has only two possible traces, one for the situation before it has terminated successfully, and the other for the situation after. These two traces are $\langle\rangle$ and $\langle\checkmark\rangle$, so the inference rule, which has no antecedents, is as follows:

$$\frac{}{SKIP \textbf{ sat } tr = \langle\rangle \vee tr = \langle\checkmark\rangle}$$

RUN

The process *RUN* is able to engage in any trace. If it is able to meet a specification, then that specification must allow all possible traces. This will therefore be an extremely weak specification, since it places no restrictions on the traces that are acceptable. This specification is equivalent to *true*:

$$\overline{\quad\quad\quad\quad\quad\quad} \atop RUN \textbf{ sat } \textit{true}(tr)$$

In fact, this rule is superfluous, since the conclusion may already be derived from the first **sat** rule given above, concerning the vacuous specification *true*. However, it is given here for the process *RUN* in order to cover that process explicitly.

External choice

The process $P_1 \;\square\; P_2$ behaves either as P_1 or as P_2. If P_1 **sat** $S(tr)$ and P_2 **sat** $T(tr)$, then the choice process $P_1 \;\square\; P_2$ satisfies the disjunction of these two specifications:

$$\frac{P_1 \textbf{ sat } S(tr) \\ P_2 \textbf{ sat } T(tr)}{P_1 \;\square\; P_2 \textbf{ sat } S(tr) \vee T(tr)}$$

Any trace of $P_1 \;\square\; P_2$ will meet either $S(tr)$ if it arises from P_1, or else $T(tr)$ if it is generated from P_2.

The indexed external choice $\square_{i \in I} P_i$ behaves in a similar way, meeting the disjunction of the specifications met by its components:

$$\frac{\forall i \in I \bullet P_i \textbf{ sat } S_i(tr)}{\square_{i \in I} P_i \textbf{ sat } \exists i \in I \bullet S_i(tr)}$$

Any trace of the indexed choice must meet at least one of the component specifications.

Internal choice

The internal choice operator has the same trace semantics as the external choice operator, so the inference rules will also be the same:

$$\frac{P_1 \textbf{ sat } S(tr) \\ P_2 \textbf{ sat } T(tr)}{P_1 \;\sqcap\; P_2 \textbf{ sat } S(tr) \vee T(tr)}$$

$$\frac{\forall i \in J \bullet P_i \textbf{ sat } S_i(tr)}{\sqcap_{i \in J} P_i \textbf{ sat } \exists i \in J \bullet S_i(tr)}$$

Parallel composition

A trace tr of the process P_1 $_A\|_B$ P_2 is comprised of a contribution from P_1 and a contribution from P_2, contained within the alphabets $A^\checkmark$ and $B^\checkmark$ respectively. In fact, the projection of the trace onto $A^\checkmark$ —$tr \restriction A^\checkmark$ —is a trace of P_1, and the projection $tr \restriction B^\checkmark$ is a trace of P_2. If P_1 **sat** $S(tr)$, then this means that $S(tr \restriction A^\checkmark)$ must hold. Similarly, if P_2 **sat** $T(tr)$, then $T(tr \restriction B^\checkmark)$ must hold. Finally, only events in $A^\checkmark$ or $B^\checkmark$ are possible for the parallel combination, so it follows that $\sigma(tr) \subseteq (A \cup B)^\checkmark$. This leads to the following proof rule:

$$\frac{\begin{array}{l} P_1 \text{ sat } S(tr) \\ P_2 \text{ sat } T(tr) \end{array}}{P_1 \, {}_A\|_B \, P_2 \text{ sat } S(tr \restriction A^\checkmark) \wedge T(tr \restriction B^\checkmark) \wedge \sigma(tr) \subseteq (A \cup B)^\checkmark}$$

This rule demonstrates the way in which parallel composition corresponds to conjunction: the constraints S and T both hold, on their respective alphabets.

For instance, the following recursive processes meet specifications as follows:

$$P_1 = b \rightarrow a \rightarrow P_1 \quad \text{sat} \quad S(tr) = (tr \downarrow a \leqslant tr \downarrow b)$$
$$P_2 = c \rightarrow b \rightarrow P_2 \quad \text{sat} \quad T(tr) = (tr \downarrow b \leqslant tr \downarrow c)$$

Then the combination $P_1 \, {}_{\{a,b\}}\|_{\{b,c\}} \, P_2$ meets the specification

$$S(tr \restriction \{a,b\}^\checkmark) \wedge T(tr \restriction \{b,c\}^\checkmark) \wedge \sigma(tr) \subseteq \{a,b,c\}^\checkmark$$

Observe that $S(tr)$ is concerned only with the occurrence of the events a and b in the trace tr, and its truth depends only on the trace restricted to those two events. Thus $S(tr) \Leftrightarrow S(tr \restriction \{a,b\}^\checkmark)$, and similarly $T(tr) \Leftrightarrow T(tr \restriction \{b,c\}^\checkmark)$. This often turns out to be the case when processes are combined in parallel, since the interface set for a process generally contains all of the events that it can perform, and specifications on such processes are usually concerned only with constraints on their performable events.

The specification is then equivalent to

$$S(tr) \wedge T(tr) \wedge \sigma(tr) \subseteq \{a,b,c\}^\checkmark$$

which reduces to

$$tr \downarrow a \leqslant tr \downarrow b \leqslant tr \downarrow c \wedge \sigma(tr) \subseteq \{a,b,c\}^\checkmark$$

The constraints imposed by P_1 and P_2 separately ensure that c must occur at least as often as a does.

The rule for the indexed parallel operator follows a similar pattern. Each component P_i with interface A_i imposes its own constraint $S_i(tr)$ on the projection of the overall trace onto the alphabet A_i.

$$\frac{\forall i \in I \bullet P_i \text{ sat } S_i(tr)}{\left\|\right\|_{A_i}^{i \in I} P_i \text{ sat } (\forall i \in I \bullet S_i(tr \restriction A_i^\checkmark)) \wedge \sigma(tr) \subseteq \left(\bigcup_{i \in I} A_i\right)^\checkmark}$$

Interleaving

An interleaved combination $P_1 \ ||| \ P_2$ performs traces tr which consist of a trace tr_1 of P_1 interleaved with a trace tr_2 of P_2. This leads to the following inference rule:

$$\frac{\begin{array}{l} P_1 \ \mathbf{sat} \ S(tr) \\ P_2 \ \mathbf{sat} \ T(tr) \end{array}}{P_1 \ ||| \ P_2 \ \mathbf{sat} \ \exists \, tr_1, tr_2 \bullet (S(tr_1) \wedge T(tr_2) \wedge tr \ \mathsf{interleaves} \ tr_1, tr_2)}$$

The resulting specification on tr met by $P_1 \ ||| \ P_2$ states that tr interleaves two traces meeting S and T respectively.

Example 5.2.1 Let $term(tr) = \checkmark \in \sigma(tr)$ denote that the trace corresponds to a terminating execution. If $P_1 \ \mathbf{sat} \ (term(tr) \Rightarrow S(tr))$ and $P_2 \ \mathbf{sat} \ (term(tr) \Rightarrow T(tr))$, then $P_1 \ ||| \ P_2$ on termination will meet the appropriate combination of S and T. For example, let $\mathsf{sum}(seq)$ be the sum of the elements of a sequence $seq \in \mathbb{Z}^*$. Then, for instance, the specification $S_n(tr) = (term(tr) \Rightarrow \mathsf{sum}(tr \Downarrow C) = n)$ states that at the time of termination, the sum of all the values passed along all the channels in the set C is n. If $P_1 \ \mathbf{sat} \ S_n(tr)$, and $P_2 \ \mathbf{sat} \ S_m(tr)$, then $P_1 \ ||| \ P_2 \ \mathbf{sat} \ S_{m+n}(tr)$: by the time of termination, the sum of the values passed by the parallel combination will be $m + n$. ∎

In practice the nature of S and T often allow this specification to be weakened to a more direct requirement $R(tr)$, by establishing the following:

$$\forall \, tr_1, tr_2 \bullet ((S(tr_1) \wedge T(tr_2) \wedge tr \ \mathsf{interleaves} \ tr_1, tr_2) \Rightarrow R(tr))$$

If $R(tr)$ holds whenever tr interleaves two traces meeting S and T, then it must hold for the particular traces tr_1 and tr_2 whose existence is asserted in the proof rule above. In such cases, it can be deduced that $P_1 \ ||| \ P_2 \ \mathbf{sat} \ R(tr)$.

This may be captured in an alternative proof rule:

$$\frac{\begin{array}{l} P_1 \ \mathbf{sat} \ S(tr) \\ P_2 \ \mathbf{sat} \ T(tr) \\ \forall \, tr_1, tr_2, tr : TRACE \bullet \left(\begin{array}{l} S(tr_1) \wedge T(tr_2) \\ \wedge \ tr \ \mathsf{interleaves} \ tr_1, tr_2 \end{array} \right) \Rightarrow R(tr) \end{array}}{P_1 \ ||| \ P_2 \ \mathbf{sat} \ R(tr)}$$

Example 5.2.2 Consider that $S(tr)$ is a specification which states that a must appear in the trace before b does. This may be captured as follows:

$$S(tr) \;=\; tr \upharpoonright a = \langle \rangle \Rightarrow tr \upharpoonright b = \langle \rangle$$

This states that if no a has occurred, then no b can have occurred. This is equivalent on processes to stating that any b event must be preceded by an a event because the trace sets of processes are prefix closed.

If both P_1 and P_2 meet specification $S(tr)$, then any b performed by one of the components of $P_1 \;|||\; P_2$ must have been preceded by an a event performed by the same component; so it appears that $P_1 \;|||\; P_2$ **sat** $S(tr)$. In order to establish this using the second proof rule for interleaving, it is necessary to check the third antecedent:

$$\left.\begin{array}{l} (tr_1 \upharpoonright a = \langle\rangle \Rightarrow tr_1 \upharpoonright b = \langle\rangle) \wedge \\ (tr_2 \upharpoonright a = \langle\rangle \Rightarrow tr_2 \upharpoonright b = \langle\rangle) \wedge \\ tr \text{ interleaves } tr_1, tr_2 \end{array}\right\} \Rightarrow (tr \upharpoonright a = \langle\rangle \Rightarrow tr \upharpoonright b = \langle\rangle)$$

This result is reasonably intuitive, but to establish it formally requires an inductive proof on tr because of the inductive definition of interleaves. ∎

Interleaved combinations $P_1 \;|||\; P_2$ are often used to make explicit the fact that the component processes have no direct interaction with one another, in cases where the alphabets of P_1 and P_2 (apart from termination) are disjoint. In such cases, it is sometimes more convenient for proof if the combination is rewritten to the form $P_1 \; _{\alpha(P_1)}\|_{\alpha(P_2)} \; P_2$ as follows:

$$P_1 \;|||\; P_2 \;\; = \;\; P_1 \; _{\alpha(P_1)}\|_{\alpha(P_2)} \; P_2 \quad \text{if } \alpha(P_1) \cap \alpha(P_2) = \{\}$$

This form is supported by the more straightforward proof rule for alphabetized parallel with its more direct relationship between the behaviour of the whole process and traces of its components.

Interface parallel

The approach to this operator is similar to the approach taken to pure interleaving. A trace tr of $P_1 \;\|_A\; P_2$ must arise from two traces tr_1 and tr_2 of P_1 and P_2 respectively, where $tr \; \text{synch}_A \; tr_1, tr_2$. This results in the following inference rule:

$$\frac{\begin{array}{l} P_1 \text{ **sat** } S(tr) \\ P_2 \text{ **sat** } T(tr) \end{array}}{P_1 \;\|_A\; P_2 \text{ **sat** } \exists tr_1, tr_2 \bullet (S(tr_1) \wedge T(tr_2) \wedge tr \; \text{synch}_A \; tr_1, tr_2)}$$

As in the case of the interleaving operator it may be possible in particular cases of S and T to show that

$$\forall tr_1, tr_2, tr \bullet (S(tr_1) \wedge T(tr_2) \wedge tr \; \text{synch}_A \; tr_1, tr_2) \Rightarrow R(tr)$$

which would allow the deduction of

$$P_1 \;\|_A\; P_2 \text{ **sat** } R(tr)$$

For example, if both P_1 and P_2 meet the specification $S(tr) = (tr \downarrow B \leqslant tr \downarrow A)$ where $B \cap A = \{\}$, then $P_1 \parallel_A P_2$ should meet the specification $R(tr) = (tr \downarrow B \leqslant 2 * tr \downarrow A)$, since events from B are performed independently by P_1 and P_2, but events from A are performed together. Indeed it is straightforward to check that

$$\forall tr_1, tr_2, tr \bullet (S(tr_1) \wedge S(tr_2) \wedge tr \, \mathsf{synch}_A \, tr_1, tr_2) \Rightarrow R(tr)$$

from which the required result follows.

Hiding

A trace of the process $P \setminus A$ arises from a trace of P simply by removing all of the events in A from the trace. Hence for any trace of $P \setminus A$ there is a corresponding trace of P. The inference rule thus takes the following form:

$$\frac{P \text{ sat } S(tr)}{P \setminus A \text{ sat } \exists tr_1 \bullet tr_1 \setminus A = tr \wedge S(tr_1)}$$

For instance, the process P might be given by $P = a \rightarrow b \rightarrow c \rightarrow P$, and the property that has been proven for P is that $tr \downarrow c \leqslant tr \downarrow b \leqslant tr \downarrow a$. The rule allows the deduction that

$$P \setminus \{b\} \quad \text{sat} \quad \exists tr_1 \bullet tr_1 \setminus \{b\} = tr \wedge tr_1 \downarrow c \leqslant tr_1 \downarrow b \leqslant tr_1 \downarrow a$$

and this specification (observe it is on tr) is equivalent to $tr \downarrow c \leqslant tr \downarrow a$, since it holds for tr precisely when this latter specification does.

In fact, the inference rule simplifies in the case where the specification $S(tr)$ is *independent* of the set A being hidden, in the sense that it holds independently of the presence or absence of events from A in the trace. A specification is A-independent if

$$\forall tr \bullet S(tr) \Leftrightarrow S(tr \setminus A)$$

For such a specification, the predicate $\exists tr_1 \bullet (S(tr_1) \wedge tr_1 \setminus A = tr)$ is equivalent to $S(tr)$, since if there is some such tr_1 then $S(tr_1 \setminus A)$—that is $S(tr)$— holds. And if there is no such tr_1, then $S(tr)$ does not hold, since tr is a candidate tr_1. The conclusion of the rule simplifies, and the resulting rule is

$$\frac{P \text{ sat } S(tr)}{P \setminus A \text{ sat } S(tr)} \quad [\, S(tr) \text{ is } A\text{-independent} \,]$$

Generally, predicates which are concerned only with certain events in the trace are likely to be good candidates for independence from other events. For example, the specification $tr \downarrow c \leqslant tr \downarrow a$ is concerned only with the projection of the trace onto the events a and c, and so it is A-independent for any set A which does not contain a or c. Hence one instantiation of the revised rule for the recursive process $P = a \to b \to c \to P$ would be

$$\frac{P \; \textbf{sat} \; tr \downarrow c \leqslant tr \downarrow a}{P \setminus \{b\} \; \textbf{sat} \; tr \downarrow c \leqslant tr \downarrow a} \qquad [\; `tr \downarrow c \leqslant tr \downarrow a` \text{ is } \{b\}\text{-independent} \,]$$

If the set A does not contain the channel c (and recall it cannot contain $\checkmark$), then a specification stating that a particular result will be provided on channel c before termination is A-independent, and so it is maintained by hiding the set A. The relevant instantiation of the rule is as follows:

$$\frac{P \; \textbf{sat} \; (term(tr) \Rightarrow tr \Downarrow c = \langle 42 \rangle)}{P \setminus A \; \textbf{sat} \; (term(tr) \Rightarrow tr \Downarrow c = \langle 42 \rangle)}$$

since the predicate '$term(tr) \Rightarrow tr \Downarrow c = \langle 42 \rangle$' is A-independent.

Observe that specifications might not be A-independent even if they do not mention events from A explicitly. The specification $term(tr) \Rightarrow \#tr > 5$, for example, states that the process must do more than 5 events before terminating. This is not A-independent (for any $A \neq \{\}$), since all events are counted towards the length of the trace; this specification is concerned with all events in Σ.

Renaming

A trace tr of a renamed process $f(P)$ will be a renamed trace $f(tr_1)$ for some tr_1 of P. The inference rule for translating specifications through a forward renaming is then as follows:

$$\frac{P \; \textbf{sat} \; S(tr)}{f(P) \; \textbf{sat} \; \exists tr_1 \bullet S(tr_1) \land f(tr_1) = tr}$$

For particular specifications $S(tr)$ it is possible to translate S through f to a specification R. This will be valid provided $R(tr)$ can be shown to translate S correctly:

$$\forall tr \bullet (S(tr) \Rightarrow R(f(tr)))$$

For example, consider the restriction of the trace to a particular set. If $P \; \textbf{sat} \; tr \downarrow A \leqslant n$, and $A = f^{-1}(B)$ for some set B (in the sense that $A = \{a \mid f(a) \in B\}$), then it might be expected that $f(P) \; \textbf{sat} \; tr \downarrow B \leqslant n$. The result that

$$\forall tr \bullet (tr \downarrow A \leqslant n \Rightarrow tr \downarrow B \leqslant n)$$

allows this conclusion to be deduced.

In the case where f is a 1–1 function, its inverse f^{-1} is also a (partial) function, and there is only one possibility for the trace tr_1 which maps under f to tr, namely $f^{-1}(tr)$. In this case the inference rule simplifies as follows:

$$\frac{P \text{ sat } S(tr)}{f(P) \text{ sat } S(f^{-1}(tr))} \quad [f \text{ injective}]$$

The specification S may often itself be transformed by f when simplifying $S(f^{-1}(tr))$. For example, consider a process B meeting the specification of a buffer:

$$B \text{ sat } tr \Downarrow out \leqslant tr \Downarrow in$$

If the channel names are renamed to *left* and *right* by the application of an injective renaming function f defined by

$$
\begin{aligned}
f(in.m) &= left.m \\
f(out.m) &= right.m \\
f(left.m) &= in.m \\
f(right.m) &= out.m
\end{aligned}
$$

then $f(B) \text{ sat } f^{-1}(tr) \Downarrow out \leqslant f^{-1}(tr) \Downarrow in$. The sequence of messages $f^{-1}(tr) \Downarrow out$ is the same as the sequence $tr \Downarrow f(out)$, that is $tr \Downarrow right$. Similarly, $f^{-1}(tr) \Downarrow in$ is equivalent to $tr \Downarrow left$, and so the result is that

$$f(B) \text{ sat } tr \Downarrow right \leqslant tr \Downarrow left$$

The inverse renaming operator is more straightforward. If tr is a trace of $f^{-1}(P)$, then $f(tr)$ is a trace of P, and so it must satisfy whatever specification P is known to satisfy. The inference rule is as follows:

$$\frac{P \text{ sat } S(tr)}{f^{-1}(P) \text{ sat } S(f(tr))}$$

For example, let P be the process $P = a \rightarrow d \rightarrow P$. Then

$$P \quad \text{sat} \quad tr \downarrow d \leqslant tr \downarrow a$$

so for any function f it follows that

$$f^{-1}(P) \quad \text{sat} \quad f(tr) \downarrow d \leqslant f(tr) \downarrow a$$

The process and the specification may be independently simplified.

If, for instance, f is the function defined by

$$\begin{aligned} f(a) = f(b) = f(c) \quad &= \quad a \\ f(d) = f(e) \quad &= \quad d \end{aligned}$$

the process $f^{-1}(P)$ reduces to

$$\begin{aligned} f^{-1}(P) \quad = \quad &a \to (d \to f^{-1}(P) \; \Box \; e \to f^{-1}(P)) \\ &\Box \; b \to (d \to f^{-1}(P) \; \Box \; e \to f^{-1}(P)) \\ &\Box \; c \to (d \to f^{-1}(P) \; \Box \; e \to f^{-1}(P)) \end{aligned}$$

which is the same as the recursively defined process

$$\begin{aligned} P' \quad = \quad &a \to (d \to P' \; \Box \; e \to P') \\ &\Box \; b \to (d \to P' \; \Box \; e \to P') \\ &\Box \; c \to (d \to P' \; \Box \; e \to P') \end{aligned}$$

by the unique fixed point law UFP_T.

Furthermore, the specification

$$f(tr) \downarrow d \leqslant f(tr) \downarrow a$$

reduces to

$$tr \downarrow f^{-1}(\{d\}) \leqslant tr \downarrow f^{-1}(\{a\})$$

which expands to

$$tr \downarrow \{d, e\} \leqslant tr \downarrow \{a, b, c\}$$

and so it is finally established that

$$P' \quad \textbf{sat} \quad tr \downarrow \{d, e\} \leqslant tr \downarrow \{a, b, c\}$$

Sequential composition

The process $P_1; P_2$ behaves entirely as P_1 until P_1 terminates, after which it behaves as P_2. Any given trace of $P_1; P_2$ admits one of two possibilities: either it is a trace of P_1 which has not yet reached termination, or else it is a trace of P_1 followed by a trace of P_2. The proof rule reflects this dichotomy:

$$\frac{\begin{array}{l} P_1 \textbf{ sat } S(tr) \\ P_2 \textbf{ sat } T(tr) \end{array}}{\begin{array}{ll} P_1; P_2 \textbf{ sat} & \neg\, term(tr) \wedge S(tr) \\ & \vee \\ & \exists\, tr_1, tr_2 \bullet tr = tr_1 \,{}^{\frown} tr_2 \wedge S(tr_1 \,{}^{\frown} \langle \checkmark \rangle) \wedge T(tr_2) \end{array}}$$

The first case covers those traces from P_1 that have not yet terminated. The second case is concerned with those traces corresponding to executions that have passed control from P_1 to P_2 at some point: in this case, $tr_1 \,{}^{\frown} \langle \checkmark \rangle$ is the part of the trace from P_1 up to termination, and tr_2 is the contribution from P_2, after control has been passed. Observe that the $\checkmark$ from P_1's termination does not appear in tr, reflecting the trace semantics of sequential composition.

A degenerate case concerns the situation where the specification $S(tr)$ for P_1 does not allow for termination: $S(tr) \Rightarrow \neg\, term(tr)$. In this case the first disjunct above reduces to $S(tr)$, and the second reduces to $false(tr)$, since $S(tr_1 \,{}^{\frown} \langle \checkmark \rangle)$ cannot hold. In other words, in the situation where P_1 cannot terminate, the result is that $P_1; P_2 \textbf{ sat } S(tr)$, corresponding to the fact that all executions will be entirely due to P_1.

Interrupt

A trace of the interrupt process $P_1 \triangle P_2$ is either a trace of P_1, or else a non-terminated trace of P_1 followed by a trace of P_2. The inference rule is as follows:

$$\frac{\begin{array}{l} P_1 \textbf{ sat } S(tr) \\ P_2 \textbf{ sat } T(tr) \end{array}}{\begin{array}{ll} P_1 \triangle P_2 \textbf{ sat} & S(tr) \\ & \vee \\ & \exists\, tr_1, tr_2 \bullet tr = tr_1 \,{}^{\frown} tr_2 \wedge \neg\, term(tr_1) \wedge S(tr_1) \wedge T(tr_2) \end{array}}$$

5.3 RECURSION INDUCTION

If process N is recursively defined by the equation $N = P$ or equivalently by $N = F(N)$ (where $F(Y) = P[Y/N]$), then a rule which is sufficient to establish that $N \textbf{ sat } S(tr)$ is the following:

$$\frac{\forall\, Y \bullet (Y \textbf{ sat } S(tr) \Rightarrow F(Y) \textbf{ sat } S(tr))}{N \textbf{ sat } S(tr)} \quad [\, S(\langle \rangle)\,]$$

This rule is sound because it provides all the ingredients for establishing by induction that $N \textbf{ sat } S(tr)$. The traces of N are those of $\bigcup_i \textsf{traces}(F^i(STOP))$, all the finite unwindings of

$F(Y)$ starting from the process *STOP*. The inductive hypothesis is that $F^i(STOP)$ **sat** $S(tr)$. The side condition $S(\langle\rangle)$ provides the base case, since it is equivalent to the statement *STOP* **sat** $S(tr)$, which is the same as $F^0(STOP)$ **sat** $S(tr)$. The antecedent of the rule provides the basis for the inductive step: that if an arbitrary process Y meets the specification $S(tr)$, then so does $F(Y)$. Hence from the fact that $F^i(STOP)$ **sat** $S(tr)$ it follows that $F(F^i(STOP))$ **sat** $S(tr)$: that is, $F^{i+1}(STOP)$ **sat** $S(tr)$. The conclusion that $\forall i \bullet F^i(STOP)$ **sat** $S(tr)$ follows by induction, and so $\forall tr \in \bigcup_i \mathsf{traces}(F^i(STOP)) \bullet S(tr)$, which means that N **sat** $S(tr)$.

Establishing the antecedent to the rule will depend on the CSP operators used in the recursive function $F(Y)$. Typically, the rules appropriate to these operators would be used.

Example 5.3.1 The recursively defined process $N = a \to b \to N$ alternates on performance of the events a and b. One specification which it meets is that the number of b events never exceeds the number of a events performed. This is expressed in the specification $S(tr) = tr \downarrow b \leqslant tr \downarrow a$.

To establish the antecedent, it is necessary to show that Y **sat** $S(tr) \Rightarrow a \to b \to Y$ **sat** $S(tr)$. Assuming that Y **sat** $S(tr)$, it follows from an application of the rule for prefix that

$$b \to Y \text{ **sat** } tr = \langle\rangle \vee (tr = \langle b\rangle \frown tr' \wedge S(tr'))$$

and so it follows from another application of that rule that

$$a \to b \to Y \text{ **sat** } tr = \langle\rangle \vee \; (tr = \langle a\rangle \frown tr'$$
$$\wedge \; (tr' = \langle\rangle \vee (tr' = \langle b\rangle \frown tr'' \wedge S(tr''))))$$

This simplifies to

$$a \to b \to Y \text{ **sat** } tr = \langle\rangle \vee tr = \langle a\rangle \vee (tr = \langle a, b\rangle \frown tr'' \wedge tr'' \downarrow b \leqslant tr'' \downarrow a)$$

which implies that

$$a \to b \to Y \text{ **sat** } S(tr)$$

as required. It is also necessary to check the side condition $S(\langle\rangle)$, which in this case is trivial. Hence the recursion induction rule allows the conclusion that N **sat** $S(tr)$.   ∎

Example 5.3.2 A definition of the mail forwarder process *NODE* of Example 2.2.4 is

$$NODE \;\; = \;\; in?x : M \to (NODE \;\|\|\; out!x \to STOP)$$

This process appears to satisfy the specification that any output v must previously have been input. This is expressed as the following predicate on traces:

$$\forall v \bullet out.v \text{ **in** } tr \Rightarrow in.v \text{ **in** } tr$$

This can be established for *NODE* by showing that the body of the definition preserves the specification: that if Y satisfies it, then so does $F(Y) = in?x : M \to (Y \,|||\, out!x \to STOP)$. This is achieved by using the rules for interleaving and input. Assuming that Y **sat** $\forall v \bullet out.v$ **in** $tr \Rightarrow in.v$ **in** tr, it follows that, for any given w,

$$Y \,|||\, out.w \to STOP \quad \textbf{sat} \quad \forall v \bullet out.v \text{ \textbf{in} } tr \Rightarrow (in.v \text{ \textbf{in} } tr \lor v = w)$$

The rule for input yields that

$$
\begin{aligned}
in?x : M \to (Y \,&|||\, out.x \to STOP) \\
\textbf{sat} \quad tr &= \langle\rangle \\
&\lor \\
head(tr) &= in.w \,\land \\
(\forall v \bullet out.v. &\text{ \textbf{in} } tail(tr) \Rightarrow (in.v \text{ \textbf{in} } tail(tr) \lor v = w))
\end{aligned}
$$

and this specification may be weakened to give the result

$$in?x : M \to (Y \,|||\, out.x \to STOP) \quad \textbf{sat} \quad \forall v \bullet (out.v \text{ \textbf{in} } tr \Rightarrow in.v \text{ \textbf{in} } tr)$$

It follows that *NODE* meets this specification. ∎

Example 5.3.3 It may happen that the specification $S(tr)$ itself is not preserved by recursive calls, even though it happens to hold of the recursively defined process. For example, the specification $S(tr) = tr \upharpoonright a = \langle\rangle \lor tr \upharpoonright b = \langle\rangle$ states that the trace tr cannot contain occurrences of both event a and event b. This holds for the process $N = a \to N$, but it is not in general preserved by the function $F(Y) = a \to Y$ defining the recursion: for instance, $b \to STOP$ **sat** $S(tr)$, but $F(b \to STOP)$ does not satisfy $S(tr)$.

One approach in such cases is to find a stronger property $T(tr)$ which is preserved by recursive calls, for which $T(tr) \Rightarrow S(tr)$.

In the case above, a suitable $T(tr)$ would be $tr \upharpoonright b = \langle\rangle$. This is preserved by the body of the recursive definition $F(Y)$, and it also implies $S(tr)$. ∎

Mutual recursion

A mutual recursion is treated in an entirely similar way to the single case, though some extra care must be taken to handle the indices of the family of defined processes.

A family of processes $N(i)$ indexed by a set I is defined by an associated family of equations $N(i) = F(i)(\underline{N})$. The entire definition is described at a stroke as $\underline{N} = \underline{F}(\underline{N})$.

In terms of specification, a family of processes may be associated with a family of specifications $S(i)(tr)$, also indexed by I. In this case, $\underline{N}$ **sat** $\underline{S}(tr)$ means that each process satisfies the associated specification: $N(i)$ **sat** $S(i)(tr)$, for each index i.

Within this framework, the inference rule for mutual recursion is similar to that for single recursion. If $\underline{N} = \underline{F}(\underline{N})$, then

$$\frac{\forall \underline{Y} \bullet \underline{Y} \text{ sat } \underline{S}(tr) \Rightarrow \underline{F}(\underline{Y}) \text{ sat } \underline{S}(tr)}{\underline{N} \text{ sat } \underline{S}(tr)} \quad [\, \forall i \in I \bullet S(i)(\langle\rangle) \,]$$

The antecedent of this rule is equivalent to the requirement for arbitrary $j \in I$ that $F(j)(\underline{Y})$ **sat** $S(j)(tr)$, under the assumption that $Y(i)$ **sat** $S(i)(tr)$ for every $i \in I$.

Example 5.3.4 Two processes defined through a mutual recursion are *LIGHT* and *ON* of Example 1.3.4:

$$
\begin{aligned}
LIGHT &= on \to ON \\
ON &= \mathit{off} \to LIGHT
\end{aligned}
$$

These may be shown to meet the respective pair of specifications

$$
\begin{aligned}
S_1(tr) &= tr \downarrow \mathit{off} \leqslant tr \downarrow on \leqslant tr \downarrow \mathit{off} + 1 \\
S_2(tr) &= tr \downarrow on \leqslant tr \downarrow \mathit{off} \leqslant tr \downarrow on + 1
\end{aligned}
$$

The proof rule for mutual recursion induction requires as its antecedent that the pair of functions preserve the pair of specifications. This means that

$$
\begin{aligned}
\forall Y \bullet (Y \text{ sat } S_2(tr) &\Rightarrow on \to Y \text{ sat } S_1(tr)) \\
\forall Y \bullet (Y \text{ sat } S_1(tr) &\Rightarrow \mathit{off} \to Y \text{ sat } S_2(tr))
\end{aligned}
$$

These may be established by an application of the proof rule for prefix, and so the conclusion *LIGHT* **sat** $S_1(tr)$ and *ON* **sat** $S_2(tr)$ follows. ∎

Example 5.3.5 The example of the family of counter processes defined in terms of each other, indexed by $\mathbb{N}$, was given in Example 4.3.10.

$$
\begin{aligned}
COUNT(0) &= increment \to COUNT(1) \\
COUNT(i) &= increment \to COUNT(i+1) \qquad \text{if } i > 0 \\
&\quad | \; decrement \to COUNT(i-1)
\end{aligned}
$$

The intention is that $COUNT(0)$ can perform no more *decrement* events that *increment* events. In general, the index of any particular $COUNT(i)$ process reached during an execution of $COUNT(0)$ records the number by which occurrences of *increment* exceed those of *decrement*.

This means that to be consistent with the requirement on $COUNT(0)$, each process $COUNT(i)$ can perform up to i more *decrement*s than *increment*s. The corresponding specifications are

$$
S(i)(tr) = tr \downarrow decrement \leqslant (i + tr \downarrow increment)
$$

To prove that each $COUNT(i)$ **sat** $S(i)(tr)$, it is sufficient to show that this claim is preserved when each process is replaced by its definition. There are essentially two cases to consider, corresponding to the two possibilities $i = 0$ and $i > 0$.

In the case $i = 0$, the definition of $COUNT(0)$ is $increment \to COUNT(1)$. Under the assumption that $COUNT(1)$ **sat** $S(1)(tr)$, an application of the inference rule for prefix yields that

$$increment \to COUNT(1)$$
$$\textbf{sat} \quad tr = \langle \rangle$$
$$\vee$$
$$head(tr) = increment \wedge$$
$$tail(tr) \downarrow decrement \leqslant (1 + tail(tr) \downarrow increment)$$

The specification can be weakened to obtain

$$increment \to COUNT(1) \quad \textbf{sat} \quad S(0)$$

The other case to consider is $i > 0$. In this case, the relevant assumptions are $COUNT(i + 1)$ **sat** $S(i + 1)(tr)$, and $COUNT(i - 1)$ **sat** $S(i - 1)(tr)$, since it is these process names that appear in the definition of $COUNT(i)$. The inference rule for prefix choice yields that

$$increment \to COUNT(i + 1) \mid decrement \to COUNT(i - 1)$$
$$\textbf{sat} \quad tr = \langle \rangle$$
$$\vee \, head(tr) = increment \wedge S(i + 1)(tail(tr))$$
$$\vee \, head(tr) = decrement \wedge S(i - 1)(tail(tr))$$

which expands to

$$increment \to COUNT(i + 1) \mid decrement \to COUNT(i - 1)$$
$$\textbf{sat} \quad tr = \langle \rangle$$
$$\vee \quad head(tr) = increment \wedge$$
$$tail(tr) \downarrow decrement \leqslant i + 1 + tail(tr) \downarrow increment$$
$$\vee \quad head(tr) = decrement \wedge$$
$$tail(tr) \downarrow decrement \leqslant i - 1 + tail(tr) \downarrow increment$$

and each disjunct implies $S(i)(tr)$, which establishes the case.

It follows that $COUNT(i)$ **sat** $S(i)(tr)$ for each $i \in I$, and so (in the special case $i = 0$) that $COUNT(0)$ **sat** $tr \downarrow decrement \leqslant tr \downarrow increment$. ∎

Example 5.3.6 The general buffer process $BUFFER = BUFFER(\langle \rangle)$ is intended to satisfy the specification $tr \Downarrow out \leqslant tr \Downarrow in$. The process $BUFFER(\langle \rangle)$ is one of a family of processes

1. Receive an initiating message from some neighbour j.

2. Send out one initiating message to each of the other neighbours, and receive initiating messages or values from them.

3. Add up all the values received, add the weight w_n, and send the result to node j.

Fig. 5.1   Behaviour of each node n in the distributed sum algorithm

indexed by sequences of messages: the sequence is intended to represent the contents of the buffer.

$$BUFFER(\langle\rangle) \quad = \quad in?x : M \rightarrow BUFFER(\langle x\rangle)$$
$$BUFFER(\langle y\rangle ^\frown s) \quad = \quad in?x : M \rightarrow BUFFER(\langle y\rangle ^\frown s ^\frown \langle x\rangle)$$
$$| \; out!y \rightarrow BUFFER(s)$$

The corresponding family of specifications is $S(s)(tr) = tr \Downarrow out \leqslant s ^\frown (tr \Downarrow in)$. The output stream of a buffer with contents s will begin with s, and continue with the sequence of messages that have been input to $BUFFER(s)$.

The family of functions defining the $BUFFER(s)$ processes preserves the family of specifications $\underline{S}(tr)$, and so $BUFFER(s)$ **sat** $S(s)(tr)$ for each sequence of messages s; and in particular, $BUFFER$ **sat** $tr \Downarrow out \leqslant tr \Downarrow in$. ∎

5.4   CASE STUDY: DISTRIBUTED SUM

This case study illustrates the use of CSP in the description, analysis, and verification of a distributed algorithm to sum a collection of values arranged in a graph. Each node follows its own procedure locally and communicates only with its neighbours, but the output of all this activity is the global sum of all the values.

Let $G = (N, E)$ be a bidirectional (symmetric) connected graph with a set of nodes N and edges $E \subseteq N \times N$. This may be viewed as a connected network of processes which may communicate only with their neighbours.

The graph G has a weight w_n associated with each node n. The algorithm of Figure 5.1 calculates the sum of all the weights. Each node n waits for one of its neighbours to send it an initiating message. It records this neighbour as its *parent*. It then sends all of its other neighbouring nodes an initiating message, and simultaneously awaits messages from all of these neighbours: some may be initiating messages, and some may be values. When all of

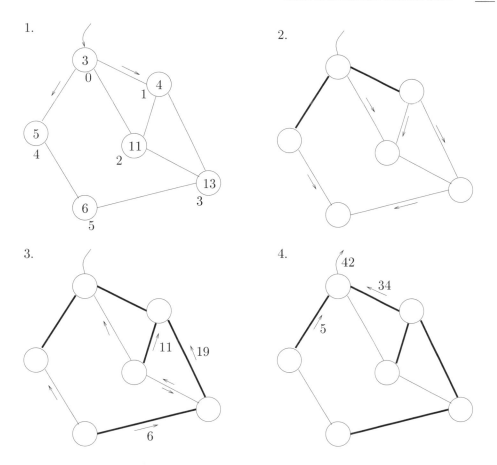

Fig. 5.2   Steps of an execution of the distributed sum algorithm; parent edges high-lighted

these have been received, the node sends to its parent the sum of all the values received and w_n, after which it terminates.

In order to start the algorithm, one special node must be initiated from outside the graph, and return its final result outside the graph: this final result will be the sum of all the weights.

An example execution is pictured in Figure 5.2, where the nodes are annotated with their weights. The associated communications are given in Figure 5.3. The top node is activated, and sends initiating messages to its neighbouring nodes, which send initiating messages to all of their neighbours in turn. Once activated, a node observes initiating messages and values arriving from other neighbours, and when it has heard from all of its neighbours it sends the sum total of the values it received plus its own weight back to its parent node. Any pairs of adjacent nodes for which neither is the parent of the other will simply exchange initiating messages.

NODE(0)	NODE(1)	NODE(2)	NODE(3)	NODE(4)	NODE(5)	
→0:i						
0→1:i	0→1:i					1
0→4:i				0→4:i		
	1→3:i		1→3:i			
	1→2:i	1→2:i				
0→2:i		0→2:i				2
			3→5:i		3→5:i	
				4→5:i	4→5:i	
				5→4:i	5→4:i	
			5→3:6		5→3:6	
		3→2:i	3→2:i			
2→0:i		2→0:i				3
		2→3:i	2→3:i			
	3→1:19		3→1:19			
	2→1:11	2→1:11				
4→0:5				4→0:5		
1→0:34	1→0:34					4
0→ :42						

Fig. 5.3   Communications associated with the execution of Figure 5.2

The execution finally ends when all nodes have communicated to their parent a value consisting of the sum of all values received from their children together with their own weight.

The algorithm will be described and verified in CSP. It is first necessary to settle some appropriate notation. The nodes are named using integers from 0 to m (where there are $m + 1$ nodes in total), so $N = \{i \mid 0 \leqslant i \leqslant m\}$, and 0 is the initial node.

For any node $i \in N$ apart from 0, its set of neighbours or adjacent nodes $adj(i)$ is given by

$$adj(i) \quad = \quad \{j \in N \mid (i,j) \in E\}$$

Node 0 also has ∞ in its set $adj(0)$ in addition to its neighbouring nodes, representing its external link.

$$adj(0) \quad = \quad \{j \in N \mid (0,j) \in E\} \cup \{\infty\}$$

The CSP description of the algorithm will describe each node as a CSP process. The nodes are connected in accordance with the graph G. Between any two neighbouring nodes i and j

there is a communication channel c_{ij} allowing messages to pass from i to j. Since the graph is symmetric, for each such channel there will be a complementary channel (c_{ji}) in the opposite direction. The channels used in the CSP implementation of the example network above are illustrated in Figure 5.4.

The values that pass along channels need to be accessed, since the algorithm is concerned with summing them. The notation v_{il} will denote the sum of all messages passed along channel c_{il}.

$$v_{il}(tr) = \mathsf{sum}(\langle tr \Downarrow c_{il}\rangle)$$

Node 0 begins in the state where it will receive a signal along channel $c_{\infty 0}$, and will then send initiating messages to all of its neighbours and await responses. When it has received all of the responses it communicates the result on the special channel $c_{0\infty}$. Its alphabet is therefore

$$
\begin{aligned}
A_0 \quad = \quad & \{c_{0l}.n \mid n \in \mathbb{N} \wedge l \in adj(0)\} \cup \{c_{l0}.n \mid n \in \mathbb{N} \wedge l \in adj(0)\} \\
& \cup c_{0\infty}.\mathbb{N} \cup c_{\infty 0}.\mathbb{N}
\end{aligned}
$$

The alphabets of the other nodes $i \neq 0$ are simply the links with their neighbours:

$$
A_i \quad = \quad \{c_{il}.n \mid n \in \mathbb{N} \wedge l \in adj(i)\} \cup \{c_{li}.n \mid n \in \mathbb{N} \wedge l \in adj(i)\}
$$

The algorithm is expressed by describing in CSP how each node should behave. One optimization is to consider each initiating message as a communication of the value 0. An active node will ignore other initiating messages, which is equivalent to adding 0 to the running total, so there is no need to distinguish between the input of an ignored initiating message and the input of a 0 which is added to the total. This identification removes the need to consider these two cases separately, and allows for a more concise treatment of node behaviour.

The system as a whole consists of a network of nodes, with all of the channels between them made internal:

$$
\begin{aligned}
DISTSUM \quad &= \quad NETWORK \setminus \{c_{ij} \mid (i,j) \in E\} \\
NETWORK \quad &= \quad \Big\|_{A_i}^{i \in N} NODE(i)
\end{aligned}
$$

The property that will be established for *DISTSUM* is that on termination the value communicated on channel $c_{0\infty}$ is indeed the sum of the weights on the nodes:

$$DISTSUM \quad \textbf{sat} \quad term(tr) \Rightarrow v_{0,\infty}(tr) = \Sigma_{i \in N} w_i$$

In order to establish this property, it is first necessary to define the component *NODE* processes. This will be done in terms of a family of processes *TOT* which keep track of the relevant

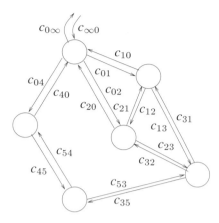

Fig. 5.4   Channels of the CSP implementation

interactions between nodes, and which sum values as they arrive. The process $TOT(i, j, M, t)$ contains in its state information:

1. the identity of its node i;

2. its parent node j;

3. the set of neighbours $M \subseteq adj(i)$ it still awaits inputs from;

4. the running total t (initially w_i).

Its behaviour will be to accept input from all the nodes listed in M, keeping track of the running total in t, and finally sending this total back to j.

The notation $\underline{F}$ will be used to refer to the function implicit in the definition of $\underline{TOT}$: the fixed point of F is $\underline{TOT}$.

The special treatment of $NODE(0)$ requires it to be defined slightly differently to the other nodes:

$$NODE(0) \quad = \quad c_{\infty 0}.0 \to (TOT(0, \infty, adj(0), w_0) \parallel (\parallel^{k \in adj(0)} c_{0k}!0 \to SKIP))$$

$$NODE(i) \quad = \quad \square_{j \in adj(i)} \, c_{ji}.0 \to (\quad TOT(i, j, adj(i) \setminus \{j\}, w_i)$$
$$\parallel \parallel^{k \in adj(i) \setminus \{j\}} c_{ik}!0 \to SKIP)$$

where the TOT processes are defined by

$$TOT(i, j, \{\}, t) \quad = \quad c_{ij}!t \to SKIP$$
$$TOT(i, j, M, t) \quad = \quad \square_{k \in M} \, c_{ki}?x \to TOT(i, j, M \setminus \{k\}, t + x) \quad \text{if } M \neq \{\}$$

The processing of the incoming values accomplished by *TOT* can be carried out concurrently with the transmission of the initiating messages to the neighbours.

The aim is first to prove that each $TOT(i,j,M,t)$ provides to its parent the sum of the values it has received together with the running total t it was initialized with. In CSP, the process must be shown to meet the $S(i,j,M,t)(tr)$ as follows:

$$TOT(i,j,M,t) \quad \textbf{sat} \quad term(tr) \Rightarrow v_{ij}(tr) = \Sigma_{l \in adj(i)} v_{li}(tr) + t$$

This is proven by recursion induction. Assume as the inductive hypothesis that $Y(i,j,M,t)$ **sat** $S(i,j,M,t)(tr)$ for each i,j,M,t. Then it is sufficient to prove for each i, j, M, and t that $\underline{F}(\underline{Y})(i,j,M,t)$ **sat** $S(i,j,M,t)(tr)$. Following the definition of *TOT* this is established by considering various cases on M.

Case $M = \{\}$: In this case $\underline{F}(\underline{Y})(i,j,\{\},t) = c_{ij}!t \rightarrow SKIP$, and

$$c_{ij}!t \rightarrow SKIP \quad \textbf{sat} \quad tr = \langle\rangle \vee tr = \langle c_{ij}.t\rangle \vee tr = \langle c_{ij}.t, \checkmark\rangle$$

and so by weakening the specification the result

$$c_{ij}!t \rightarrow SKIP \quad \textbf{sat} \quad term(tr) \Rightarrow v_{ij} = \Sigma_{l \in adj(i)} v_{li}(tr) + t$$

is obtained, since this specification is true of the trace $\langle c_{ij}.t, \checkmark\rangle$, and vacuously true for the other traces.

Case $M \neq \{\}$: In this case

$$\underline{F}(\underline{Y})(i,j,M,t) = \square_{k \in M} c_{ki}?x \rightarrow Y(i,j,M \setminus \{k\}, t+x)$$

and

$$\square_{k \in M} c_{ki}?x \rightarrow Y(i,j,M \setminus \{k\}, t+x)$$
$$\textbf{sat} \quad tr = \langle\rangle$$
$$\vee \exists k \in adj(i), v \bullet (tr = \langle c_{ki}.v\rangle \frown tr' \wedge S(i,j,M \setminus \{k\}, t+v)(tr'))$$

Consider the second disjunct of this specification. In this case $tr \neq \langle\rangle$, so $v_{ki}(tr) = v_{ki}(tr') + v$ because of the first event of tr. Observe further that $v_{li}(tr) = v_{li}(tr')$ when $l \neq k$, that $v_{ij}(tr) = v_{ij}(tr')$, and also that $term(tr) \Leftrightarrow term(tr')$. The specification is weakened to yield the following:

$$\square_{k \in M} c_{ki}.0 \rightarrow Y(i,j,M \setminus \{k\}, t)$$
$$\textbf{sat} \quad tr = \langle\rangle$$
$$\vee \exists k \in adj(i), v \bullet ((term(tr) \Rightarrow v_{ij}(tr) - \Sigma_{l \in adj(i)} v_{li}(tr) \mid t))$$

Since k and v no longer appear within the scope of the existential quantification, it may be dropped. A final weakening reveals that

$$\square_{k \in M} \, c_{ki}.0 \rightarrow Y(i,j,M \setminus \{k\},t)$$
$$\textbf{sat} \quad term(tr) \Rightarrow v_{ij}(tr) = \Sigma_{l \in adj(i)} v_{li}(tr) + t$$

This establishes that the specification is preserved by recursive calls. Since the specification is satisfiable, this means that $TOT(i,j,M,t)$ **sat** $S(i,j,M,t)$ for all i, j, M, and t.

The definition of $NODE(i)$ is also made up of components of the form $c_{ik}!0 \rightarrow SKIP$, so these will now be considered. For any arbitrary k

$$c_{ik}!0 \rightarrow SKIP \quad \textbf{sat} \quad v_{ik}(tr) = 0$$

A parallel combination of such processes satisfies the conjunction of these specifications, restricted to the appropriate alphabets:

$$\left\|_{c_{ik}}^{k \in adj(i) \setminus \{j\}} c_{ik}!0 \rightarrow SKIP \quad \textbf{sat} \quad \forall k \in adj(i) \setminus \{j\} \bullet v_{ik}(tr \Downarrow \{c_{ik}, \checkmark\}) = 0\right.$$

However, each of these specifications depends only on the events in the corresponding alphabets: $v_{ik}(tr \restriction (c_{ik}.\mathbb{N} \cup \{\checkmark\})) = 0 \Leftrightarrow v_{ik}(tr) = 0$, and $S(i,j,M,t)(tr) \Leftrightarrow S(i,j,M,t)(tr \restriction c_{ij}.\mathbb{N} \cup \{\checkmark\} \cup \bigcup\{c_{li}.\mathbb{N} \mid l \in adj(i)\}$. This means that the restrictions to the appropriate alphabets can be lifted, and the parallel combination satisfies the conjunction of the specifications on the full unrestricted trace tr.

$$TOT(i,j,M,t) \, \| \, (\|^{k \in adj(i) \setminus \{j\}} c_{ik}!0 \rightarrow SKIP)$$
$$\textbf{sat} \quad S(i,j,M,t)(tr) \wedge \forall k \in adj(i) \setminus \{j\} \bullet v_{ik}(tr) = 0$$

This specification may be weakened, resulting in

$$TOT(i,j,M,t) \, \| \, (\|^{k \in adj(i) \setminus \{j\}} c_{ik}!0 \rightarrow SKIP)$$
$$\textbf{sat} \quad term(tr) \Rightarrow \Sigma_{l \in adj(i)} v_{il}(tr) = \Sigma_{l \in adj(i) \setminus \{j\}} v_{li}(tr) + t$$

Hence for any $j \in adj(i)$, after some manipulations similar to those above, the following is obtained:

$$c_{ji}.0 \rightarrow (TOT(i,j,adj(i) \setminus \{j\}, w_i) \, \| \, (\|^{k \in adj(i) \setminus \{j\}} c_{ik}!0 \rightarrow SKIP))$$
$$\textbf{sat} \quad term(tr) \Rightarrow \Sigma_{l \in adj(i)} v_{il}(tr) = \Sigma_{l \in adj(i)} v_{li}(tr) + w_i$$

The process for each possible j allows the specification, so the choice over all $j \in adj(i)$ meets the same specification:

$$\square_{j \in adj(i)} \, c_{ji}.0 \rightarrow (TOT(i,j,adj(i) \setminus \{j\}, w_i) \, \| \, (\|^{k \in adj(i) \setminus \{j\}} c_{ik}!0 \rightarrow SKIP))$$
$$\textbf{sat} \quad term(tr) \Rightarrow \Sigma_{l \in adj(i)} v_{il}(tr) = \Sigma_{l \in adj(i)} v_{li}(tr) + w_i$$

This specification will be abbreviated by $term(tr) \Rightarrow S(i)(tr)$

Since this choice is how $NODE(i)$ is defined (for $i \neq 0$), it has now been established that

$$NODE(i) \quad \textbf{sat} \quad term(tr) \Rightarrow S(i)(tr)$$

An entirely similar train of reasoning leads to the result that

$$NODE(0) \quad \textbf{sat} \quad term(tr) \Rightarrow \Sigma_{l \in adj(0)} v_{l0}(tr) + w_0 = \Sigma_{l \in adj(0)} v_{0l}(tr) + v_{0\infty}(tr)$$

which will be abbreviated as $NODE(0)$ **sat** $term(tr) \Rightarrow S(0)(tr)$. The only difference from the specifications of the other nodes is that the extra value $v_{0\infty}$ is mentioned separately, as $c_{0\infty}$ refers to the channel that node 0 uses to communicate its result outside the graph.

Each $NODE(i)$ has an alphabet A_i. Observe that $(term(tr) \Rightarrow S(i)(tr)) \Leftrightarrow (term(tr \upharpoonright A_i^\checkmark) \Rightarrow S(i)(tr \upharpoonright A_i^\checkmark))$.

Hence the network meets the conjunction of these specifications (each suitably restricted):

$$\Big\|_{A_i} NODE(i) \quad \textbf{sat} \quad \forall i \in N \bullet term(tr \upharpoonright A_i^\checkmark) \Rightarrow S(i)(tr \upharpoonright A_i^\checkmark)$$

This specification simplifies to the form

$$term(tr) \Rightarrow \forall i \in N \bullet S(i)(tr)$$

which in turn is equivalent to

$$term(tr) \Rightarrow$$

$$
\begin{aligned}
\Sigma_{i \in N} w_i &= \Sigma_{i \in N}(\Sigma_{j \in adj(i)} v_{ij}(tr) - \Sigma_{j \in adj(i)} v_{ji}(tr)) + v_{0\infty}(tr) \\
&= \Sigma_{i \in N}(\Sigma_{j \in adj(i)} v_{ij}(tr)) - \Sigma_{i \in N}(\Sigma_{j \in adj(i)} v_{ji}(tr)) + v_{0\infty}(tr) \\
&= \Sigma_{(i,j) \in E} v_{ij}(tr) - \Sigma_{(i,j) \in E} v_{ji}(tr) + v_{0\infty}(tr) \\
&= \Sigma_{(i,j) \in E} v_{ij}(tr) - \Sigma_{(i,j) \in E} v_{ij}(tr) + v_{0\infty}(tr) \\
&= v_{0\infty}(tr)
\end{aligned}
$$

The penultimate line is justified by the fact that the set of edges E is symmetric: $(i,j) \in E \Leftrightarrow (j,i) \in E$.

This establishes that

$$NETWORK \quad \textbf{sat} \quad term(tr) \Rightarrow v_{0\infty}(tr) = \Sigma_{i \in N} w_i$$

and since this specification is $\{c_{ij} \mid (i,j) \in E\}$-independent, it follows that

$$NETWORK \setminus \{c_{ij} \mid (i,j) \in E\} \quad \textbf{sat} \quad term(tr) \Rightarrow (v_{0\infty}(tr) = \Sigma_{i \in N} w_i)$$

or in other words

$$DISTSUM \quad \textbf{sat} \quad term(tr) \Rightarrow (v_{0\infty}(tr) = \Sigma_{i \in N} w_i)$$

This completes the proof that on termination the sum of the outputs along $c_{0\infty}$ is equal to the sum of the weights on the nodes. Since $NODE(0)$ ensures that at most one value is communicated along channel $c_{0\infty}$, this value must be the sum of the weights.

What has been proven is that if an answer is given out then it will be the right one. This is a safety property: it states that the wrong answer will never be given. Observe that the connectedness of the graph was not used in establishing this property. Connectedness will be needed to show that all nodes in the graph participate in the run, and this does not need to be shown to establish the safety property. Rather, it is already assumed in the antecedent $term(tr)$, since $NETWORK$ can terminate only when *all* of its nodes are ready to do so, which requires that they all participate in the execution.

The fact that $DISTSUM$ will indeed progress towards termination, and will not deadlock or diverge, will be shown in Chapters 7 and 8, where issues of liveness are addressed.

5.5   PROCESS-ORIENTED SPECIFICATION

A specification is simply a description of acceptable or required behaviour. The property-oriented approach described thus far captures specifications in terms of requirements $S(tr)$ on traces that a process can perform. A process meets a specification if all of its traces are acceptable.

Another way of describing a set of acceptable traces is in terms of a CSP process P_0. A CSP description corresponds to a set of traces—those traces that it can exhibit. If this set of traces is taken to give precisely those traces that are acceptable, then the process P_0 itself acts as a specification. For instance, the process $RUN_{\{a,b\}}$ has as its traces all sequences whose only members are a and b events. As a specification, it captures the requirement that only a and b events are allowed.

Another process P_1 meets the specification described by P_0 if any trace of P_1 is 'allowed' by P_0, in the sense that it is a trace of P_0. P_1 is then considered to be a *refinement* of P_0. For instance, P_1 might be the recursive process $P_1 = a \rightarrow b \rightarrow P_1$ which alternates on a and b events. It meets the specification given by $RUN_{\{a,b\}}$, since it performs no events other than a's and b's. This claim is written as $P_0 \sqsubseteq_T P_1$, which is pronounced 'P_0 is refined by P_1 with respect to traces', or 'P_1 trace-refines P_0'. It is defined as follows:

$$P_0 \sqsubseteq_T P_1 \quad = \quad \mathsf{traces}(P_1) \subseteq \mathsf{traces}(P_0)$$

$$P \sqsubseteq P \qquad\qquad \langle\sqsubseteq\text{-reflex}\rangle$$

$$P_0 \sqsubseteq P_1 \wedge P_1 \sqsubseteq P_2 \Rightarrow P_0 \sqsubseteq P_2 \qquad\qquad \langle\sqsubseteq\text{-trans}\rangle$$

$$P_0 \sqsubseteq P_1 \wedge P_1 \sqsubseteq P_0 \Rightarrow P_0 = P_1 \qquad\qquad \langle\sqsubseteq\text{-anti-sym}\rangle$$

$$RUN \sqsubseteq_T P \qquad\qquad \langle\sqsubseteq_T\text{-bottom}\rangle$$

$$P \sqsubseteq_T STOP \qquad\qquad \langle\sqsubseteq_T\text{-top}\rangle$$

$$P_0 \textbf{ sat } S(tr) \wedge P_0 \sqsubseteq_T P_1 \Rightarrow P_1 \textbf{ sat } S(tr) \qquad\qquad \langle\sqsubseteq_T\text{-spec}\rangle$$

Fig. 5.5   Laws for refinement

The 'traces refinement' check of FDR (see Appendix B) checks for exactly this refinement relation.

The relation may also be captured algebraically as follows:

$$P_0 \sqsubseteq_T P_1 \quad\Leftrightarrow\quad P_0 =_T P_0 \sqcap P_1$$

Its equivalence to the definition is easily checked, though the interpretation of this characterization is a little different. It states that if P_0 is indistinguishable from $P_0 \sqcap P_1$, then any situation where P_0 is suitable must allow that $P_0 \sqcap P_1$ is suitable (since this is equal to P_0), and so P_1 must also be suitable since the internal choice could always be resolved in favour of P_1. The process P_1 is a refinement of P_0 because it will be appropriate in any environment which will find P_0 acceptable. An alternative way of thinking about the equivalence is that all of P_1's behaviours must already be allowed by P_0, since the introduction of P_1 does not introduce any new behaviours. This algebraic characterization of refinement is also appropriate for other semantic models, as will be discussed in later chapters. If the model is clear from the context then the subscript to the refinement symbol will be dropped.

Refinement satisfies a number of laws, given in Figure 5.5: it is reflexive, transitive, and anti-symmetric in all models; the process RUN is trace-refined by any other process; $STOP$ trace-refines every process; and refinement preserves **sat** specifications.

The resolution of internal choice is a refinement step: $P_0 \sqcap P_1 \sqsubseteq_T P_1$. If either P_0 or P_1 is acceptable, then certainly P_1 by itself is acceptable. Furthermore, all of the CSP operators are monotonic with respect to refinement. What this means is that for any CSP function $F(Y)$ constructed from the CSP operators, the application of F will respect the refinement relation: if $P_0 \sqsubseteq_T P_1$ then $F(P_0) \sqsubseteq_T F(P_1)$. Finally, if

$$\forall Y \bullet (F(Y) \sqsubseteq_T G(Y))$$

then $P_0 = F(P_0) \sqsubseteq_T P_1 = G(P_1)$.

Example 5.5.1 The process-oriented specification RUN_Σ specifies that termination may not occur, but imposes no other restriction. ∎

Example 5.5.2 The specification $P = a \to (P \,|||\, b \to STOP)$ specifies that only a and b events may occur, and b may not occur more often than a. This process meets the property-oriented specification $tr \downarrow b \leqslant tr \downarrow a$.

Now the function defining P may be refined as follows:

$$
\begin{aligned}
F(Y) \quad &=_T \quad a \to (Y \,|||\, b \to STOP) \\
&\sqsubseteq_T \quad a \to b \to Y
\end{aligned}
$$

and so it follows that $P \sqsubseteq_T P_1 = a \to b \to P_1$. The process that alternates on a and b refines the process that allows no more b's than a's. Since refinement preserves **sat** specifications, it follows that

$$
P_1 = a \to b \to P_1 \quad \textbf{sat} \quad tr \downarrow b \leqslant tr \downarrow a
$$

This follows from an application of Law $\sqsubseteq_T$-**spec**. ∎

Example 5.5.3 A CSP process expression can describe the behaviour required of the distributed summing network *DISTSUM* described in the case study. The resulting specification on *DISTSUM* is captured by the following refinement requirement:

$$
c_{\infty,0}.0 \to c_{0\infty}!(\Sigma_{i \in N} w_i) \to SKIP \quad \sqsubseteq_T \quad DISTSUM
$$

This states that *DISTSUM* is intended to output the appropriate value on the channel $v_{0\infty}$ before terminating. ∎

Example 5.5.4 When using CSP process expressions as specifications, it is important to ensure that no acceptable traces are excluded. For example, the requirement that a and b events should alternate (beginning with a) might use the recursive process $P = a \to b \to P$, but if no constraint is required on other events, then the acceptability of other events has to be included explicitly as a component $RUN_{\Sigma \setminus \{a,b\}}$, and the entire specification will be written

$$
P \,|||\, RUN_{\Sigma \setminus \{a,b\}}
$$

Using only P as a specification would introduce the additional constraint that no other events may occur. ∎

The model-checking tool FDR (see Appendix B) allows checks concerning the refinement relationship between two (finite state) CSP processes. This is often the quickest way to conduct process verification once the specification has been captured. The tool also assists debugging of implementations when they do not meet the specification by returning a witness trace which may be performed by the implementation but which is not possible for the specification process.

Exercises

Exercise 5.1 Specify that a lift's doors should not be open when the lift starts moving. Assume that it has events *open*, *close*, *moving*, *stopped* in its alphabet.

Exercise 5.2 Specify the hygiene requirement that hands should be washed between handling raw meat and cooked meat. Use the events *wash*, *raw*, and *cooked*, to refer to these three activities.

Does the combination $RAW \parallel_{\{wash\}} COOKED$ meet your specification?

$$RAW = raw \rightarrow wash \rightarrow RAW$$
$$COOKED = wash \rightarrow cooked \rightarrow COOKED$$

Exercise 5.3 What does the predicate $tr \leqslant \langle a, b, c \rangle \frown tr$ specify?

Exercise 5.4 What does the predicate $last(tr) = b \Rightarrow a \in \sigma(tr)$ specify?

Exercise 5.5 If P_1 **sat** $tr \downarrow a \leqslant tr \downarrow b + n$ and P_2 **sat** $tr \downarrow a \leqslant tr \downarrow b + m$, then prove that $P_1 \ ||| \ P_2$ **sat** $tr \downarrow a \leqslant tr \downarrow b + n + m$.

Exercise 5.6 Prove the statements on page 148, that

$$P_1 = b \rightarrow a \rightarrow P_1 \quad \textbf{sat} \quad S(tr) = tr \downarrow a \leqslant tr \downarrow b$$
$$P_2 = c \rightarrow b \rightarrow P_2 \quad \textbf{sat} \quad T(tr) = tr \downarrow b \leqslant tr \downarrow c$$

Exercise 5.7 Which of the following are sound proof rules for the interleaving operator?

$$\frac{P_1 \ \textbf{sat} \ tr \downarrow A \leqslant m \qquad P_2 \ \textbf{sat} \ tr \downarrow A \leqslant n}{P_1 \ ||| \ P_2 \ \textbf{sat} \ tr \downarrow A \leqslant (m + n)}$$

$$\frac{P_1 \ \textbf{sat} \ tr \downarrow a \leqslant tr \downarrow b \qquad P_2 \ \textbf{sat} \ tr \downarrow a \leqslant tr \downarrow b}{P_1 \ ||| \ P_2 \ \textbf{sat} \ tr \downarrow a \leqslant tr \downarrow b}$$

$$\frac{P_1 \ \textbf{sat} \ tr \downarrow a \leqslant tr \downarrow b \qquad P_2 \ \textbf{sat} \ tr \downarrow b \leqslant tr \downarrow c}{P_1 \ ||| \ P_2 \ \textbf{sat} \ tr \downarrow a \leqslant tr \downarrow c}$$

Exercise 5.8 Prove the claims of Example 5.3.4, that

$$\forall Y \bullet (Y \textbf{ sat } S_2(tr) \quad \Rightarrow \quad on \to Y \textbf{ sat } S_1(tr))$$
$$\forall Y \bullet (Y \textbf{ sat } S_1(tr) \quad \Rightarrow \quad off \to Y \textbf{ sat } S_2(tr))$$

Exercise 5.9 Prove by recursion induction that the process $DOOR = (open \to close \to DOOR) \,\square\, locked \to STOP$ meets the following specifications:

1. two consecutive events are not both *open*;

2. two consecutive events are not both *close* (you will have to prove something stronger);

3. $tr \downarrow close \leqslant tr \downarrow open \leqslant tr \downarrow close + 1$.

Exercise 5.10 Prove that $STACK = STACK(\langle\rangle)$ of Example 1.3.10 meets the specification

$$\forall v \bullet pop.v \textbf{ in } tr \Rightarrow push.v \textbf{ in } tr$$

Exercise 5.11 Specify the requirement that every output value (on channel *out*) must be less than or equal to some input value (on channel *in*), in both the property-oriented and the process-oriented specification styles.

Exercise 5.12 Specify the requirement that a *write* event should always occur between an *engage* event and a *release* event, as a property-oriented and as a process-oriented specification.

Exercise 5.13 Specify that a guard should never be up while a piece of machinery is switched on. A property-oriented specification should be expressed in terms of events *guard.up*, *guard.down*, *on* and *off*. Express the same specification in a process-oriented way.

Exercise 5.14 Can a node $NODE(i)$ (page 164) output its total to its parent node before it has sent out all of its initiating messages? Can it terminate before sending out all of its initiating messages?

Exercise 5.15 Show that $NODE(0)$ satisfies the following specifications:

1. $tr \Downarrow c_{0\infty} \neq \langle\rangle \Rightarrow tr \Downarrow c_{\infty0} \neq \langle\rangle$

2. $tr \upharpoonright \checkmark \neq \langle\rangle \Rightarrow tr \Downarrow c_{0\infty} \neq \langle\rangle$

3. $(tr \Downarrow c_{\infty0}) \leqslant \langle0\rangle$

4. $tr \downarrow c_{0\infty}.\mathbb{N} \leqslant 1$

Exercise 5.16 Show that $NODE(i) \textbf{ sat } \#tr \leqslant 1 + 2* \mid adj(i) \mid$

6

Stable failures

The traces model for CSP is concerned only with the sequences of events that processes may perform. Observing a process involves recording events as they occur during an execution. This view is appropriate for the analysis of safety, since the traces associated with a process provide sufficient information to verify safety properties.

Liveness properties are concerned with behaviour that processes are guaranteed to make available. Where safety properties are generally of the form 'something bad will not happen', liveness properties are of the form 'something good will happen'. With the view of processes as interacting components, a process in isolation can never by itself guarantee that any particular event will happen at any point, since its environment may always prevent the event from occurring by refusing to co-operate. However, a process might be able to guarantee the occurrence of events under particular assumptions about what its environment is prepared to allow. It is appropriate to think in terms of what the process is prepared to do rather than what it is guaranteed to do.

For example, a choice process $P_1 = a \rightarrow STOP \; \Box \; b \rightarrow STOP$ is prepared to perform both a and b, but neither of these possibilities is guaranteed to occur, since the resolution of the choice is dependent on the environment of the process, and this will not be contained in any description of the process itself. However, the process will be guaranteed to perform a if this is offered by the environment, and similarly for b.

On the other hand, if choices are made internally within the process, then some possibilities (as recorded in the traces) are not guaranteed. The internal choice process $P_2 = a \rightarrow STOP \; \Box \; b \rightarrow STOP$ has the same traces as P_1 but provides different guarantees. An environment which wishes to interact on a is not sure of doing so, and neither is an environment offering b, despite the fact that these two events are both possibilities for P_2. In fact, an environment needs to be prepared to interact on both a and b to be sure of obtaining some response from P_2, though the actual response is unpredictable. P_2 might refuse to interact if only a is offered to it, or only b, but it cannot if both a and b are simultaneously offered to it.

Trace information is in general too coarse to identify the guaranteed responses of a process. This is apparent from the fact that P_1 and P_2 have the same traces but different guaranteed behaviour, and more generally from the fact that internal and external choice have the same trace semantics, so they both give rise to the same possibilities, yet exhibit different behaviours in some contexts. Some finer form of process observation is required in order to make the necessary distinctions and provide the desired information about guaranteed process behaviour.

6.1 OBSERVING PROCESSES

Stable refusals

A process P is guaranteed to be able to respond to an offer of an event a if that event can be performed from P, provided there are no internal transitions from P which might result in withdrawal of this offer. A process P which can make no internal progress is said to be *stable*, written $P \downarrow$:

$$P \downarrow \quad = \quad \neg (P \xrightarrow{\tau})$$

Guarantees are concerned with stable states.

More generally, a stable process P can always respond in some way to the offer of a set of events $X \subseteq \Sigma^{\checkmark}$ if there is at least one $a \in X$ that P can perform. If there is no such $a \in X$, then P *refuses* the entire offer set X.

The CSP approach to semantics is to associate processes with observations of their executions, and then to use this information to understand the behaviour of the process as a whole. A single execution of a process P consisting of internal transitions leading to a stable state P' will not provide information about the events that are *guaranteed* to be offered, but will rather provide information about events that can *possibly* be refused. If no events in a set X are possible in the stable state P', then when P is initially offered X it is possible that it will reach a stable state (P') which deadlocks under that offer—no further progress can be made. In this case, the set X is termed a *refusal* of P.

A refusal might be thought of as one result of an experiment on the process P, where it is executed in an environment which offers the set X, and waits as long as necessary to see if any events in X are performed. If no events are performed, then X is considered a refusal of P, written P ref X. The assertion P ref X that P can possibly refuse the set X is defined as follows:

$$P \text{ ref } X \quad = \quad \exists P' \bullet P \xRightarrow{\langle\rangle} P' \wedge P' \downarrow \wedge \forall a \in X \bullet \neg (P' \xrightarrow{a})$$

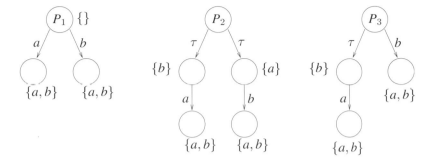

$$P_1 = a \rightarrow STOP \,\square\, b \rightarrow STOP$$
$$P_2 = a \,\rangle\, STOP \,\sqcap\, b \rightarrow STOP$$
$$P_3 = (c \rightarrow a \rightarrow STOP \,\square\, b \rightarrow STOP) \setminus \{c\}$$

Fig. 6.1   *Three processes and their stable states labelled with refusals*

Another possible result of the experiment is that some event from X is performed. This will be recorded as trace information. The final possible result is that P performs internal transitions for ever, never reaching a stable state nor performing any event. In this case, P is said to be *divergent*, written $P \uparrow$.

$$P \uparrow = \exists \langle P_i \rangle_{i \in \mathbb{N}} \bullet (P = P_0 \wedge \forall i \bullet P_i \xrightarrow{\tau} P_{i+1})$$

A process is non-divergent if it does not diverge, and it is divergence-free if none of its reachable states diverge.

The offer of a set of events A will be guaranteed some response from a non-divergent process P precisely when A is not a possible refusal set for P.

The refusals of a process P are concerned with the sets of events that might be refused by P before any visible events have occurred. Refusals thus provide information about initial behaviour. The notion of refusal also extends to other stages of an execution. In general, an observer will experiment on a process by repeatedly offering to interact on sets of events, where each offer is either accepted by the process, or not. Once they are made, offers are not withdrawn by the observer, so if an offer is not accepted by the process then the experiment ends.

Example 6.1.1 The transition graphs and associated refusal sets of the following three processes are illustrated in Figure 6.1. Each of them is able to perform only events a and b, so all other events will automatically be refused at any stable node, and are not included explicitly.

Since the refusal sets associated with a process state are subset closed, only the maximal refusal set in each case is included.

The process $P_1 = a \to STOP \,\square\, b \to STOP$ is unable to refuse either a or b in its initial state, but can refuse both of these events after it has performed something.

The process $P_2 = a \to STOP \,\sqcap\, b \to STOP$ is unstable, as there are two internal transitions that are possible for it. Each of these leads to a stable state where either a or b is possible, and the other can be refused.

The process $P_3 = (c \to a \to STOP \,\square\, b \to STOP) \setminus \{c\}$ is initially unstable, although it can perform the event b from its initial unstable state, after which it can refuse $\{a, b\}$. However, there is no refusal set associated with the initial unstable state, and the single internal transition leads to a state in which b is refused. This means that an interacting process wishing to synchronize on b might succeed, but it is also possible that the internal event will occur first and the b will then be refused. There is no guarantee that b will be accepted, since the internal transition is entirely under the control of process P_3 itself and cannot be prevented from occurring. ∎

Stable failures

It is possible that at some point during an execution an offer set X will be refused by the process P. This refusal will be recorded together with the finite sequence of events tr that were performed during the execution leading up to the refusal of X. The observation (tr, X) is called a *stable failure* of P, recording the fact that

$$\exists P'' \bullet P \stackrel{tr}{\Longrightarrow} P'' \wedge P'' \downarrow \wedge P'' \text{ ref } X$$

The process may perform the events in tr, and then reach a stable state where it refuses all of the events in the set X. If after the performance of tr it is in an environment in which events from the set X are possible but no others, then there will be no further progress.

Example 6.1.2 Figure 6.2 gives the transition graph of the process P defined as follows:

$$
\begin{aligned}
P \;=\; & (a \to (c \to STOP \,\sqcap\, d \to STOP) \,\square\, b \to STOP) \\
& \sqcap \\
& (b \to c \to STOP \,\square\, (c \to (f \to d \to STOP \,\square\, e \to STOP) \setminus f))
\end{aligned}
$$

There are two stable states P can reach purely by performing internal transitions, corresponding to the trace $\langle \rangle$. These reflect the ways the top level choice can be resolved. One of these states is able to refuse the set $\{c, d\}$, so $(\langle \rangle, \{c, d\})$ is a possible failure of P. However, $(\langle \rangle, \{b\})$ is not a failure of P, since both stable states are able to perform b—neither can refuse it. Similarly, $(\langle \rangle, \{a, c\})$ is not a failure of P since each stable state is able to perform some event from the set $\{a, c\}$, even though $\{a\}$ and $\{c\}$ can be refused separately.

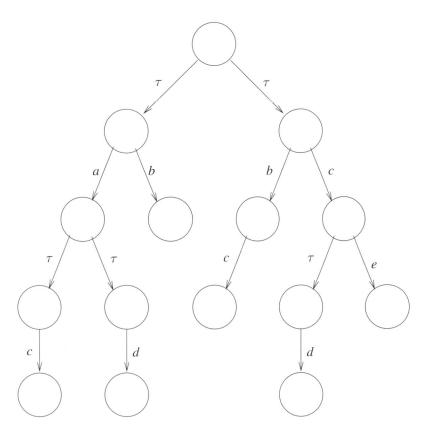

Fig. 6.2   _Transitions of process_ P _of Example 6.1.2_

Subsequent to the performance of the a event, there are again two stable states that can be reached. One of them is unable to perform any of the set $\{a, b, c\}$, so $(\langle a \rangle, \{a, b, c\})$ is a failure of P.

There are two stable states corresponding to the trace $\langle b \rangle$. One of them is able to refuse c, so $(\langle b \rangle, \{c\})$ is a failure of P. On the other hand, c is possible from the other stable state, so $\langle b, c \rangle$ is a possible trace of P, and $(\langle b, c \rangle, \{\})$ is a possible failure.

Finally, there is a single stable state subsequent to an initial c event, and e is not possible from that state, though it is transiently possible immediately after the c. Thus $(\langle c \rangle, \{e\})$ is a failure of P. ∎

Semantic model

The stable failures model for CSP identifies a process P with the traces and the stable failures that are associated with it. This model is more discriminating and hence less abstract than the traces model, but the underlying approach taken to the semantics and to specification and verification is the same. The extra information associated with processes allows them to be analysed with respect to additional specifications, such as those concerned with liveness requirements.

If two sets T and SF of traces and of stable failures respectively are to correspond to the possible behaviours of some process, there are some consistency conditions that they should meet. These are properties that must hold of any pair of sets which describe some process.

As in the traces model, the set T should meet $T1$ and $T2$ of page 92: it must be empty and prefix closed. Consistency between SF and T requires that any failure $(tr, X) \in SF$ must have its trace recorded in T:

$$SF1 \qquad (tr, X) \in SF \Rightarrow tr \in T$$

There is also a property of subset closure in the refusal component of a behaviour: if a set X can be refused after a trace tr, then any subset X' of X can also be refused after that trace.

$$SF2 \qquad (tr, X) \in SF \wedge X' \subseteq X \Rightarrow (tr, X') \in SF$$

Thirdly, if a stable state has been reached from which no events in a set X' are possible, then the refusal set can be augmented with the set X':

$$SF3 \qquad (tr, X) \in SF \wedge \forall a \in X' \bullet tr \frown \{a\} \notin T \Rightarrow (tr, X \cup X') \in SF$$

Finally, any terminating trace results in a stable state in which no further events are possible (and so any set can be refused):

$$SF4 \qquad tr \frown \langle \checkmark \rangle \in T \Rightarrow (tr \frown \langle \checkmark \rangle, X) \in F$$

6.2 PROCESS SEMANTICS

Each CSP process expression will be associated with appropriate traces and stable failures. These are defined compositionally, so the behaviours associated with a composite process will be defined in terms of the behaviours of its components. The definitions of the traces $\mathsf{traces}(P)$ associated with processes are those of the traces model given in Chapter 4 and are not repeated here. The stable failures associated with a CSP process expression P will be given by $\mathcal{SF}[\![P]\!]$.

STOP

The process *STOP* is a stable, deadlocked process. It is not able to perform any event, and can refuse anything.

$$\mathcal{SF}[\![STOP]\!] \quad = \quad \{(\langle \rangle, X) \mid X \subseteq \Sigma^{\checkmark}\}$$

Prefixing

In a stable failure of the process $a \to P$, there are two possibilities: either the event a has not occurred, in which case the trace must be $\langle\rangle$ and P is in its stable initial state, able to refuse any event other than a; or else the event a has occurred and the rest of the stable failure derives from process P.

$$\mathcal{SF}\,[\![a \to P]\!] \quad = \quad \{(\langle\rangle, X) \mid a \notin X\}$$
$$\cup$$
$$\{(\langle a\rangle \frown tr, X) \mid (tr, X) \in \mathcal{SF}\,[\![P]\!]\}$$

Prefix choice

A failure of the process $x : A \to P(x)$ is again one of two possibilities. Either no event has yet occurred, in which case any events apart from those in A can be refused; or else an event a in A has occurred, and the subsequent behaviour is that of the corresponding process $P(a)$.

$$\mathcal{SF}\,[\![x : A \to P(x)]\!] \quad - \quad \{(\langle\rangle, X) \mid A \cap X = \{\}\}$$
$$\cup$$
$$\{(\langle a\rangle \frown tr, X) \mid a \in A \wedge (tr, X) \in \mathcal{SF}\,[\![P(a)]\!]\}$$

SKIP

The atomic process *SKIP* is used to denote successful termination, and it signals this by means of the termination event $\checkmark$. This is the only event it can perform, and it is stable before and after this event. All other events will be refused before termination, and all events will be refused after termination.

$$\mathcal{SF}\,[\![SKIP]\!] \quad = \quad \{(\langle\rangle, X) \mid \checkmark \notin X\}$$
$$\cup \{(\langle\checkmark\rangle, X) \mid X \subseteq \Sigma^{\checkmark}\}$$

DIV

It is useful to identify the process which does nothing except diverge. This is *livelock*—it can perform only internal events. It is denoted *DIV*. It has the same traces as *STOP*, but it has no stable states at all, and hence no stable failures:

$$\text{traces}(DIV) \quad = \quad \{\langle\rangle\}$$
$$\mathcal{SF}\,[\![DIV]\!] \quad = \quad \{\}$$

This process was not introduced in the traces model, so its traces are also given here. It is the minimal process in the stable failures model, because this model records only stable behaviour, and *DIV* does not have any. The model turns a blind eye to divergent behaviour, so the internal activity of this process is not observed. It will be given a more accurate treatment when divergent behaviours are considered in Chapter 8.

CHAOS

The process which can do absolutely anything except diverge is *CHAOS*. This is able to accept or refuse any events, but it is at least guaranteed to stabilize. It has all possible stable failures, and the same traces as *RUN*:

$$
\begin{aligned}
\mathsf{traces}(CHAOS) &= TRACE \\
\mathcal{SF}[\![CHAOS]\!] &= TRACE \times \mathbb{P}(\Sigma^\checkmark)
\end{aligned}
$$

Chaotic behaviour may be restricted to a particular set of events $A \subseteq \Sigma^\checkmark$. The process $CHAOS_A$ allows any events in the set A to be performed or refused, but cannot perform any events outside the set A.

$$
\begin{aligned}
\mathsf{traces}(CHAOS_A) &= \{tr \mid \sigma(tr) \subseteq A\} \\
\mathcal{SF}[\![CHAOS_A]\!] &= \{(tr, X) \mid \sigma(tr) \subseteq A\}
\end{aligned}
$$

RUN

Although they have the same traces, in the stable failures model *RUN* is better behaved than *CHAOS*, always willing to interact and never refusing any interaction.

$$
\mathcal{SF}[\![RUN]\!] = \{(tr, X) \mid X = \{\} \lor \checkmark \in \sigma(tr)\}
$$

The process RUN_A parameterized by a particular set A is able to perform events in that set, and to refuse all others.

$$
\mathcal{SF}[\![RUN_A]\!] = \{(tr, X) \mid \sigma(tr) \subseteq A \land (X \cap A = \{\} \lor \checkmark \in \sigma(tr))\}
$$

If $\checkmark \notin A$ then RUN_A cannot terminate.

External choice

An observer of the choice construct $P_1 \mathbin{\square} P_2$ might observe an execution of P_1, or of P_2; there are no other possibilities. Before any events are performed and the choice resolved, any refused set must be refused by both P_1 and P_2, so both processes must be stable. After the choice is resolved, any refusal need be possible only for the process which resolved the choice.

$$\mathcal{SF}\,[\![P_1 \,\square\, P_2]\!] \;=\; \{(\langle\rangle, X) \mid ((\langle\rangle, X) \in \mathcal{SF}\,[\![P_1]\!] \cap \mathcal{SF}\,[\![P_2]\!])\}$$
$$\cup$$
$$\{(tr, X) \mid tr \neq \langle\rangle \wedge (tr, X) \in \mathcal{SF}\,[\![P_1]\!] \cup \mathcal{SF}\,[\![P_2]\!]\}$$

The properties of idempotence, associativity, and commutativity still hold for external choice in the stable failures model. Furthermore, *STOP* is still a unit, though *RUN* is no longer a zero because P might not be initially stable. Instead *RUN* $\square$ *DIV* is its zero. It has the same traces and stable failures as *RUN* apart from on the empty trace, where it is not stable.

$$P \,\square\, (RUN \,\square\, DIV) =_{SF} (RUN \,\square\, DIV) \qquad\qquad \langle\square\text{-zero}_{SF}\rangle$$

The executions of the indexed external choice $\square_{i \in I}\, P_i$ are the executions of all of its components. Its stable failures will be those of its components:

$$\mathcal{SF}\,[\![\square_{i \in I}\, P_i]\!] \;=\; \{(\langle\rangle, X) \mid ((\langle\rangle, X) \in \bigcap_{i \in I} \mathcal{SF}\,[\![P_i]\!])\}$$
$$\cup$$
$$\{(tr, X) \mid tr \neq \langle\rangle \wedge (tr, X) \in \bigcup_{i \in I} \mathcal{SF}\,[\![P_i]\!]\}$$

In the case where the choice is over the empty set of processes, the intersection $\bigcap_{i \in I} \mathcal{SF}\,[\![P_i]\!]$ is taken to include all possible stable failures, since all of them are vacuously in each of the $\mathcal{SF}\,[\![P_i]\!]$. This means that in this case, any refusal is possible on the empty trace. Furthermore, no events are possible. As in the traces model, an empty choice is equivalent to *STOP*

Internal choice

The internal choice $P_1 \sqcap P_2$ behaves either as P_1 or as P_2, and its environment exercises no control over which. The possible observations are precisely those that either P_1 or P_2 are able to exhibit.

$$\mathcal{SF}\,[\![P_1 \sqcap P_2]\!] \;=\; \mathcal{SF}\,[\![P_1]\!] \cup \mathcal{SF}\,[\![P_2]\!]$$

The stable failures of $P_1 \sqcap P_2$ differ from those of $P_1 \,\square\, P_2$ in the case where no events have been performed: before the choice has been made. When the trace is empty, a refusal of $P_1 \,\square\, P_2$ must be generated from both participants, whereas in the case of internal choice, only one of the components of $P_1 \sqcap P_2$ is required to contribute to any refusal. Hence $(\langle\rangle, \{a\})$ is a failure of $a \to STOP \sqcap b \to STOP$, but is not a failure of $a \to STOP \,\square\, b \to STOP$.

The indexed internal choice $\bigsqcap_{i \in J} P_i$ is able to behave as any of its component processes, and its behaviours will be the union of those of its constituents:

$$\mathcal{SF}\left[\!\!\left[\bigsqcap_{i \in J} P_i\right]\!\!\right] = \bigcup_{i \in J} \mathcal{SF}\left[\!\!\left[P_i\right]\!\!\right]$$

The internal choice operator also distributes over the external choice operator:

$$P_1 \sqcap (P_2 \,\square\, P_3) =_U (P_1 \sqcap P_2) \,\square\, (P_1 \sqcap P_3) \qquad \qquad \langle\square\text{-}\sqcap\text{-dist}_U\rangle$$

Any set X that is initially offered can either be accepted by one of the three component processes, or refused, either by P_1 or by both P_2 and P_3. The two extra refusal possibilities for the right-hand side—that X should be refused by both P_1 and P_2, or by both P_1 and P_3—both imply that P_1 can refuse X, and hence that the left-hand side has this as a refusal too.

Example 6.2.1 This law helps to clarify the possible behaviours associated with a drinks machine, which will either return the cash or will offer a choice between a *tea* and a *coffee*.

$$(ret \rightarrow STOP) \sqcap (tea \rightarrow STOP \,\square\, coffee \rightarrow STOP)$$
$$= \ (ret \rightarrow STOP \sqcap tea \rightarrow STOP) \,\square\, (ret \rightarrow STOP \sqcap coffee \rightarrow STOP)$$

This law states that it makes no difference whether the machine first makes its internal decision and then possibly offers a choice to the customer, or whether the customer makes the choice between tea and coffee first and the machine then decides internally whether to service that choice or return the cash. ∎

Alphabetized parallel

In the parallel combination $P_1 \,_A\|_B\, P_2$, processes P_1 and P_2 synchronize on events in $(A \cap B)^{\checkmark}$, and perform their other events independently.

As in the traces model, any trace of the parallel combination projected onto $A^{\checkmark}$ must be a trace of P_1. Further, if P_1 is able to refuse some events X in its interface $A^{\checkmark}$, then so too is the combination. Similar considerations apply to P_2. If synchronization is required for the performance of events, then either component is able independently to block them.

$$\begin{aligned}
\mathcal{SF}\left[\!\!\left[P_1 \,_A\|_B\, P_2\right]\!\!\right] = \ & \{(tr, X) \mid \ \exists X_1, X_2 : \mathbb{P}(\Sigma^{\checkmark}) \bullet \\
& \qquad X \cap (A \cup B)^{\checkmark} = (X_1 \cap A^{\checkmark}) \cup (X_2 \cap B^{\checkmark}) \\
& \qquad \wedge (tr \upharpoonright A^{\checkmark}, X_1) \in \mathcal{SF}\left[\!\!\left[P_1\right]\!\!\right] \\
& \qquad \wedge (tr \upharpoonright B^{\checkmark}, X_2) \in \mathcal{SF}\left[\!\!\left[P_2\right]\!\!\right] \\
& \qquad \wedge \sigma(tr) \subseteq (A \cup B)^{\checkmark} \}
\end{aligned}$$

All of the laws for the parallel operator given in Figure 4.5, with the exception of $\|\text{-idem}_T$, also hold for the stable failures model.

Example 6.2.2 The processes *PETE* and *DAVE* were introduced in Example 2.1.9. They both repeatedly and independently made a nondeterministic choice whether to lift a piano or a table.

$$PETE \quad = \quad lift\_piano \to PETE \sqcap lift\_table \to PETE$$
$$DAVE \quad = \quad lift\_piano \to DAVE \sqcap lift\_table \to DAVE$$

The process *DAVE* had exactly the same description.

Thus either of them can engage in any number of *lift_piano* and *lift_table* events, and then refuse either of them (but not both).

$$\mathcal{SF}\,[\![PETE]\!] \quad = \quad \{(tr, X) \mid \quad tr \in \{lift\_piano, lift\_table\}^* \\ \land \{lift\_piano, lift\_table\} \not\subseteq X\}$$

and $\mathcal{SF}\,[\![DAVE]\!] = \mathcal{SF}\,[\![PETE]\!]$.

When these two processes are composed in parallel, then they must agree on the events that appear in the trace, but a refusal will be the union of refusals of the components. If $(tr, X_1) \in \mathcal{SF}\,[\![PETE]\!]$ and $(tr, X_2) \in \mathcal{SF}\,[\![DAVE]\!]$, then $(tr, X_1 \cup X_2) \in \mathcal{SF}\,[\![PETE \parallel DAVE]\!]$. The constraints that each of *PETE* and *DAVE* must be willing to perform one of their events is not reflected in their combination, which can refuse any events at all. The constraints that $\{lift\_piano, lift\_table\} \not\subseteq X_1$ and $\{lift\_piano, lift\_table\} \not\subseteq X_2$ are not strong enough to impose any constraints on $X_1 \cup X_2$.

$$\mathcal{SF}\,[\![PETE \parallel DAVE]\!] \quad = \quad \{(tr, X) \mid tr \in \{lift\_piano, lift\_table\}^*\}$$

Any trace is still possible, but deadlock at any stage is also possible. ∎

Interleaving

An interleaving of two processes $P_1 \,|\|\, P_2$ executes each of them entirely independently of the other. Since they do not synchronize, an event (other than termination) will be refused by the combination only when it is refused by both processes independently—if one of the processes is ready to perform the event, then so is the combination. Termination requires the participation of both components, so it can be blocked by either. As in the traces model, traces of the combination appear as interleavings of traces of the two component processes.

$$\mathcal{SF}\,[\![P_1 \,|\|\, P_2]\!] \quad = \quad \{(tr, X_1 \cup X_2) \mid \exists tr_1, tr_2 \bullet \quad tr \text{ interleaves } tr_1, tr_2 \\ \land X_1 \restriction \Sigma = X_2 \restriction \Sigma \\ \land (tr_1, X_1) \in \mathcal{SF}\,[\![P_1]\!] \\ \land (tr_2, X_2) \in \mathcal{SF}\,[\![P_2]\!]\}$$

The laws given in Figure 4.9 are all true for the stable failures model as well, with the exception of $|||$-**zero**$_T$. Although all (non-terminating) traces will be possible for $P \;|||\; RUN_\Sigma$, it will not be stable unless P is. Instability is introduced by including DIV as another interleaved component, resulting in the process $RUN \;|||\; DIV$ which serves as the zero for interleaving: it has all non-terminating traces, and no stable failures.

$$P \;|||\; (RUN_\Sigma \;|||\; DIV) =_{SF} (RUN_\Sigma \;|||\; DIV) \qquad\qquad \langle|||\text{-}\mathsf{zero}_{SF}\rangle$$

This law is also true in the traces model, since $RUN_\Sigma \;|||\; DIV$ has the same traces as RUN_Σ.

Interface parallel

The process $P_1 \parallel_A P_2$ is a combination of synchronous and interleaved parallel, synchronizing on events in the set $A^\checkmark$ and interleaving outside that set.

Any stable failure of the parallel process $P_1 \parallel_A P_2$ will be a combination of stable failures of its two components.

$$\mathcal{SF}\,[\![P_1 \parallel_A P_2]\!] \;=\; \{(tr, X_1 \cup X_2) \mid \exists\, tr_1, tr_2 \bullet$$
$$tr\ \mathsf{synch}_A\ tr_1, tr_2)$$
$$\wedge\ X_1 \setminus A^\checkmark = X_2 \setminus A^\checkmark$$
$$\wedge\ (tr_1, X_1) \in \mathcal{SF}\,[\![P_1]\!]$$
$$\wedge\ (tr_2, X_2) \in \mathcal{SF}\,[\![P_2]\!]\}$$

The laws for interface parallel given in Figure 4.10 all hold in the stable failures model with the exception of $\parallel_{A_T}$ -**zero**, which requires instability to be introduced to the zero for the same reason as the zero for interleaving:

$$P \parallel_A (RUN_{\Sigma \setminus A} \;|||\; DIV) =_{SF} (RUN_{\Sigma \setminus A} \;|||\; DIV) \qquad\qquad \langle\parallel_A\text{-}\mathsf{zero}_{SF}\rangle$$

Hiding

The process $P \setminus A$ will undergo the same executions as P, but events in the set A will occur as internal events rather than as external synchronizations. This means that after any trace, a stable refusal X of $P \setminus A$ will correspond to a stable refusal of P in which not only internal

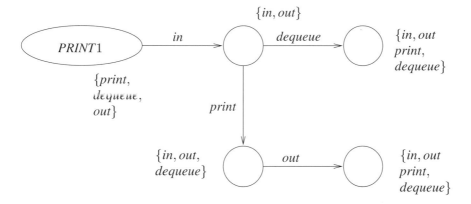

Fig. 6.3 *Transition graph for* PRINT1, *labelled with maximal refusals*

events of P but also all events in A (which have become internal events) are refused. The stable failures of $P \setminus A$ are therefore given by:

$$\mathcal{SF}[\![P \setminus A]\!] \;=\; \{(tr \setminus A, X) \mid (tr, X \cup A) \in \mathcal{SF}[\![P]\!]\}$$

Example 6.2.3 A one-shot printer queue, a cut-down version of *PRINTQ* of page 59, uses its channels as follows:

$$
\begin{aligned}
PRINT1 \;=\; & in \to (print \to out \to STOP \\
& \qquad \Box \; dequeue \to STOP)
\end{aligned}
$$

This has stable failures, illustrated in Figure 6.3, as follows:

$$
\begin{aligned}
\mathcal{SF}[\![PRINT1]\!] \;=\; & \{(\langle\rangle, X) \mid in \notin X\} \\
& \cup \{(\langle in\rangle, X) \mid \{print, dequeue\} \cap X = \{\}\} \\
& \cup \{(\langle in, print\rangle, X) \mid out \notin X\} \\
& \cup \{(\langle in, print, out\rangle, X) \mid X \subseteq \Sigma^{\checkmark}\} \\
& \cup \{(\langle in, dequeue\rangle, X) \mid X \subseteq \Sigma^{\checkmark}\}
\end{aligned}
$$

The stable failures of *PRINT1* $\setminus$ $\{print\}$ derive from the stable failures of *PRINT1* whose refusals that can be augmented with $\{print\}$. These are all failures apart from those with trace $\langle in\rangle$. The stable failures of *PRINT1* $\setminus$ $\{print\}$ are therefore derived as follows:

$$
\begin{aligned}
\mathcal{SF}[\![PRINT1 \setminus \{print\}]\!] \;=\; & \{(\langle\rangle, X) \mid in \notin X\} \\
& \cup \{(\langle in\rangle, X) \mid out \notin X\} \\
& \cup \{(\langle in, out\rangle, X) \mid X \subseteq \Sigma^{\checkmark}\} \\
& \cup \{(\langle in, dequeue\rangle, X) \mid X \subseteq \Sigma^{\checkmark}\}
\end{aligned}
$$

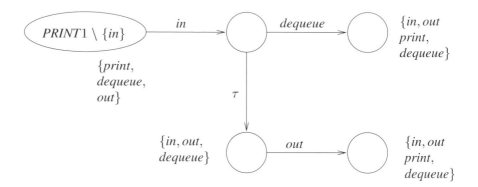

Fig. 6.4 *Transition graph for* $PRINT1 \setminus \{in\}$, *labelled with maximal refusals*

These failures are illustrated in Figure 6.4. It emerges that *out* cannot be refused after *in*, but that *dequeue* can be. ∎

Renaming

The forward renamed process $f(P)$ behaves as P, except that $f(a)$ can be performed whenever P could have performed a. It follows that the process $f(P)$ can refuse a set X if every event that f maps into X can be refused by P, since if there is some event a which P cannot refuse, then $f(P)$ would have to be open to $f(a)$. This means that $f^{-1}(X)$ must be a refusal of P whenever X is a refusal of $f(P)$.

$$\mathcal{SF}\,[\![f(P)]\!] \quad = \quad \{(f(tr), X) \mid (tr, f^{-1}(X)) \in \mathcal{SF}\,[\![P]\!]\}$$

The renaming operator in the stable failures model meets all of the laws given in Figure 4.13.

The backward renaming operator $f^{-1}(P)$ also behaves in a similar fashion to P, but any event a that is performed by $f^{-1}(P)$ corresponds to an event $f(a)$ performed by P. If a set X is offered to the process $f^{-1}(P)$, then this corresponds to $f(X)$ being offered to the underlying process P. Hence $f^{-1}(P)$ can refuse X whenever P refuses $f(X)$.

$$\mathcal{SF}\,[\![f^{-1}(P)]\!] \quad = \quad \{(tr, X) \mid (f(tr), f(X)) \in \mathcal{SF}\,[\![P]\!])\}$$

All the laws given in Figure 4.13 for backward renaming also remain valid in the stable failures model.

Sequential composition

The sequential composition $P_1; P_2$ behaves as P_1 until P_1 terminates successfully, at which point it passes control to P_2. A stable failure of $P_1; P_2$ will arise either from a failure of P_1, which also refuses to terminate and transfer control to P_2, or else from a terminating trace of P_1 followed by a failure of P_2.

$$\mathcal{SF}\llbracket P_1; P_2 \rrbracket = \{(tr, X) \mid (tr, X \cup \{\checkmark\}) \in \mathcal{SF}\llbracket P_1 \rrbracket\}$$
$$\cup \{(tr_1 \frown tr_2, X) \mid (tr_1 \frown \langle \checkmark \rangle \in \text{traces}(P_1)$$
$$\wedge (tr_2, X) \in \mathcal{SF}\llbracket P_2 \rrbracket)\}$$

Not all of the laws of sequential composition given in Figure 4.14 are valid in the stable failures model. In particular, $P; SKIP = P$ fails because of the possibility of termination in P forming one branch of a choice. For example, the process $P = SKIP \,\square\, a \to STOP$ is not able to refuse the event a, but $P; SKIP$ is able to refuse it by performing P's termination event and resolving the choice. However, all of the other laws continue to hold.

Interrupt

The process $P_1 \,\triangle\, P_2$ executes as P_1, but at any stage before termination it can begin executing as P_2. Any given stable failure (tr, X) is either a stable failure of P_1 for which (if not terminating) P_2 is also able to refuse X (since P_2 is still enabled); or else it is a non-terminating trace of P_1 followed by a failure of P_2, which must have a non-empty trace (since P_2 must perform an event to effect the interrupt).

$$\mathcal{SF}\llbracket P_1 \,\triangle\, P_2 \rrbracket = \{(tr, X) \mid (tr, X) \in \mathcal{SF}\llbracket P_1 \rrbracket$$
$$\wedge (\checkmark \in \sigma(tr) \vee (\langle \rangle, X) \in \mathcal{SF}\llbracket P_2 \rrbracket)\}$$
$$\cup \{(tr_1 \frown tr_2, X) \mid tr_1 \in \text{traces}(P_1) \wedge \checkmark \notin \sigma(tr_1)$$
$$\wedge (tr_2, X) \in \mathcal{SF}\llbracket P_2 \rrbracket$$
$$\wedge tr_2 \neq \langle \rangle\}$$

All of the laws concerning the interrupt operator that are presented in Figure 4.15 are also true in the stable failures model.

Example 6.2.4 A message authenticator will accept a message, and then either pass it on, or else reject it. It is unstable after its input. It can also be shut down at any stage during its execution.

The one-message version is described as follows:

$$AUTH = left?x : T \to (DIV \,|||\, (right!x \to STOP$$
$$\sqcap reject \to STOP))$$
$$\triangle\, shutdown \to STOP$$

The stable failures of the process inside the interrupt are simply pairs of the form $(\langle \rangle, X)$ where $X \cap left.T = \{\}$. Once the first event has occurred, the process becomes unstable and contributes no further stable failures.

The calculation of the stable failures of *AUTH* requires consideration of the traces of the first process. For example, $(\langle left.3, reject, shutdown \rangle, \{right.3\})$ arises from the trace $\langle left.3, reject \rangle$ and the stable failure $(\langle shutdown \rangle, \{right.3\})$. Only sequential composition and interrupt require knowledge of the traces of their first component in order to derive their stable failures.

In fact, the stable failures of *AUTH* will be

$$\{(\langle\rangle, X) \mid shutdown \notin X\}$$
$$\cup \{(\langle left.x, shutdown \rangle, X) \mid x \in T\}$$
$$\cup \{(\langle left.x, right.x, shutdown \rangle, X) \mid x \in T\}$$
$$\cup \{(\langle left.x, reject, shutdown \rangle, X) \mid x \in T\}$$

The refusal set in a stable failure is given by $shutdown \to STOP$ only when the trace from that component is not empty: *shutdown* must have occurred. ■

6.3 RECURSION

A recursive definition $N = P$ defines the process N in terms of a process description P which may itself contain instances of N. The stable failures model provides guarantees that any such definition is sound: that any recursive equation has a solution. It also provides a way of determining the stable failures of the appropriate solution—the smallest possible such set of stable failures. This means that any solution to the recursive equation is guaranteed to have at least those stable failures as possible observations. The traces of the appropriate solution are given in the traces model.

Example 6.3.1 The recursive equation $N = N \,\square\, a \to STOP$ has many fixed points, including $a \to STOP, a \to STOP \,\square\, b \to STOP$, and $a \to STOP \,\square\, DIV$. The least of these in the stable failures model is $a \to STOP \,\square\, DIV$, and so this will be the semantics of the process defined by the recursive equation. ■

Operational semantics

The understanding of recursion in the stable failures model requires a slightly different operational treatment of recursive unwinding than was presented in Chapter 1, in order to give a satisfactory account of divergence. In particular, unguarded recursions such as the one in Example 6.3.1 above are considered to be unstable because an infinite sequence of recursive invocations of the process N of Example 6.3.1 may occur without the occurrence of any external events. Beginning with the process N, the process $N \,\square\, a \to STOP$ is reached from a recursive invocation, and then $N \,\square\, a \to STOP \,\square\, a \to STOP$, and so on. To consider this as a divergent sequence, an internal event is associated with a recursive unwinding, resulting in the following rule for recursion in place of the original transition rule given on page 13.

$$\frac{}{N \xrightarrow{\tau} P} \quad [\, N = P \,]$$

When the process expression P is guarded in N, then this initial internal action makes no difference to the visible behaviour of P as compared with the original transition rule for recursive processes: both rules will give rise to the same traces and stable failures. In fact, the traces will be the same for all guarded and unguarded recursive process definitions, and all the results concerning the traces model remain valid if this rule for recursion is used instead. The only difference between the impact of the two rules is on the stability of unguarded recursions.

Example 6.3.2 Concerning the process $N = N \,\square\, a \to STOP$, the revised rule for recursive unwinding allows the sequence of transitions:

$$N$$
$$\downarrow \tau$$
$$N \,\square\, a \to STOP$$
$$\downarrow \tau$$
$$N \,\square\, a \to STOP \,\square\, a \to STOP$$
$$\downarrow \tau$$
$$\vdots$$

The original rule for recursion had no internal transitions for N, and only one transition, labelled by a, to $STOP$. ∎

Example 6.3.3 The process $N = STOP \,\sqcap\, b \to N$ takes an internal transition to unwind the definition, and then a further transition to resolve the internal choice. Finally, it has either reached $STOP$ or else the stable process $b \to N$. The same possibilities arise if the original transition rule for recursion is used, except that the initial internal transition is absent. The two transition graphs are compared in Figure 6.5. They are each associated with the same traces and stable failures. ∎

All of the techniques for recursion introduced in Chapter 4 for the traces model are also applicable in the stable failures model.

The traces and stable failures associated with recursively defined process expressions $N = P$ can be obtained directly from the operational semantics, or alternatively by using the denotational semantics. Both of these approaches give the same result.

The process P with free variable N corresponds to a function $F(Y) = P[Y/N]$, and successive applications of the function F will give rise to approximations to the fixed point. The

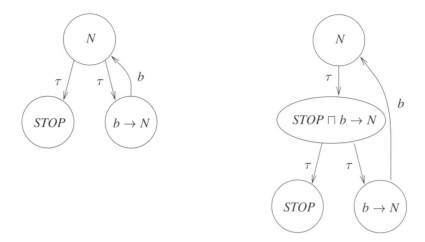

Fig. 6.5   Two transition graphs for $N = STOP \sqcap b \to N$

first approximation is the minimal process DIV, and successive approximations are $F(DIV)$, $F(F(DIV))$ and then $F^n(DIV)$ for $n \in \mathbb{N}$. The sequence of approximations $\langle F^n(DIV) \rangle_{n \in \mathbb{N}}$ will define the fixed point, which will consist of those traces and stable failures that appear in some elements of the sequence. The traces of N are those given in the traces model. The stable failures will then be

$$\bigcup_{n \in \mathbb{N}} \mathcal{SF} \, [\![F^n(DIV)]\!]$$

This process is the minimal one which contains all of the approximations.

Example 6.3.4 The process $N = STOP \sqcap b \to N$ is the fixed point of the function $F(Y) = STOP \sqcap b \to Y$. For any n, the semantics of $F^{n+1}(DIV)$ can be calculated from the semantics of $F^n(DIV)$, resulting in

$$\mathcal{SF} \, [\![F^n(DIV)]\!] \quad = \quad \{ (\langle b \rangle^i, X) \mid i < n \wedge X \subseteq \Sigma^\checkmark \}$$

The union of these approximations yields

$$\mathcal{SF} \, [\![N]\!] \quad = \quad \{ (\langle b \rangle^i, X) \mid i \in \mathbb{N} \wedge X \subseteq \Sigma^\checkmark \}$$

which is in accordance with the behaviours predicted from the operational semantics. ■

Law **recursion-unwinding** of page 120 will hold for any recursive definition $N = P$. The law **UFP** also holds: all solutions to any guarded equation must have the same stable failures.

$$(F(Y) \text{ guarded} \wedge (F(P_1) =_{SF} P_1) \wedge (F(P_2) =_{SF} P_2)) \Rightarrow P_1 =_{SF} P_2 \qquad \langle \text{UFP}_{SF} \rangle$$

For example, the function F of Example 4.3.4 is event guarded:

$$
\begin{aligned}
N &= F(N) &= (a \rightarrow N) \,\Box\, b \rightarrow STOP \\
M &= a \rightarrow M \\
P &= M \,\triangle\, (b \rightarrow STOP)
\end{aligned}
$$

Furthermore, $P =_{SF} F(P)$, and $N =_{SF} F(N)$ by definition, so it follows that $N =_{SF} P$.

Mutual recursion

Mutual recursion is a generalization of single recursion, with an appropriate generalized treatment. The operational transition rule is adjusted in a similar way, modelling the recursive unwinding of any process variable N_i as accompanied by an internal transition. As with the case for single recursion, exactly the same results concerning the traces model remain valid if this transition rule is used instead.

$$\frac{}{N_i \xrightarrow{\tau} P_i} \quad [\underline{N} = \underline{P}]$$

The stable failures associated with all of the N_i processes will be those that are predicted by the operational semantics. They will give the minimal processes that satisfy the set of defining equations—the ones with the fewest stable failures. The underlying theory of CSP guarantees that such minimal processes must exist for any set of recursive CSP definitions.

The results concerning single recursion carry over to the more general case. The semantics of the N_i are the unions of the semantics of the chain of approximations, starting from DIV. Each N_i is defined by a function $F_i(\underline{N})$. If the jth approximation to N_i is written as N_i^j, then each $N_i^0 = DIV$, and each $N_i^{j+1} = F_i(\underline{N}^j)$, where $\underline{N}^j$ is the vector of all of the jth approximations. Each approximation N_i^j is associated with a set of stable failures $\mathcal{SF}\,[\![N_i^j]\!]$. Each limit N_i will have stable failures given by

$$\mathcal{SF}\,[\![N_i]\!] = \bigcup_{j \in \mathbb{N}} \mathcal{SF}\,[\![N_i^j]\!]$$

Law **recursion-unwinding** will hold for any family of mutually recursive definitions. Whenever $N_i = P_i$ appears as a recursive definition, then $N_i =_{SF} P_i$.

Law **UFP** also generalizes to mutual recursion. In a mutually recursive definition $\underline{N} = \underline{P}$, a process variable N_i is recursive if it appears in any of the P_j. If each process definition P_i associated with any recursive N_i is event guarded in all of the process variables that appear in it, then the recursive definition is event guarded. If two families of processes both satisfy the same guarded recursive equation, then they must be equivalent:

$$(\underline{F}(\underline{Y}) \text{ guarded} \wedge (\underline{F}(\underline{P_1}) =_{SF} \underline{P_1}) \wedge (\underline{F}(\underline{P_2}) =_{SF} \underline{P_2})) \Rightarrow \underline{P_1} =_{SF} \underline{P_2} \qquad \langle \mathsf{UFP}_{SF} \rangle$$

As in the traces model, a family of process definitions may be rewritten using Law recursion-unwinding to equivalent processes whose definitions are in a form more suitable for further reasoning.

Exercises

Exercise 6.1 What are the stable failures associated with the following state machines?

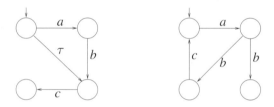

Exercise 6.2 Give the stable failures of the following processes:

1. $a \rightarrow STOP \mid b \rightarrow c \rightarrow STOP$

2. $a \rightarrow STOP \mid b \rightarrow (c \rightarrow STOP \mid d \rightarrow STOP)$

3. $a \rightarrow STOP \,\square\, a \rightarrow b \rightarrow STOP$

Exercise 6.3 What are the stable failures of the following non-recursive processes?

1. $(coin \rightarrow tea \rightarrow STOP) \,\square\, (coin \rightarrow coffee \rightarrow STOP)$

2. $(tea \rightarrow STOP) \,\sqcap\, (coffee \rightarrow STOP)$

3. $(coin \rightarrow tea \rightarrow STOP) \,\|\, (coin \rightarrow coffee \rightarrow STOP)$

4. $(coin \rightarrow tea \rightarrow STOP) \,\|\|\, (coin \rightarrow coffee \rightarrow STOP)$

5. $(coin \rightarrow ((tea \rightarrow STOP) \,\square\, (coffee \rightarrow STOP))) \setminus \{tea\}$

Exercise 6.4 What are the stable failures of the following recursive processes?

1. $VM1 = (coin \rightarrow (VM1 \sqcap choc \rightarrow VM1))$

2. $VM2 = (coin \rightarrow (VM2 \square choc \rightarrow VM2))$

3. $VM3 = VM3 \square choc \rightarrow STOP$

Exercise 6.5 Give a process P for which $P \parallel P \neq_{SF} P$.

Is $P \parallel P =_{SF} P \parallel P \parallel P$ a law of the stable failures model?

Exercise 6.6 What is the behaviour of the following processes?

1. $RUN \parallel CHAOS$

2. $RUN \parallel\parallel CHAOS$

3. $RUN_A \parallel CHAOS$

4. $RUN_A \parallel\parallel RUN_B$

5. $RUN_A \square CHAOS$

6. $RUN_A \sqcap CHAOS$

Exercise 6.7 Give a single operational rule for *DIV* which is consistent with the stable failures semantics.

Exercise 6.8 Give operational rules for *CHAOS* which are consistent with the stable failures semantics.

Exercise 6.9 Does the law $\langle \square\text{-}\sqcap\text{-dist} \rangle$ on page 182 hold in the traces model?

7

Specification and verification with failures

7.1 PROPERTY-ORIENTED SPECIFICATION

The introduction of failures information in the stable failures model allows a wider range of specification than was possible in the traces model. Specifications on behaviours describe those executions that are acceptable, and a verification of a system or process P requires an argument to establish that no behaviour of P violates such a specification. Since there are now two sets of behaviours associated with any process—traces, and stable failures—a specification will consist of two parts, each of which describes the required property of observations from the corresponding behaviour set. A specification S can be written as a pair $(S_T(tr), S_{SF}(tr, X))$. Each of the predicates S_T and S_{SF} can be expressed in any notation, though in common with specifications in the traces model first order logic and elementary set and sequence notation tend to be sufficient in practice.

$$P \text{ sat } (S_T(tr), S_{SF}(tr, X)) \quad = \quad \begin{aligned} &\forall tr \in \text{traces}(P) \bullet S_T(tr) \\ &\wedge \forall (tr, X) \in \mathcal{SF}\,[\![P]\!] \bullet S_{SF}(tr, X) \end{aligned}$$

Safety specifications, that 'nothing bad will happen', are requirements on traces, where 'nothing bad' means that no event will occur at an inappropriate point. Safety requirements are captured in this model by using the predicate S_T to constrain the traces that are permitted.

The stable failures model also contains sufficient detail to support the expression of liveness specifications, which require that 'something good will happen'. Within the context of synchronizing concurrent systems, liveness is expressed in terms of a process's willingness to participate in events. This will mean that at particular points of an execution, the process should be guaranteed to offer certain events: any stable state reached by the process should not refuse those events. These conditions are precisely what is expressed by the requirement that certain events should not appear in the refusal set X. If the process does not diverge, then it should be guaranteed to reach a stable state where the events are offered.

For example, a stable component that must always be ready for input should meet the specification that input can never be refused: $S_{SF}(tr, X) = in.T \cap X = \{\}$. Whatever trace has occurred previously, the process can never refuse input.

Example 7.1.1 (Railway crossing) The process *CROSS*, defined in Example 1.3.3, raises and lowers a barrier, and records when trains enter and leave the crossing. As well as its safety requirements, it should also meet the liveness requirement that it is ready to lower the gate whenever the gate is up and an approaching train is detected. This is a conditional liveness property, requiring an offer of a particular event only under certain conditions on the trace:

$$S_{SF}(tr, X) \quad = \quad tr = tr' ^\frown \langle gate.raise, train.approach \rangle \Rightarrow gate.lower \notin X$$

∎

Example 7.1.2 (Buffers) A common specification is that of a *buffer* or first-in-first-out queue. The safety requirements on a buffer have already been discussed in the previous chapter, but a buffer must also have some liveness requirements: that it must be ready for input when it is empty, and that it must be ready for output when it is non-empty. The specification of a buffer of type T may be expressed as a predicate on traces and on stable failures:

$$
\begin{aligned}
Buff_T(tr) \quad &= \quad tr \Downarrow out \leqslant tr \Downarrow in \\
Buff_{SF}(tr, X) \quad &= \quad tr \Downarrow out = tr \Downarrow in \Rightarrow in.T \cap X = \{\} \\
&\quad \wedge \ tr \Downarrow out < tr \Downarrow in \Rightarrow out.T \nsubseteq X
\end{aligned}
$$

The safety specification, expressed on traces, states that the sequence of outputs must match the sequence of inputs, appearing in the same order. If the sequence of inputs is equal to the sequence of outputs, then the buffer must be empty, and the liveness requirement states that no input may be refused. If the sequence of outputs does not contain all input messages, then the buffer is non-empty, and so not all outputs can be refused. The safety specification allows only one output to be possible, so any output which is not the next element of the sequence can be refused in a stable state.

The specification states nothing about the capacity of the buffer, or even whether the capacity is fixed, or finite or infinite. It also allows events along other channels, since it places no restrictions on the behaviour of the process with regard to other events. However, the specification is conventionally used to describe processes which have only input and output channels: $\sigma(P) \subseteq in.T \cup out.T$. This can be introduced into the specification, as another safety specification:

$$Buff'_T(tr) \quad = \quad Buff_T(tr) \wedge \sigma(tr) \subseteq in.T \cup out.T$$

The specification also implies that a buffer cannot terminate. It requires liveness after any trace, and terminating traces would not be exempt. ∎

7.2   VERIFICATION

The semantic equations associated with the CSP operators support a number of proof rules for reasoning about CSP process descriptions. Proof obligations are of the form P **sat** $(S_T(tr), S_{SF}(tr, X))$. These can be split into two separate obligations:

1. a traces obligation P **sat** $S_T(tr)$ which can be addressed with the proof system for the traces model presented in Chapter 5;

2. a stable failures obligation P **sat** $S_{SF}(tr, X)$, which states that all the stable failures of P meet predicate S_{SF}. Requirements of this form are the concern of this chapter.

This section will present a set of compositional proof rules for establishing stable failures specifications for processes. Two of these rules (sequential composition, and interrupt) rely on trace specifications of their component processes, reflecting the fact that the definitions of the stable failures of these processes refer to the traces of their components.

STOP

There is only one trace of the process *STOP*: the empty trace. It may be accompanied by any refusal set, so there is no restriction on the refusal X. The constraint on any stable failure is simply that its trace is empty.

$$\overline{\qquad STOP \textbf{ sat } tr = \langle\rangle \qquad}$$

The rule has no antecedents, corresponding to the fact that *STOP* has no component processes.

Prefix

A failure of the process $a \to P$ either has an empty trace, in which case a cannot be refused, or else begins with the event a followed by a failure of P. If P **sat** $S_{SF}(tr, X)$ then the part of the trace after a (that is: $tail(tr)$) together with the refusal X must meet the specification S_{SF}.

$$\frac{P \textbf{ sat } S_{SF}(tr, X)}{a \to P \textbf{ sat } \quad tr = \langle\rangle \wedge a \notin X}$$
$$\vee$$
$$head(tr) = a \wedge S_{SF}(tail(tr), X)$$

Prefix choice

The prefix choice operator generalizes the prefix operator: it contains a number of component processes, and the first event that is performed can be any one of the menu of events offered.

The antecedent to the rule assumes a family of specifications $S_a(tr, X)$, one for each of the components $P(a)$.

$$\frac{\forall\, a \in A \bullet P(a) \text{ \bf sat } S_a(tr, X)}{x : A \to P(x) \text{ \bf sat } \begin{aligned} &tr = \langle\rangle \wedge A \cap X = \{\} \\ &\vee \\ &\exists\, a \in A \bullet head(tr) = a \wedge S_a(tail(tr), X) \end{aligned}}$$

Output and input

The output process $c!v \to P$ is simply a particular kind of prefix process, and the proof rule reflects this:

$$\frac{P \text{ \bf sat } S_{SF}(tr, X)}{c!v \to P \text{ \bf sat } \begin{aligned} &tr = \langle\rangle \wedge c.v \notin X \\ &\vee \\ &head(tr) = c.v \wedge S_{SF}(tail(tr), X) \end{aligned}}$$

Similarly, the input process $c?x : T \to P(x)$ is a special form of prefix choice, and so the proof rule is very similar:

$$\frac{\forall\, v \in T \bullet P(v) \text{ \bf sat } S_v(tr, X)}{c?x : T \to P(x) \text{ \bf sat } \begin{aligned} &tr = \langle\rangle \wedge in.T \cap X = \{\} \\ &\vee \\ &\exists\, v \in T \bullet head(tr) = c.v \wedge S_v(tail(tr), X) \end{aligned}}$$

SKIP

The process *SKIP* does nothing except terminate successfully. It has only two possible stable failures, one for before termination, and one for after.

$$\frac{}{SKIP \text{ \bf sat } (tr = \langle\rangle \wedge \checkmark \notin X) \vee tr = \langle\checkmark\rangle}$$

The refusal set is hardly constrained, apart from the requirement that termination should not be refused before it occurs.

DIV

The process *DIV* has no stable failures at all, so there is no specification that it can violate. It therefore vacuously meets any specification S (even *false*). *false*(tr, X).

$$\frac{}{DIV \text{ \bf sat } S(tr, X)}$$

This apparently miraculous behaviour of *DIV*—that it can meet any specification—indicates that there is some aspect of the behaviour of *DIV* that is not considered in the stable failures model. The fact that it is divergent exempts it from any need to be concerned with stable failures.

CHAOS

The worst process, *CHAOS*, is able to perform or refuse anything. It will only meet the trivial specification $true(tr, X)$, the weakest specification.

$$\overline{CHAOS \textbf{ sat } true(tr, X)}$$

RUN

The process *RUN* is able to do any trace, but unlike *CHAOS* it is unable to refuse any event before termination.

$$\overline{RUN \textbf{ sat } \checkmark \notin \sigma(tr) \Rightarrow X = \{\}}$$

The specification met by *RUN* imposes no restrictions on the traces that it can perform, only on the refusals that may accompany those traces.

External choice

The process $P_1 \,\square\, P_2$ behaves either as P_1 or as P_2. If $P_1 \textbf{ sat } S_1(tr, X)$ and $P_2 \textbf{ sat } S_2(tr, X)$ then the choice process $P_1 \,\square\, P_2$ satisfies the disjunction of these two specifications, and their conjunction when the trace is empty:

$$\frac{P_1 \textbf{ sat } S_1(tr, X)}{P_2 \textbf{ sat } S_2(tr, X)}$$
$$P_1 \,\square\, P_2 \textbf{ sat } \quad (tr = \langle\rangle \Rightarrow S_1(tr, X) \wedge S_2(tr, X))$$
$$\wedge\, (tr \neq \langle\rangle \Rightarrow (S_1(tr, X) \vee S_2(tr, X)))$$

Any refusal of $P_1 \,\square\, P_2$ before any event has yet been performed must be a refusal of both components.

The rule generalizes to indexed external choices:

$$\frac{\forall i \in I \bullet P_i \textbf{ sat } S_i(tr, X)}{\square_{i \in I} P_i \textbf{ sat } \quad tr = \langle\rangle \Rightarrow \bigwedge_{i \in I} S_i(tr, X)}$$
$$\wedge\, tr \neq \langle\rangle \Rightarrow \bigvee_{i \in I} S_i(tr, X)$$

Any events refused before the choice has been made must be refusable by all of the components. After the choice has been made, the refusal set is the responsibility of the process in whose favour the choice was resolved.

Internal choice

The internal choice operator can behave as either of its components:

$$\frac{P_1 \textbf{ sat } S_1(tr, X)}{P_1 \sqcap P_2 \textbf{ sat } S_1(tr, X) \vee S_2(tr, X)}$$

The indexed internal choice can behave as any of its components:

$$\frac{\forall\, i \in J \bullet P_i \textbf{ sat } S_i(tr, X)}{\sqcap_{i \in J} P_i \textbf{ sat } \exists\, i \in J \bullet S_i(tr, X)}$$

Parallel composition

A failure (tr, X) of the process $P_1 \;_{A_1}\|_{A_2}\; P_2$ is comprised of a contribution from P_1 and a contribution from P_2, contained within the alphabets $A_1^{\checkmark}$ and $A_2^{\checkmark}$ respectively. In fact, the projection $tr \restriction A_1^{\checkmark}$ is a trace of P_1, and the projection $tr \restriction A_2^{\checkmark}$ is a trace of P_2. The refusal set X is a made up of X_1 and X_2 from P_1 and P_2 respectively.

$$\frac{\begin{array}{l} P_1 \textbf{ sat } S_1(tr, X) \\ P_2 \textbf{ sat } S_2(tr, X) \end{array}}{\begin{array}{ll} P_1 \;_{A_1}\|_{A_2}\; P_2 \textbf{ sat } \exists\, X_1, X_2 \bullet & S_1(tr \restriction A_1^{\checkmark}, X_1) \wedge S_2(tr \restriction A_2^{\checkmark}, X_2) \\ & \wedge\, \sigma(tr) \subseteq (A_1 \cup A_2)^{\checkmark} \\ & \wedge\, X \cap (A_1 \cup A_2)^{\checkmark} = (X_1 \cap A_1^{\checkmark}) \cup (X_2 \cap A_2^{\checkmark}) \end{array}}$$

For instance, two processes might both meet an initial liveness specification on the event a, that a must be available until it is performed, as follows:

$$P_1 \quad \textbf{sat} \quad S_1(tr, X) = a \notin \sigma(tr) \Rightarrow a \notin X$$
$$P_2 \quad \textbf{sat} \quad S_2(tr, X) = a \notin \sigma(tr) \Rightarrow a \notin X$$

Each of them meets the specification that if a has not yet occurred, then it cannot be refused.

The rule yields that the combination $P_1 \;_{\{a,b\}}\|_{\{a,c\}}\; P_2$ meets the specification

$$\begin{array}{ll} \exists\, X_1, X_2 \bullet & tr \restriction \{a, b\}^{\checkmark} = \langle\rangle \Rightarrow a \notin X_1 \\ & tr \restriction \{a, c\}^{\checkmark} = \langle\rangle \Rightarrow a \notin X_2 \\ & \wedge\, \sigma(tr) \subseteq \{a, b, c\}^{\checkmark} \\ & \wedge\, X \restriction \{a, b, c\}^{\checkmark} = (X_1 \cap \{a, b\}^{\checkmark}) \cup (X_2 \cap \{a, c\}^{\checkmark}) \end{array}$$

which implies that $a \notin \sigma(tr) \Rightarrow a \notin X$, and so

$$P_1 \;_{\{a,b\}}\|_{\{a,c\}}\; P_2 \quad \textbf{sat} \quad a \notin \sigma(tr) \Rightarrow a \notin X$$

If both components are initially live on the event a, then so is their parallel combination.

The rule for the indexed parallel operator follows a similar pattern. Each component P_i with interface A_i imposes its own constraint $S_i(tr, X)$ on the projection of the overall behaviour onto the alphabet $A_i^{\checkmark}$.

$$\frac{\forall i \in I \bullet P_i \text{ sat } S_i(tr, X)}{\left\|_{A_i} P_i \text{ sat } \exists \langle X_i \rangle \bullet \begin{array}{l} \forall i \in I \bullet S_i(tr \upharpoonright A_i^{\checkmark}, X_i) \\ \wedge\, X \cap (\bigcup_i A_i)^{\checkmark} = \bigcup_i (X_i \cap A_i^{\checkmark}) \\ \wedge\, \sigma(tr) \subseteq (\bigcup_{i \in I} A_i)^{\checkmark} \end{array}}$$

Interleaving

An interleaved combination $P_1 \;|||\; P_2$ performs traces tr which consist of a trace tr_1 of P_1 interleaved with a trace tr_2 of P_2. A refusal after such a trace must be a refusal of both processes.

$$\frac{\begin{array}{l} P_1 \text{ sat } S_1(tr, X) \\ P_2 \text{ sat } S_2(tr, X) \end{array}}{P_1 \;|||\; P_2 \text{ sat } \exists tr_1, tr_2, X_1, X_2 \bullet \begin{array}{l} (S_1(tr_1, X_1) \wedge S_2(tr_2, X_2) \wedge tr \text{ interleaves } tr_1, tr_2) \\ \wedge\, X_1 \cup X_2 = X \wedge X_1 \setminus \{\checkmark\} = X_2 \setminus \{\checkmark\} \end{array}}$$

For instance, consider a process P_1 which meets the specification given previously that the process must initially be live on $a \in \Sigma$:

$$P_1 \quad \text{sat} \quad a \notin \sigma(tr) \Rightarrow a \notin X$$

Then P_1 interleaved with any (non-divergent) process P_2 at all will still meet this specification. Firstly any such process has P_2 **sat** $true(tr, X)$, so the rule for interleaving yields that

$$P_1 \;|||\; P_2 \quad \text{sat} \quad \exists tr_1, tr_2, X_1, X_2 \bullet \begin{array}{l} a \notin \sigma(tr_1) \Rightarrow a \notin X_1 \wedge tr \text{ interleaves } tr_1, tr_2 \\ \wedge\, X_1 \cup X_2 = X \wedge X_1 \setminus \{\checkmark\} = X_2 \setminus \{\checkmark\} \end{array}$$

Furthermore, if tr **interleaves** tr_1, tr_2 then $\sigma(tr) = \sigma(tr_1) \cup \sigma(tr_2)$, so $a \notin \sigma(tr) \Rightarrow a \notin \sigma(tr_1)$. Also, $a \notin X_1 \Rightarrow a \notin X$. Thus

$$P_1 \;|||\; P_2 \quad \text{sat} \quad a \notin \sigma(tr) \Rightarrow a \notin X$$

A single component of an interleaved combination can ensure liveness.

Interface parallel

A failure (tr, X) of $P_1 \parallel_A P_2$ must arise from two failures (tr_1, X_1) and (tr_2, X_2) of P_1 and P_2 respectively, where tr synch$_A$ tr_1, tr_2, and X_1 and X_2 coincide on events P_1 and P_2 can perform independently—those outside $A^{\checkmark}$. This results in the following inference rule:

$$\frac{\begin{array}{l} P_1 \text{ sat } S_1(tr, X) \\ P_2 \text{ sat } S_2(tr, X) \end{array}}{\begin{array}{l} P_1 \parallel_A P_2 \text{ sat } \quad \exists tr_1, tr_2, X_1, X_2 \bullet \\ \qquad\qquad (S_1(tr_1, X_1) \land S_2(tr_2, X_2) \land tr \text{ synch}_A tr_1, tr_2 \\ \qquad\qquad \land X_1 \cup X_2 = X \\ \qquad\qquad \land X_1 \setminus A = X_2 \setminus A) \end{array}}$$

Hiding

A trace of the process $P \setminus A$ arises from a trace of P simply by removing all of the events in A from the trace. Hence for any trace of $P \setminus A$ with refusal set X there is a corresponding trace of P with refusal set $X \cup A$. The rule is then as follows:

$$\frac{P \text{ sat } S(tr, X)}{P \setminus A \text{ sat } \exists tr_1 \bullet (S(tr_1, X \cup A) \land tr = tr_1 \setminus A)}$$

Example 7.2.1 Consider the process P given by $P = a \to b \to c \to P$. The proof rule will be used to establish the liveness specification on $P \setminus \{b\}$ that c should be available whenever a is the last event to have occurred:

$$P \setminus \{b\} \quad \text{sat} \quad foot(tr) = a \Rightarrow c \notin X$$

A property that P satisfies is

$$S(tr, X) \quad = \quad (foot(tr) = a \Rightarrow b \notin X) \land (foot(tr) = b \Rightarrow c \notin X)$$

If (tr, X) is a stable failure of $P \setminus \{b\}$, then $\exists tr_1 \bullet S(tr_1, X \cup \{b\}) \land tr = tr_1 \setminus \{b\}$. If $foot(tr) = a$, then $foot(tr_1 \setminus \{b\}) = a$, so either $foot(tr_1) = a$ or $foot(tr_1) = b$. The first of these contradicts $S(tr_1, X \cup \{b\})$, since it implies that $b \notin X \cup \{b\}$; and the second implies that $c \notin X \cup \{b\}$, which in turn implies that $c \notin X$. The specification can thus be weakened to obtain

$$P \setminus \{b\} \quad \text{sat} \quad foot(tr) = a \Rightarrow c \notin X$$

This is the specification required. ∎

In fact, the inference rule simplifies in the case where the specification $S_{SF}(tr, X)$ is *independent* of the set A being hidden. A failures specification is A-independent if $\forall tr, X \bullet (S_{SF}(tr, X) \Leftrightarrow S_{SF}(tr \setminus A, X \setminus A))$. For such a specification, the predicate $\exists tr_1 \bullet S_{SF}(tr_1, X \cup A) \wedge tr_1 \setminus A = tr$ is equivalent to $S_{SF}(tr, X)$. The resulting rule is

$$\frac{P \text{ sat } S_{SF}(tr, X)}{P \setminus A \text{ sat } S_{SF}(tr, X)} \quad [\, S_{SF}(tr, X) \text{ is } A\text{-independent}\,]$$

This rule states that if a process P meets a specification $S_{SF}(tr, X)$ independently of the performance or refusal of any events in A, then $P \setminus A$ also meets it. Both the specification itself and P's meeting of it are completely independent of its behaviour on A.

Observe that the earlier specification $foot(tr) = a \Rightarrow c \notin X$ is not $\{b\}$-independent even though b does not appear anywhere explicitly in the specification, since in this case $foot(tr)$ is not the same as $foot(tr \setminus \{b\})$.

On the other hand, a specification that is $\{b\}$-independent is the liveness requirement that whenever the same number of a's and c's have been performed, then a should be on offer:

$$tr \downarrow \{a\} = tr \downarrow \{c\} \Rightarrow a \notin X$$

The process $P = a \rightarrow b \rightarrow c \rightarrow P$ meets this specification, and so the derived inference rule for hiding yields that $P \setminus \{b\}$ also satisfies it.

Renaming

A failure (tr, X) of a renamed process $f(P)$ will be a renamed failure $(f(tr_1), X)$ for some tr_1 for which $(tr_1, f^{-1}(X))$ is a failure of P. The inference rule for translating specifications through a forward renaming is as follows:

$$\frac{P \text{ sat } S_{SF}(tr, X)}{f(P) \text{ sat } \exists tr_1 \bullet S_{SF}(tr_1, f^{-1}(X)) \wedge f(tr_1) = tr}$$

Example 7.2.2 In Example 3.2.4 a process *OFFICE* models two staff who each answer their own phones. When both phones are mapped to the same number—$f(phone.sylvie) = f(phone.janet) = phone.janet\&sylvie$—then the best guarantee that can be provided is that someone will answer, but with no guarantees as to who it will be.

The specification used to obtain this result through the inference rule is

$$OFFICE \quad \textbf{sat} \quad foot(tr) = phone.janet \vee foot(tr) = phone.sylvie$$
$$\Rightarrow \{answer.janet, answer.sylvie\} \not\subseteq X$$

The direct result of applying the inference rule with this antecedent yields the result

$$f(OFFICE) \quad \textbf{sat} \quad \exists tr_1 \bullet (foot(tr_1) = phone.janet \vee foot(tr_1) = phone.sylvie$$
$$\Rightarrow \{answer.janet, answer.sylvie\} \not\subseteq f^{-1}(X))$$
$$\wedge f(tr_1) = tr$$

which is equivalent to the result required:

$$f(OFFICE) \quad \textbf{sat} \quad foot(tr) = phone.janet\&sylvie$$
$$\Rightarrow \{answer.janet, answer.sylvie\} \nsubseteq X$$

Observe that the specification on *OFFICE* covered all of the possible ways in which $foot(tr) = phone.janet\&sylvie$ can arise in $f(OFFICE)$, and showed that in each case the required result followed. In order to establish that $f(P)$ **sat** $R_{SF}(tr, X)$ from the fact that P **sat** $S_{SF}(tr, X)$, it is necessary for all behaviours that meet S_{SF} to satisfy R_{SF} when mapped through the alphabet renaming. Another form of this rule is:

$$\frac{\begin{array}{l} P \textbf{ sat } S_{SF}(tr, X) \\ \forall tr_1, tr, X \bullet (S_{SF}(tr_1, f^{-1}(X) \wedge f(tr_1) = tr) \Rightarrow R_{SF}(tr, X)) \end{array}}{f(P) \textbf{ sat } R_{SF}(tr, X)}$$

If S_{SF} does not constrain all traces tr_1 which map to a particular tr, then no useful conclusions will be obtained. For example, the result that

$$OFFICE \quad \textbf{sat} \quad foot(tr) = phone.sylvie \Rightarrow answer.sylvie \notin X$$

does not in itself provide any useful information about the behaviour of $f(OFFICE)$ since any trace of $f(OFFICE)$ ending in *phone.janet&sylvie* might have originated from a trace ending in *phone.janet*, and no information is provided about the behaviour in such a circumstance. ■

In the case where f is a 1–1 function, its inverse f^{-1} is well defined and there is only one possibility for the trace tr_1 which maps under f to tr, namely $f^{-1}(tr)$. In this case the inference rule simplifies as follows:

$$\frac{P \textbf{ sat } S_{SF}(tr, X)}{f(P) \textbf{ sat } S_{SF}(f^{-1}(tr), f^{-1}(X))} \quad [\, f \text{ injective} \,]$$

The backward renaming operator is more straightforward. If (tr, X) is a failure of $f^{-1}(P)$, then $(f(tr), f(X))$ is a failure of P, and so it must satisfy whatever specification P is known to satisfy. The inference rule is as follows:

$$\frac{P \textbf{ sat } S_{SF}(tr, X)}{f^{-1}(P) \textbf{ sat } S_{SF}(f(tr), f(X))}$$

The process *SALE* of Example 3.2.5 is ready to accept payment after a choice of goods has been made.

$$SALE \quad \textbf{sat} \quad foot(tr) = choose \Rightarrow pay \notin X$$

The event renaming function

$$f(cash) \quad = \quad pay$$
$$f(cheque) \quad = \quad pay$$
$$f(credit\_card) \quad = \quad puy$$

is used to expand the interface of *SALE* and accept any of these methods of payment. The inference rule yields that

$$f^{-1}(SALE) \quad \textbf{sat} \quad foot(f(tr)) = choose \Rightarrow pay \notin f(X)$$

and this is equivalent to

$$f^{-1}(SALE) \quad \textbf{sat} \quad foot(tr) = choose \Rightarrow \{cash, cheque, credit\_card\} \cap X = \{\}$$

After a choice has been made, the process is ready to accept any of the events that map to *pay*—it cannot refuse any of them.

Sequential composition

Any given failure of $P_1; P_2$ must arise from one of two possibilities: either it is a failure of P_1 which has not yet reached termination, or else it consists of a trace of P_1 followed by a failure of P_2. The proof rule reflects this:

$$\frac{\begin{array}{l} P_1 \ \textbf{sat} \ (S_T(tr), S_1(tr, X)) \\ P_2 \ \textbf{sat} \ S_2(tr, X) \end{array}}{\begin{array}{l} P_1; P_2 \ \textbf{sat} \quad \checkmark \notin \sigma(tr) \wedge S_1(tr, X \cup \{\checkmark\}) \\ \qquad\qquad \vee \\ \qquad\qquad \exists\, tr_1, tr_2 \bullet tr = tr_1 \frown tr_2 \wedge S_T(tr_1 \frown \langle\checkmark\rangle) \wedge S_2(tr_2, X) \end{array}}$$

The first case covers those failures from P_1 that have not yet terminated: in this case, $\checkmark$ must also be refusable. The second case is concerned with those failures corresponding to executions that have passed control from P_1 to P_2 at some point: in this case, $tr_1 \frown \langle\checkmark\rangle$ is the trace from P_1 up to its termination, and so it must meet P_1's trace specification $S_1(tr)$, and (tr_2, X) is the contribution from P_2.

Interrupt

A failure of the interrupt process $P_1 \triangle P_2$ is either a failure of P_1 whose refusal is also a possible initial refusal for P_2, or else a non-terminated trace of P_1 followed by a failure of P_2.

The inference rule is as follows:

$$
\begin{array}{c}
P_1 \ \mathbf{sat} \ (S_T(tr), S_1(tr, X)) \\
P_2 \ \mathbf{sat} \ S_2(tr, X) \\
\hline
\begin{aligned}
P_1 \bigtriangleup P_2 \ \mathbf{sat} \quad & S_1(tr, X) \wedge (S_2(\langle\rangle, X) \vee \checkmark \in \sigma(tr)) \\
& \vee \\
& \exists tr_1, tr_2 \bullet tr = tr_1 \frown tr_2 \ \wedge \ \checkmark \notin \sigma(tr_1) \wedge S_T(tr_1) \\
& \qquad\qquad \wedge tr_2 \neq \langle\rangle \wedge S_2(tr_2, X)
\end{aligned}
\end{array}
$$

In the second disjunct, tr_1 is the trace contribution from P_1, so it meets P_1's trace specification $S_T(tr)$.

Example 7.2.3 If *int* is a special interrupt event, and P_2 is initially enabled on this event, unable to refuse it, then

$$
P_2 \quad \mathbf{sat} \quad int \notin \sigma(tr) \Rightarrow int \notin X
$$

Then whatever form process P_1 takes, and whatever specification S_1 it satisfies, the rule yields that

$$
\begin{aligned}
P_1 \bigtriangleup P_2 \quad \mathbf{sat} \quad & S_1(tr, X) \wedge (int \notin X \vee \checkmark \in \sigma(tr)) \\
& \vee \\
& \exists tr_1, tr_2 \bullet \quad tr = tr_1 \frown tr_2 \wedge \checkmark \notin \sigma(tr_1) \wedge S_1(tr_1, \{\}) \\
& \qquad\qquad\quad \wedge tr_2 \neq \langle\rangle \wedge (int \notin \sigma(tr_2) \Rightarrow int \notin X)
\end{aligned}
$$

which can be weakened to

$$
P_1 \bigtriangleup P_2 \quad \mathbf{sat} \quad int \notin \sigma(tr) \Rightarrow (int \notin X \vee \checkmark \in \sigma(tr))
$$

The interrupt combination will have the interrupt event *int* enabled throughout an execution, until either it occurs or the execution finishes. ∎

7.3 RECURSION INDUCTION

If a recursive definition $N = F(N)$ preserves the satisfiable specification $S_{SF}(tr, X)$, then N must also meet the specification $S_{SF}(tr, X)$.

$$
\frac{\forall Y \bullet (Y \ \mathbf{sat} \ S_{SF}(tr, X) \Rightarrow F(Y) \ \mathbf{sat} \ S_{SF}(tr, X))}{N \ \mathbf{sat} \ S_{SF}(tr, X)} \quad [\, N = F(N) \,]
$$

In contrast to the rule for trace specifications, no separate check is required for satisfiability of $S_{SF}(tr, X)$, since all such specifications are met by *DIV*.

The rule generalizes to mutual recursion in exactly the same way as it does in the traces model:

$$\frac{\forall\, \underline{Y} \bullet (\underline{Y} \text{ sat } \underline{S}_{SF}(tr, X) \Rightarrow \underline{F}(\underline{Y}) \text{ sat } \underline{S}_{SF}(tr, X))}{\underline{N} \text{ sat } \underline{S}_{SF}(tr, X)} \quad [\, \underline{N} = \underline{F}(\underline{N}) \,]$$

Example 7.3.1 The light switch process has a recursive definition:

$$LIGHT \;=\; on \to off \to LIGHT$$

It appears that whenever the light is on it is ready to be turned off. The appropriate specification to verify is

$$S_{SF}(tr, X) \;=\; foot(tr) = on \Rightarrow off \notin X$$

Assume that Y **sat** $S_{SF}(tr, X)$. Then two applications of the inference rule for prefixing establish that

$$
\begin{aligned}
on \to off \to Y \quad \textbf{sat} \quad & tr = \langle \rangle \wedge on \notin X \\
& \vee\; tr = \langle on \rangle \wedge off \notin X \\
& \vee\; tr = \langle on, off \rangle \frown tr' \wedge S_{SF}(tr', X)
\end{aligned}
$$

If $foot(tr) = on$, then either $tr = on \wedge off \notin X$ or else $tr = \langle on, off \rangle \frown tr' \wedge foot(tr') = on \wedge S_{SF}(tr', X)$. In either case, $off \notin X$, so the specification weakens to $S_{SF}(tr, X)$, and so

$$on \to off \to Y \quad \textbf{sat} \quad S_{SF}(tr, X)$$

Finally, an application of the inference rule for recursion allows the conclusion that

$$LIGHT = on \to off \to LIGHT \quad \textbf{sat} \quad foot(tr) = on \Rightarrow off \notin X$$

Thus $LIGHT$ **sat** $S_{SF}(tr, X)$ as required. ∎

Example 7.3.2 (Alternating bit protocol) A communications protocol provides a service over a lower level medium which provides a lesser service. The alternating bit protocol provides a service in which messages of type T are relayed between agents without loss, over a medium in which messages can be lost, although they cannot become corrupted or reordered.

The service guaranteed by the underlying medium may be described by a two part CSP specification $Med(in, out)$:

$$
\begin{aligned}
Med_{SF}(in, out) \;=\; & tr \Downarrow out \preccurlyeq tr \Downarrow in \\
& \wedge\; in.T \cap X - \{\} \vee out.T \nsubseteq X
\end{aligned}
$$

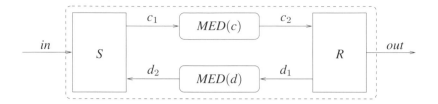

Fig. 7.1   The alternating bit protocol

Any output messages should have previously appeared as input messages, and they should appear in the same order, but some messages can be lost. The medium is always ready for either input or output.

A well-behaved process such as *COPY* satisfies the specification $Med(in, out)$, as do less well-behaved processes which can sometimes lose messages.

A medium which accepts input on c_1 and provides output on c_2 will be referred to as $MED(c)$. Such a medium does not need to be explicitly described in CSP; only the fact that it meets the specification is required for verification.

$$MED(c) \quad \textbf{sat} \quad Med(c_1, c_2)$$

The protocol itself consists of a sender component S and a receiver component R whose combined behaviour is intended to ensure that no message becomes lost from the system. The two components communicate in each direction over the unreliable medium. The system is illustrated in Figure 7.1.

The sender awaits input, and then transmits it along output channel c_1 together with a particular bit b. It will wait for an acknowledgement to arrive on channel d_2: receipt of the correct bit b indicates that the message arrived, whereas receipt of the incorrect bit $\bar{b}$ should be ignored as being associated with a previous message whose acknowledgement has already been received. The message can be resent as an alternative to waiting for acknowledgement, since it is possible that the message or its acknowledgement were lost during transmission.

$$
\begin{aligned}
S &= S(0) \\
S(b) &= in?x : T \rightarrow c_1!(x.b) \rightarrow S(b, x) \\
S(b, x) &= c_1!(x.b) \rightarrow S(b, x) \\
&\quad \square\ d_2.b \rightarrow S(\bar{b}) \\
&\quad \square\ d_2.\bar{b} \rightarrow S(b, x)
\end{aligned}
$$

The receiver process R awaits messages $x.b$ along channel c_2, and checks the bit b to see if it is the next bit expected, in which case x must be a fresh message for output. If the bit is not the one expected, then the message must be a repeated transmission, and will not be presented for output. In either case, an acknowledgement consisting of the bit received should be sent out on channel d_1.

$$
\begin{aligned}
R &= R(0) \\
R(b) &= c_2?x.b' : (T.\{b\}) \to out!x \to d_1!b \to R(\overline{b}) \\
&\quad \Box \; c_2?x.b' : (T.\{\overline{b}\}) \to d_1!\overline{b} \to R(b)
\end{aligned}
$$

The two components S and R do not synchronize on any events, and their combination is described as $S \;|||\; R$ which is equivalent to $S \;||\; R$ because of S and R's disjoint alphabets. Similarly, the two channels are independent, and their combination is described as $MED(c) \;|||\; MED(d)$. Finally, the components are composed in parallel, resulting in the following description of the alternating bit protocol:

$$
ABP \;=\; ((S \;|||\; R) \;||\; (MED(c) \;|||\; MED(d))) \setminus (c_1.\mathbb{N} \cup c_2.\mathbb{N} \cup d_1.\mathbb{N} \cup d_2.\mathbb{N})
$$

The requirement is that this system should behave as a buffer and satisfy the specification $(Buff_T(tr), Buff_{SF}(tr, X))$.

The safety and liveness aspects of the specification may each be treated in turn. The traces model can be used (see Exercise 7.9) to establish that

$$
ABP \quad \textbf{sat} \quad tr \Downarrow out \leqslant_1 tr \Downarrow in
$$

The only further property to establish is deadlock-freedom, in order to establish that the combination is a buffer in terms of liveness as well as safety. The safety specification shows that only one of *in* or *out* can ever be possible: *in* when the buffer is empty, and *out* when non-empty. Hence deadlock-freedom will establish that it must be open to inputs when empty, and ready to output when non-empty. Furthermore, the definition of the sender S is data-independent—once it is ready to accept some input, it is ready to accept any.

The system can be seen to be deadlock-free by considering a stable state. If *in* is refused in this state, then S is live on both c_1 and d_2. If these are both refused by their respective media, then both c_2 and d_1 must be enabled within the media. The receiver R cannot be willing to interact on either of these internal events, otherwise the state would not be stable, so it must be ready to provide output

Hence the required result is obtained: that ABP **sat** $Buff_{SF}(tr, X)$.   ∎

7.4 PROCESS-ORIENTED SPECIFICATION

As in the traces model, the refinement relation on processes $(T, SF) \sqsubseteq_{SF} (T, SF)$ holds when the second process has fewer possible behaviours than the first.

$$
(T_1, SF_1) \sqsubseteq_{SF} (T_2, SF_2) \quad \Leftrightarrow \quad T_2 \subseteq T_1 \wedge SF_2 \subseteq SF_1
$$

The subscript *SF* emphasizes the fact that the relationship is defined on the stable failures model.

Refinement holds between two process expressions P_1 and P_2 whenever it holds between their sets of traces and stable failures. Another way of characterizing the relationship $P_1 \sqsubseteq_{SF} P_2$ is as $P_1 =_{SF} P_1 \sqcap P_2$. The introduction of the traces and stable failures of P_2 does not introduce any new behaviours to P_1. The subscript *SF* will be elided if it is clear from the context.

The refinement relation $P_1 \sqsubseteq_{SF} P_2$ supports a process-oriented approach to specification. As in the traces model, a specification describes behaviours that are acceptable in a particular situation, and these behaviours can be described either by use of predicates, or else by means of a CSP process expression itself. A process description *SPEC* will have particular traces and stable failures associated with it, and these are taken to be all the acceptable behaviours. An implementation process *IMP* meets this specification if all of its possible behaviours are allowed by *SPEC*, or in other words, if $SPEC \sqsubseteq_{SF} IMP$.

Many common specifications can be captured in a process-oriented style, where the specification is the process with the most behaviours which meets the requirement. This means that *SPEC* should allow all possibilities that are not expressly forbidden.

The process $ALT = a \to b \to ALT$ expresses the requirement that the performance of *a*'s and *b*'s should alternate. It also contains the requirement that these events should be available, and that no other events are possible, since none appear as possibilities in *ALT*. A weaker specification which places no constraint on any other events would be $ALT \;|||\; CHAOS_{\Sigma \setminus \{a,b\}}$, which allows arbitrary behaviour on all other events, but still requires that *a* and *b* must be available when they are next in the alternating sequence. An even weaker specification, which also allows the possibility of deadlock, would be $ALT \underset{\{a,b\}}{\|} CHAOS$. Any sequence of *a*'s and *b*'s must still be alternating, but no liveness conditions on them are present.

Example 7.4.1 (Buffers) The property of being a buffer of type *T* is expressible in a process-oriented way, by means of a mutual recursion. Internal choice is used to describe the various possibilities:

$$
\begin{aligned}
NBUFF_T(\langle\rangle) &= in?x : T \to NBUFF_T(\langle x \rangle) \\
NBUFF_T(s \frown \langle y \rangle) &= out!y \to NBUFF_T(s) \\
&\quad \Box\, (STOP \sqcap in?x : T \to NBUFF_T(\langle x \rangle \frown s \frown \langle y \rangle))
\end{aligned}
$$

The parameter to *NBUFF* consists of the sequence of messages that the buffer currently contains. If this sequence is the empty sequence $\langle\rangle$, then the buffer is empty and must be ready for input. If the sequence contains some messages, then the buffer must be ready to output the next message required. It is also possible that it will accept further input, but it does not have to. These possibilities are represented by the internal choice between *STOP* and a further input.

The buffer specification $NBUFF_T = NBUFF_T(\langle\rangle)$ also specifies that the alphabet of the buffer is restricted to its input and output channels. It encapsulates the buffer specification given on page 196:

$$NBUFF \sqsubseteq_{SF} IMP \quad \Leftrightarrow \quad IMP \textbf{ sat } (Buff_T(tr), Buff_{SF}(tr, X))$$

If further events are to be possible (such as a channel which can report on whether or not the buffer is empty), then the appropriate specification will be $NBUFF_T \mathbin{|||} CHAOS_A$, where A are the other possible events. The most general specification, which corresponds to $Buff_T(tr, X)$, is given as follows:

$$NBUFF_T \mathbin{|||} CHAOS_{\Sigma \setminus (in.T \cup out.T)} \sqsubseteq_{SF} IMP$$
$$\Leftrightarrow \quad IMP \textbf{ sat } (Buff_T(tr), Buff_T(tr, X))$$

However, in general it will be more appropriate to restrict A to the particular set of events which are allowed for the buffer. ∎

One of the benefits of the process-oriented approach is provided by the availability of model-checking tools which permit automatic checking of (finite state) specifications against implementations. The FDR tool allows processes to be checked against process-oriented specifications with regard to their stable failures.

The two styles of specification can often be combined within verification. If $SPEC \sqsubseteq_{SF} IMP$ and $SPEC \textbf{ sat } Spec_{SF}(tr, X)$, then $IMP \textbf{ sat } Spec_{SF}(tr, X)$, and this result can be used within the application of a proof rule.

A process-oriented version of the proof rule for recursion induction will use $SPEC \sqsubseteq_{SF} Y$ in place of $Y \textbf{ sat } S_{SF}(tr, X)$, resulting in the following antecedent:

$$\forall Y \bullet (SPEC \sqsubseteq_{SF} Y \Rightarrow SPEC \sqsubseteq_{SF} F(Y))$$

This is equivalent to the assertion that $SPEC \sqsubseteq_{SF} F(SPEC)$. The rule becomes

$$\frac{SPEC \sqsubseteq_{SF} F(SPEC)}{SPEC \sqsubseteq_{SF} N} \quad [\, N = F(N) \,]$$

Even if the relation $SPEC \sqsubseteq_{SF} N$ cannot be checked directly by mechanical means, for example if N has infinitely many states, it can still be verified via the proof rule by checking that $SPEC \sqsubseteq_{SF} F(SPEC)$.

Example 7.4.2 The bag process *BAG* takes messages as input, and makes them available for output. It is given by a guarded recursive definition.

$$BAG \quad = \quad in?x : T \rightarrow (BAG \mathbin{|||} (out!x \rightarrow STOP))$$

One property that this process satisfies is that it is always ready for input. This specification can be captured as the process

$$INS \quad = \quad RUN_{in.T} \;|||\; CHAOS_{out.T}$$

It is not possible to check $INS \sqsubseteq_{SF} BAG$ directly using a model-checker, since the process *BAG* has an infinite number of states. However,

$$INS \quad \sqsubseteq_{SF} \quad in?x : T \rightarrow (INS \;|||\; (out!x \rightarrow STOP))$$

which can be automatically checked, since *INS* has a finite (and extremely small) number of states. This single refinement check establishes the antecedent to the inference rule for guarded recursion given above, establishing the result

$$INS \sqsubseteq_{SF} BAG$$

The process *BAG* is always ready for input. ∎

7.5   CASE STUDY: DISTRIBUTED SUM

The functional correctness of the distributed sum algorithm was established in Chapter 5. Only traces need to be considered in order to establish that any answer provided by the system of nodes must be the correct one.

However, the trace analysis does not provide any guarantees that an answer will eventually be output. This is a liveness property, so an analysis in the stable failures model is required. The main aim will be to establish deadlock-freedom of the network; more specific liveness properties will follow from this. It will also ultimately be necessary to establish that the network is free from divergence. This will be discussed in Chapter 8.

The liveness of the network as a whole will rely on the liveness properties of the individual nodes. The particular properties used to prove deadlock-freedom will be $I1$ and $I2$ concerning liveness on inputs, $O1$ and $O2$ concerning liveness on outputs, and $T1$ concerning liveness on termination. A subsidiary result $N1$ is also useful: it can be established in the traces model.

Liveness on input

All nodes will be initially live on all of their input channels. This is specified for each input channel c_{ij} as follows:

$$I1_{ij} \qquad NODE(j) \; \textbf{sat} \; tr \restriction A_j^{\checkmark} = \langle\rangle \Rightarrow c_{ij}.0 \notin X$$

Given a particular node j and edge $(i, j) \in E$, if node j has not yet communicated with any neighbour, then it must be ready for an initiating input from i.

Furthermore, any node j on any particular input channel c_{ij} will remain willing to accept input until it occurs (see Exercise 7.11).

$$I2_{ij} \qquad NODE(j) \; \textbf{sat} \; (tr \upharpoonright A_j^{\checkmark} \neq \langle \rangle \wedge tr \Downarrow c_{ij} = \langle \rangle) \Rightarrow c_{ij}.\mathbb{N} \cap X = \{\}$$

Given a particular node j and edge $(i, j) \in E$, if node j has performed some communication but has not yet received any input from its neighbour i, then it must be ready to input any possible value.

Liveness on output

The first liveness property on output is that, once some message has been received along a channel c_{ki}, then output is available along any channel c_{ij} other than the one matching the initial input. This means that a node is ready to provide output to any of its neighbours with the possible exception of the neighbour it first interacted with. The relationship between two neighbours i and j is expressed as follows:

$$O1_{ij} \qquad NODE(i) \; \textbf{sat} \quad tr \neq \langle \rangle \wedge \mathsf{channel}(head(tr)) \neq c_{ji}$$
$$\Rightarrow (tr \Downarrow c_{ij} = \langle \rangle \Rightarrow c_{ij}.0 \notin X)$$

The process $c_{ij}!0 \to SKIP$ is live on channel c_{ij} until it occurs:

$$c_{ij}!0 \to SKIP \quad \textbf{sat} \quad (tr \Downarrow c_{ij} = \langle \rangle \Rightarrow c_{ij}.0 \notin X)$$

Furthermore, the channel c_{ij} is not in the alphabet of any of the processes $c_{ik}!0 \to SKIP$ where $k \neq j$, nor of $TOT(i, k, adj(i) \setminus \{k\}, w_i)$ where $k \neq j$. It follows that the same specification is met by the parallel combination (provided $k \neq j$):

$$(TOT(i, k, adj(i) \setminus \{k\}, w_i) \; || \; (||^{l \in adj(i) \setminus \{k\}} \; c_{ij}!0 \to SKIP))$$
$$\textbf{sat} \quad (tr \Downarrow c_{ij} = \langle \rangle \Rightarrow c_{ij}.0 \notin X)$$

Prefixing this process with an input $c_{ki}.0$ will yield the required specification when $j \neq k$

$$c_{ki}.0 \to (TOT(i, k, adj(i) \setminus \{k\}, w_i) \; || \; (||^{l \in adj(i) \setminus \{k\}} \; c_{ij}!0 \to SKIP))$$
$$\textbf{sat} \quad tr \neq \langle \rangle \wedge \mathsf{channel}(head(tr)) \neq c_{ji} \Rightarrow (tr \Downarrow c_{ij} = \langle \rangle \Rightarrow c_{ij}.0 \notin X)$$

In the case where $j = k$, then the specification is vacuously satisfied since whenever $tr \neq \langle \rangle$ then $\mathsf{channel}(head(tr)) = c_{ji}$. Hence the specification is met in all cases, and $O1_{ij}$ follows from the fact that $NODE(i)$ is an indexed choice between all of these processes.

The other liveness property required on output is that once a node has received inputs from all of its neighbours, it is ready to output to the neighbour that it first communicated with. The set of input possibilities to a node i will be defined as A_i^{in}:

$$A_i^{in} \quad = \quad \{c_{ji}.n \mid c_{ji}.n \in A_i\}$$

If all the input channels are mentioned in the trace, then the node has the required liveness property:

$$O2_{ij} \qquad NODE(i) \text{ sat } \text{channels}(A_i^{in}) \subseteq \text{channels}(tr) \wedge \text{channel}(head(tr)) = c_{ji}$$
$$\Rightarrow ((tr \Downarrow c_{ij} = \langle\rangle \Rightarrow c_{ij}.\mathbb{N} \not\subseteq X))$$

The proof of this property is left as an exercise (see Exercise 7.13).

Liveness on termination

When a node has had some communication along each of its channels, it is either ready to terminate or else already terminated:

$$T1_i \qquad NODE(i) \text{ sat } \text{channels}(A_i) \subseteq \text{channels}(tr) \Rightarrow (\checkmark \text{ in } tr \vee \checkmark \notin X)$$

The proof of this property is left as Exercise 7.14.

Safety on the nodes

The safety property is simply that the first event of any process must be on one of its input channels. This may be established in the traces model.

$$N1_i \qquad NODE(i) \text{ sat } tr \neq \langle\rangle \Rightarrow \text{channel}(head(tr \upharpoonright A_i^{\checkmark})) \in A_i^{in}$$

A single application of the proof rule for input (using simply $P(x)$ **sat** $true(tr)$ as the antecedent) establishes that this specification holds for any process of the form $c?x : T \rightarrow P(x)$ for which $c \in A_i^{in}$. This is indeed the case for all channels of the form c_{ji} where $j \in adj(i)$, so the proof rule for indexed external choice yields that any process of the form

$$\square_{j \in adj(i)} \quad c_{ji}?x : T \rightarrow P(x, j)$$

must also satisfy this specification, since each of its components do. The description of $NODE(i)$ is of this form, so $N1_i$ follows without any need to consider the behaviour following the first event.

Deadlock-freedom for the network

The properties of the individual nodes given above are sufficient to establish that the process $NETWORK = \|_{A_i} NODE(i)$ is deadlock-free.

Consider a failure (tr, X) of $NETWORK$. Then the refusal set is made up of a family of refusal sets $\langle X_i \rangle_{i \in N}$, one for each $i \in N$, where $X = \bigcup_{i \in N}(X_i \cap A_i^{\checkmark})$, and $(tr \upharpoonright A_i^{\checkmark}, X_i) \in \mathcal{SF}\llbracket NODE(i) \rrbracket$. The special channels $c_{0\infty}$ and $c_{\infty 0}$ appear only in A_0. All other channels c_{ij} appear in only two alphabets, A_i and A_j. This means that if there is some value v for which $c_{ij}.v \notin X_j$ and $c_{ij}.v \notin X_i$, then $c_{ij}.v \notin X$. If it is offered by both $NODE(i)$ and $NODE(j)$, then it cannot be blocked by any other component.

To establish deadlock-freedom for $NETWORK$, all the possible cases for the trace tr will be considered, and in each case (before termination) the liveness properties will be enough to show that there is some communication which does not appear in the refusal set X.

There are essentially two cases to consider: whether or not any of the nodes are still in their initial state. The two cases each split into a number of subcases.

Case $\exists i \bullet tr \upharpoonright A_i^{\checkmark} = \langle \rangle$:

Subcase $tr \Downarrow c_{\infty,0} = \langle \rangle$: In this case $(tr \upharpoonright A_0^{\checkmark}) \Downarrow c_{\infty,0} = \langle \rangle$, and so $(\langle \rangle, X_0)$ is a failure of $NODE(0)$. It follows from $I1_{\infty 0}$ that $c_{\infty,0}.0 \notin X_0$, and so $c_{\infty 0}.0 \notin X$.

Subcase $tr \Downarrow c_{\infty,0} \neq \langle \rangle \wedge \exists j \bullet tr \upharpoonright A_j^{\checkmark} = \langle \rangle$: In this case the set of nodes can be partitioned into the nodes that have engaged in some event, and those that have not. Both sets will be non-empty:

$$
\begin{aligned}
S_1 &= \{i \in N \mid tr \upharpoonright A_i^{\checkmark} \neq \langle \rangle\} \\
S_2 &= N \setminus S_1
\end{aligned}
$$

Connectedness of the graph (N, E) implies that there must be some edge $(i, j) \in E$ connecting the two sets: $i \in S_1$ and $j \in S_2$. Then $c_{ij} \in A_j$, so $tr \Downarrow c_{ij} = \langle \rangle$ because $j \in S_2$, so $I1_{ij}$ yields that $c_{ij}.0 \notin X_j$.

Furthermore, $tr \upharpoonright A_1^{\checkmark} \neq \langle \rangle$ since $i \in S_1$, and $tr \Downarrow c_{ji} = \langle \rangle$ because $j \in S_2$, so from $O1_{ij}$ it follows that $c_{ij}.0 \notin X_i$. Thus $c_{ij}.0$ does not appear in X, which establishes the case.

Case $\forall i \bullet tr \upharpoonright A_i^{\checkmark} \neq \langle \rangle$:

In this case, every node has participated in some event in the trace tr. In each case, the first channel that a node i has interacted on will be $c_{ji} = \mathsf{channel}(head(tr \upharpoonright A_i^{\checkmark}))$ for some other node j. The set of all such channels is defined to be the set T:

$$
T = \{\mathsf{channel}(head(tr \upharpoonright A_i^{\checkmark})) \mid i \in N\}
$$

These are the channels from parent to child nodes. They form a tree.

Property $N1_i$ means that for any i the set $T \cap A_i^{in}$ contains exactly one channel: each node has exactly one parent.

If $c_{ji} \in T$ then node i will pass the sum of its inputs, together with its own weight w_i, along the complementary channel c_{ij}. The set of all such channels is defined to be T':

$$T' \;=\; \{c_{ij} \mid c_{ji} \in T\}$$

This is the set of channels from child nodes to their parent nodes. These are the channels that carry values rather than initiating messages.

The set of all channels apart from those in T' is given by

$$\overline{T'} \;=\; \left(\textstyle\bigcup_{i \in N} \text{channels}(A_i)\right) \setminus T'$$

These are the channels that carry initiating messages.

Subcase $\overline{T'} \nsubseteq \text{channels}(tr)$: The first subcase to consider is where not all initiating messages have yet occurred: not all channels in $\overline{T'}$ appear in the trace.

In this case there is a channel $c_{ij} \in \overline{T'}$ such that $tr \Downarrow c_{ij} = \langle\rangle$. This means that $c_{ji} \neq channel(head(tr \upharpoonright A_i^{\vee}))$. The property $O1_{ij}$ implies that $c_{ij}.0 \notin X_i$, and $I2_{ij}$ means that $c_{ij}.0 \notin X_j$. Hence $c_{ij}.0$ cannot appear in the refusal set X.

Any channel in $\overline{T'}$ that has not appeared in the trace cannot have 0 refused.

Subcase $\overline{T'} \subseteq \text{channels}(tr) \wedge T' \nsubseteq \text{channels}(tr)$: In this subcase, all initiating messages have occurred (all channels in $\overline{T'}$ have been used) but not all values have yet been returned: some channels in T' have not yet been used. Then the set of channels $U' \subseteq T'$ that have not been used by a child node to return its value to its parent node is non-empty:

$$U' \;=\; \{c_{ij} \in T' \mid tr \Downarrow c_{ij} = \langle\rangle\}$$

The channels in the opposite direction to those in U', from parent to child, are given by U:

$$U \;=\; \{c_{ji} \mid c_{ij} \in U'\}$$

Thus $U \subseteq T$. The sets T, T', U', and U corresponding to the point reached in Diagram 3 of Figure 5.2 are illustrated in Figure 7.2. The set U consists of those channels c_{ij} which are the first channels used by some node i such that i has not communicated its output along the corresponding channel c_{ji}. The last of those channels to have appeared in the trace is given by $\text{channel}(foot(tr \upharpoonright U)) = c_{lk}$ for some l and k. The aim is to show that $c_{kl}.\mathbb{N}$ cannot be refused.

To establish this, it is sufficient to show that all of the inputs channels A_k^{in} to node k must appear in the trace tr:

1. Firstly, all of those in $\overline{T'}$ must have occurred, since all channels in $\overline{T'}$ appear in tr in this subcase.

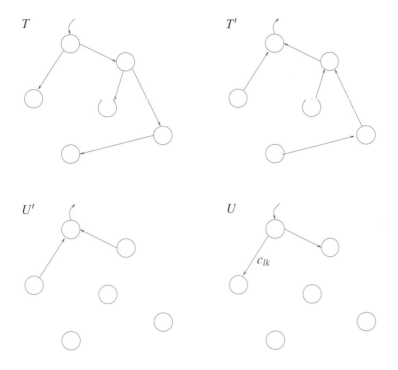

Fig. 7.2 *Example edge sets* T, T', U', *and* U

2. Secondly, all of k's input channels in T' must also appear in tr. If any of k's input channels do not appear in tr, then there is some input channel $c_{mk} \in U'$, since U' consists of those channels of T' that do not appear in tr. This means that the corresponding channel $c_{km} \in U$. Both c_{km} and c_{lk} are in the alphabet A_i of $NODE(i)$. The fact that $c_{lk} \in A_k^{in}$ means that $c_{lk} = \mathsf{channel}(head(tr \upharpoonright A_k^{\checkmark}))$, and so c_{km} must appear after c_{jk} in the trace tr. But this is impossible, since $\mathsf{channel}(foot(tr \upharpoonright U)) = c_{lk}$, so no other channel in U can appear in the trace after c_{lk}.

Thus all of k's input channels appear in tr, so $\mathsf{channels}(A_k^{in}) \subseteq \mathsf{channels}(tr \upharpoonright A_k^{\checkmark})$. Since $tr \Downarrow c_{kl} = \langle \rangle$, property $O2_{kl}$ yields that $c_{kl}.\mathbb{N} \not\subseteq X_k$, and so there is some number v for which $c_{kl}.v \notin X_k$. If $l = \infty$ (and $k = 0$) then this is sufficient to establish that $c_{kl}.v \notin X$. Otherwise, property $I2_{kl}$ yields that $c_{kl}.v \notin X_j$. Hence in either case $c_{kl}.v$ cannot appear in the refusal set X.

Subcase $\overline{T'} \subseteq \mathsf{channels}(tr) \wedge T \subseteq \mathsf{channels}(tr)$: In this case all of the channels have been used, so for any node i

$$\mathsf{channels}(A_i) \subseteq \mathsf{channels}(tr \upharpoonright A_i^{\checkmark})$$

The property $T1$ on each node yields in each case that either $\checkmark$ **in** $tr \upharpoonright A_i^{\checkmark}$ or that $\checkmark \notin X_i$.

1. If $\checkmark \notin tr$, then $\checkmark \notin tr \upharpoonright A_i^{\checkmark}$ for any node i, and so $\checkmark \notin X_i$ for any i, and hence $\checkmark \notin X$.

2. If $\checkmark \in tr$, then the execution has terminated and deadlock is no longer a concern.

Hence no possible trace of *NETWORK* is associated with a deadlock before termination, so *NETWORK* is deadlock-free.

The deadlock-freedom of *DISTSUM* allows further conclusions to be drawn about its behaviour. The alphabet of *DISTSUM* is simply $c_{0\infty}.\mathbb{N} \cup c_{\infty 0}.\mathbb{N} \cup \{\checkmark\}$. This is a subset of the alphabet of node 0, so any constraints imposed by that node on the order of these events must be respected by *DISTSUM*.

In fact (see Exercise 5.15) *NODE*(0) satisfies the following safety specifications:

$$tr \Downarrow c_{0\infty} \neq \langle \rangle \Rightarrow tr \Downarrow c_{\infty 0} \neq \langle \rangle$$
$$tr \upharpoonright \checkmark \neq \langle \rangle \Rightarrow tr \Downarrow c_{0\infty} \neq \langle \rangle$$
$$(tr \Downarrow c_{\infty 0}) \leqslant \langle 0 \rangle$$
$$(tr \downarrow c_{0\infty}) \leqslant 1$$

These together mean that any first event of *DISTSUM* must be $c_{0\infty}.0$, any second event must be a communication along the channel $c_{0\infty}$, and any third event must be termination. Deadlock-freedom means that each of these events must be available in turn, so the behaviour of *DISTSUM* is equivalent to a process

$$c_{\infty 0}.0 \to c_{0\infty}!v \to SKIP$$

for some value v. The safety specification proven in the previous chapter ensures that the value v is the sum of all the weights of the nodes, and so

$$DISTSUM \quad =_{SF} \quad c_{\infty 0}.0 \to c_{0\infty}!(\Sigma_{i \in N} w_i) \to SKIP$$

Exercises

Exercise 7.1 A cheese shop sells Stilton, Brie, Gouda, and Jarlsberg cheese. Specify that

1. all of these will always be available;

2. all of these will initially be available;

3. at any time at least three are available;

4. at any time some cheese is available;

5. after a delivery there is at least one cheese available.

Exercise 7.2 If P is deadlock-free, then prove that $P \setminus A$ is also deadlock-free.

Exercise 7.3 If P_1 and P_2 are strongly deadlock free, then prove that so too is $P_1 \underset{\{a\}}{\|} P_2$. Must $P_1 \underset{\{a,b\}}{\|} P_2$ be deadlock-free?

Exercise 7.4 Prove that if P_1 and P_2 are always live on an input *in*, then so too is $P_1 \underset{in.T}{\|} P_2$.

Exercise 7.5 Prove that

$$\forall Y \bullet (SPEC \sqsubseteq_{SF} Y \Rightarrow SPEC \sqsubseteq_{SF} F(Y))$$

is equivalent to the assertion that $SPEC \sqsubseteq_{SF} F(SPEC)$.

Exercise 7.6 Prove that $P = on \to off \to P$ **sat** $foot(tr) = off \Rightarrow on \notin X$. [You will have to strengthen the specification before the recursion rule can be applied.]

Exercise 7.7 Prove that $P_1 \sqcap P_2 \sqsubseteq_{SF} P_1 \square P_2$ for any P_1 and P_2.

Exercise 7.8 A stack process (or last-in-first-out queue) of type T must always be receptive to input elements of T along channel *push* when empty, and is always willing to output along channel *pop* when non-empty. It can accept further input when non-empty, but is not obliged to. Its output is always the item most recently input that has not yet been output. The process defined in Example 1.3.10 may be considered a process-oriented specification for the traces model.

1. Give a process-oriented specification of a stack for the stable failures model, which allows for the possibility of non-empty stacks being full.

2. Prove that $STACK_1 = push?x : \mathbb{N} \to pop!x \to STACK_1$ is a stack.

3. Prove that $push?x : T \to STACK_2(x)$ is a stack, where

$$
\begin{aligned}
STACK_2(x) \quad = \quad & pop!x \to push?y : T \to STACK_2(y) \\
& \mid push?y : T \to pop!y \to STACK_2(x)
\end{aligned}
$$

Exercise 7.9 (Hard) Prove that the alternating bit protocol of Example 7.3.2 meets its trace specification:

$$ABP \quad \textbf{sat} \quad tr \Downarrow out \leqslant_1 tr \Downarrow in$$

Exercise 7.10 If the graph of nodes in the distributed sum *NETWORK* process is not connected, which part of the liveness proof breaks down? What will be the behaviour of the network in this case, and at what point will it deadlock?

Exercise 7.11 Prove that

$$I2_{ij} \qquad NODE(j) \textbf{ sat } (tr \restriction A_j^{\checkmark} \neq \langle\rangle \land tr \Downarrow c_{ij} = \langle\rangle) \Rightarrow c_{ij}.\mathbb{N} \cap X = \{\}$$

Hint: a useful starting point is to establish by a mutual recursion induction that the *TOT* family of processes meet a corresponding family of specifications:

$$TOT(j, k, M, t) \quad \textbf{sat} \quad \begin{aligned} & i \notin M \lor \\ & (tr \Downarrow c_{ij} = \langle\rangle \Rightarrow c_{ij}.\mathbb{N} \cap X = \{\} \end{aligned}$$

Exercise 7.12 Use the traces model to prove $N1_i$ on page 214.

Exercise 7.13 (Harder) Prove $O2_{ij}$ on page 214.

Exercise 7.14 Prove $T1_i$ on page 214.

8

Failures, divergences, and infinite traces

8.1 OBSERVING PROCESSES

The stable failures model records the occurrence of events as processes perform them, and their refusal after processes stabilize. This approach is effective for processes that cannot diverge. When divergence is a possibility then the stable failures model is not discriminating enough, since it completely ignores any divergent behaviour that a process might have.

In order to analyse processes for the possibility of divergence, it is necessary to introduce the appropriate observations into the model. There are two kinds of behaviour that have a bearing on divergence: traces that lead to a divergent state, and infinite traces that might give rise to divergence. These are introduced alongside failures information to yield the *failures/divergences/infinite traces* model, which is the concern of this chapter.

Divergence

When a process executes, it may pass through a sequence of process states by means of internal τ transitions. In an unstable state, external events might be possible as well as the internal event, but there can be no assurance that they will be available to the environment of the process, since there is no way the τ transition can be prevented from firing. It is appropriate to consider guarantees on event offers only for those states which have no internal transitions leading from them.

If a process P is able to perform an infinite sequence of internal events, then there is no guarantee that it will ever reach a stable state, and in fact there is no guarantee that it will ever

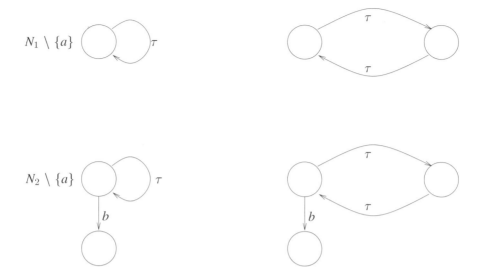

Fig. 8.1 Divergent processes

respond to any offer that its environment can make to it. As defined on page 175, P is said to be *divergent*, written $P \uparrow$.

Divergence is the worst possible behaviour that a component of a system may exhibit, since any other component waiting to synchronize with it might remain waiting for ever, in anticipation that the process will eventually reach a point where it will synchronize. Infinite computing resources will be consumed during a divergent execution. Figure 8.1 illustrates some divergent processes.

Example 8.1.1 The process $N_1 \setminus \{a\}$ has a divergent execution, where N_1 is defined recursively as $N_1 = a \to N_1$. Thus $N_1 \setminus \{a\} \uparrow$. This is pictured in Figure 8.1. ∎

Example 8.1.2 The process $N_2 \setminus \{a\}$ has a divergent execution, where N_2 is defined recursively as $N_2 = (a \to N_2 \mid b \to STOP)$. There is an infinite sequence of internal transitions that can be performed. Thus $N_2 \setminus \{a\} \uparrow$. This is pictured in Figure 8.1. ∎

If a process P is unable to diverge, this means that there are no infinite sequences of internal transitions starting from P, and so every sequence of internal transitions must eventually reach a stable state $P' \downarrow$ from which no further internal events are possible.

Divergent traces

If a divergent state is reached after a finite sequence of events, then the sequence tr is recorded as a *divergent trace* of the process. No guarantees about the behaviour of the process can be made subsequent to a divergent trace. The trace *tr* is a divergent trace of *P* if there is some divergent process P' such that $P \stackrel{tr}{\Longrightarrow} P' \wedge P' \uparrow$. For example, the process $N_2 \setminus \{a\}$ of Example 8.1.2 has $\langle \rangle$ as a divergent trace.

Infinite traces

If an infinite sequence of offers are all accepted, then an infinite trace *u* will be recorded. No refusal information will appear since there is no point at which offers are refused. If the trace $u = \langle a_0, a_1, a_2 \ldots \rangle$ then *u* will be an infinite trace of *P* if there is an infinite sequence $\langle P_i \rangle_{i \in \mathbb{N}}$ such that

$$P = P_0 \wedge \forall i \bullet P_i \stackrel{\langle a_i \rangle}{\Longrightarrow} P_{i+1}$$

For example, the process $P = a \to P$ has $\langle a, a, a, \ldots \rangle$ as an infinite trace—in fact its only one.

The set of all possible infinite traces is denoted *ITRACE*, and the variable *u* is used to range over *ITRACE*. It is the set of all infinite sequences of events from Σ. Such sequences cannot contain the termination event $\checkmark$ if termination occurs at some point in a trace then it must be last.

Failures

The stable failures of a process will continue to be recorded. However, a divergent process is also able to refuse any set of offered events by default, since it is able to ignore permanently any offers made to it simply by following the divergent execution. Observations of such behaviour will also be recorded as failures.

For example, the process $N_2 \setminus \{a\}$ of Example 8.1.2 has $(\langle \rangle, \{a, b\})$ as a possible (unstable) failure, since it can engage in a divergent execution after the empty trace, and hence refuse $\{a, b\}$.

The inclusion of both stable and unstable failures as observations means that the traces of a process no longer need to be recorded separately. Unlike the stable failures model, all traces of a process will appear in the failure set. Every trace of a process will either be divergent, or will lead to a stable state. In either case, it will be associated with the refusal $\{\}$, either from a stable refusal of the empty set (which is possible for any stable state, since no events are offered), or else for an unstable refusal. Hence whenever *tr* is a trace of a process, then $(tr, \{\})$ will be a failure of that process.

Example 8.1.3 The process N_3 pictured in Figure 8.2 has $\langle c \rangle$ and $\langle a, b, c \rangle$ as two of its possible divergent traces. It has $(\langle a, b \rangle, \{b\})$ as a possible failure, and $\langle a, b, a, b, \ldots \rangle$ as an infinite trace. ∎

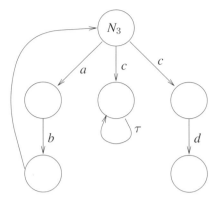

Fig. 8.2   Divergent processes

Semantic model

The failures, divergences, and infinite traces model (abbreviated as the FDI model) for CSP identifies a process P with the failures, divergences, and infinite traces that may be observed of it. This model is even more discriminating than the stable failures model, as it takes account of divergent and infinite behaviour as well as stable failures, but the underlying approach taken to the semantics and to specification and verification is the same as in all the models for CSP.

If three sets F, D, and I are to correspond respectively to the possible failures, divergences, and infinite traces of some process, there are some consistency conditions that they should meet, both within and between the sets. These are properties that must hold of any triple of sets which describe some process.

Firstly, the set F should not be empty: there must always be some observation. Although each of D and I can be empty (since it is reasonable for processes to have no divergent or infinite traces) any experiment on a process will give some response. In fact, it is possible to be more specific: if the empty set of events is initially offered to any process, then it will be refused, since the empty set can always be refused. This is described by the failure $(\langle\rangle, \{\})$, which must therefore appear in any process's set of failures.

$$F1 \qquad (\langle\rangle, \{\}) \in F$$

The second property is also inherited from the traces model, although it is formulated differently because of the presence of refusal sets. If a failure (tr, X) is in the set F of failures associated with a process, then that process must be able to perform any prefix tr' of the trace tr. Although the failure gives no information about possible refusals after the trace tr', the empty refusal set $\{\}$ must always be possible after tr'.

$$F2 \qquad (tr, X) \in F \wedge tr' \leqslant tr \Rightarrow (tr', \{\}) \in F$$

There is also a property of subset closure in the refusal component of a behaviour: if a set X can be refused after a trace tr, then any subset X' of X can also be refused after that trace.

$$F3 \qquad (tr, X) \in F \wedge X' \subseteq X \Rightarrow (tr, X') \in F$$

The final property of the failures component F is concerned with the relationship between refusals and events that are not possible. If $(tr, X) \in F$, and no event from X' can follow the trace tr, then the set X' can augment the refusal set. Events are either possible or refusable.

$$F4 \qquad (tr, X) \in F \wedge \forall a \in X' \bullet (tr \frown \{a\}, \{\}) \notin F \Rightarrow (tr, X \cup X') \in F$$

Since $\checkmark$ is always the last event in a trace, $F4$ means that any set of events can be refused after $\checkmark$ has occurred, since the trace cannot be extended beyond $\checkmark$. A terminating trace can be associated with all refusal sets.

The FDI model takes a pessimistic approach to recording process behaviours. In order to guarantee that certain behaviours are not possible, which will be required for verification, it is necessary to allow for the possibility of all behaviours that cannot be definitely excluded. Behaviours are known to be possible if they can actually be observed during some interaction with the process, and correspond directly to some execution. Certainly these behaviours cannot be excluded. However, divergence complicates the picture, because an extremely negative view is taken of divergent processes.

Any process P which is attempting to interact with a divergent process P_D can guarantee nothing about the results of any attempted interaction, or even about its own independent progress, since the divergent execution might take precedence over any activity that P would prefer, and the parallel combination of P and P_D is also divergent. Since nothing can be guaranteed about any future behaviour, nothing can be excluded. The possibility of divergence masks all other possible executions, so once a process is divergent then all other behaviours should be allowed as possible observations. Any process or environment interacting with a purely divergent process which can only loop has no guarantees about further interactions, just as if it were interacting with a divergent process that has some other well-defined executions. Even the possibility of divergence is considered to be catastrophic. This is true in a precise testing sense, as will be discussed at the end of this chapter. The reason for recording divergence within the FDI model is because it is a phenomenon that may arise, so the possibility must be incorporated in order to provide a framework which can establish that it has not arisen in particular systems.

Hence once a divergence has occurred, then no behaviour can be excluded from the possibilities associated with a process, so any behaviour prefixed by a divergent trace will be included in the semantics of a process. This means that any trace which contains a divergent trace as a prefix will also be in the set of possible divergences:

$$D1 \qquad tr \in D \wedge tr \leqslant tr' \Rightarrow tr' \in D$$

Any possible divergence can be associated with any refusal set X, and appear in the set of possible refusals:

$$D2 \qquad tr \in D \wedge X \subseteq \Sigma^{\checkmark} \rightarrow (tr, X) \in F$$

Any infinite trace which has a divergent trace as a prefix cannot be excluded as a possible behaviour:

$$D3 \qquad tr \in D \wedge tr \leqslant u \Rightarrow u \in I$$

Once a process has diverged then nothing can be ruled out.

Finally, the relationship between divergence and termination is as follows:

$$D4 \qquad tr \,^\frown \langle \checkmark \rangle \in D \Rightarrow tr \in D$$

A process cannot diverge on termination—if it is divergent after termination, then this must be because it was already divergent.

Determinism

In sequential programming, determinism is associated with programs which give the same result each time they are executed from the same initial state. This characterization is not entirely appropriate for concurrent programs, since their execution is dependent to some extent on their environment. Furthermore, such components are often non-terminating, since they are designed to provide some ongoing service rather than to perform a specific computation and return a result. Rather than focus on initial and final states, it is necessary to consider the interactions that a process can perform, and whether an environment will achieve the same interactions every time it offers events.

There are three possible results that may be obtained from offering an event to a process: it might accept the event, it might refuse it, or it may diverge and not give a response at all. If the same response is guaranteed every time the offer is made, then the process will be considered to be deterministic on this event. Hence a process will be deterministic if it only ever has one possible response to an offer, after any given previous interaction. This means that if a trace can be extended with some event, then that event cannot also be refused. A process (F, D, I) is *deterministic* if

$$\forall tr, a \bullet ((tr \,^\frown \langle a \rangle, \{\}) \in F \Rightarrow (tr, \{a\}) \notin F)$$

It follows from this definition that no divergent process can be deterministic, since after divergence all failures are possible.

Deterministic processes are completely characterized by their traces: once their traces are known, then their failures can be deduced from the fact that they are deterministic, together with (the contrapositive of) the property $F4$. The refusals associated with a trace tr will be precisely those events that do not extend tr. All the possible infinite traces will be present: the infinite traces will be the limits of all the chains of finite traces.

If T is the set of traces of a deterministic process, then its failures, divergences, and infinite traces will be given by

$$
\begin{aligned}
F_T &= \{(tr, X) \mid tr \in T \wedge \forall a \in X \bullet tr ^\frown \langle a \rangle \notin T\} \\
D_T &= \{\} \\
I_T &= \{u \mid \forall tr \leqslant u \bullet \#tr < \infty \Rightarrow tr \in T\}
\end{aligned}
$$

Each process in the traces model corresponds to a deterministic process in the FDI model.

For example, if

$$
F = \{(\langle a \rangle^n, X) \mid a \notin X\}
$$

then F gives the failures of a process which can only ever perform a events, and can never refuse them. The only trace set T with $F_T \subseteq F$ is

$$
T = \{\langle a \rangle^n \mid n \in \mathbb{N}\}
$$

Thus $I_T = \{\langle a \rangle^\omega\}$.

Infinite traces

The relationship between the infinite traces and the finite traces of a process has implications in both directions. Firstly, the presence of an infinite trace u requires that the finite prefixes of u, must appear as traces in the set of failures.

$$
I1 \qquad u \in I \wedge tr < u \Rightarrow (tr, \{\}) \in F
$$

For example, if $\langle a \rangle^\omega \in I$, then $(\langle a \rangle^n, \{\}) \in F$ for any n.

Secondly, the presence of some infinite traces may be deduced from failures information about sequences of events that can be forced from a process.

The *closure* $\overline{(F, D, I)}$ of a set of behaviours (F, D, I) includes all the infinite traces that are consistent with the finite traces which appear in the refusal set.

$$
\overline{(F, D, I)} \quad = \quad (F, D, \{u \mid \forall tr \leqslant u \bullet (tr, \{\}) \in F\})
$$

A set of behaviours is *closed* if it is equal to its closure.

If a process is closed then that means that any set of finite approximations to an infinite trace could have come from the same execution. Not all processes are closed; for instance, those with infinite choice such as $\bigsqcap_{i \in \mathbb{N}} P_n$ are able to perform arbitrary length finite sequences of a events, but no infinite sequences of a's. (Recall that $P_0 = STOP$, and $P_{i+1} = a \rightarrow P_i$.)

In this case the a can be refused at any stage, so an infinite sequence cannot be forced. Deterministic processes are closed. This means that their infinite traces I_T can be deduced from their set of finite traces T.

Any process P has a deterministic refinement, since in principle all of its internal choices can be resolved in advance of execution. Hence at any point of a process's execution, having exhibited a trace tr and reached a process state P, there is a deterministic refinement of P with set of traces T.

$I2 \qquad \forall (tr, X) \in F, \exists T \bullet$

$$\{(tr \frown tr', X') \mid (tr', X') \in F_T\} \subseteq F \wedge \{tr \frown u \mid u \in I_T\} \subseteq I$$

This property allows the inference of infinite traces from finite ones, since it asserts that a particular set of infinite traces are contained in I. For example, a process whose set of failures is $\{(\langle a \rangle^n, X) \mid n \in \mathbb{N} \wedge a \notin X\}$ has the set $T = \{\langle a \rangle^n \mid n \in \mathbb{N}\}$ as the only possible deterministic refinement (after the empty trace). If it has any fewer traces, then the set F_T will allow the refusal of a at some point, and this contradicts $I2$'s requirement that $F_T \subseteq F$. Since it has all possible traces of a, the set $I_T = \{\langle a \rangle^\omega\}$, and so $\langle a \rangle^\omega$ must be a trace of I. This follows purely from the set of finite failures and $I2$.

There are different degrees of nondeterminism that it is useful to distinguish. Processes that only ever make internal choices between finitely many alternatives are said to be *finitely nondeterministic*, and they will be characterized by their finite behaviours. This means that once their finite traces and divergences are known, together with a finite set of refusals for each trace, then their remaining behaviours can be derived. Such processes will be closed: their infinite traces will be the limits of all the infinite chains of their traces. Furthermore, their refusal behaviour will be deduced from their refusal behaviour on a finite number of sets. This property is called *FMMR* (finitely many maximal refusals), and a process is *FMMR* if:

$$\forall (tr, \{\}) \in F, \exists G \in \mathbb{F}(\mathbb{P}(\Sigma^\checkmark)) \bullet ((tr, X) \in F \Leftrightarrow \exists Y \in G \bullet X \subseteq Y)$$

This states that after any trace tr, there are only a finite number of maximal refusals, given by the finite set G. All refusals of the process (F, D, I) after tr must be contained in one of these refusals.

A process is finitely nondeterministic precisely when it is both closed and *FMMR*.

A useful property slightly weaker than *FMMR* is *compactness*, which allows all refusal information to be deduced from refusals of finite size. A process (F, D, I) is said to be *compact* if whenever it is able to refuse all finite subsets of a set, then it will also be able to refuse the entire set:

$$(\forall X' \subseteq^{fin} X \bullet (tr, X') \in F) \Rightarrow (tr, X) \in F$$

Processes that are not closed, or which do not have the property *FMMR*, are *infinitely nondeterministic*: at some stage they will contain some internal choice over an infinite number of possibilities.

Since the property *FMMR* is stronger than compactness, any process which exhibits only finite nondeterminism must also be compact. Contrapositively, any process which is not compact must be infinitely nondeterministic. This fact is useful in identifying infinite nondeterminism, since compactness is often easier to identify than *FMMR*.

For example, the process $\bigsqcap_{i \in \mathbb{N}} (i \to STOP)$ will internally choose a single number i to offer, and will refuse all others. This process can refuse any finite subset of $\mathbb{N}$, but will be unable to refuse all of $\mathbb{N}$, so it is not compact, and hence not *FMMR*. (Note, however, that it is closed.)

On the other hand, the process $\bigsqcap_{i \in \mathbb{N}} P_i$ described earlier, where

$$P_0 = STOP$$
$$P_{n+1} = a \to P_n$$

does meet *FMMR*, since after any trace it will always be able to refuse everything apart from a, and may refuse a as well. In this case, $G = \{\Sigma^\checkmark\}$. However, it is not closed, since it can perform any finite number of a events, but not an infinite sequence. This process is also infinitely nondeterministic.

8.2 PROCESS SEMANTICS

Each CSP process expression will be associated with appropriate failures, divergences, and infinite traces in the FDI model. These are defined compositionally, so the behaviours associated with a composite process will be defined in terms of the behaviours of its components. The failures associated with a CSP process expression P will be given by $\mathcal{F}[\![P]\!]$, the divergences by $\mathcal{D}[\![P]\!]$, and the infinite traces by $\mathcal{I}[\![P]\!]$.

There is a close relationship between the traces semantics, the stable failures semantics, and the FDI semantics of any process expression P which does not have any divergences. In this case, the set of traces predicted by the trace semantics $\mathsf{traces}(P)$ is the same as the traces appearing in the failures $\mathcal{F}[\![P]\!]$ of P:

$$\mathcal{D}[\![P]\!] = \{\} \quad \Rightarrow \quad \{tr \mid (tr, \{\}) \in \mathcal{F}[\![P]\!]\} = \mathsf{traces}(P)$$

Any trace appearing with some refusal set in $\mathcal{F}[\![P]\!]$ will also appear with the empty refusal set, by property *F3*, so the set of traces appearing with the empty refusal is precisely the set of traces appearing in the failures set.

Furthermore, the set of stable failures predicted in the stable failures is the same as the failures given in the FDI model:

$$\mathcal{D}[\![P]\!] = \{\} \quad \Rightarrow \quad \mathcal{F}[\![P]\!] = \mathcal{SF}[\![P]\!]$$

The definitions of $\mathcal{F}[\![P]\!]$ generally correspond to the definitions of $\mathcal{SF}[\![P]\!]$ with an extra clause which includes the additional failures introduced as a result of divergences of P.

STOP

The process *STOP* is a deadlocked process. It is able to perform nothing and can refuse anything. It has no infinite traces (or finite traces apart from $\langle\rangle$), and it does not diverge.

$$
\begin{aligned}
\mathcal{F}\llbracket STOP \rrbracket &= \{(\langle\rangle, X) \mid X \subseteq \Sigma^{\checkmark}\} \\
\mathcal{D}\llbracket STOP \rrbracket &= \{\} \\
\mathcal{I}\llbracket STOP \rrbracket &= \{\}
\end{aligned}
$$

Prefixing

In a failure of the process $a \to P$, there are two possibilities: either the event a has not occurred, in which case the trace must be $\langle\rangle$ and any events other than a can be refused, or else the event a has occurred and the rest of the failure derives from process P.

$$
\begin{aligned}
\mathcal{F}\llbracket a \to P \rrbracket = \ &\{(\langle\rangle, X) \mid a \notin X\} \\
&\cup \\
&\{(\langle a \rangle \frown tr, X) \mid (tr, X) \in \mathcal{F}\llbracket P \rrbracket\}
\end{aligned}
$$

It does not diverge initially, so any divergence will be a divergence of P, prefixed with the initial a:

$$
\mathcal{D}\llbracket a \to P \rrbracket = \{\langle a \rangle \frown tr \mid tr \in \mathcal{D}\llbracket P \rrbracket\}
$$

Its infinite traces will be those of P, prefixed with the initial a:

$$
\mathcal{I}\llbracket a \to P \rrbracket = \{\langle a \rangle \frown u \mid u \in \mathcal{I}\llbracket P \rrbracket\}
$$

Prefixing preserves determinism: if P is deterministic, then so too is $a \to P$.

Prefix choice

A failure of the process $x : A \to P(x)$ is again one of two possibilities. Either no event has yet occurred, in which case no event from A can be refused; or else an event a in A has occurred, and the subsequent behaviour is that of the corresponding process $P(a)$.

$$
\begin{aligned}
\mathcal{F}\llbracket x : A \to P(x) \rrbracket = \ &\{(\langle\rangle, X) \mid A \cap X = \{\}\} \\
&\cup \\
&\{(\langle a \rangle \frown tr, X) \mid a \in A \wedge (tr, X) \in \mathcal{F}\llbracket P(a) \rrbracket\}
\end{aligned}
$$

The prefix choice does not initially diverge, so any divergence will arise from behaviours of the $P(a)$ components; and infinite traces will also be generated by the $P(a)$ processes.

$$\mathcal{D}\,[\![x : A \to P(x)]\!] \;\;=\;\; \{a \frown tr \mid a \in A \land tr \in \mathcal{D}\,[\![P(a)]\!]\}$$
$$\mathcal{I}\,[\![x : A \to P(x)]\!] \;\;=\;\; \{a \frown u \mid a \in A \land u \in \mathcal{I}\,[\![P(a)]\!]\}$$

Prefix choice also preserves determinism.

SKIP

The atomic process *SKIP* is used to denote successful termination, and it signals this by means of the termination event $\checkmark$. This is the only event it can perform. It cannot diverge, and it has no infinite traces. All other events will be refused before termination, and all events will be refused after termination.

$$\mathcal{F}\,[\![SKIP]\!] \;\;=\;\; \{(\langle\rangle, X) \mid \checkmark \notin X\}$$
$$\cup \{(\langle\checkmark\rangle, X) \mid X \subseteq \Sigma^{\checkmark}\}$$
$$\mathcal{D}\,[\![SKIP]\!] \;\;=\;\; \{\}$$
$$\mathcal{I}\,[\![SKIP]\!] \;\;=\;\; \{\}$$

All of the laws given earlier concerning the behaviour of *SKIP* in parallel combinations remain valid in the FDI model.

DIV

The process that can immediately diverge, and hence provides no guarantees about any behaviour, is denoted *DIV*. This process has all possible failures, divergences, and infinite traces.

$$\mathcal{F}\,[\![DIV]\!] \;\;=\;\; \{(tr, X) \mid tr \in TRACE \land X \subseteq \Sigma^{\checkmark}\}$$
$$=\;\; TRACE \times \mathbb{P}(\Sigma^{\checkmark})$$
$$\mathcal{D}\,[\![DIV]\!] \;\;=\;\; TRACE$$
$$\mathcal{I}\,[\![DIV]\!] \;\;=\;\; ITRACE$$

CHAOS

The process which can do absolutely anything except diverge is *CHAOS*. This is able to accept or refuse any events, but it is at least guaranteed to stabilize. It has all possible failures and infinite traces, but no divergences.

$$\mathcal{F}[\![CHAOS]\!] = TRACE \times \mathbb{P}(\Sigma^{\checkmark})$$
$$\mathcal{D}[\![CHAOS]\!] = \{\}$$
$$\mathcal{I}[\![CHAOS]\!] = ITRACE$$

Chaotic behaviour may be restricted to a particular set of events $A \subseteq \Sigma^{\checkmark}$. The process $CHAOS_A$ allows any events in the set A to be performed or refused, but cannot perform any events outside the set A.

$$\mathcal{F}[\![CHAOS_A]\!] = \{(tr, X) \mid \sigma(tr) \subseteq A\}$$
$$\mathcal{D}[\![CHAOS_A]\!] = \{\}$$
$$\mathcal{I}[\![CHAOS_A]\!] = \{u \mid \sigma(u) \subseteq A\}$$

RUN

Both *CHAOS* and *DIV* have the same traces as *RUN*, so there was no need to introduce them in the traces model. In the FDI model, it is *RUN* that is the best behaved, always willing to interact, and never refusing any interaction, before termination.

$$\mathcal{F}[\![RUN]\!] = \{(tr, X) \mid X = \{\} \vee \checkmark \in \sigma(tr)\}$$
$$\mathcal{D}[\![RUN]\!] = \{\}$$
$$\mathcal{I}[\![RUN]\!] = ITRACE$$

This process is deterministic.

The process RUN_A parameterized by a particular set A is able to perform events in that set, and to refuse all others.

$$\mathcal{F}[\![RUN_A]\!] = \{(tr, X) \mid \sigma(tr) \subseteq A \wedge (X \cap A = \{\} \vee \checkmark \in \sigma(tr))\}$$
$$\mathcal{D}[\![RUN_A]\!] = \{\}$$
$$\mathcal{I}[\![RUN_A]\!] = \{u \mid \sigma(u) \subseteq A\}$$

If $\checkmark \notin A$ then RUN_A cannot terminate.

External choice

An observer of the choice construct $P_1 \ \square \ P_2$ might observe an execution of P_1, or of P_2; there are no other possibilities. Before any events are performed and the choice resolved, any refused set must be refused by both P_1 and P_2, unless the choice has already diverged in which case any refusal is possible. After the choice is resolved, any refusal need only be possible for the process in whose favour the choice was resolved.

$$\mathcal{F} \llbracket P_1 \square P_2 \rrbracket = \{(\langle\rangle, X) \mid ((\langle\rangle, X) \in \mathcal{F} \llbracket P_1 \rrbracket \cap \mathcal{F} \llbracket P_2 \rrbracket) \vee \langle\rangle \in \mathcal{D} \llbracket P_1 \square P_2 \rrbracket\}$$
$$\cup$$
$$\{(tr, X) \mid tr \neq \langle\rangle \wedge (tr, X) \in \mathcal{F} \llbracket P_1 \rrbracket \cup \mathcal{F} \llbracket P_2 \rrbracket\}$$

The divergences and infinite traces of a choice are simply the unions of the component behaviours.

$$\mathcal{D} \llbracket P_1 \square P_2 \rrbracket = \mathcal{D} \llbracket P_1 \rrbracket \cup \mathcal{D} \llbracket P_2 \rrbracket$$
$$\mathcal{I} \llbracket P_1 \square P_2 \rrbracket = \mathcal{I} \llbracket P_1 \rrbracket \cup \mathcal{I} \llbracket P_2 \rrbracket$$

The properties of idempotence, associativity, and commutativity still hold for external choice in the FDI model. Furthermore, *STOP* is still a unit, though *RUN* is no longer a zero because *P* might diverge whereas *RUN* does not. In the FDI model, the zero of external choice is *DIV*, which has the same traces as *RUN* but minimal guaranteed behaviour.

$P \square DIV =_{FDI} DIV$ $\langle\square\text{-zero}_{FDI}\rangle$

In fact the zero in the stable failures model, *RUN* $\square$ *DIV*, is also a zero in this model since here it is equivalent to *DIV*.

The executions of the indexed external choice $\square_{i \in I} P_i$ are the executions of all of its components. Its failures, divergences, and infinite traces will be those of its components:

$$\mathcal{F} \llbracket \square_{i \in I} P_i \rrbracket = \{(\langle\rangle, X) \mid ((\langle\rangle, X) \in \bigcap_{i \in I} \mathcal{F} \llbracket P_i \rrbracket) \vee \langle\rangle \in \mathcal{D} \llbracket \square_{i \in I} P_i \rrbracket\}$$
$$\cup$$
$$\{(tr, X) \mid tr \neq \langle\rangle \wedge (tr, X) \in \bigcup_{i \in I} \mathcal{F} \llbracket P_i \rrbracket\}$$
$$\mathcal{D} \llbracket \square_{i \in I} P_i \rrbracket = \bigcup_{i \in I} \mathcal{D} \llbracket P_i \rrbracket$$
$$\mathcal{I} \llbracket \square_{i \in I} P_i \rrbracket = \bigcup_{i \in I} \mathcal{I} \llbracket P_i \rrbracket$$

In the case where the choice is over the empty set of processes, the intersection $\bigcap_{i \in I} \mathcal{F} \llbracket P_i \rrbracket$ is taken to include all possible failures, since all of them are vacuously in each of the $\mathcal{F} \llbracket P_i \rrbracket$. This means that in this case, any refusal is possible on the empty trace. Furthermore, no events are possible, and there are no divergences or infinite traces. As in the traces model, an empty choice is equivalent to *STOP*.

Internal choice

The internal choice $P_1 \sqcap P_2$ behaves either as P_1 or as P_2, and its environment exercises no control over which, at any point. The possible observations are precisely those that either P_1 or P_2 are able to exhibit.

$$
\begin{aligned}
\mathcal{F}\llbracket P_1 \sqcap P_2 \rrbracket &= \mathcal{F}\llbracket P_1 \rrbracket \cup \mathcal{F}\llbracket P_2 \rrbracket \\
\mathcal{D}\llbracket P_1 \sqcap P_2 \rrbracket &= \mathcal{D}\llbracket P_1 \rrbracket \cup \mathcal{D}\llbracket P_2 \rrbracket \\
\mathcal{I}\llbracket P_1 \sqcap P_2 \rrbracket &= \mathcal{I}\llbracket P_1 \rrbracket \cup \mathcal{I}\llbracket P_2 \rrbracket
\end{aligned}
$$

The indexed internal choice $\sqcap_{i \in J} P_i$ is able to behave as any of its component processes, and its behaviours will be the union of those of its constituents:

$$
\begin{aligned}
\mathcal{F}\llbracket \textstyle\sqcap_{i \in J} P_i \rrbracket &= \bigcup_{i \in J} \mathcal{F}\llbracket P_i \rrbracket \\
\mathcal{D}\llbracket \textstyle\sqcap_{i \in J} P_i \rrbracket &= \bigcup_{i \in J} \mathcal{D}\llbracket P_i \rrbracket \\
\mathcal{I}\llbracket \textstyle\sqcap_{i \in J} P_i \rrbracket &= \bigcup_{i \in J} \mathcal{I}\llbracket P_i \rrbracket
\end{aligned}
$$

Indexed internal choice over an infinite set is one of the few operators which can introduce infinite nondeterminism into a process description.

Alphabetized parallel

An alphabetized parallel combination $P_1 \; {}_A\|_B \; P_2$ consists of P_1 performing events in $A^{\checkmark}$, and P_2 performing events in $B^{\checkmark}$. Processes P_1 and P_2 synchronize on events in $(A \cap B)^{\checkmark}$, and perform the other events independently.

The definition of the failures of a parallel combination resembles that of the stable failures model, though divergences must also be included:

$$
\begin{aligned}
\mathcal{F}\llbracket P_1 \; {}_A\|_B \; P_2 \rrbracket = \; &\{(tr, X) \mid \; \exists X_1, X_2 : \mathbb{P}(\Sigma^{\checkmark}) \bullet \\
&\quad X \cap (A \cup B)^{\checkmark} = (X_1 \cap A^{\checkmark}) \cup (X_2 \cap B^{\checkmark}) \\
&\quad \wedge (tr \upharpoonright A^{\checkmark}, X_1) \in \mathcal{F}\llbracket P_1 \rrbracket \\
&\quad \wedge (tr \upharpoonright B^{\checkmark}, X_2) \in \mathcal{F}\llbracket P_2 \rrbracket) \\
&\quad \wedge \sigma(tr) \subseteq (A \cup B)^{\checkmark} \} \\
\cup \; &\{(tr, X) \mid tr \in \mathcal{D}\llbracket P_1 \; {}_A\|_B \; P_2 \rrbracket\}
\end{aligned}
$$

Failures will also be present as a result of divergence of the combination.

When one of the components has reached a divergent state, then the entire combination is divergent. In order to reach a divergent state, co-operation may be required from the other component, though once the divergence is reached then no further co-operation is required.

$$
\mathcal{D} \, [\![P_1 \,{}_A\|_B\, P_2]\!] \;=\; \{ tr \frown tr' \mid \; \sigma(tr) \subseteq (A \cup B)^{\checkmark}) \wedge tr' \in \mathit{TRACE} \wedge
$$
$$
(tr \restriction A^{\checkmark} \in \mathcal{D} \, [\![P_1]\!] \wedge (tr \restriction B^{\checkmark}, \{\}) \in \mathcal{F} \, [\![P_2]\!]
$$
$$
\vee \; tr \restriction B^{\checkmark} \in \mathcal{D} \, [\![P_2]\!] \wedge (tr \restriction A^{\checkmark}, \{\}) \in \mathcal{F} \, [\![P_1]\!]) \}
$$

The infinite traces of $P_1 \,{}_A\|_B\, P_2$, apart from those arising as a result of divergence, will be those whose projections onto the interface sets $A^{\checkmark}$ and $B^{\checkmark}$ are behaviours of P_1 and P_2. The projections could individually be finite, in which case they will appear in the failure of the corresponding process, or infinite, appearing as an infinite trace.

$$
\mathcal{I} \, [\![P_1 \,{}_A\|_B\, P_2]\!] \;=\; \{ u \mid \; \sigma(u) \subseteq A \cup B \wedge
$$
$$
u \downarrow A = \infty \Rightarrow u \restriction A \in \mathcal{I} \, [\![P_1]\!] \wedge
$$
$$
u \downarrow A < \infty \Rightarrow (u \restriction A, \{\}) \in \mathcal{F} \, [\![P_1]\!] \wedge
$$
$$
u \downarrow B = \infty \Rightarrow u \restriction B \in \mathcal{I} \, [\![P_2]\!] \wedge
$$
$$
u \downarrow B < \infty \Rightarrow (u \restriction B, \{\}) \in \mathcal{F} \, [\![P_2]\!] \}
$$
$$
\cup \{ tr \frown u \mid tr \in \mathcal{D} \, [\![P_1 \,{}_A\|_B\, P_2]\!] \}
$$

All of the laws for the parallel operator given in Figures 4.5 and 4.8, with the exception of the laws ||-idempotence and ||-zero, also hold for the FDI model.

The zero for parallel composition in the FDI model is the immediately divergent process *DIV*, and the law is

---

$P \parallel DIV =_{FDI} DIV$ $\langle \|\text{-zero}_{FDI} \rangle$

If both P_1 and P_2 are divergence-free, then so too is their parallel combination. Furthermore, if both P_1 and P_2 are deterministic, then so is their parallel combination: synchronized parallel combination preserves determinism.

Interleaving

An interleaving of two processes $P_1 \; \||| \; P_2$ executes each component entirely independently of the other. Traces of the combination appear as interleavings of traces of the two component processes. Since they do not synchronize, an event (other than termination) will be refused by the combination only when it is refused by both processes independently—if only one of the processes is able to refuse the event, then the combination will still perform it when offered the opportunity.

$$
\begin{aligned}
\mathcal{F}\llbracket P_1 \;|||\; P_2 \rrbracket \;=\; & \{(tr, X_1 \cup X_2) \mid \exists\, tr_1, tr_2 \bullet \; tr \text{ interleaves } tr_1, tr_2 \\
& \qquad\qquad\qquad\qquad \wedge\; X_1 \restriction \Sigma = X_2 \restriction \Sigma \\
& \qquad\qquad\qquad\qquad \wedge\; (tr_1, X_1) \in \mathcal{F}\llbracket P_1 \rrbracket \\
& \qquad\qquad\qquad\qquad \wedge\; (tr_2, X_2) \in \mathcal{F}\llbracket P_2 \rrbracket \} \\
& \cup\, \{(tr, X) \mid tr \in \mathcal{D}\llbracket P_1 \;|||\; P_2 \rrbracket \}
\end{aligned}
$$

An interleaved combination diverges as soon as one of its components does:

$$
\begin{aligned}
\mathcal{D}\llbracket P_1 \;|||\; P_2 \rrbracket \;=\; & \{tr \frown tr' \mid \exists\, tr_1, tr_2 \bullet \; tr \text{ interleaves } tr_1, tr_2 \;\wedge \\
& \qquad (tr_1 \in \mathcal{D}\llbracket P_1 \rrbracket \wedge (tr_2, \langle\rangle) \in \mathcal{F}\llbracket P_2 \rrbracket \\
& \qquad \vee\, (tr_2 \in \mathcal{D}\llbracket P_2 \rrbracket \wedge (tr_1, \langle\rangle) \in \mathcal{F}\llbracket P_1 \rrbracket)) \}
\end{aligned}
$$

The infinite traces are the infinite interleavings of finite or infinite traces of the two components, provided at least one of the components makes an infinite contribution. Infinite traces may also be present as a consequence of the combination's divergence.

$$
\begin{aligned}
\mathcal{I}\llbracket P_1 \;|||\; P_2 \rrbracket \;=\; & \{u \mid \;\; \exists\, u_1, u_2 \bullet \; u \text{ interleaves } u_1, u_2 \\
& \qquad\qquad\qquad \wedge\; u_1 \in \mathcal{I}\llbracket P_1 \rrbracket \wedge u_2 \in \mathcal{I}\llbracket P_2 \rrbracket \\
& \qquad \vee\, \exists\, u_1, tr_2 \bullet \; u \text{ interleaves } u_1, tr_2 \\
& \qquad\qquad\qquad \wedge\; u_1 \in \mathcal{I}\llbracket P_1 \rrbracket \wedge (tr_2, \{\}) \in \mathcal{F}\llbracket P_2 \rrbracket \\
& \qquad \vee\, \exists\, tr_1, u_2 \bullet \; u \text{ interleaves } tr_1, u_2 \\
& \qquad\qquad\qquad \wedge\; (tr_1, \{\}) \in \mathcal{F}\llbracket P_1 \rrbracket \wedge u_2 \in \mathcal{I}\llbracket P_2 \rrbracket \} \\
& \cup\, \{tr \frown u \mid tr \in \mathcal{D}\llbracket P_1 \;|||\; P_2 \rrbracket \}
\end{aligned}
$$

The interleaving condition involving infinite traces is defined as a limit of interleaving on finite traces. If there are three sequences of traces, $\langle tr_i \rangle_{i \in \mathbb{N}}$, $\langle tr_i' \rangle_{i \in \mathbb{N}}$, $\langle tr_i'' \rangle_{i \in \mathbb{N}}$, whose limits are w, w', and w'' respectively, then w interleaves w', w'' if tr_i interleaves tr_i', tr_i'' for each $i \in \mathbb{N}$. This definition is applicable both for finite and infinite w, w', and w''. If all sequences are infinite then it ensures that all of the events in both w' and w'' appear in w.

The laws given in Figure 4.9 are all true for the FDI model as well, with the exception of $|||$-zero$_T$. Although all of the *traces* of RUN_Σ will be possible for $P \;|||\; RUN_\Sigma$, if P is divergent then it will be able to refuse arbitrary offers after it has diverged and hence will not be equivalent to RUN_Σ. The zero for interleaving in the FDI model is the immediately divergent process DIV, and the law is

$$
P \;|||\; DIV =_{FDI} DIV \qquad\qquad\qquad\qquad \langle |||\text{-zero}_{FDI} \rangle
$$

Interface parallel

The process $P_1 \parallel_A P_2$ is a combination of synchronous and interleaved parallel, synchronizing on events in the set $A^\checkmark$ and interleaving outside that set.

Any failure of the parallel process $P_1 \parallel_A P_2$ will be a combination of failures of its two components.

$$
\begin{aligned}
\mathcal{F}\,[\![P_1 \parallel_A P_2]\!] \;=\; &\{(tr, X_1 \cup X_2) \mid \; \exists\, tr_1, tr_2 \bullet \\
&\qquad\qquad tr\ \mathsf{synch}_A\ tr_1, tr_2) \\
&\qquad\qquad \wedge X_1 \setminus A^\checkmark = X_2 \setminus A^\checkmark \\
&\qquad\qquad \wedge (tr_1, X_1) \in \mathcal{F}\,[\![P_1]\!] \\
&\qquad\qquad \wedge (tr_2, X_2) \in \mathcal{F}\,[\![P_2]\!]\} \\
&\cup \{(tr, X) \mid tr \in \mathcal{D}\,[\![P_1 \parallel_A P_2]\!]\}
\end{aligned}
$$

Divergences will arise from divergences of either component:

$$
\begin{aligned}
\mathcal{D}\,[\![P_1 \parallel_A P_2]\!] \;=\; &\{tr \frown tr' \mid \exists\, tr_1, tr_2 \bullet \; tr\ \mathsf{synch}_A\ tr_1, tr_2 \wedge \\
&\qquad (tr_1 \in \mathcal{D}\,[\![P_1]\!] \wedge (tr_2, \{\}) \in \mathcal{F}\,[\![P_2]\!] \\
&\qquad \vee tr_2 \in \mathcal{D}\,[\![P_2]\!] \wedge (tr_1, \{\}) \in \mathcal{F}\,[\![P_1]\!]\}
\end{aligned}
$$

Infinite traces will arise from infinite traces of the components, or from divergences:

$$
\begin{aligned}
\mathcal{I}\,[\![P_1 \parallel_A P_2]\!] \;=\; &\{u \mid \; \exists\, u_1, u_2 \bullet \; u\ \mathsf{synch}_A\ u_1, u_2 \\
&\qquad\qquad \wedge u_1 \in \mathcal{I}\,[\![P_1]\!] \wedge u_2 \in \mathcal{I}\,[\![P_2]\!] \\
&\qquad \vee \exists\, u_1, tr_2 \bullet \; u\ \mathsf{synch}_A\ u_1, tr_2 \\
&\qquad\qquad \wedge u_1 \in \mathcal{I}\,[\![P_1]\!] \wedge (tr_2, \{\}) \in \mathcal{F}\,[\![P_2]\!] \\
&\qquad \vee \exists\, tr_1, u_2 \bullet \; u\ \mathsf{synch}_A\ tr_1, u_2 \\
&\qquad\qquad \wedge (tr_1, \{\}) \in \mathcal{F}\,[\![P_1]\!] \wedge u_2 \in \mathcal{I}\,[\![P_2]\!]\} \\
&\cup \{tr \frown u \mid tr \in \mathcal{D}\,[\![P_1 \parallel_A P_2]\!]\}
\end{aligned}
$$

The synch_A operator for an infinite trace w is defined in a similar way to the corresponding operation for interleaving. If there are three sequences of traces, $\langle tr_i \rangle_{i \in \mathbb{N}}$, $\langle tr_i' \rangle_{i \in \mathbb{N}}$, $\langle tr_i'' \rangle_{i \in \mathbb{N}}$, whose limits are w, w', and w'' respectively (where w' and w'' can be finite or infinite, though at least one of them will be infinite), then $w\ \mathsf{synch}_A\ w', w''$ if $tr\ \mathsf{synch}_A\ tr_i', tr_i''$ for each $i \in \mathbb{N}$. The predicate $w\ \mathsf{synch}_A\ w', w''$ will hold for precisely those traces which have an appropriate sequence of approximations.

The laws for interface parallel given in Figure 4.10 all hold in the FDI model with the exception of $\parallel$-zero$_T$, which does not hold for divergent processes, although $P \parallel_A STOP = STOP$ for any non divergent process P with $\alpha(P) \subseteq A$. The general zero for interface parallel is

DIV, since immediate divergence is propagated:

$$P \parallel_{A} DIV =_{FDI} DIV \qquad\qquad \langle \parallel_{A}\text{-zero}_{FDI} \rangle$$

Hiding

The process $P \setminus A$ will undergo the same executions as P, but with all events in the set A as internal events rather than external synchronizations. This means that any stable refusal X of $P \setminus A$ will correspond to a refusal of P in which not only internal events but also all events in A are refused. The failures of $P \setminus A$ are constructed around this possibility:

$$\begin{aligned} \mathcal{F}[\![P \setminus A]\!] \quad=\quad & \{(tr \setminus A, X) \mid (tr, X \cup A) \in \mathcal{F}[\![P]\!]\} \\ & \cup \{(tr, X) \mid tr \in \mathcal{D}[\![P \setminus A]\!]\} \end{aligned}$$

Failures arising as a result of divergence must also be included in the failure set.

The process $P \setminus A$ may diverge because P does, but the abstraction of A may also result in some fresh divergent behaviour. If P may perform an infinite sequence of events from the set A, then once those events are internalized the process P is able to perform a divergent trace. The infinite traces of P contain the requisite information.

$$\begin{aligned} \mathcal{D}[\![P \setminus A]\!] \quad=\quad & \{(tr \setminus A) \frown tr' \mid tr \in \mathcal{D}[\![P]\!]\} \\ & \cup \{(u \setminus A) \frown tr' \mid u \in \mathcal{I}[\![P]\!] \wedge \#(u \setminus A) < \infty\} \end{aligned}$$

If the trace $u \setminus A$ is finite when $u \in \mathcal{I}[\![P]\!]$ is infinite, then u must end with an infinite sequence of events from A, and this becomes a divergent sequence of $P \setminus A$. Hiding is the only operator, apart from recursion, that is able to introduce a divergence when applied to a non-divergent process.

The infinite traces of $P \setminus A$ are those infinite traces of P that are still infinite when A is hidden:

$$\mathcal{I}[\![P \setminus A]\!] \quad=\quad \{u \setminus A \mid u \in \mathcal{I}[\![P]\!] \wedge \#(u \setminus A) = \infty\}$$

All of the laws for hiding given in Figure 4.12 are also true in the FDI model.

Together with infinite choice and infinite-to-one alphabet renaming, hiding of an infinite set is one of the few ways in which infinite nondeterminism can be introduced into a process description. For example, the process *CH* defined below offers the choice of any natural number, and then performs that number of *a* events before stopping. This process is deterministic, and so finitely nondeterministic.

$$CH = n : \mathbb{N} \to P_n$$
$$P_0 = STOP$$
$$P_{n+1} = a \to P_n$$

If all of the initial events $\mathbb{N}$ are hidden, then the choice becomes internal, and the resulting process $CH \setminus \mathbb{N} = \bigsqcap_{i \in \mathbb{N}} P_i$ is infinitely nondeterministic: it can perform any finite sequence of *a* events, but not an infinite sequence, so it is not closed.

Example 8.2.1 Consider a one-time transmission process which polls two input channels repeatedly until it receives an input, upon which it outputs the value received and terminates. This might be described as follows:

$$POLL1 = in_1 \to out \to STOP$$
$$\square \; switch \to \; in_2 \to out \to STOP$$
$$\square \; switch \to POLL1$$

Its FDI semantics will be:

$$
\begin{aligned}
\mathcal{F}[\![POLL1]\!] = \; & \{(tr, X) \mid \; \exists n \bullet tr = \langle switch \rangle^{2n} \wedge \{switch, in_1\} \cap X = \{\} \\
& \vee \; \exists n \bullet tr = \langle switch \rangle^{2n+1} \wedge \{switch, in_2\} \cap X = \{\} \\
& \vee \; \exists n \bullet tr = \langle switch \rangle^{2n} \frown \langle in_1 \rangle \wedge out \notin X \\
& \vee \; \exists n \bullet tr = \langle switch \rangle^{2n+1} \frown \langle in_2 \rangle \wedge out \notin X \\
& \vee \; \exists n \bullet tr = \langle switch \rangle^{2n} \frown \langle in_1, out \rangle \\
& \vee \; \exists n \bullet tr = \langle switch \rangle^{2n+1} \frown \langle in_2, out \rangle \}
\end{aligned}
$$

$$\mathcal{D}[\![POLL1]\!] = \{\}$$
$$\mathcal{I}[\![POLL1]\!] = \{\langle switch \rangle^{\omega}\}$$

If the *switch* between channels is abstracted, the result is $POLL1 \setminus \{switch\}$. This process can perform an infinite sequence of internal *switch* events from its initial state, so it is immediately divergent. This is reflected in the semantics by the fact that the infinite trace of *POLL1* becomes the empty trace when *switch* is hidden:

$$\mathcal{D}[\![POLL1 \setminus \{switch\}]\!] =$$
$$\{((\langle switch \rangle^{\omega}) \setminus \{switch\} \frown tr' \mid \#(\langle switch \rangle^{\omega} \setminus \{switch\}) < \infty\}$$
$$= \; TRACE$$

Therefore $POLL1 \setminus \{switch\}$ also contains all infinite traces, and all possible failures, and is thus equivalent to *DIV*. ∎

Renaming

The forward renamed process $f(P)$ behaves as P, except that $f(a)$ can be performed whenever P could have performed a. It can refuse a set X if every event that f maps into X can be refused by P. This means that $f^{-1}(X)$ must be a refusal of P for X to be a refusal of $f(P)$.

$$\begin{aligned}
\mathcal{F}[\![f(P)]\!] &= \{(f(tr), X) \mid (tr, f^{-1}(X)) \in \mathcal{F}[\![P]\!]\} \\
&\cup \{(tr, X) \mid tr \in \mathcal{D}[\![f(P)]\!]\}
\end{aligned}$$

Failures arising from divergence are also included.

The divergences will be generated by those divergent traces of P, mapped through the renaming function f:

$$\mathcal{D}[\![f(P)]\!] = \{f(tr) ^\frown tr' \mid tr \in \mathcal{D}[\![P]\!]\}$$

Finally, the infinite traces of $f(P)$ will be generated by the infinite traces of P, and by the divergences of $f(P)$:

$$\begin{aligned}
\mathcal{I}[\![f(P)]\!] &= \{f(u) \mid u \in \mathcal{I}[\![P]\!]\} \\
&\cup \{tr ^\frown u \mid tr \in \mathcal{D}[\![f(P)]\!]\}
\end{aligned}$$

Infinite-to-one renaming is one of the few operators that can introduce infinite nondeterminism from a finitely nondeterministic process. For example, the function f which maps each number $n \in \mathbb{N}$ to the same event b, and $f(a)$ to a, might be applied to the process CH described above. The result $f(CH)$ is a process for which b followed by any finite number of a events is a possible trace of $f(P)$, but b followed by an infinite number of a's is not. The application of f has introduced infinite nondeterminism, since the resulting process $f(P)$ is not closed.

Finite-to-one renaming cannot introduce infinite nondeterminism, though it might introduce some nondeterminism even when applied to a deterministic process. However, if f is a one-one renaming, then it will preserve determinism.

The renaming operator in the FDI model meets all of the laws given in Figure 4.13.

The backward renaming operator $f^{-1}(P)$ also behaves in a similar fashion to P, but any event a in $f^{-1}(P)$ corresponds to an event $f(a)$ in P.

$$\begin{aligned}
\mathcal{F}[\![f^{-1}(P)]\!] &= \{(tr, X) \mid (f(tr), f(X)) \in \mathcal{F}[\![P]\!])\} \\
&\cup \{(tr, X) \mid tr \in \mathcal{D}[\![f^{-1}(P)]\!]\}
\end{aligned}$$

The divergences of $f^{-1}(P)$ will be generated by the divergences of P:

$$\mathcal{D}[\![f^{-1}(P)]\!] = \{tr \mid f(tr) \in \mathcal{D}[\![P]\!]\}$$

The infinite traces of $f^{-1}(P)$ will be generated by the infinite traces of P:

$$\mathcal{I}[\![f^{-1}(P)]\!] \quad = \quad \{u \mid f(u) \in \mathcal{I}[\![P]\!]\}$$

All the laws given in Figure 4.13 for backward renaming remain valid.

Sequential composition

The sequential composition $P_1; P_2$ behaves as P_1 until P_1 terminates successfully, at which point it passes control to P_2. A failure of $P_1; P_2$ will arise either from a failure of P_1, whose stability means that it also refuses to transfer control to P_2, or else from a terminating trace of P_1 followed by a failure of P_2.

$$\begin{aligned}
\mathcal{F}[\![P_1; P_2]\!] \quad = \quad & \{(tr, X) \mid (tr, X \cup \{\checkmark\}) \in \mathcal{F}[\![P_1]\!]\} \\
& \cup \{(tr_1 \frown tr_2, X) \mid (\ tr_1 \frown \langle\checkmark\rangle, \{\}) \in \mathcal{F}[\![P_1]\!] \\
& \qquad\qquad\qquad\qquad \wedge (tr_2, X) \in \mathcal{F}[\![P_2]\!]\} \\
& \cup \{(tr, X) \mid tr \in \mathcal{D}[\![P_1; P_2]\!]\}
\end{aligned}$$

A divergence of $P_1; P_2$ arises either from a divergence of P_1, or from a trace of P_1 followed by a divergence of P_2:

$$\mathcal{D}[\![P_1; P_2]\!] \quad = \quad \mathcal{D}[\![P_1]\!] \cup \{tr \frown tr' \mid (tr \frown \langle\checkmark\rangle, \{\}) \in \mathcal{F}[\![P_1]\!] \wedge tr' \in \mathcal{D}[\![P_2]\!]\}$$

An infinite trace of $P_1; P_2$ also arises in ways similar to divergences: either from an infinite trace of P_1, or else from a trace of P_1 followed by an infinite trace of P_2:

$$\mathcal{I}[\![P_1; P_2]\!] \quad = \quad \mathcal{I}[\![P_1]\!] \cup \{tr \frown u \mid (tr \frown \langle\checkmark\rangle, \{\}) \in \mathcal{F}[\![P_1]\!] \wedge u \in \mathcal{I}[\![P_2]\!]\}$$

The same laws for sequential composition are valid in the FDI model as in the stable failures model (see Figure 4.14).

Interrupt

The process $P_1 \triangle P_2$ executes as P_1, but at any stage before termination (or divergence) it can begin executing as P_2. Its failures will be given by these behaviours together with those included from divergence.

$$\begin{aligned}
\mathcal{F}[\![P_1 \triangle P_2]\!] \quad = \quad & \{(tr, X) \mid (tr, X) \in \mathcal{F}[\![P_1]\!] \wedge \\
& \qquad\qquad\quad (\checkmark \in \sigma(tr) \vee (\langle\rangle, X) \in \mathcal{F}[\![P_2]\!])\} \\
& \cup \{(tr_1 \frown tr_2, X) \mid (tr_1, \{\}) \in \mathcal{F}[\![P_1]\!] \wedge \checkmark \notin \sigma(tr_1) \\
& \qquad\qquad\qquad\qquad \wedge (tr_2, X) \in \mathcal{F}[\![P_2]\!] \\
& \cup \{(tr, X) \mid tr \subset \mathcal{D}[\![P_1 \triangle P_2]\!]\}
\end{aligned}$$

The divergences are either divergences of P_1, or else traces of P_1 followed by divergences of P_2:

$$\mathcal{D}\,[\![P_1 \,\triangle\, P_2]\!] \;\;=\;\; \mathcal{D}\,[\![P_1]\!] \cup \{tr_1 \,^\frown\, tr_2 \mid (\, tr_1, \{\}) \in \mathcal{F}\,[\![P_1]\!]$$
$$\wedge \,\checkmark \notin \sigma(tr_1)$$
$$\wedge \, tr_2 \in \mathcal{D}\,[\![P_2]\!]\}$$

Similarly, the infinite traces are either infinite traces of P_1, or else finite non-terminating traces of P_1 followed by infinite traces of P_2:

$$\mathcal{I}\,[\![P_1 \,\triangle\, P_2]\!] \;\;=\;\; \mathcal{I}\,[\![P_1]\!] \cup \{tr_1 \,^\frown\, tr_2 \mid (tr_1, \{\}) \in \mathcal{F}\,[\![P_1]\!]$$
$$\wedge \,\checkmark \notin \sigma(tr)$$
$$\wedge \, tr_2 \in \mathcal{I}\,[\![P_2]\!]\}$$

All of the laws concerning the interrupt operator that are presented in Figure 4.15 are also true in the FDI model.

8.3 RECURSION

The understanding of recursion in the FDI model requires the same operational treatment of recursion as given for the stable failures model in Chapter 6: that recursions unwind via an internal τ event.

The failures, divergences, and infinite traces associated with recursively defined process expressions $N = P$ can be obtained directly from the operational semantics, or alternatively by using the denotational semantics. Both of these approaches give the same result.

A recursive definition $N = P$ defines the process N in terms of a process description which may itself contain instances of N. The FDI model provides guarantees that any recursive definition equation has a solution. It also provides a way of determining the failures, divergences, and infinite traces of the appropriate solution.

The FDI model is concerned with the guarantees that can be made regarding process behaviour. This means that the more possible behaviours a process has associated with it, the less can be guaranteed about it in any particular context. The process DIV has the most possible behaviours of any process, and as a result nothing can be guaranteed about how it will execute. More generally, any process of the form $P_1 \sqcap P_2$ will have more behaviours than P_1 alone, and so less can be guaranteed about how it will execute.

As in the traces model, the refinement ordering $(F_1, D_1, I_1) \sqsubseteq_{FDI} (F_2, D_2, I_2)$ between processes holds when the second process has fewer possible behaviours than the first.

$$(F_1, D_1, I_1) \sqsubseteq_{FDI} (F_2, D_2, I_2) \;\;\Leftrightarrow\;\; F_2 \subseteq F_1 \wedge D_2 \subseteq D_1 \wedge I_2 \subseteq I_1$$

The subscript *FDI* signifies that the relationship is defined on the FDI model.

Refinement holds between two process expressions P_1 and P_2 whenever it holds between their sets of failures, divergences, and infinite traces. Another way of characterizing the relationship $P_1 \sqsubseteq_{FDI} P_2$ is as $P_1 =_{FDI} P_1 \sqcap P_2$. The introduction of the behaviours of P_2 does not introduce any new behaviours to P_1. The subscript *FDI* will be elided if it is clear from the context.

In the FDI model, refinement amounts to reducing nondeterminism in processes. The minimal process with respect to this ordering, refined by all other processes, is *DIV*. The maximal processes in the refinement ordering will be the deterministic processes: no deterministic process can be further refined. Unlike the traces model and the stable failures model, there is no single maximal process.

Any recursive CSP equation $N = P$ will have a least fixed point: a solution which is refined by any other solutions that might exist. The least solution provides the fewest guarantees, and all guarantees that it does provide are also true for any of the other solutions. It is appropriate to use the least solution of $N = P$ as the semantics of N, since the only observations that can be guaranteed of N will be those that follow from the fact that it is a solution of the equation $N = P$. In contrast to the approaches taken in the traces and stable failures model, approximation in the FDI model begins with as many behaviours as possible, and only excludes those behaviours whose absence is guaranteed by unfolding the recursive definition.

Example 8.3.1 The recursive equation $N = N \Box a \to STOP$ has many fixed points in the FDI model, including $a \to STOP$, $a \to STOP \Box b \to STOP$, and *DIV*. The least of these in the FDI model is *DIV*, and so this will be the semantics of the process defined by the recursive equation. The equation does not exclude the possibility of initial divergence, so that possibility must be allowed, resulting in no guarantees at all concerning useful behaviour. The possibility of divergence leads to its semantics being different to its stable failures semantics given in Example 6.3.1. ∎

The process P with free variable N corresponds to a function $F(Y) = P[Y/N]$, and successive applications of the function F will give rise to approximations to the fixed point. The first approximation is the weakest process of all, *DIV*, and successive approximations are $F^n(DIV)$ for $n \in \mathbb{N}$. Each of these will be refined by any fixed point, since if $N = F(N)$, then

- $DIV \sqsubseteq_{FDI} N$; and

- if $F^n(DIV) \sqsubseteq_{FDI} N$ then $F(F^n(DIV)) \sqsubseteq_{FDI} F(N) = N$ because all of the CSP operators comprising F are monotonic with respect to the refinement order $\sqsubseteq$.

If the function F does not introduce any infinite nondeterminism—in other words P does not contain any infinite internal choice, infinite hiding, or infinite-to-one renaming—then the sequence of approximations $\langle F^n(DIV) \rangle_{n \in \mathbb{N}}$ will define the fixed point, which will consist of those failures, divergences, and infinite traces that are in the behaviours of all elements of the sequence. The fixed point will then be given by the triple:

$$(\bigcap_{n \in \mathbb{N}} \mathcal{T} [\![F^n(DIV)]\!], \bigcap_{n \in \mathbb{N}} \mathcal{D} [\![F^n(DIV)]\!], \bigcap_{n \in \mathbb{N}} \mathcal{I} [\![F^n(DIV)]\!])$$

This process must refine all of the approximations, since it is contained in each of them. Furthermore, any other process which refines all of the approximations will also refine this process, which is therefore the least fixed point of F: it will be refined by any other fixed point of F.

Example 8.3.2 The process $N = STOP \sqcap a \to N$ is the fixed point of the function $F(Y) = STOP \sqcap a \to Y$. For any n, the semantics of $F^{n+1}(DIV)$ can be calculated from the semantics of $F^n(DIV)$, resulting in

$$
\begin{aligned}
\mathcal{F}\llbracket F^n(DIV) \rrbracket &= \{ (\langle a \rangle^i, X) \mid i < n \wedge X \subseteq \Sigma^{\checkmark} \} \\
&\quad \cup \{ (\langle a \rangle^n \frown tr, X) \mid tr \in TRACE \wedge X \subseteq \Sigma^{\checkmark} \} \\
\mathcal{D}\llbracket F^n(DIV) \rrbracket &= \{ \langle a \rangle^n \frown tr \mid tr \in TRACE \} \\
\mathcal{I}\llbracket F^n(DIV) \rrbracket &= \{ \langle a \rangle^n \frown u \mid u \in ITRACE \}
\end{aligned}
$$

The only behaviours that are in all of the corresponding sets are those that have only a's in their traces. There is no trace that appears in all of the divergence sets, and the only trace that appears in all the infinite trace sets is the trace $\langle a \rangle^{\omega}$. The intersections of the three components reduces to

$$
\begin{aligned}
\mathcal{F}\llbracket N \rrbracket &= \{ (\langle a \rangle^i, X) \mid i \in \mathbb{N} \wedge X \subseteq \Sigma^{\checkmark} \} \\
\mathcal{D}\llbracket N \rrbracket &= \{\} \\
\mathcal{I}\llbracket N \rrbracket &= \{ \langle a \rangle^{\omega} \}
\end{aligned}
$$

which is in accordance with the behaviours predicted from the operational semantics.

In fact, the function F has two fixed points:

$$
(\{ (\langle a \rangle^n, X) \mid n \in \mathbb{N} \wedge X \subseteq \Sigma^{\checkmark} \}, \{\}, \{\})
$$

and

$$
(\{ (\langle a \rangle^n, X) \mid n \in \mathbb{N} \wedge X \subseteq \Sigma^{\checkmark} \}, \{\}, \langle a \rangle^{\omega})
$$

Both processes have the same failures: any finite sequence of a's is possible, and any refusal is also possible at any stage. However, one of the fixed points has an infinite sequence of a's possible, whereas the other one does not. If nothing is known about N other than the fact that it satisfies the equation above, then it is inappropriate to exclude the infinite trace, since its absence cannot be guaranteed. The appropriate semantics for N defined by the recursive definition $N = STOP \sqcap a \to N$ will be the second process, with the infinite trace, as calculated. ∎

Example 8.3.3 The unguarded process $N = N \,\square\, a \to STOP$ corresponds to the function $F(Y) = Y \,\square\, a \to STOP$. Since the possibility of divergence is preserved by external choice, it follows from the semantics of the external choice operator that $F(DIV)$ has the same semantics as DIV. This means that the entire sequence $\langle F^n(DIV)\rangle_{n\in\mathbb{N}}$ is simply $\langle DIV\rangle_{n\in\mathbb{N}}$, so the limit of this sequence is DIV. Hence $N = DIV$, as predicted by the operational semantics. ∎

If the function F does contain infinite nondeterminism, then some further work may be required, as the intersection of the approximations might not give the fixed point. If F is guarded, then the intersection will at least give the finite behaviours of the fixed point: the failures and divergences. However, it may be too pessimistic on the infinite traces and further approximations may be required. Hence if $N = F(N)$ for guarded F, then the FDI semantics of N satisfy

$$
\begin{aligned}
\mathcal{F}\llbracket N\rrbracket &= \bigcap_{n\in\mathbb{N}} \mathcal{F}\llbracket F^n(DIV)\rrbracket \\
\mathcal{D}\llbracket N\rrbracket &= \bigcap_{n\in\mathbb{N}} \mathcal{D}\llbracket F^n(DIV)\rrbracket \\
\mathcal{I}\llbracket N\rrbracket &\subseteq \bigcap_{n\in\mathbb{N}} \mathcal{I}\llbracket F^n(DIV)\rrbracket
\end{aligned}
$$

Example 8.3.4 The process N defined by

$$
\begin{aligned}
N &= (STOP \sqcap a \to N) \parallel A \\
A &= \bigsqcap_{n\in\mathbb{N}} A(n) \\
A(0) &= STOP \\
A(n+1) &= a \to A(n)
\end{aligned}
$$

is prevented from performing any infinite sequence of a's, though it can perform any arbitrarily long finite sequence of them. Each of the approximations $F^n(DIV)$ has the same behaviours as the approximations in Example 8.3.2:

$$
\begin{aligned}
\mathcal{F}\llbracket F^n(DIV)\rrbracket &= \{(\langle a\rangle^i, X) \mid i < n \wedge X \subseteq \Sigma^\checkmark\} \\
&\quad \cup \{(\langle a\rangle^n \frown tr, X) \mid tr \in TRACE \wedge X \subseteq \Sigma^\checkmark\} \\
\mathcal{D}\llbracket F^n(DIV)\rrbracket &= \{\langle a\rangle^n \frown tr \mid tr \in TRACE\} \\
\mathcal{I}\llbracket F^n(DIV)\rrbracket &= \{\langle a\rangle^n \frown u \mid u \in ITRACE\}
\end{aligned}
$$

and so the intersection of all the approximations will contain $\langle a\rangle^n$ as an infinite trace. The intersection is in a sense the ωth approximation to the fixed point, and will be denoted $F^\omega(DIV)$. In each approximation $F^n(DIV)$ the infinite trace $\langle a\rangle^\omega$ arises as a result of the divergence $\langle a\rangle^n$.

$$
\begin{aligned}
\mathcal{F}\llbracket F^\omega(DIV)\rrbracket &= \{(\langle a\rangle^i, X) \mid i \in \mathbb{N} \wedge X \subseteq \Sigma^\checkmark\} \\
\mathcal{D}\llbracket F^\omega(DIV)\rrbracket &= \{\} \\
\mathcal{I}\llbracket F^\omega(DIV)\rrbracket &= \{\langle a\rangle^\omega\}
\end{aligned}
$$

The limit process has no divergences, and so one further application of F will remove the infinite trace and result in the fixed point (which also happens to be the semantics of the process A).

$$
\begin{aligned}
\mathcal{F}\,[\![N]\!] &= \{(\langle a\rangle^i, X) \mid i \in \mathbb{N} \land X \subseteq \Sigma^\checkmark\} \\
\mathcal{D}\,[\![N]\!] &= \{\} \\
\mathcal{I}\,[\![N]\!] &= \{\}
\end{aligned}
$$

The function F is guarded, and so the sets $\mathcal{F}\,[\![N]\!]$ and $\mathcal{D}\,[\![N]\!]$ must be reached by the ωth approximation, as the intersection of the finite approximations: $\mathcal{F}\,[\![N]\!] = \mathcal{F}\,[\![F^\omega(DIV)]\!]$ and $\mathcal{D}\,[\![N]\!] = \mathcal{D}\,[\![F^\omega(DIV)]\!]$. Only the infinite traces may require more than ω iterations, but even they must eventually be reached. ∎

If a function F is not guarded, then the number of approximations required to determine the failures and divergences of the fixed point may be more than ω (see Exercise 8.12).

Law **recursion-unwinding** will hold for any recursive definition $N = P$. However, the law **UFP** does not hold in general, since even guarded recursive definitions can admit more than one fixed point. For example, the (guarded) function $F(Y) = STOP \sqcap a \to Y$ has both the least fixed point calculated in Example 8.3.2, and the process A of Example 8.3.4 as solutions to the equation $F(Y) = Y$. However, all solutions to any guarded equation must have the same failures and divergences.

A more restricted unique fixed point law holds in the FDI model. The infinite traces of finitely nondeterministic processes are determined completely by their failures and divergences. This means that if $F(P_1) = P_1$ and $F(P_2) = P_2$ where P_1 and P_2 are finitely nondeterministic, and F is guarded, they must have exactly the same behaviours: $P_1 =_{FDI} P_2$. The second law for recursion in the FDI model can now be given:

$(P_1$ finitely nondeterministic $\land\ P_2$ finitely nondeterministic

$\land\ F$ event guarded $\land\ (F(P_1) =_{FDI} P_1) \land (F(P_2) =_{FDI} P_2))$

$$\Rightarrow P_1 =_{FDI} P_2 \qquad\qquad \langle \mathsf{UFP}_{FDI}\rangle$$

In particular, if a guarded F itself contains no infinite nondeterminism, then the recursively defined process $P_1 = F(P_1)$ will be finitely nondeterministic, and hence equivalent to any other such process P_2 for which $P_2 =_{FDI} F(P_2)$.

For example, the finite nondeterminism conditions hold for both N and M of Example 4.3.4, and hence for P defined below as well:

$$
\begin{aligned}
N &= F(N) &= (a \rightarrow N) \,\square\, b \rightarrow STOP \\
M &= a \rightarrow M \\
P &= M \,\triangle\, (b \rightarrow STOP)
\end{aligned}
$$

and $P =_{FDI} F(P)$, so it follows that $N =_{FDI} P$.

Mutual recursion

Mutual recursion generalizes single recursion in the same way as in the models already introduced. The operational transition rule is adjusted in a similar way, modelling the recursive unwinding of any process variable N_i as accompanied by an internal transition. As with the case for single recursion, exactly the same results concerning the traces model remain valid if this transition rule is used instead.

$$
\frac{\rule{3cm}{0.4pt}}{N_i \overset{\tau}{\rightarrow} P_i} \quad [\,\underline{N} = \underline{P}\,]
$$

The failures, divergences, and infinite traces associated with all of the N_i processes will be those that are predicted by the operational semantics. They will give the most nondeterministic processes that satisfy the set of defining equations—the ones with the most failures, divergences, and infinite traces. The theory of CSP guarantees that such processes must exist for any set of recursive CSP definitions.

The results concerning single recursion carry over to the more general case:

- If all of the recursive calls are event guarded, and none of the recursive definitions contains any infinite nondeterminism, then the semantics of the N_i are the intersections of the semantics of the chain of approximations, starting from DIV. Each N_i is defined by a function $F_i(\underline{N})$. If the jth approximation to N_i is written as N_i^j, then each $N_i^0 = DIV$, and each $N_i^{j+1} = F_i(N^j)$, where N^j is the vector of all of the jth approximations. Each approximation N_i^j is associated with failures $\mathcal{F}\,[\![N_i^j]\!]$, divergences $\mathcal{D}\,[\![N_i^j]\!]$, and infinite traces $\mathcal{I}\,[\![N_i^j]\!]$. The limit N_i will have failures, divergences, and infinite traces given by

$$
\begin{aligned}
\mathcal{F}\,[\![N_i]\!] &= \bigcap_{j \in \mathbb{N}} \mathcal{F}\,[\![N_i^j]\!] \\
\mathcal{D}\,[\![N_i]\!] &= \bigcap_{j \in \mathbb{N}} \mathcal{D}\,[\![N_i^j]\!] \\
\mathcal{I}\,[\![N_i]\!] &= \bigcap_{j \in \mathbb{N}} \mathcal{I}\,[\![N_i^j]\!]
\end{aligned}
$$

- If all of the recursive calls are event guarded, then the finite behaviours—the failures and divergences—will be given even if infinite nondeterminism is present:

$$\mathcal{F}\,\llbracket N_i \rrbracket \;=\; \bigcap_{j \in \mathbb{N}} \mathcal{F}\,\llbracket N_i^j \rrbracket$$
$$\mathcal{D}\,\llbracket N_i \rrbracket \;=\; \bigcap_{j \in \mathbb{N}} \mathcal{D}\,\llbracket N_i^j \rrbracket$$

However, the infinite traces may not be accurate, though they will be contained in the intersection of those of the finite approximations:

$$\mathcal{I}\,\llbracket N_i \rrbracket \;\subseteq\; \bigcap_{j \in \mathbb{N}} \mathcal{I}\,\llbracket N_i^j \rrbracket$$

Law **recursion-unwinding** will hold for any family of mutually recursive definitions. Whenever $N_i = P_i$ appears as a recursive definition, then $N_i =_{FDI} P_i$.

Law **UFP**$_{FDI}$ also generalizes to mutual recursion. In a mutually recursive definition $\underline{N} = \underline{P}$, a process variable N_i is recursive if it appears in any of the P_j. If each process definition P_i associated with any recursive N_i is event guarded in all of the process variables that appear in it, then the recursive definition is event guarded. If two families $\underline{P}$ and $\underline{P}'$ of finitely nondeterministic processes both satisfy the same guarded recursive equation, then they must be equivalent:

$$
\begin{array}{ll}
(\underline{P} \text{ finitely nondeterministic and } \underline{P}' \text{ finitely nondeterministic} & \\
\quad \wedge\ \underline{F} \text{ event guarded} \wedge (\underline{F}(\underline{P}) =_{FDI} \underline{P}) \wedge (\underline{F}(\underline{P}') =_{FDI} \underline{P}')) & \\
\qquad\qquad\qquad\qquad\qquad\qquad \Rightarrow \underline{P} =_{FDI} \underline{P}' & \langle \text{UFP}_{FDI} \rangle
\end{array}
$$

8.4   SPECIFICATION AND VERIFICATION

Property-oriented specification

The inclusion of refusal, divergence, and infinite trace information in the FDI model allows a wider range of specification to be presented than was possible in the traces model or the stable failures model. Since there are three sets of behaviours associated with any process, the most general form of specification will consist of three parts which each describe the required property of observations from the corresponding behaviour set. A specification S can be written as a triple $(S_F(tr, X), S_D(tr), S_I(u))$.

$$
\begin{array}{rl}
P \text{ sat } (S_F(tr, X), S_D(tr), S_I(u)) \;=\; & \forall (tr, X) \in \mathcal{F}\,\llbracket P \rrbracket \bullet S_F(tr, X) \\
& \wedge\ \forall\, tr \in \mathcal{D}\,\llbracket P \rrbracket \bullet S_D(tr) \\
& \wedge\ \forall\, u \in \mathcal{I}\,\llbracket P \rrbracket \bullet S_I(u)
\end{array}
$$

The most basic form of liveness is divergence-freedom, which requires that at any stage of an execution the process should at least eventually reach a stable state. The appropriate specification $S_D(tr)$ on the divergence set of a process states simply that no divergence should occur. This is captured by requiring that $S_D(tr)$ should be false for any trace tr. Divergence-freedom is then the specification

$$\text{divergence-free} \quad = \quad (true(tr, X), false(tr), true(u))$$

It is satisfied by any process which has no divergences, and by no process that can diverge at any stage. The most nondeterministic process which satisfies it is *CHAOS*.

Example 8.4.1 A buffer $B(N)$ of size N is guaranteed not to diverge provided it is not overloaded. It provides no guarantees about its behaviour if it is ever supplied with more than N pieces of data. In this case, the specification $S_D(tr)$ that it meets will be

$$S_D(tr) \quad = \quad \exists\, tr' \leqslant tr \bullet tr' \downarrow in > tr' \downarrow out + N$$

This states that any divergence tr must begin with a sequence tr' witnessing the fact that too many inputs occurred. In order to guarantee divergence-freedom of a system which contains such a component, the rest of the system will have to ensure that the buffer is never asked to carry more items than its capacity N.

Divergence here is associated with a limitation on the capabilities of the component. A manufacturer would be unlikely to provide a component which is sure to diverge when its capacity is exceeded. It is more likely that the manufacturer simply makes no claims about the component in this case. For example, a bridge with a weight limit of 44 tonnes does not claim to support a heavier load: any weight which does collapse the bridge should be heavier than 44 tonnes. ∎

Example 8.4.2 (Deadlock-freedom) Deadlock-freedom is captured by the specification

$$\text{strong deadlock-free}(tr, X) \quad = \quad X \neq \Sigma^{\checkmark}$$

Whatever trace has already occurred, the process cannot refuse the entire set of events $\Sigma^{\checkmark}$. A deadlock-free process must therefore be divergence-free, since all events could be refused on divergence.

A weaker form of deadlock-freedom, which allows the possibility of termination, is expressed as

$$\text{deadlock-free}(tr, X) \quad = \quad \checkmark \notin \sigma(tr) \Rightarrow X \neq \Sigma^{\checkmark}$$

Deadlock-freedom for a process P can be established in the stable failures model provided P can also be shown to be divergence-free in the FDI model, since in that case $\mathcal{SF}[\![P]\!] = \mathcal{F}[\![P]\!]$.

It also follows that if a divergence-free process P **sat** strong deadlock-free(tr, X) in the stable failures model, then this must also be true in the FDI model. ∎

The relationship between the traces model and the FDI model, on divergence-free processes, means that results concerning safety obtained using the traces model can be imported into the FDI model. If $S_T(tr)$ is a predicate on traces, then a corresponding predicate on failures can be defined to hold whenever S_T holds on the trace component: $S_F(tr, X) \Leftrightarrow S_T(tr)$. If P is known to be divergence-free, then the traces model can be used to verify any safety specification, and the result can be imported into the FDI model, since the semantics in the two models give the same traces. In particular, if P **sat** divergence-free, then

$$P \text{ sat } S_T(tr) \quad \Rightarrow \quad P \text{ sat } (S_F(tr, X), false(tr), true(u))$$

This allows reasoning from the traces model and the FDI model to be combined within a single system's analysis.

Example 8.4.3 (Buffers) As well as respecting the order on messages passing through the system, and offering to receive input and provide output as appropriate, a buffer should also be divergence-free. This means that the specification of a buffer in the FDI model combines the trace specification and the stable failures specification into a requirement on the FDI failures:

$$
\begin{aligned}
Buff_F(tr, X) \quad = \quad & tr \Downarrow out \leqslant tr \Downarrow in \\
& \wedge \; tr \Downarrow out = tr \Downarrow in \Rightarrow in.T \cap X = \{\} \\
& \wedge \; tr \Downarrow out < tr \Downarrow in \Rightarrow out.T \nsubseteq X
\end{aligned}
$$

The restriction on traces and failures means that any process satisfying this predicate cannot diverge, since any divergence will give rise to failures which violate the specification. ∎

Specifications on infinite traces will often be concerned with some kind of progress requirement or fairness constraint. For example, any infinite sequence of tosses of a fair coin should contain infinitely many heads and infinitely many tails:

$$u \downarrow heads = \infty \wedge u \downarrow tails = \infty$$

All finite sequences of heads and tails will be permitted in the failures of a process representing such a coin, but the infinite traces will be constrained. Stronger requirements can also be expressed, such as the expectation that the proportion of heads will approach 0.5 as the length of the trace increases:

$$S_I(u) \quad = \quad \lim_{n \to \infty} (((u \upharpoonright n) \downarrow heads)/n) = 0.5$$

Example 8.4.4 Resource allocation by a scheduler is often subject to fairness requirements with regard to its servicing of requests from various processes. If a request of process i is represented by an event req_i, and an allocation to process i is represented by $alloc_i$, then one possible requirement is that no request should be ignored for ever. This may be captured as the specification

$$S_I(u) \quad = \quad \forall i \bullet (u \downarrow req_i = \infty \Rightarrow u \downarrow alloc_i = \infty)$$

In order to ensure that processes are not prevented from making their request by another process starving them out with an infinite sequence of resource allocations, it might be appropriate to ensure that the req_i events are entirely under the control of the processes themselves and so cannot be blocked by the scheduler or other processes.   ∎

Example 8.4.5 A communications medium which can sometimes lose messages might be used as the basis for a link between two peers that wish to communicate reliably. They will be able to do this provided the medium can guarantee some form of progress, namely that it can never lose an infinite sequence of messages, and must eventually provide output if a message is input sufficiently often.

The possibility of messages being lost, but not duplicated or reordered, is captured by the trace specification $tr \Downarrow out \preccurlyeq tr \Downarrow in$: the sequence of output messages must be a subsequence of the input messages, so everything that is output was previously input. However, not all inputs are guaranteed to be successfully transmitted.

Liveness might be captured as deadlock-freedom: the medium must always be ready to input or output.

The progress property is then described as

$$S_I(u) \quad = \quad u \downarrow in = \infty \Rightarrow u \downarrow out = \infty$$

Any infinite traces of a process must be consistent with the finite traces, which meet the safety property, so it is not necessary to specify that the outputs of the infinite sequence must be a subsequence of the inputs. This follows from the corresponding property on the finite traces.   ∎

Admissible specifications

The infinite traces of a process must be consistent with its finite ones, as described by property $I1$. If a process is required to meet a progress or fairness condition, then its infinite traces must be examined and checked against the specification $S_I(u)$. However, specifications are often expressed only in terms of their failures, and no constraints are placed explicitly on the infinite traces except those required by consistency with the constrained finite behaviours. For example, deadlock-freedom is concerned with refusal information after finite traces, and buffer specifications are concerned with maintaining the order between inputs and outputs, and with liveness at finite stages of the execution. Such specifications are easier to check, since they are dependent only on the finite behaviours of processes, and these are often more straightforward to calculate and reason about. They are known as *admissible* specifications, and are equivalent to specifications of the form $(S_F(tr, X), S_D(tr), true(u))$.

Verification

The semantic equations associated with the CSP operators can support a number of proof rules for reasoning about CSP process descriptions, but in practice the most common form of specification is concerned with divergence-freedom. Once this is established, the stable failures model can be used to analyse the requirements on the failures of the process. This section will be concerned with conditions for establishing divergence-freedom of process descriptions.

Processes can be shown to be divergence-free by calculating their semantics directly, in particular their set of divergences. However, there are some common techniques for making sure that divergence is not introduced at any stage of a process description, resulting in a process that is divergence-free by construction.

The only operators that can introduce divergence into a process description are *DIV*, the hiding operator, and recursion. All of the other operators preserve the property of 'divergence-freedom': if their components satisfy **divergence-free** then so too will their combination. These three operators will be considered in turn.

DIV

This process is divergent, and any use of it will introduce divergence into the process description. It is therefore best avoided when constructing divergence-free processes.

Hiding

If P **sat** **divergence-free**, then a divergence of the process $P \setminus A$ must arise from a trace u of P which ends in an infinite sequence of events from A. In order for $P \setminus A$ to satisfy **divergence-free** it is necessary to ensure that this possibility cannot arise.

This will be guaranteed if any trace $tr \setminus A$ of $P \setminus A$ is associated with some bound on the length that the original trace tr can be. This will ensure that $tr \setminus A$ cannot be generated from any infinite trace of P, and so there is no possibility of divergence. The bound associated with a trace $tr \setminus A$ will be given by a bounding function $\beta : TRACE \to \mathbb{N}$: P should satisfy the specification that the length of any of its traces tr must be no greater than the bound $\beta(tr \setminus A)$. This means that there is a bound on the length of all of the traces that could have given rise to $tr \setminus A$. If P is divergence-free, then this may be established in the traces model.

The rule is as follows:

$$\frac{P \text{ sat divergence-free} \\ P \text{ sat } \#tr \leqslant \beta(tr \setminus A)}{P \setminus A \text{ sat divergence-free}}$$

Example 8.4.6 Consider the process P given by $P = a \to b \to c \to P$ discussed in Example 7.2.1. The proof rule will be used to establish that $P \setminus \{b\}$ **sat divergence-free**.

The set $\{b\}$ is to be hidden, so it is necessary to find a bounding function. In fact, $\beta(tr') = 2 * \#tr'$ is such a function, in that P **sat** $\#tr \leqslant 2 * \#(tr \setminus \{b\})$—any trace of $P \setminus \{b\}$ of length n must have come from a trace of P of length no greater than $2n$.

The existence of the bounding function yields that $P \setminus \{b\}$ **sat** divergence-free. ∎

8.5 RECURSION INDUCTION

Recursive definitions have the potential to introduce divergent behaviours, so the possibility of divergence must be addressed within a verification of a recursive process.

If a recursive definition $N = F(N)$ is event guarded, and F preserves divergence-freedom, then N will be divergence-free.

$$\frac{\forall Y \bullet (Y \text{ sat divergence-free} \Rightarrow F(Y) \text{ sat divergence-free})}{N \text{ sat divergence-free}} \quad \begin{bmatrix} N = F(N) \\ F \text{ guarded} \end{bmatrix}$$

The event guard means that the unfolding of the recursive definition will not itself introduce a divergent loop. The antecedent that F preserves divergence-free means that F does not introduce any divergences itself. This is required to exclude functions such as

$$F(Y) = a \rightarrow (Y \,|||\, b \rightarrow DIV)$$

which is guarded but does not preserve divergence-free, since $F(STOP)$ has a divergent trace.

Example 8.5.1 The light switch process of Example 7.3.1 has a guarded recursive definition:

$$LIGHT = on \rightarrow off \rightarrow LIGHT$$

It can be seen to be divergence-free by observing that the function $F(Y) = on \rightarrow off \rightarrow Y$ is guarded, and that it does not introduce divergence since it contains only operators that do not introduce divergence. ∎

A more general recursion induction rule allows an explicit treatment of divergence. In this case there are no constraints on the form of the recursive function F, so in particular it need not be guarded. This rule instead requires that each recursive unfolding of F increases the length of any possible divergence. The fixed point of F thus cannot have any divergence of finite length.

Let $Spec_n = (true(tr, X), \#tr \geqslant n, true(u))$: this specification requires that any divergence is of length at least n.

The $Spec_n$ specifications are progressively stronger as n increases, with a limit of divergence-free. In order to check if a process meets a specification $Spec_n$, only those behaviours with traces of length less than n need be considered. So any process will meet any $Spec_0$.

$$\frac{\forall\, n, Y \bullet (Y \text{ sat } Spec_n \Rightarrow F(Y) \text{ sat } Spec_{n+1})}{N \text{ sat divergence-free}} \quad [\, N = F(N) \,]$$

If recursive calls allow the approximations $Spec_n$ to get closer to **divergence-free**, then in the limit the specification **divergence-free** will itself be met by the recursive process.

In order to establish the antecedent, more general proof rules would be required than those given in this section, since there is also a need to consider divergences explicitly. This may be done by a direct appeal to the semantics of the CSP function F, or alternatively by developing from the semantics a more detailed collection of rules that handle more general specifications on divergence.

Example 8.5.2 The definition of a buffer whose capacity expands as it accepts messages is given as follows:

$$EXPBUFF \quad = \quad in?x : T \to ((out!x \to EXPBUFF) \gg COPY)$$

Each time an input is provided, a fresh buffer *COPY* is spawned and added to the chain, and the input value is passed to it. The definition of the body of the recursion $F(Y) = in?x : T \to ((out!x \to Y) \gg COPY)$ is not guarded, since there is an implicit hiding operator within the chaining operator. However, divergence-freedom can be proved by the recursion induction rule for divergence-freedom.

Let tr be a divergence of Y of length at least n giving rise to a divergence $\langle in.v \rangle \frown tr'$ of $F(Y)$. Then $\langle out.x \rangle \frown tr$ is a divergence of $out!x \to Y$, and there is some trace tr'' of *COPY* whose inputs match the outputs of $\langle out.x \rangle \frown tr$: $tr'' \Downarrow in = (\langle out.x \rangle \frown tr) \Downarrow out$. Recall that

$$COPY \quad \textbf{sat} \quad tr \Downarrow out \leqslant_1 tr \Downarrow in$$

so $tr'' \downarrow out.T \geqslant tr'' \downarrow in.T - 1$.

The events in tr' will be the inputs of tr and the outputs of tr''. So

$$
\begin{aligned}
\#tr' \quad &= \quad tr \downarrow in.T + tr'' \downarrow out.T \\
&\geqslant \quad tr \downarrow in.T + (tr'' \downarrow in.T - 1) \\
&= \quad tr \downarrow in.T + (((\langle out.x \rangle \frown tr) \downarrow out.T - 1) \\
&= \quad tr \downarrow in.T + tr \downarrow out.T \\
&= \quad \#tr \\
&\geqslant \quad n
\end{aligned}
$$

and so $\#\langle in.v \rangle \frown tr' \geqslant n+1$. Thus the antecedent to the inference rule is true. If all divergences of Y are of length at least n, then those of $F(Y)$ are of length at least $n+1$. Applying a recursive call increases the length of a divergent trace, and so the rule allows the deduction that the process cannot diverge.   ■

Process-oriented specification

As well as its use in identifying fixed points, the refinement relation $P_1 \sqsubseteq_{FDI} P_2$ supports a process-oriented approach to specification, similar to that taken in the traces model and stable failures model. A specification describes behaviours that are acceptable in a particular situation, and these behaviours can be described either by use of predicates, or else by means of a CSP process expression itself. A process description *SPEC* will have particular failures, divergences, and infinite traces associated with it, and these are taken to be all the acceptable behaviours. An implementation process *IMP* meets this specification if all of its possible behaviours are allowed by *SPEC*, or in other words, if $SPEC \sqsubseteq_{FDI} IMP$.

The specification is the most nondeterministic process which meets the requirement. This means that *SPEC* should allow all possibilities that are not expressly forbidden.

The specification for divergence-freedom is *CHAOS*: any non-divergent behaviour is permitted, but *CHAOS* does not admit any divergences.

The FDR tool allows processes to be checked against process-oriented specifications with regard to their failures and divergences. The behaviour sets associated with finite state processes are closed, since no such processes can have any infinite nondeterminism, so the infinite traces do not need to be checked separately: if the failures and divergences are all acceptable, then the infinite traces must also be.

Example 8.5.3 (Alternating bit protocol) The alternating bit protocol of Example 7.3.2 was verified with regard to its traces and stable failures. It remains to establish divergence-freedom.

Since the medium is not itself described as a CSP process, further properties need to be described in the FDI model in order to establish divergence-freedom. Firstly, that the medium is itself divergence-free. Secondly, a fairness assumption is required to ensure that the medium does not simply lose messages for ever. These assumptions cannot be expressed in the stable failures model.

$$Med_I(in, out)(u) \quad = \quad \#(u \Downarrow in) = \infty \Rightarrow \#(u \Downarrow out) = \infty$$
$$Med_D(in, out)(tr) \quad = \quad false$$

The predicate on infinite traces requires that enough messages pass through the medium: if infinitely many have been input, then infinitely many must be output. The requirement that there are no divergences is a consequence of the other requirements: if some divergence is possible, then the other requirements would be violated by the arbitrary behaviours following divergence.

The system can then be shown to be divergence-free. The components themselves are individually divergence-free, and the internalizing of the communications over the channels does not introduce divergence. If there were some infinite sequence u of internal actions on the c and d channels without any inputs or outputs, then u would have to contain an infinite sequence of transmissions along channel c_1, since the other channels can only see as many messages as c_1. This would have to end with an infinite sequence of the same message

$x.b$, since they all arise from the state $S(b, x)$. Hence by Med_I and Med_F there would be an infinite number of occurrences of $x.b$ on channel c_2, and infinitely many acknowledgements b sent along d_1, and so infinitely many acknowledgements b received along d_2. But this is impossible, since receipt of b in state $S(b, x)$ means that S becomes ready for the next input, and does not engage in any further internal activity until this arrives.

This permits the conclusion that the alternating bit protocol is divergence-free, and hence that it is a buffer. ∎

8.6   CASE STUDY: DISTRIBUTED SUM

The final property required of the distributed summing network *DISTSUM* is divergence-freedom.

The effect of abstracting the internal channels must be considered.

$$DISTSUM \quad = \quad NETWORK \setminus \{c_{ij} \mid (i,j) \in E\}$$

If *NETWORK* can be shown to be divergence-free, and a bound on the length of its traces can be found, then it follows that *DISTSUM* is divergence-free.

All the recursive definitions for the family of processes *TOT* are guarded, and none of the definitions uses either *DIV* or the hiding operator, so all the *TOT* processes are divergence-free. This means that all of the *NODE*(i) processes are divergence-free, since they are composed of divergence-free processes, and hence that *NETWORK* is divergence-free, being a parallel combination of divergence-free processes.

There is also a bound on the number of communications each node can be involved in. It will communicate on each channel at most once, and can terminate at most once.

$$N2_i \qquad NODE(i) \text{ sat } \#tr \leqslant \# \text{ channels}(A_i) + 1$$

This may be established in the traces model (see Exercise 5.16), and imported into the FDI model using the fact that each *NODE*(i) is divergence-free.

This places a bound on the length of a trace tr of *NETWORK* number of internal events that may occur. The property $N2$ on each node i identifies a bound on the length of the trace $tr \upharpoonright A_i^{\checkmark}$, and $tr = tr \upharpoonright (\bigcup_i A_i)^{\checkmark}$, so $\#tr \leqslant \Sigma_i(tr \downarrow A_i^{\checkmark}) \leqslant \Sigma_{i \in N}(2* \mid adj(i) \mid +1)$.

Hence an appropriate bounding function $\beta(tr)$ is simply the constant function $\beta(tr) = \Sigma_{i \in N}(2* \mid adj(i) \mid +1)$: no more than this number of internal events can ever occur. It follows that *DISTSUM* is divergence-free.

8.7   MUST TESTING AND FDI EQUIVALENCE

The FDI model is equivalent to another form of testing equivalence which can be defined directly on the operational semantics. In contrast to may testing, which was concerned with the *possibility* of a process passing a test, the form of testing appropriate for the FDI model is one which considers when processes are *guaranteed* to pass tests. This is known as *must testing*.

A process P is tested in the same way as described in Section 4.4: P is placed in parallel with a test T, and all of the events in Σ are hidden. Since this form of testing is concerned with the guarantees about a process's execution, only the maximal executions of $(P \parallel_\Sigma T) \setminus \Sigma$ are considered, to allow the process the opportunity to exhibit the desired behaviour.

The maximal executions are those sequences of states and transitions that cannot be extended, either because they reach a final state from which no further events are possible, or else because they consist of an infinite sequence of transitions. For example, the process

$$N \quad = \quad P = a \to N \,\square\, b \to c \to STOP$$

has $\langle N, \tau, P, a, N, \tau, P, b, (c \to STOP), c, STOP \rangle$ and $\langle N, \tau, P, a, N, \tau, P, a, N, \ldots \rangle$ as maximal executions. On the other hand, $\langle N, a, N, b, (c \to STOP) \rangle$ is not a maximal execution.

The process P passes a test T if *all* of the maximal executions of $(P \parallel_\Sigma T) \setminus \Sigma$ pass through some state in which a success event ω was possible. This is written P **must** T.

Two processes are considered to be equivalent if they must pass exactly the same tests:

$$P_1 \equiv_{must} P_2 \quad = \quad \forall T \bullet P_1 \text{ \bf must } T \Leftrightarrow P_2 \text{ \bf must } T$$

The requirement that only maximal executions are considered allows the identification of refusal behaviour, since a finite maximal execution must end in a deadlocked state. In such a state, any events not refused by the testing process must be refused by the process under test.

Must testing also allows the distinction of internal from external choice. For example, the two processes

$$P_1 \quad = \quad a \to STOP \,\square\, b \to STOP$$
$$P_2 \quad = \quad a \to STOP \,\sqcap\, b \to STOP$$

are distinguished by the test $T = b \to SUCCESS$. The first process P_1 must pass this test, since it is unable to refuse to synchronize on the initial b. The empty execution is not maximal for $(P_1 \parallel_\Sigma T) \setminus \Sigma$; its only maximal execution indeed passes through a success state. The other process P_2 might not pass the test, since one of its possibilities is to resolve the choice in favour of $a \to STOP$, resulting in a deadlock and the inability of the test to reach its success state.

The must approach to testing also results in the treatment of divergence as catastrophic, and the equivalence of all processes that might possibly diverge. If $N = (a \to N) \setminus \{a\}$, then the divergent process N is equivalent under must testing to a process P_3 which has the possibility of diverging among other possibilities:

$$P_3 \quad = \quad P_3 \,\square\, b \to STOP$$

If a test T is not initially in a success state, then the infinite execution

$$\langle (P_3 \underset{\Sigma}{\parallel} T) \setminus \Sigma, \ \tau, \ (P_3 \underset{\Sigma}{\parallel} T) \setminus \Sigma, \ \tau, \ (P_3 \underset{\Sigma}{\parallel} T) \setminus \Sigma, \ \ldots \rangle$$

is a maximal execution which does not take T through a success state. The possibility of divergence in P_3 ensures that P_3 does not always pass T, and so $P_3 \equiv_{must} N$. No guarantees can be provided about the behaviour of a process that might diverge.

This notion of testing equivalence turns out to correspond exactly to equivalence in the FDI model:

$$P_1 \equiv_{must} P_2 \quad \Leftrightarrow \quad (\mathcal{F}\,[\![P_1]\!], \mathcal{D}\,[\![P_1]\!], \mathcal{I}\,[\![P_1]\!]) = (\mathcal{F}\,[\![P_2]\!], \mathcal{D}\,[\![P_2]\!], \mathcal{I}\,[\![P_2]\!])$$

If two processes have different semantics in the FDI model, so there is some behaviour of one that is not a behaviour of the other, then a test can be constructed which distinguishes them; and conversely, if there is a test that distinguishes two processes, then there is some behaviour in the FDI semantics of one that is not in the semantics of the other (see Exercises 8.23 and 8.24). The FDI model is fully abstract with respect to must testing.

Must testing also gives rise to a natural notion of refinement:

$$P_1 \sqsubseteq_{must} P_2 \quad = \quad \forall T \bullet (P_1 \text{ must } T) \Rightarrow (P_2 \text{ must } T)$$

If the specification process P_1 provides some guarantees concerning its behaviour within a particular context, then any implementation of it P_2 must meet these guarantees.

Must testing refinement is equivalent to refinement in the FDI model:

$$P_1 \sqsubseteq_{must} P_2 \quad \Leftrightarrow \quad P_1 \sqsubseteq_{FDI} P_2$$

8.8   NOTES

The traces model for CSP was first introduced by Hoare in [46]. The failures model [13] refined the traces model with the introduction of failure observations, but it modelled divergence as allowing arbitrary failures. This approach is not altogether satisfactory for a number of technical reasons: some of the expected algebraic laws do not hold, and the semantics of recursive definitions are not always in accordance with the operational semantics. This was resolved by Brookes and Roscoe with the introduction of divergences, resulting in the failures-divergences model [14, 12, 100].

Brookes also provided the first *algebraic semantics* for CSP [12] , in which a set of algebraic laws on process terms are actually taken to define equivalence between processes. A more recent presentation of algebraic semantics for CSP can be found in [103]. This is also the primary semantic approach taken by the process algebra ACP [5].

Neither the failures model nor the failures-divergences model is able to model infinite nondeterminism, because the refusal sets essentially have to be finite in order to ensure that the model is a complete partial order, required for defining recursive processes. This limitation forces certain restrictions on the language of CSP: alphabet renaming has to be finite-to-one; hiding must be restricted to finite sets; and only finite nondeterministic choices are permitted. These restrictions were all enforced in [47] by the requirement that process alphabets should be finite. The FDI model [101] introduced the ability to model arbitrary nondeterminism with the introduction of infinite traces as additional observations. See [103] for an alternative presentation. The technical property $I2$ of that model is defined rigorously and discussed fully there and in [9]. A different fixed point theory, proposed by Roscoe [101] and refined by Barrett [6] (also presented in [79]), is needed for this model as the standard approaches are not applicable (see [101]).

The stable failures model for CSP [103] is a relatively recent development, arising from a collaboration between Jategoankar, Meyer and Roscoe. A similar model was presented by Valmari [118]. Rather than attempt to model divergence within a failures model, the insight behind the stable failures model is that divergence can often usefully be ignored.

The traces model and the stable failures model both form a complete lattice (and hence a complete partial order) under the subset order. In both cases all of the CSP operators are monotonic and continuous, with *STOP* as the bottom element of the traces model, and *DIV* as the bottom element of the stable failures model. This ensures that all recursive definitions have a least fixed point, which means that all recursive processes are well-defined. Furthermore, they each form a complete metric space with the distance function

$$d(P, P') \quad = \quad \inf\{2^{-n} \mid P \upharpoonright n = P' \upharpoonright n\}$$

where in the traces model $P \upharpoonright n = \{tr \in traces(P) \mid \#tr < n\}$ and in the stable failures model $P \upharpoonright n = \{(tr, X) \in \mathcal{SF} \, [\![P]\!] \mid \#tr < n\}$. In each case, the longer it takes to tell P from P', the closer together they are. In this metric space, all guarded CSP functions correspond to contraction mappings, and hence have a *unique* fixed point.

The FDI model also has the partial order structure and the same results hold for it. However, this structure is weaker than those of the other models, and so more effort is required to ensure that all the processes have the correct semantics. [21] provides an introduction to the lattices and partial order structures involved. Introductory material on metric spaces can

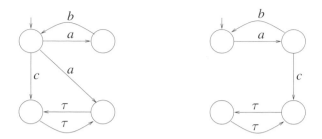

Fig. 8.3 *Two recursive processes*

be found in [115]. Appendix A of [103] also discusses both kinds of structures with particular emphasis on their use in CSP.

Note that the terminology of *CHAOS* follows the more recent treatment given in [103] and differs from [47]. In the latter book, *CHAOS* was the immediately divergent process (what we call *DIV*) and there was no special name for the most nondeterministic divergence-free process.

The distributed sum algorithm is due to [18]; it is a variant of Segall's Propagation of Information with Feedback protocol [112]. The first formal verification of the algorithm was given by Vaandrager [117]. Groote has also provided a formal verification [39].

Exercises

Exercise 8.1 What are the failures, divergences, and infinite traces associated with the finite state machines in Figure 8.3?

Exercise 8.2 What are the FDI semantics of:

1. $N_1 = (a \rightarrow N_1) \;\Box\; b \rightarrow STOP$

2. $N_2 = b \rightarrow a \rightarrow DIV$

3. $N_1 \parallel N_2$

4. $N_1 \underset{\{b\}}{\parallel} N_2$

5. $N_1 \;|||\; N_2$

6. $N_1 \setminus \{a\}$

7. $N_3 = (a \rightarrow (N_3; b \rightarrow SKIP) \;\Box\; c \rightarrow SKIP)$

8. $N_4 = (a \rightarrow N_4) \;\triangle\; b \rightarrow STOP$

9. $N_4 \setminus \{b\}$

10. $N_4 \setminus \{a\}$

Exercise 8.3 Does the law $\langle \Box\text{-}\sqcap\text{-}\mathbf{dist}\rangle$ on page 182 hold in the FDI model?

Exercise 8.4 Are the operational rules you gave in Exercises 6.7 and 6.8 for *DIV* and *CHAOS* consistent with their FDI semantics? If not, give rules which are consistent with both the stable failures and the FDI semantics.

Exercise 8.5

1. Give a deterministic process P for which $P \setminus A$ is nondeterministic.

2. Can a nondeterministic process P have that $P \setminus A$ is deterministic?

3. Give a process P for which $P \parallel P \neq_{FDI} P$.

4. Give a nondeterministic process P for which $P \parallel P =_{FDI} P$.

5. Give two nondeterministic processes P_1 and P_2 for which $P_1 \parallel\parallel P_2$ is deterministic.

6. If P is nondeterministic, can $P \parallel\parallel P$ be deterministic?

7. Find a deterministic P for which $P \parallel\parallel P$ is nondeterministic.

Exercise 8.6 Give operational rules for *DIV* and *CHAOS* which are consistent with their FDI semantics given in Section 8.2.

Exercise 8.7 Capture the following specifications in either the property-oriented or the process-oriented style of specification:

1. A process cannot diverge if it has accepted at least as many coins as it has dispensed chocolates.

2. A process can diverge only if it accepts three consecutive inputs without providing output.

3. A process will not diverge if all of its inputs are less that $2^{32} - 1$.

4. On average, no more than $\frac{1}{3}$ of messages should be lost.

5. Any infinite trace must contain an 'a' at some point.

6. Every request is eventually serviced.

7. Every execution eventually terminates.

Exercise 8.8 Find an *FMMR* process P such that $P \setminus A$ is not *FMMR*.

Exercise 8.9 Find an *FMMR* process P such that $f(P)$ is not *FMMR*.

Exercise 8.10 Which of the following variants of the process *EXPBUFF* of Example 8.5.2 are divergence-free?

$$
\begin{aligned}
EXPBUFF2 &= in?x : T \to (COPY \gg out!x \to EXPBUFF2) \\
EXPBUFF3 &= in?x : T \to (COPY \gg out!x \to EXPBUFF3 \gg COPY) \\
EXPBUFF4 &= COPY \gg (in?x : T \to out!x \to EXPBUFF4) \\
EXPBUFF5 &= in?x : T \to (out!x \to EXPBUFF5 \gg EXPBUFF5)
\end{aligned}
$$

Which of them can never refuse input?

Exercise 8.11 Which of the following processes are deterministic? Which are *FMMR*? Which are closed?

1. $BAG = in?x : T \to (BAG \ ||| \ out!x \to STOP)$

2. *DISTSUM* of page 163

3. *ABP* of Example 7.3.2

4. $INN = in?n \to A(n)$ where
$$
\begin{aligned}
A(0) &= b \to STOP \\
A(n+1) &= a \to A(n)
\end{aligned}
$$

5. $INN \setminus in.\mathbb{N}$

6. $f(INN)$, where $f(in.n) = b$ for any n

7. $INN \setminus in.\mathbb{N} \cup \{a\}$

8. $ND = a \to ND \sqcap b \to ND \sqcap a \to b \to ND$

9. *DIV*

10. *CHAOS*

Exercise 8.12 If α is an ordinal number, identified with the set of ordinals less than α, then for each $\beta \in \alpha$ define

$$
P_\beta = \gamma : \beta \to RUN_\alpha
$$

This process allows any ordinal less than β as its initial event, and then allows all sequences of ordinals less than α. The recursive definition

$$
N = \beta : \alpha \to ((P_\beta \ || \ N) \setminus \alpha)
$$

is not guarded, because of the use of the hiding operator within the definition.

1. Can N diverge?

2. How long will the chain of approximations $F^\beta(DIV)$ be before it reaches the fixed point? How many of these approximations can diverge?

Deduce that for any ordinal α, if $\alpha \subseteq \Sigma$ then there are recursions that require at least α approximations before the set of failures and divergences is fixed.

Exercise 8.13 The following processes are defined:

$$
\begin{aligned}
P_1 &= a \to STOP \sqcap b \to c \to STOP \\
P_2 &= a \to STOP \;\Box\; b \to c \to STOP \\
P_3 &= a \to STOP \;\Box\; P_3 \\
P_4 &= a \to STOP \;\Box\; b \to RUN
\end{aligned}
$$

Which of them must pass which of the following tests:

$$
\begin{aligned}
T_1 &= a \to SUCCESS \\
T_2 &= b \to c \to SUCCESS \\
T_3 &= a \to SUCCESS \;|||\; b \to SUCCESS \\
T_4 &= (a \to SUCCESS) \setminus \{a\} \\
T_5 &= SUCCESS
\end{aligned}
$$

Exercise 8.14 Find a test which distinguishes $a \to STOP$ from $STOP \sqcap a \to STOP$.

Exercise 8.15 Find a test which distinguishes $a \to b \to STOP$ from $a \to STOP \;|||\; b \to STOP$.

Exercise 8.16 Using your operational rule for DIV from Exercise 8.4, find a test that distinguishes DIV from $STOP$.

Exercise 8.17 Using your operational rules for $CHAOS$ from Exercise 8.4, find a test that distinguishes $CHAOS$ from RUN.

Exercise 8.18 Find a test that distinguishes $P_1 = \bigsqcap_{n \in \mathbb{N}} A(n)$ from $P_2 = P_1 \sqcap (N = a \to N)$, where $A(0) = STOP$ and $A(n + 1) = a \to A(n)$.

Exercise 8.19 Find a test T such that P **must** T if and only if $\langle a, b, c \rangle \notin \mathcal{D}[\![P]\!]$.

Exercise 8.20 Find a test T such that P **must** T if and only if $(\langle a, b, c\rangle, \{d, e\}) \notin \mathcal{F}\,[\![P]\!]$.

Exercise 8.21 Find a pair of processes that are equivalent under may testing but distinguished by must testing.

Exercise 8.22 Find a pair of processes that are equivalent under must testing but distinguished by may testing.

Exercise 8.23

1. Given $tr \in \mathcal{D}\,[\![P_1]\!]$ and $tr \notin \mathcal{D}\,[\![P_2]\!]$, find a test T such that $\neg(P_1$ **must** $T)$ and $(P_2$ **must** $T)$.

2. Given $\mathcal{D}\,[\![P_1]\!] = \mathcal{D}\,[\![P_2]\!]$ and $(tr, X) \in \mathcal{F}\,[\![P_1]\!]$ and $(tr, X) \notin \mathcal{F}\,[\![P_2]\!]$, find a test T such that $\neg(P_1$ **must** $T)$ and $(P_2$ **must** $T)$.

3. Given $\mathcal{D}\,[\![P_1]\!] = \mathcal{D}\,[\![P_2]\!]$ and $u \in \mathcal{I}\,[\![P_1]\!]$ and $u \notin \mathcal{I}\,[\![P_2]\!]$, find a test T such that $\neg(P_1$ **must** $T)$ and $(P_2$ **must** $T)$.

4. Deduce that if $P_1 \equiv_{must} P_2$ then $P_1 =_{FDI} P_2$.

Exercise 8.24 Assume that $\neg(P_1$ **must** $T)$ and P_2 **must** T. Show that there is some divergence, failure, or infinite trace of P_1 which is not also in the semantics of P_2.

Part III

Introducing time

9

The timed language

The language of CSP and the semantic models introduced thus far are appropriate for describing and analysing systems in terms of their possible sequences of events. The traces model is concerned only with the order in which events can occur; and the stable failures and FDI models are also concerned with liveness. All of these models have deliberately abstracted away concerns about timing such as the precise time at which events occur or the delay before an event is made available. This allows reasoning at the appropriate level of abstraction with regard to untimed safety and liveness properties: when systems are correct by virtue of the order in which they perform events, analysis and verification is possible in the appropriate untimed model.

The facility to reason about timing behaviour in processes may be introduced for a variety of reasons. There may be a requirement to analyse a CSP process description with regard to its real-time behaviour, to understand how long executions may be expected to last, or to check conditions for scheduling. In this case, presenting a timed interpretation of the CSP language is necessary, to describe operator behaviour at a more concrete, timed, level. Furthermore, it may be desirable to introduce new constructs such as timeouts and delays into the language of CSP itself, in order to support the precise description of time-sensitive behaviour. Systems whose correct operation is due to their precise timing behaviour can only be analysed with respect to a model which includes a notion of time.

Time will be introduced into CSP in both these ways. In this chapter the language is extended to include new timing constructs to permit the description of time-sensitive behaviour. These new constructs are timeout, delay, and timed interrupt, which are introduced in Sections 9.4 and 9.8. Timed transitions are used to describe execution steps of timed CSP processes, in terms of event transitions and delay transitions. In Chapter 10 the structure of the execution patterns possible for timed CSP processes is explored in more depth, and used to motivate the nature of the timed observations underpinning the timed semantic model presented in Chapter 11. This model provides a timed interpretation for the entire language, which defines the new constructs, and reinterprets the language already introduced in a timed context. This will provide a foundation for the specification of timing behaviour, as presented in Chapter 12. Finally, Chapter 13 covers the relationships between the timed and the un-timed semantic models, and considers how the links can be exploited in the development and verification of timed systems.

9.1 TIMED COMPUTATIONAL MODEL

The following five assumptions are used in the timed computational model:

Instantaneous events: The treatment of events as synchronizations means that it is appropriate to consider their occurrence as instantaneous, performed by a process at the precise point it becomes committed to the event. CSP is designed to consider systems in terms of synchronizing processes, and so the treatment of events as instantaneous naturally follows. Actions which take some time to complete may be modelled in terms of an event at which they begin, and an event at which they end, in analogy with the way geometric figures may be described in terms of their boundaries.

Newtonian time: Time passes with reference to a single conceptual global clock. Time progresses at the same rate in all components of the system, as measured by this global clock. The occurrence of any event in any process is at a single precise time, and events in different processes can be judged for simultaneity. Processes themselves do not have read-access to the clock, rather it is used in the semantic framework for the analysis and description of processes.

Real-time: Time is modelled as the non-negative real numbers. This means that there is no minimal level of granularity, and there is no minimum delay between events occurring at two different times.

Maximal parallelism: There are always sufficient resources for processes to execute, so effectively each process is executed on its own dedicated processor. This amounts to the assumption that concurrent processes are not in competition for processor time or memory, and so there are no implicit scheduling considerations. If a scheduling analysis is required then it should be made explicit.

Maximal progress: An event occurs when all participants are willing to engage in it. This means that an event must occur at the instant that all participants are ready. In the case of an external event of a system, both the system and its environment must be ready: if a system does not perform an event it is ready to perform, then this must be because its environment is not yet ready. For example, an automated teller machine may be ready to return a card, but this event will not occur until a customer is ready to remove it from the slot. Once the customer does attempt to remove an offered card from the slot, then it happens.

An internal event of a system, such as a message passing from one component to another, should also occur as soon as the participants are ready. Such events do not require the participation of the environment since the fact that an event is internal to a system means precisely that the environment is not a participant in that event. The transmission of a print job being sent to a print spooler will occur as soon as both the sending process is ready to send it and the spooler is ready to receive it.

Maximal progress follows from the observation that responsibility and control are most effective when they appear together: agents who are given the responsibility for ensuring that a task is completed should be given control over that task, and conversely if an agent has control over a task then responsibility for the correct performance of that task should also be accepted. If a cleaner has a key to an office, then he or she has control over the door and can be given responsibility for relocking it. Conversely, there is no point requiring the cleaner to have responsibility for locking the door if he or she does not have a key, since in that case there is no control over the door lock.

In the world of events as synchronizations, processes do not have complete control over the performance of external events, since these are also dependent on the co-operation of their environments. It follows that processes should not have the responsibility for performing those events, so it is inappropriate to require a process to perform an event at a particular time, since any event can always be blocked. On the other hand, processes do have complete control over their internal events, since they do not synchronize with any other agents. Processes are therefore given the accompanying responsibility to ensure that internal events are performed when they become possible.

These assumptions encapsulate the approach taken to the understanding of processes in the context of time.

9.2 TRANSITIONS

Transitions will be used to describe the possible executions of CSP processes. The decision to treat events as instantaneous means that transitions describing the performance of events are not associated with the passage of time. *Evolution* transitions will instead be used to describe the passage of time. The first step in the execution of a process will be given in terms of the events it can immediately perform at the time the process begins execution, and in terms of the evolutions that it can undergo. Timed transition systems, which describe the allowable combinations of event transitions and evolutions, and the constraints on them, will be introduced in the next chapter.

This separation of time and events allows timing behaviour to be introduced to the operators of the untimed language without interfering with their behaviour on events. Delays and durations in a process description must then be given explicitly, and are not implicitly bound up with individual operators.

Event transitions

The labelled transition $Q \xrightarrow{\mu} Q'$ will be understood at the timed level as asserting that the timed CSP process Q may immediately and instantaneously perform event μ and behave subsequently as the timed CSP process Q'. Such a transition takes no time: the time on the global clock immediately after the transition is the same as the time immediately before it is performed. This understanding of a labelled transition in the timed context is more concrete than its interpretation in the untimed context, which is neutral with regard to time: a transition $P \xrightarrow{\mu} P'$ in an untimed context is understood simply to indicate that μ is a possible next event for P to perform. The question of whether μ is immediately possible or whether it would be preceded or followed by some delay does not arise at the untimed level. In fact both possibilities are described by the same transition.

Evolution transitions

The passage of time will be described by an *evolution* transition $Q \xrightarrow{d} Q'$, where d can be any strictly positive real-time value: $d > 0$. This is understood as Q progressing simply by allowing time to pass, so that after a delay d it will have evolved to process Q'. The transition takes d units of time, in that the time on the global clock will be advanced by d units of time during the course of this transition: the time immediately after the transition has occurred is d greater than the time immediately before. No internal or external event is performed at any point during this transition. If Q is able to evolve through a sequence of states $\{Q_i\}$ over all time without performing any events, then the abbreviation $Q \xrightarrow{\infty}$ will be used to denote this. Formally, the abbreviation is defined as follows:

$$Q \xrightarrow{\infty} \quad = \quad \exists \{Q_i\}_{i\in\mathbb{N}}, \{d_i\}_{i\in\mathbb{N}} \bullet (\Sigma_i d_i = \infty \wedge Q = Q_0 \wedge \forall i \bullet Q_i \xrightarrow{d_i} Q_{i+1})$$

Observe that $Q \xrightarrow{\infty}$ is not an evolution transition, since an infinite evolution can never be completed. If $Q \xrightarrow{\infty}$ appears in a process execution, then this must be at the end. In this case Q is said to be *stable*, since it will not perform any internal transitions.

9.3   PERFORMING EVENTS

STOP

The CSP process *STOP* represents deadlock, but its interpretation must now be given in the timed setting. It remains unable to perform any internal or external events, so there will be no transitions of the form *STOP* $\xrightarrow{\mu} Q$ for any event μ and process Q. On the other hand, its state can be recorded as time passes. A process which can never make progress must still be in the same state after any delay has occurred. The inference rule for deriving the time transitions is therefore as follows:

$$\frac{\rule{3cm}{0.4pt}}{STOP \overset{d}{\leadsto} STOP}$$

This states that the process *STOP* can allow any amount of time d to elapse, and that the resulting state will still be *STOP*. The fact that no event transitions are provided for it means that this trivial progress is the only kind of progress that it can make. Observe that $STOP \overset{1}{\leadsto} STOP \overset{1}{\leadsto} STOP \overset{1}{\leadsto} \ldots$, so it follows that $STOP \overset{\infty}{\leadsto}$.

Event prefix

The CSP expression $a \rightarrow Q$ describes a process which is prepared to engage in the event a, after which it will behave as Q. It remains in its initial state until the event a is performed, continually offering this event to its environment until the offer is accepted. The understanding that events are instantaneous means that on occurrence of the event a control is instantly passed to process Q. Alternatively, some time may elapse without the event a being accepted. In this case the process remains in the same state, patiently maintaining the offer. These two possibilities are described by the transitions which are given for this construct by the following rules:

$$\frac{\rule{3cm}{0.4pt}}{(a \rightarrow Q) \overset{a}{\rightarrow} Q}$$

$$\frac{\rule{3cm}{0.4pt}}{(a \rightarrow Q) \overset{d}{\leadsto} (a \rightarrow Q)}$$

A delayed event prefix $a \overset{d}{\rightarrow} Q$ will be introduced on page 278.

Example 9.3.1 The one-shot printer of Example 1.2.1 is described as

$$PRINTER0 \quad = \quad accept \rightarrow print \rightarrow STOP$$

Initially it is only able to accept a job, but if no job is forthcoming immediately, then some time will pass instead. Eventually perhaps a job is accepted, after which some further time may elapse before the job is printed. After the job is printed, then no further events are possible, although time will still pass. One possible execution is described by

$$(accept \rightarrow print \rightarrow STOP)$$
$$\quad \wr 3$$
$$(accept \rightarrow print \rightarrow STOP)$$
$$\quad \downarrow accept$$
$$(print \rightarrow STOP)$$
$$\quad \wr 2$$
$$(print \rightarrow STOP)$$
$$\quad \downarrow print$$
$$STOP$$
$$\quad \wr \infty$$

Not all executions have to alternate evolutions and event transitions, however, or run for all time. Another possible execution for $PRINTER0$ is given by

$$(accept \rightarrow print \rightarrow STOP)$$
$$\quad \wr 3$$
$$(accept \rightarrow print \rightarrow STOP)$$
$$\quad \wr 7$$
$$(accept \rightarrow print \rightarrow STOP)$$
$$\quad \downarrow accept$$
$$(print \rightarrow STOP)$$
$$\quad \downarrow print$$
$$STOP$$

However, Section 10.1 discusses why all sequences of evolutions may be collapsed to a single evolution.

A third execution of $PRINTER0$ is given by $PRINTER0 \overset{\infty}{\leadsto}$. This execution describes a run in which the printer was never provided with a job. ∎

Timed event prefix

A more general form of event prefix allows the process to record the amount of time which has elapsed between the initial event's offer and its occurrence. This information may then be used by the subsequent process. The timed prefix operator is written as

$$a@u \rightarrow Q$$

(pronounced 'a at u then Q'), where u is a time variable which is allowed to appear free within time expressions in Q: such occurrences become bound by this construction. This form of prefix offers the event a continually until it occurs, in the same way as event prefix, and the subsequent behaviour once a occurs is described by Q. The time variable u within Q takes the value of the time d at which a occurs relative to the time a was first offered, and so all free occurrences of u within Q are replaced with this time once the a has occurred. The substitution notation $Q[d/u]$ denotes the process expression Q with every free occurrence of u replaced by d.

The transitions for this operator are therefore given as follows:

$$(a@u \rightarrow Q) \overset{a}{\rightarrow} Q[0/u]$$

$$(a@u \rightarrow Q) \overset{d}{\rightsquigarrow} (a@u \rightarrow Q[(u+d)/u])$$

Events occur instantaneously without any associated passing of time, and execution of a process begins at time 0. Immediate occurrence of the event a accordingly assigns the time 0 to the variable u, so the subsequent execution is that of process Q with time 0 replacing all occurrences of u.

The process may also delay for any length of time. Following an evolution transition, it must continue to offer the same event, but the process describing the subsequent behaviour must be updated to reflect the passage of time. Once d units of time have passed, the resulting process must have all occurrences of the time variable u replaced by the expression $u + d$.

Example 9.3.2 Let Q be a process which has two free time variables u and u'. The prefix

$$a@u \rightarrow b@u' \rightarrow Q$$

has the following as a possible execution:

$$
\begin{aligned}
&a@u \rightarrow b@u' \rightarrow Q \\
&\quad \wr 5 \\
&a@u \rightarrow b@u' \rightarrow Q[(u+5)/u] \\
&\quad \downarrow a \\
&b@u' \rightarrow (Q[(u+5)/u])[0/u] \\
&\quad \wr 6 \\
&b@u' \rightarrow (Q[5/u])[(u'+6)/u'] \\
&\quad \downarrow b \\
&Q[5/u][6/u'] \\
&\quad \vdots
\end{aligned}
$$

The process offers the event a continually until it is accepted, and will fix the variable u to the time at which a occurs. In this execution this occurred at time 5. The substitution $[u + 5/u]$

followed by $[0/u]$ results in substituting $0 + 5$ for u. Once a has occurred b is offered until it occurs, whereupon u' is set to the length of time b was on offer. In the execution above this is the value 6, so the resulting process Q has u set to 5 and u' set to 6. Observe that the time u' is not the time since the start of the entire execution (which would be 11), it is the length of time b was available. The timer for u' is not started until the prefix $b@u' \rightarrow \ldots$ is reached.

If neither u nor u' appear free in Q, then the substitution $Q[5/u][6/u']$ is equivalent to performing no substitution, and in this case the entire process is equivalent to $a \rightarrow b \rightarrow Q$. Observing the time of an event's occurrence and then forgetting it is equivalent to ignoring the time completely. ∎

Example 9.3.3 A machine designed to test human reaction time has a user place a finger on a sensor pad. The machine switches on a green light, and then the user lifts the finger from the pad. The machine records the delay between the light and the finger movement, and displays it to an accuracy of one thousandth of a second. This may be described by the following process, where the time units are seconds:

$$REACT \quad = \quad greenlight \rightarrow lift@u \rightarrow display!(round(u, 3)) \rightarrow STOP$$

The function $round(u, 3)$ returns the value of u to three decimal places. The value to be output along channel $display$ is dependent on the delay between $greenlight$—the point $lift$ is enabled—and $lift$—the point at which it occurs.

An example execution of $REACT$ is given by

$$
\begin{aligned}
&REACT \\
&\quad \downarrow greenlight \\
&lift@u \rightarrow display!round(u, 3) \rightarrow STOP \\
&\quad \updownarrow 0.0127 \\
&lift@u \rightarrow display!round(u + 0.0127, 3) \rightarrow STOP \\
&\quad \downarrow lift \\
&display!round(0 + 0.0127, 3) \rightarrow STOP \\
&\quad \downarrow display.0.013 \\
&STOP \\
&\quad \vdots
\end{aligned}
$$

The $display$ output occurs at time 0.0127. ∎

Choosing between events

The menu choice process $x : A \rightarrow Q(x)$ behaves in a similar way to the event prefix with regard to time. When an event $a \in A$ is chosen then control immediately and instantaneously passes to the corresponding process $Q(a)$. The choice is resolved instantly, at the moment the event is performed. Until some event is chosen, the process remains in the initial state, patiently offering all events in the set A. This behaviour is described by the transition semantics:

$$\frac{}{(x : A \to Q(x)) \overset{a}{\to} Q(a)} \quad [\, a \in A \,]$$

$$\frac{}{(x : A \to Q(x)) \overset{d}{\leadsto} (x : A \to Q(x))}$$

Successful termination

The CSP process *SKIP* is the immediately terminating process. Since the event $\checkmark$ is used to denote termination, the transitions for *SKIP* are firstly that it is immediately ready to perform $\checkmark$, and secondly that it remains ready as time passes.

$$\frac{}{SKIP \overset{\checkmark}{\to} STOP} \qquad \frac{}{SKIP \overset{d}{\leadsto} SKIP}$$

The process *SKIP* is ready to terminate at the very instant it begins execution. If it is prevented from terminating, then it may undergo an evolution transition, remaining in the terminating state. In fact, it is possible that termination may never occur, as witnessed by the execution $SKIP \overset{\infty}{\leadsto}$.

9.4 CHOICE

Timeout

The timeout operator introduces a way of describing time-sensitive process behaviour. It is written as

$$Q_1 \overset{d}{\triangleright} Q_2$$

and pronounced 'Q_1 timeout d Q_2'. The time value d can be any time expression—an arithmetic expression which evaluates to a non-negative real number. A timeout construction cannot be executed if its time expression evaluates to anything other than a non-negative real, or if it involves free time variables.

A timeout process offers a time-sensitive choice between Q_1 and Q_2. Initially the process Q_1 is available, which means that control is with process Q_1 when execution begins.

If Q_1 performs some external event before d units of time have elapsed, then the timeout choice is resolved in favour of Q_1, and Q_2 is discarded without ever being made available. The process Q_1 may also perform internal events, but these do not resolve the choice. If Q_1 does not engage in any visible event in the first d units of time, then the timeout occurs, the choice is resolved against Q_1 which is discarded, and the execution continues with Q_2. Hence the timeout choice must always be resolved within d units of time. The process Q_1 is given d units of time to resolve the choice, and if it has not done so within its allotted time then the choice is resolved in favour of Q_2.

The transition rules for this operator introduce the mechanism which ensures that internal events are urgent, in accordance with maximal progress. The timeout event will be an internal event, and it is imperative that it occurs at the moment the timeout period has expired. This is guaranteed within the transition semantics by ensuring that no evolution transition is possible which will reach a point beyond the time of the timeout. This forces the internal event to occur at the point it becomes enabled, since once that point is reached no further time can elapse until the internal event occurs.

Any evolution reduces the time remaining on the timeout: a timeout $Q_1 \overset{d}{\triangleright} Q_2$ has d units of time remaining before the timeout occurs. If this construct evolves for d' units of time, then the time remaining for the timeout becomes $(d - d')$, so the resulting process will be of the form $Q_1' \overset{d-d'}{\triangleright} Q_2$.

$$\frac{Q_1 \overset{a}{\to} Q_1'}{Q_1 \overset{d}{\triangleright} Q_2 \overset{a}{\to} Q_1'} \qquad\qquad \frac{Q_1 \overset{d'}{\rightsquigarrow} Q_1'}{Q_1 \overset{d}{\triangleright} Q_2 \overset{d'}{\rightsquigarrow} Q_1' \overset{d-d'}{\triangleright} Q_2} \quad [\, 0 < d' \leqslant d \,]$$

$$\frac{Q_1 \overset{\tau}{\to} Q_1'}{Q_1 \overset{d}{\triangleright} Q_2 \overset{\tau}{\to} Q_1' \overset{d}{\triangleright} Q_2}$$

$$\frac{}{Q_1 \overset{0}{\triangleright} Q_2 \overset{\tau}{\to} Q_2}$$

The first d time units of any execution will have transitions identical to an execution of Q_1, since all transitions before the timeout occurs correspond to transitions of Q_1. This is the expected behaviour of the timeout operator, which allows Q_1 to execute at least until the moment the timeout occurs.

Example 9.4.1 A timed printer *TPRINTER*1 offers a choice between accepting a job or shutting down. Unlike the untimed printer *PRINTER*1 of Example 1.5, the timed printer is ready to accept a job only for a limited amount of time, 300 seconds, before timing out and offering the alternative option of shutting down. This behaviour is expressed by the description

$$TPRINTER1 \;\; = \;\; (accept \to print \to STOP) \overset{300}{\triangleright} shutdown \to STOP$$

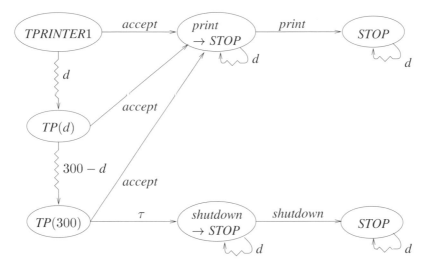

Fig. 9.1 *Transitions and evolutions of* TPRINTER1

This process may evolve for any amount of time d up to 300s, after which it will behave as the process $TP(d) = (accept \to print \to STOP) \overset{300-d}{\triangleright} shutdown \to STOP$. It may perform an *accept* event either initially, or after some evolution, and after performing this event the resulting process is $print \to STOP$. Alternatively, it can continue to evolve until there is no time left on the timeout, becoming the process $(accept \to print \to STOP) \overset{0}{\triangleright} shutdown \to STOP$. At this point, no further evolutions are possible, since there is no rule given which allows further evolution transitions to be derived. The only possibilities are that an *accept* event occurs, or else an internal τ action corresponding to the timeout occurs. If the environment of the printer is not prepared to engage in an *accept* event, then the internal event is the only possible transition, and time cannot continue to pass until the internal event has occurred. The internal event is urgent: time will be blocked until it (or some alternative such as *accept*) is performed.

The transitions and evolutions of *TPRINTER1* are illustrated in Figure 9.1. The process can evolve for a total of 300 seconds; this evolution can be made up of any number of smaller steps, though only two steps are illustrated in the diagram. During the evolution *TPRINTER1* passes through a continuum of states, where it is in the state $TP(d)$ after d seconds.

Internal events are urgent, since they are completely under the control of their host process, and so cannot be blocked. ■

Delay

The timeout operator can be used to introduce delays into process descriptions. A waiting process which delays for exactly d time units before terminating can be defined using this construction:

$$WAIT\ d \quad = \quad STOP \overset{d}{\triangleright} SKIP$$

The process $WAIT\ d$ can perform no events for the first d time units of its execution, but after that delay it terminates and its subsequent behaviour is that of $SKIP$. This is delayed termination.

The process

$$STOP \overset{d}{\triangleright} Q$$

delays the execution of Q for d units of time. Initially the process $STOP$ is executed. Since this can perform no events, the timeout cannot be resolved in its favour, so after a delay of d the timeout occurs, and control passes to Q, which begins execution, d time units after the process $STOP \overset{d}{\triangleright} Q$ was invoked. The construction $WAIT\ d; Q$ discussed on page 305 provides the same behaviour.

A delay immediately following the occurrence of an event occurs frequently enough in process descriptions to warrant its own abbreviated forms:

$$a \overset{d}{\to} Q \quad = \quad a \to (STOP \overset{d}{\triangleright} Q)$$
$$x : A \overset{d_x}{\to} Q(x) \quad = \quad x : A \to (STOP \overset{d_x}{\triangleright} Q(x))$$

In the first process description, the event a occurs at any point in time, and control passes to Q after a further d time units have elapsed. The process cannot perform any other events between the occurrence of the event a and the subsequent execution of process Q. The second definition is a simple extension of this to prefix choice; and the delay may depend on the chosen event.

Example 9.4.2 The service offered by a restaurant waiter may be described as

$$WAITER \quad = \quad coat \overset{2}{\to} order \overset{20}{\to} meal \overset{60}{\to} bill \overset{0.001}{\to} tip \to coat \to STOP$$

where the time units in this example are minutes.

Initially, the waiter is prepared to take the customer's coat, and will remain ready to do this until a customer arrives. The waiter takes 2 minutes to hang the coat, after which time he will be ready to accept an order from the customer. After the order is received, the meal will be offered to the customer 20 minutes later, and the bill will be offered to the customer 60 minutes after the meal has been delivered. The waiter is ready to receive a tip 0.001 minutes after the bill, after which he immediately returns the coat. The events in the description of $WAITER$ are synchronizations between him and the customer, so the delays following the various events should not be interpreted as delays between the events, but rather the minimum delay imposed by the waiter before the next event can occur. If the customer is not ready to order until 10 minutes after his coat is taken, then the *order* event cannot occur until then. If the customer is ready to order immediately, then he must wait 2 minutes until the waiter is ready. ∎

Timeouts are often used for exception handling: a course of action is expected, and the timeout is invoked only if it does not occur.

Example 9.4.3 A postman delivering a parcel to a house will ring on the doorbell and wait for an answer. If there is no answer within 1 minute then a note will be delivered explaining that the parcel is being held for collection. This scenario may be described as follows:

$$DELIVERY =$$
$$ring \rightarrow ((answer \rightarrow deliver \rightarrow STOP) \overset{1}{\triangleright} note \overset{180}{\rightarrow} collect \rightarrow STOP)$$

The *ring* on the doorbell may occur at any point. The timer for the timeout begins when the *ring* occurs, and there is a 1 minute window of opportunity for the door to be answered, followed by subsequent delivery of the parcel. If the door is not answered, then the note will be delivered and the parcel will be ready for collection 3 hours later. ∎

Example 9.4.4 A watchdog timer monitors another process by waiting for a *reset* signal, which should be received within a certain period of time d. If the signal is not received, then an *alarm* should be raised. This is typically repeated for the lifetime of the monitored process.

The action on a single period may be described by the process

$$WATCHDOG \quad = \quad (reset \rightarrow SKIP) \overset{d}{\triangleright} alarm \rightarrow SKIP$$

The *reset* event is expected, but if it has not occurred within d then the *alarm* signal is enabled. ∎

Timeouts are also used to offer opportunities for disagreement. In such cases, the usual or expected behaviour is described by the process after the timeout, but some delay is introduced to permit possible interruption to prevent normal continuation.

Example 9.4.5 A book club offers its members the opportunity to buy books at a discount every month. When the catalogue is sent out, the 'editor's choice' book is highlighted as a particular recommendation, and will automatically be sent out with an invoice after 7 days unless the club receives notification that the book is not wanted. Normally, the book would be sent, but it is possible to prevent this by swift action. The interaction each month between the club and a customer with regard to the editor's choice is described by

$$OFFER \quad = \quad recommendation \rightarrow ((reject \rightarrow STOP)$$
$$\overset{7}{\triangleright} send\_book \rightarrow payment \rightarrow STOP)$$

∎

The time expression for the timeout must not contain free time variables when the timeout is invoked. For example, the process $Q_1 \overset{3+u}{\triangleright} Q_2$ cannot properly be executed if u is not bound to some value. However, a timeout may contain time variables provided they have all been instantiated with real-time values by the stage control is passed to the timeout. The timed event prefix operator is the one which instantiates values for variables. Care must be taken to ensure that any possible combinations of values which can be substituted for the time variables will result in the time expression evaluating to a non-negative real.

Example 9.4.6 Although the expression $Q_1 \overset{u}{\triangleright} Q_2$ cannot be executed if u is a time variable, it is perfectly acceptable within the process expression $a@u \to (Q_1 \overset{u}{\triangleright} Q_2)$, since u will be replaced by some particular non-negative time value d when the timeout is actually executed.

On the other hand, execution of the process $a@u \to (Q_1 \overset{5-u}{\triangleright} Q_2)$ might result in a negative value for the time expression, in the case where more than 5 time units pass before the event a is performed. If the intention is that Q_2 should be executed subsequent to a occurring after time 5, then this should be described by the process

$$(a@u \to (Q_1 \overset{5-u}{\triangleright} Q_2)) \overset{5}{\triangleright} a \to Q_2$$

Here the variable u cannot obtain a value greater than 5, since the timed event prefix will be discarded by the timeout if its initial event has not occurred by time 5. ∎

External choice

The external choice operator offers a choice between processes, which is resolved at the instant the first visible event occurs, in favour of the process which performs it. In contrast to the prefix choice construct, which offers a stable choice between events, the external choice operator allows each of its arguments to execute independently, making events available and withdrawing them as time progresses, until the choice is resolved. At the untimed level this entails retaining the choice between processes when they progress via internal events; in the context of time, it also requires that the choice is preserved when processes evolve. Since time passes for both processes at the same rate, they both participate in any evolution.

The rules for deriving transitions of a choice are given as follows:

$$\frac{Q_1 \overset{a}{\to} Q_1'}{\begin{array}{c} Q_1 \,\square\, Q_2 \overset{a}{\to} Q_1' \\ Q_2 \,\square\, Q_1 \overset{a}{\to} Q_1' \end{array}} \qquad \frac{Q_1 \overset{d}{\rightsquigarrow} Q_1' \quad Q_2 \overset{d}{\rightsquigarrow} Q_2'}{Q_1 \,\square\, Q_2 \overset{d}{\rightsquigarrow} Q_1' \,\square\, Q_2'}$$

$$\frac{Q_1 \overset{\tau}{\to} Q_1'}{\begin{array}{c} Q_1 \,\square\, Q_2 \overset{\tau}{\to} Q_1' \,\square\, Q_2 \\ Q_2 \,\square\, Q_1 \overset{\tau}{\to} Q_2 \,\square\, Q_1' \end{array}}$$

The choice is resolved only by an external event of one of the participating processes. All other progress retains the choice, and progress by evolution must involve both processes.

The choice $Q_1 \square Q_2$ has as its initial offers all events offered by either Q_1 or Q_2, at the times that those processes offer them. If an event is chosen at a particular time, then the process that was offering it at that time must be the one chosen, even if the other process offered the same event at some other times. If both processes are able to perform the same event at the same time, then the resulting choice between those processes becomes nondeterministic, as it was in the untimed case.

Example 9.4.7 Example 1.4.1 describes a bus journey from A to B in terms of the events *board*, *pay*, and *alight*. The timeout operator allows timing information to be incorporated into the description to capture the transience of particular offers. This timed example will consider a simplified version of the service: boarding a bus commits the passenger to the journey on that bus. (Exercise 9.4 is concerned with a more detailed timed service.)

$$TIMED\_BUS\_37$$
$$= \quad board.37.A \rightarrow \quad pay.90 \overset{35}{\rightarrow} ((alight.37.B \rightarrow STOP) \overset{1}{\triangleright} STOP)$$
$$\overset{3}{\triangleright} STOP$$

The bus is present at the bus stop at A for 3 minutes, during which time it is possible to board the bus. If this opportunity is missed, then the bus departs and no further interactions with the bus are possible. Departure of the bus is modelled by the occurrence of the timeout.

If the bus is successfully boarded, then the driver waits until payment is received before continuing on the journey. The other significant event is the possibility of alighting at B, which is reached 35 minutes later. The bus waits for 1 minute at this stop, before continuing on its journey. If departure from the bus does not occur by this point, then it will no longer be possible to alight at B. Since the description of the bus service is concerned only with the journey from A to B, the possibilities of alighting from the bus at other stops, or of being ejected from the bus at the terminus, have not been included explicitly in the description.

The alternative service may be elaborated in the same way. The reason for the cheaper fare becomes clear: the bus is not an express.

$$TIMED\_BUS\_111$$
$$= \quad board.111.A \rightarrow \quad pay.70 \overset{80}{\rightarrow} (\quad (alight.111.B \rightarrow STOP)$$
$$\overset{2}{\triangleright} STOP)$$
$$\overset{5}{\triangleright} STOP$$

If the 111 bus leaves 15 minutes before the 37 bus, then the service offered by the two buses is described by

$$TIMED\_BUS\_111 \square (WAIT \ 15; TIMED\_BUS\_37)$$

The second bus is ready to take passengers after 15 minutes. In this case, the event *board*.111.*A* is available from time 0 to time 5, and the event *board*.37.*A* is available from time 15 to time 18. These two possibilities comprise the complete boarding opportunities offered by the two buses.

Example 1.4.2 considered the same bus service from the point of view of a passenger unable to read the bus number. In that case the descriptions are simply

$$TIMED\_BUS\_1 \quad = \quad board.A \rightarrow pay.90 \stackrel{35}{\rightarrow} ((alight.B \rightarrow STOP) \stackrel{1}{\triangleright} STOP)$$
$$\stackrel{3}{\triangleright} STOP$$

and

$$TIMED\_BUS\_2 \quad = \quad board.A \rightarrow pay.70 \stackrel{80}{\rightarrow} ((alight.B \rightarrow STOP) \stackrel{2}{\triangleright} STOP)$$
$$\stackrel{5}{\triangleright} STOP$$

In this case, the same form of choice

$$TIMED\_BUS\_2 \ \square \ (WAIT \ 15; \ TIMED\_BUS\_1)$$

offers the single event *board*.*A* between times 0 and 5 and between times 15 and 18. If the choice is taken in the first interval, then a fare of 70 is guaranteed; if it is taken in the second interval, then a fare of 90 is guaranteed. Even though both choices offer the same event, the distinct times these events are offered ensures that the choice is always resolved in a deterministic way. A traveller who cannot read the number on a bus, but who is able to tell the time, can still catch whichever bus is required.

If there is some overlap of the times at which the two buses offer the first event, as in the choice

$$TIMED\_BUS\_2 \ \square \ (WAIT \ 3; \ TIMED\_BUS\_1)$$

then a choice at any point of overlap will be made nondeterministically. Between times 3 and 5 both buses are present, so a decision to board one during that interval will result in the choice of bus being made nondeterministically: an inability to distinguish the buses means that either could be boarded. Boarding before time 3 will still guarantee that the cheaper bus is boarded, and boarding after time 5 will guarantee that the faster bus is taken. The nondeterminism is present only during the interval where both processes make the same event available. These possibilities are illustrated in Figure 9.2. ∎

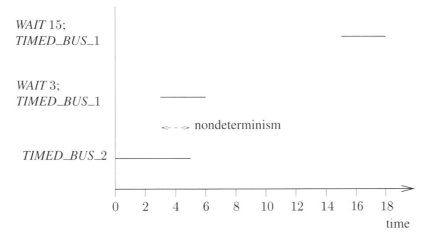

Fig. 9.2   Opportunities for boarding buses: availability of *board.A*

Internal choice

Internal choice is a specification construct: it describes a process in terms of possibilities for its behaviour, but does not give the environment of the process any control over which of these possibilities will arise. The process $Q_1 \sqcap Q_2$ is guaranteed to behave as Q_1 or as Q_2, but no control is offered over which will be chosen, or indeed how the choice will be made. It could be made by the implementor when the process is coded, it could be made at run-time when the process is invoked, or it could be delayed until the point where the choice must be made, when an interaction is offered that is possible for one of the processes but not for the other.

In providing an operational semantics, a decision is taken concerning resolution of the internal choice. At the untimed level, the choice is resolved as soon as execution begins. This is not a decision about how to implement internal choice, but rather a decision about how to represent it within a labelled transition system. Internal choice resolved in this way includes all of the possible ways it can actually be implemented.

For example, the process $a \rightarrow STOP \sqcap b \rightarrow STOP$ may actually be implemented by some random mechanism at the point an a or a b is offered. If nothing is offered until a b at time 5 then either the b will be accepted, or refused, at that time. This cannot be distinguished from the situation where the same choice was instead made at time 0 when the process began execution. As another example, an observer opening the box containing Shrödinger's cat[1] at

---

[1]This is a quantum physics thought experiment in which a cat in a box has an equal chance of being alive or dead at the point the box is opened.

time 5 cannot tell whether the choice between life and death for the cat was made at time 5, or at some earlier time.

The timed transition semantics will reflect the untimed: that the choice will be modelled as being resolved immediately and internally.

$$\frac{\rule{3cm}{0.4pt}}{\begin{array}{c} Q_1 \sqcap Q_2 \xrightarrow{\tau} Q_1 \\ Q_1 \sqcap Q_2 \xrightarrow{\tau} Q_2 \end{array}}$$

There are no evolution transitions, since the choice is to be made immediately: time cannot pass until one of the internal events accompanying resolution of the choice has occurred. Once the choice has been made, then the subsequent behaviour is that of Q_1 or of Q_2.

Indexed internal choice

The internal choice operator generalizes in the expected way. Resolution of an indexed choice is modelled as immediate, and in favour of any one of its component processes.

$$\frac{\rule{3cm}{0.4pt}}{\displaystyle\bigsqcap_{i \in J} Q_i \xrightarrow{\tau} Q_j}$$

The absence of any evolution transitions again forces the choice to be resolved immediately.

Indexed internal choice can be used to describe uncertain delays within a process. Timing requirements on processes often allow some lassitude with regard to the precise time of the offer or occurrence of some event, and are instead concerned that it meets some deadline or is placed within some interval.

Example 9.4.8 A one-shot buffer which accepts a message of type T, and then offers it for output d seconds later can be described as

$$ONE\_SHOT_d \quad = \quad in?x : T \xrightarrow{d} out!x \to STOP$$

If the delay d must be between 3 and 5 seconds, then this constraint can be imposed on d:

$$3 \leqslant d \leqslant 5$$

To specify that the one-shot buffer should make the output available sometime between 3 and 5 seconds after input, the indexed internal choice can be used:

$$ONE\_SHOT_{[3,5]} \quad = \quad \bigcap_{d \in [3,5]} ONE\_SHOT_d$$

This describes a buffer with a nondeterministic delay between input and output of any time between 3 and 5 seconds. It may be taken as a description of a particular system, where the delay might in fact be completely determined by the underlying system. Lower level implementation details have been abstracted at this level of description, resulting in nondeterminism within the process description.

Alternatively, the description may be considered as a specification, expressing the range of acceptable delays. A minimum throughput of 3 seconds is required for flow control, and a maximum of 5 seconds is required for liveness. ∎

A nondeterministic delayed prefix is often useful. The non-empty interval D describes the range of allowed delays. The delayed prefix is simply the nondeterministic composition of all the possible delayed prefix possibilities.

$$a \overset{D}{\to} Q \quad = \quad \bigcap_{d \in D} a \overset{d}{\to} Q$$

An alternative description of $ONE\_SHOT_{[3,5]}$ would then be

$$in?x : T \overset{[3,5]}{\to} out!x \to STOP$$

Example 9.4.9 The reaction timer *REACT* given in Example 9.3.3 can be elaborated. The user is first required to press a button to initiate the test. The green light goes on after a random delay, and the test proceeds. This may be described by the process

$$REACT2 \quad = \quad button \overset{[1,20]}{\to} greenlight \to lift@u \to display!round(u,3) \to STOP$$

The nondeterministic delay in this example is due to run-time randomness. Indeed, it is imperative that the user does not know in advance how long the delay will be, or else the test will be compromised. The nondeterminism in this example is intended to represent a decision to be taken at run-time, and must not be refined away. ∎

The nondeterministic delayed prefix generalizes naturally to prefix choice. In the delayed prefix choice a delay is chosen nondeterministically from the (non-empty) range of possibilities D_x raised by the first event x.

$$x : A \overset{D_x}{\to} Q(x) \quad = \quad x : A \to \bigcap_{d \in D_x} (WAIT\ d; Q(x))$$

The amount of time the one-shot buffer may take to output a message may depend on the length of the message. It may take between one and three seconds per kilobyte, so the interval of possibilities D_x associated with a message x is $[s(x), 3s(x)]$, where $s(m)$ is the size of the message in kilobytes. The revised version is described by ONE_SHOT2, defined by

$$ONE\_SHOT2 \quad = \quad in?x : T \overset{D_x}{\leadsto} out!x \to STOP$$

The indexed internal choice operator can also be used to generalize delays, to allow delays which are nondeterministic over some interval. If D is a time interval, then a process which terminates nondeterministically at some point during the interval can be described as $WAIT\ D$, defined as

$$WAIT\ D \quad = \quad \bigsqcap_{d \in D} WAIT\ d$$

Making the choice at the beginning of execution is equivalent to the choice being made internally as the process executes. This description states that the delay process is guaranteed to terminate at some point during the interval D, but allows its environment no control over when it will be. The choice of termination time is entirely with the process itself.

The process which instead offers the choice of when to terminate to its environment is $WAIT(\min(D))$ (provided D has a least element). The external choice operator is not required since only one event is offered, in this case $\checkmark$; the choice offered to the environment concerns the time at which it will occur. This is offered by a delay process which makes termination a possibility at the earliest time and hence allows its environment control over precisely when it will occur.

9.5 RECURSION

Recursive process definitions $N = Q$ consist of a process name N, and a CSP process description Q which may contain instances of that name. The original untimed transition rule allowed N precisely those transitions that could be deduced for Q. This is also the approach taken in the timed setting, where evolutions are allowed in addition to transitions.

$$\frac{Q \overset{\mu}{\to} Q'}{N \overset{\mu}{\to} Q'} \ [\,N = Q\,] \qquad\qquad \frac{Q \overset{d}{\leadsto} Q'}{N \overset{d}{\leadsto} Q'} \ [\,N = Q\,]$$

The recursive call is modelled as taking no time: the result of dereferencing the process name N has exactly the same transitions as N itself. Any delay required for recursive calls should therefore be explicitly included in the relevant process description. In this way the treatment of recursion is separated from timing considerations, and there are no implicit delays inherent in a recursive description. A recursive definition $N = Q$ really does equate N with Q.

Example 9.5.1 A process which polls on two input channels by repeatedly enabling each of them in turn may be described using recursion together with timeout. This process offers a choice between two events, but is able to offer only one at a time.

$$POLLING \quad = \quad (in_1?x : T \to Q_1(x))$$
$$\overset{2}{\triangleright} ((in_2?x : T \to Q_2(x))$$
$$\overset{2}{\triangleright} POLLING)$$

If the input arrives on in_1 then it will be output on out, and similarly if it arrives on in_2. The process $POLLING$ executes its cycle every 4 time units, either for ever or until some input is accepted.

One possible execution is

$$POLLING$$
$$\quad \overset{\ }{\{}2$$
$$(in_1?x : T \to Q_1(x)) \overset{0}{\triangleright} ((in_2?x : T \to Q_2(x)) \overset{2}{\triangleright} POLLING)$$
$$\quad \downarrow \tau$$
$$(in_2?x : T \to Q_2(x)) \overset{2}{\triangleright} POLLING$$
$$\quad \{2$$
$$(in_2?x : T \to Q_2(x)) \overset{0}{\triangleright} POLLING$$
$$\quad \downarrow \tau$$
$$POLLING$$
$$\quad \downarrow in_1.17$$
$$Q_1(17)$$
$$\quad \vdots$$

These evolution and event transitions are possible for $POLLING$ because they may be deduced for the corresponding process definition.   ■

Example 9.5.2 A message held in a buffer is associated with a lifetime, which is provided as input with the message. If the message has not been accepted for output after its lifetime has expired then it is discarded. The lifetime t provided with message x is used to control a timeout on the message, which forces a hard real-time deadline on the agent receiving the output.

$$HARDBUFF \quad = \quad in?x.t : M.\mathbb{R}^+ \to ((out!x \overset{1}{\to} HARDBUFF)$$
$$\overset{t}{\triangleright} WAIT\ 1; HARDBUFF)$$

Observe that time values can be passed along channels as data values, and then used in the control structure of a process.   ∎

Example 9.5.3 A transmitter which repeatedly sends a given message x until it receives an acknowledgement may be modelled using recursion together with the timeout operator:

$$TRANSMIT(x) \quad = \quad send!x \rightarrow ((ack \rightarrow STOP) \overset{3}{\triangleright} TRANSMIT(x))$$

If $TRANSMIT(x)$ is in an environment which is always ready to accept a *send* message, then it will send the message every 3 time units until an *ack* message is received.   ∎

Example 9.5.4 A timed one-place buffer process might have some restrictions on the minimum delay $l > 0$ and maximum delay $u \geqslant l$ on throughput.

$$TCOPY \quad = \quad in?x : T \overset{[l,u]}{\rightarrow} out!x \rightarrow TCOPY$$

The minimum time that one pass through the recursive definition will take is l, though even if the environment is co-operative, a single pass might take as long as u.   ∎

All of the examples presented above have a minimal non-zero amount of time required for the recursively defined process $N = Q$ to traverse its body Q and reach a fresh instance of N within Q. If a process is able to reach a fresh recursive call in no time at all, then the danger arises of performing infinitely many recursive calls in no time, which is undesirable. For example, the process $N = a \rightarrow N$ is able to perform the event a at time 0 and then immediately loop, allowing an infinite sequence of a events in no time. To avoid the possibility of introducing infinitely fast processes, it is sufficient to require that any recursive definition is *time-guarded*—that there is some non-zero time which provides a lower bound for the time taken to reach a fresh recursive call. Time-guardedness will be discussed in greater depth in Section 10.3, once the entire language of timed CSP has been introduced.

Mutual recursion

The mutual recursion construction is that of the untimed language, where a collection of process names are collectively bound to a collection of process definitions which may refer to those names. Any name appearing in a process definition should be bound. The transition rules are identical to those for single recursion, though the surrounding context of process definitions may differ. If $N = Q$ is one of the recursive definitions, then the transitions for N are given by

$$\frac{Q \overset{\mu}{\rightarrow} Q'}{N \overset{\mu}{\rightarrow} Q'} \; [\, N = Q \,] \qquad\qquad \frac{Q \overset{d}{\rightsquigarrow} Q'}{N \overset{d}{\rightsquigarrow} Q'} \; [\, N = Q \,]$$

These rules provide the transitions for each process name bound in one of the process definitions.

Example 9.5.5 A transmitter *TRANS* repeatedly receives messages x from an application, and repeatedly sends it until an acknowledgement is received. There are two kinds of state the transmitter is in: handling a message, or awaiting input.

$$TRANS \quad = \quad in?x : T \xrightarrow{1} TRANS(x)$$

$$TRANS(x) \quad = \quad send!x \rightarrow ((ack \xrightarrow{1} TRANS) \overset{3}{\triangleright} TRANS(x))$$

This provides a collection of definitions, one for each $x \in T$. The definition of *TRANS* is in terms of all of the *TRANS(x)*, and each of those definitions is in terms of itself and of *TRANS*. The collection of definitions is mutually recursive.

An example execution is

$$TRANS$$
$$\quad \downarrow in.3$$
$$STOP \overset{1}{\triangleright} TRANS(3)$$
$$\quad \wr 1$$
$$STOP \overset{0}{\triangleright} TRANS(3)$$
$$\quad \downarrow \tau$$
$$TRANS(3)$$
$$\quad \wr 7$$
$$send!3 \rightarrow ((ack \xrightarrow{1} TRANS) \overset{3}{\triangleright} TRANS(3))$$
$$\quad \downarrow send.3$$
$$(ack \xrightarrow{1} TRANS) \overset{3}{\triangleright} TRANS(3)$$
$$\quad \wr 2$$
$$(ack \xrightarrow{1} TRANS) \overset{1}{\triangleright} TRANS(3)$$
$$\quad \downarrow ack$$
$$STOP \overset{1}{\triangleright} TRANS$$
$$\quad \vdots$$

The transitions from *TRANS* and *TRANS*(3) are deduced from the corresponding process definitions.   ∎

Example 9.5.6 A digital stopwatch accurate to one hundredth of a second can be started, stopped, and reset. When stopped, it can also display the time it currently holds: this takes one second. The watch is defined by

$$STOPWATCH = STOPPEDWATCH(0)$$

where $STOPPEDWATCH(t)$ and $STOPWATCH(t)$ are defined by a set of mutually recursive definitions:

$$
\begin{aligned}
STOPPEDWATCH(t) \quad &= \quad start \overset{0.01}{\to} STOPWATCH(0.01) \\
&\quad \Box \ time!t \overset{1}{\to} STOPPEDWATCH(t) \\
STOPWATCH(t) \quad &= \quad (halt \overset{0.01}{\to} STOPPEDWATCH(t + 0.01) \\
&\qquad \overset{0.01}{\rhd} STOPWATCH(t + 0.01)) \\
&\quad \Box \ reset \overset{0.01}{\to} STOPWATCH(0)
\end{aligned}
$$

There is a latency of 0.01 seconds following any of the buttons on the watch: *start*, *halt*, and *reset*. Display of the time, modelled by the output *time!t*, takes a full second, and is possible only when the watch is stopped. ∎

As in the case of single recursion, mutually recursive definitions should be time-guarded to avoid infinitely fast executions. There should be a minimum delay between successive recursive calls throughout the process definition. For a collection of definitions this means that there should be a single non-zero time guard which is a lower bound on all of the process definitions for when they will next reach the next recursively bound process name. This is discussed in greater depth in Section 10.3.

9.6 CONCURRENCY

Many of the aspects of the computational model concerning the timed behaviour of processes—durationless events, maximal parallelism, maximal progress, Newtonian time—have an impact on the modelling of concurrent processes. The transitions given for all of the parallel operators below directly reflect these properties. Concurrent processes must always agree on the performance of evolution transitions. This is due to a combination of the maximal parallelism property and the Newtonian time assumption, which require that concurrent processes are executed together rather than scheduled one after the other, and that time passes at the same rate in all processes.

The durationless nature of event transitions is reflected in the fact that if a concurrent component is not participating in an event of a concurrent combination, then it makes no progress, through time or otherwise, while the event occurs. When concurrent components do synchronize on an event, then no delays are introduced: the combination is ready to engage in the event at the instant all the participants are ready, in accordance with maximal progress.

Alphabetized parallel

The alphabetized parallel operator provides interfaces A and B for its two component processes Q_1 and Q_2, and they synchronize on events common to both interfaces, but are independently able to perform events outside this intersection. They must also synchronize on termination. The event transitions in the timed context are identical to the untimed transitions, though the understanding of them here is that they describe the possible first steps of the process at the very first instant of execution. The single timed transition simply requires that time progresses at the same rate in both Q_1 and Q_2.

$$\frac{Q_1 \xrightarrow{\mu} Q_1'}{Q_1 \, _A\|_B \, Q_2 \xrightarrow{\mu} Q_1' \, _A\|_B \, Q_2} \quad [\, \mu \in (A \cup \{\tau\} \setminus B) \,]$$

$$\frac{Q_2 \xrightarrow{\mu} Q_2'}{Q_1 \, _A\|_B \, Q_2 \xrightarrow{\mu} Q_1 \, _A\|_B \, Q_2'} \quad [\, \mu \in (B \cup \{\tau\} \setminus A) \,]$$

$$\frac{Q_1 \xrightarrow{a} Q_1' \qquad Q_2 \xrightarrow{a} Q_2'}{Q_1 \, _A\|_B \, Q_2 \xrightarrow{a} Q_1' \, _A\|_B \, Q_2'} \quad [\, a \in (A \cap B)^{\checkmark} \,]$$

$$\frac{Q_1 \stackrel{d}{\rightsquigarrow} Q_1' \qquad Q_2 \stackrel{d}{\rightsquigarrow} Q_2'}{Q_1 \, _A\|_B \, Q_2 \stackrel{d}{\rightsquigarrow} Q_1' \, _A\|_B \, Q_2'}$$

Two processes can synchronize on an event they both perform only at a time when both are ready. This is a consequence of the fact that time progresses at the same rate in both processes, together with the requirement that both processes must be ready for synchronization at the same instant. The set of times at which a common event can occur in a parallel combination will be the intersection of the sets of times at which each process can perform it.

As in untimed CSP, the combination $Q_1 \parallel Q_2$ is understood as $Q_1 \, _{\alpha Q_1}\|_{\alpha Q_2} \, Q_2$.

Example 9.6.1 If Helen is expecting a meeting and will wait up to 30 minutes before giving up and finding something else to do, and Carl will be ready for a meeting in 15 minutes, then it is possible that they will meet since there is an overlap in the times that they are available.

$$HELEN \;\; = \;\; (meet \xrightarrow{30} work \to STOP) \stackrel{30}{\triangleright} work \to STOP$$

$$CARL \;\; = \;\; WAIT \, 15; \, ((meet \xrightarrow{30} home \to STOP) \stackrel{45}{\triangleright} home \to STOP)$$

The parallel combination

$$HELEN \parallel CARL$$

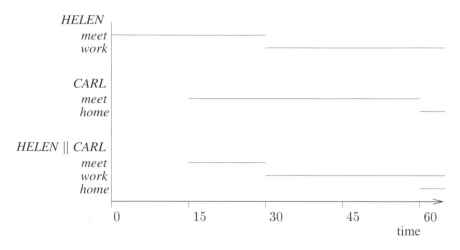

Fig. 9.3   Possible initial events for Helen and Carl

describes the situation where *HELEN* works independently, but requires *CARL* to participate in a meeting. The default alphabets for *HELEN* and *CARL* are {*meet*, *work*} and {*meet*, *home*} respectively. Although no meeting is possible in the first 15 minutes because *CARL* will not perform the event *meet*, after 15 minutes *CARL* becomes able to perform *meet* and there is a window of 15 minutes before *HELEN* will give up and return to work. The event *meet* is enabled during that 15 minutes. If it does not occur then *CARL* will wait a further 30 minutes before giving up on the meeting and returning home. These possibilities are illustrated in Figure 9.3.

If Carl is 30 minutes behind schedule, then his behaviour would be described by

$$LATECARL \quad = \quad WAIT\ 45; ((meet \xrightarrow{30} home \rightarrow STOP) \overset{45}{\triangleright} home \rightarrow STOP)$$

In this case there is no possibility of synchronizing for the meeting. By the time *LATECARL* is ready to perform *meet*, *HELEN* has already given up waiting and has returned to her work. Although *HELEN* and *LATECARL* are each able to engage in the event *meet* as their first event, they are unable to synchronize on that event in the combination

$$HELEN \parallel LATECARL$$

because they cannot agree on a time for it to occur.   ■

The style of introducing constraints to a specification by means of the parallel operator extends to timing requirements. A minimum delay may be expressed by means of a delayed prefix. The requirement that *b* should be offered at least 5 seconds after *a* is captured in the description

$$C1 \quad = \quad a \xrightarrow{5} b \rightarrow STOP$$

In this process, there is a delay of 5 seconds after the occurrence of the a event before the b becomes possible, forcing a minimum delay of 5 after the a.

A maximum delay between occurrence of events in a process-oriented specification is expressed by a timeout. A maximum delay of 8 seconds between occurrence of a and occurrence of b is described by

$$C2 \quad = \quad a \rightarrow ((b \rightarrow STOP) \overset{8}{\triangleright} STOP)$$

In this process, if a and b both occur then they must do so within 8 seconds of each other. The combination of minimum and maximum delay together can be expressed as $C1 \parallel C2$, or alternatively as

$$C3 \quad = \quad a \overset{5}{\rightarrow} ((b \rightarrow STOP) \overset{3}{\triangleright} STOP)$$

Neither $C1$ nor $C2$ require that b must occur, since it is an external event and hence can always be blocked by an unco-operative environment. Both constraints simply describe some restriction on b's availability.

A maximum delay before an event is *offered* is expressed by means of a nondeterministic delayed prefix. If b may be offered as soon as 5 seconds after the a, and must be offered within 6 seconds, then this is described by the constraint

$$C4 \quad = \quad a \overset{[5,6]}{\rightarrow} b \rightarrow STOP$$

This constraint does not place a constraint of the maximum delay between the occurrences of a and b—a timeout would be required for that—simply between the occurrence of a and the offer of b.

In contrast, the minimum required delay between the occurrence of a and the offer of b must always be the same as the minimum possible delay between their occurrences: if b occurs then it must have been offered, and if it is offered then its occurrence is possible.

Example 9.6.2 After supper, Kate's bedtime routine is that either she has a 15 minute bath followed by bed, or else goes straight to bed. These choices are described as follows:

$$KATE\_BED \quad = \quad supper \rightarrow ((bath \overset{15}{\rightarrow} bed \rightarrow STOP) \;\square\; bed \rightarrow STOP)$$

There are also timing constraints on the relationships between these events. She should not have a bath for at least 20 minutes after supper, and also no more than 90 minutes after supper. This combines a maximum and a minimum delay requirement, and is described by $K1$. Furthermore, she should not go to bed for at least 80 minutes after supper, as described by $K2$.

$$K1 \quad = \quad supper \overset{20}{\rightarrow} ((bath \rightarrow STOP) \overset{70}{\triangleright} STOP)$$
$$K2 \quad = \quad supper \overset{80}{\rightarrow} bed \rightarrow STOP$$

The combined requirements are described by

$$K \quad = \quad K1 \parallel K2$$

where $K1$ and $K2$ impose constraints only on those events in their alphabets.

The complete description of the expected behaviour is

$$K \parallel KATE\_BED$$

This combined behaviour would be difficult to express without the parallel operator, and also harder to understand. The use of the parallel operator permits separation of requirements which are conceptually distinct.   ∎

Indexed parallel

The indexed parallel operator $\left\Vert_{A_i}^{i \in I} Q_i\right.$ behaves exactly as expected. It is defined in terms of multiple applications of the binary parallel operator in Section 2.1. This definition means that it can perform an event whenever all relevant components are able to perform it, and it can evolve precisely when all of its component processes can evolve.

Example 9.6.3 A chain of n processes which act simply as buffers passing on information was introduced in Example 2.1.11. Each process in the chain simply inputs a message and passes it on. This example may be elaborated by the introduction of a timed specification concerning the message throughput for each node. The requirement is that following input of a message, it must be available for output 2 microseconds later, and must be accepted within 12 microseconds, or not at all. This is expressed by means of a delayed prefix and a timeout.

For every i between 0 and $n-1$, the timed buffer TQ_i and its interface A_i is given by the following definition,

$$A_i \quad = \quad c_i.\mathbb{Z} \cup c_{i+1}.\mathbb{Z}$$
$$TQ_i \quad = \quad c_i?x : \mathbb{Z} \xrightarrow{2} ((c_{i+1}!x \to TQ_i) \overset{10}{\triangleright} STOP)$$

The interfaces are identical to those in the untimed version, as is the description of the chain of buffers:

$$TCHAIN \quad = \quad \left\Vert_{A_i}^{i \in \{0 \ldots n-1\}} TQ_i\right.$$

There are n nodes in the chain, and each introduces a delay of at least 2 microseconds. Any message input along c_0 cannot be offered as output on c_n until a minimum of $2n$ microseconds have elapsed. Furthermore, if it is to be offered as output then this must occur within $12n$ microseconds.

The input rate can be as fast as one message every 2 microseconds if all the events in the system occur as soon as possible. There is no minimum input rate. The chain may hold as many as n pieces of data, all of which will be lost if an output on c_n does not occur during the 10 microsecond window it is available.   ∎

Interleaving

The introduction of time to the interleaving operator is entirely similar to the approach taken for the parallel composition. In an interleaved combination each internal or external event is performed by precisely one of the components, while the other component makes no progress at all, reflecting the decision to treat events as having no duration. The passage of time occurs at the same rate in both processes, so they must agree on timed transitions.

The rules for deriving the transitions for an interleaved combination are as follows:

$$
\frac{Q_1 \overset{\mu}{\to} Q_1'}{\begin{array}{c} Q_1 \;|||\; Q_2 \overset{\mu}{\to} Q_1' \;|||\; Q_2 \\ Q_2 \;|||\; Q_1 \overset{\mu}{\to} Q_2 \;|||\; Q_1' \end{array}} \; [\, \mu \neq \checkmark \,]
\qquad
\frac{Q_1 \overset{d}{\rightsquigarrow} Q_1' \quad Q_2 \overset{d}{\rightsquigarrow} Q_2'}{Q_1 \;|||\; Q_2 \overset{d}{\rightsquigarrow} Q_1' \;|||\; Q_2'}
$$

$$
\frac{Q_1 \overset{\checkmark}{\to} Q_1' \quad Q_2 \overset{\checkmark}{\to} Q_2'}{Q_1 \;|||\; Q_2 \overset{\checkmark}{\to} Q_1' \;|||\; Q_2'}
$$

The event transitions are the same as in the untimed case, and the timed transition is derived from the same timed transition in each component.

In the context of time it is easy to see that two interleaved copies of a process which performs a particular task will be faster than a single copy of that process—the task will be performed more times over any given interval.

Example 9.6.4 The fax machine of Example 2.2.3 can be elaborated to include timing information. It will take 20 seconds to print each page of a fax message. If $\#d$ is the number of pages of message d, then the behaviour of the timed fax machine *TFAX* may be described as follows:

$$
TFAX \;=\; accept?d : DOCUMENT \to print!d \overset{20\#d}{\to} TFAX
$$

Thus a single *TFAX* machine can print off one page every 20 seconds. A bank of four faxes

$$
TFAXES \;=\; (TFAX \;|||\; TFAX) \;|||\; (TFAX \;|||\; TFAX)
$$

is able to print off up to four pages every 20 seconds, and so in this sense it is faster. However, the improvement is apparent only if many fax messages arrive together, since different messages can then be processed concurrently, compared to the sequential processing possible for a single machine. The bank of faxes will not process a single message any quicker, since only one fax machine will be used for any particular message. ∎

Indexed interleaving

The timed interleaving operator is both associative and commutative, so the indexed form

$$\left|\right|\right|_{i \in I} Q_i$$

is well-defined for a finite indexing set I. It behaves as expected, performing events at any point where any component process can do so, and passing time at the same rate in all components.

Interface parallel

The hybrid form of parallel composition also takes the same approach to time, performing events at points where the relevant participating processes are able to do so, and forcing them all to pass time together at the same rate. The operational semantics is straightforward:

$$\frac{Q_1 \xrightarrow{a} Q_1' \quad Q_2 \xrightarrow{a} Q_2'}{Q_1 \underset{A}{\|} Q_2 \xrightarrow{a} Q_1' \underset{A}{\|} Q_2'} \quad [\, a \in A \,]$$

$$\frac{Q_1 \xrightarrow{\mu} Q_1'}{\begin{array}{c} Q_1 \underset{A}{\|} Q_2 \xrightarrow{\mu} Q_1' \underset{A}{\|} Q_2 \\[4pt] Q_2 \underset{A}{\|} Q_1 \xrightarrow{\mu} Q_2 \underset{A}{\|} Q_1' \end{array}} \quad [\, \mu \notin A^{\checkmark} \,]$$

$$\frac{Q_1 \overset{d}{\rightsquigarrow} Q_1' \quad Q_2 \overset{d}{\rightsquigarrow} Q_2'}{Q_1 \underset{A}{\|} Q_2 \overset{d}{\rightsquigarrow} Q_1' \underset{A}{\|} Q_2'}$$

The processes Q_1 and Q_2 co-operate on any event drawn from A, and interleave on events not in A. They must also co-operate on time transitions.

Indexed interface parallel

The timed version of interface parallel, for a given set of common events A, is associative and commutative, so the generalisation of the interface parallel operator is well-defined when the indexing set I is finite and each process Q_i is defined for each $i \in I$.

$$\underset{A_{i \in I}}{\|} Q_i$$

The timed behaviour of this combination follows exactly the same pattern as the other parallel operators. Any event in A can occur only when all the processes are ready to participate in it, though events outside A can occur whenever any single process wishes to perform it. Any time transition must involve all the component processes.

9.7 ABSTRACTION

Hiding

When an event is made internal, then the environment of the system is no longer required to participate in that event. The encapsulation achieved by the hiding operation is to identify *all* participants in the event. Removing the event from the interface closes off the opportunity for any other processes to become involved.

The property of maximal progress requires an event to occur when all of its participants are ready. This forces hidden events to become urgent, occurring at the instant they are enabled, since all the participants of an internal event are identified in the process description. The process

$$Q = (a \rightarrow b \rightarrow STOP) \setminus \{a\}$$

should perform the a, internally, at the instant the process begins execution. This will enable the event b at time 0. Encapsulation of the event a means that Q has complete control over it, taking responsibility for its occurrence.

Example 9.7.1 Example 2.1.10 introduced a CSP description of a meeting composed of a group of people who all had to participate in the event *meeting*. Timing information may be introduced into the description: it takes 1 minute to enter or leave, and once the meeting starts nobody is allowed to leave for 10 minutes.

$$TPERSON_{name} = enter.name \xrightarrow{1} TPRESENT_{name}$$

$$TPRESENT_{name} = leave.name \xrightarrow{1} TPERSON_{name}$$
$$\square \; meeting \xrightarrow{10} TPRESENT_{name}$$

A meeting between Alice and Bob could be described as $AB = TPERSON_{alice} \parallel TPERSON_{bob}$. They synchronize on *meeting*, but perform their *enter* and *leave* events independently. However, this description leaves open the possibility that other people may also attend the meeting, since further *TPERSON* processes may be introduced in parallel with AB. The meeting can go ahead only with the consent of AB's environment.

The hiding operator is used to describe the situation where there are to be no further participants in the meeting. The encapsulation $AB \setminus \{meeting\}$ removes the possibility of involvement of any other processes, and ensures that the meeting goes ahead as soon as Alice and Bob are both ready. This will be 1 minute after the second of them performs their *enter* event. ∎

Urgency is captured in the timed transition system by ensuring that time cannot pass while an urgent event is enabled. This is built into the transition rules for the hiding operator, which give the transitions for the process $Q \setminus A$.

$$\frac{Q \xrightarrow{a} Q'}{Q \setminus A \xrightarrow{\tau} Q' \setminus A} \quad [\, a \in A \,] \qquad\qquad \frac{Q \stackrel{d}{\rightsquigarrow} Q' \quad \forall a \in A \bullet \neg(Q \xrightarrow{a})}{Q \setminus A \stackrel{d}{\rightsquigarrow} Q' \setminus A}$$

$$\frac{Q \xrightarrow{\mu} Q'}{Q \setminus A \xrightarrow{\mu} Q' \setminus A} \quad [\, \mu \notin A \,]$$

The rule for the timed transitions allows an evolution to occur only if there are no outstanding internal events. Section 10.2 will discuss the property that the set of events on offer by a process does not change simply with the passage of time; any change must be accompanied by some internal or external event. This means that if no events from the set A are possible for Q at the beginning of an evolution $Q \stackrel{d}{\rightsquigarrow} Q'$, then they will not be possible at any point during that evolution, and indeed will not be possible for Q'. This property of the transition system ensures that maximal progress is not violated by the evolution transition rule for hiding; there is no possibility of any hidden events becoming enabled during the evolution.

The rule for evolution of abstracted processes introduces the feature of a *negative premiss*, where an evolution is possible only if some other transitions are not possible. The only other operator for which this will occur is sequential composition, which also introduces a special form of urgency on the ✓ event. All of the operators seen so far in this chapter have had their evolution transitions derived from the evolutions of their components, or else given without premisses at all. The evolution rule given here is dependent on the *absence* of some other event transitions from the timed transition system. This means that all of the event transitions of Q must first be known in order to deduce whether or not $Q \setminus A$ is able to evolve.

The transition rules for all of the operators are given in such a way that event transitions are defined only in terms of other event transitions, without any conditions about evolution transitions appearing in any of their premisses. The timed transition system for timed CSP is accordingly defined in two steps. The event transitions are all defined in the first step, and so all of the event transitions possible for each process are already determined by the stage the evolution transitions are derived in the second step.

Example 9.7.2 The process $c \to b \to STOP$ has only one event transition

$$(c \to b \to STOP) \xrightarrow{c} (b \to STOP)$$

in addition to the evolution transitions $(c \rightarrow b \rightarrow STOP) \overset{d}{\leadsto} (c \rightarrow b \rightarrow STOP)$.

Any evolution transition for the process $(c \rightarrow b \rightarrow STOP) \setminus \{c\}$ will be derived from the inference rule

$$\frac{Q \overset{d}{\leadsto} Q' \\ \forall a \in A \bullet \neg(Q \overset{a}{\rightarrow})}{Q \setminus A \overset{d}{\leadsto} Q' \setminus A}$$

but although the first premiss is true—the process can itself evolve—the second premiss requiring the absence of a c transition is false. It follows that there are no evolution transitions for the process when c is hidden. On the other hand, the first inference rule for event transitions yields the single internal transition

$$((c \rightarrow b \rightarrow STOP) \setminus \{c\}) \overset{\tau}{\rightarrow} ((b \rightarrow STOP) \setminus \{c\})$$

The fact that there are no evolutions ensures that this transition is urgent. In fact it is the only transition that is possible for the process $(c \rightarrow b \rightarrow STOP) \setminus \{c\}$.

The process $(b \rightarrow STOP) \setminus \{c\}$ has both event and evolution transitions. The negative premiss $\neg((b \rightarrow STOP) \overset{c}{\rightarrow})$ is true, so the evolutions for the process $(b \rightarrow STOP)$ give rise to evolutions for the process $(b \rightarrow STOP) \setminus \{c\}$. Furthermore the b transition is not made internal, but remains as an external event when c is abstracted.

A typical execution of the process $(c \rightarrow b \rightarrow STOP) \setminus \{c\}$ might then be

$$(c \rightarrow b \rightarrow STOP) \setminus \{c\}$$
$$\downarrow \tau$$
$$(b \rightarrow STOP) \setminus \{c\}$$
$$\wr 5$$
$$(b \rightarrow STOP) \setminus \{c\}$$
$$\downarrow b$$
$$STOP \setminus \{c\}$$
$$\wr 3$$
$$STOP \setminus \{c\}$$
$$\vdots$$

The internal event must occur at time 0, enabling the event b which will then remain enabled until it occurs.   ■

The fact that hidden events become urgent means that if a process is prepared to engage in a choice of different events, then the hidden event that is first enabled must be chosen. A choice will be resolved in favour of the first available event. For example, in the process

$$((a \rightarrow Q_1) \; \Box \; (WAIT \; 1; b \rightarrow Q_2)) \setminus \{a, b\}$$

both a and b are offered as alternatives of the choice, but b will not be available for 1 second, whereas a is available immediately. The abstraction of a and b means that the internal a becomes urgent and must occur at time 0, resolving the choice before b becomes possible.

Example 9.7.3 Two well-known algorithms for finding the minimal spanning tree over a graph are Prim's algorithm and Kruskal's algorithm. The relative efficiency of each is dependent on the properties of the input graph. Rather than perform some precalculation on an input to decide which algorithm is most appropriate to invoke, it is possible to run both algorithms concurrently and simply accept the first answer returned by either of them.

The algorithms for graphs up to a given maximum number of nodes are encoded within the processes *PRIM* and *KRUSKAL*, whose interface behaviour is given by

$$PRIM = in?g : GRAPH \overset{[5,250]}{\to} out_1!sp_1(g) \to STOP$$

$$KRUSKAL = in?g : GRAPH \overset{[2,300]}{\to} out_2!sp_2(g) \to STOP$$

The functions sp_1 and sp_2 calculate the minimal spanning tree of a graph according to Prim's and Kruskal's algorithm respectively. The precise description of the algorithms are not included in the descriptions of the processes, since such internal computation is orthogonal to the descriptions of the interactions each process may be involved in. However, the possible time associated with the execution of the algorithm is included in the delay following an input. Prim's algorithm will take at least 5 seconds to return a result, but will be sure to finish with $250s$. On the other hand, Kruskal's algorithm might return a result within 2 seconds, but may take as long as 300.

A 'shortest path server' which takes in a query on channel *query* and returns an answer on channel *answer* is written to make use of both of these algorithms to obtain the fastest result.

$$SP = query?g : GRAPH \to in!g \to \quad out_1?t : TREE \to answer!t \to STOP$$
$$\square$$
$$out_2?t : TREE \to answer!t \to STOP$$

The entire service is illustrated in Figure 9.4 and is described as

$$(SP \underset{in,out_1,out_2}{\|} (PRIM \underset{in}{\|} KRUSKAL)) \setminus \{in, out_1, out_2\}$$

The first answer to be offered on channel out_1 or out_2 will be accepted and will resolve the choice at the instant it is offered. ■

Example 9.7.4 A print spooler accepts print jobs along an input channel and passes them on to the printer. The printer receives jobs from the spooler and prints them out. The delays between input and output imposed by each of these processes varies nondeterministically

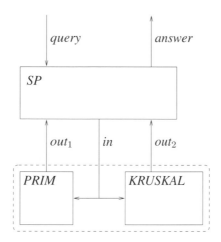

Fig. 9.4   A minimal spanning tree server

depending on factors such as the size of the job and whether the paper tray requires refilling on the printer.

$$SPOOL = in?j : JOB \overset{[2,10]}{\to} mid!j \overset{1}{\to} SPOOL$$

$$PRINT = mid?j : JOB \overset{[1,30]}{\to} print!j \overset{[5,100]}{\to} PRINT$$

The channel *mid* is used to pass jobs from *SPOOL* to *PRINT*: the appropriate description places these two components in parallel, and then makes the channel *mid* internal to indicate that it is a channel between precisely those two components.

$$(SPOOL \parallel PRINT) \setminus mid.JOB$$

In some circumstances, *SPOOL* may be ready to send a job on *mid* but *PRINT* is not yet ready. This possibility arises, for example, if the previous job is taking a long time to print and *SPOOL* has already accepted the next job. In this case, the time at which the message passes will depend on the time that *PRINT* becomes ready to accept it. In other situations, *PRINT* is ready to receive the message but *SPOOL* has not yet made it available. In this case, the time of the *mid* event will depend upon *SPOOL*'s behaviour.

In this example, neither *SPOOL* nor *PRINT* has control over when the *mid* event should occur, so neither of them can individually be given the responsibility for ensuring that it is performed. However, responsibility lies with the combination. Maximal progress ensures that the job is passed along *mid* as soon as both processes are ready for this to occur.   ■

Example 9.7.5 Timeout was crudely modelled in the untimed language by means of a timeout event. Example 3.1.7 introduced a special offer which lapsed at a particular point, whereupon it was replaced by the standard offer.

$$OFFER \quad = \quad ((cheap \to STOP) \ \Box \ (lapse \to standard \to STOP)) \setminus \{lapse\}$$

The timed language allows the delay before the *lapse* event to be made explicit. If the special offer is to last 10 days, then there should be a delay of 10 before the event *lapse*:

$$TOFFER =$$
$$((cheap \to STOP) \ \Box \ (WAIT \ 10; lapse \to standard \to STOP)) \setminus \{lapse\}$$

This means that the *cheap* offer will stand for 10 days, and will be replaced by a standard offer if it has not been taken up by that time.

This process is equivalent to the timeout process

$$(cheap \to STOP) \ \overset{10}{\triangleright} \ standard \to STOP$$

A timeout can be constructed from an external choice in this way. A delayed special event is made available as part of the choice, and the hiding operator is used to make that special event urgent and thus resolve the choice at the required time, if it has not already been resolved.

■

Example 9.7.6 Example 3.1.10 described a process which polled two data channels, checking each of them repeatedly in turn until one of them provided input.

$$POLL \quad = \quad in.1?x : T \to out!x \to POLL$$
$$\Box \ switch \to (\ in.2?x : T \to out!x \to POLL$$
$$\Box \ switch \to POLL)$$

The lack of timing information in this description means that the possibility of divergence cannot be excluded when the *switch* event is hidden. A refined version of *POLL* which includes timing information makes it clear that the process is well-behaved when *switch* is hidden:

$$TPOLL \quad = \quad in.1?x \overset{1}{\to} out!x \overset{1}{\to} TPOLL$$
$$\Box \ WAIT \ 2; switch \to (\ in.2?x \overset{1}{\to} out!x \overset{1}{\to} TPOLL$$
$$\Box \ WAIT \ 2; switch \to TPOLL)$$

Each input is checked for 2 seconds before the *switch* event is enabled, allowing attention to be transferred to the other input. The process $TPOLL \setminus \{switch\}$ makes the event *switch* urgent, so each input channel is monitored for exactly 2 seconds in turn until some input is performed. This timeout behaviour arises through the combination discussed in the previous example: choice, delay, and hiding.

The use of the internal *switch* event in the process description is as a timeout event. Input is awaited for a particular interval, and if it is not forthcoming then the urgent *switch* event removes control and passes it to the next phase of the process. In fact the process *TPOLL* \ {*switch*} is indistinguishable from the process *POLLING* defined in Example 9.5.1.

There is no notion of fairness between the two input channels: if *in*.1 is always supplied with input, then *in*.2 will never be examined. This might be appropriate if *in*.1 is the main input channel, and *in*.2 is a backup input channel which does not need to be read while the main channel is operating as expected. ■

Event renaming

The event renaming operators allow synchronization events to be replaced in a process execution. The operators do not affect any timing behaviour, and leave evolution transitions unchanged. As in the untimed language, in each case the renaming is by means of a function $f : \Sigma \to \Sigma$ for which $f(\checkmark) = \checkmark$—termination must be preserved.

The case of forward renaming allows the process $f(Q)$ to perform the event $f(a)$ whenever Q could perform a.

$$\frac{Q \xrightarrow{a} Q'}{f(Q) \xrightarrow{f(a)} f(Q')} \qquad \frac{Q \overset{d}{\rightsquigarrow} Q'}{f(Q) \overset{d}{\rightsquigarrow} f(Q')}$$

$$\frac{Q \xrightarrow{\tau} Q'}{f(Q) \xrightarrow{\tau} f(Q')}$$

As in the untimed case, the function f need not be injective: different events may be renamed to the same resulting event. In this case the identity of the originating event is abstracted, and nondeterminism may be introduced as a result. In the timed context nondeterminism may arise even if it does not appear in the untimed behaviour, by affecting the timing behaviour of the resulting process. For example, a process $(a \xrightarrow{3} c \to STOP) \; \square \; (b \xrightarrow{5} c \to STOP)$ might be renamed via a function that maps both a and b to d. At the untimed level the result is a deterministic process that can initially perform d and then perform c. When the timing behaviour is considered, the result is equivalent to the process $d \xrightarrow{3} c \to STOP \sqcap d \xrightarrow{5} c \to STOP$. It is nondeterministic whether or not c will be available 4 seconds after d.

Backward renaming allows $f^{-1}(Q)$ to perform a whenever Q can perform $f(a)$. This operator also has no impact on the timing behaviour of a process, leaving evolution transitions unchanged.

$$
\frac{Q \xrightarrow{f(a)} Q'}{f^{-1}(Q) \xrightarrow{a} f^{-1}(Q')}
\qquad\qquad
\frac{Q \overset{d}{\rightsquigarrow} Q'}{f^{-1}(Q) \overset{d}{\rightsquigarrow} f^{-1}(Q')}
$$

$$
\frac{Q \xrightarrow{\tau} Q'}{f^{-1}(Q) \xrightarrow{\tau} f^{-1}(Q')}
$$

This operator does not introduce any new nondeterminism, even in the presence of time.

9.8   FLOW OF CONTROL

Sequential composition

Sequential composition allows control to pass to a second process when the first one terminates successfully, as indicated by the occurrence of the termination event $\checkmark$. In the process

$$Q_1 ; Q_2$$

control must pass immediately and urgently to Q_2 on termination of Q_1. This means that if Q_1 is able to perform a $\checkmark$ event then it cannot delay before performing it. This is expressed by using the mechanism for making events urgent: evolution transitions must be blocked whenever Q_1's termination event is enabled.

$$
\frac{Q_1 \xrightarrow{\mu} Q_1'}{Q_1 ; Q_2 \xrightarrow{\mu} Q_1' ; Q_2} \quad [\, \mu \neq \checkmark \,]
\qquad\qquad
\frac{Q_1 \overset{d}{\rightsquigarrow} Q_1' \quad \neg(Q_1 \xrightarrow{\checkmark})}{Q_1 ; Q_2 \overset{d}{\rightsquigarrow} Q_1' ; Q_2}
$$

$$
\frac{Q_1 \xrightarrow{\checkmark} Q_1'}{Q_1 ; Q_2 \xrightarrow{\tau} Q_2}
$$

The rule for evolutions of $Q_1 ; Q_2$ has a negative premiss concerning the transitions of Q_1, as did the rule for hiding. This is used to ensure that evolutions cannot occur when termination is possible.

The passing of control is urgent. The process $SKIP; Q$ should behave exactly as Q, and the possibility of $SKIP$'s immediate termination ensures that Q indeed begins execution at time 0 in the process $SKIP; Q$. A delayed process $WAIT\ d; Q$ relies on the fact that passage of control will occur at the instant $WAIT\ d$ is first ready to terminate, ensuring that Q begins execution after precisely d time units.

If one branch of an external choice is simply a delay, then it may be used with a sequential composition to produce timeout behaviour. The process

$$a \rightarrow Q\ \square\ WAIT\ d$$

offers the event a from time 0, and also raises the possibility of termination at time d if the choice has not already been resolved. If termination is made urgent, then the offer of the a event will timeout at time d.

The construction $(Q_1\ \square\ WAIT\ d); Q_2$ is initially prepared to behave as Q_1, but if no event occurs by time d then control passes to Q_2. The difference between this construction and timeout is that if the choice is resolved in Q_1's favour by an event before time d, then Q_2 is not discarded but is retained for execution after termination of Q_1. It is equivalent to $Q_1; Q_2$ timing out to Q_2.

$$(Q_1\ \square\ WAIT\ d); Q_2\ =\ Q_1; Q_2 \overset{d}{\triangleright} Q_2$$

This construction is useful in cases where the second process Q_2 must occur, and the first Q_1 should be given an opportunity before Q_2 is executed.

Example 9.8.1 A bus will visit 17 stops on its route. At each stop, it will wait for 10 seconds to see if anyone wishes to *alight* from or *board* the bus. Each of these activities can take any time between 30 seconds and 3 minutes (180 seconds). There is a 2 minute journey between stops, so there will be a delay of 120 seconds between the time the bus leaves one stop and the time it reaches the next.

The behaviour between the ith stop and the $i + 1$th stop is given by

$$BUS\_STOP_i\ =\ (((alight \overset{[30,180]}{\rightarrow} SKIP)\ \square\ WAIT\ 10)$$
$$|||\ ((board \overset{[30,180]}{\rightarrow} SKIP)\ \square\ WAIT\ 10));\ WAIT\ 120$$

Here there are two possibilities which may time out: alighting from and boarding the bus. In each case, if the event does not occur within 10 seconds, then the choice will be resolved against it. Either can independently occur, and if it does then there will be a delay of between half a minute and 3 minutes before the bus is able to resume its journey, modelled by control passing to the final delay process $WAIT\ 120$, which represents the journey to the next stop.

The entire bus journey may be described by

$$BUS\_STOP_1; BUS\_STOP_2; \ldots; BUS\_STOP_{16}; BUS\_STOP_{17}$$

All of the bus stops will be visited in turn, and at each the possibility for passengers to alight and board will be made available. However, at each stop the same subsequent process will follow whether or not that possibility is taken up, so a standard timeout for those events is inappropriate and the construction using sequential composition is preferable. ∎

Interrupt

The interrupt construction $Q_1 \bigtriangleup Q_2$ allows the first process Q_1 to execute, but it may be interrupted at any time by an event from process Q_2. The timed interpretation of this operator permits greater control over precisely when interrupts may occur, since it allows the interrupting process Q_2 to raise and lower the possibility of interrupt events while Q_1 is executing. In effect, Q_2 is executed concurrently with Q_1 until either Q_1 terminates the execution, or else Q_2 performs an interrupt event.

Unlike sequential composition, in the interrupt construction both Q_1 and Q_2 evolve together. The process Q_2 is also able to perform internal events without triggering the interrupt, which means that external interrupt events may be offered and retracted by Q_2 as the execution unfolds.

The transition rules are as follows:

$$\frac{Q_1 \xrightarrow{\mu} Q_1'}{Q_1 \bigtriangleup Q_2 \xrightarrow{\mu} Q_1' \bigtriangleup Q_2} \quad [\,\mu \neq \checkmark\,] \qquad \frac{Q_1 \overset{d}{\rightsquigarrow} Q_1' \quad Q_2 \overset{d}{\rightsquigarrow} Q_2'}{Q_1 \bigtriangleup Q_2 \overset{d}{\rightsquigarrow} Q_1' \bigtriangleup Q_2'}$$

$$\frac{Q_1 \xrightarrow{\checkmark} Q_1'}{Q_1 \bigtriangleup Q_2 \xrightarrow{\checkmark} Q_1'}$$

$$\frac{Q_2 \xrightarrow{\tau} Q_2'}{Q_1 \bigtriangleup Q_2 \xrightarrow{\tau} Q_1 \bigtriangleup Q_2'}$$

$$\frac{Q_2 \xrightarrow{a} Q_2'}{Q_1 \bigtriangleup Q_2 \xrightarrow{a} Q_2'}$$

A static interrupting process Q_2 which does not change as Q_1 progresses can be achieved by means of using a prefix or a prefix choice process as an interrupting process. The interrupting events in that case would be initially available, and would remain possible as long as necessary. Processes prefixed by events do not make progress initially, they simply allow time to pass, remaining in the same state until their event is performed.

Example 9.8.2 Many trains offer passengers the means to stop the train in an emergency. There is an 'emergency stop' handle in each carriage which can be used as a brake for the train. This offers passengers the opportunity to interrupt the train journey. It is a static interrupt, in the sense that it does not evolve with time but rather offers the same interrupt event throughout the journey, with the same effect whenever it is performed. If *JOURNEY* describes the normal behaviour of the train during a journey, and *EMERGENCY* describes the behaviour subsequent to the emergency handle being pulled, then the availability of the emergency stop is described by

$$JOURNEY \; \triangle \; (handle \rightarrow EMERGENCY)$$

In this case the interrupt behaviour itself is not time-dependent, though the processes *JOURNEY* and *EMERGENCY* might be. ∎

Example 9.8.3 A late-night party begins at 9pm. After 11pm, there is the possibility that the party will be closed down due to the level of noise. There are 2 hours of the party where there is no danger of interruption, but after that interval the possibility of being closed down arises. This is naturally described by

$$PARTY \; \triangle \; (WAIT \; 2; \, close \rightarrow SKIP)$$

The interrupting event *close* becomes enabled after 2 hours, allowing the party to be closed down if necessary. The interrupting event does not have to occur, and if the noise level is sufficiently low then the party may continue. Observe also that if the party finishes early, then the entire process terminates and the interrupt is no longer required. ∎

Example 9.8.4 Eleanor and Kate have access to a photocopier. Eleanor demands access to the copier, modelled by *in.eleanor*, whenever she needs to use it, though she only ever copies one item at a time. Kate has general use of the copier, on the understanding that she can be interrupted at any time by Eleanor. Kate's and Eleanor's usage of the photocopier is described by

$$KATE \;\; = \;\; in.kate?j : JOB \stackrel{[2,30]}{\rightarrow} out!j \rightarrow KATE$$
$$ELEANOR \;\; = \;\; in.eleanor?j : JOB \stackrel{1}{\rightarrow} out!j \rightarrow SKIP$$

The overall usage of the photocopier is that Kate can use it until such time as Eleanor has some input, at which point Kate's use is interrupted. When Eleanor has finished, the copier is ready for general use again.

$$COPIER \;\; = \;\; KATE \; \triangle \; (ELEANOR; \, COPIER)$$

Observe that the interrupt can occur at any time, as Eleanor demands. If it occurs after an *in.kate* event, then Kate will not obtain the output and will have to restart the job after Eleanor has finished.

The copier scenario has been described from a point of view which can distinguish *in.kate* from *in.eleanor*. The copier itself cannot distinguish between its users, and would consider all inputs identically. A description from this point of view might take the form

$$K = in?j : JOB \overset{[2,30]}{\rightarrow} out!j \rightarrow K$$

$$COPIER2 = K \triangle (in?j : JOB \overset{1}{\rightarrow} out!j \rightarrow SKIP); COPIER2$$

This description is equivalent to renaming both of the *in* channels in *COPIER* to a single channel *in*. In this case the interrupting event *in.j* is also possible for the interruptible process *K*, and if it occurs at a point where both are possible then it is nondeterministic which of the two possibilities has actually occurred. The subsequent behaviour might provide output in 1 second, or it might refuse it for a minimum of 2 seconds. This situation arises when the copier is not being used, and then receives an input: the input might have been provided by either Eleanor or Kate, and the distinction cannot be made at the input. ■

Interrupt provides another way in which delays can be combined with sequential composition to control the execution of a process. A delay *WAIT d* placed to interrupt an executing process will allow the combination to terminate from time *d* if it has not already done so. A sequential composition will force this to occur at time *d*. In other words, the construction

$$(Q_1 \triangle WAIT d); Q_2$$

will execute Q_1 either until Q_1 terminates, or until time *d*, whichever happens first. Control will then be passed to Q_2, and execution continues. For example, a lecture intended to last for 50 minutes is to be followed by questions. This may be described by the process

$$(LECTURE \triangle WAIT 50); QUESTIONS$$

where *LECTURE* will describe the behaviour of the lecturer, and *QUESTIONS* will describe the behaviour of the question session. A strict chairman will step in if the lecture is not finished by that time, and begin the question session anyway. However, if the lecture finishes earlier, then the question session can begin earlier.

Timed interrupt

The introduction of time allows an alternative approach to the interruption of processes. If the process is permitted to run for no more than a particular length of time, then the passage of time can itself trigger an interrupt to remove control from a process. Whereas the event-driven interrupt above might never occur if the environment of the process does not wish to perform the interrupt event, a timed interrupt is predestined to occur, since the environment of the process is not involved and so cannot prevent it.

A timed interrupt is written as

$$Q_1 \triangle_d Q_2$$

pronounced 'Q_1 timed interrupt d then Q_2'. It allows the execution of Q_1 for precisely d units of time, after which control is passed to Q_2, unless Q_1 has terminated previously. There is no need for Q_2 to execute concurrently with Q_1 since it will not be invoked until time d, and any state of Q_2 cannot affect the interrupt possibilities or the behaviour of Q_1. The timed interrupt is similar to sequential composition in this regard, in contrast to the event-driven interrupt which provides greater expressive power by allowing the interrupting process to execute throughout.

The transitions for the timed interrupt are given by the following rules:

$$\frac{Q_1 \xrightarrow{\mu} Q_1'}{Q_1 \triangle_d Q_2 \xrightarrow{\mu} Q_1' \triangle_d Q_2} \quad [\, \mu \neq \checkmark \,]$$

$$\frac{Q_1 \xrightarrow{\checkmark} Q_1'}{Q_1 \triangle_d Q_2 \xrightarrow{\checkmark} Q_1'}$$

$$\frac{}{Q_1 \triangle_0 Q_2 \xrightarrow{\tau} Q_2}$$

$$\frac{Q_1 \stackrel{d'}{\rightsquigarrow} Q_1'}{Q_1 \triangle_d Q_2 \stackrel{d'}{\rightsquigarrow} Q_1' \triangle_{d-d'} Q_2} \quad [\, d' \leqslant d \,]$$

The time remaining before the interrupt decreases with evolution, and does not alter when events occur, reflecting the fact that events are instantaneous.

Example 9.8.5 A party which must be closed down after 2 hours, independently of the noise level, can be described with a timed interrupt:

PARTY $\triangle_2$ *SKIP*

The description of the party in Example 9.8.3 raised the possibility of the interrupt event *close* occurring after 2 hours, but since the interrupt is triggered by an event, it is possible that it may not happen when it becomes enabled. If the authorities required that the party be closed down at the first available opportunity, then this might be achieved by abstracting the *close* event, making it the responsibility of the party organizers to perform it as an urgent action. This achieves the same effect as the timed interrupt (provided $close \notin \alpha(PARTY)$):

$$(PARTY \mathbin{\triangle} (WAIT\ 2; close \to SKIP)) \setminus \{close\} \quad = \quad PARTY \mathbin{\triangle_2} SKIP$$

Once control over the interrupt event is lost, it might as well be considered as a timed interrupt.
∎

Example 9.8.6 A time server that increments its value every one hundredth of a second can be described by means of a mutual recursion and a timed interrupt:

$$CLOCK(n) \quad = \quad (time!(n/100) \to STOP) \mathbin{\triangle_{0.01}} CLOCK(n+1)$$

The clock can provide any output value once along channel *time*, at any point during the time interval $[n/100, (n+1)/100]$. This output does not affect the accuracy of the clock, whose time value progresses independently of any output it provides. Observe that if an output is requested at the very instant $(n+1/100)$ that the value of the clock changes, then it is nondeterministic whether the value passed along *time* at time $(n+1)/100$ will be $n/100$ or $(n+1)/100$.
∎

Exercises

Exercise 9.1 Describe in timed CSP the process of becoming committed to a life assurance policy: after signing the policy, a 14 day cooling off period is allowed during which the policy may be cancelled without charge; after that, the customer is committed to the policy.

Exercise 9.2 Use the timeout operator to describe the opportunity for disagreement offered at the stage where the official states 'speak now or for ever hold your peace'.

Exercise 9.3 A quiz competition is between two teams. Whenever a question is asked, the first team to press their buzzer are allowed to answer the question. If they fail to answer it correctly, or if 10 seconds expires, then the other side is offered the question. Describe these possibilities in CSP.

Exercise 9.4 Construct a version of the service offered by the two buses of Example 9.4.7 in which the passenger may alight from the bus as an alternative to paying (as in the untimed version of Example 1.4.1). In this case, you should include the possibility that alighting from one bus allows for the possibility of catching a later bus.

Exercise 9.5 Write a process which can be placed in parallel with *COPIER* of Example 9.8.4 to prevent Eleanor from interrupting a job when Kate is actually on the machine: it will prevent *in.eleanor* from occurring between *in.kate* and *out*.

Exercise 9.6 Write a process which can be placed in parallel with *COPIER* which only allows Eleanor to interrupt after Kate has been on the machine for 10 minutes, so Kate is guaranteed an uninterrupted 10 minutes on the machine. This opportunity should occur no more than once per hour.

Exercise 9.7 What is the difference between $(Q_1 \triangle_d SKIP); Q_2$ and $Q_1 \triangle_d Q_2$?

Exercise 9.8 Give an operational semantics for timed prefix choice: $x : A@u \to Q(x, u)$.

Exercise 9.9 Process $a \overset{[3,7]}{\to} b \to STOP$ will offer the b nondeterministically at some point after occurrence of the a: between 3 and 7 time units after its performance. Which process will allow its environment to make that choice?

Exercise 9.10 Construct a sequence of transitions for *HELEN* $\|$ *CARL* of Example 9.6.1 describing the execution where they have a meeting after 20 minutes, Helen returns to work after 1 hour, and Carl goes home after 3 hours.

Exercise 9.11 Express the following constraints as timed CSP processes:

1. A machine should offer a response between 1 and 15 seconds after a button is pressed.

2. A machine should respond between 1 and 15 seconds after a button is pressed, or not at all. (For example, a cash card offered back to the customer.)

Exercise 9.12 Use the inference rules to identify all of the possible initial transitions of the process

$$((a \to STOP) \ \square \ (WAIT \ 1; b \to STOP)) \setminus \{b\}$$

When is the a possible? What events are possible at time 1?

10

Timed transition systems

The transition rules given for all of the timed CSP process constructors and processes define a timed labelled transition system which describes all of the possible executions of CSP processes. The transition system has some useful properties concerning the relationships between the different transitions that may appear. These properties include the assumptions of the computational model described at the beginning of the previous chapter, as well as other properties which ensure that processes behave in expected and reasonable ways. Some properties are concerned with the way processes evolve through time, and others are concerned with the relationship between evolution transitions and possible event transitions. Together they allow a picture of the nature or shape of process executions to be built up. This understanding will be important when extracting observational information about processes in order to design a compositional semantics for timed CSP.

10.1 EVOLUTION

Time determinism

The first important property of timed CSP processes is that evolution is deterministic. This means that there is only ever one possible result that a process can reach simply by allowing time to pass. Any alternative courses of action must therefore be accompanied by an event transition.

$$\forall Q, Q', Q'' : CSP;\ d : \mathbb{R}^+ \bullet (Q \overset{d}{\rightsquigarrow} Q' \land Q \overset{d}{\rightsquigarrow} Q'') \Rightarrow Q' \equiv Q''$$

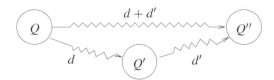

Fig. 10.1   Time additivity and time interpolation

where the relation '$\equiv$' is syntactic equivalence on process expressions. This expresses time determinism by stating that if Q is able to evolve to both Q' and Q'' under the same evolution transition, then the two resulting process expressions must be the same. An equivalent statement of this property is that if $Q \stackrel{d}{\leadsto} Q'$ then for any other $Q'' \not\equiv Q'$, Q cannot also evolve to Q'': $\neg(Q \stackrel{d}{\leadsto} Q'')$. Once the result of an evolution from Q has been identified, then no other process can be the result of the same evolution from Q.

Time additivity

If a process Q is able to evolve for d time units, and then for a further d' time units resulting in the final process Q'', it is natural to expect Q to be able to evolve for $d + d'$ time units directly to reach Q''. The property of time additivity states that all of the evolution transitions for any CSP process reflect this expectation.

$$\forall Q, Q', Q'' : CSP; \ d, d' : \mathbb{R}^+ \bullet (Q \stackrel{d}{\leadsto} Q' \wedge Q' \stackrel{d'}{\leadsto} Q'') \Rightarrow Q \stackrel{d+d'}{\leadsto} Q''$$

This property expresses that the state reached by a process after a delay of $d+d'$ is independent of whether or not an intermediate state of the process was recorded during that delay. This is illustrated in Figure 10.1: if the two successive transitions from Q to Q'' via Q' are possible, then the direct transition from Q to Q'' is also possible.

Time interpolation

The converse of time additivity is time interpolation: that whenever a process is able to evolve for some length of time, there must be an intermediate state at any instant during that evolution:

$$\forall Q, Q'' : CSP; \ d, d' : \mathbb{R}^+ \bullet Q \stackrel{d+d'}{\leadsto} Q'' \Rightarrow (\exists Q' : CSP \bullet Q \stackrel{d}{\leadsto} Q' \wedge Q' \stackrel{d'}{\leadsto} Q'')$$

An intermediate state is one which is reachable from the first process, and from which the second can be reached in the remaining time. This is also illustrated by Figure 10.1: if the direct evolution from Q to Q'' is possible, then there must be some Q' at time d that the evolution passes through.

This property together with time determinism means that there must be precisely one intermediate process for any given point during the evolution. An evolution of duration d passes through a unique continuum of process states.

Time closure

An infinite sequence of evolutions may be described in terms of an infinite sequence of processes $\{Q_i\}_{i \in \mathbb{N}}$ and delays $\{d_i\}_{i \in \mathbb{N}}$ such that for each i we have $Q_i \overset{d_i}{\leadsto} Q_{i+1}$. It is called a *Zeno sequence* if it is also the case that the sum of times is finite:

$$\Sigma_{i=0}^{\infty} d_i = d < \infty$$

Such a sequence of evolutions describes the process Q_0 evolving towards d but not reaching it. The sequence provides evidence that any evolution less than d is possible, but it does not provide evidence that an evolution of duration d itself is possible. Time closure allows this conclusion: that any CSP process able to evolve for all durations less than d is also able to evolve for d.

$$\forall Q : CSP;\ d : \mathbb{R}^+ \bullet ((\ \forall d' : \mathbb{R}^+ \bullet d' < d \Rightarrow \exists Q' : CSP \bullet Q \overset{d'}{\leadsto} Q')$$
$$\Rightarrow \exists Q'' \bullet Q \overset{d}{\leadsto} Q'')$$

This means that Zeno sequences of evolutions must have a limit process.

The property of time interpolation means that the set of delays possible for a process must be an interval of the positive real numbers, whose lower bound is 0. Time closure means that this set cannot be a finite open interval of the form $(0, d)$, since the supremum d of such a set of delays must also be a possible evolution, and hence should also appear in the interval. The only possibilities are either that a process is able to evolve for all time, or else that there is a final point that it can reach simply by evolving.

10.2 EXECUTIONS

Event transitions and evolution transitions correspond to steps in a process execution. Finite and infinite sequences of such transitions, where the final process of one transition is the initial process of the next, generally describe a way of stepping through a process execution. Initial segments of such executions have appeared in the examples in the last chapter.

The results concerning the behaviour of evolution transitions means that some economy can be introduced into the description of an execution. Time additivity allows two adjacent evolution transitions

$$Q \overset{d}{\leadsto} Q' \overset{d'}{\leadsto} Q''$$

to be collapsed to a single one

$$Q \overset{d+d'}{\rightsquigarrow} Q''$$

An infinite sequence of evolution transitions with initial process Q can also be collapsed into a single one, either by using the abbreviation $Q \overset{\infty}{\rightsquigarrow}$ when the sum of the delays is infinite, or by use of the time closure property to provide a transition of the form $Q \overset{d}{\rightsquigarrow} Q'$ for some Q' in the case where the sum of the delays is $d < \infty$.

Additivity and time closure together mean that any process execution can be described in terms of a sequence of transitions which contains no pairs of adjacent evolution transitions. Accordingly the definition of a process *execution* will be a sequence of processes and transition labels (events or delays) which contains no two delays as successive transitions.

An *execution* e of a process Q is a finite or infinite sequence $e = \langle s_0, s_1, s_2, \ldots \rangle$ satisfying the following conditions

- $s_0 \equiv Q$;

- if $2n < \#e$ then s_{2n} is a CSP process;

- if $2n + 1 < \#e$ then s_{2n+1} is either an event $\mu \in \Sigma^{\checkmark, \tau}$ or a time $d \in \mathbb{R}^+ \cup \{\infty\}$;

- if $s_{2n+1} = \mu \in \Sigma^{\checkmark, \tau}$ then $s_{2n} \overset{\mu}{\rightarrow} s_{2n+2}$;

- if $s_{2n+1} = d \in \mathbb{R}^+$ then $s_{2n} \overset{d}{\rightsquigarrow} s_{2n+2}$ and $s_{2n+3} \notin \mathbb{R}^+ \cup \{\infty\}$;

- if $s_{2n+1} = \infty$ then $s_{2n} \overset{\infty}{\rightsquigarrow}$ and $\#e = 2n + 2$;

- if e is finite then it finishes either with a process or with the value ∞.

These conditions state the following:

- the execution begins with Q;

- even positions are occupied by CSP process states;

- the positions between them are labels: events or delays;

- $\langle Q, \mu, Q' \rangle$ in the execution corresponds to a valid step $Q \overset{\mu}{\rightarrow} Q'$;

- similarly with delays, but two successive evolution transitions cannot appear;

- $\langle Q, \infty \rangle$ in the execution must appear at the end, and $Q \overset{\infty}{\rightsquigarrow}$.

The set *executions*(Q) is the set of all executions e meeting these conditions.

A *maximal execution* will be an execution sequence that cannot be extended. If it is infinite then it will contain an infinite number of event transitions, interspersed with time transitions; and if it is finite then it will either finish with the value ∞, or with a process for which no evolution or event transitions are possible. Sequences of transitions which end with an infinite sequence of evolutions are not considered as maximal executions, or indeed as appropriate descriptions of executions at all.

The *duration* of an execution e is the sum of the values of its delay transitions. This is denoted duration(e).

Events and evolutions

For CSP processes, in addition to the properties concerning their delay transitions, there is also a strong relationship between the event transitions that they can perform and the delay transitions that they can undergo. This relationship is described by several properties concerning process behaviour.

Urgent internal actions

One of the consequences of the maximal progress assumption is that internal events must occur as soon as they are enabled. If a process is able to perform an internal event then it should not also be possible for that process to delay. This is captured as the following property on the transitions possible for a CSP process.

$$\forall Q : CSP \bullet Q \xrightarrow{\tau} \Rightarrow (\forall d : \mathbb{R}^+ \bullet \neg (Q \overset{d}{\rightsquigarrow}))$$

No time may pass whenever an internal event is enabled. This encapsulates the mechanism by which internal events are treated as urgent within the operational semantics. This is illustrated particularly by the operational semantics of internal choice, hiding, and sequential composition.

Constancy of offers

An indication that CSP processes are well-behaved is that the set of visible event transitions possible for a process remains constant as time progresses. When Q evolves to Q', any events possible for Q must also be possible for Q', and conversely any events possible for Q' must also have been possible for Q.

$$\forall Q, Q' : CSP; \ d : \mathbb{R}^+ \bullet Q \overset{d}{\rightsquigarrow} Q' \Rightarrow (\forall a : \Sigma^\checkmark \bullet Q \xrightarrow{a} \Leftrightarrow Q' \xrightarrow{a})$$

The passage of time does not introduce any new events as possibilities, nor does it allow the withdrawal of any offers. Any such alterations in the set of offered events must therefore be accompanied by an event transition.

It is this property that underwrites the transition rule for evolution under hiding. The negative premiss $\forall a : A \bullet \neg(Q \xrightarrow{a})$ concerning the process Q is used to allow the derivation of an evolution $Q \setminus A \overset{d}{\rightsquigarrow} Q' \setminus A$ from the evolution $Q \overset{d}{\rightsquigarrow} Q'$. This does not contravene maximal progress because none of the events in A will become enabled at any point during the evolution: there is no danger of failing to perform an enabled urgent event. Similar reasoning justifies the transition rule for evolution of a sequential composition.

Termination

The final property is simply a sensible condition concerning termination: that any execution (maximal or otherwise) cannot contain any event transitions subsequent to a $\checkmark$ transition. This means that any execution containing the terminating event finishes either with the state reached following the $\checkmark$ transition, or else with a single subsequent evolution.

Unrealistic executions

Normally a complete or maximal execution of a process can be expected to have infinite duration: the process can be observed indefinitely. In the world of implementations, Newtonian time progresses at a constant rate and cannot be blocked, whatever the behaviour of any particular process. It is this march of time coupled with the blockage of a time transition when an internal event is enabled which actually forces the urgency of internal events. However, the blockage of a time transition for a particular process is no more than a mechanism for expressing this urgency. It does not constitute reasonable behaviour in its own right, since it conflicts with the unstoppable passage of time.

For the same reason, complete executions with finite duration are not consistent with this view of time. A maximal execution is a record of a complete sequence of steps that a process can pass through during an execution. If this execution only reaches a finite time, and yet it cannot be extended, then it is inconsistent with the expectation of time progressing beyond that point.

There are a number of ways a maximal execution can have a finite duration. These are illustrated in Figure 10.2.

1. A maximal execution could consist of a finite number of transitions. A finite duration execution cannot end with a $Q' \overset{\infty}{\rightsquigarrow}$ evolution, so there must be a final process Q for which neither evolution nor event transitions are possible. Such a process is termed a *timestop*.

2. A maximal execution might contain infinitely many transitions, but only finitely many evolution transitions. These must necessarily sum to a finite duration. The execution must finish with an infinite sequence of event transitions. Such a sequence is termed a *spin execution*, performing infinitely many events at a single instant. A *spin divergence*

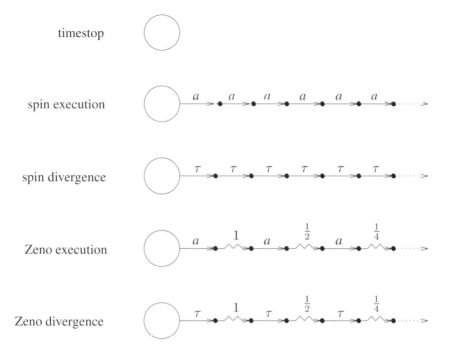

Fig. 10.2   Maximal executions of finite duration

is a spin execution with only finitely many external event transitions: it must end with an infinite sequence of internal events.

3. A maximal execution could contain infinitely many evolution transitions, but the sum of their durations is finite. Such an execution is called a *Zeno execution*, since it approaches a time but never reaches it. A *Zeno divergence* is a Zeno execution with only finitely many external event transitions: it must end with an infinite sequence of τ transitions interspersed with evolutions.

All of these possibilities can arise within the transition system given for timed CSP (in the context of non-time-guarded recursion).

Timestops

A new CSP timestop process *TIMESTOP* could be defined directly by stating that there are no rules for generating its transitions, and concluding that it is a process with no event or evolution transitions. However, a timestop can also arise within the language of timed CSP given already, through an unguarded recursion:

$$TIMESTOP = TIMESTOP$$

No transitions are deducible for this process, so it will behave as a timestop, blocking the passage of time.

Arbitrarily fast processes

An infinite sequence of event transitions describes an execution in which infinitely many events are performed at the same instant. A recursively defined process which does not include any delay between successive unfoldings may give rise to such behaviour. For example, the process

$$FASTLIGHT = on \rightarrow off \rightarrow FASTLIGHT$$

is able to perform *on* and *off* an arbitrary number of times at any instant. Although the definition appears to allow simply that as soon as the light is switched on it is in a state where it is ready to be switched off, and vice versa, this allows the infinitely fast execution as a consequence. The process is likely to be placed in a slower environment which will prevent infinitely fast executions, but this cannot be guaranteed. It might instead have these events abstracted, in which case both *on* and *off* will be forced to occur urgently as internal events. The process $FASTLIGHT \setminus \{on, off\}$ will never allow time to pass, and furthermore it will consume computing resources; it is worse than *TIMESTOP*.

Arbitrarily fast processes can be useful in specification. Generally they are useful when it would be inappropriate to specify a lower limit on a particular delay, but where there is confidence that such a lower limit will be imposed elsewhere.

Example 10.2.1 A bicycle speedometer receives *click* signals from a detector which tracks the frequency of rotation of the wheel by means of a magnet attached to a spoke. The circumference of the wheel is 216 cm, so if u seconds is the length of time the wheel takes to rotate once, then the speed of the bicycle can be calculated as $(7.776/u)$ km h^{-1}. This value is displayed on the electronic speedometer (rounded to the nearest whole number). The value is updated on each rotation of the wheel. This may be described using the mutually recursive definition

$$SPEEDO(n) \quad = \quad (display!n \rightarrow STOP)$$
$$\triangle$$
$$click@u \rightarrow SPEEDO\lfloor(7.776/u, 0)\rfloor$$

The display of the current value n is possible, and remains so until the next *click* event signalling another rotation of the wheel. At that point the value to be displayed is recalculated and the process continues with that new value.

It is clear from the informal understanding of the description that an infinite number of *click* events at a single instant would not be expected, since a physical bicycle wheel must have some bound on its rotation speed. However, the CSP description allows for the recursive calls to occur one after the other without any delay, which can lead to an infinite sequence of *click* events. If *click* were made internal (though it is hard to imagine what this might mean in the context of the bicycle) then a spin divergence would result.

In fact, the manufacturer guarantees the speedometer only up to a speed of 200 km h^{-1}, which means that a minimum wheel rotation time of 0.03888 seconds can be assumed. In order to ensure that the description does not admit infinitely fast executions, this delay can be introduced before the *click* event. This in turn necessitates an alteration to the calculation of the display value.

$$
\begin{aligned}
SPEEDO'(n) \quad = \quad & (display!n \rightarrow STOP) \\
& \triangle \\
& WAIT\ 0.03888; \\
& \quad click@u \rightarrow SPEEDO'(\lfloor 7.776/(u+0.03888) \rfloor)
\end{aligned}
$$

This process will not accept *click* events faster than every 0.03888 seconds.   ■

Zeno behaviour

Many processes which have spin executions also have Zeno executions which may be obtained from the spin execution by introducing delays between successive events so that the sum of the delays introduced is finite. For example, the *SPEEDO* process in the example above is able to receive *click* events where the nth click is preceded by a delay of 2^{-n}.

Zeno executions can also be introduced by recursive processes which reduce the delays between successive recursive calls, though such processes will avoid spin executions. The most natural description is in terms of a mutually recursive definition:

$$
Z(n) \quad = \quad a \xrightarrow{2^{-n}} Z(n+1)
$$

Each occurrence of an a event is followed by some delay, but the sum of the delays is finite. A possible Zeno execution for $Z(0)$ is

$$
\begin{array}{l}
Z(0) \\
\quad \downarrow a \\
(STOP \overset{1}{\triangleright} Z(1)) \\
\quad \updownarrow 1 \\
(STOP \overset{0}{\triangleright} Z(1)) \\
\quad \downarrow \tau \\
Z(1) \\
\quad \downarrow a \\
(STOP \overset{0.5}{\triangleright} Z(2)) \\
\quad \updownarrow 0.5 \\
(STOP \overset{0}{\triangleright} Z(2)) \\
\quad \downarrow \tau \\
Z(2) \\
\quad \downarrow a \\
(STOP \overset{0.25}{\triangleright} Z(3)) \\
\quad \updownarrow 0.25 \\
(STOP \overset{0}{\triangleright} Z(3)) \\
\quad \downarrow \tau \\
Z(3) \\
\quad \vdots
\end{array}
$$

In this particular execution each a occurs at the moment it is enabled. This means that if a is hidden then this execution will give rise to a Zeno divergence. The time passed during the execution will approach 2 seconds, but will never quite reach it.

The process $Z(0)$ also has some perfectly well-behaved executions: for example, it has an execution where the event a occurs once per second. On the other hand, the process $Z(0) \setminus \{a\}$ has no well-behaved complete executions.

Time-guarded CSP

All of the finite duration maximal executions of timed CSP discussed above arise from recursive definitions $N = Q$ and $N_i = Q_i$ which do not introduce a sufficient delay between recursive calls. Instantaneous recursions can give rise to timestops and spin executions, and recursive calls separated by ever reducing delays might give rise to Zeno behaviour. There could be reasons external to a process as to why such unrealistic executions will not be possible, as was the case with the example *SPEEDO* process. However, it may be preferable to use the process description itself to guarantee the absence of these executions.

These possible deviant executions are all prevented by ensuring that there is some minimum positive delay t between the time a recursive definition Q or Q_i begins execution and the time it reaches a recursive invocation marked by a process name N or N_i. A single or mutually recursive definition is said to be t-*guarded* if this is the case.

Informally, a process term is t-guarded when any execution of that term cannot reach a recursive call in less than t units of time. A number of conditions are provided for deducing t-guardedness for process expressions.

- Any CSP process expression Q is 0-guarded (including process names N).

- The processes *STOP* and *SKIP* are t-guarded, for any $t \in \mathbb{R}^+$.

- If Q is t-guarded, then so too are $a \rightarrow Q$, $Q \setminus A$, $f(Q)$, and $f^{-1}(Q)$; and $a \xrightarrow{d} Q$ is $t + d$-guarded. None of the unary CSP operations reduces the value of any time guards; and delayed prefix increases any guard by the value of the delay.

- If Q_1 and Q_2 are t-guarded, then so too are $Q_1 \ \square \ Q_2$, $Q_1 \ \sqcap \ Q_2$, $Q_1 \ _A\|_B \ Q_2$, $Q_1 \ ||| \ Q_2$, $Q_1 \ \underset{A}{\|} \ Q_2$, $Q_1 ; Q_2$, and $Q_1 \ \triangle \ Q_2$.

- If I is a finite indexing set and Q_i is t-guarded for all $i \in I$, then so too are $\square_{i \in I} \ Q_i$, $\|_{A_i}^{i \in I} \ Q_i$, and $|||_{i \in I} \ Q_i$. In fact these all follow from the fact that the corresponding binary operators preserve t-guardedness.

- If Q_1 is t-guarded for $t \leqslant d$, then $Q_1 \ \overset{d}{\triangleright} \ Q_2$ and $Q_1 \ \triangle_d \ Q_2$ are t-guarded. The second argument Q_2 in each case will not be reached before time t, so the nature of Q_2 is irrelevant to the question of t-guardedness of the combinations.

- If Q_1 is $(t + d)$-guarded, and Q_2 is t-guarded, then $Q_1 \ \overset{d}{\triangleright} \ Q_2$ is $(t + d)$-guarded.

- If Q_1 is $(d + \epsilon)$-guarded for some $\epsilon > 0$, and Q_2 is t-guarded, then $Q_1 \ \triangle_d \ Q_2$ is $(d + t)$-guarded. Q_1 will be interrupted before it reaches any recursive calls, and control will pass to Q_2 at time d, so any guard of Q_2 is added to the time taken to reach Q_2.

- If $Q(x)$ is t-guarded for every $x \in A$, then $x : A \rightarrow Q(x)$ is t-guarded.

- If Q_i is t-guarded for each $i \in J$ then $\sqcap_{i \in J} \ Q_i$ is t-guarded.

It follows from these rules that if a process is t-guarded, then it is also t'-guarded for any $t' < t$.

A process term Q is *time-guarded* if there is some time $t > 0$ such that Q is t-guarded. A collection of process terms Q_i is *uniformly time-guarded* if there is a single time $t > 0$ for which all of the Q_i are t-guarded.

A CSP recursively defined process $N = Q$ is *time-guarded* if there is some time $t > 0$ such that Q is t-guarded. All of a set of mutually recursively defined processes $\{N_i = Q_i\}_{i \in J}$ are *time-guarded* if there is some $t > 0$ such that whenever a name N_j appears in the body of any of the definitions, then the corresponding Q_j is t-guarded. In other words, those terms that are recursively invoked should be t-guarded. The binding of a name N_k not appearing in any of the definition bodies will not affect the mutual recursion, and so need not itself be time-guarded. No recursive calls will be made to N_k.

Example 10.2.2 The following mutually recursive set of definitions is indexed by the integers. Each of the process definitions for the $LEVEL(n)$ processes is 1-guarded.

$$
\begin{aligned}
LEVEL(n) \quad = \quad & up \xrightarrow{1} LEVEL(n+1) \\
& \square\ level!n \xrightarrow{3} LEVEL(n) \\
& \square\ down \xrightarrow{2} LEVEL(n-1)
\end{aligned}
$$

This set is 1-guarded. The definition $LEVEL = LEVEL(0)$ can be added to the mutually recursive family of process definitions. The process name $LEVEL$ does not appear in any of the process bodies, so the resulting set of definitions remains 1-guarded. The body of the definition of $LEVEL$ is not time-guarded, but the fact that none of the other process definitions refers to it means that it does not impact on the time-guardedness of the set. ■

In a mutually recursive definition, any occurrence of a process name N_i appearing in any of the defining process terms may be replaced by the process term Q_i it is bound to, to yield an equivalent definition. This fact may sometimes be used to rewrite a mutually recursive set of definitions which is not time-guarded to a semantically equivalent form which is time-guarded. The aim of such a rewriting of the definitions is to obtain time-guardedness by

1. expanding the definitions of unguarded process terms, and

2. removing names bound to unguarded terms from all process terms.

Example 10.2.3 It may happen that recursive definitions are given in a form which does not meet the conditions for time-guardedness. One situation where this will arise is when different states of a process are represented by different processes, and it is possible to move from some states to some others in zero time. The following set of definitions is not time-guarded, because the process definitions for $STANDBY$ and $READY$ are not t-guarded for any $t > 0$. Guardedness of the process definition for TOY is irrelevant since TOY does not appear in any of the right-hand process terms.

$$
\begin{aligned}
TOY \quad &= \quad power \rightarrow STANDBY \\
STANDBY \quad &= \quad brake\_off \rightarrow READY \\
READY \quad &= \quad on \rightarrow MOVING \\
MOVING \quad &= \quad off \xrightarrow{1} READY
\end{aligned}
$$

The state space corresponding to this set of definitions is illustrated in Figure 10.3.

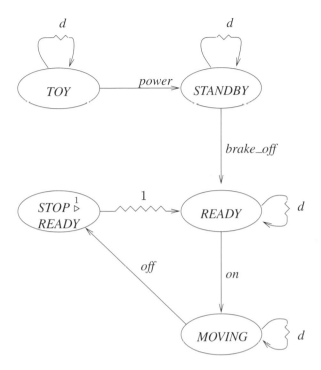

Fig. 10.3   State space for *TOY*

If the occurrences of the names *STANDBY* and *MOVING* in the right-hand side processes are replaced by their process definitions, then the following set of definitions results:

$$
\begin{aligned}
TOY &= power \to brake\_off \to READY \\
STANDBY &= brake\_off \to READY \\
READY &= on \to off \overset{1}{\to} READY \\
MOVING &= off \overset{1}{\to} READY
\end{aligned}
$$

The definition of *READY* has been elaborated by replacing the unguarded name *MOVING* with its definition, resulting in a 1-guarded process term. The name *STANDBY* has been removed from all process terms, so the fact that it is bound to an unguarded term no longer has a bearing on the guardedness of the set of recursive definitions. These two rewrites do not affect the possible executions of any of the defined processes, but they yield a set of definitions which is 1-guarded. The only name appearing on the right-hand side is *READY*, so the only term which needs to be checked for time-guardedness is $on \to off \overset{1}{\to} READY$.   ■

Guardedness and termination

The rules given above for t-guardedness do not take into account the delay which might be introduced by a process before it terminates and passes control to the second process. In fact, both *SKIP* and *WAIT d* are t-guarded for any t, but the latter introduces a time guard when it precedes another process. In addition to time guards, it is necessary to identify the minimum time that must elapse before a process can terminate: in the case of *SKIP* it will be 0, whereas for *WAIT d* it will be d. A second notion is required—that of t-activity.

A process Q is t-*active* if it cannot terminate before t units of time. In other words, any execution starting from Q which contains a $\checkmark$ event must have a duration $t' \geqslant t$. This provides a final rule for guardedness:

- If Q_1 is t-active and $(t+t')$-guarded, and Q_2 is t'-guarded, then $Q_1 ; Q_2$ is $(t+t')$-guarded.

This rule allows the deduction that *WAIT d*; Q_2 is d-guarded, since *WAIT d* is d-active and d-guarded, and Q_2 will always be 0-guarded. Preceding a process with a delay ensures that it the result is time-guarded.

A t-activity property for process expressions can be deduced from t-activity of its components:

- any CSP process Q is 0-active.

- *STOP* is t-active for any $t \in \mathbb{R}^+$.

- If Q_1 is t-active, then so are $a \to Q_1, Q_1 \;_A\|_B Q_2, Q_2 \;_B\|_A Q_1, Q_1 \;|||\; Q_2, Q_1 \;\|_A Q_2$ and $Q_2 \;\|_A Q_1, Q_1 \setminus A, f(Q_1),$ and $f^{-1}(Q_1)$; and $a \xrightarrow{d} Q_1$ is $(t+d)$-active.

- If Q_1 and Q_2 are t-active, then so too are $Q_1 \;\Box\; Q_2, Q_1 \;\sqcap\; Q_2$, and $Q_1 \;\triangle\; Q_2$.

- Indexed internal choice, external choice, and interleaving all preserve the property t-active.

- If Q_1 is t-active and Q_2 is t'-active, then $Q_1 ; Q_2$ is $(t + t')$-active.

- If Q_1 is t-active for $t \leqslant d$, then $Q_1 \overset{d}{\triangleright} Q_2$ and $Q_1 \;\triangle_d\; Q_2$ are t-active.

- If Q_1 is $(t + d)$-active, and Q_2 is t-active, then $Q_1 \overset{d}{\triangleright} Q_2$ is $(t + d)$-active.

- If Q_1 is $(d+\epsilon)$-active for some $\epsilon > 0$, and Q_2 is t-active, then $Q_1 \;\triangle_d\; Q_2$ is $(d+t)$-active.

- If $Q(x)$ is t-active for every $x \in A$, then $x : A \to Q(x)$ is t-active.

- If Q_i is t-active for each $i \in J$ then $\bigsqcap_{i \in J} Q_i$ is t-active.

If a process is t-active, then it is also t'-active for any $t' < t$.

10.3   WELL-TIMED PROCESSES

A timed CSP process is *well-timed* if all associated single and mutual recursive definitions $\{N_i = Q_i\}_{i \in J}$ are time-guarded. Well-timedness of a process term is therefore dependent on its context of recursive process definitions. For example, the name N is well-timed in the context of the definition $N = a \xrightarrow{2} N$, but not well-timed in the context of $N = a \to N$. If no recursive definitions are required to define a process then it must be well-timed. On the other hand, if the process is defined through recursive definitions, then it will be well-timed if the definitions can be presented in a form which is time-guarded.

Well-timed processes can only have well-behaved executions, and can never exhibit timestops, spin executions, or Zeno executions. This means that if Q is well-timed then all of its maximal executions have infinite duration.

This result means that the executions of any well-timed process have two extra properties which a number of less well-behaved processes lack. The first is the guaranteed absence of timestops, and the second is *finite variability*, which states that an execution should only perform finitely many events in any finite interval.

No timestops

Any process whose maximal executions all have infinite duration must always be able to make progress in an execution. This means that a timestop cannot be reached at any point.

$$\forall Q : CSP \bullet Q \text{ well-timed} \Rightarrow Q \xrightarrow{\tau} \lor \exists d, Q' \bullet Q \overset{d}{\rightsquigarrow} Q'$$

A process cannot guarantee to perform an external event, since its environment may not co-operate in this. In order to ensure that some progress can always be made, either an internal transition or an evolution must be possible. The urgency of internal events always means that at most one of these will be possible.

Finite variability

The property of finite variability states that any finite time interval of an execution should contain only finitely many events. This is a property required of any process which is ultimately to be implemented. It is most easily expressed as the contrapositive: that infinitely many events take infinitely long to occur.

$$\forall Q : CSP \bullet Q \text{ well-timed} \land e \in \mathsf{executions}(Q) \land \#e = \infty \Rightarrow \mathsf{duration}(e) = \infty$$

For any process, its executions of infinite length are precisely those with infinitely many event transitions. This result states that for well-timed processes, all such executions (which are necessarily maximal) must take for ever to be performed.

The shape of an execution

The results given in this chapter regarding the relationship between processes and transitions reveal much information about the structure of process executions.

Urgency of internal events together with time determinism means that there is at most one time at which a process can perform its first internal transition. It can delay up to that time, but not beyond it. During this delay, it passes through a continuum of process states: in each of these the same set of events is enabled, and they differ only with regard to their clock values. This means that a process enables this set of events over the entire interval up to the time the internal event occurs. In the case where no internal event will occur, any amount of delay is possible for a well-timed process, and the same set of events will be enabled over all time until one of them occurs.

Events can occur whenever they are enabled. Successive events may occur at the same instant, but if there is a delay between them then the same set of events must have been enabled throughout that delay, since the enabled set can change only on performance of some event.

The maximal executions of a well-timed process must be of infinite duration. This means that at every time $t \in \mathbb{R}^+$ there will be some corresponding process state during this execution, and an enabled set of events at that time. The execution will therefore be associated with a total function from times to sets of enabled events, which will have the structure of a step function since its value can change only finitely often in a finite time.

Example 10.3.1 The process

$$Q = ((a \rightarrow STOP) \overset{5}{\triangleright} (b \rightarrow STOP)) \triangle_8 (c \rightarrow STOP)$$

has the singleton $\{a\}$ as its set of initially enabled events. There is an internal event possible for this process at time 5, so the set will remain enabled until that time (unless an a occurs beforehand). Execution passes through a continuum of states up to time 5, where the process state after a delay of $t \leqslant 5$ is

$$((a \rightarrow STOP) \overset{5-t}{\triangleright} (b \rightarrow STOP)) \triangle_{8-t} (c \rightarrow STOP)$$

If the enabled a is performed during this time, the resulting process is

$$STOP \triangle_{8-t} (c \rightarrow STOP)$$

which has no events enabled. No events will be enabled until the internal event occurs after a further $8 - t$, resulting in the process

$$c \rightarrow STOP$$

No internal event is possible for this process, so it can delay for ever. The singleton $\{c\}$ is enabled and will remain so for ever, or until the c occurs.

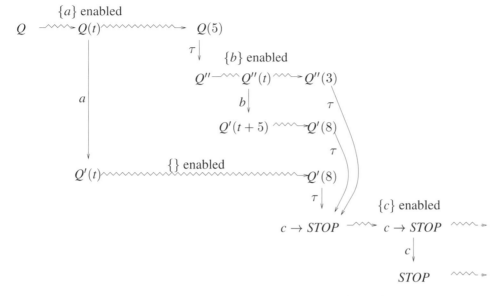

Fig. 10.4   Events enabled during executions of Q

If a does not occur, then the b will become enabled at time 5 and will remain so for 3 time units or until it occurs if this is sooner. In either case the c event will again become enabled at time 8.

The graph of possibilities is illustrated in Figure 10.4. Each path beginning at Q corresponds to an execution, and is associated with a step function of enabled sets of events.

■

10.4   NOTES

There have been a number of timed extensions proposed for CSP. The earliest was [61], and other examples include [126, 36, 58, 85, 125]. The timed CSP on which this book is based was first presented in [97], in which the *WAIT* statement is the single new language construct. Other common time constructs such as timeout, timed interrupt, and event interrupt, were defined elaborately using delays and other CSP operators [107]. More recently, they have entered the language in their own right and been given their own semantics directly, since the complexity of their definitions made reasoning more cumbersome than necessary. The original operational semantics for timed CSP appeared in [109], and was recast in [110] in the notation of [80] for consistency with the presentation of the majority of the other timed process algebras.

Numerous timed extensions to other process algebras, and new timed process algebras, were developed during the same period as timed CSP. They have naturally had an influence on the development of the language of timed CSP and on the presentation of its operational semantics. Most timed process algebras are defined operationally in terms of the event transitions and the time transitions (or delays, or evolutions) that processes can perform. They all add time constructs to the language—delays, timeouts, and timed interrupts—resulting in a language that is powerful enough to express time-sensitive behaviour. The introduction of time may also have an impact on the existing untimed operators. For example, in the case of the choice operator it is necessary to decide whether the passage of time should resolve the choice or not, or whether to introduce two choice operators to cover both possibilities, as was done by Moller and Tofts in [80].

Timed process algebras can differ in a variety of ways, reflecting the possible decisions taken during their design. Some of the main factors which will influence the design of the language are the following:

- whether the time domain is discrete or dense;

- whether to allow timestops, and how the language operators should treat them;

- how to handle Zeno behaviour;

- whether to allow urgent visible events;

- whether to aim for compatibility with an untimed process algebra, where the event transitions of untimed processes are the same in the timed and untimed semantics, and where processes equivalent in the untimed world should remain equivalent under their timed semantics. These properties are called *semantics conservation* and *isomorphism* respectively [82];

- which semantic underpinning will be used: bisimulation, testing, denotational, or algebraic;

- whether a complete axiomatization of semantic equivalence (of finite processes) is desired.

In [82] Nicollin and Sifakis compare and catalogue many of the timed process algebras mentioned below with respect to criteria such as these. Wang Yi [122] and Nicollin and Sifakis [82] also introduced much of the terminology of properties of timed transition systems used in this chapter. Further discussion and comparison of two such properties is provided in [60].

Timed extensions to CCS (Calculus of Communicating Systems) have been presented by Wang Yi [123], Moller and Tofts [80], Liang Chen [72], and Hansson [40]. These all introduce additional timing operators into the language and use timed bisimulation for the semantic theory, where equivalent processes must match on both event transitions and time transitions. Other operators are also introduced as necessary. In particular, Wang Yi [122] first introduced the timed event prefix, which has since been imported into CSP. Fencott [30] provides a good introduction to the timed CCS of Moller and Tofts. In addition, synchronous

CCS [77, 38] may be considered as a discrete timed extension of CCS, though in rather a different style: all concurrent components execute at the same rate (in lockstep).

Other timed extensions of process algebras include Baeten and Bergstra's ACP$_\rho$ [3], a timed extension of ACP Communicating Processes) [7] which takes an axiomatic approach to the semantics; Hennessy and Regan's TPL [43], a timed extension of Hennessy's EPL [42]; and a number of timed extensions of LOTOS, from Quemada et al. [94, 93], Bolognesi and Lucidi [11], and Leduc and Léonard's ET-LOTOS [70]. The last of these is closest in spirit to timed CSP, as demonstrated by the similarity of their semantics [16] for the well-timed subset. It goes beyond timed CSP in allowing instant recursion which makes a significant semantic difference [69].

New process algebras developed specifically for reasoning about time have also been introduced: Nicollin and Sifakis' Algebra of Timed Processes (ATP) [83]; The PARTY language from Ho-Stuart et al. [44]; and Jeffrey's more general framework [59]. The UPPAAL tool [67] provides automated support for verification of timed systems.

In addition to the process algebraic tradition, there are many other methods which have been developed for describing and analysing real-time systems. Collections and surveys of the main approaches can be found in [41, 63, 27]. All the approaches essentially require a language for describing timed systems, a way of capturing specifications on such systems, and a relationship between systems and specifications. System descriptions are often expressed in terms of a programming language that contains explicit timing (and often concurrency) constructs, such as ESTEREL [8] or an idealized programming language [49]. The semantics of such programs can be given for example in terms of timed automata [2], or timed Petri nets [75]. Specifications can be expressed using a real-time extension of temporal logic [65, 86] or other real-time logic [57], the duration calculus [124], or by using the programming language itself (akin to the style of process-oriented specifications). Verification is then achieved by establishing that the execution paths in the semantics are all acceptable in terms of the specification, either by using a proof system as in [49], by model-checking (for finite-state systems) [1], or by establishing a simulation relation between the implementation and the abstract program representing the specification [74]. It is also possible to translate such techniques to process-algebraic system descriptions, and this has been done in the context of ATP [84].

Exercises

Exercise 10.1 Which properties ensure that no evolution can ever pass beyond a point where an internal event was possible, i.e. that $Q \overset{d+d'}{\leadsto} Q''$ and $Q \overset{d}{\leadsto} Q' \overset{\tau}{\rightarrow}$ is never possible for $d' > 0$?

Exercise 10.2 Using a single recursion but no mutual recursion give a process which has Zeno executions but no spin executions.

Exercise 10.3 Find a process which is not t-guarded for any $t > 0$, but which contains no unrealistic executions.

Exercise 10.4 Hiding interferes with event guards in the untimed model. How does it interact with time guards in the timed model?

Exercise 10.5 Give transitions for a process construction '$(a > 0) \rightarrow Q$' which offers the event a at all times greater than 0, but not at 0 itself, and whose subsequent behaviour is that of Q. Which of the well-behaved properties of transition systems does it violate? What would be the transitions of $((a > 0) \rightarrow b \rightarrow STOP) \setminus a$? If the internal event is urgent, at what times can it occur?

Part IV

Timed analysis

$$11$$

Semantics of timed CSP

The language of Communicating Sequential Processes considers processes as interacting system components. Although processes may have widely differing internal behaviour, they should be judged only in terms of their external behaviour. It is only activity at the interface which can have any effect on a context in which processes might be placed. In particular, if two processes cannot be told apart within any CSP environment, then they should be considered equivalent.

In the timed world, contexts can be more sensitive to the behaviour of their components than at the untimed level. Not only is a component's ability to perform or refuse events important, but the extended language's ability to describe processes with time-sensitive behaviour means that different timing behaviour of components can also be distinguished. For example, the processes $Q_1 = a \rightarrow STOP$ and $Q_2 = WAIT\, 2; a \rightarrow STOP$ are both able to perform the event a, and both processes will have the same traces, failures, divergences, and infinite traces. However, the times at which the a is on offer are different, so the processes should be distinguished on the basis of their timed behaviour. If placed in parallel with the time-sensitive process $(a \rightarrow STOP) \overset{1}{\triangleright} STOP$ the first resulting system is able to perform the event a but the second is not. A timed semantics must differentiate Q_1 from Q_2.

Conversely, a consideration of the two processes

$$(WAIT\, 2; a \rightarrow STOP) \sqcap (WAIT\, 2; b \rightarrow STOP)$$

and

$$WAIT\, 2; ((a \rightarrow STOP) \sqcap (b \rightarrow STOP))$$

reveals that they have very different executions: one resolves the internal choice at time 0, and the other does not resolve it until time 2. However, no context is able to distinguish these two processes: if one is appropriate for use as a component of a system, then so is the other. They both have the same interactions possible, each being able to perform an a or a b event after time 2, but also able to refuse either of them.

This chapter introduces a semantic model for well-timed processes which makes exactly the distinctions required. It is a compositional model which considers processes as sets of *timed failures*. A timed failure is a record of an execution, consisting of a *timed trace* which contains information about events performed, and a *timed refusal* which contains information about when events could be refused. Timed failures information captures exactly those aspects of a process's behaviour that can be observed by interacting with it.

11.1 TIMED OBSERVATIONS

When a well-timed process executes, it performs events at its interface. A *timed trace* is a record of performed events, together with the times at which they were performed relative to the beginning of the process execution. Internal events are not recorded in the timed trace, since they are not visible at the interface and their occurrence cannot have any direct effect on any other process.

A *timed event* is a pair drawn from $\mathbb{R}^+ \times \Sigma$, consisting of a time and an event. For example, the pairs $(3, coin)$, $(7, in.4)$, $(3.1, print.j)$, and $(\pi, start)$ are all timed events. A timed trace is a sequence of timed events in which the times are non-decreasing: the events are recorded in temporal order. Thus $\langle (3, on), (5, off), (9, on) \rangle$ and $\langle (2, on), (4, off), (4, left), (6, on) \ldots \rangle$ are both timed traces, but $\langle (5, off), (3, on) \rangle$ is not a timed trace since the events are recorded in reverse order.

A trace may be a record of a finite or an infinite duration execution. In the first case, finite variability means that the length of the trace must be finite. In the second case, the length of the trace may be finite, if only finitely many external events occurred. Alternatively, it may be infinite, in which case the infinite duration of the execution means that the times in the trace are not bounded.

The set TT of all possible timed traces that might be associated with an execution of a well-timed process is defined as follows:

$$
\begin{aligned}
TT \;=\; & \{ s \in (\mathbb{R}^+ \times \Sigma^{\checkmark})^* \mid\; \forall t_1, t_2 : \mathbb{R}^+ ;\; a_1, a_2 : \Sigma^{\checkmark} \bullet \\
& \qquad\qquad \langle (t_1, a_1), (t_2, a_2) \rangle \preccurlyeq s \Rightarrow t_1 \leqslant t_2 \wedge a_1 \neq \checkmark \} \\
& \cup \\
& \{ s \in (\mathbb{R}^+ \times \Sigma)^{\omega} \mid\; \forall t_1, t_2 : \mathbb{R}^+ ;\; a_1, a_2 : \Sigma \bullet \\
& \qquad\qquad \langle (t_1, a_1), (t_2, a_2) \rangle \preccurlyeq s \Rightarrow t_1 \leqslant t_2 \\
& \qquad\qquad \wedge \forall t \in \mathbb{R}^+ \bullet \exists t_1 > t;\; a_1 : \Sigma \bullet (t_1, a_1)\; \mathbf{in}\; s \}
\end{aligned}
$$

The set of timed traces TT consists of all finite sequences of timed events which are ordered in time, together with the infinite sequences of timed events which are ordered and unbounded in time. Infinite sequences cannot contain ✓ events, and finite sequences can only contain it at the end.

The projection of a trace onto an interval D is written $s \uparrow D$, pronounced 's during D', and defined by the following sequence comprehension:

$$s \uparrow D \quad = \quad \langle (t,a) \mid (t,a) \; \langle \; s, t \subset D \rangle$$

The interval D can be finite or infinite.

Strict and non-strict forms of 'before' and 'after' operators can be defined in terms of the 'during' operator:

$$s \lceil t \quad = \quad s \uparrow [0,t]$$
$$s \Vert t \quad = \quad s \uparrow [0,t)$$
$$s \rceil t \quad = \quad s \uparrow [t,\infty)$$
$$s \Vert t \quad = \quad s \uparrow (t,\infty)$$

For example, if

$$s_0 = \langle (1,on), (3,off), (6,on) \rangle$$

then $s_0 \lceil 3 = \langle (1,on), (3,off) \rangle$, $s_0 \Vert 3 = \langle (1,on) \rangle$, $s_0 \rceil 3 = \langle (3,off), (6,on) \rangle$, and $s_0 \Vert 3 = \langle (6,on) \rangle$.

A timed trace may also be projected onto a particular set of events: $s \restriction A$ is the subsequence of s consisting of its events from A; $s \restriction a$ is the sequence of a events from s; $s \downarrow A$ is the number of A events in s; $s \downarrow a$ is the number of occurrences of a; $s \setminus A$ is the trace with all elements of A removed; and $strip(s)$ is the sequence of events in s with the times removed. So $s_0 \restriction on = \langle (1,on), (6,on) \rangle$, $s_0 \downarrow on = 2$, $s_0 \setminus \{on\} = \langle (3,off) \rangle$, and $strip(s_0) = \langle on, off, on \rangle$.

A trace may also be translated through time, so $s + t$ is the timed trace s with all the times increased by t; and $s - t$ is the timed trace with all times reduced by t. Traces cannot begin before time 0, so any trace translated back in time will be truncated where necessary, in order to ensure that all times associated with events are non-negative. Thus $s_0 + 3 = \langle (4,on), (6,off), (9,on) \rangle$, and $s_0 - 3 = \langle (0,off), (3,on) \rangle$.

Particular elements of a non-empty trace can also be extracted: $head(\langle (t,a) \rangle \frown s) = (t,a)$, $tail(\langle (t,a) \rangle \frown s) = s$, $begin(\langle (t,a) \rangle \frown s) = t$, and $first(\langle (t,a) \rangle \frown s) = a$. So $head(s_0) = (1,on)$, $tail(s_0) = \langle (3,off), (6,on) \rangle$, $begin(s_0) = 1$, and $first(s_0) = on$.

Furthermore, the following operations are defined on finite non-empty traces: $foot(s \frown \langle (t,a) \rangle) = (t,a)$, $init(s \frown \langle (t,a) \rangle) = s$, $end(s \frown \langle (t,a) \rangle) = t$, and $last(s \frown \langle (t,a) \rangle) = a$. So $foot(s_0) = (6,on)$, $init(s_0) = \langle (1,on), (3,off) \rangle$, $end(s_0) = 6$, and $last(s_0) = on$.

For an infinite trace s, $init(s) = s$ and $end(s) = \infty$. The last element of an infinite trace s is not defined, so (for notational convenience) when s is infinite, $last(s) \neq a$ for any event $a \in \Sigma$.

For the empty trace, $begin(\langle \rangle)$ and $end(\langle \rangle)$ are defined to be ∞ and 0 respectively. The operations $head$, $tail$, $first$, $foot$, $init$, and $last$, are not defined on the empty trace.

Timed traces

The timed traces associated with a process can be determined from its executions. An execution e is an alternating sequence of processes and transitions, so it contains information about events that are performed and their associated times. In an execution, two successive processes should be related by the transition between them: whenever $\langle Q_i, \mu_i, Q_{i+1} \rangle$ appears as a contiguous subsequence of e for some event $\mu \in \Sigma^{\checkmark, \tau}$, then $Q_i \xrightarrow{\mu_i} Q_{i+1}$ should be a possible transition; and whenever $\langle Q_i, d_i, Q_{i+1} \rangle$ appears as a contiguous subsequence of e for some duration $d_i \in \mathbb{R}^+$, then $Q_i \xrightarrow{d_i} Q_{i+1}$ should be a possible evolution. The duration ∞ cannot occur between two processes, though an execution can end with $\langle Q_i, \infty \rangle$, provided $Q_i \xrightarrow{\infty}$.

The executions of a timed CSP process Q, denoted timed executions(Q), is the set of those executions e whose first element is the process term Q. Internal τ events do appear in executions, even though they will not be recorded in the corresponding trace.

For example, one execution of the process $a \xrightarrow{2} STOP$ is the sequence

$$\langle (a \xrightarrow{2} STOP), \ 3, \ (a \xrightarrow{2} STOP), \ a,$$
$$(STOP \xrightarrow{2}_{\triangleright} STOP), \ 2, \ (STOP \xrightarrow{0}_{\triangleright} STOP), \ \tau, \ STOP \rangle$$

Since time is recorded with reference to the beginning of the execution, the initial transition occurs at time 0. The ith transition in an execution e is actually the $2i + 1$th element of e because processes and transitions alternate. The notation $trans_e(i)$ identifies this transition:

$$trans_e(i) \ = \ e@(2i + 1)$$

The time of the 0th transition is 0. At any stage in the execution, the time the $i + 1$th transition occurs depends on whether the ith was an event transition, in which case no time has elapsed, or an evolution transition, in which case the time d associated with that delay has elapsed. The time $time_e(i)$ of the ith transition $trans_e(i)$ can thus be determined as follows:

$$time_e(0) \ = \ 0$$
$$time_e(i + 1) \ = \ \begin{cases} time_e(i) & \text{if } trans_e(i) \in \Sigma^{\checkmark, \tau} \\ time_e(i) + trans_e(i) & \text{if } trans_e(i) \in \mathbb{R}^+ \cup \{\infty\} \end{cases}$$

The $i + 1$th transition is the $2i + 1$th element of the execution sequence e because that sequence alternates processes and transitions. The time at which the ith transition ends and the $i + 1$th transition begins execution is the sum of the time transitions that have occurred up to that point. If $trans_e(i)$ is a visible event whose occurrence should be recorded in the trace, then $(time_e(i), trans_e(i))$ will appear in the trace.

A finite or infinite execution e of length $\#e$ will have $\lfloor \#e/2 \rfloor$ transitions associated with it: an execution with an odd length $2n + 1$ will begin and end with a process, and will have n

$$e = \langle Q_0, 3, Q_1, a, Q_2, 2, Q_3, b, Q_4, c, Q_5, 2, Q_6 \rangle$$
$$\mathsf{ttrace}(e) = \langle (3, a), (5, b), (5, c) \rangle$$

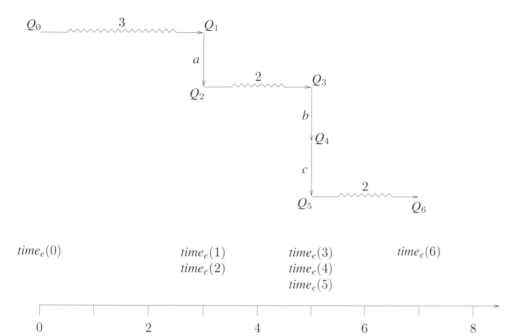

Fig. 11.1   *An execution e and its timed trace*

transitions; an execution with an even length $2n$ will end with an infinite evolution and have n transitions in total (including the final one); and an execution with infinite length will have an infinite number of transitions—$\lfloor \infty/2 \rfloor = \infty$. The timed trace associated with an execution e of any of these kinds is then given by

$$\mathsf{ttrace}(e) \quad = \quad \langle (time_e(i), trans_e(i)) \mid i \leftarrow \langle 0, 1 \ldots \lfloor \#e/2 \rfloor - 1 \rangle, trans_e(i) \in \Sigma^{\checkmark} \rangle$$

This definition extracts the external events occurring in the execution e, together with the times that they occur. Figure 11.1 provides an illustration of an execution and its associated timed trace.

The timed traces associated with a process Q are those associated with its executions.

$$\mathsf{timed\ traces}(Q) \quad = \quad \{ \mathsf{ttrace}(e) \mid e \in \mathsf{timed\ executions}(Q) \}$$

Timed refusals

Processes interact with each other by synchronizing on events at particular times. When a process is offered the opportunity to perform an event, it can make one of two possible responses. It can either perform the event, resulting in a transition to another process state, or else it can refuse to perform it. The timed trace is the record of the timed events that were performed during an execution; and a *timed refusal* will be a record of those timed events that were refused.

In the untimed model, an untimed refusal indicates that the process has either reached a stable state, in which no further internal transitions are possible and where none of the refused events is possible; or that it is diverging, performing an infinite sequence of internal transitions and never reaching a stable state. A timed analysis is more discriminating, since it considers event refusals at particular times and not simply at the end of the execution. Finite variability ensures that divergence by any time is not possible, so the refusal of an event a at a time t will simply reflect the fact that a is not possible for the state reached at time t. If the execution records the performance of any events at time t, passing through several states, then the refusal information is associated with the last of these states. At any particular instant, the refusal information is subsequent to the events performed at that time. Refusal information about intermediate states at that instant is not available.

The states of an execution associated with refusal information are those states which are followed by an evolution. Timed refusal information is associated with evolutions rather than with event transitions.

For example, the execution e_1 described by

$$((a \to c \to STOP) \;\square\; d \to STOP) \overset{3}{\rhd} b \to STOP \quad (1)$$
$$\wr 3$$
$$((a \to c \to STOP) \;\square\; d \to STOP) \overset{0}{\rhd} b \to STOP \quad (2)$$
$$\downarrow \tau$$
$$b \to STOP \quad\quad\quad\quad\quad\quad\quad\quad\quad\quad\quad (3)$$
$$\wr \infty$$

reaches an unstable state (2) at time 3 from which it immediately performs an internal event to the state $b \to STOP$. The process state (2) has an a transition but no b transition, but it is not stable since it also has an immediate τ transition. The state (3) does have a b transition enabled, so b cannot be refused. On the other hand, this state has no a transition, so a can be refused at time 3. If the event a is offered to the process at time 3, then it is possible that the process will refuse to perform it, preferring the internal transition. Of course, it is also possible that the a will be accepted at time 3, if the timeout has not yet occurred. This is an example of *point nondeterminism*, where an event is both possible and refusable at the instant its offer is withdrawn.

Another execution e_2 of the process has the event a occurring at time 1:

$$((a \to c \to STOP) \,\square\, d \to STOP) \overset{3}{\triangleright} b \to STOP \quad (1)$$
$$\downarrow 1$$
$$((a \to c \to STOP) \,\square\, d \to STOP) \overset{2}{\triangleright} b \to STOP \quad (2)$$
$$\downarrow a$$
$$c \to STOP \quad\quad\quad\quad\quad\quad\quad\quad\quad\quad (3)$$
$$\downarrow \infty$$

There are two states this execution passes through at time 1, one before and one after the a has been performed. If the d is offered to the process at time 1, it might be accepted in preference to the a, but in this execution the a has been performed, so d will instead be refused at that time. Conversely, given that this sequence of transitions has occurred, the c event cannot be refused at time 1, since the stable state at that time within this execution is state (3), subsequent to the performance of the event. A key feature of a timed analysis is that refusal information is available throughout an execution and not simply at the end as was the case with untimed refusal information.

A refusal set $\aleph$ is simply a set of timed events. If the pair (t, a) appears in a refusal set associated with a particular execution, then this means that the state from which an evolution occurs at time t (i.e. the state at which no further events occur) has no a transition. A set of timed events appearing within a single refusal set indicates that none of the events could be performed by their corresponding stable state during the execution.

Since refusals accompany evolutions, and event offers are constant over evolutions, the same set of events will be refusable throughout an evolution. Refusal sets can therefore be structured so that the set of refused events is finitely variable with respect to time. This means that a refusal set will record intervals over which sets of events are refused. The appropriate intervals are half-open, corresponding to the stable states along the evolution: an evolution $Q \overset{d}{\rightsquigarrow} Q'$ will correspond to a refusal of the set A (provided Q can perform no event from A) over the interval $[0, d)$. The time d itself is not included since the evolution contains no information about whether Q' itself evolves. All the states at the times in $[0, d)$ are stable relative to this execution fragment, but Q' may not be.

A *refusal token* is a special kind of refusal set: a set of events A being refused along a half-open interval of the form $[t_1, t_2)$. These will be the building blocks from which refusal sets will be constructed. The set of all possible refusal tokens is denoted *RTOK*:

$$RTOK \quad = \quad \{[t_1, t_2) \times A \mid t_1 \leqslant t < t_2 \wedge A \subseteq \Sigma^\checkmark\}$$

$$R \in RTOK \quad \Leftrightarrow \quad \exists t_1 : \mathbb{R}^+;\ t_2 : \mathbb{R}^+ \cup \infty;\ A \subseteq \Sigma^\checkmark \bullet$$
$$t_1 < t_2 \wedge R = \{(t, a) \mid t_1 \leqslant t < t_2 \wedge a \in A\}$$

For example, the set

$$\{(t, a) \mid 2 \leqslant t < 5 \wedge (a = on \vee a = off)\} \quad (= [2, 5) \times \{on, off\})$$

is a refusal token, corresponding to the refusal of both events *on* and *off* over the interval from 2 to 5.

Refusal sets are simply combinations of refusal tokens, constructed to ensure that finite variability is guaranteed:

$$Y \in FRSET \quad \Leftrightarrow \quad \exists R : \mathbb{F}(RTOK) \bullet Y = \bigcup R$$

$$FRSET \quad = \quad \{\bigcup R \mid R \subseteq^{fin} RTOK\}$$

$$\aleph \in RSET \quad \Leftrightarrow \quad \aleph \subseteq \mathbb{R}^+ \times \Sigma^{\checkmark} \wedge \forall t : \mathbb{R}^+ \bullet \{(t', a) \in \aleph \mid t' < t\} \in FRSET$$

The set *FRSET* is the set of those timed refusal sets which change only finitely often over time. These can be described as finite unions of refusal tokens. *RSET* is the set of all refusal sets: the finite variability condition is that only finitely many changes can have occurred up to any finite time, which is expressed as the requirement that the refusal set up to any time t must be a member of *FRSET*.

The notation $\aleph \uparrow I$ stands for the projection of the refusal set onto the interval I: the set of timed events whose times fall in I. If I is a single point interval $[t, t]$ then the notation may be overloaded and the time t used in place of the interval. $\aleph \Vert t$ is the refusal set $\aleph$ strictly before t, and $\aleph \uparrow t$ is the refusal set $\aleph$ at and after the time t.

Other projections and translations through time are also defined: $\aleph \upharpoonright A$ restricts the refusal set to events in A, whereas $\aleph \setminus A$ removes all the events in A from the refusal set. $\aleph + t$ increases by t all the times associated with the events in $\aleph$, and $\aleph - t$ decreases the times by t. If a refusal set is shifted back through time, then it is truncated so no refusals before time 0 can appear. Finally, $\sigma(\aleph)$ is the set of events that appear at some time in $\aleph$, $begin(\aleph)$ is the first time an event appears in $\aleph$, and $end(\aleph)$ is the point from which no further refusals are recorded.

Example 11.1.1 If $\aleph_0 = [2, 5) \times \{on, off\} \cup [4, 7) \times \{up\}$, then

$$
\begin{aligned}
\aleph_0 \uparrow [4, 5) &= [4, 5) \times \{on, off, up\} \\
\aleph_0 \Vert 4 &= [2, 4) \times \{on, off\} \\
\aleph_0 \uparrow 4 &= [4, 5) \times \{on, off\} \cup [4, 7) \times \{up\} \\
\aleph_0 \upharpoonright \{on\} &= [2, 5) \times \{on\} \\
\aleph_0 \setminus \{on\} &= [2, 5) \times \{off\} \cup [4, 7) \times \{up\} \\
\aleph_0 + 4 &= [6, 9) \times \{on, off\} \cup [8, 11) \times \{up\} \\
\aleph_0 - 4 &= [0, 1) \times \{on, off\} \cup [0, 3) \times \{up\} \\
\sigma(\aleph_0) &= \{on, off, up\} \\
begin(\aleph_0) &= 2 \\
end(\aleph_0) &= 7
\end{aligned}
$$

■

A refusal set $\aleph \in RSET$ is *consistent with* an execution e if every timed event (t, a) in the refusal set can be refused during the execution. This means that an a transition is not possible for the particular process state reached at t during the execution. Refused events are associated with evolution transitions, and the delay transition $trans_e(i)$ is associated with the interval $[time_e(i), time_e(i + 1))$. If t falls within this interval, then the process state reached at t will be able to refuse a precisely when the process $Q_e(i) = e@2i$ at the beginning of that delay cannot perform it, since offers and hence refusals do not change during an evolution. Formally, $\aleph$ is consistent with an execution e if

$$\forall (t, a) \in \aleph \bullet \exists i : \mathbb{N} \bullet time_e(i) \leqslant t < time_e(i + 1) \wedge \neg(Q_e(i) \xrightarrow{a})$$

The process $Q_e(i)$ is the process reached at the beginning of the delay during which (t, a) is refused, so $Q_e(i)$ must itself be unable to perform the event a.

A number of different refusal sets will be consistent with any particular execution, and in particular the empty refusal set $\{\}$ will vacuously be consistent with any execution. Every execution will have a unique maximal refusal set consistent with it, consisting of all possible refused events for the duration of the execution. A set $\aleph \in RSET$ will be consistent with an execution if and only if it is a subset of the maximal refusal set.

For example, the execution e_1 given on page 340 is consistent with the refusal set

$$[0, 3) \times \{b, c\} \cup [3, 17) \times \{a\}$$

but not with

$$[0, 5) \times \{b, c\}$$

since the state reached after three units of time is $b \to STOP$, which cannot refuse the event b. Hence the elements (t, b) in the refusal set are not consistent with the execution when $t \geqslant 3$.

The maximal refusal set consistent with e_1 is

$$([0, 3) \times \{b, c\}) \cup ([3, \infty) \times \{a, c, d\}) \cup ([0, \infty) \times \Sigma^{\checkmark} \setminus \{a, b, c, d\})$$

All events in $\Sigma^{\checkmark}$ apart from a, b, c, and d can be refused throughout the execution, since they are never possible. There is a single event transition, at time 3, and the events that were possible before that were a and d (so b and c were refusable before that time). After that transition only b is possible, so all other events can be refused.

Timed failures

Processes are considered in terms of the possible observations that can be made of their executions. These will be described in terms of timed traces and timed refusals. An execution makes it clear what events have been performed, so there can be only one possible trace ttrace(e) associated with an execution e. On the other hand, the events observed to be refused during the execution are not explicit in the transitions. Possible refusal sets are those that are consistent with the execution, but the observation of a refusal set will depend on what was offered to the process during the execution: if nothing was offered, then no events will be observed to be refused. A shop that requests of its customers 'please do not ask for credit as a refusal often offends' does not actually refuse credit unless a customer asks for it. A refusal can be observed only if it is requested of the process. An outside recorder cannot know that it was the *process* that refused an event unless it also knows that this event was not blocked by the environment.

An observation of an execution will consist of a timed trace and a timed refusal. This pair $(s, \aleph)$ is termed a *timed failure*. The trace s will be the sequence of events occurring in the execution, and the refusal set $\aleph$ will be some consistent set of timed events which could be refused during the execution. The refusal set is a record of refusals *during* the performance of the trace, and not simply at the end. A natural way to understand the pair $(s, \aleph)$ as an observation of a process is as evidence that it is able to perform the sequence of events s, and to refuse all events in the set $\aleph$ if offered them while performing s. In general it is a partial record of an execution. The timed failure $(\langle (1, a) \rangle, [2, 3) \times \{b\})$ records that during the execution the process engaged in the event a at time 1, and refused the event b over the interval from 2 to 3.

A dual way to consider the pair $(s, \aleph)$ is from the point of view of the process's environment. The environment offers events at particular times to the process: these offers are either accepted, in which case they appear in the trace, or else they are refused, in which case they are recorded in the refusal set. The timed failure thus provides a record of all events that were offered to the process during the observation, indicating whether they were accepted or refused. It may be considered as a record of an experiment conducted by the environment on the process, offering particular events and eliciting responses. From this point of view, the timed failure $(\langle (1, a) \rangle, [2, 3) \times \{b\})$ is a record that an a was offered at time 1, and it was accepted; and that the event b was offered over the interval from 2 to 3, but it was refused. Since the environment can make arbitrary offers, any process will have timed failures corresponding to all possible offers.

Timed failures may contain enough information to indicate urgency of some events. If an event a is refused over a particular interval, and performed at the end of that interval, then that occurrence of a must be urgent within the execution. The timed failure $(\langle (3, a) \rangle, [0, 3) \times \{a\})$ associated with the process *WAIT* 3; $a \xrightarrow{2} a \rightarrow STOP$ indicates that the a event was offered continually up until time 3, at which point it was accepted. The earlier refusal establishes that it was not possible before time 3 during this execution, so the occurrence at time 3 is an urgent one. This information is obtained directly from the timed failure itself, and does not require explicit reference to the underlying execution.

It is also possible that the environment offers two copies of the event a to the process: it will maintain its offer of a until it has occurred twice. The refusal set does not need to identify how many copies it is refusing: if the process is unable to perform a then it will refuse both offers as easily as it refuses one. When the process is able to perform a then it will appear in the trace. In this case refusal of the second a can follow occurrence of the first. The timed failure

$(\langle(3, a)\rangle, [3, 5) \times \{a\})$ has an a occurring at time 3 but a subsequently being refused from time 3 to time 5. The occurrence and subsequent refusal of a at time 3 indicates that having performed the event a no further occurrences were possible at that time. This is analogous to the untimed failure $(\langle a \rangle, \{a\})$ which indicates that a is both possible and refusable—but the refusability is subsequent to the performance of a. In the timed setting, the refusal of events at any instant is subsequent to the events performed.

Urgent events can be refused up until the time that they actually occur, and then having occurred further occurrences may be refused from that time onwards. A timed failure $(\langle(3, a)\rangle, [0, 5) \times \{a\})$ is best understood from the dual point of view of environmental offers: the event a is offered between times 0 and 5, so any occurrences during that interval will be urgent, by maximal progress. In this case it was performed at time 3, but the environment continued with an offer of further a's after this occurrence. Any events occurring during or at the end of a refusal token contained in $\aleph$ (though not necessarily at the beginning) must be urgent. If it is known that the environment is ready to engage in events during particular intervals, then maximal progress dictates that the events must occur as soon as the process enables them. In the extreme case, if an event is in a refusal set throughout all time, so $[0, \infty) \times \{a\} \subseteq \aleph$, then this indicates that all occurrences of a in the trace s of $(s, \aleph)$ are urgent: the environment is always willing to engage in as many a events as the process can perform, and is permanently offering further copies of a. All a's must occur as soon as they are enabled by the process.

Some of the projection functions on timed traces and timed refusals above lift to timed failures, as follows: $(s, \aleph) + t = (s+t, \aleph+t)$; $(s, \aleph) - t = (s-t, \aleph-t)$; $(s, \aleph) \upharpoonright A = (s \upharpoonright A, \aleph \upharpoonright A)$; $(s, \aleph) \parallel t = (s \parallel t, \aleph \parallel t)$; and $(s, \aleph) \lceil t = (s \lceil t, \aleph \parallel t)$. The last of these definitions is anomalous, but reflects the fact that an observation of an execution up to and including time t but not beyond it will include the events reported in the trace at time t, but not the events recorded in the refusal.

The timed failures model

Any well-timed CSP process will be associated with a set of timed failures, corresponding to all the possible records of all its executions. Not every arbitrary set of timed failures will represent a CSP process, and there are some properties *TF*1–*TF*4 (discussed below) which must hold for any set of timed failures corresponding to some CSP process. The timed failures model for timed CSP will consist of all sets of failures which meet these properties.

Timed failures contain varying amounts of information about the capabilities of a process, and they may be ordered according to how much information they contain. The information order $\preccurlyeq$ on $TT \times RSET$ is defined as follows:

$$(s', \aleph') \preccurlyeq (s, \aleph) \quad \Leftrightarrow \quad \exists s'' \bullet s = s' \frown s'' \wedge \aleph' \subseteq \aleph \parallel begin(s'')$$

A process P that is capable of exhibiting $(s, \aleph)$ must have some execution e in which the events in s are performed, and during which the events in $\aleph$ are refused. It follows that any prefix e' of that execution must also be a possible execution for P, so its corresponding trace $s' \leqslant s$ must be a possible trace, and up to the time where s' and s differ e' and e are the same execution so the same events (and hence any subset $\aleph'$) can be refused. If $(s, \aleph)$ is a failure of P, then any behaviour $(s', \aleph') \preccurlyeq (s, \aleph)$ is also sure to be a failure of P.

A set of timed failures which represents a CSP process must satisfy certain properties. Firstly, it must contain the empty observation, corresponding to the possibility that a process might never be observed. This observation records an experiment in which no event was ever offered to the process, either for it to accept or for it to refuse. This experiment with an empty result is possible for any process.

Secondly, any set of timed failures corresponding to a timed process must contain all the observations whose presence can be deduced from behaviours known already to be present. The set of timed failures should be *downwards closed* under the information ordering.

Furthermore, any timed failure is associated with an execution, which will have a complete set of possible refusals accompanying the sequence of transitions. This means that the refusal set $\aleph$ already exhibited can be augmented with further refusal information to obtain a *complete* refusal $\aleph' \supseteq \aleph$, which contains all the other events that could have been refused during the execution. Completeness of $\aleph'$ means that for any time t, any event a not appearing in $\aleph'$ must have been offered at that time during the execution, and hence must have been possible for the process. This manifests itself in two ways:

C1 any timed event (t, a) that does not appear in the refusal set $\aleph'$ must provide a possible alternative continuation to the trace. Refusal information at t is subsequent to the trace up to and including that time, so the event (t, a) follows the trace up to and including t.

C2 If an event a is not refused as time t is approached, then it is possible throughout the evolution leading up to time t, so a must also be possible at the point the execution first reaches t by the constancy of event offers and time closure for evolutions. This means that it must be possible at that time in place of any other events that occur then.

These considerations are all captured as the following properties on a set S of timed failures:

$TF1.$ $(\langle\rangle, \{\}) \in S$

$TF2.$ $((s, \aleph) \in S \wedge (s', \aleph') \preccurlyeq (s, \aleph)) \Rightarrow (s', \aleph') \in S$

$TF3.$ $(s, \aleph) \in S \Rightarrow$
$$\exists \aleph' \in RSET \bullet \quad \aleph \subseteq \aleph' \wedge (s, \aleph') \in S \wedge \forall (t, a) \in \mathbb{R}^+ \times \Sigma \bullet$$
$$(C1) \qquad (t, a) \notin \aleph' \Rightarrow (s \upharpoonright t \frown \langle (t, a) \rangle, \aleph' \parallel t) \in S$$
$$\wedge$$
$$(C2) \qquad (t > 0 \wedge \neg \exists \varepsilon > 0 \bullet ([t - \varepsilon, t) \times \{a\} \subseteq \aleph'))$$
$$\Rightarrow (s \parallel t \frown \langle (t, a) \rangle, \aleph' \parallel t) \in S$$

The property $TF3$ is the timed analogue of $SF3$ in the stable failures model, or $F4$ in the FDI model. All of them essentially require that events should be either possible or refusable.

A further property $TF4$ can be considered as an infinitary version of $TF3$, allowing the deduction of infinite failures corresponding to complete executions of the process. In this sense it is a timed analogue of the property $I2$ concerned with infinite traces in the FDI model.

The set of all possible infinite failures associated with a set S will be contained in $\overline{S}$, the *closure* of S. This is defined to include all the infinite behaviours of S that are consistent with its finite behaviours:

$$\overline{S} \;=\; \{(s, \aleph) \mid \forall t \in \mathbb{R}^+ \bullet (s, \aleph) \parallel t \in S\}$$

A set S is *closed* if it is equal to its closure. Any process which does not contain infinite nondeterminism will have a closed set of timed failures. This means that once all of its finite duration timed failures are known, the infinite duration ones are also known. The property $TF4$ predicts the presence of infinite timed failures for any process, but in general, when infinite nondeterminism may be present, this need not be all of those in $\overline{S}$.

11.2   TIMED FAILURES SEMANTICS

The timed failures $\mathcal{TF}\,[\![Q]\!]$ associated with any timed CSP process Q can be obtained directly from those of its constituents, without the need to extract the information directly from the executions. The compositional semantics has a clause for each CSP construct.

STOP

The process *STOP* is unable to perform any events, and can refuse any offers that are made.

$$\mathcal{TF}\,[\![STOP]\!] \;=\; \{(\langle\rangle, \aleph) \mid \aleph \in RSET\}$$

This set of observations can also be understood as the process *STOP* responding to any offers with the empty trace.

Event prefix

When an event a is offered by a process $a \xrightarrow{d} Q$, then the executions of that process fall into two classes. Firstly the event a may never be performed. This will be due to the environment never offering the event, since any offer would certainly be accepted. This means that a cannot appear in the refusal set $\aleph$, though it can contain any other events at any times. Secondly, the event a may be performed at some time t. In this case it could not have been offered before t, since any offer before that time would also have been accepted. The behaviour subsequent to the a will be that of the subsequent process Q, except that it has been delayed by $t + d$ time units.

These two possibilities are reflected in the two clauses defining the set of timed failures of $a \overset{d}{\to} Q$.

$$\mathcal{TF}[\![a \overset{d}{\to} Q]\!] = \{(\langle\rangle, \aleph) \mid a \notin \sigma(\aleph)\}$$
$$\cup$$
$$\{(\langle(t, a)\rangle \frown (s + (t + d)), \aleph) \mid \quad t \in \mathbb{R}^+$$
$$\wedge \, a \notin \sigma(\aleph \| t)$$
$$\wedge \, (s, \aleph - (t + d)) \in \mathcal{TF}[\![Q]\!]\}$$

The process $a \to Q$ is equivalent to $a \overset{0}{\to} Q$; the behaviour of Q begins at the instant a occurs.

Timed event prefix

The executions of the timed event prefix fall into the same two categories as the previous operator. The only difference concerns the identity of the process subsequent to an a event occurring at time t. In that case the time variable u becomes bound to t in the resulting process.

$$\mathcal{TF}[\![a@u \to Q]\!] = \{(\langle\rangle, \aleph) \mid a \notin \sigma(\aleph)\}$$
$$\cup$$
$$\{(\langle(t, a)\rangle \frown s + t, \aleph) \mid \quad t \in \mathbb{R}^+ \wedge$$
$$a \notin \sigma(\aleph \| t) \wedge$$
$$(s, \aleph - t) \in \mathcal{TF}[\![Q[t/u]]\!]\}$$

If u does not appear free in the subsequent process Q, then $Q[t/u] = Q$ and the set of timed failures is exactly that of $a \to Q$ as would be expected.

Choosing between events

If a set of events A is offered by a process $x : A \to Q(x)$, then either no event is ever performed, in which case none of the events in the set A can be refused, or else some event $a \in A$ is performed at some time t as the first event of the execution, and the subsequent behaviour is provided by $Q(x)$ shifted through t time units.

$$\mathcal{TF}[\![x : A \to Q(x)]\!] = \{(\langle\rangle, \aleph) \mid A \cap \sigma(\aleph) = \{\}\}$$
$$\cup$$
$$\{(\langle(t, a)\rangle \frown (s + t), \aleph) \mid$$
$$a \in A \wedge t \geqslant 0 \wedge A \cap \sigma(\aleph \| t) = \{\}$$
$$\wedge \, (s, \aleph - t) \in \mathcal{TF}[\![Q(x)]\!]\}$$

Successful termination

The process *SKIP* is immediately ready to terminate, and remains in that state, unable to refuse termination, until and unless it does so. If it terminates at time t, then this can only be because its environment was not prepared to allow it to terminate beforehand, encapsulated in the fact that ✓ cannot appear in the refusal set before time t.

$$\mathcal{TF}[\![SKIP]\!] = \{(\langle\rangle, \aleph) \mid ✓ \notin \sigma(\aleph)\}$$
$$\cup$$
$$\{(\langle(t, ✓)\rangle, \aleph) \mid t \in \mathbb{R}^+ \wedge ✓ \notin \sigma(\aleph \parallel t)\}$$

There are no restrictions on the refusal set after the ✓ event has been performed.

Timeout

A choice between processes will have a number of alternative ways of exhibiting timed failures. The time-sensitive choice $Q_1 \overset{d}{\triangleright} Q_2$ either resolves the choice in favour of Q_1 by performing some event by time d, or else resolves the choice in favour of Q_2. There will be timed failures corresponding to each of these possibilities. Those behaviours of Q_1 whose first event recorded in the trace occurs before time d will appear as behaviours of $Q_1 \overset{d}{\triangleright} Q_2$. The other behaviours will be those where the timeout is reached. The first d time units remain the responsibility of Q_1, so the refusal over that initial interval must be a refusal of Q_1. The behaviour following the timeout is that of Q_2, translated through d time units.

$$\mathcal{TF}[\![Q_1 \overset{d}{\triangleright} Q_2]\!] = \{(s, \aleph) \mid begin(s) \leqslant d \wedge (s, \aleph) \in \mathcal{TF}[\![Q_1]\!]\}$$
$$\cup$$
$$\{(s, \aleph) \mid begin(s) \geqslant d \wedge (\langle\rangle, \aleph \parallel d) \in \mathcal{TF}[\![Q_1]\!]$$
$$\wedge (s, \aleph) - d \in \mathcal{TF}[\![Q_2]\!]\}$$

There are a number of laws associated with the timeout operator, and these are given in Figure 11.2. Timeout exhibits a form of associativity, although the time of the second timeout will depend on the bracketing of the operators, which affects whether it starts at time d or at time 0. Timeout also distributes over both internal and external choices. Finally, it reduces or expires when its first argument delays.

Delay

The delay construct *WAIT d* is a derived construct defined as $STOP \overset{d}{\triangleright} SKIP$, so its semantics can be deduced from those of *STOP*, *SKIP*, and timeout. The result is the following:

$$\mathcal{TF}[\![WAIT\ d]\!] = \{(\langle\rangle, \aleph) \mid ✓ \notin \sigma(\aleph \uparrow d)\}$$
$$\cup$$
$$\{(\langle(t, ✓)\rangle, \aleph) \mid t \geqslant d \wedge ✓ \notin \sigma(\aleph \uparrow [d, t))\}$$

$$Q_1 \overset{d}{\triangleright} (Q_2 \overset{d'}{\triangleright} Q_3) = (Q_1 \overset{d}{\triangleright} Q_2) \overset{d+d'}{\triangleright} Q_3 \qquad\qquad \langle\triangleright\text{-assoc}\rangle$$

$$(Q_1 \sqcap Q_2) \overset{d}{\triangleright} Q_3 = (Q_1 \overset{d}{\triangleright} Q_3) \sqcap (Q_2 \overset{d}{\triangleright} Q_3) \qquad\qquad \langle\triangleright\text{-left-dist}\rangle$$

$$Q_1 \overset{d}{\triangleright} (Q_2 \sqcap Q_3) = (Q_1 \overset{d}{\triangleright} Q_2) \sqcap (Q_1 \overset{d}{\triangleright} Q_3) \qquad\qquad \langle\triangleright\text{-right-dist}\rangle$$

$$(Q_1 \square Q_2) \overset{d}{\triangleright} Q_3 = (Q_1 \overset{d}{\triangleright} Q_3) \square (Q_2 \overset{d}{\triangleright} Q_3) \qquad\qquad \langle\triangleright\text{-}\square\text{-left-dist}\rangle$$

$$Q_1 \overset{d}{\triangleright} (Q_2 \square Q_3) = (Q_1 \overset{d}{\triangleright} Q_2) \square (Q_1 \overset{d}{\triangleright} Q_3) \qquad\qquad \langle\triangleright\text{-}\square\text{-right-dist}\rangle$$

$$STOP \overset{d}{\triangleright} Q_1 = WAIT\, d; Q_1 \qquad\qquad \langle\triangleright\text{-delay}\rangle$$

$$(WAIT\, d; Q_1) \overset{d+d'}{\triangleright} Q_2 = WAIT\, d; (Q_1 \overset{d'}{\triangleright} Q_2) \qquad\qquad \langle\triangleright\text{-delay-1}\rangle$$

$$(WAIT(d + d'); Q_1) \overset{d}{\triangleright} Q_2 = WAIT\, d; Q_2 \qquad\qquad \langle\triangleright\text{-delay-2}\rangle$$

Fig. 11.2   Laws for timeout

$$WAIT\, d;\ WAIT\, d' = WAIT(d + d') \qquad\qquad \langle\text{delay-sum}\rangle$$

$$a \overset{d}{\rightarrow} P = a \rightarrow WAIT\, d; P \qquad\qquad \langle\text{delay-prefix}\rangle$$

Fig. 11.3   Laws for delay

Termination is not possible before time d, and until it happens it cannot be refused after time d.

The laws for the delay operator state that delays may be combined, and that they may be used in place of delays in event prefix. They are given in Figure 11.3.

External choice

The refusals of an external choice between processes are the joint responsibility of both processes before the choice is resolved. The choice executes both of its arguments concurrently until the first event occurs, so any events that are refused before this point must be refused by both processes. Dually, if the choice is offered an event when both components are enabled, then both components are individually offered the event.

A timed failure $(s, \aleph)$ of a choice may be considered in terms of whether it corresponds to an execution in which the choice has been resolved in favour of Q_1, or of Q_2, or to one where the choice has not yet been resolved. If the choice has been resolved in favour of one of the processes then $s \neq \langle\rangle$, and the other process must have participated in the refusal up to *begin*(*s*). If the choice has not yet been made, then $s = \langle \rangle$ and the refusal must be possible for both processes.

There is a concise way of capturing this information:

$$\mathcal{TF} \llbracket Q_1 \,\square\, Q_2 \rrbracket \;=\; \{(s, \aleph) \mid (s, \aleph) \in \mathcal{TF} \llbracket Q_1 \rrbracket \cup \mathcal{TF} \llbracket Q_2 \rrbracket$$
$$\wedge$$
$$(\langle \rangle, \aleph \parallel begin(s)) \in \mathcal{TF} \llbracket Q_1 \rrbracket \cap \mathcal{TF} \llbracket Q_2 \rrbracket \}$$

Every behaviour must derive from either Q_1 or Q_2, depending on which way the choice is resolved. Furthermore, its projection onto the interval up to the point where the choice is resolved must also be a behaviour of both processes. Finally, the case where the trace is empty and the choice has not yet been made is already taken care of: the second clause requires that both processes can exhibit the timed failure, and in fact the first clause follows from the second when $s = \langle \rangle$.

Internal choice

An internal choice can behave either as Q_1 or as Q_2. Its observations are simply those observations that accompany any execution of Q_1 or of Q_2.

$$\mathcal{TF} \llbracket Q_1 \,\sqcap\, Q_2 \rrbracket \;=\; \mathcal{TF} \llbracket Q_1 \rrbracket \cup \mathcal{TF} \llbracket Q_2 \rrbracket$$

The fact that timed refusal information is recorded throughout the trace allows processes to be distinguished on the basis of *refusal testing* information. A timed environment can probe a timed process by offering events and have its subsequent behaviour dependent on whether the events were accepted or refused. For example, an environment $(a \rightarrow Q_1) \overset{2}{\triangleright} Q_2$ will continue with Q_1 if a is accepted, and with Q_2 if a is refused.

This possibility is reflected in the failure of the following untimed law to hold in the timed model:

$$(P_1 \,\square\, P_2) \sqcap P_3 \;\;=_U\;\; (P_1 \sqcap P_3) \,\square\, (P_2 \sqcap P_3)$$

If refusal testing is available, then some of the possibilities of the right-hand side cannot be matched by the left-hand side. For example, the first event of P_1 might be refused, followed by the occurrence of the first event of P_2. This is not possible for the left-hand process. For example, the process $((a \rightarrow STOP) \sqcap STOP) \,\square\, ((b \rightarrow STOP) \sqcap STOP)$ can exhibit the timed failure $(\langle (1, b) \rangle, [0, 1) \times \{a\})$, whereas $(((a \rightarrow STOP) \,\square\, (b \rightarrow STOP)) \sqcap STOP)$ cannot.

The law holds in the untimed models because refusal information is available only after the trace has been performed, so a refusal can occur only at the end of an execution. An untimed process cannot offer an event and subsequently withdraw it if not accepted. The lack of control over time means that a process might withdraw an event too quickly, so it cannot guarantee that its environment was unwilling to perform it. The introduction of time sensitive CSP operators allows a greater degree of control and enables process contexts to carry out refusal testing.

Indexed internal choice

An indexed internal choice can behave as any of its arguments. Its associated timed failures are accordingly all of those timed failures associated with any of its constituent processes.

$$\mathcal{TF} \left[\!\left[\sqcap_{i \in J} Q_i \right]\!\right] \quad = \quad \bigcup_{i \in J} \mathcal{TF} \left[\!\left[Q_i \right]\!\right]$$

This operator does not preserve closedness: it may yield a process which is not closed, even if all of its arguments are closed. For example, if $Q_0 = a \rightarrow STOP$ and $Q_{i+1} = a \overset{1}{\rightarrow} Q_i$ then each of the $\mathcal{TF}\left[\!\left[Q_i \right]\!\right]$ is closed, but $\mathcal{TF}\left[\!\left[\sqcap_{i \in \mathbb{N}} Q_i \right]\!\right]$ is not closed, since it can perform any finite number of a events, but cannot perform an infinite number. Thus $(\langle (n, a) \mid n \leftarrow \mathbb{N} \rangle, \{\})$ is not a timed failure of $\sqcap_{i \in \mathbb{N}} Q_i$, even though all of its finite projections are.

Alphabetized parallel

In the parallel combination $Q_1 \,_A\|_B\, Q_2$, the execution projected onto the set $A^{\checkmark}$ is due to Q_1, and onto the set $B^{\checkmark}$ is due to Q_2. Where A and B intersect, both Q_1 and Q_2 must agree on events in the trace, since they synchronize on events, but if either of them refuses an event then the combination will refuse it—either can prevent an event in $(A \cap B)^{\checkmark}$ from occurring.

$$\mathcal{TF} \left[\!\left[Q_1 \,_A\|_B\, Q_2 \right]\!\right] \quad = \quad \{(s, \aleph) \mid \exists \aleph_1, \aleph_2 \bullet$$
$$\aleph \restriction (A \cup B)^{\checkmark} = (\aleph_1 \restriction A^{\checkmark}) \cup (\aleph_2 \restriction B^{\checkmark})$$
$$\wedge \; s = s \restriction (A \cup B)^{\checkmark}$$
$$\wedge \; (s \restriction A^{\checkmark}, \aleph_1) \in \mathcal{TF} \left[\!\left[Q_1 \right]\!\right]$$
$$\wedge \; (s \restriction B^{\checkmark}, \aleph_2) \in \mathcal{TF} \left[\!\left[Q_2 \right]\!\right] \}$$

The combination can only perform events that either of its components can perform, so no events can occur outside the set $(A \cup B)^{\checkmark}$. This means that all such events can be refused, which is why there are no restrictions on the refusal set outside $(A \cup B)^{\checkmark}$.

Interleaving

In an interleaved combination, each event involves the participation of precisely one of the component processes. This means that up until termination an event can be refused only when both components can refuse it. The refusal part of any timed failure before termination must be a refusal for both processes. The timed trace will be an interleaving of the two component timed traces.

$$\mathcal{TF}[\![Q_1 \mid\mid\mid Q_2]\!] \;=\; \{(s, \aleph_1 \cup \aleph_2) \mid \exists s_1, s_2 \bullet \; s \; \text{interleaves} \; s_1, s_2$$
$$\wedge \; (s_1, \aleph_1) \in \mathcal{TF}[\![Q_1]\!]$$
$$\wedge \; (s_2, \aleph_2) \in \mathcal{TF}[\![Q_2]\!]$$
$$\wedge \; \aleph_1 \restriction \Sigma = \aleph_2 \restriction \Sigma\}$$

The interleaves relation on traces is lifted to timed traces by requiring that at each instant the trace should be an interleaving of the two component traces in the sense of the definition on page 105:

$$s \; \text{interleaves} \; s_1, s_2 =$$
$$\forall t : \mathbb{R}^+ \bullet strip(s \uparrow t) \; \text{interleaves} \; strip(s_1 \uparrow t), strip(s_2 \uparrow t)$$

Each timed event $a \in \Sigma$ in s arises from exactly one of the traces; and $\checkmark$ must be present in both.

Interface parallel

The interface parallel operator $Q_1 \parallel_A Q_2$ combines the features of the interface parallel and the interleaving operators, requiring synchronization on events from the interface event set A, and interleaving on events not in that set. This means that events within the set A can be refused by either process, but events outside that set can only be refused when both processes refuse them.

$$\mathcal{TF}[\![Q_1 \parallel_A Q_2]\!] \;=\; \{(s, \aleph_1 \cup \aleph_2) \mid \; \exists s_1, s_2 \bullet$$
$$s \; \text{synch}_A \; s_1, s_2$$
$$\wedge \; \aleph_1 \setminus A^{\checkmark} = \aleph_2 \setminus A^{\checkmark}$$
$$\wedge \; (s_1, \aleph_1) \in \mathcal{TF}[\![Q_1]\!]$$
$$\wedge \; (s_2, \aleph_2) \in \mathcal{TF}[\![Q_2]\!]\}$$

The relation synch_A on traces lifts to timed traces as follows:

$$s \; \text{synch}_A \; s_1, s_2 \;=\; \forall t \bullet strip(s \uparrow t) \; \text{synch}_A \; strip(s_1 \uparrow t), strip(s_2 \uparrow t)$$

The laws for untimed parallel combinations given in Figures 4.5 and 4.8 remain true in the timed context, and the introduction of delays into the timed language introduces some fresh laws concerning their interaction with the parallel operators. These are given in Figure 11.4. The first three state that delays distribute over each of the parallel operators. The last two are concerned with the interaction between a process which can only delay, and one which is ready to perform an event. If both processes must participate in the event then an initial delay is inevitable. Otherwise, the event may be performed while the delay is unfolding. Similar laws may be formulated and generalized for the other parallel combinations (see Exercise 11.12).

$$(WAIT\ d;\ Q_1)\ _A\|_B\ (WAIT\ d;\ Q_2) = WAIT\ d;\ (Q_1\ _A\|_B\ Q_2) \qquad \langle\text{delay-}\|\text{-dist}\rangle$$

$$(WAIT\ d;\ Q_1)\ |||\ (WAIT\ d;\ Q_2) = WAIT\ d;\ (Q_1\ |||\ Q_2) \qquad \langle\text{delay-}|||\text{-dist}\rangle$$

$$(WAIT\ d;\ Q_1)\ \|_A\ (WAIT\ d;\ Q_2) = WAIT\ d;\ (Q_1\ \|_A\ Q_2) \qquad \langle\text{delay-}\|\text{-dist}\rangle$$

$$a \in B \cap A \Rightarrow \qquad\qquad\qquad\qquad\qquad\qquad\qquad\qquad \langle\text{delay-}\|\text{-step-1}\rangle$$
$$(WAIT\ d;\ Q_1)\ _A\|_B\ (a \to Q_2) = WAIT\ d;\ (Q_1\ _A\|_B\ a \to Q_2)$$

$$a \in B \setminus A \Rightarrow \qquad\qquad\qquad\qquad\qquad\qquad\qquad\qquad \langle\text{delay-}\|\text{-step-2}\rangle$$
$$(WAIT\ d;\ Q_1)\ _A\|_B\ (a \to Q_2) =$$
$$\quad (a@u \to (WAIT(d - u);\ Q_1\ _A\|_B\ Q_2))$$
$$\quad\quad \overset{d}{\triangleright} (Q_1\ _A\|_B\ a \to Q_2)$$

Fig. 11.4 Laws for delays interacting with parallel operators

Hiding

When a set of events A is abstracted from the interface of a process P, the process itself is given control and responsibility over the performance of events from A, with the maximal progress requirement that all occurrences should be performed urgently. The nature of refusal information means that whenever the set of events A is seen to have been refused over an interval $[b, e)$ then all occurrences of events from A that appear in the corresponding trace during the half-closed interval $(b, e]$ (i.e. immediately preceded by an interval in $[b, e)$) are urgent: the refusal information means that they were not enabled before the instant they occurred. If A is refused over the entire time domain $[0, \infty)$ then all occurrences of events from A during the entire execution must be urgent.

The dual view of refusal sets as records of offers from the environment considers the information as a record that the environment of the process offered A over the interval $[b, e)$. Maximal progress means that any events from A enabled during that interval must be performed urgently. If A is offered over the entire interval $[0, \infty)$, then the corresponding trace must correspond to an execution in which all events in A are performed urgently. This is exactly the situation when A is abstracted. From the point of view of the process P, it is in an environment which is always prepared to allow it to perform events from A, but where it must still synchronize on events not in A.

The timed failures for $P \setminus A$ are obtained by firstly identifying those timed failures of P throughout which A is performed urgently. These are precisely those that can be augmented to include $[0, \infty) \times A$ in the refusal set. The trace will have all occurrences of A removed, since they now occur internally within $P \setminus A$ and are no longer synchronizations.

$$\mathcal{TF}[\![P \setminus A]\!] \quad = \quad \{(s \setminus A, \aleph) \mid (s, \aleph \cup ([0, \infty) \times A) \in \mathcal{TF}[\![P]\!]\}$$

$$(WAIT\ d;\ Q) \setminus A = WAIT\ d;\ (Q \setminus A) \qquad\qquad \langle\text{hide-delay}\rangle$$

$$(f(WAIT\ d;\ Q)) = WAIT\ d;\ f(Q) \qquad\qquad \langle f(.)\text{-delay}\rangle$$

$$(f^{-1}(WAIT\ d;\ Q)) = WAIT\ d;\ (f^{-1}(Q)) \qquad\qquad \langle f^{-1}(.)\text{-delay}\rangle$$

Fig. 11.5   Delays and abstraction

The untimed laws for hiding given in Figure 4.12 remain valid in the timed world. In particular, the law $(a \to Q) \setminus A = Q \setminus A$ if $a \in A$ remains true, corresponding in the timed setting to the fact that the internal a occurs urgently: no delays are introduced. The interaction with delays is straightforward, as shown in Figure 11.5: that delays are unaffected by hiding.

Event renaming

The event renaming operators have an entirely similar semantics to the failures of their untimed counterparts, simply lifted to include the timing information.

The forward renamed process $f(Q)$ maps each event that is performed through the function f, so the timed trace has each event transformed by f, leaving the times unchanged. Similarly, an event a can be refused by $f(Q)$ at some time only when Q can refuse all events that map to a.

$$\mathcal{TF}\,[\![f(Q)]\!] \quad = \quad \{(f(s), \aleph) \mid (s, f^{-1}(\aleph)) \in \mathcal{TF}\,[\![Q]\!]\}$$

The backward renamed process $f^{-1}(P)$ performs events a whenever P can perform $f(a)$, and refuses a whenever P refuses $f(a)$. The timed failures of this process directly reflect this understanding.

$$\mathcal{TF}\,[\![f^{-1}(P)]\!] \quad = \quad \{(s, \aleph) \mid (f(s), f(\aleph)) \in \mathcal{TF}\,[\![P]\!]\}$$

The transformations on s and $\aleph$ are defined as follows:

$$
\begin{aligned}
f(s) &= \langle (t, f(a)) \mid (t, a) \leftarrow s \rangle \\
f(\aleph) &= \{(t, f(a)) \mid (t, a) \in \aleph\} \\
f^{-1}(\aleph) &= \{(t, a) \mid (t, f(a)) \in \aleph\}
\end{aligned}
$$

Neither of these forms of abstraction has any effect on delays that are present in their argument processes. The appropriate laws are given in Figure 11.5.

Sequential composition

A composition of two processes running sequentially executes the first process until it terminates, at which point control is passed to the second. Termination of the first process is entirely within its control, which means that the first process cannot delay termination once it is enabled. It must terminate urgently, since the sequential composition provides the environment which is awaiting the $\checkmark$ termination event.

Any behaviour of Q_1 within the composition $Q_1; Q_2$ must therefore be urgent on $\checkmark$. This means that it should be possible to augment a timed failure with additional information which states that $\checkmark$ is refused right up to the moment it is performed as Q_1 terminates, or dually, that Q_1 is executed in an environment which is always ready to allow the $\checkmark$ event.

A timed failure of $Q_1; Q_2$ is generated either by a non-terminating behaviour of Q_1, or by a terminating behaviour of Q_1 followed by a behaviour of Q_2. These two possibilities are reflected in the definition.

$$
\begin{aligned}
\mathcal{TF}[\![Q_1; Q_2]\!] \;=\; & \{(s, \aleph) \mid \; \checkmark \notin \sigma(s) \wedge \\
& \qquad (s, \aleph \cup ([0, \infty) \times \{\checkmark\})) \in \mathcal{TF}[\![Q_1]\!]\} \\[4pt]
& \cup \\[4pt]
& \{(s_1 \frown s_2, \aleph) \mid \\
& \quad \exists t \bullet \; \checkmark \notin \sigma(s_1) \\
& \qquad \wedge (s_2, \aleph) - t \in \mathcal{TF}[\![Q_2]\!] \\
& \qquad \wedge (s_1 \frown \langle(t, \checkmark)\rangle, \aleph \upharpoonright t \cup ([0, t) \times \{\checkmark\})) \in \mathcal{TF}[\![Q_1]\!]\}
\end{aligned}
$$

The first clause states that the timed failure corresponds to a non-terminating execution: $\checkmark$ does not appear in the trace, and the refusal can be augmented with $\checkmark$ refused over the entire interval. The second possibility arises when Q_1 exhibits a behaviour which terminates at time t, indicated by the $\checkmark$ at that time and the refusal of it beforehand. In this case Q_1's $\checkmark$ does not appear in the overall trace since it should not be taken as termination of the overall construct. The subsequent behaviour is that of Q_2, beginning at time t rather than time 0.

Interrupt

The process $Q_1 \triangle Q_2$ begins executing as Q_1. The events of Q_2 are enabled alongside those of Q_1, and the occurrence of any of them results in the interruption of Q_1 and transfer of control from Q_1 to Q_2. Observations of $Q_1 \triangle Q_2$ will correspond either to uninterrupted timed failures of Q_1, or else to timed failures of Q_1 followed by timed failures of Q_2 subsequent to some interruption. In either case the refusal while Q_1 is executing must be possible also for Q_2. The two possibilities are both described by a single clause, and they correspond to the cases where the trace s_2 of Q_2 is empty and non-empty respectively. In the case where it is empty, $begin(s_2) = \infty$ and the situation where Q_1 runs without interruption is described. In the case where it is non-empty then control is passed at $begin(s_2)$, the time of Q_2's first event.

$$
\begin{aligned}
\mathcal{TF}[\![Q_1 \triangle Q_2]\!] \;=\; & \{(s_1 \frown s_2, \aleph) \mid \; (s_1, \aleph \upharpoonright begin(s_2)) \in \mathcal{TF}[\![Q_1]\!] \wedge \\
& \qquad (s_2, \aleph \upharpoonright begin(s_1 \upharpoonright \{\checkmark\})) \in \mathcal{TF}[\![Q_2]\!]\}
\end{aligned}
$$

$$Q_1 \, \triangle_d \, (Q_2 \, \triangle_{d'} \, Q_3) = (Q_1 \, \triangle_d \, Q_2) \, \triangle_{d+d'} \, Q_3 \qquad\qquad \langle \triangle_d\text{-assoc} \rangle$$

$$(Q_1 \sqcap Q_2) \, \triangle_d \, Q_3 = (Q_1 \, \triangle_d \, Q_3) \sqcap (Q_2 \, \triangle_d \, Q_3) \qquad\qquad \langle \triangle_d\text{-left-dist} \rangle$$

$$Q_1 \, \triangle_d \, (Q_2 \sqcap Q_3) = (Q_1 \, \triangle_d \, Q_2) \sqcap (Q_1 \, \triangle_d \, Q_3) \qquad\qquad \langle \triangle_d\text{-right-dist} \rangle$$

$$(Q_1 \,\square\, Q_2) \, \triangle_d \, Q_3 = (Q_1 \, \triangle_d \, Q_3) \,\square\, (Q_2 \, \triangle_d \, Q_3) \qquad\qquad \langle \triangle_d\text{-}\square\text{-left-dist} \rangle$$

$$STOP \, \triangle_d \, P = WAIT \, d; Q_1 \qquad\qquad \langle \text{stop-}\triangle_d\text{-delay} \rangle$$

$$(WAIT \, d; Q_1) \, \triangle_{d+d'} \, Q_2 = WAIT \, d; (Q_1 \, \triangle_{d'} \, Q_2) \qquad\qquad \langle \triangle_d\text{-delay-1} \rangle$$

$$(WAIT(d + d'); Q_1) \, \triangle_d \, Q_2 = WAIT \, d; Q_2 \qquad\qquad \langle \triangle_d\text{-delay-2} \rangle$$

Fig. 11.6   Laws for timed interrupt

The sequence $s_1 \frown s_2$ is a timed trace, so if s_1 terminates then the only possible trace for s_2 is $\langle\rangle$, since the resulting sequence must have s_1's $\checkmark$ as its last event. Also, the refusal associated with Q_2 is relevant only before the time of Q_1's termination.

If Q_1 does not terminate then $\aleph \parallel begin(s_1 \upharpoonright \{\checkmark\}) = \aleph$ and the entire refusal $\aleph$ will be a refusal for Q_2.

Timed interrupt

In a timed interrupt $Q_1 \, \triangle_d \, Q_2$, the first process Q_1 runs for d units of time and then control passes to Q_2 if Q_1 has not already terminated. A timed failure of such a process will consist of two parts, the first part being a timed failure exhibited by Q_1 up to time d, and the second part being the subsequent contribution from Q_2.

$$\mathcal{TF}[\![Q_1 \, \triangle_d \, Q_2]\!] = \{(s_1 \frown (s_2 + d), \aleph) \mid$$
$$end(s_1) \leqslant d \,\wedge$$
$$(s_1, \aleph \parallel d) \in \mathcal{TF}[\![Q_1]\!] \,\wedge$$
$$\checkmark \notin \sigma(s_1) \Rightarrow (s_2, \aleph - d) \in \mathcal{TF}[\![Q_2]\!]\}$$

If $\checkmark \in \sigma(s_1)$ then the fact that $s_1 \frown s_2 + d$ is a timed trace means that $s_2 = \langle\rangle$.

The laws given for timed interrupt in Figure 11.6 are very similar to those given for the timeout operator, the only difference being that timed interrupt does not distribute from the right over external choice (see Exercise 11.13).

11.3   RECURSION

The recursive definition $N = Q$ corresponds to an equation in N. When the process variable N appears in Q then N is defined in terms of itself, and it is necessary to provide some way of solving the equation. This is achieved by imposing some structure on the timed failures model. This section discusses how this is done using the refinement order and the theory of metric spaces.

The refinement order introduced in Chapter 8 related processes in terms of the behaviours that they could exhibit. The more behaviours a process can exhibit in the FDI model, the more nondeterministic it is. Hence Q_1 is said to be less deterministic than Q_2, or alternatively Q_1 is refined by Q_2, written $Q_1 \sqsubseteq Q_2$, if the set of observations of Q_1 contains the observations of Q_2. An alternative characterization is the equation $Q_1 \sqcap Q_2 = Q_1$, which states that the nondeterministic possibility of Q_2 does not in fact introduce any behaviours not already present in Q_1.

This characterization remains natural for the timed failures model. The most nondeterministic process will correspond to the set of all possible timed failures. The most deterministic processes will be the maximal processes under this nondeterminism partial order '$\sqsubseteq_{TF}$' on the timed failures model. These are the processes that cannot have any further nondeterminism refined away.

In fact any well-timed CSP equation $N = Q$ will have a *least* solution under the nondeterminism ordering. This solution is the natural one to consider as the timed failures associated with N, since a pessimistic approach to timed failures semantics includes all behaviours that cannot be ruled out. If processes are fit for purpose under this assumption then any refinement or implementation is sure to be appropriate. It turns out that the least fixed point in the timed failures model contains precisely the failures information which can be extracted from the transition system, so the operational and denotational semantics correspond precisely.

The partial order structure imposed by the nondeterminism ordering can be combined with a metric space structure to pinpoint the timed failures of recursively defined processes in a clearer way. A *distance* between processes will be defined in such a way that the longer it takes to tell them apart, the closer together they are.

The behaviours of a process S up to time $t \in \mathbb{R}^+$ are defined by lifting the 'strictly before' operator:

$$S \restriction t = \{(s, \aleph) \in S \mid (s, \aleph) = (s, \aleph) \restriction t\}$$

This gives all of those timed failures of S which contain only trace and refusal information about behaviour before time t. Together they contain all of the information about what S might be able to exhibit before time t, but no information at or after that time.

The set $S \restriction \infty$ is defined slightly differently

$$S \restriction \infty = \{(s, \aleph) \in S \mid end(s, \aleph) < \infty\}$$

This is the set of all behaviours of S which have finite duration.

If $S \parallel t = T \parallel t$ then S and T will be indistinguishable up to time t. Any observer who wishes to tell S and T apart by finding an observation that distinguishes them will have to wait at least t time units in order to do so.

The distance function d is defined on processes as follows:

$$d(S, T) \quad = \quad \inf\{2^{-t} \mid t \in \mathbb{R}^+ \wedge S \parallel t = T \parallel t\}$$

The distance between any two processes can be at most 1, and this will be when they can be distinguished at time 0. If the distance between two processes S and T is 0, then they must have exactly the same set of finite duration timed failures: $S \parallel \infty = T \parallel \infty$. In this case, if S and T are not the same process then it is only by means of the infinite duration behaviours that they can be distinguished.

Example 11.3.1

- The distance between $\mathcal{TF} \llbracket a \rightarrow STOP \rrbracket$ and $\mathcal{TF} \llbracket b \rightarrow STOP \rrbracket$ is 1.

- $\mathcal{TF} \llbracket WAIT\ 1;\ a \rightarrow STOP \rrbracket$ and $\mathcal{TF} \llbracket WAIT\ 1;\ b \rightarrow STOP \rrbracket$ have a distance of $\frac{1}{2}$ between them.

- There is a distance of 0 between $\mathcal{TF} \llbracket \sqcap_{t \in \mathbb{R}^+} WAIT\ t;\ a \rightarrow STOP \rrbracket$ and $\mathcal{TF} \llbracket STOP \sqcap \sqcap_{t \in \mathbb{R}^+} WAIT\ t;\ a \rightarrow STOP \rrbracket$, since they have exactly the same finite duration timed failures. However, they are not the same, since the second process can refuse a over all time, whereas the first is unable to do this—they differ on their infinite duration behaviours.

- The distance between $\mathcal{TF} \llbracket N = a \xrightarrow{1} N \rrbracket$ and $\mathcal{TF} \llbracket M = a \xrightarrow{1} a \xrightarrow{1} M \rrbracket$ is 0, and in fact these processes have the same semantics.

■

The *finite timed failures* (FTF) model is introduced to identify the sets of finite duration timed failures associated with processes. Its introduction is useful in the presentation of the fixed point theory. It is the projection of the timed failures model onto finite duration observations. A set S will be in the finite timed failures model precisely when there is some set T in the timed failures model such that $S = T \parallel \infty$. Any two processes Q_1 and Q_2 whose distance apart is 0 will correspond to the same element of the FTF model, written $Q_1 =_{FTF} Q_2$; and any two distinct elements of the FTF model will be some non-zero distance apart. This is because if two sets S and T in the FTF model are different, then one will have some timed failure $(s, \aleph)$ that is not in the other. This timed failure will have some finite duration $end(s, \aleph) = t$ and so $S \parallel (t + 1) \neq T \parallel (t + 1)$, so $d(S, T) \geqslant 2^{-(t+1)} > 0$. In fact the FTF model together with the distance function d forms a *complete metric space* [115], which means that some powerful general results about fixed points are available.

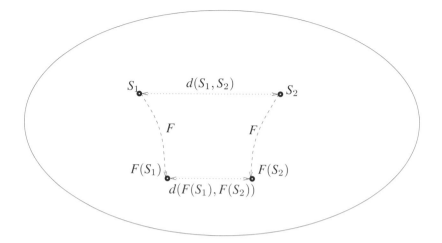

Fig. 11.7   A contraction mapping

A *contraction mapping f* on a complete metric space M with distance function d is one which reduces the distance between two elements by a minimum of some factor, as illustrated in Figure 11.7. More precisely, there is some $\alpha < 1$ such that $\forall S, T : M \bullet d(f(S), f(T)) \leqslant \alpha d(S, T)$. A key result is that any contraction mapping must have exactly one fixed point $m = f(m)$ in the metric space. It cannot have two distinct fixed points $m \neq m'$, since an application of f would have to reduce the distance between them, and so could not leave them both unchanged. One way of finding the fixed point is to pick *any* element $n \in M$, and then consider the sequence $\langle n, f(n), f^2(n), f^3(n), \ldots \rangle$. Successive elements become closer, and the sequence is a Cauchy sequence which must have a limit—the fixed point of f—because of completeness of the metric space. All such sequences, starting from any n, must have the same limit.

Any well-timed recursive process definition $N = Q$ is t-guarded for some time $t > 0$. The function F_Q on the FTF model[1] corresponding to Q is a contraction mapping, since its t-guardedness means that if $S \parallel u = T \parallel u$ then $F_Q(S) \parallel (u + t) = F_Q(T) \parallel (u + t)$, and so $d(F_Q(S), F_Q(T)) \leqslant 2^{-t}.d(S, T)$. There is therefore only one set of finite duration timed failures that can be associated with N, since F_Q has a unique fixed point in the FTF model. This set must be the finite duration timed failures of the semantics of N in the timed failures model. Furthermore, the set can be obtained by a sequence of approximations which give successively longer duration timed failures of N. A sequence corresponding to repeated applications of the recursive definition will be $\{Q_n\}_{n \in \mathbb{N}}$. It can start from any process Q_0 whatsoever, and successive processes are defined in terms of the previous one, as illustrated in Figure 11.8:

---

[1]Defined as $F_Q(S) = \mathcal{TF}[\![Q[I_S/N]]\!] \upharpoonright \infty$, where I_S is a CSP term whose semantics in the timed failures model is the set $\bar{S}$.

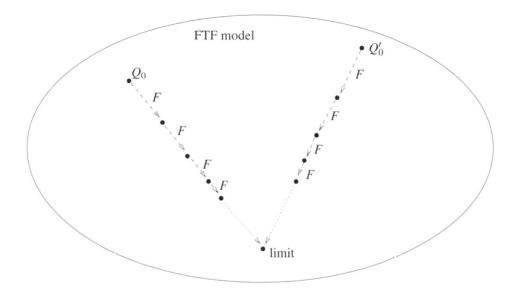

Fig. 11.8 *Approaching the unique fixed point in the FTF model*

$Q_{n+1} = Q[Q_n/N]$. The limit of the sequence gives the finite behaviours of $\mathcal{TF}[\![N]\!]$:

$$\mathcal{TF}[\![N]\!] \restriction \infty = \bigcup_{n\in\mathbb{N}}(\mathcal{TF}[\![Q_n]\!] \restriction nt)$$

Provided Q contains no infinite nondeterminism, the time closure $\overline{\bigcup_{n\in\mathbb{N}}(\mathcal{TF}[\![Q_n]\!] \restriction nt)}$ of this set will be the least fixed point of the function F_Q. This means that

$$\mathcal{TF}[\![N]\!] = \overline{\bigcup_{n\in\mathbb{N}}(\mathcal{TF}[\![Q_n]\!] \restriction nt)}$$

if the defining process term Q does not contain any of the operators which can introduce infinite nondeterminism—infinite nondeterministic choice, hiding of infinite sets and infinite-to-one renaming. Otherwise, it is possible that this set is not a fixed point of Q in the timed failures model. In any case it will contain all the timed failures of N, and will agree with N on the finite duration timed failures.

$$\mathcal{TF}[\![N]\!] \restriction \infty = \bigcup_{n\in\mathbb{N}}(\mathcal{TF}[\![Q_n]\!] \restriction nt)$$
$$\mathcal{TF}[\![N]\!] \subseteq \overline{\bigcup_{n\in\mathbb{N}}(\mathcal{TF}[\![Q_n]\!] \restriction nt)}$$

Even in this case there will still be a least fixed point S under the nondeterminism ordering $\sqsubseteq_{TF}$, and S will correspond exactly to the operational semantics.

The uniqueness of the fixed point in the FTF model leads to the corresponding law:

$(Q_1$ finitely nondeterministic $\wedge$ Q_2 finitely nondeterministic

$\quad \wedge$ F time-guarded $\wedge$ $(F(Q_1) =_{TF} Q_1) \wedge (F(Q_2) =_{TF} Q_2))$

$$\Rightarrow Q_1 =_{TF} Q_2 \qquad\qquad \langle \text{UFP} \rangle$$

Example 11.3.2 If N is defined by the 2-guarded equation $N = a \xrightarrow{2} N$, then approximations to the timed failures of N can be generated starting from $Q_0 = STOP$. Then for each n, $Q_{n+1} = a \xrightarrow{2} Q_n$, and so

$$
\begin{aligned}
\mathcal{TF}[\![Q_n]\!] \parallel 2n \;=\; \{(s, \aleph) \mid \;& end(s) < 2n \wedge end(\aleph) \leqslant 2n \\
& \wedge\; \sigma(s) \subseteq \{a\} \\
& \wedge\; \forall t \bullet \#(s \uparrow [t, t+2)) \leqslant 1 \\
& \wedge\; \forall t \bullet (t, a) \in \aleph \Rightarrow a \in s \uparrow (t-2, t]\}
\end{aligned}
$$

The behaviours of Q_n before $2n$ are those timed failures before $2n$ whose trace can contain only a's, no more than one a in any interval of length 2, and which can only refuse a at a time if it was performed within the last 2 time units.

The union of all such approximations is

$$
\begin{aligned}
\{(s, \aleph) \mid \;& end(s, \aleph) < \infty \\
& \wedge\; \sigma(s) \subseteq \{a\} \\
& \wedge\; \forall t \bullet \#(s \uparrow [t, t+2)) \leqslant 1 \\
& \wedge\; \forall t \bullet (t, a) \in \aleph \Rightarrow a \in s \uparrow (t-2, t]\}
\end{aligned}
$$

and these are all of the finite length timed failures of N. Since the process expression $a \xrightarrow{2} N$ contains no constructs which introduce infinite choice, the set of infinite behaviours of $N = a \xrightarrow{2} N$ is simply the closure of this set:

$$
\begin{aligned}
\mathcal{TF}[\![N]\!] \;=\; \{(s, \aleph) \mid \;& \sigma(s) \subseteq \{a\} \\
& \wedge\; \forall t \bullet \#(s \uparrow [t, t+2)) \leqslant 1 \\
& \wedge\; \forall t \bullet (t, a) \in \aleph \Rightarrow a \in s \uparrow (t-2, t]\}
\end{aligned}
$$

∎

Mutually recursive definitions are treated in exactly the same way. There will only be one possible set of finite duration timed failures associated with each N_i defined through a well-timed family of process definitions $\langle N_i = Q_i \rangle_{i \in I}$, where each Q_i is t-guarded. They can be obtained from the sequences of processes which converge towards them. The definitions of these sequences are intertwined. For each $i \in I$, an initial CSP process $Q_{i,0}$ is chosen. For each $n \in \mathbb{N}^+$ and $i \in I$, the process $Q_{i,n+1} = Q_i[Q_{j,n}/N_j]$ is the definition process Q_i with all of the previous elements $Q_{j,n}$ replacing the corresponding process variable N_j wherever they appear in Q_i. The finite behaviours of N_i are obtained from the elements of the sequence $\langle Q_{i,0}, Q_{i,1}, Q_{i,2}, \ldots \rangle$:

$$\mathcal{TF}[\![N_i]\!] \parallel \infty \;=\; \bigcup_{n \in \mathbb{N}} ((\mathcal{TF}[\![Q_{i,n}]\!]) \parallel nt)$$

If none of the Q_i contain any infinite nondeterminism, then the semantics in the timed failures model of the N_i must be the closure of this set:

$$\mathcal{TF}[\![N_i]\!] \;=\; \overline{\bigcup_{n \in \mathbb{N}} ((\mathcal{TF}[\![Q_{i,n}]\!]) \parallel nt)}$$

Otherwise, in each case the semantics will be contained in the closure, with the same set of finite behaviours, and will again correspond to the timed failures which can be obtained directly from the operational semantics.

Uniqueness of fixed points generalizes to mutual recursion:

$(\underline{Q}$ finitely nondeterministic and $\underline{Q}'$ finitely nondeterministic

$\quad \wedge\ \underline{F}$ time-guarded $\wedge\ (\underline{F}(\underline{Q}) =_{TF} \underline{Q}) \wedge (\underline{F}(\underline{Q}') =_{TF} \underline{Q}'))$

$$\Rightarrow \underline{Q} =_{TF} \underline{Q}' \qquad\qquad \langle\text{UFP}\rangle$$

11.4 TESTING AND TIMED FAILURES EQUIVALENCE

The two forms of testing introduced for untimed CSP are directly applicable to the timed language. Executions of the process $(Q \parallel_{\Sigma} T) \setminus \Sigma$ are considered, and tests T (as well as the processes Q) are drawn from the timed language. Must testing will consider the combination's maximal executions as defined in Section 10.2.

The processes under test, and the tests themselves, are required to be well-timed processes. It then turns out that equivalence under must testing is the same as timed failures equivalence: the timed failures model is fully abstract with respect to must testing.

May testing is slightly weaker than must testing, identifying more processes. If two processes Q_1 and Q_2 are the same on all of their finite duration timed failures, so $d(Q_1, Q_2) = 0$, then they will be the same under may testing; otherwise they will be distinguished. The FTF model is fully abstract with respect to may testing equivalence, and in fact this is the weakest non trivial congruence in the richer setting of the timed CSP language.

The enriched language of tests means that some untimed CSP processes that were indistinguishable under untimed testing can be distinguished by more sophisticated timed tests. For example, the fact that timed tests can perform some refusal testing allows the following pair of processes to be distinguished:

$$Q_1 \;=\; (a \to STOP) \sqcap (b \to STOP \;\square\; c \to STOP)$$
$$Q_2 \;=\; (a \to STOP \sqcap b \to STOP) \;\square\; (a \to STOP \sqcap c \to STOP)$$

The test

$$T = (b \rightarrow SUCCESS) \overset{1}{\triangleright} (c \rightarrow STOP \; \square \; a \rightarrow SUCCESS)$$

suffices. The event b is internal to the combination and offered by T over the first time unit. Internal events are urgent, so if b does not occur, then this must be due to the tested process's refusal to perform it. T will reach a success state unless the refusal of b can be followed by the performance of c. Thus Q_1 **must** T but $\neg(Q_2 \textbf{ must } T)$.

Since Q_1 and Q_2 are distinguished after some finite time, this means that they can also be told apart by may testing. In this case, a dual test

$$T' = (b \rightarrow STOP) \overset{1}{\triangleright} (c \rightarrow SUCCESS \; \square \; a \rightarrow STOP)$$

will be used. This one can succeed only if the refusal of b can be followed by the performance of c, so $\neg(Q_1 \textbf{ may } T')$ and $Q_2 \textbf{ may } T'$. The sensitivity of timed may testing to failures information contrasts with the coarseness of untimed may testing which yields only untimed traces equivalence.

As in the untimed models, may and must testing also give rise to related notions of refinement:

$$Q_1 \sqsubseteq_{must} Q_2 \;\; = \;\; \forall T \bullet (Q_1 \textbf{ must } T) \Rightarrow (Q_2 \textbf{ must } T)$$
$$Q_1 \sqsubseteq_{may} Q_2 \;\; = \;\; \forall T \bullet \neg (Q_1 \textbf{ may } T) \Rightarrow \neg (Q_2 \textbf{ may } T)$$

Once again, the notions of refinement defined operationally are equivalent to refinement in the associated semantic model. Thus must testing refinement is the same as refinement in the failures model, and may testing equivalence is refinement in the FTF model:

$$Q_1 \sqsubseteq_{must} Q_2 \;\; \Leftrightarrow \;\; Q_1 \sqsubseteq_{TF} Q_2$$
$$Q_1 \sqsubseteq_{may} Q_2 \;\; \Leftrightarrow \;\; Q_1 \sqsubseteq_{FTF} Q_2$$

Exercises

Exercise 11.1 Which of the following are legitimate refusal sets?

1. $[3, 6) \times \{a, b\}$

2. $[0, \infty) \times \{on\}$

3. $(3, on)$

4. $[4, 7] \times \{off\}$

5. $\{\}$

6. $\{(4, on), (5, off)\}$

Exercise 11.2 Which of the following refusal sets are consistent with the execution

$$\langle (a \xrightarrow{2} b \to STOP), \ 3, \ (a \xrightarrow{2} b \to STOP), \ a, \ (STOP \overset{2}{\triangleright} b \to STOP), \ 2,$$
$$(STOP \overset{0}{\triangleright} b \to STOP), \ \tau, \ (b \to STOP), \ \infty \rangle$$

1. $[0, 3) \times \{a\}$

2. $[3, 6) \times \{a\}$

3. $[3, 6) \times \{b\}$

4. $[3, 5) \times \{a, b\}$

5. $[7, \infty) \times \{a\}$

6. $[7, \infty) \times \{b\}$

7. $\{\}$

Exercise 11.3 Which of the following timed failures are consistent with the process $a \xrightarrow{2} b \to$ *STOP*?

1. $(\langle \rangle, \{\})$

2. $(\langle (1, a) \rangle, [0, 3) \times \{b\})$

3. $(\langle (0, a) \rangle, [0, 3) \times \{b\})$

4. $(\langle (1, a) \rangle, [0, \infty) \times \{a\})$

5. $(\langle (0, a) \rangle, [0, \infty) \times \{a\})$

6. $(\langle (1, a), (2, b) \rangle, [0, 2) \times \{b\})$

Exercise 11.4 Can a timed failure record an event being performed and refused at the same instant, with (t, a) appearing both in the trace and in the refusal set?

Exercise 11.5 What are the timed failures of

$$wake \xrightarrow{10} shower \xrightarrow{10} eat \xrightarrow{5} leave \to SKIP$$

Exercise 11.6 What are the timed failures of

$$wake \xrightarrow{10} shower \xrightarrow{10} (eat \xrightarrow{5} leave \rightarrow SKIP$$
$$\xrightarrow{10}{\triangleright} leave \rightarrow SKIP)$$

Exercise 11.7 What are the timed failures of

$$WATCH \quad = \quad (reset \xrightarrow{1} WATCH) \overset{10}{\triangleright} alarm \rightarrow STOP$$

Exercise 11.8 Would it make any difference to the timed failures of a recursive process if recursion took a τ to unwind, i.e. if the rule for recursion was

$$\frac{}{N \xrightarrow{\tau} Q} \quad [N = Q]$$

(and no evolutions were possible for N) ?

Exercise 11.9

1. Is $STOP \sqcap a \rightarrow STOP \sqsubseteq (a \xrightarrow{2} STOP) \overset{2}{\triangleright} STOP$?

2. Is $STOP \sqcap a \rightarrow STOP \sqsubseteq WAIT\ 2; a \rightarrow STOP$?

Exercise 11.10 (Hard) Prove that $(\langle\rangle, \{\}) \in \mathcal{TF} [\![Q \setminus A]\!]$ for any process Q.

Exercise 11.11 (Hard) Prove that the law **hide-combine** given in Figure 4.12 is true in the timed failures model. In other words,

$$\mathcal{TF} [\![(Q \setminus A) \setminus B]\!] = \mathcal{TF} [\![Q \setminus (A \cup B)]\!]$$

for any process Q.

Exercise 11.12 Give laws that reduce the process expressions $WAIT\ d; Q_1 \ |||\ a \rightarrow Q_2$ and $WAIT\ d; Q_1 \ \|_A\ a \rightarrow Q_2$ in the style of the $\|$-**step** laws of Figure 11.4. Use the 'timed prefix choice' generalization of the timed event prefix $a : C@u \rightarrow Q(a)$ (with the obvious semantics) to give a law that reduces $WAIT\ d; Q_1 \ _A\|_B\ a : C \rightarrow Q(a)$. Give similar laws for the other two parallel operators.

Exercise 11.13 Give an example to show that in general

$$Q_1 \triangle_d (Q_2 \square Q_3) \neq (Q_1 \triangle_d Q_2) \square (Q_1 \triangle_d Q_3)$$

Exercise 11.14 Use the operational semantics to construct the timed failures set S associated with the (ill-timed) process *WAIT* 1; N, where $N = a \rightarrow N$. Extract the timed failure set of (*WAIT* 1; N) \ {a} from the operational semantics, and compare it with the result obtained from applying the definition of the hiding operator to the set S. Are they the same?

Exercise 11.15 What happens if the timed test T of Section 11.4 is recast into the untimed language (so the timeout construction $Q_1 \overset{d}{\triangleright} Q_2$ is replaced by an 'untimed timeout' ($Q_1 \sqcap$ *STOP*) $\square$ Q_2). Does the resulting process still distinguish Q_1 from Q_2?

Exercise 11.16 (Very hard) Non well-timed processes have well-defined operational semantics, and so the definitions of may and must testing can be applied to them. The following pathological processes are defined:

$$
\begin{aligned}
SPIN &= SKIP; SPIN \\
TIMELOCK &= TIMELOCK \\
ZENO(t) &= WAIT(\frac{t}{2}); ZENO(\frac{t}{2})
\end{aligned}
$$

1. Which notion of maximal execution is appropriate in the context of Zeno processes, spin processes, and timestops?

2. Consider the following process definitions:

$$
\begin{aligned}
Q_1 &= WAIT\ 2; SPIN \\
Q_2 &= ZENO(2) \\
Q_3 &= WAIT\ 2; TIMELOCK \\
Q_4 &= \sqcap_{t>2} WAIT\ t; TIMELOCK \\
Q_5 &= (WAIT\ 2; TIMELOCK) \square a \rightarrow STOP \\
Q_6 &= (WAIT\ 2; SPIN) \square a \rightarrow STOP \\
Q_7 &= ZENO(2) \square a \rightarrow STOP
\end{aligned}
$$

   Which of these are the same under may testing? Under must testing?

3. What observations are required of a process in order to give a characterization of may testing equivalence?

4. What observations are required of a process in order to give a characterization of must testing equivalence?

5. What is the congruence associated with each of these forms of equivalence?

12

Timed specification and verification

12.1 SPECIFICATION

A timed specification is a predicate $S(s, \aleph)$ on timed failures. It describes the behaviour required of a process in terms of constraints on its timed traces and timed refusals. A process Q meets a specification $S(s, \aleph)$ if S holds of every timed failure associated with Q. This is written Q **sat** $S(s, \aleph)$.

$$Q \ \mathbf{sat} \ S(s, \aleph) \quad \Leftrightarrow \quad \forall (s, \aleph) \in \mathcal{TF}[\![Q]\!] \bullet S(s, \aleph)$$

Specifications $S(s, \aleph)$ are often expressed in terms of projections of traces and refusals onto events and intervals.

Example 12.1.1 The operating system for a circular saw allows it to be switched *on* or *off*, and controls a guard around the blade which can be taken up or down, modelled by the events *guard.up* and *guard.down* respectively.

The timed safety requirement that the guard should never be taken up within 5 time units of the *off* event is captured as the specification

$$\forall t \in \mathbb{R}^+ \bullet (t, guard.up) \ \mathbf{in} \ s \Rightarrow off \notin \sigma(s \uparrow (t - 5, t + 5))$$

Untimed safety requirements are also expressible on timed traces. The expectation that the guard alternates between its two positions, beginning in the down position, is captured as

$$s \downarrow \{guard.down\} \leqslant s \downarrow \{guard.up\} \leqslant s \downarrow \{guard.down\} + 1$$

The requirement that *on* and *off* alternate is similarly expressed.

In the context of the previous property, the requirement that the saw should never be switched on when the guard is up means that whenever the saw is on then the guard must be down.

$$\neg\, \mathsf{off}(s) \Rightarrow \mathsf{guard\text{-}down}(s)$$

where

$$
\begin{aligned}
\mathsf{guard\text{-}down}(s) \quad &\Leftrightarrow \quad s \downarrow \mathit{guard.down} = s \downarrow \mathit{guard.up} \\
\mathsf{off}(s) \quad &\Leftrightarrow \quad s \downarrow \mathit{on} = s \downarrow \mathit{off}
\end{aligned}
$$

The guard is down whenever the number of *guard.up* and *guard.down* events match; and the machine is off whenever the number of *on* and *off* events match.

Given that $\neg\, \mathsf{off}(s) \Rightarrow \mathsf{guard\text{-}down}(s)$, the requirement that the guard should have been down for at least 8 time units whenever the saw is switched on may be expressed as

$$
\begin{aligned}
\neg\, \mathsf{off}(s) \Rightarrow \quad &\mathit{end}(s \upharpoonright \{\mathit{guard.down}\}) + 8 \leqslant \mathit{end}(s \upharpoonright \{\mathit{on}\}) \\
&\vee\, s \upharpoonright \{\mathit{guard.down}\} = \langle\rangle
\end{aligned}
$$

The projection $\mathit{end}(s \upharpoonright \{\mathit{guard.down}\})$ identifies the time at which the event *guard.down* most recently occurred. The fact that *guard.down*(s) is true for the trace *s* means that the guard must have been down from that point onwards.

Liveness properties are expressed in terms of inability to refuse events in particular circumstances: if timed events cannot appear in a refusal set associated with a particular trace, then they must be on offer.

The saw must initially be ready to be switched on. This is expressed as a liveness requirement associated with the empty trace.

$$s = \langle\rangle \Rightarrow on \notin \sigma(\aleph)$$

This states that if nothing has yet occurred, then *on* cannot be refused, but must be made available by the process.

The contrapositive formulation of this requirement is

$$on \in \sigma(\aleph) \Rightarrow s \neq \langle\rangle$$

This is best understood through the dual interpretation of refusals, as environmental offer sets. It states that if the environment is known to have offered the event *on*, then some event must have occurred—either an *on* in response, or else perhaps some other event (such as *guard.up*).

A second liveness requirement is that the saw must be available to be switched *on* after 10 time units of the guard being consistently down. This may be expressed as follows:

$$\mathsf{guard\text{-}down}(s) \wedge \mathsf{off}(s) \Rightarrow on \notin \sigma(\aleph \upharpoonright (end(s \upharpoonright guard.down) + 10))$$

The time $end(s \upharpoonright guard.down) + 10$ is 10 units of time after the guard went down. If the guard is down and the saw is off at the end of the trace, then *on* cannot be refused after that time.

A dual formulation of this requirement is as follows:

$$\mathsf{guard\text{-}down}(s) \wedge on \in \sigma(\aleph \upharpoonright end(s \upharpoonright guard.down) + 10) \Rightarrow \neg\, \mathsf{off}(s)$$

If the environment offers *on* after the guard has been consistently down for over 10 time units, then the saw cannot be off—it must have responded to the environment's offer.   ■

A specification $S(s, \aleph)$ is *admissible* if it holds on timed failures of infinite length precisely whenever it holds of all their finite approximations. Admissible specifications can be checked of processes simply by checking that all of the finite duration timed failures meet the predicate S. The precise definition of an admissible specification $S(s, \aleph)$ is one for which

$$(\forall t \bullet S(s \upharpoonright t, \aleph \upharpoonright t)) \Rightarrow S(s, \aleph)$$

If a predicate's failure to hold of a timed behaviour will always show up in a finite time, then that predicate corresponds to an admissible specification. All of the requirements in Example 12.1.1 above are admissible. Inadmissible predicates are those which may hold for all finite prefixes of a timed failure $(s, \aleph)$ but not for $(s, \aleph)$ itself. Examples include $\#s < \infty$ and $\exists t \bullet (t, a) \notin \aleph$.

Specification macros

Writing specifications directly as predicates upon traces s and refusals $\aleph$ can become cumbersome. Furthermore, there are many similar specification patterns for safety, liveness, and commonly occurring assumptions about the environment of the process. It is often convenient to define a number of specification macros or building blocks as a shorthand for these patterns and for use with proof rules to reason about specifications at a higher level of abstraction. The macros given in this section are not intended to provide a complete set, but rather to provide some building blocks from which more application-specific macros can be developed. The fact that they are all firmly grounded in traces and refusals means that relationships between the macros can be identified, allowing reasoning about specifications at the level of macros rather than directly at the nuts and bolts level of traces and refusals. The macros are given in terms of the free variables s and $\aleph$.

The first macro simply expresses that the event a is recorded in the trace as having occurred at time t:

$$a \text{ at } t \quad = \quad \langle (t, a) \rangle \preccurlyeq s$$

This may be weakened to express that a occurs at some point during an interval I, without specifying precisely which point.

$$a \text{ at } I \quad = \quad \exists\, t \in I \bullet a \text{ at } t$$

It may be further weakened to express that some event from A occurs somewhere along the interval I:

$$A \text{ at } I \quad = \quad \exists\, a \in A \bullet a \text{ at } I$$

The macros stating that only events from some set A may ever appear in the trace, or that no events from A may appear in the trace, may both be defined in terms of **at**:

$$
\begin{aligned}
\text{only } A \quad &= \quad \neg(\Sigma^\checkmark \setminus A) \text{ at } [0, \infty) \\
\text{no } A \quad &= \quad \neg(A \text{ at } [0, \infty))
\end{aligned}
$$

If A is a singleton set $\{a\}$, then the brackets may be elided, allowing **only** a and **no** a as macros.

The liveness of a process at time t with regard to a particular event a can be manifested in one of two ways. Either the event is performed (which is clear evidence of liveness), in which case it will appear in the trace, or else it should not appear in the refusal set:

$$a \text{ live } t \quad = \quad a \text{ at } t \vee (t, a) \notin \aleph$$

This definition is equivalent to $(t, a) \in \aleph \Rightarrow a \text{ at } t$, which states that if a is offered by the environment, then it must occur. This is precisely what is meant by liveness in CSP.

More intricate aspects of liveness can be characterized. A process might enable an event a at some time t, and continue to offer it at least until some event in A occurs. Usually the event a will be a member of the set A, since occurrence of a should discharge the obligation to continue offering it. The specification for this property and its generalization to a set B (usually contained in A) is

$$
\begin{aligned}
a \text{ live from } t \text{ until } A \quad &= \quad ([t, begin(s \restriction t \restriction A)) \times \{a\}) \cap \aleph = \{\} \\
B \text{ live from } t \text{ until } A \quad &= \quad ([t, begin(s \restriction t \restriction A)) \times B) \cap \aleph = \{\} \\
B \text{ live from } t \text{ until } A \text{ or } t' \quad &= \quad ([t, \min\{t', begin(s \uparrow [t, \infty) \restriction A)\}) \times B) \cap \aleph = \{\}
\end{aligned}
$$

The time $begin(s \restriction t \restriction A)$ is the time of the first occurrence of an A event after t.

The first definition states that between t and the first occurrence of a subsequent event from A, the event a cannot be refused. The second definition generalizes this to a set B. The last definition is appropriate to the case where the offer of B can be withdrawn once a particular time t' is reached as well as on occurrence of A. The time $\min\{t', begin(s \uparrow [t, \infty) \restriction A)\}$ is the earlier of t' and the time of the first A after t. The definition states that B cannot be refused between t and that time.

The time at which the event will be offered may only be known to come from some interval rather than being known precisely. If a will be offered within δ of t then it might occur any time after t, but is not guaranteed to be offered until $t + \delta$:

$$a \text{ live within } \delta \text{ of } t \text{ until } A \;=\; A \text{ at } [t, t + \delta) \vee a \text{ live from } t + \delta \text{ until } A$$
$$a \text{ live within } \delta \text{ of } t \text{ until } A \text{ or } t' \;=\; A \text{ at } [t, t + \delta) \vee a \text{ live from } t + \delta \text{ until } A \text{ or } t'$$

Whenever δ increases or t' decreases, then the specification is weakened: if $\delta \leqslant \delta'$ and $t' \geqslant t''$ then $(a \text{ live within } \delta \text{ of } t \text{ until } A \text{ or } t') \Rightarrow (a \text{ live within } \delta' \text{ of } t \text{ until } A \text{ or } t'')$.

When δ is 0, the specification can drop the 'within δ' component: $a \text{ live within } 0 \text{ of } t \text{ until } A = a \text{ live from } t \text{ until } A$.

Assumptions about the environment of the process are also used in specifications. An interface event a is open at a time t if the environment of the process will not block the occurrence of the event (t, a). This means that if the event does not occur, it is due to the process's refusal to perform it, so (t, a) will appear in $\aleph$ as evidence. The alternative view of refusals as environmental offers corroborates this interpretation: the appearance of (t, a) in $\aleph$ means that a was offered to the process at time t.

$$a \text{ open } t \;=\; a \text{ at } t \vee (t, a) \in \aleph$$

Either a is actually performed at time t, which provides clear evidence that the environment of the process was open to the occurrence of a; or it appears in the refusal set.

The characterization of the environmental open assumption extends to sets of events, and to intervals. The environment is open to a set of events A at some time t if it is prepared for any one of the events in A to occur. In this case, either some such event does occur, or else they are all refused. This second possibility is expressed as $A \subseteq \sigma(\aleph \uparrow t)$: A is a subset of the set of events refused at t.

$$A \text{ open } t \;=\; A \text{ at } t \vee A \subseteq \sigma(\aleph \uparrow t)$$

If the environment is open on the set A over an interval I, this means that all of A should appear in the refusal set during I, until some event from A actually occurs. The trace projection $(s \restriction A) \uparrow I$ gives the sequence of events from s of events in A that occur during the interval I, so the time of the first such event can be retrieved as the time of the first event in this trace, provided it is non-empty. If it is empty, then A will be refused over the whole of I.

$$A \text{ open } I \;=\; (I \times A \subseteq \aleph) \vee ((I \cap [0, \mathit{begin}(s \restriction A \uparrow I))) \times A \subseteq \aleph)$$

A more extreme form of environmental assumption is that it is prepared to allow all occurrences of events from A that the process wishes to perform, at any time. In this case the set A will be offered to the process at all times, even times at which events from A are also performed, since further copies of A are offered. Such an environment will make a process *active* on the set A, since it will perform all occurrences of A urgently.

$$A \text{ active } = [0, \infty) \times A \subseteq \aleph$$

The environment might not be prepared to allow events to occur at particular times. In this case, the evidence is that the events cannot appear in the trace. Refusal information cannot be obtained, since the environment is not offering the appropriate events to the process.

$$a \text{ closed } t = \neg(a \text{ at } t)$$
$$A \text{ closed } I = \neg(A \text{ at } I)$$

These can be directly expressed in terms of previously defined macros, but they are included within the macro language to allow the specifier to separate environmental assumptions from expectations on processes.

Example 12.1.2 The timed requirements on the circular saw of Example 12.1.1 are also expressible in the macro language. The requirement that the guard should not be taken up within 5 time units of *off* can be expressed as

$$\forall t \in \mathbb{R}^+ \bullet \mathit{guard.up} \text{ at } t \Rightarrow \neg \mathit{off} \text{ at } (t - 5, t + 5)$$

The other timed safety requirement was that the guard should not have moved for at least 8 time units whenever the saw is switched on. This is naturally expressed as

$$\forall t \in \mathbb{R}^+ \bullet \mathit{on} \text{ at } t \Rightarrow \neg\{\mathit{guard.up}, \mathit{guard.down}\} \text{ at } (t - 8, t]$$

The liveness requirement that the saw must initially be ready to be switched on is captured as

$$\mathit{on} \text{ live from } 0 \text{ until } \Sigma^{\checkmark}$$

The event *on* is available until some event (from $\Sigma^{\checkmark}$) occurs.

This may also be expressed using an environmental assumption:

$$\forall t \in \mathbb{R}^+ \bullet (\mathit{on} \text{ open } t \Rightarrow \Sigma^{\checkmark} \text{ at } [0, t])$$

If the environment is open on the event *on* at time t, then either some event must have already occurred, or else some event must occur at time t. In particular, if no other event (such as *guard.up*) disables *on* by time t then it will occur. This exemplifies a common pattern in specification: an environmental assumption as the antecedent to some activity of the process. This style considers process behaviour in terms of responses to offered events.

The other liveness requirement addresses when the unit can be switched on.

$$\forall t \in \mathbb{R}^+ \bullet \quad \textsf{guard-down}(s \upharpoonright t) \wedge \neg\{\textit{guard.up}, \textit{guard.down}\} \textsf{ at } (t, t + 10]$$
$$\wedge \textsf{ off}(s \Vert t + 10)$$
$$\Rightarrow \textit{on} \textsf{ live from } t + 10 \textsf{ until } \Sigma^{\checkmark}$$

It states that if the saw is off then it should be ready to be switched on after the guard has been down for 10 time units. ∎

Relationships between different macros can be identified and established by appealing to their definitions. These can be useful in reasoning about specifications and manipulating them.

A straightforward relationship exists between open, live, and at specifications. If a live t and a open t both hold for a timed failure $(s, \aleph)$, then so does a at t: if the process and its environment are both ready for a to occur, then it will occur. Conversely, if a at t then it immediately follows that a live t and a open t: if a occurs then both the process and its environment were ready for it to occur.

$$(a \textsf{ live } t \wedge a \textsf{ open } t)(s, \aleph) \quad \Leftrightarrow \quad a \textsf{ at } t(s, \aleph)$$

This may be generalized: if an event a is enabled from time t until it occurs, and the environment will allow it at time $t' \geqslant t$ then it must occur sometime between t and t':

$$a \textsf{ live from } t \textsf{ until } \{a\} \wedge a \textsf{ open } t' \wedge t' \geqslant t \quad \Rightarrow \quad a \textsf{ at } [t, t']$$

12.2 VERIFICATION

It is possible to prove that a candidate CSP implementation meets a specification by checking that every one of its timed failures meets the specifying predicate. But it is generally more convenient to use a more structured approach to verification.

The semantic equations underpin a set of compositional proof rules. A specification satisfied by a composite process can be deduced from specifications of the components. A rule is given for the timed CSP operators, relating specifications of the component processes to a specification for their combination.

STOP

The strongest specification satisfied by *STOP* states that no event can ever occur.

$$STOP \textsf{ sat only}\{\}$$

Event prefix

If Q **sat** $S(s, \aleph)$, then the behaviour of $a \xrightarrow{d} Q$ subsequent to the occurrence of the a event, after a further delay d, will satisfy S; and the behaviour up to the occurrence of the first a will be to offer it continually until it is accepted. The first event in the trace must be a.

$$\frac{Q \textbf{ sat } S(s, \aleph)}{\begin{array}{l} a \xrightarrow{d} Q \textbf{ sat } \quad a \text{ live from } 0 \text{ until } \{a\} \\ \qquad \wedge s \neq \langle\rangle \Rightarrow \\ \qquad\qquad \mathit{first}(s) = a \wedge \mathit{begin}(\mathit{tail}(s)) \geqslant \mathit{begin}(s) + d \\ \qquad\qquad \wedge S((\mathit{tail}(s), \aleph) - (\mathit{begin}(s) + d)) \end{array}}$$

The simple event prefix $a \rightarrow Q$ is the same as $a \xrightarrow{0} Q$, and the proof rule is similar except that the clause of the resulting specification '$\mathit{begin}(\mathit{tail}(s)) \geqslant \mathit{begin}(s) + 0$' is vacuously true and can be dropped.

Timed event prefix

For a timed event prefix, the process $P[t/u]$ executed after the first event is dependent on the time t at which that event occurred. Different possible instantiations for t may meet different specifications, so in general there will be a family of specifications S_t indexed by times, such that S_t is satisfied by the process obtained when the first event occurs at time t. Otherwise, the inference rule is similar to that for event prefix:

$$\frac{\forall t \in \mathbb{R}^+ \bullet Q[t/u] \textbf{ sat } S_t(s, \aleph)}{\begin{array}{l} a@u \rightarrow Q \textbf{ sat } \quad a \text{ live from } 0 \text{ until } \{a\} \\ \qquad \wedge s \neq \langle\rangle \Rightarrow \\ \qquad\qquad \mathit{first}(s) = a \\ \qquad\qquad \wedge S_{\mathit{begin}(s)}(\mathit{tail}(s) - \mathit{begin}(s), \aleph - \mathit{begin}(s)) \end{array}}$$

If all the subsequent processes meet the same specification S, so that $S_t = S$ for all $t \in \mathbb{R}^+$, then the time at which the first event is performed is irrelevant to the subsequent behaviour.

Example 12.2.1 A timed event prefix $a@u \rightarrow \mathit{WAIT}\ u; b \rightarrow \mathit{STOP}$ will have a minimal delay between the a and the b governed by the initial delay before the a occurs. The rules may be used to establish that the end time is at least twice the beginning time—that it meets the specification $b \in \sigma(s) \Rightarrow \mathit{end}(s) \geqslant 2 * \mathit{begin}(s)$. The time $\mathit{end}(s)$ will be the time of b's occurrence, and $\mathit{begin}(s)$ will be the time of a's occurrence.

Firstly, a delayed event prefix $\mathit{WAIT}\ t; b \rightarrow \mathit{STOP}$ satisfies the specification $S_t(s, \aleph)$, which states that if (the only possible event) b has occurred then it must be after the delay t:

$$\mathit{WAIT}\ t; b \rightarrow \mathit{STOP} \quad \textbf{sat} \quad b \in \sigma(s) \Rightarrow \mathit{end}(s) \geqslant t$$

The rule for timed event prefix then allows the deduction

$$a@u \rightarrow WAIT\ u; b \rightarrow STOP$$
$$\textbf{sat} \quad a \text{ live from } 0 \text{ until } \{a\}$$
$$\wedge s \neq \langle\rangle \Rightarrow$$
$$first(s) = a$$
$$\wedge\ b \in \sigma(tail(s) - begin(s)) \Rightarrow end(tail(s) - begin(s)) \geqslant begin(s)$$

which can be weakened to

$$a@u \rightarrow WAIT\ u; b \rightarrow STOP \quad \textbf{sat} \quad b \in \sigma(s) \Rightarrow end(s) \geqslant 2 * begin(s)$$

The time at which b occurs must be at least twice that of a. ■

Choosing between events

In the process $x : A \rightarrow Q(x)$, the entire set A is initially offered until one of its events is chosen, and the subsequent behaviour is dependent on the identity of this event.

$$\frac{\forall x : A \bullet Q(x)\ \textbf{sat}\ S_x(s, \aleph)}{x : A \rightarrow Q(x)\ \textbf{sat}\ A \text{ live from } 0 \text{ until } A}$$
$$\wedge s \neq \langle\rangle \Rightarrow$$
$$first(s) \in A$$
$$\wedge\ S_{first(s)}(tail(s) - begin(s), \aleph - begin(s))$$

Successful termination

The process *SKIP* is immediately ready to terminate, and remains in that state until termination occurs. No events other than $\checkmark$ are possible at any time: there can be at most one event in the trace.

$$\overline{SKIP\ \textbf{sat}\ (\checkmark \text{ live from } 0 \text{ until } \{\checkmark\} \wedge \#s \leqslant 1 \wedge \text{only}\{\checkmark\})}$$

The last clause states that no event other than $\checkmark$ is ever possible. This is redundant, but is included for explicitness. It may be deduced for processes that satisfy the other clauses of the specification: the fact that the process is live on $\checkmark$ until it occurs means that any trace not containing $\checkmark$ can be augmented with it. If a process meeting this specification has a non-empty trace, then appending $\checkmark$ will yield a trace of length greater than 1, violating the second clause.

Timeout

A behaviour of $Q_1 \overset{d}{\rhd} Q_2$ is either an observation of Q_1 whose first event occurs before time d, or else an observation of Q_2 delayed by d units of time, in which case the refusal before time d should still be possible for Q_1.

$$
\frac{
\begin{array}{l}
Q_1 \text{ sat } S_1(s, \aleph) \\
Q_2 \text{ sat } S_2(s, \aleph)
\end{array}
}{
\begin{array}{l}
Q_1 \overset{d}{\rhd} Q_2 \text{ sat } \quad (begin(s) \leqslant d \wedge S_1(s, \aleph) \\
\qquad\qquad\qquad \vee\ (begin(s) \geqslant d \wedge S_1(\langle\rangle, \aleph \parallel d) \wedge S_2(s - d, \aleph - d)))
\end{array}
}
$$

A special case of this rule concerns the case where $Q_1 = STOP$, since then $Q_1 \overset{d}{\rhd} Q_2 = WAIT\ d; Q_2$. This results in the following rule:

$$
\frac{
Q \text{ sat } S(s, \aleph)
}{
WAIT\ d; Q \text{ sat } begin(s) \geqslant d \wedge S(s - d, \aleph - d)
}
$$

Any specification met by Q, translated through d units of time, will be met by $WAIT\ d; Q$.

Delay

The delay construct $WAIT\ d$ can do nothing except be ready to terminate any time after d. There can only ever be one event in the trace.

$$
\frac{}{
WAIT\ d \text{ sat } (\checkmark \text{ live from } d \text{ until } \{\checkmark\} \wedge \#s \leqslant 1 \wedge only\{\checkmark\})
}
$$

External choice

The rule for external choice directly reflects the semantic equation for that operator.

$$
\frac{
\begin{array}{l}
Q_1 \text{ sat } S_1(s, \aleph) \\
Q_2 \text{ sat } S_2(s, \aleph)
\end{array}
}{
\begin{array}{l}
Q_1 \ \square\ Q_2 \text{ sat } \quad (S_1(s, \aleph) \vee S_2(s, \aleph)) \\
\qquad\qquad\qquad \wedge\ S_1(\langle\rangle, \aleph \parallel begin(s)) \wedge S_2(\langle\rangle, \aleph \parallel begin(s))
\end{array}
}
$$

Any behaviour of $Q_1 \ \square\ Q_2$ is a behaviour of Q_1 or Q_2 and before the first event is performed, it must be a behaviour of both and hence must meet both specifications.

Internal choice

An internal choice can behave either as Q_1 or as Q_2. Any behaviour of $Q_1 \sqcap Q_2$ will be a behaviour of one of its components, so it must meet the corresponding specification.

$$\frac{Q_1 \ \textbf{sat} \ S_1(s, \aleph) \\ Q_2 \ \textbf{sat} \ S_2(s, \aleph)}{Q_1 \sqcap Q_2 \ \textbf{sat} \ S_1(s, \aleph) \vee S_2(s, \aleph)}$$

Indexed internal choice

An indexed internal choice can behave as any of its arguments, so the specification it meets must be the disjunction of all the specifications met by its components.

$$\frac{\forall i : J \bullet Q_i \ \textbf{sat} \ S_i(s, \aleph)}{\sqcap_{i \in J} Q_i \ \textbf{sat} \ \exists i : J \bullet S_i(s, \aleph)}$$

Alphabetized parallel

In the parallel combination $Q_1 \ {}_A\|_B \ Q_2$, any behaviour $(s, \aleph)$ is a combination of a timed failure $(s_1, \aleph_1)$ and $(s_2, \aleph_2)$ from its two components. Only events in the interfaces A and B can be performed, and events in an interface can be refused by the corresponding component.

$$\frac{\begin{array}{l} Q_1 \ \textbf{sat} \ S_1(s, \aleph) \\ Q_2 \ \textbf{sat} \ S_2(s, \aleph) \end{array}}{Q_1 \ {}_A\|_B \ Q_2 \ \textbf{sat} \ \exists \aleph_1, \aleph_2 \bullet \begin{array}{l} S_1(s \upharpoonright A^\checkmark, \aleph_1) \\ \wedge \ S_2(s \upharpoonright B^\checkmark, \aleph_2) \\ \wedge \ \text{only}(A \cup B)^\checkmark \\ \wedge \ \aleph \upharpoonright (A \cup B)^\checkmark = (\aleph_1 \upharpoonright A^\checkmark) \cup (\aleph_2 \upharpoonright B^\checkmark) \end{array}}$$

Example 12.2.2 Example 9.6.1 introduced Helen and Carl, who were hoping to arrange a meeting.

$$HELEN \ = \ (meet \xrightarrow{30} work \rightarrow STOP) \overset{30}{\triangleright} work \rightarrow STOP$$

$$CARL \ = \ WAIT \ 15; ((meet \xrightarrow{30} home \rightarrow STOP) \overset{45}{\triangleright} home \rightarrow STOP)$$

Helen is ready for a meeting from time 0, but will not wait beyond time 30:

$$HELEN \quad \textbf{sat} \quad meet \ \text{live from} \ 0 \ \text{until} \ \{meet\} \ \text{or} \ 30$$

Carl is ready for a meeting from time 15, and will not wait beyond time 45:

$$CARL \quad \textbf{sat} \quad meet \text{ live from } 15 \text{ until } \{meet\} \text{ or } 45$$

Each of these specifications can be weakened so that *meet* will be ready within 15 of 0, until either *meet* occurs or time 30 is reached:

$$HELEN \quad \textbf{sat} \quad meet \text{ live within } 15 \text{ of } 0 \text{ until } \{meet\} \text{ or } 30$$
$$CARL \quad \textbf{sat} \quad meet \text{ live within } 15 \text{ of } 0 \text{ until } \{meet\} \text{ or } 30$$

The inference rule allows the deduction that $HELEN \parallel CARL$ satisfies the specification

$$\exists \aleph_1, \aleph_2 \bullet$$
$$meet \text{ live within } 15 \text{ of } 0 \text{ until } \{meet\} \text{ or } 30 \, [(s \upharpoonright \{meet, work\})/s, \aleph_1/\aleph]$$
$$\wedge \, meet \text{ live within } 15 \text{ of } 0 \text{ until } \{meet\} \text{ or } 30 \, [(s \upharpoonright \{meet, home\})/s, \aleph_2/\aleph]$$
$$\wedge \, \text{only}\{meet, work, home\}$$
$$\wedge \, \aleph \upharpoonright \{meet, work, home\} = (\aleph_1 \upharpoonright \{meet, work\}) \cup (\aleph_2 \upharpoonright \{meet, home\})$$

Expanding the definitions, this may be weakened to

$$HELEN \parallel CARL \quad \textbf{sat} \quad meet \text{ live within } 15 \text{ of } 0 \text{ until } \{meet\} \text{ or } 30$$

This reasoning reflects the understanding that if both components cannot refuse *meet* (if it has not already occurred) then their combination is unable to refuse it. Both processes are guaranteed to wait at least up to time 30, so the combination also guarantees this. ∎

This example illustrates a useful instance of the inference rule for parallel. If both processes satisfy a liveness specification on events in both of their interfaces, then the combination satisfies the same liveness specification.

$$\frac{Q_1 \textbf{ sat } C \text{ live within } \delta \text{ of } t \text{ until } D \text{ or } t' \quad}{Q_1 \,_A\|_B \, Q_2 \textbf{ sat } C \text{ live within } \delta \text{ of } t \text{ until } D \text{ or } t'} \qquad [\, (C \cup D) \subseteq (A \cap B)^\checkmark \,]$$

In the example above, the specifications for *HELEN* and *CARL* were weakened to the same result, so that this inference rule could be applied.

Much simpler rules for parallel combinations can be derived. For example, if P and Q are both live on some event they must synchronize on, then so is their parallel combination.

$$\frac{Q_1 \textbf{ sat } a \text{ live } t \quad}{Q_1 \,_A\|_B \, Q_2 \textbf{ sat } a \text{ live } t} \qquad [\, a \in (A \cap B)^\checkmark \,]$$

If the processes do not synchronize on event a, and the process responsible for it is live, then so is the combination, irrespective of the behaviour of the other process.

$$\frac{Q_1 \text{ sat } a \text{ live } t}{Q_1 \ _A\|_B \ Q_2 \text{ sat } a \text{ live } t} \quad [\, a \in A \setminus B \,]$$

There are many ways of combining specifications in parallel, justified as particular instances of the inference rule for the parallel combination. The timed failures underpinning all of the definitions ensures that candidate rules can be shown to be sound and consistent with the CSP semantics.

Indexed parallel

The inference rule for the parallel operator generalizes naturally to the indexed form.

$$\frac{\forall i : I \bullet Q_i \text{ sat } S_i(s, \aleph)}{\begin{array}{l} \left\|_{A_i} Q_i \text{ sat } \exists \aleph_{i_1}, \dots, \aleph_{i_n} \bullet \quad \forall i : I \bullet S_i(s \upharpoonright A_i^\checkmark, \aleph_i) \\ \qquad\qquad\qquad\qquad \wedge \text{ only}(\bigcup_{i \in I} A_i)^\checkmark \\ \qquad\qquad\qquad\qquad \wedge \aleph \upharpoonright (\bigcup_{i \in I} A_i)^\checkmark = \bigcup_{i \in I}(\aleph_i \upharpoonright A_i^\checkmark) \end{array}}$$

Interleaving

An interleaved combination of processes also performs an aggregation of behaviours contributed by each of its components. In this case, the trace will be an interleaving of the component traces, and the refusal must be possible for both processes.

$$\frac{\begin{array}{l} Q_1 \text{ sat } S_1(s, \aleph) \\ Q_2 \text{ sat } S_2(s, \aleph) \end{array}}{\begin{array}{l} Q_1 \, ||| \, Q_2 \text{ sat } \exists s_1, s_2, \aleph_1, \aleph_2 \bullet \quad s \text{ interleaves } s_1, s_2 \\ \qquad\qquad\qquad\qquad \wedge \aleph_1 \upharpoonright \{\checkmark\} \cup \aleph_2 \upharpoonright \{\checkmark\} = \aleph \upharpoonright \{\checkmark\} \\ \qquad\qquad\qquad\qquad \wedge \aleph_1 \setminus \{\checkmark\} = \aleph_2 \setminus \{\checkmark\} = \aleph \setminus \{\checkmark\} \\ \qquad\qquad\qquad\qquad \wedge S_1(s_1, \aleph) \wedge S_2(s_2, \aleph) \end{array}}$$

Interface parallel

The interface parallel operator combines both interleaving and synchronous parallel. A behaviour of a combination of processes is once again made up of behaviours of each of the components, combined in the appropriate way. Each of the component behaviours will meet the corresponding specification predicate.

$$\frac{\begin{array}{l} Q_1 \text{ sat } S_1(s, \aleph) \\ Q_2 \text{ sat } S_2(s, \aleph) \end{array}}{\begin{array}{l} Q_1 \underset{A}{\|} Q_2 \text{ sat } \exists s_1, s_2, \aleph_1, \aleph_2 \bullet \ s \text{ synch}_A \ s_1, s_2 \\ \qquad \land \aleph_1 \upharpoonright A^{\checkmark} \cup \aleph_2 \upharpoonright A^{\checkmark} = \aleph \upharpoonright A^{\checkmark} \\ \qquad \land \aleph_1 \setminus A^{\checkmark} = \aleph_2 \setminus A^{\checkmark} = \aleph \setminus A^{\checkmark} \\ \qquad \land S_1(s_1, \aleph_1) \land S_2(s_2, \aleph_2) \end{array}}$$

Hiding

When considering the specification which an abstracted process $P \setminus A$ will meet, only the behaviours of P which are active on A are relevant. The inference rule most closely corresponding to the timed failures definition of hiding will be the following:

$$\frac{Q \text{ sat } S(s, \aleph)}{Q \setminus A \text{ sat } \exists s_1 \bullet s = s_1 \setminus A \land S(s_1, \aleph \cup [0, \infty) \times A)}$$

If Q is known to satisfy some specification which is independent of A, under the environmental assumption that A is active, then a more specialized rule can be deployed:

$$\frac{Q \text{ sat } (\text{active } A \Rightarrow S(s, \aleph))}{Q \setminus A \text{ sat } S(s, \aleph)} \quad [\, \forall s, \aleph \bullet S(s, \aleph) \Leftrightarrow S(s \setminus A, \aleph \setminus A) \,]$$

This rule makes use of results concerning Q activated on A. If the specification S is concerned only with events that are not hidden, then the resulting process $Q \setminus A$ will also meet the specification S.

Example 12.2.3 The print spooler combination $SPOOL \| PRINT$ of Example 9.7.4 satisfies the specification

$$\text{active } mid.JOB \Rightarrow \forall t : \mathbb{R}^+ \bullet in \text{ at } t \Rightarrow print \text{ live within } 130 \text{ of } t \text{ until } print$$

If the channel *mid* is active, then whenever a job is submitted to the spooler, it should be available on the printer within 130 seconds.

The consequent of this implication is independent of the event *mid*, so the rule allows the conclusion

$$(SPOOL \| PRINT) \setminus mid.JOB$$
$$\text{sat} \quad \forall t : \mathbb{R}^+ \bullet in \text{ at } t \Rightarrow print \text{ live within } 130 \text{ of } t \text{ until } print$$

The combination will be ready to print a job within 130 seconds of its submission. ■

Event renaming

The inference rules for the event renaming operators are entirely straightforward:

$$\frac{Q \text{ sat } S(s, \aleph)}{f(Q) \text{ sat } \exists s_1 \bullet f(s_1) = s \wedge S(s_1, f^{-1}(\aleph))}$$

$$\frac{Q \text{ sat } S(s, \aleph)}{f^{-1}(Q) \text{ sat } S(f(s), f(\aleph))}$$

Example 12.2.4 An initial design of a cash dispenser is described as $card \rightarrow DISPENSE$. This describes a process that is initially ready to accept a card:

$$card \rightarrow DISPENSE \quad \textbf{sat} \quad card \text{ live from } 0 \text{ until } \{card\}$$

It is able to accept *Switch* and *Delta* direct debit cards, so its interface can be expanded through a backwards alphabet renaming. If

$$\begin{aligned} f(switch) &= card \\ f(delta) &= card \end{aligned}$$

then the resulting process is described as $f^{-1}(card \rightarrow DISPENSE)$, and the inference rule for backwards renaming yields that

$$f^{-1}(card \rightarrow DISPENSE) \quad \textbf{sat} \quad card \text{ live from } 0 \text{ until } \{card\}[f(s)/s, f(\aleph)/\aleph]$$

Expanding the definition of the specification yields

$$[0, begin(f(s) \upharpoonright \{card\})) \times \{card\} \cap f(\aleph) = \{\}$$

which simplifies to

$$[0, begin(s \upharpoonright \{switch, delta\})) \times \{switch, delta\} \cap \aleph - \{\}$$

giving the result that

$$f^{-1}(card \rightarrow DISPENSE) \quad \textbf{sat} \quad \{switch, delta\} \text{ live from } 0 \text{ until } \{switch, delta\}$$

The process is ready to accept both cards, until one of them is provided. ∎

Sequential composition

A behaviour of a sequential composition $Q_1 ; Q_2$ is either a non-terminating timed failure of the process Q_1 which must be active on $\checkmark$, or else a terminating behaviour of Q_1, active on $\checkmark$ until termination, followed by a behaviour of Q_2.

$$Q_1 \textbf{ sat } S_1(s, \aleph)$$
$$Q_2 \textbf{ sat } S_2(s, \aleph)$$

$$\begin{aligned}
Q_1 ; Q_2 \textbf{ sat } \quad &\textsf{no} \checkmark \wedge S_1(s, \aleph \cup [0, \infty) \times \{\checkmark\}) \vee \\
&\exists s_1, s_2, t \bullet \ s = s_1 \frown (s_2 + t) \wedge (\textsf{no}\{\checkmark\}[s_1/s]) \\
&\qquad\qquad \wedge S_1(s_1 \frown \langle(t, \checkmark)\rangle, \aleph \parallel t \cup [0, t) \times \{\checkmark\}) \\
&\qquad\qquad \wedge S_2(s_2, \aleph - t)
\end{aligned}$$

The macro $\textsf{no}\{\checkmark\}$ applies to s_1 rather than s, so this substitution is made in the specification for $Q_1 ; Q_2$.

Interrupt

The process $Q_1 \triangle Q_2$ executes as Q_1, concurrently with Q_2 available to interrupt such an execution and take control. The inference rule directly reflects the formulation used to give the timed failures semantics of this operator.

$$Q_1 \textbf{ sat } S_1(s, \aleph)$$
$$Q_2 \textbf{ sat } S_2(s, \aleph)$$

$$\begin{aligned}
Q_1 \triangle Q_2 \textbf{ sat } \exists s_1, s_2 \bullet \ &s = s_1 \frown s_2 \wedge \\
&S_1(s_1, \aleph \parallel begin(s_2)) \wedge \\
&S_2(s_2, \aleph \parallel begin(s_1 \upharpoonright \{\checkmark\}))
\end{aligned}$$

Example 12.2.5 If Q_1 cannot terminate, and the interrupting process Q_2 is continually live on an interrupt event *int* from time 0 onwards, then the combination must also be live on this event. The information available is that $Q_1 \textbf{ sat } \textsf{no} \checkmark$, and $Q_2 \textbf{ sat } int$ live from 0 until $\{int\}$. An application of the rule yields that

$$\begin{aligned}
Q_1 \triangle Q_2 \quad \textbf{sat} \quad \exists s_1, s_2 \bullet \ &s = s_1 \frown s_2 \wedge \\
&\textsf{no} \checkmark [s_1/s, \aleph \parallel begin(s_2)/\aleph] \wedge \\
&int \text{ live from } 0 \text{ until } \{int\}[s_2/s, \aleph \parallel begin(s_1 \upharpoonright \{\checkmark\})/\aleph]
\end{aligned}$$

This specification can be weakened to

$$int \text{ live from } 0 \text{ until } \{int\}$$

for the combined timed failure $(s, \aleph)$, since $begin(s_1 \upharpoonright \{\checkmark\}) = \infty$, and if *int* cannot be refused before it occurs in s_2 then it certainly cannot be refused before it occurs in s.

Processes respect weakening of specifications, so it follows that

$$Q_1 \bigtriangleup Q_2 \quad \textbf{sat} \quad int \text{ live from } 0 \text{ until } \{int\}$$

The interrupt event *int* will always be available while it has not yet occurred.   ■

Timed interrupt

The timed interrupt combination $Q_1 \bigtriangleup_d Q_2$ behaves initially as Q_1, and then after d units of time its behaviour is that of Q_2. The formulation of this rule reflects the timed failures definition for timed interrupt.

$$\frac{Q_1 \textbf{ sat } S_1(s, \aleph) \qquad Q_2 \textbf{ sat } S_2(s, \aleph)}{\begin{array}{l} Q_1 \bigtriangleup_d Q_2 \textbf{ sat } \exists s_1, s_2 \bullet \quad s = s_1 \frown (s_2 + d) \wedge end(s_1) \leqslant d \wedge \\ \qquad\qquad\qquad\qquad\qquad S_1(s_1, \aleph \upharpoonright d) \wedge \\ \qquad\qquad\qquad\qquad\qquad \mathsf{no}\{\checkmark\}[s_1/s] \Rightarrow S_2(s_2, \aleph - d) \end{array}}$$

12.3   RECURSION INDUCTION

If $N = Q$ is a well-timed recursive definition, then the finite duration behaviours of N are uniquely determined. An admissible specification S which is satisfiable by some process Q_0, and which is preserved by recursive calls $F(Y) = Q[Y/N]$, will also be satisfied by N. The proof rule encapsulating this is the following:

$$\frac{\forall Y \bullet (Y \textbf{ sat } S(s, \aleph) \Rightarrow F(Y) \textbf{ sat } S(s, \aleph))}{N \textbf{ sat } S(s, \aleph)} \qquad \left[\begin{array}{l} \exists Q_0 \bullet Q_0 \textbf{ sat } S(s, \aleph) \\ S(s, \aleph) \text{ is admissible} \\ N = F(N) \end{array} \right]$$

If there is some Q_0 that meets the specification, then each $F^i(Q_0)$ satisfies the specification, where $F^0(Y) = Y$ and $F^{i+1}(Y) = F(F^i(Y))$ define successive recursive calls. This is because the antecedent states that S is preserved by the application of the function F. This means that all the behaviours $(s, \aleph)$ of all of the $F^i(Q_0)$ meet the predicate S. Each of the finite behaviours of N is contained in at least one of the $F^i(Q)$, since

$$\mathcal{TF}[\![N]\!] \upharpoonright \infty \quad = \quad \bigcup_{n \in \mathbb{N}} (\mathcal{TF}[\![F^i(Q_0)]\!] \upharpoonright nt)$$

so all of those behaviours meet S. Any infinite timed failure $(s, \aleph)$ of N must have all of its finite approximations $(s \upharpoonright t, \aleph \upharpoonright t)$ as finite behaviours of N. The specification S will hold of all of these finite approximations, and since S is admissible it must also hold for the infinite timed failure $(s, \aleph)$ itself. In other words, S holds of all the timed failures of N, finite and infinite: $N \textbf{ sat } S(s, \aleph)$.

Example 12.3.1 A simple timed switch with a built-in delay may be defined recursively:

$$TSWITCH \;\; = \;\; on \xrightarrow{3} off \xrightarrow{5} TSWITCH$$

Whenever the switch is turned off, it should not have been turned on in the preceding 3 seconds. Since the switch can never perform two events at exactly the same time (see Exercise 12.6), this may be captured as the specification

$$Light(s, \aleph) \;\; = \;\; \forall t : \mathbb{R}^+ \bullet on \text{ at } t \Rightarrow \neg(off \text{ at } [t, t+3))$$

This specification is admissible: if a particular timed failure $(s, \aleph)$ violates it, then this will be detected at some finite time, since there will be some (t, off) appearing in the trace too close to its preceding *on*. Furthermore, the specification is trivially satisfied by *STOP*, or indeed by any process which is unable to perform *off*.

The side conditions of the rule are thus met, and it remains only to establish the antecedent. Assuming the X **sat** $Light(s, \aleph)$, it is sufficient to show that $on \xrightarrow{3} off \xrightarrow{5} X$ **sat** $Light(s, \aleph)$.

An application of the delayed prefix rule yields that

$$off \xrightarrow{5} X \quad \textbf{sat} \quad
\begin{aligned}
& off \text{ live from } 0 \text{ until } \{off\} \\
& \wedge \; s \neq \langle\rangle \Rightarrow \\
& \qquad first(s) = off \wedge begin(tail(s)) \geqslant begin(s) + 5 \\
& \qquad \wedge \; Light((tail(s), \aleph) - (begin(s) + 5))
\end{aligned}$$

which weakens to

$$off \xrightarrow{5} X \quad \textbf{sat} \quad Light(s, \aleph)$$

since on the one hand any occurrence of *off* in *tail(s)* cannot occur within 3 seconds of any previous *on* event in *tail(s)* and therefore in *s*, and on the other hand the initial *off* in *s* does not follow an *on* event at all.

A second application of the rule for delayed prefix yields that

$$on \xrightarrow{3} off \xrightarrow{5} X \quad \textbf{sat} \quad
\begin{aligned}
& on \text{ live from } 0 \text{ until } \{on\} \\
& \wedge \; s \neq \langle\rangle \Rightarrow \; first(s) = on \\
& \qquad\qquad\qquad \wedge \; begin(tail(s)) \geqslant begin(s) + 3 \\
& \wedge \; s \neq \langle\rangle \Rightarrow Light((tail(s), \aleph) - (begin(s) + 3))
\end{aligned}$$

which may be weakened to

$$on \xrightarrow{3} off \xrightarrow{5} X \quad \textbf{sat} \quad
\begin{aligned}
& s = \langle\rangle \vee first(s) = on \\
& \wedge \; begin(tail(s)) \geqslant begin(s) + 3 \\
& \wedge \; Light((tail(s), \aleph))
\end{aligned}$$

which itself implies

$$on \xrightarrow{3} off \xrightarrow{5} X \quad \textbf{sat} \quad Light(s, \aleph)$$

since any *off* event in *tail(s)* must be at least 3 seconds after any *on* event in *tail(s)*, and must also be at least 3 seconds after the initial *on* event. Thus

$$TSWITCH \quad \textbf{sat} \quad Light(s, \aleph)$$

A second specification met by *TSWITCH* is that *off* cannot occur more than once every 8 seconds:

$$TSWITCH \quad \textbf{sat} \quad \forall t : \mathbb{R}^+ \bullet off \text{ at } t \Rightarrow \neg off \text{ at } (t - 8, t + 8)$$

However, this specification is not preserved by recursive calls of *TSWITCH* in general. For example, it is true for the process $off \rightarrow STOP$ but not for the process $on \xrightarrow{3} off \xrightarrow{5} off \rightarrow STOP$. The recursion induction rule is not directly applicable with this specification. As in the untimed case, it is sometimes necessary to strengthen the specification in order to ensure that it is preserved by recursive calls.

The specification can be strengthened to one which is preserved by recursive calls.

$$\forall t : \mathbb{R}^+ \bullet off \text{ at } t \Rightarrow \neg off \text{ at } (t - 8, t + 8) \wedge \neg off \text{ at } [0, 3)$$

The fact that *off* is also prevented from occurring during the first 3 seconds of a process run ensures that recursive calls preserve the desired property above. This fact must be incorporated into the application of the proof rule. ∎

Mutual recursion

The generalization to mutual recursion follows the approach taken in the untimed case. A family of process definitions $N_i = Q_i$ indexed by J is abbreviated as a recursive definition of a vector of processes: $\underline{N} = \underline{Q}$ where the vectors are indexed by J.

A vector of processes $\underline{Q}$ satisfies a vector of specification $\underline{S}$ if every process meets its corresponding specification:

$$\underline{Q} \text{ sat } \underline{S}(s, \aleph) \quad = \quad \forall i : J \bullet \underline{Q}_i \text{ sat } \underline{S}(s, \aleph)_i$$

A vector of specifications is admissible if each of its component specifications is admissible.

If $\underline{F}$ is the function corresponding to the process bodies $\underline{Q}$, then the recursion induction rule is

$$\frac{\forall \underline{Y} \bullet (\underline{Y} \textbf{ sat } \underline{S}(s, \aleph) \Rightarrow \underline{F}(\underline{Y}) \textbf{ sat } S(s, \aleph))}{\underline{N} \textbf{ sat } \underline{S}(s, \aleph)} \qquad \left[\begin{array}{l} \exists \underline{Y} \bullet \underline{Y} \textbf{ sat } \underline{S}(s, \aleph) \\ \underline{S}(s, \aleph) \text{ is admissible} \\ \underline{N} = \underline{F}(\underline{N}) \end{array} \right]$$

The process definitions Q_i contain recursive calls to a number of the N_j. The antecedent to the rule requires that all such recursive calls for all the Q_i should preserve the specification.

Example 12.3.2 The switch of the previous example can be defined in terms of a mutual recursion:

$$\begin{aligned} \textit{TSWITCH} &= \quad on \xrightarrow{3} \textit{ON} \\ \textit{ON} &= \quad \textit{off} \xrightarrow{5} \textit{TSWITCH} \end{aligned}$$

In order to prove that *TSWITCH* cannot perform two *off* events within 8 seconds of each other, it is sufficient to prove that the vector of functions

$$F(\left\langle \begin{array}{c} X \\ Y \end{array} \right\rangle) \quad = \quad \left\langle \begin{array}{c} on \xrightarrow{3} Y \\ \textit{off} \xrightarrow{5} X \end{array} \right\rangle$$

preserves the vector of specifications

$$\left\langle \begin{array}{l} \forall t : \mathbb{R}^+ \bullet \textit{off at } t \Rightarrow \neg\textit{off at } (t - 8, t + 8) \wedge \neg\textit{off at } [0, 3) \\ \forall t : \mathbb{R}^+ \bullet \textit{off at } t \Rightarrow \neg\textit{off at } (t - 8, t + 8) \end{array} \right\rangle$$

This requires establishing two results:

$$\begin{aligned} &Y \textbf{ sat } \forall t : \mathbb{R}^+ \bullet \textit{off at } t \Rightarrow \neg\textit{off at } (t - 8, t + 8) \\ &\Rightarrow \quad on \xrightarrow{3} Y \textbf{ sat } \forall t : \mathbb{R}^+ \bullet \textit{off at } t \Rightarrow \neg\textit{off at } (t - 8, t + 8) \wedge \neg\textit{off at } [0, 3) \end{aligned}$$

and

$$\begin{aligned} &X \textbf{ sat } \forall t : \mathbb{R}^+ \bullet \textit{off at } t \Rightarrow \neg\textit{off at } (t - 8, t + 8) \wedge \neg\textit{off at } [0, 3) \\ &\Rightarrow \quad \textit{off} \xrightarrow{5} X \textbf{ sat } \forall t : \mathbb{R}^+ \bullet \textit{off at } t \Rightarrow \neg\textit{off at } (t - 8, t + 8) \end{aligned}$$

Each of these may be discharged using an application of the inference rule for delayed prefix. ∎

12.4 ILL-TIMED PROCESSES

All CSP processes, including those that are not well-timed, have an operational semantics and hence will have a set of associated timed failures. Such processes are often well-understood and can be useful, particularly as components of constraint-oriented specifications. They may be legitimately used as CSP descriptions, though their timed failures must be derived explicitly from the possible transition sequences. The resulting set will always meet properties $TF1$ and $TF2$ (non-empty, and downwards closed under the information order respectively). However, it need not meet $TF3$ (such as the sets associated with the recursive definitions $N = N$ or $N = (a \rightarrow STOP) \mathbin{|||} N$, which have no behaviours beyond time 0).

The compositional definitions of the timed failures associated with CSP operators do not extend to processes that fail to meet properties $TF1$–$TF4$. The resulting set of timed failures will not necessarily correspond to the operational semantics (see Exercise 11.14). Ill-timed processes should be avoided where possible, since verifications which involve them will be lengthier and at a less abstract level. However, they can occasionally play a role in specification.

Example 12.4.1 (J. J. Zic) The following requirements are identified for a particular process:

- it should act as a buffer or first-in-first-out queue;

- it should have a minimum throughput time of 5 seconds;

- it should have a minimum separation of 2 seconds between inputs;

- it should be live on input within 10 seconds of the previous input;

- it should have a minimum separation of 4 seconds between outputs;

- it must be live on output within 10 seconds of the previous output.

These requirements may be captured as specifications, or alternatively using the constraint-oriented specification style. The latter option will capture various of the properties as CSP processes, and then combine them in parallel.

The FIFO queue constraint places no restrictions on the timed behaviour of the process— it is simply concerned with the order of events. It also places no constraints on the ability of the process to accept inputs. It is defined in the standard mutually recursive way, indexed on the sequence of messages contained in the buffer:

$$
\begin{aligned}
BUFF(\langle\rangle) &= in?x \rightarrow BUFF(\langle x \rangle) \\
BUFF(\langle x \rangle \mathbin{\frown} tr) &= in?y \rightarrow BUFF(\langle x \rangle \mathbin{\frown} tr \mathbin{\frown} \langle y \rangle) \\
&\quad \square\ out!x \rightarrow BUFF(tr)
\end{aligned}
$$

This definition is not well-timed, since the recursive calls are not time-guarded. The process $BUFF = BUFF_{\langle\rangle}$ in isolation would be able to perform infinitely fast executions.

The requirement that each input has a minimum throughput of 5 seconds can be described by the process

$$
THROUGH = in?x \rightarrow ((WAIT\ 5;\ out!x \rightarrow STOP) \mathbin{|||} THROUGH)
$$

This process is always ready to input, and will be ready for the corresponding output after 5 seconds. It is also not well-timed, since there is no time-guard for the recursive call on *THROUGH*.

The minimum and maximum times at which successive inputs should become enabled are together encapsulated in the process

$$IN \quad = \quad in?x \stackrel{[2,10]}{\rightarrow} IN$$

This process is concerned only with the delays between inputs. The definition is well-timed.

Similarly, the constraints on delays between outputs are described by the process

$$OUT \quad = \quad out?x \stackrel{[4,10]}{\rightarrow} OUT$$

This process will allow any output at all, at the prescribed times; it is not concerned with the value passed along the *out* channel. This process is well-timed.

The entire set of constraints is then given as

$$BUFF(\langle\rangle) \parallel THROUGH \parallel (IN \parallel\parallel OUT)$$

Although the first two components are not well-timed, the restrictions imposed by *IN* and *OUT* slow them down in such a way that all the infinitely fast executions are prevented from occurring, and the resulting combination is well-timed, and meets all of the properties of the timed failures model. ∎

12.5 CASE STUDY: FISCHER'S PROTOCOL

An algorithm attributed to Fischer makes use of delays in order to guarantee mutual exclusion. A collection of processes interact by means of a single shared variable, which they can all read from. They all also have write access to this shared variable, so its value might be changed between a process writing to it and reading from it.

If the value contained in the variable is 0 then the critical region is understood to be free and any process can request access. A process does this by writing its own identifier i to the variable within some delay δ_i of discovering that the variable contains value 0. It then waits at least a further ϵ_i before reading the variable again: if it still contains the value i then that process is granted access to the critical region. As long as each of the ϵ_i delays are greater than all of the δ_i delays then only one process at a time can ever gain access. The algorithm is presented in Figure 12.1.

An example execution is illustrated in Figure 12.2. It contains two participants Q_1 and Q_2 each with a δ delay of 3 and an ϵ delay of 4. Initially the variable contains value 0. At

$$x := 0$$
$$\textbf{cobegin } [i = 1..n]$$
$$\quad \textbf{if } x = 0 \ \rightarrow \ \langle x := i \rangle_{\text{within } \delta_i} \textbf{ fi}$$
$$\quad \textbf{delay}_{\geq \epsilon_i}$$
$$\quad \textbf{if } x = i \ \rightarrow \ \textit{enter critical section } \textbf{fi}$$
$$\textbf{coend}$$

Fig. 12.1   Pseudo-code for Fischer's algorithm

	Process Q_1	Process Q_2
0	req.1, read.0	req.2
2		read.0
	write.1	
4		
		write.2
6		
	read.2	
8		
		read.2
10		enter.2
12		exit.2

Fig. 12.2   An example run of Fischer's algorithm

time 0, Q_1 reads value 0 from the variable. At time 2, Q_2 reads value 0 from the variable. At time 3, Q_1 sets the value of the variable to 1. At time 5, Q_2 sets the value of the variable to 2. At time 7, Q_1 reads the variable again, and learns that it does not contain the value 1, so Q_1 does not access the critical region. Because of the relationships between the delays, Q_1 could not have re-read the variable before Q_2 updated it. At time 9, Q_2 reads the variable again and learns that it contains the value 2, so Q_2 is permitted access to the critical region.

The combination of processes is illustrated in Figure 12.3. A component Q_i accepts a request *req.n* from a client process, and then executes the algorithm to service that request. The client will use the events *enter.n* and *exit.n* to move into and out of the critical region, and the process Q_i will restrict these events so that they can occur only when it is safe. Q_i writes values to the shared variable by means of a *write* event, and reads values by means of the event *read*. For a single run of the protocol, the component processes Q_i may be described within

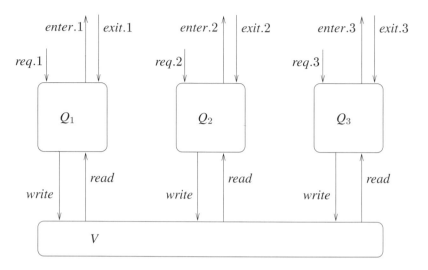

Fig. 12.3   An architecture for Fischer's algorithm

CSP as follows:

$$Q_i \quad = \quad req.i \to read?x : \mathbb{N} \to$$

$$\mathbf{if}\ x \neq 0$$
$$\mathbf{then}\ STOP$$
$$\mathbf{else}\ (\ write!i \xrightarrow{\epsilon_i} read?y : \mathbb{N} \to$$
$$\mathbf{if}\ y \neq i$$
$$\mathbf{then}\ STOP$$
$$\mathbf{else}\ enter.i \to exit.i \to STOP) \overset{\delta_i}{\triangleright} STOP$$

The maximum delay between reading a value 0 and writing a value i is δ_i, so there is a timeout in the process description to prevent i being written beyond that time. The minimum delay between writing the value i and reading the value of the variable is ϵ_i, so this appears as the delay associated with the prefix choice. If the process times out or receives an undesired value, then it will not reach the critical region in this run, so no further action is taken.

The Q_i components execute completely independently:

$$QS \quad = \quad {\vert\vert\vert}_{n \in N} Q_n$$

The system as a whole is described by introducing a shared variable V, with alphabet $read.\mathbb{N} \cup write.\mathbb{N}$:

$$FISCHER \quad = \quad QS \parallel V$$

The aim is to establish that

$$FISCHER \quad \textbf{sat} \quad s \downarrow enter.\mathbb{N} \leqslant 1 \tag{12.1}$$

The shared variable V should exhibit certain sensible properties, but it does not need to be described in CSP beyond that. In order to establish the above requirement for mutual exclusion, that at no time do two processes have access to the critical region, the only property required of V is that any value read at any time should be the most recent value written (or 0 if no value has yet been written).

$$V \quad \textbf{sat} \quad s = s_1 \frown \langle (t, read.j) \rangle \frown s_2 \Rightarrow last(s_1 \upharpoonright write) = write.j$$

for any $j \neq 0$.

$$V \quad \textbf{sat} \quad s = s_1 \frown \langle (t, read.0) \rangle \frown s_2 \Rightarrow (\quad s_1 \upharpoonright write = \langle \rangle$$
$$\vee \, last(s_1 \upharpoonright write) = write.0)$$

Since these are safety specifications which constrain only the occurrence of *read*s and *write*s in timed traces, the proof rule for parallel composition can be used to establish that they will also be true for the composite process *FISCHER*:

$$FISCHER \quad \textbf{sat} \quad s = s_1 \frown \langle (t, read.j) \rangle \frown s_2 \Rightarrow last(s_1 \upharpoonright write) = write.j \tag{12.2}$$

for any $j \neq 0$.

$$FISCHER \quad \textbf{sat} \quad s = s_1 \frown \langle (t, read.0) \rangle \frown s_2$$
$$\Rightarrow s_1 \upharpoonright write = \langle \rangle \vee last(s_1 \upharpoonright write) = write.0$$

This second specification can be weakened so that

$$FISCHER \quad \textbf{sat} \quad read.0 \text{ at } t \Rightarrow \text{no } write.\mathbb{N} \text{ at } [0, t) \vee write.0 \text{ in } s \tag{12.3}$$

The crucial property exhibited by the Q_i components concerns the timing relationships between readings of the shared variable and writing to it. In order to reach the critical region (by performing *enter.i*), the delay between the first *read* and the *write* should be no more than δ_i, and the delay between the *write* and the second *read* should be at least ϵ_i. This is expressed by the specification T_i, illustrated in Figure 12.4:

$$Q_i \quad \textbf{sat} \quad T_i = \quad enter.i \text{ in } s \Rightarrow \exists t_i, t_i', t_i'' \, \bullet$$
$$read.0 \text{ at } t_i \wedge write.i \text{ at } t_i' \wedge read.i \text{ at } t_i'' \wedge$$
$$t_i' - \delta_i \leqslant t_i \leqslant t_i' \leqslant t_i'' - \epsilon_i$$

Fig. 12.4   Illustration of the specification T_i

For any i, if Q' is any process for which $enter.i \notin \sigma(Q')$, then an application of the proof rule for interleaving yields that

$$Q_i \ ||| \ Q' \quad \textbf{sat} \quad T_i$$

because any occurrence of $enter.i$ in $Q_i \ ||| \ Q'$ must be due to the component Q_i.

Now $i \neq j \Rightarrow enter.i \notin \sigma(Q_j)$, so $enter.i \notin \sigma(|||_{j \neq i} Q_j)$, and so

$$QS \quad \textbf{sat} \quad T_i$$

and hence for any i:

$$FISCHER \quad \textbf{sat} \quad T_i \qquad\qquad (12.4)$$

Two other properties used in the proof are (1) that any component writes only its own identifier, and (2) that each component writes only once:

$$Q_i \quad \textbf{sat} \quad \sigma(s \upharpoonright write) \subseteq \{write.i\} \qquad\qquad (12.5)$$
$$Q_i \quad \textbf{sat} \quad s \downarrow write.i \leqslant 1 \qquad\qquad (12.6)$$

Since Line 12.5 implies that each Q_i **sat** no $write.0$ in s, it follows that

$$QS \quad \textbf{sat} \quad \text{no} \ write.0 \ \text{in} \ s$$

and so

$$FISCHER \quad \textbf{sat} \quad \text{no} \ write.0 \ \text{in} \ s$$

It therefore follows from Line 12.3 that

$$FISCHER \quad \textbf{sat} \quad read.0 \ \text{at} \ t \Rightarrow \text{no} \ write.\mathbb{N} \ \text{at} \ [0, t) \qquad\qquad (12.7)$$

Since $i \neq j \Rightarrow write.i \notin \sigma(Q_j)$, any $write.i$ appearing in QS must be due to Q_i. Line 12.6 yields for any i that

$$QS \quad \textbf{sat} \quad s \downarrow write.i \leqslant 1$$

Hence for any i

$$FISCHER \quad \textbf{sat} \quad s \downarrow write.i \leqslant 1 \qquad (12.8)$$

Now fix a trace s_0 of *FISCHER*. The aim is to prove that no more than one *enter* event can appear in s_0. If this is true for an arbitrary trace s_0 of *FISCHER* then the safety requirement 12.1 will be established.

Assume for a contradiction that *enter.i* in s_0 and *enter.j* in s_0 for $i \neq j$. Then from Line 12.4 for i and j there are $t_i, t_i', t_i'', t_j, t_j', t_j''$ such that

$$
\begin{aligned}
&read.0 \text{ at } t_i \wedge write.i \text{ at } t_i' \wedge read.i \text{ at } t_i'' \wedge \\
&read.0 \text{ at } t_j \wedge write.j \text{ at } t_j' \wedge read.j \text{ at } t_j'' \wedge \\
&t_i' - \delta_i \leqslant t_i \leqslant t_i' \leqslant t_i'' - \epsilon_i \wedge && (12.9) \\
&t_j' - \delta_j \leqslant t_j \leqslant t_j' \leqslant t_j'' - \epsilon_j && (12.10)
\end{aligned}
$$

Assume without loss of generality that $write.j$ occurred after $write.i$:

$$write.j \quad = \quad last(s_0 \restriction \{write.i, write.j\}) \qquad (12.11)$$

Since the trace s_0 has $read.0$ at t_j and $write.i$ at t_i' it follows from Line 12.7 that

$$t_j \leqslant t_i' \qquad (12.12)$$

The specification given in Line 12.2 together with the fact that $read.i$ in s_0 yields that there are s_1 and s_2 such that

$$s_0 = s_1 \frown \langle (t_i'', read.i) \rangle \frown s_2 \quad \wedge \quad write.i = last(s_1 \restriction write)$$

Now $write.j$ appears after $write.i$ in the trace s_0 (from Line 12.11, it cannot appear in s_1, and Line 12.8 states that it appears in total only once), so it must appear in s_2. Since traces are temporally ordered, the time t_j' at which $write.j$ occurs cannot be earlier than t_i'':

$$t_i'' \quad \leqslant \quad t_j' \qquad (12.13)$$

The facts that have been established thus far are sufficient to establish the contradiction. They are

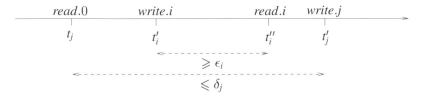

Fig. 12.5   Contradictory conditions

1. $t_j \leqslant t_i'$ (Line 12.12);

2. $t_i'' \leqslant t_j'$ (Line 12.13);

3. $\epsilon_i > \delta_j$, by the conditions on the ϵ and δ delays.

The situation is illustrated in Figure 12.5. The following chain of inequalities yields the contradiction that $t_j < t_j$:

$$
\begin{aligned}
t_j \;\; &\leqslant \;\; t_i' &&\text{Line 12.12} \\
&\leqslant \;\; t_i'' - \epsilon_i &&\text{Line 12.9} \\
&\leqslant \;\; t_j' - \epsilon_i &&\text{Line 12.13} \\
&< \;\; t_j' - \delta_j &&\text{since } \delta_j < \epsilon_i \\
&\leqslant \;\; t_j &&\text{Line 12.10}
\end{aligned}
$$

The initial assumption was false, and hence s_0 cannot contain two *enter* events, and hence $s_0 \downarrow enter.\mathbb{N} \leqslant 1$. Since s_0 was an arbitrary trace of *FISCHER*, this establishes the required result that

$$FISCHER \quad \textbf{sat} \quad s \downarrow enter.\mathbb{N} \leqslant 1$$

Exercises

Exercise 12.1 Specify the following properties:

1. No more than two patients are seen every 5 minutes.

2. The doctor is ready to see the next patient within 2 minutes of the previous one leaving.

3. A *pizza* should be available within 10 minutes of *payment*.

4. A *beat* event should occur every 5 seconds, as long as the environment never blocks it.

5. If a *cancellation* is not received within 14 days, then the contract will stand.

6. The bank card should be offered back to the customer within 12 seconds of the cash being taken from the machine.

Exercise 12.2 Specify that the event *eat* should be available (live) after 10 minutes of the occurrence of *shower*. Prove that the process of Exercise 11.5 meets this specification.

Exercise 12.3 Specify that *alarm* should be live following a 10 second interval in which *reset* does not occur (provided it has not already occurred). Does the process *WATCH* of Exercise 11.7 meets this specification?

Exercise 12.4 Prove that

$$N = a \stackrel{3}{\rightarrow} (N \;|||\; N) \quad \textbf{sat} \quad S(s, \aleph) = \forall n : \mathbb{N} \bullet \#(s \restriction 3n) \leqslant 2^n - 1$$

Deduce that N **sat** $\forall t : \mathbb{R}^+ \bullet \#(s \restriction 3t) \leqslant 2^{\lceil t \rceil} - 1$.

Exercise 12.5 Show that $(\forall t \in I \bullet A \text{ at } (I \restriction t) \vee A \text{ open } t)$ is equivalent to $A \text{ open } I$.

Exercise 12.6 Give a specification that states that no two events may ever be performed at the same time. Does *TSWITCH* of page 388 meet your specification?

Exercise 12.7 Adapt the CSP description of the Q_i in *FISCHER* on page 392 so the system can engage in repeated runs of the protocol: once Q_i exits the critical region, it should reset the shared variable to 0 and return to its initial state. Also, if Q_i does not reach the critical region, then it should continually re-attempt to do so.

Does the resulting protocol satisfy the following specifications?

1. $s \downarrow exit \leqslant s \downarrow enter$

2. $s \downarrow enter \leqslant s \downarrow exit + 1$

13

Timewise refinement

The semantic models for untimed CSP and for timed CSP together allow analysis of systems at different levels of abstraction. The relationships between the models can be exploited to combine results obtained in the various models. In particular, untimed safety and liveness properties of a timed system may be verifiable in the untimed models and then used in a timed analysis. This allows the results of untimed CSP model-checking or more abstract proofs to be used whenever possible, and the more intricate timed failures model need be used for analysis only where timed behaviour is critical. The approach also supports a design method of starting with an untimed system description and adding time constraints where needed, in a way that preserves correctness.

This chapter is concerned with the relationship between untimed and timed processes. At the level of the CSP language it is concerned with relating untimed CSP process descriptions to timed ones which are considered as *timewise refinements*, since they contain more information about timing behaviour. These are not refinements in the classical sense: normally refinements hold between processes within a single semantic model. However, the approach is the same: an untimed process description imposes constraints on the ordering and ultimate availability of events, and allows all timed behaviours that are consistent with its description. A timewise refinement of such a process must be consistent with the untimed description, and will impose further constraints upon the timed behaviour.

Timewise refinement also allows specifications to be translated between semantic models, so a specification in the traces model, the stable failures model, or the FDI model will correspond to some specification on timed failures. If an untimed process satisfies an untimed specification, then any timewise refinement of it must meet the corresponding timed specification. This allows the results of untimed verifications to be mapped directly into the timed model.

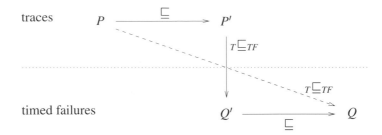

Fig. 13.1   Timewise refinement and transitivity

A timed CSP process will be consistent with an untimed CSP process if its timed failures are consistent with the untimed process's semantics. There will be three forms of consistency, one for each of the untimed models, giving rise to the three relationships of *trace timewise refinement*, *failures timewise refinement*, and *FDI timewise refinement*.

13.1   TRACE TIMEWISE REFINEMENT

Classical refinement in the traces model states that P is refined by P' if any trace of P' is also a trace of P. In this sense, P is considered as a description of the traces that are allowable, and then P' is a refinement if all of its traces are allowed by P.

Following this approach, a process Q will be a trace timewise refinement of P if all of its timed traces are 'allowed' by P. An untimed trace tr of P is simply a sequence of events which P is able to perform. An observation of Q contains a timed trace s which is a sequence of events that Q is able to perform, together with associated times. The sequence of events $strip(s)$ is extracted from the timed trace by removing the times. Then Q will refine P if any finite trace of Q corresponds to a trace of P.

The trace timewise relation is written '$P\ _T{\sqsubseteq}_{TF}\ Q$' where P is an untimed CSP process term, and Q is a timed CSP process term. It is defined as

$$P\ _T{\sqsubseteq}_{TF}\ Q\ =\ \forall (s, \aleph) \in \mathcal{TF}\,[\![Q]\!] \bullet \#s < \infty \Rightarrow strip(s) \in \mathsf{traces}(P)$$

The traces of an untimed process P do not include infinite traces, so no restriction is placed upon the infinite timed traces of Q. However, this does not mean that Q can have arbitrary infinite traces: downward closure of Q's timed failures means that all finite prefixes of any infinite trace of Q must be consistent with P.

The trace timewise refinement relation interacts with the refinement relations within the traces model and timed failures model, giving a form of transitivity:

$$P \sqsubseteq_T P'\ _T{\sqsubseteq}_{TF}\ Q' \sqsubseteq_{TF} Q\ \Rightarrow P\ _T{\sqsubseteq}_{TF}\ Q$$

This relationship is illustrated in Figure 13.1.

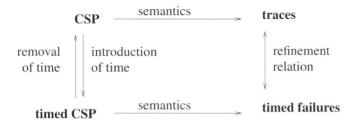

Fig. 13.2   Introducing and removing time in process descriptions

This means that a sequence of refinement steps in the traces model starting from process *P*, followed by a timewise refinement, followed by a sequence of refinement steps in the timed failures model resulting finally in a process *Q*, will ensure that *Q* is a timewise refinement of *P*.

Relating process descriptions

The refinement relation between processes can always be investigated through a direct analysis of their semantics. There are also a number of results which support refinement at the level of the process languages. These results give circumstances in which

- timed versions of process descriptions can be derived from untimed descriptions by the introduction of delays and timeouts; and

- untimed versions can be projected from timed ones by the removal of timing information and the replacement of timed operators with untimed ones: the resulting untimed process will be refined by the original timed one.

These possibilities are illustrated in Figure 13.2.

For example, $a \rightarrow STOP \; {}_T\sqsubseteq_{TF} \; a \xrightarrow{1} STOP$ and $b \rightarrow STOP \; {}_T\sqsubseteq_{TF} \; b \xrightarrow{2} STOP$. The untimed interrupt operator $\triangle$ can be trace timewise refined by a timed interrupt operator $\triangle_d$, which means that the refinement is preserved when the untimed and timed processes are combined with their respective operators:

$$a \rightarrow STOP \triangle b \rightarrow STOP \quad {}_T\sqsubseteq_{TF} \quad a \xrightarrow{1} STOP \triangle_d b \xrightarrow{2} STOP$$

Sequences of events of the timed process can contain either an *a* before time *d* followed by a *b* after time *d*, or else can contain only the *b* event. These possibilities are also allowed by the untimed description, so the refinement relation holds. The use of the timed operator carries more detail than its untimed counterpart concerning the possible executions of the process.

There are a number of general rules concerning conditions under which the trace timewise refinement relation holds. All of the CSP operators preserve this relation.

Firstly, it holds for the atomic processes as follows:

$$P \quad {}_T\sqsubseteq_{TF} \quad STOP \text{ for any untimed CSP process } P$$
$$RUN \quad {}_T\sqsubseteq_{TF} \quad Q \text{ for any timed CSP process } Q$$
$$SKIP \quad {}_T\sqsubseteq_{TF} \quad SKIP$$
$$SKIP \quad {}_T\sqsubseteq_{TF} \quad WAIT\ d \text{ for any time } d$$
$$SKIP \quad {}_T\sqsubseteq_{TF} \quad WAIT\ I \text{ for any interval } I$$

The unary CSP operators all preserve trace timewise refinement: if $P\ {}_T\sqsubseteq_{TF}\ Q$, then

$$a \rightarrow P \quad {}_T\sqsubseteq_{TF} \quad a \xrightarrow{d} Q \text{ for any delay } d$$
$$a \rightarrow P \quad {}_T\sqsubseteq_{TF} \quad a \xrightarrow{I} Q \text{ for any interval } I$$
$$P \setminus A \quad {}_T\sqsubseteq_{TF} \quad Q \setminus A \text{ for any set of events } A$$
$$f(P) \quad {}_T\sqsubseteq_{TF} \quad f(Q) \text{ for any alphabet renaming } f$$
$$f^{-1}(P) \quad {}_T\sqsubseteq_{TF} \quad f^{-1}(Q) \text{ for any alphabet renaming } f$$
$$P \quad {}_T\sqsubseteq_{TF} \quad WAIT\ d; Q \text{ for any delay } d$$
$$P \quad {}_T\sqsubseteq_{TF} \quad WAIT\ I; Q \text{ for any interval } I$$

The last two rules are used to justify the introduction of delays into process descriptions in a way that preserves the refinement relation.

Furthermore, if $P\ {}_T\sqsubseteq_{TF}\ Q[d/u]$ for any time d, then

$$a \rightarrow P \quad {}_T\sqsubseteq_{TF} \quad a@u \rightarrow Q$$

The binary CSP operators also preserve this refinement relation: if $P_1\ {}_T\sqsubseteq_{TF}\ Q_1$ and $P_2\ {}_T\sqsubseteq_{TF}\ Q_2$, then

$$P_1 \,\square\, P_2 \quad {}_T\sqsubseteq_{TF} \quad Q_1 \,\square\, Q_2$$
$$P_1 \,\square\, P_2 \quad {}_T\sqsubseteq_{TF} \quad Q_1 \overset{d}{\triangleright} Q_2 \text{ for any time } d$$
$$P_1 \,\sqcap\, P_2 \quad {}_T\sqsubseteq_{TF} \quad Q_1 \,\sqcap\, Q_2$$
$$P_1 \,{}_A\|_B\, P_2 \quad {}_T\sqsubseteq_{TF} \quad Q_1 \,{}_A\|_B\, Q_2$$
$$P_1 \,|||\, P_2 \quad {}_T\sqsubseteq_{TF} \quad Q_1 \,|||\, Q_2$$
$$P_1 \,\|_A\, P_2 \quad {}_T\sqsubseteq_{TF} \quad Q_1 \,\|_A\, Q_2$$
$$P_1; P_2 \quad {}_T\sqsubseteq_{TF} \quad Q_1; Q_2$$
$$P_1 \,\triangle\, P_2 \quad {}_T\sqsubseteq_{TF} \quad Q_1 \,\triangle\, Q_2$$
$$P_1 \,\triangle\, P_2 \quad {}_T\sqsubseteq_{TF} \quad Q_1 \,\triangle_d\, Q_2$$

Finally, the indexed operators preserve the refinement relation: if $P(a) \ _T\sqsubseteq_{TF} Q(a)$ for every $a \in A$, then

$$x : A \to P(x) \quad _T\sqsubseteq_{TF} \quad x : A \xrightarrow{d} Q(x)$$

and if $P_i \ _T\sqsubseteq_{TF} Q_i$ for every $i \in J$, then

$$\bigsqcap_{i \in J} P_i \quad _T\sqsubseteq_{TF} \quad \bigsqcap_{i \in J} Q_i$$

The other indexed operators are defined in terms of the appropriate binary operators, and so they inherit the property of preserving trace timewise refinement.

Timed process descriptions may also be amenable to untimed analysis by extracting the timed aspects of the process description. A timed process Q may be translated to an untimed process P by removing all delays associated with any event prefix, removing all *WAIT* constructs, replacing timeout with external choice, and timed interrupt with event interrupt. The resulting process P will be trace timewise refined by the original process Q.

Example 13.1.1 In Example 9.6.1, Helen and Carl are attempting to meet up.

$$HELEN \;=\; (meet \xrightarrow{30} work \to STOP) \overset{30}{\rhd} work \to STOP$$

$$CARL \;=\; WAIT\ 15; ((meet \xrightarrow{30} home \to STOP) \overset{45}{\rhd} home \to STOP)$$

Some properties of the interacting processes *HELEN* $\|$ *CARL* will be dependent on the timed behaviour of the components, and will therefore not be susceptible to an untimed analysis. Other properties, such as the fact that a meeting will not occur once Carl has gone home, are independent of the timing behaviour and true simply because of the order in which events occur. Such a property could be established in the traces model, on an untimed version of the process. Removing all of the timing information and replacing timeout with choice yields

$$UHELEN \;=\; (meet \to work \to STOP) \;\Box\; work \to STOP$$

$$UCARL \;=\; (meet \to home \to STOP) \;\Box\; home \to STOP$$

and

$$UHELEN \;\|\; UCARL \quad _T\sqsubseteq_{TF} \quad HELEN \;\|\; CARL$$

In some cases, untimed properties are a result of timed behaviour and will not be appropriate for untimed analysis. For example, the combination *HELEN* $\|$ *LATECARL* in the same example has Carl 30 minutes behind schedule, and so a meeting will not be possible since there is no time that both participants can agree on. The combination meets the untimed safety specification '*meet* will never occur'. However, the untimed versions of these two processes are exactly the processes *UHELEN* and *UCARL*, and their combination allows the event *meet* because the timing information has become lost. In this case, there are some untimed traces that do not correspond to any timed traces of the timed system. This is because the more refined description contains further information as to why some events cannot occur. Refinement allows behaviours to be removed by providing more detail about processes, and in this case the provision of timed information does allow the possibility of the *meet* event to be excluded. ∎

Refinement is also preserved by recursion. Let $M = P$ be an untimed recursive definition, and $N = Q$ a timed one. If the bodies P and Q of the recursive definitions respect the refinement relation, then the resulting processes will also be related. In the case of a single recursion, this means that if $P[X/M] \sqsubseteq_{TF} Q[Y/N]$ whenever $X \sqsubseteq_{TF} Y$, then the conclusion $M \sqsubseteq_{TF} N$ follows:

$$\frac{\forall X;\ Y \bullet (X \sqsubseteq_{TF} Y \Rightarrow P[X/M] \sqsubseteq_{TF} Q[Y/N])}{M \sqsubseteq_{TF} N} \quad \left[\begin{array}{l} M = P \\ N = Q \end{array} \right]$$

Furthermore, if the body of Q preserves the property of being a refinement of some process P, then N itself will be a refinement of P: if $P \sqsubseteq_{TF} Y \Rightarrow P \sqsubseteq_{TF} Q[Y/N]$, then $P \sqsubseteq_{TF} N$.

$$\frac{\forall Y \bullet P \sqsubseteq_{TF} Y \Rightarrow P \sqsubseteq_{TF} Q[Y/N]}{P \sqsubseteq_{TF} N} \quad [\, N = Q \,]$$

Example 13.1.2 The fax machine of Example 2.2.3 is described as

$$FAX \quad = \quad accept?d : DOC \rightarrow print!d \rightarrow FAX$$

It is clear from an analysis of the traces of *FAX* that it must alternate on receiving and printing documents. A timed description consistent with this untimed one may be obtained by introducing delays throughout the description. One such result is

$$TFAX \quad = \quad WAIT\, 2;\, accept?d : DOC \stackrel{[1,15]}{\rightarrow} print!d \stackrel{[10,180]}{\rightarrow} TFAX$$

The traces of *TFAX* are consistent with those of *FAX*.

It may also be a requirement that the fax machine will be switched off if it does not receive any fax for 24 hours (86,400 seconds). If this occurs then no activity will occur.

The rules for preservation of refinement state that $STOP \sqsubseteq_{TF} STOP$, and also that an external choice may be replaced by a timeout. This means that

$$FAX \,\square\, STOP \quad \sqsubseteq_{TF} \quad TFAX \stackrel{86,400}{\triangleright} STOP$$

The introduction of *STOP* into the untimed process description has no effect, since $P \mathbin{\square} STOP = P$ for any CSP process P. However, the introduction of the timeout into the timed process description does remove some traces, but timewise refinement is preserved because no fresh traces are introduced. Hence the process $TFAX \overset{86,400}{\vartriangleright} STOP$ is also a trace timewise refinement of *FAX*. It is a timed description of the fax machine that is consistent with the more abstract description given by *FAX*.   ∎

The results generalize to mutual recursion. An untimed mutual recursion is of the form $\underline{M} = \underline{P}$, and a timed mutual recursion is of the form $\underline{N} = \underline{Q}$. If for each i the relation $P_i[\underline{X}/\underline{M}] \ _T{\sqsubseteq}_{TF} \ Q_i[\underline{Y}/\underline{N}]$ holds whenever $X_j \ _T{\sqsubseteq}_{TF} \ Y_j$ for all indices j, then this means that the vector of process definitions preserves the refinement relation. The recursively defined processes will also be related: $M_i \ _T{\sqsubseteq}_{TF} \ N_i$ for each i.

The fact that all of the process operators preserve timewise refinement means that the refinement process is compositional: a system may be refined by introducing timing information to each of its components independently. Any untimed process description P can be translated to a timed process description Q by introducing delays of any length into any event prefix, and by introducing *WAIT d* or *WAIT I* into any point where they are required. Furthermore, external choices may be translated into timeout choices.

Untimed recursive definitions will not contain any timed constructs, and so when considered as timed CSP descriptions they will not be well-timed. It is necessary to introduce some time guards into recursive definitions in order to perform a timed analysis.

Translating specifications

If a process P satisfies a particular specification $S(tr)$, then every trace of P meets S. The traces of any timewise refinement Q of P will be consistent with those of P. This means that all of the finite traces of Q will be traces of P once the times have been stripped away, and so will themselves meet the specification S. This means that Q meets the timed specification $\#s < \infty \Rightarrow S(strip(s))$. In other words, any timed failure $(s, \aleph)$ of Q meets this predicate: that if the trace is finite then S holds of the sequence of events described in s. No constraint is placed on the refusal set.

$$P \text{ sat } S(tr) \wedge P \ _T{\sqsubseteq}_{TF} \ Q \quad \Rightarrow \quad Q \text{ sat } (\#s < \infty \Rightarrow S(strip(s)))$$

The specification $\#s < \infty \Rightarrow S(strip(s))$ is the timed translation of $S(tr)$, mapping the abstract predicate on sequences of events to a predicate on the more detailed timed failures. An untimed specification is *admissible* if it is true of an infinite trace whenever it is true of all its finite approximations. For admissible specifications, the translation is even more straightforward:

$$S(strip(s))$$

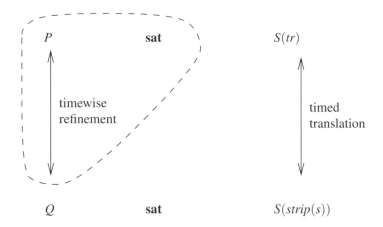

Fig. 13.3 Completeness for timewise refinement

and the result for admissible specifications is

$$P \text{ sat } S(tr) \wedge P \ {}_T\!\sqsubseteq_{TF} Q \quad \Rightarrow \quad Q \text{ sat } S(strip(s))$$

Most untimed safety specifications are admissible, so this translation is usually straightforward.

The converse is a kind of completeness result: if a timed specification can be expressed in the form $S(strip(s))$, so it is dependent only on the sequence of events in the timed trace s, then whenever $Q \text{ sat } S(strip(s))$ there must be some untimed CSP process $P \ {}_T\!\sqsubseteq_{TF} Q$ such that $P \text{ sat } S(tr)$. This form of completeness is illustrated in Figure 13.3: if Q and S are known, then there must be some untimed process P which allows the diagram to be completed.

Completeness allows the results of reasoning in the timed model to map to the untimed world and be used in more abstract analysis: there is always a process P which is an untimed version of a timed system Q and which meets the untimed version of the timed specification. Process P is then appropriate for use in further analysis at the untimed level, perhaps as a component of a larger system. The reasoning does not need to know the process P itself, only the fact that it meets $S(tr)$.

The fact that timewise refinement preserves trace specifications allows verifications to be translated from the untimed traces model to the timed model. Together with completeness, this means that an analysis of a system can move freely between the timed and the untimed models.

Example 13.1.3 The specification that *accept* and *print* events alternate is admissible:

$$Alt_{accept,print}(tr) \quad = \quad tr \downarrow print \leqslant tr \downarrow accept \leqslant tr \downarrow print + 1$$

This means that if *FAX* **sat** $Alt_{accept,print}(tr)$ and *FAX* $_T\sqsubseteq_{TF}$ *TFAX* then the result *TFAX* **sat** $Alt_{accept,print}(strip(s))$ immediately follows. This is written out in full as

$$TFAX \quad \textbf{sat} \quad strip(s) \downarrow print \leqslant strip(s) \downarrow accept \leqslant strip(s) \downarrow print + 1$$

The length of the sequence $strip(s)$ is the same as the length of s itself, so the result simplifies to

$$TFAX \quad \textbf{sat} \quad s \downarrow print \leqslant s \downarrow accept \leqslant s \downarrow print + 1$$

The timing out fax machine $TFAX \overset{86,400}{\triangleright} STOP$ is also guaranteed to meet this specification by virtue of refining *FAX*. ∎

Example 13.1.4 The requirement that any occurrence of the event *meet* must take place before the event *home* is captured by the admissible specification

$$Home(tr) \quad = \quad (foot(tr) = meet \Rightarrow home \notin \sigma(tr))$$

If the last event in the trace is *meet*, then *home* cannot yet have appeared in the trace.

It is easy to prove that *UHELEN* || *UCARL* **sat** $Home(tr)$, so it follows that

$$HELEN \parallel CARL \quad \textbf{sat} \quad foot(strip(s)) = meet \Rightarrow home \notin \sigma(strip(s))$$

which simplifies to

$$HELEN \parallel CARL \quad \textbf{sat} \quad last(s) = meet \to home \notin \sigma(s)$$

It has also been established that if Carl is running late, then he and Helen will not meet:

$$HELEN \parallel LATECARL \quad \textbf{sat} \quad meet \notin \sigma(s)$$

If Simon is also aiming to join the meeting, this result enables an untimed analysis to conclude that no such meeting will take place. Completeness allows the deduction that there is some untimed process P which is refined by *HELEN* || *LATECARL* and which satisfies the untimed translation of the specification:

$$P \quad \textbf{sat} \quad meet \notin \sigma(tr)$$

An untimed analysis establishes that $P \parallel RUN$ **sat** $meet \notin \sigma(tr)$. Any timed description *SIMON* will refine the untimed process *RUN*, so

$$P \parallel RUN \quad _T\sqsubseteq_{TF} \quad (HELEN \parallel LATECARL) \parallel SIMON$$

and the timed process satisfies the specification *meet* $\notin \sigma(s)$. This will be true for any particular description, such as

$$SIMON \quad = \quad WAIT\ 10; ((meet \rightarrow STOP) \overset{60}{\triangleright} coffee \rightarrow STOP)$$

which overlaps on meeting times with each of Helen and Carl.

The analysis of the three-way parallel combination must involve consideration of the timed behaviours at some stage, since the impossibility of the meeting is a result of time mismatches between some of the participants; a purely untimed analysis would be too coarse. The theory of timewise refinement allows the timed analysis to be localized to the appropriate part of the system, and completeness allows the reasoning to continue at the untimed level.

■

Example 13.1.5 (Mutual exclusion) In Exercise 12.7 the CSP description of Fischer's algorithm was adapted to allow repeated runs, while maintaining the mutual exclusion property: *enter* and *exit* events were guaranteed to alternate. Although this property is a result of the timed behaviour of the components, the specification itself may be expressed as a timed translation of the untimed specification

$$Alt_{enter,exit}(tr) \quad = \quad tr \downarrow exit \leqslant tr \downarrow enter \leqslant tr \downarrow exit + 1$$

This means that there is some untimed process *UFISCHER* which is refined by *FISCHER* and which satisfies this specification.

Even though the only information about the process *UFISCHER* is its specification, this is enough to allow it to be used as a component in the untimed development and verification of a system. The analysis can all take place in the traces model, secure in the knowledge that the untimed property is ensured by the implementation of *UFISCHER*. The timed analysis is confined to the process *FISCHER*, the only part of the system where the timed behaviour ensures correctness. This is illustrated in Figure 13.4 with regard to P_1 and P_2 described below.

For example, two processes P_1 and P_2 each have access to a modem and wish to transmit a message. It is important to ensure that only one process at a time is sending its message in order to avoid interference. Each process P_i can input a message x consisting of a finite sequence of letters from the alphabet A along channel *in.i*. Having received x, it attempts to obtain control of the modem in order to transmit the message one letter at a time.

$$P_i \quad = \quad in.i?x : A^* \rightarrow req.i \rightarrow enter.i \rightarrow TRANS(x); exit.i \rightarrow P_i$$

where the *TRANS* processes are defined by

$$TRANS(\langle\rangle) \quad = \quad SKIP$$
$$TRANS(\langle a\rangle \frown as) \quad = \quad send!a \rightarrow TRANS(as)$$

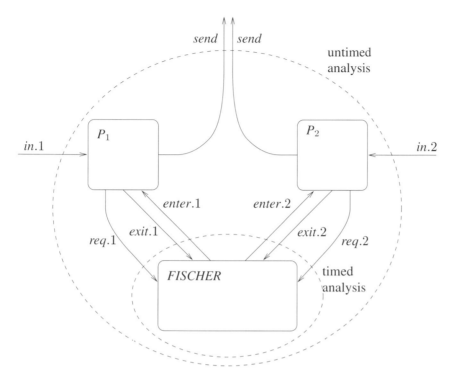

Fig. 13.4   Localizing timed analysis

An untimed analysis in the traces model can establish that the combination

$$(P_1 \,|||\, P_2) \,\|\, \textit{UFISCHER}$$

does not merge the sequences that P_1 and P_2 wish to transmit, but transmits each sequence in its entirety. This may be specified as

$$\exists\, tr_0 \bullet tr_0 \text{ interleaves } (tr \Downarrow in_1), (tr \Downarrow in_2) \wedge tr \Downarrow send \leqslant \textit{flatten}(tr_0)$$

The specification states that there is some ordering tr_0 of the sequences arriving on in_1 and in_2 which corresponds to the letters output along *send*: tr_0 is a sequence of sequences, and *flatten*(tr_0) is the concatenation of all those sequences into a single sequence of elements output along *send*.

Only the mutual exclusion specification of *UFISCHER* is required in order to establish that the combination meets the sequence specification. The results of the analysis mean that however P_1 and P_2 are implemented with regard to their timed behaviour, the resulting system will not allow them to interfere, since the timed implementation of *UFISCHER* guarantees mutual exclusion. ∎

13.2   FAILURES TIMEWISE REFINEMENT

Analysis of a system using the stable failures model includes consideration of liveness aspects of behaviour in addition to the safety aspects described by the traces information. A timewise refinement of a process with respect to the stable failures model will have to be consistent with the stable failures information. This requires an understanding of untimed information within the context of the timed model.

A stable failure (tr, X) represents the observation of the sequence of events listed in tr, followed by the eventual arrival at a stable state from which none of the events in the refusal set X can be performed. Unlike a timed failure, no information is contained in the untimed failure (tr, X) concerning the refusal of events during the performance of the trace; the only refusal information follows the end of the trace.

A timed failure $(s, \aleph)$ of a process Q has either a finite or an infinite trace. If it is finite, then there are a number of possible untimed behaviours consistent with $(s, \aleph)$. The sequence of events $tr = strip(s)$ must be the untimed trace, but the timed refusal might contain a number of different refusal tokens of the form $[t, \infty) \times X$, so for each of these $[t, \infty) \times X \subseteq \aleph$. In each case this indicates that the associated set of events X could eventually be refused for ever after the performance of $strip(s)$. Thus any of the failures $(strip(s), X)$ are consistent with $(s, \aleph)$.

The timed process Q will be a failures timewise refinement of the untimed process P (written P $_{SF}\sqsubseteq_{TF}$ Q) if all of its timed traces are allowed by the untimed traces of P, and all of its timed failures are allowed by the stable failures of P. The timed failures of Q will contain certain observations that would appear as particular untimed observations if recorded in an untimed context; and P should permit all of these observations. This is formally defined as follows:

$$
\begin{aligned}
P \ _{SF}\sqsubseteq_{TF} Q \ = \ & \forall (s, \aleph) \in \mathcal{TF}[\![Q]\!] \ \bullet \\
& \#s < \infty \Rightarrow \\
& \quad strip(s) \in \mathsf{traces}(P) \wedge \\
& \quad (\exists t : \mathbb{R}^+ ; \ X \subseteq \Sigma \bullet ([t, \infty) \times X) \subseteq \aleph \\
& \quad \quad \Rightarrow (strip(s), X) \in \mathcal{SF}[\![P]\!])
\end{aligned}
$$

Example 13.2.1 If for any $x \in T$ the untimed process $P(x)$ is failures timewise refined by the process $Q(x)$, then the untimed process $in?x : T \rightarrow P(x)$ will be refined by the process $WAIT\ 5; in?x : T \rightarrow Q(x)$. Although this process can initially refuse to input, it cannot refuse input for ever. An untimed offer of a synchronization corresponds to an eventual offer in the timed setting. If the environment is ever prepared to wait long enough to synchronize on an event, then eventually its offer must be accepted—it cannot be refused for ever.

Conversely, the timed process $(in?x : T \rightarrow Q(x)) \overset{5}{\triangleright} STOP$ does not refine the untimed inputting process. Although it is initially ready to accept input, it will retract that offer at time 5 and refuse input after that time. A partner offering input at time 8 will not have its input accepted, even if it waits for ever.

On the other hand, it is a trace timewise refinement of the untimed choice, since the refusal information is not relevant, and it is only the untimed liveness behaviour that is not preserved by the timeout choice. ∎

Example 13.2.2 The untimed choice

$$INPUTS \quad = \quad in_1?x : T \rightarrow out!x \rightarrow INPUTS$$
$$\square \; in_2?x : T \rightarrow out!x \rightarrow INPUTS$$

is initially prepared to accept input along either of two channels in_1 and in_2. The choice is external and so neither channel can be refused. An obvious refinement is obtained by reproducing the external choice:

$$INPUTS \quad _{SF}\sqsubseteq_{TF} \quad TINPUTS = \quad in_1?x : T \xrightarrow{1} out!x \rightarrow TINPUTS$$
$$\square \; in_2?x : T \xrightarrow{1} out!x \rightarrow TINPUTS$$

This timed process makes both in_1 and in_2 available over all time, until some input occurs. A timewise refinement of the choice does not require quite such strong availability, only that in_1 and in_2 can never be refused for ever. Any environment which wishes to provide an input, and is prepared to wait long enough, should be guaranteed to do so as long as nothing else occurs first. This allows a weaker form of choice, whereby each input channel is polled in turn until one of them provides the input. The *POLLING* process of Example 9.5.1 is also a refinement of *INPUTS*:

$$INPUTS \quad _{SF}\sqsubseteq_{TF} \quad POLLING$$

Neither in_1 nor in_2 can ever be refused for more than two time units.

Observe that *POLLING* itself is not stable. Timed failures information contains no information about stability, as the more detailed refusal information makes this unnecessary. ∎

The failures timewise refinement relation interacts with the refinement relations within the failures model and timed failures model in the same way as the trace timewise refinement relation does:

$$P \sqsubseteq_{SF} P' \; _{SF}\sqsubseteq_{TF} Q' \sqsubseteq_{TF} Q \quad \Rightarrow P \; _{SF}\sqsubseteq_{TF} Q$$

Relating process descriptions

Most of the relationships between untimed and timed CSP operators that hold for trace timewise refinement also hold for failures timewise refinement, though there are some exceptions, the most significant being parallel composition.

Failures timewise refinement holds for the atomic processes, with the exception of *DIV*, which cannot be failures timewise refined by any process because it has no stable failures at all.

$$CHAOS \quad _{SF}\sqsubseteq_{TF} \quad Q \text{ for any timed CSP process } Q$$
$$STOP \quad _{SF}\sqsubseteq_{TF} \quad STOP$$
$$SKIP \quad _{SF}\sqsubseteq_{TF} \quad SKIP$$
$$SKIP \quad _{SF}\sqsubseteq_{TF} \quad WAIT \, d \text{ for any time } d$$
$$SKIP \quad _{SF}\sqsubseteq_{TF} \quad WAIT \, I \text{ for any interval } I$$

The unary CSP operators all preserve failures timewise refinement: if $P \; _{SF}\sqsubseteq_{TF} \; Q$, then

$$a \to P \quad _{SF}\sqsubseteq_{TF} \quad a \xrightarrow{d} Q \text{ for any delay } d$$
$$a \to P \quad _{SF}\sqsubseteq_{TF} \quad a \xrightarrow{I} Q \text{ for any interval } I$$
$$P \setminus A \quad _{SF}\sqsubseteq_{TF} \quad Q \setminus A$$
$$f(P) \quad _{SF}\sqsubseteq_{TF} \quad f(Q)$$
$$f^{-1}(P) \quad _{SF}\sqsubseteq_{TF} \quad f^{-1}(Q)$$
$$P \quad _{SF}\sqsubseteq_{TF} \quad WAIT \, d; Q \text{ for any delay } d$$
$$P \quad _{SF}\sqsubseteq_{TF} \quad WAIT \, I; Q \text{ for any interval } I$$

Furthermore, if $P \; _{SF}\sqsubseteq_{TF} \; Q[d/u]$ for any time d, then

$$a \to P \quad _{SF}\sqsubseteq_{TF} \quad a@u \to Q$$

Most binary CSP operators also preserve this refinement relation, though any forms of synchronizing parallel combinations do not, and so neither do their indexed forms. Their failure to preserve refinement will be discussed in Section 13.3. Furthermore, once refusals are taken into account, timeout choice does not refine external choice, though it does refine the untimed form of timeout choice. Finally timed interrupt does not refine event interrupt (see Exercise 13.1).

If $P_1 \; _{SF}\sqsubseteq_{TF} \; Q_1$ and $P_2 \; _{SF}\sqsubseteq_{TF} \; Q_2$, then

$$P_1 \, \Box \, P_2 \quad _{SF}\sqsubseteq_{TF} \quad Q_1 \, \Box \, Q_2$$
$$(P_1 \, \sqcap \, STOP) \, \Box \, P_2 \quad _{SF}\sqsubseteq_{TF} \quad Q_1 \overset{d}{\rhd} Q_2 \text{ for any time } d$$
$$P_1 \, \sqcap \, P_2 \quad _{SF}\sqsubseteq_{TF} \quad Q_1 \, \sqcap \, Q_2$$
$$P_1; P_2 \quad _{SF}\sqsubseteq_{TF} \quad Q_1; Q_2$$
$$P_1 \, \triangle \, P_2 \quad _{SF}\sqsubseteq_{TF} \quad Q_1 \, \triangle \, Q_2$$

The indexed operators preserve the refinement relation: if $P(a)$ $_{SF}\sqsubseteq_{TF}$ $Q(a)$ for every $a \in A$, then

$$x : A \to P(x) \quad _{SF}\sqsubseteq_{TF} \quad x : A \to Q(x)$$

and if P_i $_{SF}\sqsubseteq_{TF}$ Q_i for every $i \in J$, then

$$\bigsqcap_{i \in J} P_i \quad _{SF}\sqsubseteq_{TF} \quad \bigsqcap_{i \in J} Q_i$$

Indexed external choice and indexed interleaving both preserve failures timewise refinement, because their binary forms do.

Finally, for divergence-free processes, refinement is again preserved by recursion. This means that if the bodies of the recursive definitions $M = P$ and $N = Q$ respect the refinement relation, then the resulting processes will also be related. This means that if $P[X/M]$ $_{SF}\sqsubseteq_{TF}$ $Q[Y/N]$ whenever X $_{SF}\sqsubseteq_{TF}$ Y, then M $_{SF}\sqsubseteq_{TF}$ N:

$$\frac{\forall X, Y \bullet (X \;_{SF}\sqsubseteq_{TF} Y \Rightarrow P[X/M] \;_{SF}\sqsubseteq_{TF} Q[Y/N])}{M \;_{SF}\sqsubseteq_{TF} N} \qquad \left[\begin{array}{l} M \text{ divergence-free} \\ M = P \\ N = Q \end{array} \right]$$

The generalization to mutual recursion also holds, for an untimed mutually recursive definition $\underline{M} = \underline{P}$, and a timed mutual recursion $\underline{N} = \underline{Q}$. If for each i the relation $P_i[\underline{X}/\underline{M}]$ $_{SF}\sqsubseteq_{TF}$ $Q_i[\underline{Y}/\underline{N}]$ holds whenever X_j $_{SF}\sqsubseteq_{TF}$ Y_j for all indices j, then the recursively defined processes will also be related by this relation: M_i $_{SF}\sqsubseteq_{TF}$ N_i for each i.

However, unlike the case for trace timewise refinement, if the body of a recursive definition $N = Q$ preserves the property of failures timewise refining an untimed process P, this does not necessarily mean that P $_{SF}\sqsubseteq_{TF}$ N, even if P is divergence-free. For example, $WAIT\ 1; N$ will preserve refinement of any untimed process P: if P $_{SF}\sqsubseteq_{TF}$ N then P $_{SF}\sqsubseteq_{TF}$ $WAIT\ 1; N$. However, the fixed point N is equivalent to $STOP$, which certainly does not failures timewise refine any arbitrary P such as $a \to STOP$.

13.3 REFINEMENT AND PARALLEL COMPOSITION

A process Q is considered to offer an event a if any environment that is eventually willing to wait for long enough can be sure of interacting on that event. However, the process Q itself need not be prepared to wait continuously; it may not have the patience expected of its environment. This means that two processes which are each always guaranteed to offer a eventually may not be able to agree on a single time at which they can both simultaneously offer the event a. For example, a process which offers a for 1 second of every 4 may be defined as

$$Q_1 \quad = \quad (a \to STOP) \stackrel{1}{\rhd} WAIT\ 3; Q_1$$

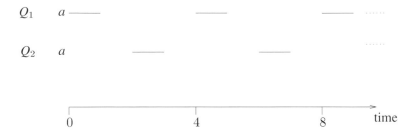

Fig. 13.5 Offers of two timed processes

This process is a timewise refinement of the simple process which is ready to perform an a:

$$a \to STOP \quad _{SF}\sqsubseteq_{TF} \quad Q_1$$

The process $Q_2 = WAIT\ 2; Q_1$ is also a refinement of $a \to STOP$. However, when these two processes are required to synchronize on a, there is no time they can agree to do so, as illustrated in Figure 13.5, and so their parallel combination is able to refuse a over all time. This means that $Q_1 \parallel Q_2$ is not a refinement of $a \to STOP \parallel a \to STOP$ despite the fact that the refinement relation holds between the components of the two parallel combinations. Parallel composition does not always preserve failures timewise refinement.

Non-retraction

Parallel composition fails to preserve timewise refinement when neither of the timed processes is prepared to wait for the other, and each periodically withdraws offers. If each of the timed processes were to provide a more patient environment for the other, then timewise refinement would be preserved by parallel composition. A parallel component need not be patient on all of its activity, simply on those parts of it that involve the other party.

The critical property required for a process is *non-retraction*, that once an event is made available then it should remain on offer at least until some event occurs. A non-retracting process is one that does not withdraw offers after it is guaranteed to have made them. If an event cannot be refused at a particular time after some behaviour, then it must be on offer at that time, and so non-retraction requires that it should still be on offer at any later time.

Viewed contrapositively in terms of refusals, this means that if a particular event can be refused by a non-retracting process Q at some time t'', then it should be possible for the process to have refused that event continually since the time t at which the previous event occurred. Figure 13.6 illustrates this. The possibility of augmenting the refusal indicates that it might not have been on offer at all during that period of time. If it had been on offer at some instant t' between t and t'', then it could not have been refused at t''.

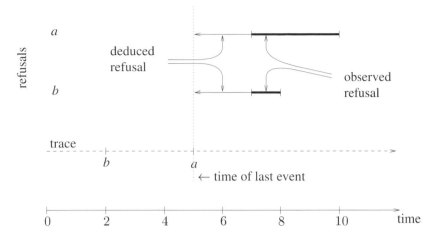

Fig. 13.6 Non-retraction on a timed failure

A process Q is said to be non-retracting if every timed failure $(s, \aleph)$ can be augmented with the appropriate additional refusal information:

$$(s, \aleph) \in \mathcal{TF}\,[\![Q]\!] \Rightarrow$$
$$(s, \aleph \cup \{(t, a) \mid \exists t' \bullet (t', a) \in \aleph \wedge end(s) \leqslant t < t'\}) \in \mathcal{TF}\,[\![Q]\!]$$

This is illustrated on the timed failure $(\langle (2, b), (5, a) \rangle, \ [7, 10) \times \{a\} \cup [7, 8) \times \{b\})$ in Figure 13.6. Some time after the performance of the two events in the trace, the events a and b are refused by the process. This indicates that a previous unretracted offer cannot have occurred, so the process must also have been able to refuse a and b between the end of the trace and the observed refusal set. The definition requires that

$$(\langle (2, b), (5, a) \rangle, \ [5, 10) \times \{a\} \cup [5, 8) \times \{b\})$$

is also a timed failure of the process.

This definition is concerned only with guaranteed offers of events, rather than with possible offers of events. Once a time is reached when an event is guaranteed to have been offered, then that event must be on offer from then on, so it cannot then be refused.

Example 13.3.1 The waiter process ($WAIT\ 2$; $order \rightarrow MEAL$) is non-retracting (assuming $MEAL$ is) because any refusal of the event $order$ must occur before 2 minutes have elapsed, and may be preceded by earlier refusals of $order$. Once $order$ is guaranteed to be offered, at time 2, then it cannot subsequently be refused.

A waiter serving two tables at the same time, though at different speeds, might be described as

$$WAITER1 \quad = \quad (WAIT\ 2; order_1 \rightarrow MEAL_1) \ \square \ (WAIT\ 4; order_2 \rightarrow MEAL_2)$$

Although the events on offer change as time progresses, the offers are always enhanced and no offer is retracted.

A less attentive waiter might return to the kitchen if the order is not placed within 5 minutes, refusing further interactions with the customer. The process

$$WAITER2 \quad = \quad (WAIT\ 2;\ order \rightarrow MEAL) \overset{5}{\triangleright} STOP$$

fails to be non-retracting, since it exhibits the failure $(\langle\rangle, [5, 6) \times \{order\})$ but not the failure $(\langle\rangle, [0, 6) \times \{order\})$; the definition of non-retraction requires the presence of the second if the first is possible. This corresponds to the fact that the waiter is guaranteed to accept an order sometime during the interval $[0, 5)$ but not afterwards.

The waiter who might never even arrive to take an order could be described as follows:

$$WAITER3 \quad = \quad STOP \sqcap ((WAIT\ 2;\ order \rightarrow MEAL) \overset{5}{\triangleright} STOP)$$

This process is not guaranteed to accept *order* at all (though it might during the interval $[2, 5)$), and so it is considered as non-retracting—the refusal of *order* over the interval $[5, 6)$ could be associated with a run of *STOP*, and so there is no evidence of a definite offer having previously been available. If the event *order* does occur, then this provides evidence that it was indeed on offer during that particular execution, but its very occurrence results in a different execution, one in which *order* is not retracted but performed instead. It is not possible to obtain evidence that *order* was on offer unless it is actually performed.

These examples illustrate that non-retraction is not preserved by refinement within the timed failures model. Refinement generally provides more guarantees about the offer of events over particular intervals, but non-retraction on such guarantees requires the presence of other guarantees which might not themselves be introduced during refinement. For example, *WAITER3* $\sqsubseteq$ *WAITER2*, but *WAITER3*'s non-retraction is not retained by *WAITER2*. *WAITER3* guarantees nothing and so is vacuously non-retracting. The refinement to *WAITER2* introduces guarantees over the interval $[2, 5)$, but then non-retraction requires that *order* should not be retracted after time 5 in *WAITER2*. No such obligation is placed upon *WAITER3*, since *order* was not guaranteed to be available at any point.   ∎

If two timed processes Q_1 and Q_2 are both non-retracting, then any form of parallel combination respects their timewise refinement relationships with untimed processes. This means that if $P_1 \ _{SF}\!\sqsubseteq_{TF} Q_1$ and $P_2 \ _{SF}\!\sqsubseteq_{TF} Q_2$, then $P_1 \parallel P_2 \ _{SF}\!\sqsubseteq_{TF} Q_1 \parallel Q_2$ and $P_1 \ _A\!\parallel_B$ $P_2 \ _{SF}\!\sqsubseteq_{TF} Q_1 \ _A\!\parallel_B Q_2$. Any offers that are made by Q_1 and Q_2 will remain until some event occurs, and so they will be sure to synchronize on any offers that their untimed counterparts are bound to make.

Furthermore, non-retraction is preserved when processes are combined in parallel: if Q_1 and Q_2 are non-retracting, then so are $Q_1 \parallel Q_2$ and $Q_1 \ _A\!\parallel_B Q_2$. This means that timewise refinement is also preserved for indexed parallel combinations of non-retracting processes.

Eventual non-retraction

The property of non-retraction may be generalized to allow some initial transient activity before a process settles down to make stable offers. A process will be *eventually non-retracting* if after any trace there is some point beyond which any offers made by the process will not be retracted. Offers may be made and then withdrawn before that point is reached.

A process Q is eventually non-retracting if

$$(s, \aleph) \in \mathcal{TF} \llbracket Q \rrbracket \wedge \#s < \infty \Rightarrow$$
$$\exists t \geqslant end(s) \bullet (s, \aleph \cup \{(t', a) \mid \exists (t'', a) \in \aleph \bullet t \leqslant t' < t''\}) \in \mathcal{TF} \llbracket Q \rrbracket$$

The time t is the point after which guaranteed offers cannot be retracted: if an event is refused at some time t' after t, then it must have been possible to continually refuse it between t and t'. For a non-retracting process, the time t will be $end(s)$, so any process which is non-retracting will also be eventually non-retracting.

Eventual non-retraction is an extremely robust property, as it is preserved by almost all of the timed CSP operators. The basic processes *STOP*, *SKIP*, *WAIT d*, and *WAIT I* for any d are all eventually non-retracting. If Q is eventually non-retracting, then so too is $a \rightarrow Q$, *WAIT d*; Q, *WAIT I*; Q, $f(Q)$, and $f^{-1}(Q)$. If Q_1 and Q_2 are eventually non-retracting, then so too are $Q_1 \; \Box \; Q_2$, $Q_1 \; \sqcap \; Q_2$, $Q_1 \; \overset{d}{\triangleright} \; Q_2$, $Q_1 \; {}_A\|_B \; Q_2$, $Q_1 \; \||| \; Q_2$; $Q_1 \; \|_A \; Q_2$, $Q_1 \; \triangle \; Q_2$, and $Q_1 \; \triangle_d \; Q_2$. If each $Q(a)$ is eventually non-retracting then so too is $x : A \rightarrow Q(x)$, and if each Q_i is eventually non-retracting, then so is $\sqcap_{i \in J} Q_i$. The indexed versions of external choice and the parallel operators all preserve eventual non-retraction because their binary versions do. Finally, if $Q[d/u]$ is eventually non-retracting for any time d, then $a@u \rightarrow Q$ is also eventually non-retracting.

In fact, the only operators which fail to preserve the property of eventual non-retraction are the hiding operator, sequential composition, and those instances of recursion which either contain hiding or sequential composition, or which have recursive calls not guarded by an event. If the body Q of a recursive definition $N = Q$ preserves eventual non-retraction (so that $Q[X/N]$ is eventually non-retracting whenever X is) and all instances of the variable name N are event guarded, then N itself is eventually non-retracting. This is also true for mutual recursion, where all instances of any process variable in any process body must be event guarded.

The stronger property of non-retraction is not preserved by the timeout operator or the timed interrupt operator, but is preserved by all of the other operators which preserve eventual non-retraction. Furthermore, if non-retraction is preserved by the body of a recursive definition $N = Q$ or $N_i = Q_i$, then the recursively defined process must be non-retracting (and thus eventually non-retracting), even in the absence of event guardedness.

An important result concerning eventual non-retraction is its interaction with timewise refinement: if two processes Q_1 and Q_2 are eventually non-retracting, then they will preserve failures timewise refinement through all forms of parallel composition.

Eventual non-retraction may be further generalized. When two processes Q_1 and Q_2 are combined in a form of synchronized parallel such as $Q_1 \parallel_A Q_2$ they are required to co-operate on the performance of events in their common interface A. In order for the parallel combination to preserve timewise refinements $P_1 \ {}_{SF}\sqsubseteq_{TF} \ Q_1$ and $P_2 \ {}_{SF}\sqsubseteq_{TF} \ Q_2$ the timed processes must together be able to offer events whenever the corresponding untimed processes are able to do so. The co-operation is required only on the set $A^\checkmark$. The offer and refusal of events outside the set $A^\checkmark$ is dependent on the two components individually rather than on how they might jointly perform events, and so their offers are already guaranteed by the individual relationships $P_1 \ {}_{SF}\sqsubseteq_{TF} \ Q_1$ and $P_2 \ {}_{SF}\sqsubseteq_{TF} \ Q_2$. Non-retraction properties are not required on such events.

A further weakening of eventual non-retraction is possible. A process Q is *eventually non-retracting on* $A \subseteq \Sigma^\checkmark$ if

$$
(s, \aleph) \in \mathcal{TF} \ [\![Q]\!] \wedge \#s < \infty \Rightarrow
$$
$$
\exists t \geqslant end(s) \bullet
$$
$$
(s, \aleph \cup \{(t', a) \mid \exists (t'', a) \in \aleph \bullet \quad t \leqslant t' < t'' \wedge a \in A\}) \in \mathcal{TF} \ [\![Q]\!]
$$

Only offers of events in the set A need eventually be stable, so it is only refusals of such events which will augment the refusal set.

If a process is eventually non-retracting on both A and B, then it will also be eventually non-retracting on $A \cup B$ and on any subset of it.

Non-retraction on the common interface is all that is required to preserve timewise refinement. If processes are both non-retracting on their common interface, then their parallel combination will preserve timewise refinement. In other words, if $P_1 \ {}_{SF}\sqsubseteq_{TF} \ Q_1$ and $P_2 \ {}_{SF}\sqsubseteq_{TF} \ Q_2$, then

- $P_1 \parallel_A P_2 \ {}_{SF}\sqsubseteq_{TF} \ Q_1 \parallel_A Q_2$ if Q_1 and Q_2 are eventually non-retracting on $A^\checkmark$;

- $P_1 \ {}_A\|_B P_2 \ {}_{SF}\sqsubseteq_{TF} \ Q_1 \ {}_A\|_B Q_2$ if Q_1 and Q_2 are eventually non-retracting on $(A \cap B)^\checkmark$;

- $P_1 \ ||| \ P_2 \ {}_{SF}\sqsubseteq_{TF} \ Q_1 \ ||| \ Q_2$ if Q_1 and Q_2 are eventually non-retracting on $\{\checkmark\}$.

This is illustrated in Figure 13.7.

Provided the possibility of termination cannot be withdrawn, a timed process will be non-retracting on $\{\checkmark\}$. In such cases, interleaving will preserve timewise refinement. This is vacuously true for non-terminating processes.

Example 13.3.2 The input process *TINPUTS* of Example 13.2.2 is non-retracting, and so it is eventually non-retracting.

If only one input channel can be live at any time, then the external choice might be replaced by a timeout:

$$
TINPUTS2 \quad = \quad in_1?x : T \xrightarrow{1} out!x \rightarrow TINPUTS2
$$
$$
\overset{3}{\triangleright} in_2?x : T \xrightarrow{2} out!x \rightarrow TINPUTS2
$$

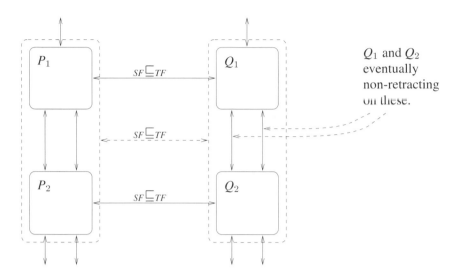

Fig. 13.7 **_Eventual non-retraction on an interface set preserves timewise refinement_**

This process is no longer non-retracting, since the offer of input along in_1 is withdrawn at time 3 if it has not been accepted. On the other hand, the process is eventually non-retracting, since any offers made after 3 seconds of *TINPUTS2* becoming enabled will not be withdrawn.

Polling provides an alternative way of checking for input:

$$TINPUTS3 \quad = \quad in_1?x : T \xrightarrow{2} out!x \rightarrow TINPUTS3$$
$$\overset{3}{\triangleright} in_2?x : T \xrightarrow{2} out!x \rightarrow TINPUTS3$$
$$\overset{3}{\triangleright} TINPUTS3$$

In this process definition there is an instance of a recursive call, the final *TINPUTS3* reached after two timeouts, which is not event guarded. Accordingly, *TINPUTS3* is not eventually non-retracting, since offers on both in_1 and in_2 will always be withdrawn. However, it is eventually non-retracting on the channel *out*.

The untimed process *INPUTS* of Example 13.2.2 is refined by both *TINPUTS* and *TINPUTS3*, but not by *TINPUTS2*. A transformation process

$$TRANS \quad = \quad out?x : T \rightarrow out_2!f(x) \rightarrow TRANS$$

is refined by the timed process

$$TTRANS \quad = \quad out?x : T \overset{[1,5]}{\rightarrow} out_2!f(x) \rightarrow TTRANS$$

This process is non-retracting, and hence eventually non-retracting on *out*. It follows that the parallel combination of *TINPUTS*3 and *TTRANS* will be a timewise refinement of *INPUTS* combined with *TRANS*:

$$INPUTS \parallel_{out} TRANS \quad _{SF}\sqsubseteq_{TF} \quad TINPUTS3 \parallel_{out} TTRANS$$

The eventual non-retraction property guarantees that *out* in the timed version of the process will always be available when predicted by the untimed version. The fact that the combination is not eventually non-retracting on the in_i channels does not affect the timewise refinement, since their availability as required by the untimed combination is guaranteed by the fact that $INPUTS \ _{SF}\sqsubseteq_{TF} TINPUTS3$. ∎

Promptness

It will often be the case that only one of the component processes needs to have a non-retracting property in order for timewise refinement to carry through parallel combinations: it will patiently wait for the other. However, this is not always sufficient. For example, consider the following two process descriptions. The alphabet renaming *succ* maps events of the form $mid.n$ to $mid.n + 1$ where $n \in \mathbb{N}$, and leaves other events unchanged.

$$OFFERS \quad = \quad (mid!0 \rightarrow STOP \ \square \ WAIT\ 1; succ(OFFERS))$$

$$WITHDRAWS \quad = \quad (mid?n : \mathbb{N} \rightarrow STOP) \overset{1}{\triangleright} succ(WITHDRAWS)$$

The process *WAIT* 2; *OFFERS* waits for 2 seconds, and then begins to offer outputs along channel *mid*, introducing a new possibility every second. No offer is ever withdrawn, and each recursive call introduces a new offer, so that by any time $n + 2$ it will be able to output any of the values from 0 to n. Furthermore, *WAIT* 2; *OFFERS* is a refinement of an untimed process which offers all of the possible outputs along channel *mid*:

$$UOFFERS = mid.n : mid.\mathbb{N} \rightarrow STOP \quad _{SF}\sqsubseteq_{TF} \quad WAIT\ 2; OFFERS$$

There is no output that the timed process can refuse for ever, and all the possible traces of the timed process are allowed by the untimed one.

The process *WITHDRAWS* is initially prepared to accept any value along the channel *mid*, but after each recursive call the lowest value still acceptable is withdrawn, so after $n + 1$ seconds it is no longer prepared to accept any value between 0 and n. This process most definitely fails to be non-retracting, or even eventually non-retracting. At any particular time, only finitely many possible inputs will have been withdrawn, so *WITHDRAWS* will refine an untimed process which can refuse finite sets of events:

$$UWITHDRAWS \quad _{SF}\sqsubseteq_{TF} \quad WITHDRAWS$$
$$UWITHDRAWS \quad = \quad \bigsqcap_{F \subseteq^{fin} \mathbb{N}} mid.n : mid.(\mathbb{N} \setminus F) \rightarrow STOP$$

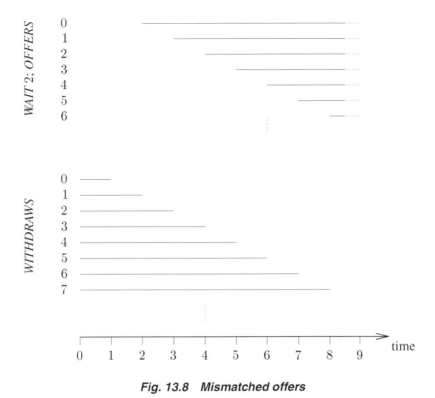

Fig. 13.8   Mismatched offers

This untimed process can perform any of the possible inputs, and can also refuse any finite subset of them. However, it cannot refuse all of them simultaneously.

When the two timed processes are placed in parallel, there is no event that they can agree on, since *WITHDRAWS* retracts the possibility of events before *WAIT* 2; *OFFERS* enables them, as illustrated in Figure 13.8. This means that the parallel combination can refuse all events over all time.

However, $UOFFERS \parallel_{mid.\mathbb{N}} UWITHDRAWS$ is not able to refuse all events, so it is not refined by $OFFERS \parallel_{mid.\mathbb{N}} WITHDRAWS$. The timed combination has a behaviour not allowed by the untimed. The processes are unable to interact because the offers made by the process *OFFERS* take for ever to be made available. This can be avoided by requiring all offers to be made by some specific time.

A process which guarantees to make all of its offers within some specific time is said to be *prompt*. Any process which has both non-retracting properties and promptness properties will guarantee to preserve failures timewise refinement through parallel composition, without any constraints on the other parallel process. The fact that a process Q_1 is guaranteed to have made all of its offers within some particular time, and is guaranteed not to retract them, means

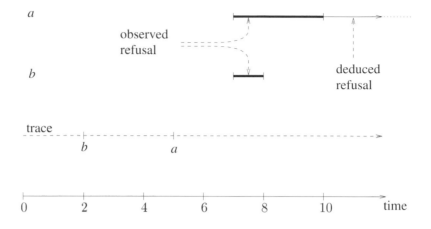

Fig. 13.9 *3-promptness on a timed failure*

that any inability of Q_1 and Q_2 to interact will be entirely the responsibility of Q_2 and so it will already be allowed in the untimed process P_2 that is refined by Q_2.

A process is defined to be *prompt* if after any trace the environment of the process need only wait some finite time for any events that the process is going to offer. Any events not offered during that time may be refused for ever.

A process Q is prompt if:

$$(s, \aleph) \in \mathcal{TF}\,[\![Q]\!] \quad \Rightarrow \quad \exists t : \mathbb{R}^+ \bullet \forall t' : \mathbb{R}^+; \ A \subseteq \Sigma^{\checkmark} \bullet$$
$$[t', t' + t) \times A \subseteq \aleph \wedge t' \geqslant end(s)$$
$$\Rightarrow (s, \aleph \cup [t', \infty) \times A) \in \mathcal{TF}\,[\![Q]\!]$$

If a set of events A can be refused after the end of the trace for an interval of length t, then A can be refused for ever after that point. Any offers from a prompt process Q have to be made within t, so a refusal over t time units indicates that such offers will not be forthcoming.

A process is said to be *d-prompt* if the same value d will serve as the appropriate time t for any observation $(s, \aleph) \in \mathcal{TF}\,[\![Q]\!]$.

The definition is illustrated in Figure 13.9. If the process exhibiting the timed failure is 3-prompt, then the observation of a's refusal for 3 time units allows the conclusion that a can be refused for ever from that point on. The refusal of b for one time unit is insufficient to allow further refusals to be deduced concerning b.

Promptness may be restricted to a particular set of events, since to preserve timewise refinement it will only be required on the interface set. A process is *prompt on a set* $A \subseteq \Sigma^{\checkmark}$ if there is some finite length of time necessary to wait for events from the set A, but there need be no restrictions on other events. The definition is obtained by replacing the set $\Sigma^{\checkmark}$ in the definition of 'prompt' by the set A, restricting concern only to those sets that are contained in A.

If a process is prompt on a set A_1 and on another set A_2, then it will also be prompt on their union $A_1 \cup A_2$ and on any subset of it.

For example, the waiter process $WAIT\ d;\ order \stackrel{10}{\rightarrow} serve \rightarrow STOP$ will be prompt for any d, since there is some time $d + 1$ within which any initial offer is guaranteed to be made. However, the arbitrary choice of the initial delay d loses promptness: $\sqcap_{d \in \mathbb{R}+} WAIT\ d;\ order \stackrel{10}{\rightarrow} serve \rightarrow STOP$ is no longer prompt, since there is no time by which the initial event is guaranteed to have been offered, but neither can it be refused for all time. However, it is prompt on $serve$ since this event is always guaranteed to be offered after 10 minutes of placing the order.

Many of the timed CSP operators preserve the property of promptness, and of promptness on a set A. Those that do not are the hiding operator, infinite internal choice, infinite-to-one alphabet renaming, sequential composition, synchronizing parallel operators, and those recursive definitions that either contain any of these operators or else are not event guarded. Unbounded nondeterminism does not preserve promptness, since each component may have some time by which a response is guaranteed without there being a uniform time for all of the components.

As discussed earlier, processes which are non-retracting and prompt will be useful in ensuring that timewise refinement is preserved by parallel combination. In particular, if Q_1 is both eventually non-retracting on the set $A^\checkmark$ and prompt on the set $A^\checkmark$, and $P_1\ _{SF}\sqsubseteq_{TF} Q_1$ and $P_2\ _{SF}\sqsubseteq_{TF} Q_2$, then

- $Q_1 \parallel_A Q_2$ will be a failures timewise refinement of $P_1 \parallel_A P_2$;

- $Q_1\ _B\parallel_C Q_2$ will be a failures timewise refinement of $P_1\ _B\parallel_C P_2$ if $A = B \cap C$.

These results place no conditions upon Q_2, which can be an arbitrary timed refinement of P_2. This is useful in cases where very little is known about Q_2. Such a situation might arise where Q_2 is known only to be a timewise refinement of P_2, and there is no separate timed process description. The process Q_1 takes all the responsibility for ensuring that the timed processes synchronize whenever they are expected to.

It need not be necessary for a single process to take responsibility for all of the inter-actions between the two processes. Each process might take responsibility for part of the interface, guaranteeing that the required interactions for some subset of the synchronizing events. If Q_1 is eventually non-retracting and prompt on $A_1^\checkmark$, and Q_2 is eventually non-retracting and prompt on A_2, then Q_1 and Q_2 are guaranteed to synchronize successfully on all of these events whenever their untimed versions require it, and

$$P_1 \parallel_{(A_1 \cup A_2)} P_2\ _{SF}\sqsubseteq_{TF} Q_1 \parallel_{(A_1 \cup A_2)} Q_2$$

For example, if all timed processes are eventually non-retracting and prompt on all of their input channels, and each channel connects exactly two processes—one sending process and one receiving process for that channel—then a network of such processes is guaranteed to

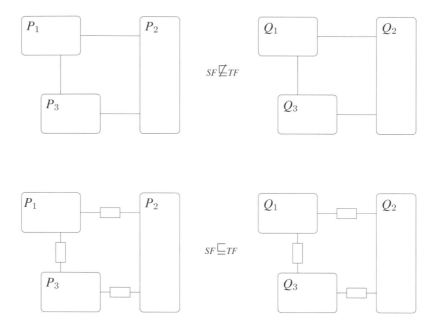

Fig. 13.10 *Introducing buffers to preserve refinement*

preserve timewise refinement. A similar result holds for the situation where all processes are non-retracting and prompt on output, as is the case in the programming language occam2. Timewise refinement can also be achieved for an arbitrary network of processes by replacing every channel between processes by a prompt and non-retracting buffer such as *TCOPY*. This is illustrated in Figure 13.10. Each version of *TCOPY* is non-retracting and prompt on both of its channels, and every synchronization in the network involves one of the *TCOPY* processes, so the result will refine the same transformation at the untimed level.

Finite interfaces

If the interface $A^{\checkmark}$ between two processes is finite, then eventual non-retraction of a process Q on the set $A^{\checkmark}$ implies that Q is also prompt on $A^{\checkmark}$. Once the point where offers will not be retracted is reached, each event a in A is either refusable for ever, or else must be offered by some time t_a. Finiteness of A means that there is a maximal t_a, and this is the time after which all events in A that will be offered at all are guaranteed to be offered. This means that if Q_1 is eventually non-retracting on the finite set $A^{\checkmark}$, then failures timewise refinement will be preserved for parallel combinations involving Q_1 whenever the synchronization set is A. If Q_1 is eventually non-retracting, then it will preserve timewise refinement in any parallel combination where the interface set is finite.

The same result holds if the synchronization set A can be partitioned into two sets A_1 and A_2 so that Q_1 is non-retracting on $A_1^{\checkmark}$ and Q_2 is non-retracting on A_2.

The result also extends to cases where the interface set A consists of a finite number of channels, provided firstly that each channel in A is associated with exactly two processes, one sending and one receiving, and each channel c has one of the component processes non-retracting on it; and secondly that the timed processes do not discriminate on input. This means that whenever any input is possible then all inputs must be possible: and if any input can be refused at some point, then all inputs can be refused at that point. For example, the process $in?n : \mathbb{N} \rightarrow out!n \rightarrow STOP$ does not discriminate on input, whereas the process $in?n : \mathbb{N} \rightarrow in?m : (\mathbb{N} \setminus \{n\}) \rightarrow out!n \rightarrow STOP$ does, since the permitted second input is dependent on the first input that occurred. To achieve non-discrimination on input, any input construction of the form $c?x : T \rightarrow P(x)$ should only use the type of the channel c as the set T of permitted inputs.

Compactness

A final condition for preservation of timewise refinement is *compactness* in untimed processes. This means that all the information about the refusals of a process are contained in its finite refusal sets: an infinite set X can be refused precisely when all of its finite subsets can be. For example, the process *UOFFERS* defined on page 420 is compact, but the process *WITHDRAWS* is not. In fact, any untimed process with no infinite nondeterminism will be compact. Since infinite nondeterminism is introduced only by infinite internal choice, hiding, and infinite-to-one renaming, any untimed process description which contains none of these operators must be compact.

Eventual non-retraction of a timed process Q_1 on a set A will imply promptness on all finite subsets of A. In the case of a compact untimed process P_1 timewise refined by Q_1, this means that timed refusals of $Q_1 \underset{A}{\|} Q_2$ involving only finitely many events will be reflected in $P_1 \underset{A}{\|} P_2$. This means that an arbitrary timed refusal of $Q_1 \underset{A}{\|} Q_2$ will have all of its finite subsets allowed by the untimed parallel combination, and so by compactness the entire refusal will also be allowed.

Hence, when the untimed processes are compact, then timewise refinement will be preserved whenever one of the timed processes is eventually non-retracting, or alternatively whenever the synchronization set can be partitioned so that each timed component is non-retracting on one of the partition sets.

Summary

The results discussed above are summarized in Figure 13.11 for $P_1 \ _{SF}\sqsubseteq_{TF} Q_1$ and $P_2 \ _{SF}\sqsubseteq_{TF} Q_2$, where $A_1 \cup A_2 = A = A_3 \cap A_4$ as illustrated in Figure 13.12. Figure 13.11 gives sufficient conditions for refinement to be preserved by the parallel combinations: $P_1 \ _{A_3}\|_{A_4} P_2 \ _{SF}\sqsubseteq_{TF} Q_1 \ _{A_3}\|_{A_4} Q_2$, and $P_1 \underset{A}{\|} P_2 \ _{SF}\sqsubseteq_{TF} Q_1 \underset{A}{\|} Q_2$. The special case $A = A_1, A_2 = \{\}$ is applicable even when no guarantees can be made about the behaviour of Q_2.

P_1	P_2	Q_1	Q_2	A
—	—	eventually non-retracting on $A^\checkmark$	eventually non-retracting on $A^\checkmark$	—
—	—	eventually non-retracting on $A_1^\checkmark$ and prompt on $A_1^\checkmark$	eventually non-retracting on A_2 and prompt on A_2	$A = A_1 \cup A_2$
—	—	eventually non-retracting on $A_1^\checkmark$	eventually non-retracting on A_2	A finite, $A = A_1 \cup A_2$
—	—	eventually non-retracting on $A_1^\checkmark$, non-discriminating on all channels in A_1	eventually non-retracting on A_2, non-discriminating on all channels in A_2	A finite set of channels, $A = A_1 \cup A_2$
compact	compact	eventually non-retracting on $A_1^\checkmark$	eventually non-retracting on A_2	$A = A_1 \cup A_2$

Fig. 13.11 *Conditions for synchronization on A to preserve failures timewise refinement*

Example 13.3.3 (Chaining timed buffers) The untimed specification *NBUFF* introduced in Chapter 6 was used to specify buffers by means of the refinement relation. A non-divergent process B is a buffer precisely when $NBUFF \sqsubseteq_{SF} B$. The process *NBUFF* may also be used to specify timed buffers by means of timewise refinement: a timed CSP process TB is a buffer if and only if $NBUFF \; {}_{SF}\sqsubseteq_{TF} TB$. This means that TB must behave as a first-in-first-out queue, and should never be able permanently to refuse input when empty, nor be able permanently to refuse output when non-empty.

Roscoe's first buffer law states that the chaining together of two buffers produces another buffer. This is not always true in the timed world, since the output of the first buffer might never synchronize with the input of the second, even though both components individually will always eventually offer to communicate. On the other hand, if one of the buffers is eventually non-retracting on their common channel, then their composition will result in another buffer. This is justified by the general results about timewise refinement.

Consider two timed buffers TB_1 and TB_2 of type T, which are both timewise refinements of *NBUFF*, and where TB_1 is eventually non-retracting on $out.T^\checkmark$. Their composition under chaining is equivalent to

$$(swap_{out,mid}(TB_1) \parallel swap_{in,mid}(TB_2)) \setminus mid.T$$

This definition involves one-one alphabet renaming, parallel composition, and abstraction.

The alphabet renaming preserves timewise refinement, so

$$swap_{out,mid}(NBUFF) \quad {}_{SF}\sqsubseteq_{TF} \quad swap_{out,mid}(TB_1)$$

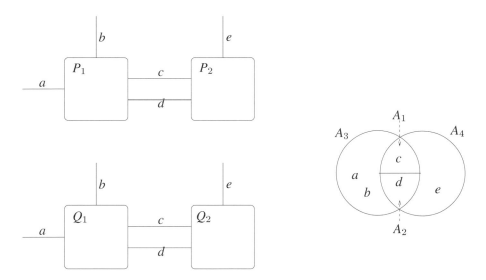

Fig. 13.12   *Interfaces of a parallel combination*

and

$$swap_{mid,in}(NBUFF) \quad _{SF}\sqsubseteq_{TF} \quad swap_{mid,in}(TB_2)$$

It also preserves eventual non-retraction, though it translates the non-retracting set of events, so $swap_{out,mid}(TB_1)$ is eventually non-retracting on $swap_{out,mid}(out.T) = mid.T$.

The untimed process *NBUFF* is compact, and compactness is also preserved by one-one renaming. Furthermore, the two components only synchronize on *mid*, on which the first component is eventually non-retracting, so the conditions are present for the timewise refinements to be preserved by the parallel composition:

$$swap_{out,mid}(NBUFF) \parallel swap_{in,mid}(NBUFF)$$
$$_{SF}\sqsubseteq_{TF} \quad swap_{out,mid}(TB_1) \parallel swap_{in,mid}(TB_2)$$

Finally, abstraction preserves timewise refinement, so hiding the channel *mid* in both the untimed and the timed process descriptions yields the definitions of chaining again:

$$NBUFF \gg NBUFF \quad _{SF}\sqsubseteq_{TF} \quad TB_1 \gg TB_2$$

The untimed buffer law states that $NBUFF \sqsubseteq_{SF} NBUFF \gg NBUFF$, so it follows that $NBUFF \ _{SF}\sqsubseteq_{TF} TB_1 \gg TB_2$: the chaining of the two timed buffers produces another buffer.

A longer chain of timed buffers will thus form a buffer if all of the components are non-retracting on output, or if all of them are non-retracting on input, or if alternate buffers are non-retracting on both input and output. This last observation means that if a stable buffer such as *TCOPY* is placed between all adjacent timed buffers in a chain, then the result is guaranteed to be another timed buffer.   ∎

Translating specifications

A specification in the stable failures model consists of two parts: a predicate $S_T(tr)$ on traces, and a predicate $S_F(tr, X)$ on stable failures. A process P satisfies such a specification if the behaviours in the three sets that make up its semantics all meet the appropriate predicate. Whenever $P \;_{SF}\!\sqsubseteq_{TF} Q$ then all the behaviours of the timed process Q must be permitted by P, which means that they will be constrained by the specification S.

The presence in the semantics of Q of a timed failure $(s, \aleph)$ with a finite timed trace s, and containing some infinite refusal token $[t, \infty) \times A \subseteq \aleph$, means that the untimed failure $(strip(s), A)$ must be present in the failures $\mathcal{SF}[\![P]\!]$. Thus $S_T(strip(s))$ and $S_F(strip(s), A)$ must hold. In this way the constraints on the behaviours of P translate to a constraint on the finite trace observations of Q.

The timed translation of an untimed specification $S = (S_T(tr), S_F(tr, X))$ is therefore

$$\#s < \infty \Rightarrow \; \begin{aligned} &S_T(strip(s)) \wedge \\ &(\forall t : \mathbb{R}^+ ; \; A \subseteq \Sigma^{\checkmark} \bullet ([t, \infty) \times A \subseteq \aleph \Rightarrow S_F(strip(s), A)) \end{aligned}$$

If P **sat** S and $P \;_{SF}\!\sqsubseteq_{TF} Q$ then Q will satisfy the timed translation of S.

Example 13.3.4 (Deadlock-freedom) The untimed specification of deadlock-freedom simply requires that the refusal set should never be all events: $S_F(tr, X) = X \neq \Sigma^{\checkmark}$. No restrictions are imposed on traces (so $S_T(tr)$ is always true).

The timed translation of deadlock-freedom is equivalent to

$$\#s < \infty \Rightarrow (\forall t : \mathbb{R}^+ ; \; A \subseteq \Sigma^{\checkmark} \bullet [t, \infty) \times A \subseteq \aleph) \Rightarrow A \neq \Sigma^{\checkmark}$$

which reduces to

$$\forall t : \mathbb{R}^+ \bullet t > end(s) \Rightarrow [t, \infty) \times \Sigma^{\checkmark} \not\subseteq \aleph$$

There is no point after the end of a trace from which $\Sigma^{\checkmark}$ may be permanently refused. Some interaction will always eventually be offered by the process. Deadlock-freedom is preserved by timewise refinement: if P is deadlock-free, and $P \;_{SF}\!\sqsubseteq_{TF} Q$, then Q is deadlock-free.   ∎

Example 13.3.5 (Buffers) The untimed specification of a buffer is expressed as follows:

$$\begin{aligned} Buff_T(tr) &= tr \Downarrow out \leqslant tr \Downarrow in \\ Buff_F(tr, X) &= tr \Downarrow out = tr \Downarrow in \Rightarrow X \cap in.T = \{\} \wedge \\ &\quad\; tr \Downarrow out < tr \Downarrow in \Rightarrow out.T \not\subseteq X \end{aligned}$$

The translation of the buffer specification into a timed specification results in

$$
\begin{aligned}
TBuff(s, \aleph) \quad = \quad & s \Downarrow out \leqslant s \Downarrow in \wedge \\
& s \Downarrow out = s \Downarrow in \Rightarrow \forall t : \mathbb{R}^+ ;\ v : T \bullet [t, \infty) \times \{in.v\} \not\subseteq \aleph \wedge \\
& s \Downarrow out < s \Downarrow in \Rightarrow \forall t : \mathbb{R}^+ \bullet [t, \infty) \times out.T \not\subseteq \aleph
\end{aligned}
$$

This states that the output sequence of values should match the input sequence, that all possible input should always eventually be offered if the buffer is empty, and that the appropriate output should always eventually be offered if the buffer is non-empty. ∎

If a timed specification is expressible as a translation of an untimed specification, then there is a completeness result as for trace timewise refinement, asserting the existence of an untimed process meeting the untimed specification. If a timed specification $S(s, \aleph)$ can be expressed in a form

$$
\#s < \infty \Rightarrow (S_T(strip(s)) \wedge \forall t : \mathbb{R}^+ ;\ A \subseteq \Sigma \bullet S_F(strip(s), A)))
$$

then it is dependent only on the sequences of events in the (finite) timed trace s and on sets that can be refused for ever after the end of the trace. Then whenever Q **sat** $S(s, \aleph)$ there is some (divergence-free) untimed CSP process $P \ _{SF}\sqsubseteq_{TF} Q$ such that P **sat** $(S_T(tr), S_F(tr, X))$.

Completeness again allows results to be translated freely between the untimed failures model and the timed model, permitting each stage of the analysis of a system to be carried out at the most suitable level of abstraction.

Conversely, properties which are not expressible in terms of specifications on individual process behaviours might not be preserved or translated by refinement. The property of being deterministic, for example, is expressed in terms of the relationships between different behaviours in a process's semantics, rather than as a property which must be met by all behaviours. Thus an untimed process may be deterministic, but have a nondeterministic timewise refinement. The untimed waiter process $order \rightarrow serve \rightarrow STOP$ is deterministic. A timed version such as $WAIT[0, 20]; order \overset{10}{\rightarrow} serve \rightarrow STOP$ refines the untimed version, yet it introduces some nondeterminism in the time dimension: at time 5, the order might be taken or it might be refused. The untimed version is blind to this distinction, requiring only that the waiter eventually be ready to take the order.

Example 13.3.6 (Timed alternating bit protocol) Example 7.3.2 gave an untimed verification of the alternating bit protocol. The implementation of the protocol might involve some timing considerations, and it will be necessary to ensure that the timed implementation preserves the correctness result previously established.

The sender process includes the possibility of retransmitting the tagged message as an alternative to receiving the acknowledgement. An implementation would aim to delay this retransmission for some optimal time. If transmission of messages is expensive then retransmission may be delayed until after an acknowledgement is expected. If transmission of messages is relatively cheap, the medium unreliable, and the round trip for a message relatively lengthy, then it may send several copies of the message before an acknowledgement is expected. Acknowledgements on the other hand are more likely to be accepted at any time.

One possible timed version of the sender process is as follows:

$$
\begin{aligned}
TS &= TS(0) \\
TS(b) &= in?x : T \xrightarrow{1} c_1!(x.b) \xrightarrow{1} TS(b,x) \\
TS(b,x) &= WAIT\,15; c_1!(x.b) \xrightarrow{1} TS(b,x) \\
&\quad\ \square\ d_2.b \xrightarrow{1} TS(\bar{b}) \\
&\quad\ \square\ d_2.\bar{b} \xrightarrow{1} TS(b,x)
\end{aligned}
$$

This is a failures timewise refinement of the untimed sender process S, and furthermore it is non-retracting and prompt. The delay before retransmission has been set at 15 time units, though the analysis to follow will be appropriate for any delay.

A timed version of the receiver process might simply introduce the delays between successive events:

$$
\begin{aligned}
TR &= TR(0) \\
TR(b) &= c_2?x.b' : T.\{b\} \xrightarrow{1} out!x \xrightarrow{1} d_1!b \xrightarrow{1} TR(\bar{b}) \\
&\quad\ \square\ c_2?x.b' : T.\{\bar{b}\} \xrightarrow{1} d_1!\bar{b} \xrightarrow{1} TR(b)
\end{aligned}
$$

This process is also non-retracting and prompt, and $R \ _{SF}\sqsubseteq_{TF}\ TR$. Hence the combination $TS \ |||\ TR$ is both non-retracting and prompt.

The timed specification for the two media will simply be the translation of the untimed specifications $Med(c_1,c_2)$ and $Med(d_1,d_2)$. However, non-retraction properties are not guaranteed. Some timed properties such as d-promptness might be pertinent in the timed analysis to decide the optimal delay before retransmission, but they are not necessary to establish functional correctness. The (non-terminating) timed media $TMED(c)$ and $TMED(d)$ will refine some untimed media $MED(c)$ and $MED(d)$ which satisfy the untimed specifications $Med(c_1,c_2)$ and $Med(d_1,d_2)$ respectively, as a consequence of the completeness result. The combination of the timed media thus refines the combination of the untimed:

$$
MED(c) \ |||\ MED(d) \quad _{SF}\sqsubseteq_{TF} \quad TMED(c) \ |||\ TMED(d)
$$

so the non-retraction and promptness of the sender and receiver means that

$$
\begin{aligned}
&(S \ |||\ R) \ ||\ (MED(c) \ ||\ MED(d)) \\
&_{SF}\sqsubseteq_{TF}\ \ (TS \ |||\ TR) \ ||\ (TMED(c) \ |||\ TMED(d))
\end{aligned}
$$

and hence that

$$ABP \quad {}_{SF}\sqsubseteq_{TF} \quad ((TS \;|||\; TR) \;||\; (TMED(c) \;|||\; TMED(d))) \setminus \left(\begin{array}{c} c_1.T \cup c_2.T \\ \cup\, d_1.T \cup d_2.T \end{array} \right)$$

Since *ABP* is a buffer, it follows that the timed version is also a buffer.

If the choice between transmission of a message and receipt of an acknowledgement is implemented by polling, alternating repeatedly on the two possibilities, then timewise refinement is not guaranteed. Indeed, since the media are not guaranteed to be non-retracting, the sender might never successfully pass the message to *TMED(c)* and so never make any progress. ∎

13.4 CASE STUDY: A RAILWAY CROSSING

This example gives an extremely simple model of a railway crossing which is nevertheless complex enough to illustrate a number of aspects of the modelling and verification of timed systems and the role that timewise refinement can play.

The system is described as consisting of three components: a train, a gate, and a gate controller. The gate should be up to allow traffic to pass when no train is approaching, but should be lowered to obstruct traffic when a train is close to reaching the crossing. It is the task of the controller to monitor the approach of a train, and to instruct the gate to be lowered within the appropriate time. The train is modelled at a high level of abstraction: the only relevant aspects of the train's behaviour are when it is nearing the crossing, when it is entering it, when it is leaving it; and the minimum delays between these events.

A number of safety conditions are formulated. These require the gate to be down when the train enters the crossing; the gate not to change state for 10 time units before the train enters the crossing; and the train to have left the crossing by the time the gate goes up. The liveness property that the crossing is deadlock-free is also required. A system that deadlocked with the gate down would meet the safety conditions, but would not be satisfactory.

The analysis begins with an untimed description of the system, to investigate which of these properties may be verified at the untimed level. The process descriptions are kept as simple as possible, including only those events that are relevant to consideration of these properties.

The gate controller *CONTROLLER* receives two types of signal from the crossing sensors: *near.ind*, which informs the controller that the train is approaching, and *out.ind*, which indicates that the train has left the crossing. It sends two types of signal to the crossing gate mechanism: *down.command*, and *up.command*, which instruct the gate to go down and up respectively. It also receives a confirmation *confirm* from the gate. These five events form the alphabet *C* of the controller.

The gate, modelled by *GATE*, responds to the commands sent by the controller. The additional events *up* and *down* are included to model the position of the gate. These two events, together with *up.command* and *down.command* and the confirmation *confirm*, form the alphabet *G* of the gate.

This results in the following description of the crossing mechanism:

$$CROSSING \quad = \quad CONTROLLER \;_C\|_G\; GATE$$

The controller responds to sensory inputs by issuing gate command signals:

$$CONTROLLER \quad = \quad near.ind \rightarrow down.command \rightarrow confirm \rightarrow CONTROLLER$$
$$\square$$
$$out.ind \rightarrow up.command \rightarrow confirm \rightarrow CONTROLLER$$

The gate process responds to the controller's signals by raising and lowering the gate.

$$GATE \quad = \quad down.command \rightarrow down \rightarrow confirm \rightarrow GATE$$
$$\square$$
$$up.command \rightarrow up \rightarrow confirm \rightarrow GATE$$

To reason about the behaviour of the system as a train approaches and reaches the crossing, the effect of such a happening is modelled via the crossing sensors. The train triggers the sensors by means of the *near.ind* and *out.ind* events. The events *train.near*, *enter.crossing*, and *leave.crossing* model respectively the situations where the train is close to the crossing, the train enters the crossing, and the train leaves the crossing. These five events are all that are required for the sake of this analysis: they form the alphabet *T* of the train.

The process *TRAIN* will be used to model the approach of the train, and its effect upon the crossing system.

$$TRAIN \quad = \quad train.near \rightarrow near.ind \rightarrow enter.crossing \rightarrow$$
$$leave.crossing \rightarrow out.ind \rightarrow TRAIN$$

The crossing system, in conjunction with the train, is described as follows, and illustrated in Figure 13.13.

$$SYSTEM \quad = \quad TRAIN \;_T\|_{C \cup G}\; CROSSING$$

The properties given earlier can now be expressed in terms of the events chosen to model the system.

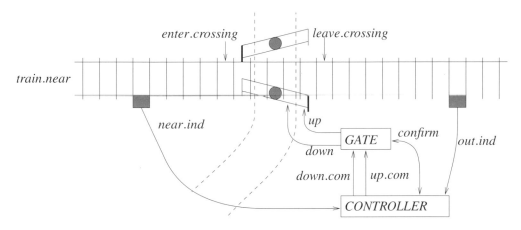

Fig. 13.13   The railway crossing system

If the train enters the crossing, then the gate should have gone down more recently than it went up:

$$Safety1(tr) \quad = \quad last(tr) = enter.crossing \Rightarrow last(tr \upharpoonright \{down, up\}) = down$$

If the train enters the crossing at time t, then no *down* or *up* events should have occurred in the preceding 10 time units; the projection of the trace to those events over that interval is empty.

$$Safety2(s, \aleph) \quad = \quad \forall t : \mathbb{R}^+ \bullet enter.crossing \text{ at } t \Rightarrow \text{no}\{down, up\} \text{ at } [t - 10, t]$$

If the gate goes up, then the train must have left the crossing more recently than it entered it:

$$Safety3(tr) \quad = \quad last(tr) = up \Rightarrow$$
$$last(tr \upharpoonright \{enter.crossing, leave.crossing\}) = leave.crossing$$

Finally, the system must be deadlock-free.

$$Liveness1(tr, X) \quad = \quad X \neq \Sigma$$

Each of these properties has been expressed at the highest possible level of abstraction. In each case, the simplest model has been used to capture the required property. Safety properties 1 and 3 are expressible in the untimed traces model. Safety property 2 concerns explicit timing issues, so the timed model is required in order to express it. Deadlock-freedom is expressible using the untimed failures model.

Safety properties 1 and 3, and the liveness property, are candidates for being established by the untimed system description. They may be established by use of algebraic laws, or by use of proof rules. An alternative approach would be to use model-checking to examine these properties directly. The states of the system are shown in Figure 13.14. Examination of the diagram reveals that at any point where *up* is possible, there must have been a *leave.crossing* event more recently than an *enter.crossing* event. Thus *Safety*3 is satisfied. On the other hand, there are *enter.crossing* transitions where *up* is more recent than *down*, showing that in fact *Safety*1 is not satisfied. Even though it is expressible as an untimed requirement, it turns out that its validity rests upon the timing properties of the system, in particular that the gate goes down in less time than it takes for the train to reach the crossing. Finally, every state has some transition out of it, so the system is deadlock-free, meeting the liveness requirement. Both *Safety*3 and *Liveness*1 are easily checked by the Failures Divergences Refinement model-checker FDR (see Appendix B).

Timewise refinement allows timing information to be added to the description of the system while preserving the properties already established. The timing information we have about the train is firstly included: that it takes at least 5 minutes from triggering the *near.ind* sensor to reach the crossing; and that it takes at least 20 seconds to get across the crossing.

$$TTRAIN = train.near \to near.ind \overset{300}{\to} enter.crossing \overset{20}{\to}$$
$$leave.crossing \to out.ind \to TTRAIN$$

The controller takes a negligible amount of time ϵ from receiving a signal from a sensor to relaying the corresponding instruction to the gate.

$$TCONTROLLER = near.ind \overset{\epsilon}{\to} down.command \to confirm \to TCONTROLLER$$
$$\square$$
$$out.ind \overset{\epsilon}{\to} up.command \to confirm \to TCONTROLLER$$

The timed gate process *TGATE* process takes a non-negligible amount of time to get the gate into position following an instruction:

$$TGATE = down.command \overset{100}{\to} down \to confirm \to TGATE$$
$$\square$$
$$up.command \overset{100}{\to} up \to confirm \to TGATE$$

However, this is still considerably less time than it takes for the train to reach the crossing, so the timed description is sufficiently detailed to establish *Safety*1, under the additional assumptions that the events *up* and *down* are entirely under the control of the *GATE*, and the commands *up.command* and *down.command* are urgent. These assumptions are captured as

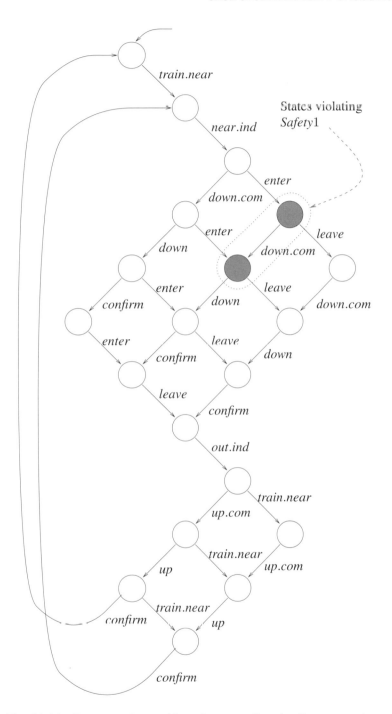

Fig. 13.14 States and transitions for an untimed railway crossing

$\{up, down, up.command, down.command\}$ active, and so the specification met by the system is

$$\{up, down, up.command, down.command\} \text{ active} \Rightarrow \mathit{Safety}1(strip(s))$$

The timed description is also sufficient to establish $\mathit{Safety}2$ provided up and $down$ and their corresponding commands are active.

The timed process descriptions are simply the untimed process descriptions with times added. The timed system trace timewise refines the untimed one, ensuring that the timed system meets $\mathit{Safety}3(strip(s))$.

Finally, the three component timed processes are all non-retracting and have finite interfaces. This ensures that the system consisting of their parallel combination is a failures timewise refinement of the untimed system, so it retains the untimed property $\mathit{Liveness}1$.

13.5 FDI TIMEWISE REFINEMENT

A timewise refinement of a process with respect to the FDI model will have to be consistent with the untimed failures, divergences, and infinite traces information. This requires an understanding of this untimed information within the context of the timed model.

An untimed divergence tr of a process P indicates that there is some sequence of events $tr' \leqslant tr$ which can be performed by P, followed by the possibility of an infinite sequence of internal transitions corresponding to some form of internal loop, or divergence. In the absence of timing information this is considered pessimistically as catastrophic, since it is possible that this execution will consume all available computing resources and thereby block any other activity. In the context of time, a more precise view is taken of infinite sequences of internal actions: they may be categorized as time divergences if they all occur at one instant, as Zeno divergences if they approach some finite time, or as well-timed if it takes for ever for the entire sequence to occur. Only the last is possible for well-timed processes, for which divergences are not catastrophic. There is no behaviour of a well-timed process that requires a treatment of divergence as pessimistic as the treatment in the FDI model. Indeed, this is the reason why divergences do not appear in the timed failures model. From the point of view of refinement, if a divergent process is acceptable in the untimed world, then any timed process will be acceptable, and hence will be a timewise refinement.

An untimed failure (tr, X) in the FDI model can be associated with P for one of two reasons. It may be that tr is a divergence of P, and so (tr, X) is included in the set of failures of P because any behaviour after divergence is acceptable. Alternatively, if tr is not a divergence of P then (tr, X) represents the observation of the sequence of events listed in tr, followed by the eventual arrival into a stable state from which none of the events in the refusal set X can be performed. The fact that tr is not a divergence of P means that only a finite number of internal actions can occur before a stable state is reached, and the set X is a refusal of one of these states that might possibly be reached. Unlike a timed failure, no information is contained in the untimed failure (tr, X) concerning the refusal of events during the performance of the trace; the only refusal information follows the end of the trace.

Infinite sequences of internal events do not require special consideration within the context of time, since they will always be associated with well-behaved executions. The timed understanding of the failure (tr, X) is that following occurrence of the sequence of events in tr, if no other visible events are performed then the execution will eventually reach a point after which all events in X can be refused for the remainder of the execution. In other words, it should be possible to associate with the execution a timed refusal set of the form $[t, \infty) \times X$. This allows for stable states (reached at time t) which can only evolve and never perform internal events. It also includes those well-timed infinite sequences of internal events which can eventually reach a sequence of states in which X is always refused. The distinction between stable and unstable states is not so critical in the timed world, and a timed understanding of an untimed refusal is given in different terms.

The timed understanding of an untimed infinite timed trace u of P is more immediate: the sequence of events recorded in u should correspond to the sequence of visible events performed during some timed execution of the timed process.

A timed failure $(s, \aleph)$ of a process Q either has a finite or an infinite trace. If $\#s = \infty$ then the untimed behaviour consistent with $(s, \aleph)$ will be the infinite trace $u = strip(s)$. There will not be any untimed refusal information associated with it, since the trace is infinite.

If $\#s < \infty$, then there are a number of possible untimed behaviours consistent with $(s, \aleph)$. As in the stable failures case, if $[t, \infty) \times A \subseteq \aleph$ then $(strip(s), X)$ is consistent with $(s, \aleph)$.

The timed process Q will be an FDI timewise refinement of the untimed process P (written $P \,_{FDI}\sqsubseteq_{TF} Q$) if all of its timed failures are allowed by the untimed failures and infinite traces of P. The timed failures of Q will contain certain observations that would appear as particular untimed observations if recorded in an untimed context; and P should permit all of these observations. This is formally defined as follows:

$$
\begin{aligned}
P \,_{FDI}\sqsubseteq_{TF} Q \quad = \quad & \forall (s, \aleph) \in \mathcal{F}_{TI} \, [\![Q]\!]. \\
& \#s = \infty \Rightarrow strip(s) \in \mathcal{I} \, [\![P]\!] \\
& \wedge \; (\#s < \infty \wedge \exists t : \mathbb{R}^+ ; \; X \subseteq \Sigma \bullet ([t, \infty) \times X) \subseteq \aleph \\
& \qquad \Rightarrow (strip(s), X) \in \mathcal{F} \, [\![P]\!])
\end{aligned}
$$

Timed observations do not contain information about untimed divergences, so the divergences of the untimed process P do not appear directly in the definition. However, an untimed divergence does give rise to a set of failures and infinite traces, which will admit any refinement since all failures and infinite traces are present. For example, the untimed divergent process DIV has all possible failures and infinite traces, and so it will be timewise refined by any timed process Q. The process $a \to DIV$ allows any behaviour after the event a, so it will be timewise refined by any process whose first event must be a, and which cannot refuses a for ever before any events have occurred.

If P is divergence-free and closed, then the two failures timewise refinement relations are equivalent:

$$P \ _{SF}\sqsubseteq_{TF} Q \quad \Leftrightarrow \quad P \ _{FDI}\sqsubseteq_{TF} Q$$

If P is closed, then

$$P \ _{SF}\sqsubseteq_{TF} Q \quad \Rightarrow \quad P \ _{FDI}\sqsubseteq_{TF} Q$$

(since $\mathcal{SF}\,[\![P]\!] \subseteq \mathcal{F}\,[\![P]\!]$). It is only on the infinite traces that the FDI model can impose more constraints on a timed process Q than can be imposed from the stable failures model. For example, if $P(0) = STOP$) and $P(n+1) = a \rightarrow P(n)$, then

$$\bigsqcap_{n} P(n) \quad _{SF}\sqsubseteq_{TF} \quad N = a \stackrel{1}{\rightarrow} N$$

but the FDI timewise relationship does not hold between these two processes, since in that case the untimed process also requires that no infinite sequences of a events are possible.

Many of the results concerning failures timewise refinement are also applicable to FDI timewise refinement.

The FDI timewise refinement relationship holds between DIV and any timed process:

$$DIV \quad _{FDI}\sqsubseteq_{TF} \quad Q \text{ for any timed CSP process } Q$$

All of the other relationships, discussed on pages 412–413 also hold for FDI timewise refinement. With regard to parallel compositions, all of the conditions given in Figure 13.11 are also sufficient to guarantee that parallel compositions preserve FDI timewise refinement.

Refinement is again preserved by recursion, and from the FDI model the rule holds even when the untimed process M can diverge. This means that if the bodies of the recursive definitions $M = P$ and $N = Q$ respect the refinement relation, then the resulting processes will also be related. This means that if $P[X/M] \ _{FDI}\sqsubseteq_{TF} Q[Y/N]$ whenever $X \ _{FDI}\sqsubseteq_{TF} Y$, then $M \ _{FDI}\sqsubseteq_{TF} N$:

$$\frac{\forall X, Y \bullet (X \ _{FDI}\sqsubseteq_{TF} Y \Rightarrow P[X/M] \ _{FDI}\sqsubseteq_{TF} Q[Y/N])}{M \ _{FDI}\sqsubseteq_{TF} N} \quad \left[\begin{array}{l} M = P \\ N = Q \end{array} \right]$$

The generalization to mutual recursion also holds for arbitrary processes.

Translating specifications

A specification in the FDI model consists of three parts: a predicate $S_F(tr, X)$ on failures, a predicate $S_D(tr)$ on divergences, and a predicate $S_F(u)$ on infinite traces.

The presence in the semantics of Q of a timed failure $(s, \aleph)$ with a finite timed trace s, and containing some infinite refusal token $[t, \infty) \times A \subseteq \aleph$, means that the untimed behaviour $(strip(s), A)$ must be present in the failures $\mathcal{F}[\![P]\!]$, and hence that $S_F(strip(s), A)$ must hold. In this way the constraint on the failures of P translates to a constraint on the finite trace observations of Q.

The infinite traces of Q must also be present in the semantics of P, and will be constrained by the part of the untimed specification which is concerned with infinite traces. This means that if $\#s = \infty$, then $strip(s)$ will be in $\mathcal{I}[\![P]\!]$, and so $S_I(strip(s))$ must hold.

The third component of the untimed specification, $S_D(tr)$, does not impose any restrictions on the behaviours of Q, since none of those behaviours predict the presence of any divergences of P.

The timed translation of an FDI specification $S = (S_F(tr, X), S_I(u), S_D(tr))$ is therefore

$$\#s < \infty \Rightarrow (\forall t : \mathbb{R}^+; \ A \subseteq \Sigma \bullet ([t, \infty) \times A \subseteq \aleph \Rightarrow S_F(strip(s), A))$$
$$\wedge \ \#s = \infty \Rightarrow S_I(strip(s))$$

If P **sat** S and $P \ {}_{FDI}\!\sqsubseteq_{TF} Q$, then Q will satisfy the timed translation of S.

There is also a completeness result as for trace timewise refinement, asserting the existence of an untimed process meeting the untimed specification. If a timed specification $S(s, \aleph)$ can be expressed in a form

$$\#s < \infty \Rightarrow \forall t : \mathbb{R}^+; \ A \subseteq \Sigma^\checkmark \bullet S_F(strip(s), A))$$
$$\wedge \ \#s = \infty \Rightarrow S_I(strip(s))$$

then it is dependent only on the (finite and infinite) sequence of events in the timed trace s and on sets that can be refused for ever after the end of the trace. Then whenever Q **sat** $S(s, \aleph)$ there is some divergence-free untimed CSP process $P \ {}_{SF}\!\sqsubseteq_{TF} Q$ such that P **sat** $(S_F(tr, X), S_D(tr), S_I(u))$ for any arbitrary divergence specification $S_D(tr)$.

As in the stable failures case, completeness allows results to be translated freely between the untimed FDI model and the timed model, permitting each stage of the analysis of a system to be carried out at the most suitable level of abstraction.

13.6   TESTING AND TIMEWISE REFINEMENT

Testing equivalences in the forms of may and must testing have been given in earlier chapters for both untimed and timed CSP. May and must testing are also associated with refinement relations at both the untimed and the timed levels:

$$P_1 \sqsubseteq_{may} P_2 \quad = \quad \forall T \bullet \neg (P_1 \textbf{ may } T) \Rightarrow \neg (P_2 \textbf{ may } T)$$

$$P_1 \sqsubseteq_{must} P_2 \quad = \quad \forall T \bullet P_1 \textbf{ must } T \Rightarrow P_2 \textbf{ must } T$$

If P_1, P_2 and T all range over untimed CSP process expressions, then the refinement relation given by **may** testing is traces refinement, and that given by **must** testing is *FDI* refinement. If P_1, P_2 and T all range over timed CSP processes, then the relation given by **may** testing is finite timed failures refinement, and that given by **must** testing is full timed failures refinement.

Timewise refinement is concerned with the relationships between untimed CSP processes and timed CSP processes. A testing characterization of a timewise refinement $P \sqsubseteq Q$ between an untimed process P and a timed process Q will need to consider timed tests for Q and corresponding untimed tests for P.

One way of achieving this is to define a 'time removing' operator Θ which extracts an untimed transition semantics from the timed operational semantics for a timed CSP process. If a timed process T can perform an event transition, possibly after some evolution, then the corresponding untimed process $\Theta(T)$ is defined to ensure that it can also perform that event. The operation Θ is not a new CSP operator, it is rather a mechanism for executing a timed process in an untimed way, or providing an untimed view of a timed process.

$$\frac{T \xrightarrow{\mu} T'}{\Theta(T) \xrightarrow{\mu} \Theta(T')}$$

$$\frac{T \overset{d}{\rightsquigarrow} T' \qquad T' \xrightarrow{\mu} T''}{\Theta(T) \xrightarrow{\mu} \Theta(T'')}$$

For example, if

$$T_0 \quad = \quad a \to STOP \overset{4}{\vartriangleright} b \to SUCCESS$$

then $\Theta(T_0)$ can either perform an a event, or else a τ event followed by b followed by ω. No timing information is retained in $\Theta(T_0)$.

The projection Θ allows may and must notions of refinement to be defined between untimed and timed process expressions P and Q respectively. May testing gives rise to the following definition:

$$P \sqsubseteq_{may}^{time} Q \quad = \quad \forall T \bullet \neg (P \textbf{ may } \Theta(T)) \Rightarrow \neg (Q \textbf{ may } T)$$

In this definition, Q and T both range over timed CSP process expressions, and P ranges over untimed CSP process expressions. Hence the operational semantics used to evaluate

P **may** $\Theta(T)$ are the untimed operational semantics of Chapters 1–3, and the operational semantics used to judge *Q* **may** *T* are the timed operational semantics of Chapter 9.

The definition states that if the specification process *P* is unable to pass the untimed version of a test, then no timed implementation should be able to pass the timed version, since this would require a behaviour that is not allowed by the specifying process. For example, test $\Theta(T_0)$ will only succeed for a process which can perform *b* as its first visible action. The timed version T_0 also requires that this first event *b* should be possible after time 4, and that *a* should be refusable up to that time. Thus for example

$$\neg(a \rightarrow b \rightarrow STOP \textbf{ may } \Theta(T_0))$$

and

$$\neg(WAIT\, 3; a \rightarrow STOP \textbf{ may } T_0)$$

It turns out that this characterization of a may testing refinement relation between untimed and timed processes is exactly the same relation as that given by trace timewise refinement:

$$P \sqsubseteq_{may}^{time} Q \quad \Leftrightarrow \quad P \,_T\!\sqsubseteq_{TF} Q$$

The only way timewise may testing refinement between processes can fail is if *Q* can exhibit a finite sequence of events that is not possible in *P*. In such a case a test *T* which can succeed only after this sequence will bear witness to the failure of the $\sqsubseteq_{may}^{time}$ relation.

The natural must testing timewise refinement relation is defined in analogy with the definitions for must testing:

$$P \sqsubseteq_{must}^{time} Q \quad = \quad \forall T \bullet P \textbf{ must } \Theta(T) \Rightarrow Q \textbf{ must } T$$

As in the previous case, process expressions *T* and *Q* range over timed process expressions, and *P* over untimed process expressions, so *P* **must** $\Theta(T)$ is evaluated in the untimed operational semantics, and *Q* **must** *T* uses the timed operational semantics.

The definition requires that if every execution of the specification process *P* under test $\Theta(T)$ is guaranteed to succeed, then this requirement, translated to the timed world, is imposed on the process *Q* under the timed version *T* of the test.

In fact, this definition captures exactly the same relation as FDI timewise refinement:

$$P \sqsubseteq_{must}^{time} Q \quad \Leftrightarrow \quad P \,_{SF}\!\sqsubseteq_{TF} Q$$

If $P \,_{SF}\!\sqsubseteq_{TF} Q$ does not hold, then there is some execution of *Q* which is not matched by *P*, and it is always possible to construct a test *T* which will fail for that execution but succeed otherwise in such a way that *P* **must** $\Theta(T)$ (see Exercise 13.9). Conversely, if there is some test T such that P **must** $\Theta(T)$ but $\neg(Q$ **must** $T)$, then there is some execution of Q which fails the test T, and so it cannot be matched by any execution in P, since all P's executions pass the untimed version of the test.

For example, if $P_0 = a \rightarrow b \rightarrow STOP$ and $Q_0 = a \rightarrow (b \rightarrow STOP \overset{3}{\triangleright} STOP)$, then Q_0 is able eventually (in fact after 3 units of time) to refuse b after the occurrence of the a, when the timeout period has elapsed. For example, Q_0 has $(\langle(0,a)\rangle, [3, \infty) \times \{b\})$ as a possible timed failure. However, P_0 cannot refuse b after the occurrence of a. A test that will not succeed if this timed failure is present is the following:

$$T_1 \quad = \quad a \overset{4}{\rightarrow} b \rightarrow SUCCESS$$

At the untimed level, P_0 **must** $\Theta(T_1)$. However, at the timed level $\neg(Q_0$ **must** $T_1)$, since the timed behaviour does not allow for a synchronization on the b event. Hence T_1 is a test that witnesses the fact that $\neg(P_0 \sqsubseteq_{must}^{time} Q_0)$.

These two natural operational testing constructions for timewise refinement, by means of may and must testing, give rise to trace timewise refinement and FDI timewise refinement respectively. Although these definitions are not abstract enough to use practically, they provide an alternative understanding of the timewise refinement relations.

13.7 NOTES

In [97, 98, 95, 96, 99] Reed and Roscoe developed a number of timed and untimed models for CSP, which were first presented in a hierarchy (see Figure 13.15) in [95]. The observations on which the timed models were built were combinations of finite timed traces, finite duration timed refusal sets, and *stability values*, which indicated the time by which internal activity following the end of the trace must have ceased. The most detailed model, at the top of the hierarchy, was the *timed failures-stabilities* model [98], in which observations consisted of trace-refusal-stability triples $(s, \aleph, \alpha)$. In this model, each trace-refusal pair of a process is associated with a unique stability value . For example, the triple $(\langle(1,a)\rangle, [0,3) \times \{b\}, 4)$ is a behaviour of $a \overset{3}{\rightarrow} STOP$, whereas the triple $(\langle(1,a)\rangle, [0,3) \times \{b\}, 1)$ is a behaviour of $a \rightarrow STOP$. The first process does not stabilize until 3 seconds after the occurrence of a, whereas the second process stabilizes on occurrence of the a. Unstable processes could have infinite stability values. If $LOOP = WAIT\ 1; LOOP$, then $a \rightarrow LOOP$ would exhibit the triple $(\langle(1,a)\rangle, [0,3) \times \{b\}, \infty)$. All three of these processes have identical timed failures, and are distinguished only by their different stability values.

Stability is used to provide strong links between the different models—in a sense it is the glue that holds the hierarchy together, by giving a finite way of considering a process's refusals over all time: once a process is stable its possible next events will not change. Refusal information after stability correlates with untimed refusal information. The model TM_{FS}^* records only refusals after stability, together with timed traces and stability values, and thus provides a link to the untimed models. However, considering processes in terms of

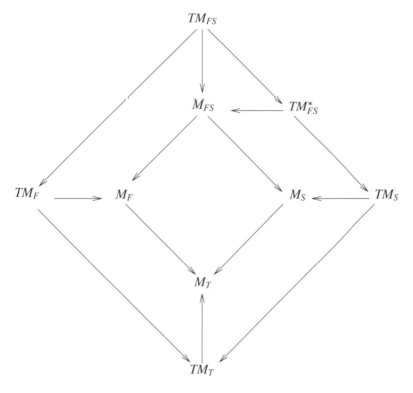

Fig. 13.15   Reed's hierarchy of models for CSP

their stability behaviour treats unstable processes rather harshly, effectively treating them as divergent even if their behaviour at the timed level is perfectly satisfactory. This means that the mappings between the models can be exploited only for stable processes.

Extending the original timed failures model to allow observations of infinite duration [108, 79] provides a way to obtain the information required to relate timed and untimed models which has a more satisfactory treatment of unstable processes. The model is discussed fully in [79]. This 'infinite timed failures' model (which this book refers to as the *timed failures* model) provides the basis for the theory of timewise refinement and this was the primary motivation for its development. Since it includes infinite observations, it also supports the modelling of arbitrary nondeterminism.

The timed language and its semantics have also evolved since they were first introduced, under the influence of related work in other timed process algebras. The original models did not allow causality or precedence between simultaneous events, and so the prefix operator $a \rightarrow Q$ was associated with a 'delay constant' $\delta > 0$ between the occurrence of a and the execution of Q. In practice this delay made process descriptions clumsier and harder to read (a delay of 3 would be expressed as $a \stackrel{3-\delta}{\rightarrow} Q$) and it has now been elided from the language. Recursion was also associated with this delay, essentially to guarantee that all recursive definitions were guarded. The delay has been elided from recursion as well, at the expense of needing to ensure explicitly that recursive definitions are time-guarded. It simplifies equational reasoning (if N is defined recursively to be Q, then instant recursion allows the conclusion $N = Q$ whereas delayed recursion means that $N = WAIT\,\delta; Q$). These two adjustments to the language also mean that no operator has any implicit delays associated with it, and so any delays in a process description must appear explicitly. A study of single and mutual recursion was presented in [25], where the metric space approach to the fixed point theory is reviewed, and a number of proof techniques for verifying recursively defined processes are given.

The proof system for the (finite) timed failures model was presented in [24, 107, 22]. It gave a complete set of rules for verifying process descriptions compositionally, in the style of the rules given here. The specification macro language was introduced by Davies in [22]. At the same time, Jackson [55, 56], developed a proof system for linear temporal logic specifications for CSP. These specifications are built up from atomic statements of the form $\mathbf{O}_a$ ('a is offered') and $\mathbf{P}_a$ ('a is performed'), using standard real-time temporal logic connectives to write real-time specifications. For example, the specification $\Box(\Box_{\leqslant 5}\neg\mathbf{P}_a \Rightarrow (\Diamond_{=8}\mathbf{O}_a \vee \mathbf{O}_b))$ states that whenever 5 seconds go by without a being performed, either a or b will be offered after a further 3 seconds.

The theory of timed CSP has also been extended in other directions. A timed probabilistic model for CSP developed by Lowe [73] allows descriptions and analysis of probabilistic aspects of a system's behaviour. A model which included a form of urgent events called *signals* was presented in [23, 22]. In order to avoid timestops, the parallel operators in this presentation are adapted so that urgent events cannot be blocked, though they can still be used to synchronize with other processes. This results in a form of broadcast concurrency similar to Prasad's [92].

Timed CSP has been applied to many examples: the alternating bit protocol, a sliding window protocol [107], a watchdog timer and a railroad crossing [26]. It has also been used for other case studies such as the design of control software for aircraft engines [54], real-time robotics [105, 113, 120], the specification of a telephone switching network [64, 114], the verification of a local area network protocol [22], the specification of asynchronous neural nets [37], the verification of the Futurebus+ distributed arbitration protocol [50], and the verification of the fault-tolerant recovery block mechanism [121].

The theory of timewise refinement for CSP was presented in [107, 111]. The notion of non-retraction is similar to (though slightly weaker than) the notion of *non-pre-emptive* given in [20], although that definition is given in operational terms, essentially requiring that internal transitions should preserve the possibility of performing any particular visible transition. There has also been some work in the area of abstracting timed processes in the context of CCS and of timed ACP. Larsen and Yi [68] proposed a notion of *time-abstracting* bisimulation which specifies when two processes are equivalent modulo timing behaviour. This may be used to verify the functional behaviour of a timed system. Baeten and Bergstra [4] consider an embedding of untimed ACP into real-time ACP , and translate certain identities of ACP into the timed framework, allowing reasoning at an untimed level to be incorporated alongside timed reasoning.

The railroad crossing example was originally formulated by Leveson and Stolzy in [71]. The timed CSP version was first presented in [26]. There is also a treatment in [103] in the style of untimed CSP described in Appendix A. Fischer's protocol is presented in [106], where it is attributed via Lamport to Fischer. The alternating bit protocol is an example of a stop-and-wait protocol requiring only one control bit, and has become a *de facto* benchmark case study for process algebras. The particular treatment presented in this chapter was first presented in [32].

Exercises

Exercise 13.1 Give an example of two pairs of processes P_1 $_{SF}\sqsubseteq_{TF}$ Q_1 and P_2 $_{SF}\sqsubseteq_{TF}$ Q_2 such that $\neg(P_1 \bigtriangleup P_2$ $_{SF}\sqsubseteq_{TF}$ $Q_1 \bigtriangleup_d Q_2)$.

Exercise 13.2 Give two prompt processes whose parallel composition is not prompt.

Exercise 13.3 Which of the following are non-retracting, and which are eventually non-retracting?

1. *STOP*

2. *STOP* $\sqcap$ $a \to$ *STOP*

3. *STOP* $\sqcap$ $a \to$ *STOP* $\sqcap$ $(a \to$ *STOP* $\overset{2}{\triangleright}$ *STOP*$)$

4. *TINPUTS* $\setminus$ $in_2.T$, where *TINPUTS* is given in Example 13.2.2

5. *TINPUTS* $\overset{4}{\triangleright}$ $in_1?x : T \to$ *STOP*

Exercise 13.4 Show that

$$a \to b \to STOP \,|||\, c \to STOP \quad _T\sqsubseteq_{TF} \quad a \overset{2}{\to} (b \to STOP \,\square\, c \to STOP)$$

Are the processes related by a failures timewise refinement?

Exercise 13.5 Is *MORNING* $_{SF}\sqsubseteq_{TF}$ *TMORNING*, where

$$
\begin{aligned}
MORNING \;=\; & wake \to ((SKIP \sqcap shower \to SKIP) \\
& \underset{\{\checkmark\}}{\|} (SKIP \sqcap eat \to SKIP); out \to SKIP \\[1em]
TMORNING \;=\; & ((wake \overset{5}{\to} shower \to STOP) \\
& \| (wake \overset{10}{\to} eat \to SKIP)) \\
& \bigtriangleup_{25} out \to SKIP \\
& \| \\
& ((eat \overset{10}{\to} out \to SKIP) \overset{25}{\triangleright} out \to SKIP)
\end{aligned}
$$

Either show that the refinement holds, or else (if it does not) provide a behaviour of *TMORNING* not allowed by the untimed process.

Exercise 13.6 Show that *TICKETS* $_{SF}\sqsubseteq_{TF}$ *TTICKETS*, where

$$TICKETS = issue \rightarrow ((STOP \sqcap TICKETS) ||| collect \rightarrow STOP)$$

$$TTICKETS = |||_{i=1}^{70,000} issue \xrightarrow{40} collect \rightarrow STOP$$
$$|| (ISSUE ||| COLLECT)$$

where $ISSUE = issue \xrightarrow{12} ISSUE$ and $COLLECT = collect \xrightarrow{2} COLLECT$.

Exercise 13.7 If the sender process of the timed alternating bit protocol of Example 13.3.6 has a timeout on awaiting acknowledgement (instead of a choice) as described below, does $S(0)$ $_{SF}\sqsubseteq_{TF}$ TS' hold? Is the protocol resulting from this change still guaranteed to provide a buffer?

$$TS' = TS'(0)$$
$$TS'(b) = in?x : T \xrightarrow{1} c_1!(x.b) \xrightarrow{1} TS'(b, x)$$
$$TS'(b, x) = (\square \, d_2.b \xrightarrow{1} TS'(\bar{b})$$
$$\square \, d_2.\bar{b} \xrightarrow{1} TS'(b, x))$$
$$\overset{15}{\triangleright} c_1!(x.b) \xrightarrow{1} TS'(b, x)$$

Exercise 13.8 The dining philosophers of Exercise 3.10 suffer from the propensity to deadlock. One possible solution is to persuade each philosopher $PHIL_i$ to replace a chopstick on the table if they have not obtained the second one within a specified time d_i.

Adapt the descriptions of the $PHIL_i$ processes to incorporate this suggestion. How is the whole system *COLLEGE* of Exercise 3.10 described in timed CSP?

Let *TCOLLEGE* be your timed version of the system.

1. Are there any conditions on the timeout delays d_i which are required to make the system $TCOLLEGE \setminus (pick.\mathbb{N}.\mathbb{N} \cup put.\mathbb{N}.\mathbb{N})$ deadlock-free?

2. Under these conditions, does $TCOLLEGE \setminus (pick.\mathbb{N}.\mathbb{N} \cup put.\mathbb{N}.\mathbb{N})$ **sat** *enter.i* at $t \Rightarrow \exists t' > t \bullet eat.i$ **live** t'?

3. Under these conditions, does $TCOLLEGE \setminus (pick.\mathbb{N}.\mathbb{N} \cup put.\mathbb{N}.\mathbb{N})$ **sat** *enter.*$\mathbb{N}$ at $t \Rightarrow \exists i, t' > t \bullet eat.i$ **live** t'?

Exercise 13.9 If P is a stable process and $\neg(P \,_{SF}\sqsubseteq_{TF} Q)$ then construct a test T which P but not Q must pass: P **must** $\Theta(T)$ but $\neg(Q$ **must** $T)$.

Appendix A:
Event-based time

It is natural to ask how far the well-established untimed language and theory for CSP can be applied to the analysis of timed systems, by taking the approach of using an event to mark the passage of time.

Time is introduced into untimed CSP by means of an event *tock* (since *tick* may be confused with $\checkmark$, which is already used for another purpose) whose occurrence represents the passing of (one unit of) time. This eliminates the need for a separate consideration of process evolution, and essentially allows a unit of evolution to be considered on a par with other events. It may be thought of in two ways:

- *tock* represents the unit evolution, and takes one time unit to occur. This means that all other events are instantaneous and can occur only at discrete points in time: all events between two successive *tock* events are simultaneous;

- *tock* events occur every time unit but are instantaneous, and events can occur between them at different times. This views the occurrence of *tock* as analogous to the internal clock used in computers, or a drum beat, marking particular points in time.

In fact, although these views are different, they both lead to the same treatment of the language.

The most immediate change from timed CSP is that the passage of time becomes discrete rather than continuous. This change does not make such a large impact as might be expected, because timed CSP works equally well with a discrete time domain, in which the language and semantics are allowed only discrete time values. Furthermore, the time units can be considered as small as necessary for any particular application, thus essentially retaining the expressivity of timed CSP.

This special *tock* event also brings a change of perspective on how time is considered within a process description. Untimed CSP deliberately abstracts away time, and is neutral as to its passing. The prefix process *start* → *P* is understood to represent a process which awaits the opportunity to engage in an event *start*, and whose subsequent behaviour is that of process *P*; any amount of time may pass before the occurrence of *start*. The timed CSP semantics reflects this understanding: any evolution for this process is possible, and it will remain in the same state. However, the use of the *tock* event to mark the passage of time means that time does not pass unless *tock* occurs, and hence that *start* → *P* must perform *start* before any time passes. The introduction of *tock* as a special event alters the way in which process behaviour is understood in the context of time. There are two ways in which *tock* can be introduced, and these will both be considered in this appendix.

The first approach will consider the use of the untimed language and theory of CSP as it stands, simply augmented with the new event *tock*. This brings the benefits of making timed process descriptions easier to understand without the need to learn a new notation. It also means that existing analysis tools are applicable. Indeed, some machine-assisted analysis of timed systems has already been carried out in this way, so it is important to understand the relationship between that approach and timed CSP, and the tradeoffs involved. In particular, we are interested in the extent to which an event marking the passage of time can be considered as a timed CSP unit delay, and the consequences of considering it on a par with other events.

The second approach aims to link into timed CSP, using an event-based approach as an additional way to reason about timed CSP processes. The aim is to translate timed CSP descriptions into event-based process descriptions in order to make reasoning about them simpler. Results about the event-based descriptions translate back to results concerning the original timed process. In this approach, the links between the timed and the untimed semantics need to be understood in order to exploit them. It turns out that in the presence of an explicit time-passing event, the semantics of some of the untimed operators need to be altered to make them consistent with their timed counterparts. The reasons why this is necessary also shed light on some of the limitations of the first approach.

A.1   STANDARD CSP AND TOCK

The first approach uses the standard CSP language with one new event *tock* which has a timed interpretation. The consideration of the passage of time as simply one event among others has a number of implications which it is important to be aware of when treating time in this way.

Example A.1.1 The one-shot printer example of Examples 1.2.1 and 9.3.1 is described as

$$PRINTER0 \quad = \quad accept \rightarrow print \rightarrow STOP$$

This process must perform *accept* and then *print* before any time can pass. In fact, even after these events have been performed, no time can pass because *STOP* is unable to perform the *tock* event. This highlights a trap for the unwary: absence of *tock* events does not mean that the process is indifferent to the passage of time (as is the case in CSP and in timed CSP), but that the process cannot allow the passage of time.

An attempt at a more suitable description might be

$$PRINTER1 \quad = \quad accept \rightarrow print \rightarrow RUN_{tock}$$

Having performed the two events, the process cannot perform any more, but will at least allow time to pass. However, the absence of a *tock* event before these events occur means that those events are *urgent*: they must be performed at the very first instant, before any time passes. Urgent external events are sometimes termed *signals*. This is in contrast to timed CSP which does not allow signals, though urgency is required of internal events.

It is likely that the printer is more relaxed about the performance of these events. In this case, the possibility of time passing must be included explicitly in the process description:

$$PRINTER2 \quad = \quad (accept \rightarrow PRINT) \;\square\; (tock \rightarrow PRINTER2)$$
$$PRINT \quad = \quad (print \rightarrow RUN_{tock}) \;\square\; (tock \rightarrow PRINT)$$

The events *accept* and *print* in *PRINTER2* are no longer urgent.

It is also possible to include some urgent events in a process description while leaving the others non-urgent. The printer might be able to wait for an *accept* event, but once that has occurred then it should *print* after two time units:

$$PRINTER3 \quad = \quad (accept \rightarrow tock \rightarrow tock \rightarrow print \rightarrow RUN_{tock})$$
$$\square\; (tock \rightarrow PRINTER3)$$

Appropriate modelling of urgent events within a process description will generally be associated with a corresponding environmental assumption: that the process will not be blocked from performing that event. ∎

The process *PRINTER0* illustrated that it is very easy to write timestop processes. Timestops may also arise as a result of blocking urgent events: since external events are synchronizations, an unco-operative environment may prevent an urgent event from occurring, and this will result in the prevention of further *tock* events. For example, if the process *PRINTER1* is not supplied with a print job immediately, then no events can occur. The parallel combination

$$PRINTER1 \parallel tock \rightarrow tock \rightarrow accept \rightarrow RUN_{tock}$$

cannot perform any events, not even *tock*, and is equivalent to a timestop. This may be the result of poor modelling of the system, or it may arise during analysis of the system as an indication that two timing assumptions are incompatible: in this example, the contradictory assumptions that *accept* should occur at time 0 and that it should not occur until time 2.

Other anomalous behaviours are also possible. Processes which are infinitely fast are easily described using recursion, even if they do not contain urgent events:

$$
\begin{aligned}
FASTCOPY &= (in?x : T \rightarrow FASTCOPYOUT(x)) \\
&\quad \square\ tock \rightarrow FASTCOPY \\
FASTCOPYOUT(x) &= (out!x \rightarrow FASTCOPY) \\
&\quad \square\ tock \rightarrow FASTCOPYOUT(x)
\end{aligned}
$$

The solution here, as in the case of timed CSP, is to require that recursively defined processes are time-guarded: that every recursive loop contains at least one *tock* event.

Checking well-timedness

The absence of infinitely fast executions in a process P can be checked by examining the process $P \setminus (\Sigma \setminus \{tock\})$. If this process is divergence-free, then P can never perform infinitely many events between two *tock* events. Furthermore, if the process is also deadlock-free, then P is free of timestops as well (assuming it is allowed to perform all its urgent events). For non-terminating processes, the following equivalence establishes both divergence- and deadlock-freedom:

$$
P \setminus (\Sigma \setminus \{tock\}) \quad =_{FDI} \quad RUN_{tock}
$$

This is a sensible first check to perform on a process description, and a process which passes it is said to be *well-timed*.

Example A.1.2 As a larger example, we will consider how the railway crossing of Section 13.4 would be modelled. Each of the components can be separately described, and the system is their parallel composition.

The controller transforms sensory inputs into gate commands:

$$
\begin{aligned}
CONTROLLER_{tock} &= \quad near.ind \rightarrow tock \\
&\qquad \rightarrow down.command \rightarrow CONFIRM_{tock} \\
&\quad \square \\
&\quad out.ind \rightarrow tock \\
&\qquad \rightarrow up.command \rightarrow CONFIRM_{tock} \\
&\quad \square \\
&\quad tock \rightarrow CONTROLLER_{tock} \\
CONFIRM_{tock} &= \quad confirm \rightarrow CONTROLLER_{tock} \\
&\quad \square \\
&\quad tock \rightarrow CONFIRM_{tock}
\end{aligned}
$$

The description resembles that in Section 13.4, with the possibility of time passing mentioned explicitly. This component is well-timed, and is not urgent on either of the sensor events *near.ind* or *out.ind*, nor on *confirm*. On the other hand, it is urgent on the gate commands, and so when the components are combined it will be necessary to confirm that the gate is able to accept these commands whenever they are sent.

The gate must be ready to accept *down.command* and *up.command* whenever they are presented, so it will be described as follows:

$$
\begin{aligned}
GATE_{tock} \quad = \quad & down.command \rightarrow MOVE_{tock}(down, 100) \\
& \square\ up.command \rightarrow MOVE_{tock}(up, 100) \\
& \square\ tock \rightarrow GATE_{tock}
\end{aligned}
$$

$$
\begin{aligned}
MOVE_{tock}(a, 0) \quad = \quad & a \rightarrow confirm \rightarrow GATE_{tock} \\
MOVE_{tock}(a, n+1) \quad = \quad & tock \rightarrow MOVE_{tock}(a, n) \\
& \square\ down.command \rightarrow MOVE_{tock}(down, 100) \\
& \square\ up.command \rightarrow MOVE_{tock}(up, 100)
\end{aligned}
$$

The delay of 100 time units between the instruction to move the gate and its effect is described in terms of the explicit occurrence of 100 *tock*s, which is achieved by the recursive definition of $MOVE_{tock}$. An *up.command* or *down.command* can be received during this time; this is treated as a fresh instruction to the gate. Observe that this contrasts with the timed CSP description, which did not consider the commands *down.command* and *up.command* from the controller process as urgent. In that situation, if the gate process was not ready to receive a command, then the controller process would have to wait until it became ready.

The urgency of the events *down* and *up* correspond to the assumption that the environment of the system will always allow them to occur, which in this case means that the gates to the crossing are not physically prevented from moving.

The crossing is described as the parallel combination of these two processes. They are required to synchronize on the passage of time, as well as on their common events:

$$
CROSSING_{tock} \quad = \quad CONTROLLER_{tock} \parallel GATE_{tock}
$$

A description of the train's behaviour is needed in order to establish that the crossing is safe. The requirements on the train times are concerned with the minimum possible delay between particular events. The train is rendered as follows:

$$
\begin{aligned}
TRAIN_{tock} &= train.near \rightarrow APPROACHING_{tock} \\
&\quad \Box\ tock \rightarrow TRAIN_{tock} \\[4pt]
APPROACHING_{tock} &= near.ind \rightarrow ENTERING_{tock}(300) \\
&\quad \Box\ tock \rightarrow APPROACHING_{tock} \\[4pt]
ENTERING_{tock}(n+1) &= tock \rightarrow ENTERING_{tock}(n) \\
ENTERING_{tock}(0) &= enter.crossing \rightarrow ON_{tock}(20) \\
&\quad \Box\ tock \rightarrow ENTERING_{tock}(0) \\[4pt]
ON_{tock}(n+1) &= tock \rightarrow ON_{tock}(n) \\
ON_{tock}(0) &= leave.crossing \rightarrow out.ind \rightarrow TRAIN_{tock} \\
&\quad \Box\ tock \rightarrow ON_{tock}(0)
\end{aligned}
$$

In its initial state, the train can indicate that it is near the crossing at any time, followed by the signal *near.ind* to the crossing sensor. It must allow at least 300 *tock* events before entering the crossing. Similarly, it will be at least 20 *tock*s before it leaves the crossing, and when it finally does so the signal *out.ind* should also occur at the same time.

The overall system is the train in parallel with the crossing:

$$
SYSTEM_{tock} = TRAIN_{tock} \parallel CROSSING_{tock}
$$

This system should firstly be checked for well-timedness to ensure that all of the timing assumptions contained in the component descriptions are consistent.

The system may then be investigated with respect to the behavioural requirements on the system. For example, the requirement that concerns the status of the gate when the train enters the crossing is as follows:

$$
Safety1(tr) = last(tr) = enter.crossing \Rightarrow last(tr \upharpoonright \{down, up\}) = down.
$$

This can be verified for the traces of $SYSTEM_{tock}$.

The second safety property is concerned with the timing behaviour: it requires that any time the train enters the crossing, the gate should not have moved in the preceding 10 seconds. This can be specified as follows:

$$
\begin{aligned}
Safety2_{tock}(tr) = \quad &(tr = tr_0 \frown tr_1 \frown \langle enter.crossing \rangle) \wedge tr_1 \downarrow tock < 10 \\
&\Rightarrow tr_1 \upharpoonright \{up, down\} = \langle \rangle
\end{aligned}
$$

This can be verified directly on the traces of $SYSTEM_{tock}$, using the traces model.

This safety property can also be specified as a CSP process which places a constraint on when the event *enter.crossing* can occur, but does not constrain any other events:

$$
\begin{aligned}
SAFETY2_{tock} &= SAFETY2(0) \; ||| \; RUN_{\Sigma \setminus \{tock, up, down, enter.crossing\}} \\
SAFETY2(n+1) &= tock \rightarrow SAFETY2(n) \\
&\quad \square \; down \rightarrow SAFETY2(10) \\
&\quad \square \; up \rightarrow SAFETY2(10) \\
SAFETY2(0) &= tock \rightarrow SAFETY2(n) \\
&\quad \square \; enter.crossing \rightarrow SAFETY2(0) \\
&\quad \square \; down \rightarrow SAFETY2(10) \\
&\quad \square \; up \rightarrow SAFETY2(10)
\end{aligned}
$$

The safety requirement can then be expressed as a simple trace refinement: that

$$
SAFETY2_{tock} \; \sqsubseteq_T \; System_{tock}
$$

This check is an appropriate candidate for mechanical verification. ∎

This example illustrates that timed systems can be described and analysed within this dialect of CSP. It is a stand-alone approach, in that it does not link into timed CSP. The process descriptions are quite different in style, and it is essentially a distinct formalism. The main difference with the timed CSP approach is that it allows urgency of events to be expressed, which brings with it a different way of thinking about timed events. Urgency can be useful: the emergence of unexpected timestops can identify conflicting timing requirements. The treatment of the passage of time as just one more event means that many properties that are built into timed CSP do not automatically hold here. For example, the fact that processes are deterministic under the passage of time need not hold. The explicit control over the passing of time which is introduced by the *tock* event means that the specifier has to take more care to ensure that it is used in a sensible way, and this will often need to be checked explicitly (such as the well-timed check).

Some untimed operators do not sit naturally with the *tock* approach to time. As will be discussed in the next section, *tock* as an event means that it resolves external choice and interrupt, and hiding and sequential composition cannot treat internal events urgently. These components of the language are thus not available for supporting design decisions: processes cannot naturally be described as the external choice of two components, or as a component with internal structure; when these operators are used, they can give rise to behaviour that is quite different to how they are generally understood. One consequence of this unsuitability of some operators is that descriptions of timed systems can be more cumbersome than in timed CSP, and tend to be quite low-level.

A.2 TRANSLATING FROM TIMED CSP

The preceding section is concerned with the use of CSP with *tock*s as a language for specifying and describing time-sensitive processes. A complementary view of the event-based approach is to use CSP with tocks as a target language for translation from timed CSP, rather than as a design language in its own right. Timed CSP is the language used to capture the system specification and design, and the translation is used to enable simpler analysis. As mentioned above, some of the timed operators do not translate well to existing operators, and some new untimed operators are therefore required. The target language, with these new operators, will be designated 'tock-CSP'.

The aim is to provide a translation mechanism Ψ which can transform timed processes to event-based processes incorporating *tock*. Since tock-CSP is discrete, we will translate only those timed CSP processes Q whose timeouts, delays, and timed interrupt values are all integers. This subset of timed CSP will be referred to as *discrete timed CSP*.

The translation aims for $\Psi(Q)$ to be refined by Q in some sense, so that results established about $\Psi(Q)$ can be translated immediately to results concerning Q. In contrast to the theory of timewise refinement which removes all timing information, the process $\Psi(Q)$ does have time-dependent behaviour and can be investigated with respect to timed specifications.

The translation function Ψ takes timed CSP processes and translates them to tock-CSP processes by introducing the possible time passing events *tock* explicitly. For example, prefixing and prefix choice will be translated as follows:

$$\Psi(a \to Q) \quad = \quad P_0 = \begin{array}[t]{l} a \to \Psi(Q) \\ \square \; tock \to P_0 \end{array}$$

$$\Psi(a : A \to Q(a)) \quad = \quad P_0 = \begin{array}[t]{l} a : A \to \Psi(Q(a)) \\ \square \; tock \to P_0 \end{array}$$

for some new process variables P_0. Delayed prefixes $a \overset{n}{\to} Q$ and $a : A \overset{n_a}{\to} Q(a)$ will be handled by rewriting to $a \to WAIT\, n; Q$ and $a : A \to WAIT\, n_a Q(a)$ respectively.

Basic processes have their *tock* events given explicitly:

$$\begin{aligned} \Psi(STOP) \quad &= \quad RUN_{tock} \\ \Psi(SKIP) \quad &= \quad P_0 = (SKIP \; \square \; tock \to P_0) \\ \Psi(WAIT\, 0) \quad &= \quad \Psi(SKIP) \\ \Psi(WAIT\, n + 1) \quad &= \quad tock \to \Psi(WAIT\, n) \end{aligned}$$

Parallel combinations are required to synchronize on *tock*:

$$\Psi(Q_1 \underset{A}{\parallel} Q_2) \quad = \quad \Psi(Q_1) \underset{A \cup \{tock\}}{\parallel} \Psi(Q_2)$$

Internal choice is resolved immediately:

$$\Psi(Q_1 \sqcap Q_2) \quad = \quad \Psi(Q_1) \sqcap \Psi(Q_2)$$

Renaming and recursive definitions are straightforwardly translated, where the alphabet renaming function f is extended to map *tock* to itself:

$$
\begin{aligned}
\Psi(f(Q)) &= f(\Psi(Q_1)) \\
\Psi(f^{-1}(Q)) &= f^{-1}(\Psi(Q)) \\
\Psi(N) &= N_T \\
\Psi(N = Q) &= N_T = \Psi(Q)
\end{aligned}
$$

Process variables are subscripted with a T (for *tock*) simply to distinguish timed processes N from their translation N_T.

Choice

There is a difficulty with external choice, essentially because in the timed world the passage of time does not resolve choice. Yet standard external choice will be resolved by the passage of time if it is modelled in terms of an event. For example, if the choice

$$a \rightarrow Q_1 \;\square\; b \rightarrow Q_2$$

is translated to

$$\Psi(a \rightarrow Q_1) \;\square\; \Psi(b \rightarrow Q_2)$$

then the choice will be resolved on the occurrence of the first *tock* by either side, which does not reflect the timed behaviour. In this particular case it happens that there is a straightforward definition as P_0:

$$
\begin{aligned}
P_0 \quad = \quad & a \rightarrow \Psi(Q_1) \\
& \square\; b \rightarrow \Psi(Q_2) \\
& \square\; tock \rightarrow P_0
\end{aligned}
$$

The operation that actually corresponds to timed external choice is not included as part of the standard untimed language. It is a choice operator that requires synchronization with regard to *tock* events (up to the point the choice is made), but is resolved by any other (external) event. The symbol $\square_{tock}$ will be used to represent this tock-CSP operator. It can be defined via an elaborate construction in terms of the standard CSP operators (see [88]). Its operational semantics are easily given:

$$
\frac{P_1 \xrightarrow{a} P_1'}{\begin{array}{l} (P_1 \;\Box_{tock}\; P_2) \xrightarrow{a} P_1' \\ (P_2 \;\Box_{tock}\; P_1) \xrightarrow{a} P_1' \end{array}} \quad [\, a \neq tock \,]
$$

$$
\frac{P_1 \xrightarrow{\tau} P_1'}{\begin{array}{l} (P_1 \;\Box_{tock}\; P_2) \xrightarrow{\tau} P_1' \;\Box_{tock}\; P_2 \\ (P_2 \;\Box_{tock}\; P_1) \xrightarrow{\tau} P_2 \;\Box_{tock}\; P_1' \end{array}}
$$

$$
\frac{P_1 \xrightarrow{tock} P_1' \qquad P_2 \xrightarrow{tock} P_2'}{(P_1 \;\Box_{tock}\; P_2) \xrightarrow{tock} P_1' \;\Box_{tock}\; P_2'}
$$

An external choice will then be translated as follows:

$$
\Psi(Q_1 \;\Box\; Q_2) \quad = \quad \Psi(Q_1) \;\Box_{tock}\; \Psi(Q_2)
$$

Translation of the timeout and interrupt operators suffers from the same difficulties as external choice: timeout is to be resolved in favour of the first process on the occurrence of its first non-tock event. However, it is possible to make use of the following equivalence (where *timeout* is a fresh event outside the alphabets of Q_1 and Q_2):

$$
Q_1 \overset{n}{\triangleright} Q_2 \quad = \quad (Q_1 \;\Box\; WAIT\ n; timeout \to Q_2) \setminus \{timeout\}
$$

Then $\Psi(Q_1 \overset{n}{\triangleright} Q_2)$ is simply defined to be $\Psi((Q_1 \;\Box\; WAIT\ n; timeout \to Q_2) \setminus \{timeout\})$.

For essentially the same reasons, a new tock-CSP interrupt operator also needs to be defined—the standard CSP interrupt operator will trigger on *tock* events from its interrupting process, and this does not express the desired behaviour.

Hiding and sequential composition

In the case of hiding and sequential composition, there is a more fundamental difficulty: the urgency of internal events cannot be provided by any of the standard CSP semantics. In untimed CSP, whenever there is a choice between an internal event and an external event, the opportunity to perform the external event is nondeterministic: it might be performed, but it also might be refused. This will therefore be the case even if the external event is a *tock* event. This allows internal events to become delayed even when they are possible. For example, in the recursive process

$$P \;=\; (a \to RUN_{tock}) \,\square\, (b \to RUN_{tock}) \,\square\, tock \to P$$

the *a* event is non-urgent, and any number of *tock* events can happen before it occurs. In the process $P \setminus \{a\}$, this event becomes internal, and the resulting process in the standard CSP semantics is given by

$$P \setminus \{a\} \;=\; (tock \to P \setminus \{a\}) \,\square\, (b \to RUN_{tock} \sqcap STOP)$$

Any number of *tock* events is possible, and at any stage a *b* event might also be possible. The *b* event cannot be guaranteed, since the internal *a* might have occurred. In contrast, the urgency of internal events required in timed CSP would force the internal *a* to occur before the first *tock*, in effect giving it priority over the *tock* event and preventing *b* from ever occurring after a *tock*. An urgent treatment of internal events would result in $P \setminus \{a\}$ behaving like

$$RUN_{tock} \,\square\, (b \to RUN_{tock} \sqcap STOP)$$

Observe that this is a refinement of the process $P \setminus \{a\}$ given above: the urgency has excluded some executions.

For the same reason, this problem is also manifested in sequential composition, where the termination event that passes control from the first process to the second should be treated urgently. The translation $\Psi(SKIP)$ is able to perform either $\checkmark$ or *tock*, so in the combination $\Psi(SKIP); P$ it may delay arbitrarily before terminating. In order to treat sequential composition in the way it would be expected to behave, the operator will need to treat termination urgently.

In order to enforce urgency, a different operational semantics will need to be given for these two operators of tock-CSP. As might be expected, these rules are similar to the timed rules given for these operators.

For hiding, an extra clause has been introduced. This requires that *tock* can occur only if there are no possible hidden events.

$$\frac{P \xrightarrow{a} P'}{P \setminus_{tock} A \xrightarrow{\tau} P' \setminus_{tock} A} \quad [\, a \in A \,]$$

$$\frac{P \xrightarrow{\mu} P'}{P \setminus_{tock} A \xrightarrow{\mu} P' \setminus_{tock} A} \quad [\, \mu \notin A, \mu \neq tock \,]$$

$$\frac{P \xrightarrow{tock} P' \quad \forall a \in A \bullet (\neg P \xrightarrow{a})}{P \setminus_{tock} A \xrightarrow{tock} P' \setminus_{tock} A}$$

The new clause for sequential composition requires that time cannot pass for the first process if it can terminate.

$$\frac{P_1 \xrightarrow{\mu} P_1'}{P_1 ;_{tock} P_2 \xrightarrow{\mu} P_1' ;_{tock} P_2} \quad [\, \mu \neq tock, \mu \neq \checkmark \,]$$

$$\frac{P_1 \xrightarrow{tock} P_1' \quad \neg(P_1 \xrightarrow{\checkmark})}{P_1 ;_{tock} P_2 \xrightarrow{tock} P_1' ;_{tock} P_2}$$

$$\frac{P_1 \xrightarrow{\checkmark} P_1'}{P_1 ;_{tock} P_2 \xrightarrow{\tau} P_2}$$

Denotational semantics

The operators required to achieve a faithful translation to tock-CSP have thus far been described operationally. In order to reason about them compositionally in the CSP style, an equivalent denotational semantics needs to be provided. This can be done for all the above operators within the standard untimed models, with the exception of hiding and sequential composition. These two operators require information about the unavailability of internal events in order to determine whether the *tock* event is possible, and none of the untimed models introduced thus far carries this kind of information.

For example, the two processes

$$P_1 = a \to RUN_{tock} \;\square\; (tock \to (b \to RUN_{tock} \;\sqcap\; RUN_{tock}))$$
$$P_2 = a \to RUN_{tock} \;\sqcap\; (tock \to (b \to RUN_{tock} \;\square\; RUN_{tock}))$$

have exactly the same traces. However, $P_1 \setminus_{tock} \{a\}$ must perform the internalized event a before any time can pass, since that event must be available. On the other hand, $P_2 \setminus_{tock} \{a\}$ can avoid performing the internal a by selecting the other branch of the choice, making b available after a *tock*. This means that the traces of a process $P \setminus_{tock} \{a\}$ are not completely determined by the traces of P: the traces model cannot provide a suitable definition of the $\setminus_{tock}$ operator.

A more complex example illustrates why failures information is also insufficient. Consider the following two processes P_3 and P_4, defined in terms of *TEA* and *COFFEE*:

$$
\begin{aligned}
TEA &= tea \to RUN_{tock} \;\square\; tock \to TEA \\
COFFEE &= coffee \to RUN_{tock} \;\square\; tock \to COFFEE \\
P_3 &= TEA \;\sqcap\; COFFEE \\
P_4 &= (coffee \to RUN_{tock} \;\square\; (tock \to TEA)) \\
&\quad \sqcap (tea \to RUN_{tock} \;\square\; (tock \to COFFEE))
\end{aligned}
$$

The two processes P_3 and P_4 have the same set of failures: they can both perform any number of *tock*s followed by a *tea* or a *coffee* (followed by further *tock*s); and at any stage either *tea* or *coffee*, but not both, can be refused.

However, there is a difference in their behaviour: P_3 is always committed to the drink it first chooses to offer, whereas after one *tock* P_4 switches the drink it offers. Failures information, even in the FDI model, is not detailed enough to identify this difference.

This difference in behaviour means that $P_3 \setminus_{tock} \{tea\}$ can provide a *coffee* after a *tock* event, whereas $P_4 \setminus_{tock} \{tea\}$ cannot—the internal *tea* will occur either immediately or after one *tock*, in both cases preventing the possibility of *coffee* after *tock*. Hence the failures (and divergences and infinite traces) of a process P are not sufficient to determine even the traces of $P \setminus_{tock} A$, let alone the failures (and divergences and infinite traces).

The information that is required to give a satisfactory treatment of hiding and sequential composition in tock-CSP is *refusal testing* information, which records events that are refused in stable states during an execution, rather than simply at the end as in the failures model.

The refusal testing model for CSP uses *refusal traces* as its basic observations. A refusal trace *rt* is an alternating sequence of refusal sets and events, corresponding to executions in which the events are performed, and the interleaved refusal sets are observations of stable states along the way. It is also necessary to allow for the possibility that an event was performed

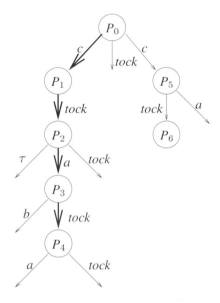

Fig. A.1   A process execution

from an unstable state, so the symbol $\bullet$ is used to represent the absence of refusal information. In this model, $\bullet$ is distinct from the empty refusal set $\{\}$, which indicates stability.

For example, the refusal trace

$$rt = \langle \{a,b\},\ c,\ \{a\},\ tock,\ \bullet,\ a,\ \{a\},\ tock,\ \{c\} \rangle$$

is associated with the execution illustrated in Figure A.1. The corresponding trace $trace(rt) = \langle c, tock, a, tock \rangle$ is simply the sequence of events extracted from the refusal trace. The initial state P_0 is stable, and the set $\{a,b\}$ can be refused. The event c can be performed from P_0 and reach a stable state P_1 in which a is refused. The event $tock$ is then possible, reaching a state P_2 from which a is possible, reaching P_3. The absence of refusal information recorded in P_2 (indicated by the $\bullet$) is necessary because P_2 is not a stable state, since τ is possible from it. Observe that at this point in the refusal trace, having performed c and $tock$, the process cannot be in state P_6 because a was refused after the c, which is not possible for the intermediate state P_5. Trace information alone would not allow this deduction: refusal information recorded during the trace does provide additional information.

The denotational characterization of $P \setminus_{tock} A$ will be concerned only with the refusal traces of P that contain the refusal of A (possibly among other events) before any $tock$ event. These are the observations in which A events occur urgently with respect to $tock$. This characterization is similar to the definition of hiding in the timed failures model.

In a similar way, the definition of $P_1 ;_{tock} P_2$ will consider only those refusal traces of P_1 that observe the refusal of $\checkmark$ before any $tock$ event. This restricts the behaviour of P_1 to the case where $\checkmark$ is urgent with respect to $tock$.

Specification

All of the standard CSP operators and the operators of tock-CSP can be given a refusal testing semantics which corresponds to their operational semantics. Specifications on such processes are therefore in terms of the possible refusal traces of a process, though in practice it is generally the traces, and perhaps the final refusal, that is of interest in specification. Although the intermediate refusal information is required in order to deduce the behaviour of the process, there are rarely requirements on this aspect of a process's behaviour.

There is a strong relationship between the traces of discrete timed CSP processes Q and the traces of their translation $\Psi(Q)$ (given in the refusal testing model). The *discrete timed traces* of a process Q will be those timed traces s which satisfy $\mathsf{discrete}(s)$: they have only integer time values. For example, the discrete timed traces of $a \rightarrow (b \rightarrow STOP \overset{1}{\triangleright} STOP) \overset{1}{\triangleright} STOP$ will be

$$\{\langle\rangle, \langle(0,a)\rangle, \langle(1,a)\rangle,$$
$$\langle(0,a),(0,b)\rangle, \langle(0,a),(1,b)\rangle,$$
$$\langle(1,a),(1,b)\rangle, \langle(1,a),(2,b)\rangle\}$$

A trace of a tock-CSP process can be transformed via the function $\mathsf{tocktimed}$ into a discrete timed trace by associating each event with the total number of *tock* events that precede it in the trace (in other words, the amount of time that has passed), and then removing the *tock* events. For example,

$$\mathsf{tocktimed}(\langle c, tock, a, tock, tock, b\rangle) \quad = \quad \langle(0,c),(1,a),(3,b)\rangle$$

The discrete timed traces of a tock-CSP process will be the set of all of its traces transformed in this way.

The discrete timed traces provide the link between the untimed and the timed versions of the same process views of a process. It turns out that the set of discrete timed traces of a discrete timed CSP process Q is the same as the set of discrete timed traces of its translation $\Psi(Q)$, as given via the refusal testing model for CSP. This means that results established about $\Psi(Q)$ apply directly to the discrete timed traces of Q.

For example, it might be established for $\Psi(Q)$ that any a event must occur after at least 5 *tock*s:

$$\Psi(Q) \quad \mathbf{sat} \quad (n,a) \text{ in } \mathsf{tocktimed}(trace(rt)) \Rightarrow n \geqslant 5$$

It can then be immediately deduced that all discrete timed traces of Q meet this specification:

$$Q \quad \mathbf{sat} \quad \mathsf{discrete}(s) \wedge (n,a) \text{ in } s \Rightarrow n \geqslant 5$$

Finally, we will exploit the relationship between Q's discrete timed traces and the rest of its timed traces in order to establish the safety property for Q overall. If s is an arbitrary timed trace, then int(s) will be the same sequence of events, but with the times associated with them rounded down. For example,

$$\text{int}(\langle (1.9, a), (\pi, b), (4, c), (4.3, d) \rangle) \;=\; \langle (1, a), (3, b), (4, c), (4, d) \rangle$$

The valuable result which holds for any discrete timed CSP process Q is that if any trace s is a trace of Q, then so too is int(s). (Note that this does not hold for arbitrary timed CSP processes.) This result allows specifications S on the discrete traces of Q to impose requirements on all the traces of Q: any s must have its discretisation int(s) allowed by the specification S. The example given above results in

$$Q \quad \textbf{sat} \quad \text{discrete}(\text{int}(s)) \wedge (n, a) \text{ in int}(s) \Rightarrow n \geqslant 5$$

Since discrete$(\text{int}(s))$ is always true, its inclusion is superfluous, and the specification simplifies to

$$Q \quad \textbf{sat} \quad a \text{ at } t \Rightarrow t \geqslant 5$$

The process Q cannot perform a before time 5. If it could perform a at some earlier time $t < 5$, then there would also be an earlier integer time $n \leqslant t$ at which it could perform a, and this has been ruled out by the untimed analysis.

In summary, if S is a specification on discrete timed traces, then to establish that Q **sat** $S(\text{int}(s))$ it is sufficient to establish that $\Psi(Q)$ **sat** $S(\text{tocktimed}(trace(rt)))$. This safety specification $S(\text{int}(s))$ will often translate to a more readable specification directly on timed traces s.

Example A.2.1

- The specification $(n, a) \text{ in int}(s) \Rightarrow n < 5$ is equivalent to $(t, a) \text{ in } s \Rightarrow t < 5$: they both state that any a that occurs should do so before time 5.

- The specification

$$(n, a) \text{ in int}(s) \wedge (n', b) \text{ in int}(s) \Rightarrow n' > n + 3$$

  states that if a and b both occur, then there should be more than 3 time units between them, with b occurring after a. This is equivalent to the specification

$$(t, a) \text{ in } s \wedge (t', b) \text{ in } s \Rightarrow t' > t + 3$$

  on arbitrary timed traces s.

- Care should be taken in translating such specifications. The previous discrete specification is equivalent to

$$(n, a) \text{ in int}(s) \wedge (n', b) \text{ in int}(s) \Rightarrow n' \geqslant n + 4$$

but this does not translate to

$$(t, a) \text{ in } s \wedge (t', b) \text{ in } s \Rightarrow t' \geqslant t + 4$$

For example, the trace $\langle (0.99, a), (4.01, b) \rangle$ meets the discrete specification, but not the incorrect translation.

■

Example A.2.2 A timed CSP process *PRINTER* is made up of two components, *SPOOL* and *PRINT*, with an architecture as follows:

$$PRINTER = (SPOOL \underset{mid.T}{\parallel} PRINT) \setminus mid.T$$

The components are recursively defined:

$$SPOOL = in?x \overset{3}{\to} mid!x \overset{1}{\to} SPOOL$$
$$PRINT = mid?y \overset{1}{\to} print!y \to PRINT$$

The aim is to analyse this process at the level of tock-CSP, and to translate the results back to timed CSP. The time units used in this example are seconds, so each *tock* will represent the passage of one second of time.

The first step is to transform *PRINTER* by means of the Ψ translation function:

$$\Psi(PRINTER) = \Psi((SPOOL \underset{mid.T}{\parallel} PRINT) \setminus mid.T)$$
$$= (SPOOL_T \underset{mid.T}{\parallel} PRINT) \setminus_{tock} mid.T$$

The recursive definitions for *SPOOL* and *PRINT* also require translation. For example, $\Psi(SPOOL = in?x \overset{3}{\to} mid!x \to SPOOL)$ yields

$$SPOOL_T = P_0 = in?x \to \Psi(WAIT\ 3; mid!x \to SPOOL)$$
$$\square\ tock \to P_0$$
$$= P_0 = in?x \to tock \to tock \to tock \to \Psi(mid!x \to SPOOL)$$
$$\square\ tock \to P_0$$

where

$$\Psi(mid!x \to SPOOL) = P_1 = mid!x \to SPOOL_T$$
$$\square\ tock \to P_1$$

The transition graph for the resulting process $\Psi(SPOOL)$ is given in Figure A.2. The translation $\Psi(PRINT)$ is carried out in a similar way (see Exercise A.3). The resulting process

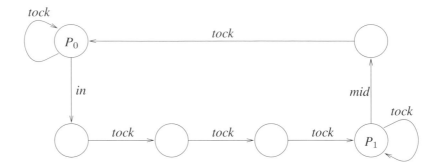

Fig. A.2 *Transitions of* $\Psi(SPOOL)$ **(message values elided)**

$\Psi(PRINTER)$ (see Exercise A.4) has the transition graph given in Figure A.3. The τ transition in that graph corresponds to a print job being passed along the print channel. Observe that the (unstable) state in which that internal event is enabled has no *tock* transition, reflecting the urgency of the τ. All other states are stable, and all have precisely one *tock* transition enabled. An analysis of the tock-timed process—either directly in terms of its refusal traces, or else by considering the transition graph—establishes that more than 3 *tock*s must occur between an input and the corresponding output. This may be captured as the following specification on refusal traces:

$$TP(rt) \;=\; (n, print.m) \textbf{ in } \mathsf{tocktimed}(trace(rt))$$
$$\Rightarrow \exists\, n' < n - 3 \bullet (n', in.m) \textbf{ in } \mathsf{tocktimed}(trace(rt))$$

and $\Psi(PRINTER)$ **sat** $TP(rt)$ is easily established for any arbitrary m.

Since *PRINTER* is a discrete timed CSP process, it follows that

$$PRINTER \quad \textbf{sat} \quad TP(\mathsf{int}(s))$$

which establishes that the throughput specification holds for all timed traces of *PRINTER*:

$$PRINTER \quad \textbf{sat} \quad (t, print.m) \textbf{ in } s \Rightarrow \exists\, t' < t - 3 \bullet (t', in.m) \textbf{ in } s$$

The more abstract tock-CSP analysis has established that there must be at least 3 seconds between the input of a job and the corresponding output.

In fact, a direct analysis in the timed failures model will establish that the throughput delay must be at least 4 seconds, but the translation to tock-CSP results in a coarser system description with a corresponding loss of precision with regard to precise timing of events. This coarsening can be reduced as much as necessary by making the time units smaller, thereby increasing the granularity of the tock-CSP description. Since the translation of the tock-CSP specification will only ever be out by a maximum of one time unit, smaller time units will result in a higher degree of precision.

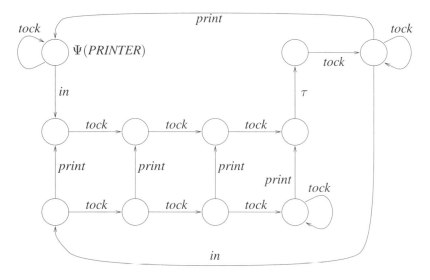

Fig. A.3 *Transitions of* $\Psi(PRINTER)$ *(message values elided)*

For instance, if there were 10 time units to the second, then the components of *PRINTER* would be described as

$$SPOOL' \quad = \quad in?x \xrightarrow{30} mid!x \xrightarrow{10} SPOOL'$$
$$PRINT' \quad = \quad mid?y \xrightarrow{10} print!y \rightarrow PRINT'$$

and the same analysis would yield that

$$PRINTER \quad \textbf{sat} \quad (t, print.m) \textbf{ in } s \Rightarrow \exists t' < t - 39 \bullet (t', in.m) \textbf{ in } s$$

This means that there must be a throughput delay of at least 3.9 seconds. Of course, this description of *PRINTER* requires a larger state space, and there will always be a tradeoff between the degree of precision provided by the tock-CSP analysis and the complexity of the analysis. ■

A.3 NOTES

The approach to introducing *tock* into CSP as simply one new event is introduced in some detail by Roscoe in [103]. The use of tock-CSP to provide a discrete treatment of timed CSP is discussed by Ouaknine in [87, 88]. He takes a dual approach to the translation of specifications, preferring to start with a timed process Q and a timed specification S, and translating both of these to tock-CSP P and S' in such a way that a verification of P **sat** S' in tock-CSP implies that Q **sat** S in timed CSP. This approach is equivalent, since it will only work for those timed specifications that are translations of tock-CSP ones.

Refusal testing was first investigated by Phillips in [90], and the refusal testing model for CSP was given by Mukkaram in [81]. The example of two vending machines that require refusal testing to distinguish them was first given by Langerak [66] though in the original example they responded to a *kick* rather than a *tock*.

Exercises

Exercise A.1 It is claimed in Example A.1.2 that $GATE_{tock}$ must always be ready to accept any command. If $GATE_{tock}$ is instead described as follows, show that the overall system might reach a timestop. Which timing assumptions are shown to be incompatible by this timestop?

$$GATE_{tock} = \begin{array}{l} down.command \to MOVE_{tock}(down, 100) \\ \square\ up.command \to MOVE_{tock}(up, 100) \\ \square\ tock \to GATE_{tock} \end{array}$$

$$MOVE_{tock}(a, 1) = tock \to a \to GATE_{tock}$$
$$MOVE_{tock}(a, n + 2) = tock \to MOVE_{tock}(a, n + 1)$$

Exercise A.2 Does $SYSTEM_{tock}$ of Example A.1.2 meet the specification *Safety*3 given on page 433?

Exercise A.3 Give the tock-CSP translation $\Psi(PRINT)$ of Example A.2.2.

Exercise A.4 Remove the parallel and hiding operators to simplify the tock-CSP translation of $\Psi(PRINTER)$ of Example A.2.2.

Exercise A.5 Describe in the tock-CSP style an automated barrier to a car park, which accepts tickets when the barrier is down, and raises the barrier exactly 2 time units after dispensing the ticket. It lowers the barrier 1 second after receiving a *through* signal. If no such signal has been received after 20 time units of raising the barrier, it emits a *beep* once per time unit until *through* or *reset* is received. The barrier is lowered 1 second after the occurrence of either of these events.

Exercise A.6

1. Describe in the tock-CSP style a thermostat which monitors ambient temperature and controls a valve to enable or disable a heating system. It is triggered by input of the events *too.hot* and *too.cold*, and is required to send a signal *turn.off* or *turn.on* in response to these respective inputs, within 2 time units.

2. Describe a valve controller which can receive signals *turn.off* and *turn.on*, and which is able to switch the valve *off* and *on* within 10 time units of the instruction. It cannot handle further inputs in the meantime.

3. How can the combination of the valve and the thermostat lead to a timestop?

4. Express as a tock-CSP process an assumption on the occurrences of *too.hot* and *too.cold* which ensures that their combination cannot timestop.

Exercise A.7 (Very hard) How do the refusals in the refusal traces of $\Psi(Q)$ relate to the timed refusals of Q? What kind of results about the refusals of Q can be established by analysing $\Psi(Q)$?

Appendix B:
Model-checking with FDR

This appendix provides a brief overview of the operation and use of the model-checking tool FDR[1], which provides automated analysis and verification of CSP process descriptions. Section B.1 describes the use of the FDR tool; Section B.2 is concerned with the theory underlying the implementation of the tool; and Section B.3 introduces the form of machine readable CSP required to provide input to the tool.

Some understanding of the workings of FDR is required in order to make best use of the tool. However, for large and complex systems it supports a number of sophisticated techniques which are beyond the scope of this appendix, and the interested reader can find further information in [102, 103, 104, 33].

FDR stands for 'Failures Divergences Refinement checker'. It is a software tool for carrying out automatic analysis of (untimed) CSP processes. Its main operation is in checking whether or not one CSP process refines another. This provides a surprisingly powerful analysis mechanism, since many important questions about processes can be expressed in terms of refinement by employing the process-oriented approach to specification, as discussed in Sections 5.5, 7.4, and 8.5. FDR provides refinement checking for each of the untimed models presented in this book. It also permits analysis for particular common properties, such as deadlock, divergence (livelock), and determinism.

---

[1]Developed and marketed by Formal Systems (Europe) Ltd.

FDR has a companion tool, ProBE [34], which stands for 'Process Behaviour Explorer'. This tool interprets and animates CSP process descriptions, allowing the user to interact with a process and thus explore its behaviour patterns. It allows the user to synchronize on events, to observe the available options at each stage, to backtrack, and to watch the trace being constructed as the process is executed. ProBE does not provide formal analysis; it does provide a better informal understanding of CSP process descriptions. It is simple to use: it can input the same CSP files as FDR, and the user interacts with a process through a window interface by selecting events to perform from the menus of events that are offered. An exploration of Example B.3.2 is illustrated in Figure B.1. Unexplored events are marked with a '+'. Any event that has been performed is marked with a '−', and followed by a description of the process reached by performing it. For example, subsequent to the performance of *enter.kate* is the process *PERSON*(*eleanor*) ∥ *PERSON*(*isabella*) ∥ *PRESENT*(*kate*). The menu of events that this combination offers is listed immediately below it:

> *enter.eleanor*
> *leave.kate*
> *enter.isabella*

ProBE then offers the opportunity to explore any of these events.

B.1 INTERACTING WITH FDR

FDR allows automatic refinement checking between (finite state) processes. In order to apply FDR, it is necessary to supply both the specification process and the implementation process. This is accomplished by loading a CSP *script* into FDR. This is simply a text file containing a collection of CSP process definitions. On loading such a script, FDR identifies all of the potential processes within it.

FDR offers the opportunity to do a number of checks on any of the processes that have been loaded. There are specific options to check for deadlock, livelock, and determinism. In addition, refinement checks between processes can be carried out. The interface is illustrated in Figure B.2.

In requesting a refinement check, it is necessary to provide FDR with three pieces of information:

- The specification process. This can be any of the processes that have been loaded in as part of the CSP script, or a process definition typed directly into the 'Specification' box. In Figure B.2, the process *SPEC* has been selected.

- The implementation process. This can also be any of the processes that have been loaded, or a process typed into the 'Implementation' box. In Figure B.2, *SYSTEM* has been selected.

- The model in which the refinement relation is to be checked. There are three choices: traces, failures, and failures/divergences. These correspond to the three untimed models

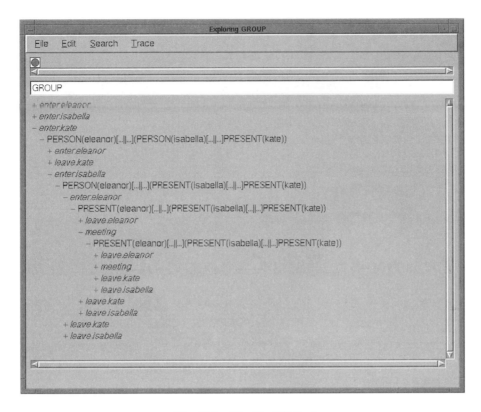

Fig. B.1   The ProBE tool

for CSP presented in Part II of this book. (The failures/divergences model is the same as the FDI model for finite-state processes.) In Figure B.2, the model selected is the failures model.

The CSP script loaded into FDR should therefore in general contain both the specification process and the implementation to be checked against it. There will usually be a number of checks of interest (perhaps a number of properties to check of an implementation, or a number of implementations to check), and so the script will need to contain all of the definitions required for these. The checks to be carried out (refinements or specific options) are either entered into the relevant window in FDR, or they can be included directly in the script as assertions. This enables them to be loaded into FDR alongside the processes, and FDR will list them when the script is loaded. In Figure B.2, a refinement check has been entered directly into the refinement window. Furthermore, four checks have loaded directly from the script: deadlock-freedom assertions on three different processes, and one traces refinement assertion.

If a check is successful, then this is reported by the tool with a √ alongside the verified assertion. If the check fails, reported by a ×, then this will be because the tool has identified a particular erroneous behaviour of the implementation process that violates the assertion.

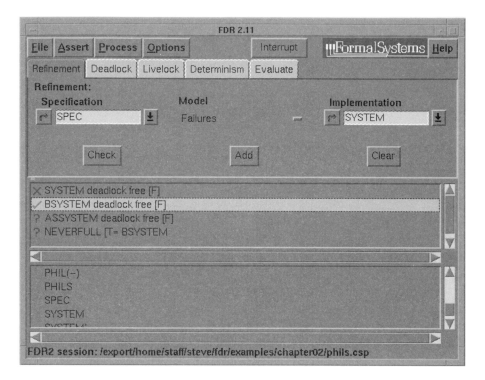

Fig. B.2   The FDR 2.11 main screen

In this case, the tool will identify the behaviour and provide it as feedback to the user. For example, with _SYSTEM_ as a description of the dining philosophers combination checked for deadlock-freedom, the feedback window provided when it identifies a possible deadlock is given in Figure B.3. The trace leading to it is given in the 'Performs' box towards the right-hand side.

Deadlock is shown by the fact that the resulting state has an empty acceptance set as shown in the 'Accepts' box, which means that all possible events can be refused.

The process tree labelled 'SYSTEM' shows the concurrent components of the process _SYSTEM_. It is possible to pick out the contribution of particular subcomponents to the erroneous behaviour. For example, the contribution $\langle enter.2, picks.2.2 \rangle$ of $PHIL(2)$ can be extracted by clicking on $PHIL(2)$.

This feedback is useful for debugging purposes. In establishing how a concurrent system is able to reach an incorrect state, design mistakes can be understood and corrected.

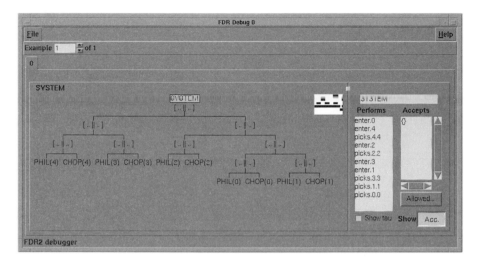

Fig. B.3   Feedback from FDR

B.2   HOW FDR CHECKS REFINEMENT

FDR checks refinement claims of the form $SPEC \sqsubseteq IMP$, where $SPEC$ is a process-oriented specification. This is achieved by exploring the state space given by the operational semantics of the process IMP, and checking for each state that all of the possibilities of event performance (as well as refusals and divergences where appropriate) for the implementation IMP are allowed by the specification $SPEC$. This is achieved by matching IMP's transitions in $SPEC$, and examining what $SPEC$ will allow in each state that IMP can reach. Since $SPEC$ is considered as a specification, $SPEC$'s behaviours are taken to be all of the behaviours that are permitted for any refinement IMP.

In order to use $SPEC$ effectively in tracking the transitions of IMP, it is necessary to identify, for any given trace that IMP could potentially perform, all of the possible events that $SPEC$ can allow next, and also all of the refusals that $SPEC$ will permit. FDR achieves this by determinizing the transition graph of $SPEC$, and adding refusal and divergence information to obtain a 'normalized' graph. Determinization involves removing all τ events, and coalescing sets of states that can all be reached via the same sequence of visible events. Thus in the determinized state space, each state will correspond to a set of states in the original state space. Any event will appear on at most one transition out of each node, and so for any particular trace of $SPEC$ there is a unique node that can be reached in the determinized graph. For example, the determinization of

$$VMSPEC \quad = \quad coin \rightarrow ((tea \rightarrow VMSPEC)$$
$$\sqcap (coffee \rightarrow VMSPEC))$$
$$\sqcap water \rightarrow VMSPEC$$

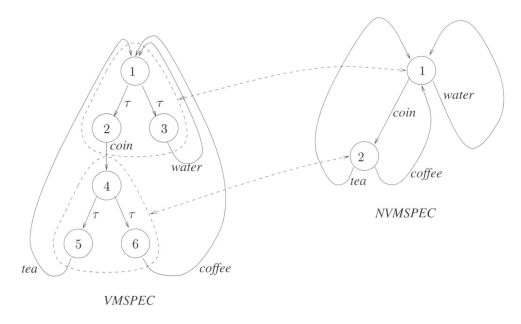

Fig. B.4   Determinizing a state graph

to the graph *NVMSPEC* is illustrated in Figure B.4.

Divergent states are also detected during this procedure, and labelled explicitly as such.

Refusal information is not contained in the transitions of the determinized graph alone, since transitions from different states of the original graph are all possible from their coalesced state. For example, states 5 and 6 of the *VMSPEC* graph of Figure B.4 are both part of state 2 of *NVMSPEC*, from which both *tea* and *coffee* are possible. The information that *tea* and *coffee* are also refusable in those states cannot be derived simply from the transitions of *NVMSPEC*.

The refusal possibilities thus need to be recorded explicitly with the nodes of the determinized graph. The complete normalization of *VMSPEC* is given in Figure B.5.

Although the process of normalizing a CSP process is exponential in the number of states in the worst case (since each state in the normalized graph will correspond to a set of states in the original graph), it has been found that in practice the worst case arises very rarely. This is partly because specification processes *SPEC* are often very simple, so that usually the size of the normalized graph is the same size or even smaller than the original graph.

FDR checks a process *IMP* by identifying for each reachable state the corresponding state of (the normalized) *SPEC* that indicates what is permitted. In exploring the state space of *IMP*, it checks for each reached state IMP_0 that all of the transitions $IMP_0 \xrightarrow{\mu} IMP_0'$ possible from that state are also possible from the corresponding state $SPEC_0$ of *SPEC*. If μ is an external event then there must be some (unique) $SPEC_0'$ for which $SPEC_0 \xrightarrow{\mu} SPEC_0'$, and the state IMP_0' will need to be checked against $SPEC_0'$. The case where $\mu = \tau$ is a special

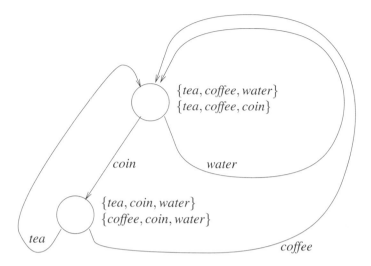

Fig. B.5 **The state graph** *NVMSPEC* **labelled with maximal refusals**

case—the matching state in *SPEC* is still $SPEC_0$, since the visible trace is not changed by this transition. Thus in this case IMP_0' must be checked against $SPEC_0$.

With regard to refusal information, FDR also performs additional checks on the stable states of *IMP*: that the refusable sets of events are possible refusal sets for *SPEC*.

Example B.2.1 The transition graph of the implementation

$$VMIMP \quad = \quad (coin \rightarrow tea \rightarrow water \rightarrow VMIMP)$$

is given in Figure B.6. It will be checked against the transition graph *NVMSPEC*.

Firstly, state 1 of *VMIMP* is checked against state 1 of *NVMSPEC*. In this state *coin* can be performed, and this is possible for the corresponding state of *NVMSPEC*. Furthermore, only subsets of $\{tea, coffee, water\}$ can be refused by *VMIMP*, and these refusals are permitted by *NVMSPEC*.

In covering the state space of *VMIMP*, the transition *coin* is followed, which requires state 2 of *VMIMP* to be checked against state 2 of *NVMSPEC*. This check is also successful: the refusal sets of *VMIMP* are allowed, and the single transition *tea* is permitted, taking *VMIMP* to state 3, matched by the transition of *NVMSPEC* back to state 1. In this state, the refusals are all permitted by the possible refusals in *NVMSPEC*, and the single transition *water* can be matched, returning both *VMIMP* and *NVMSPEC* to their initial states. Since this pair of states has already been checked, the exploration of the state graph for *VMIMP* is complete and the refinement relation *VMSPEC* $\sqsubseteq_{failures}$ *VMIMP* is confirmed. At this point FDR will confirm that the refinement relation holds. ∎

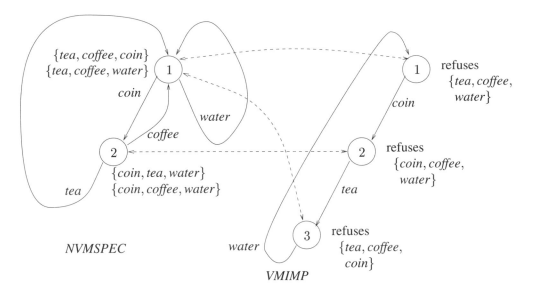

Fig. B.6   Checking *VMIMP* **against** *NVMSPEC*

Example B.2.2 An alternative implementation

$$VMIMP2 \quad = \quad (coin \rightarrow tea \rightarrow SKIP \mid\mid\mid water \rightarrow SKIP); VMIMP2$$

fails to refine *NVMSPEC*. The pairs of states that are checked is illustrated in Figure B.7. When checking *VMIMP2* state 2 against *NVMSPEC* state 2, we find a *water* transition that is not permitted by the specification. This means that the implementation can perform a trace that is not allowed by the specification: the trace $\langle coin, water \rangle$. In this way the model-checking provides a witness trace which demonstrates that *VMIMP2* is not a trace refinement of *NVMSPEC*. When FDR finds that a refinement fails to hold, it provides the counterexample which it has discovered. The feedback window that it provides for this example appears in Figure B.8. It simply provides the trace $\langle coin, water \rangle$ which fails the specification.

The checks that are carried out when the state space is explored depend on the semantic model under consideration.

Traces model: Checking for refinement in the traces model means checking that all the possible traces of the implementation are allowed by the specification. The refusal and divergence information in the normalized system is ignored. This is appropriate for checking safety properties.

Failures model: In this case, stable states that are reached while exploring the implementation are checked with respect to the refusal information recorded in the normalized specification.

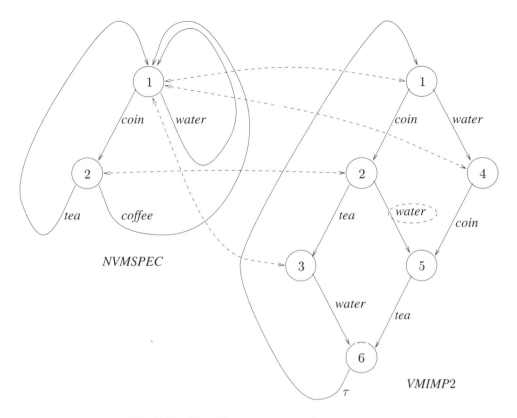

Fig. B.7   **Checking** *VMIMP2* **against** *NVMSPEC*

The failures model completely ignores divergence, and so the possibility of divergence in the implementation is simply ignored. This means that if some states are divergent, then they will not be checked with regard to refusal information.

Failures/Divergences model: In this case, states in the implementation are also checked for divergence, which will correspond to τ loops. This can add some considerable overhead to the state space exploration. In practice, implementations will not contain divergences, so it will generally be more efficient to check an implementation specifically for divergence-freedom first (using the specific 'livelock check' option). Once this has been established then a check in the failures model will be equivalent to a check in the failures/divergences model and the faster failures refinement check can be carried out.

Compression

When the state space of the implementation becomes large, it is often advantageous to reduce it before carrying out the state space exploration. FDR provides a number of ways of compressing

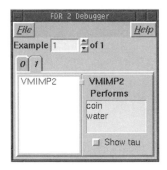

Fig. B.8   Feedback on VMIMP2 **from FDR**

the state space of a process to another (smaller) graph which has the same CSP semantics, and which will take less time to explore. We mention the main mechanisms briefly here.

One example of graph transformation is the normalization that FDR applies to the specification process of a refinement, though in this case more states may result. Many of the compression mechanisms, such as *diamond elimination* and τ-*loop elimination* are concerned with the elimination of τ events in a semantics-preserving way. Other mechanisms factor a graph by some semantic equivalence. This means that all nodes which have the same semantics are represented by a single node. This reduction can be done efficiently for strong bisimulation (which is stronger than all the CSP semantic equivalences). Its computational expense for other semantic equivalences is rather greater.

There are other mechanisms which achieve some compression but do not in general preserve the semantics, and should therefore be used with extreme care. The *chase* operator will select internal τ transitions over external ones, possibly removing some of the nondeterminism present and resulting in a refinement of the system it is applied to. It will therefore preserve the semantics of a deterministic system, but may not preserve semantics in general. The *priority* operator (still under development) also alters the operational semantics by removing some of the possible transitions when those of a higher priority are present. This does not even result in a refinement (except in the traces model), since some new refusals may be introduced by the removal of external transitions.

The compression mechanisms are discussed in more detail in [103, 104].

B.3   MACHINE READABLE CSP

A CSP script defines a number of processes. Channels used by the processes in a CSP script must be typed, where the types are either predefined types or else defined explicitly within the script. For example, the set of dining philosophers and their chopsticks can be defined by

```
nametype Phils = {0..4}
```

Operator	Syntax	ASCII form
Stop	$STOP$	STOP
Run	RUN_A	RUN(A)
Chaos	$CHAOS_A$	CHAOS(A)
Prefixing	$a \to P$	a -> P
Prefix choice	$x : A \to P(x)$	[] a : A @ a -> P(a)
Output	$c!v \to P$	c!v -> P
Input	$c?m : T \to P(m)$	c?m:T -> P(m) channel c : S where $T \subseteq S$
Recursion	$N = P$	N = P
Mutual recursion	$N(e) = P(e)$	N(e) = P(e)
Choice of process definitions	$\begin{cases} P_1 & \text{if } b \\ P_2 & \text{otherwise} \end{cases}$	if b then P_1 else P_2
External choice	$P_1 \,\square\, P_2$	P_1 [] P_2
General external choice	$\square_{i \in I} P_i$	[] i : I @ P_i
Internal choice	$P_1 \sqcap P_2$	P_1 ⌐⌐ P_2
General internal choice	$\sqcap_{i \in J} P_i$	⌐⌐ i : J @ P_i

Fig. B.9 The ASCII representation of CSP: prefix and choice

```
nametype Chops = {0..4}
```

All events and channels that are used by any CSP process in the script must be declared explicitly. Simple events are treated as channels which do not carry messages. For example, the following declarations may appear in a CSP script:

```
channel coin, tea, copy

channel in, out : {0,1}

channel picks : Phils.Chops
```

The first declares three events, so `tea` will be permitted as a process event; the second declares two channels `in` and `out` which both carry bits, so an example communication along

Operator	Syntax	ASCII form
Alphabetized parallel	$P_1 {}_A\|_B P_2$	`P`$_1$ `[ A || B ] P`$_2$
General alphabetized parallel	$\|_{A_i}^{i \in I} P_i$	`|| i : I @ [A`$_i$`] P`$_i$
Interleaving	$P_1 \|\|\| P_2$	`P`$_1$ `||| P`$_2$
General interleaving	$\|\|\|_{i \in I} P_i$	`||| i : I @ P`$_i$
Interface parallel	$P_1 \underset{A}{\|} P_2$	`P`$_1$ `[| A |] P`$_2$
General interface parallel	$\|_{A_{i \in I}} P_i$	`[| A |] i : I @ P`$_i$
Hiding	$P \setminus A$	`P \ A`
Forward renaming	$f(P)$	`P[[f]]`
Labelling	$l : P$	`P[[f`$_l$`]]`
Backward renaming	$f^{-1}(P)$	`P[[f`$^{-1}$`]]`
Chaining	$P_1 \gg P_2$	`P`$_1$ `[out <-> in] P`$_2$
General chaining	$\gg_{i=1}^{n} P_i$	`[out <-> in] i : <1..n> @ P`$_i$

Fig. B.10   The ASCII representation of CSP: concurrency and abstraction

these channels would be `out.1`; and the third declares a channel `picks` which carries two values—a value from `Phils` and a value from `Chops`—so an example event on this channel would be `picks.3.4`.

Once the channels are declared, the CSP processes themselves are given. An ASCII form of CSP is used to enable machine readability. Figures B.9, B.10, and B.11 give the main constructs of the ASCII form of CSP.

Mathematical style expressions can be used in the manipulation of process parameters and data variables, and the definition of indexing sets and data types. FDR also handles notation for arithmetic, sets, and sequences, and permits functional style definitions.

Example B.3.1 An bounded N place version of the buffer given in Example 1.3.9, may be defined using a mutual recursion indexed by sequences of messages. In this example, it will have type $T = \{high, low, middle\}$.

$$
\begin{aligned}
B(\langle\rangle) &= in?x : T \to B(\langle x \rangle) \\
B(\langle x \rangle ^\frown tr) &= (in?y : T \to B(\langle x \rangle ^\frown tr ^\frown \langle y \rangle)) \\
&\quad \square\ out!x \to B(s) \qquad\qquad \text{if } \#(\langle x \rangle ^\frown tr)) < N \\
&\quad out!x \to B(s) \qquad\qquad\ \text{otherwise}
\end{aligned}
$$

Operator	Syntax	ASCII form
Successful termination	*SKIP*	SKIP
Sequential composition	$P_1; P_2$	P_1 ; P_2
Interrupt	$P_1 \triangle P_2$	P_1 /\ P_2
Event interrupt	$P_1 \triangle e \rightarrow P_2$	int (P_1, e, P_2)

Fig. B.11   *The ASCII representation of CSP: flow of control*

This definition involves pattern matching on the sequence parameter to the process B, as well as the manipulation of sequence expressions. It may be rendered into a CSP script as shown below.

```
N = 5

datatype Message = high | low | middle

channel in, out : Message

B(<>) = in?x -> B(<x>)

B(<x>^tr) = if # (<x>^tr) < N
            then (in?y -> B(<x>^tr^<y>) [] out!x -> B(tr))
            else (out!x -> B(tr))
```

In order to check a process, values have to be provided for N and T. The value for N is simply declared, whereas T is instantiated by the enumerated type Message ∎

Example B.3.2 Example 2.1.10 is concerned with conditions under which a meeting of a group of people is considered to be quorate. It consists of a number of people who can each enter or leave the meeting independently, but who are required to synchronize on the common event *meeting*. It may be given in machine readable form as follows:

```
datatype NAMES = kate | eleanor | isabella

channel enter, leave : NAMES

channel meeting

A(n) = {enter.n, leave.n, meeting}
```

```
PERSON(n) = enter.n -> PRESENT(n)

PRESENT(n) = (leave.n -> PERSON(n)) [] (meeting -> PRESENT(n))

GROUP = || name : NAMES @ [A(name)] PERSON(name)
```

Observe that the process GROUP could also have been defined by means of an interface parallel construction:

```
GROUP = [| {meeting} |] name : NAMES @ PERSON(name)
```

In order to check that at any stage either a meeting is possible or else someone can enter, the following specification will be used.

```
SPEC = MEETENT ||| CHAOS({|leave|})

MEETENT = (meeting -> MEETENT |~| enter?x -> MEETENT)
```

The specification SPEC must always allow one of meeting and enter to be offered. It places no restrictions on occurrences of leave, reflecting the fact that it is not concerned with such events.

The following assertion captures the failures refinement check to be carried out on GROUP:

```
assert SPEC [F= GROUP
```

A CSP script to verify GROUP would need to contain all of these components.   ■

Exercises

Exercise B.1 Give a machine readable version of the cloakroom system of Example 2.1.3, whose components are as follows:

$$ATT \quad = \quad coat.off \rightarrow store \rightarrow ATT$$
$$\square \; retrieve \rightarrow coat.on \rightarrow ATT$$
$$CUST \quad = \quad enter \rightarrow coat.off \rightarrow eat \rightarrow coat.on \rightarrow CUST$$

Use FDR to check whether $ATT \underset{coat}{\parallel} CUST$ is deadlock-free.

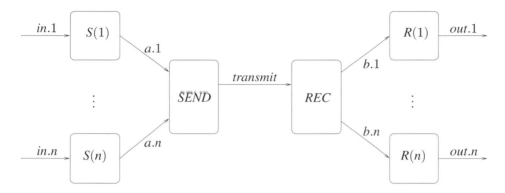

Fig. B.12   A multiplexing scheme

Exercise B.2 Give a machine readable version of the payment system of the bookshop of Example 2.2.5. Alter the description of *CHIT* and *RECEIPT* (to *CHIT*$_4$ and *RECEIPT*$_4$) so they allow only four chits and receipts to circulate. Use your description to check whether

$$CASHIER \parallel BOOK \parallel CHIT_4 \parallel RECEIPT_4$$

is deadlock-free. Do the results of your analysis apply to the case where there are an unlimited number of chits and receipts?

Exercise B.3 Use FDR to check that the railway crossing system *TRAIN* $\parallel$ *CROSSING* of Example 13.4 cannot deadlock. Check further that the gate can only ever move up when the train is not on or entering the crossing. Obtain a trace from FDR that shows that the train can enter the crossing when the gate is down.

Exercise B.4 A multiplexing scheme for a family of buffers over a single transmission channel *transmit* is illustrated in Figure B.12. The network is intended to behave as an interleaved collection of buffer processes $BUFFERS(N) = \big\vert\big\vert\big\vert_{i \in I} BUFF(i, N)$, where $BUFF(i, N)$ is the general (nondeterministic) specification of a buffer with maximum capacity N, on channels *in.i* and *out.i*.

The components are described as follows:

$$
\begin{aligned}
S(i) &= in.i?m \rightarrow a.i!m \rightarrow S(i) \\
R(i) &= b.i?m \rightarrow out.i!m \rightarrow R(i) \\
SEND &= a?j?m \rightarrow transmit!j!m \rightarrow SEND \\
RECEIVE &= transmit?j?m \rightarrow b.j!m \rightarrow RECEIVE
\end{aligned}
$$

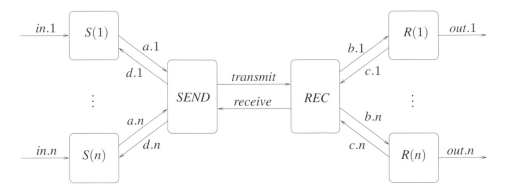

Fig. B.13   An alternative multiplexing scheme

Use FDR to check that the combination system (with the internal channels hidden) is a trace refinement of $BUFFERS(N)$ for a suitably large N. Is it a failures refinement? Is it deadlock-free? Is it a trace refinement of $BUFFERS(1)$? What is the fundamental problem with this multiplexing scheme?

Exercise B.5 In order to overcome some of the shortcomings of the multiplexing scheme given in Exercise B.4, message acknowledgement is added to the protocol, as illustrated in Figure B.13.

1. The components are now described as follows:

$$
\begin{aligned}
S(i) &= in.i?m \rightarrow a.i!m \rightarrow d.i \rightarrow S(i) \\
R(i) &= b.i?m \rightarrow out.i!m \rightarrow c.i \rightarrow R(i) \\
SEND &= a?j?m \rightarrow transmit!j!m \rightarrow SEND \\
&\quad \Box \ receive?j \rightarrow d.j \rightarrow SEND \\
RECEIVE &= transmit?j?m \rightarrow b.j!m \rightarrow RECEIVE \\
&\quad \Box \ c?j \rightarrow receive!j \rightarrow RECEIVE
\end{aligned}
$$

Use FDR to check that the combination system (with the internal channels hidden) is a trace refinement of $BUFFERS(1)$. Is it a failures refinement?

2. Place a one-place buffer on the *transmit* channel so the communication between *SEND* and *RECEIVE* becomes asynchronous. Is the resulting system divergence-free? Is it a failures refinement of *BUFFERS*?

References

1. R. Alur, C. Courcoubetis, and D. Dill. Model-checking in dense real-time. *Information and Computation*, 104(1):2–34, 1993.

2. R. Alur and D. Dill. A theory of timed automata. *Theoretical Computer Science*, 126:183–235, 1994.

3. J. C. M. Baeten and J. A. Bergstra. Real time process algebra. *Formal Aspects of Computing*, 3(2):142–188, 1991.

4. J. C. M. Baeten and J. A. Bergstra. Discrete time process algebra. Technical Report P9208b, University of Amsterdam, 1992.

5. J. C. M. Baeten and W. P. Weijland. *Process Algebra*. Cambridge University Press, 1990.

6. G. Barrett. The fixed-point theory of unbounded nondeterminism. *Formal Aspects of Computing*, 3:110–128, 1991.

7. J. A. Bergstra and J. W. Klop. Process algebra for synchronous communication. *Information and Control*, 60:109–137, 1984.

8. G. Berry and G. Gonthier. The Esterel synchronous programming language: Design, semantics, implementation. *Science of Computer Programming*, 19(2):87–152, 1992.

9. S. R. Blamey. The soundness and completeness of axioms for CSP processes. In *Topology and Category Theory in Computer Science*. Oxford University Press, 1991.

10. T. Bolognesi and E. Brinksma. Introduction to the ISO specification language LOTOS. *Computer Networks and ISDN Systems*, 14(1):25–59, 1987.

11. T. Bolognesi and F. Lucidi. A timed full LOTOS with time/action tree semantics. In T. Rus and C. Rattray, (eds), *Theories and Experiences for Real-Time System Development*, volume 2 of *AMAST Series in Computing*. World Scientific, 1995.

12. S. D. Brookes. *A Model for Communicating Sequential Processes*. D. Phil thesis, Oxford University, 1983.

13. S. D. Brookes, C. A. R. Hoare, and A. W. Roscoe. A theory of communicating sequential processes. *Journal of the ACM*, 31(3):560–599, 1984.

14. S. D. Brookes and A. W. Roscoe. An improved failures model for CSP. In *Pittsburgh Seminar on Concurrency*. Springer, LNCS 197, 1985.

15. S. D. Brookes, A. W. Roscoe, and D. J. Walker. An operational semantics for CSP. Technical Report, Oxford, 1988.

16. J. Bryans, J. W. Davies, and S. A. Schneider. Towards a denotational semantics for ET-LOTOS. In *CONCUR '95*. Springer, LNCS 962, 1995.

17. A. J. Camellieri. Mechanizing CSP trace theory in higher order logic. *IEEE Transactions on Software Engineering*, 16(9):993–1004, 1990.

18. C-T. Chou. Practical use of the notions of events and causality in reasoning about distributed algorithms. Technical Report 940035, UCLA, 1994.

19. R. Cleaveland, J. Parrow, and B. Steffen. The concurrency workbench: a semantics based verification tool for the verification of concurrent systems. *ACM Transactions on Programming Languages and Systems*, 15(1):36–72, 1993.

20. R. Cleaveland and A. E. Zwarico. A theory of testing for real-time. Technical Report, North Carolina S.U. and Johns Hopkins, 1992.

21. B. Davey and H. Priestley. *Introduction to Lattices and Order*. Cambridge University Press, 1990.

22. J. W. Davies. *Specification and Proof in Real-time CSP*. Cambridge University Press, 1993.

23. J. W. Davies, D. M. Jackson, and S. A. Schneider. Broadcast communication for real-time processes. In *Proceedings of the Symposium on Real-time and Fault-tolerant Systems*. Springer, LNCS 571, 1992.

24. J. W. Davies and S. A. Schneider. Factorising proofs in timed CSP. In *Proceedings of the Fifth International conference on the Mathematical Foundations of Programming Semantics*. Springer, LNCS 442, 1990.

25. J. W. Davies and S. A. Schneider. Recursion induction for real-time processes. *Formal Aspects of Computing*, 5(6):530–553, 1993.

26. J. W. Davies and S. A. Schneider. Real-time CSP. In T. Rus and C. Rattray, (eds), *Theories and Experiences for Real-Time System Development*, volume 2 of *AMAST Series in Computing*. World Scientific, 1995.

27. J. W. de Bakker, C. Huizing, W. P. de Roever, and G. Rozenberg, (eds). *Real-Time: Theory in Practice*. Springer, LNCS 600, 1991.

28. R. de Nicola and M. Hennessy. Testing equivalences for processes. *Theoretical Computer Science*, 34(1):83–134, 1987.

29. B. Dutertre and S. A. Schneider. Using a PVS embedding of CSP to verify authentication protocols. In *Theorem Proving in Higher Order Logics*. Springer, LNCS 1775, 1997.

30. C. Fencott. *Formal Methods for Concurrency*. International Thomson Computer Press, 1996.

31. J-C. Fernandez, H. Garavel, A. Kerbrat, R. Mateescu, L. Mounier, and M. Sighireanu. CADP: A protocol validation and verification toolbox. In *8th Conference on Computer-Aided Verification*. Springer, LNCS 1102, 1996.

32. Formal Systems (Europe) Ltd. Real-time concurrency. Formal Systems Information Pack, 1991.

33. Formal Systems (Europe) Ltd. *Failures-Divergences Refinement: FDR2 Manual*, 1997.

34. Formal Systems (Europe) Ltd. *Process Behaviour Explorer User Manual*, 1998.

35. H. Garavel. An overview of the Eucalyptus toolbox. In *COST247 International Workshop in Applied Formal Methods in System Design*. University of Maribor, 1996.

36. R. Gerth and A. Boucher. A timed model for extended communicating processes. In *ICALP '87*, pages 157–183. Springer, LNCS 267, 1987.

37. P. Gibbins, A. Kay, and S. A. Schneider. Asynchronous perceptrons in real-time CSP. ESPRIT CONCUR2 project deliverable, 1993.

38. D. Gray. *Introduction to the Formal Design of Real-Time Systems*. Springer, 1999.

39. J. F. Groote and J. Springintveld. Algebraic verification of a distributed summation algorithm. Technical Report CS-R9640, University of Amsterdam, 1996.

40. H. Hansson. *A Calculus for Communicating Systems with Time and Probabilities*. PhD thesis, University of Uppsala, 1991.

41. C. Heitmeyer and D. Mandrioli (eds). *Formal Methods for Real-Time Computing*. Wiley, 1996.

42. M. Hennessy. *Algebraic Theory of Processes*. MIT Press, 1988.

43. M. Hennessy and T. Regan. A process algebra for timed systems. *Information and Computation*, 117(2):221–239, 1995.

44. C. J. Ho-Stuart, H. Zedan, M. Fang, and C. M. Holt. PARTY: A process algebra with real-time from York. Technical Report YCS-92-177, University of York, 1992.

45. C. A. R. Hoare. Communicating sequential processes. *Communications of the ACM*, 21(8):666–677, 1978.

46. C. A. R. Hoare. A model for communicating sequential processes. In R. McKeag and J. MacNaughton, (eds), *On the Construction of Programs*. Cambridge University Press, 1980.

47. C. A. R. Hoare. *Communicating Sequential Processes*. Prentice-Hall, 1985.

48. C. A. R. Hoare and He Jifeng. *Unifying Theories of Programming*. Prentice-Hall, 1998.

49. J. Hooman. Compositional verification of real-time systems using extended Hoare triples. In de Bakker et al. [27].

50. F. Howles. Distributed arbitration in the Futurebus protocol. Master's thesis, Oxford University, 1993.

51. Inmos Ltd. OCCAM2 *Reference Manual*. Prentice-Hall, 1988.

52. ISO/IEC-JTC1/SC21/WG1/FDT/C, IPS-OSI-LOTOS. A formal description technique based on the temporal ordering of observational behaviour, ISO standard 8807, 1989.

53. ISO/IEC-JTC1/SC21/WG7. Working draft on enhancements to LOTOS, 1997.

54. D. M. Jackson. The specification of aircraft engine control software in timed CSP. Master's thesis, Oxford University, 1989.

55. D. M. Jackson. Specifying timed communicating sequential processes using temporal logic. Technical Report TR–5–90, Programming Research Group, Oxford University, 1990.

56. D. M. Jackson. *Logical Verification of Reactive Software Systems*. D. Phil thesis, Oxford University, 1992.

57. F. Jahanian and A. Mok. Safety analysis of timing properties in real-time systems. *IEEE Transactions on Software Engineering*, 12(9):890–904, 1986.

58. A. Jeffrey. Discrete timed CSP. Technical Report PMG-78, Chalmers University of Technology, 1990.

59. A. Jeffrey. *Observation Spaces and Timed Processes*. D.Phil thesis, Oxford University, 1991.

60. A. Jeffrey, S. A. Schneider, and F. Vaandrager. A comparison of two axioms for timed transition systems. Technical Report CS-R9366, University of Amsterdam, 1993.

61. G. Jones. *A Timed Model of Communicating Processes*. D. Phil thesis, Oxford University, 1982.

62. G. Jones and M. H. Goldsmith. *Programming in* OCCAM2. Prentice-Hall, 1988.

63. M. Joseph (ed.). *Real-Time Systems.* Prentice-Hall, 1995.

64. A. Kay and J. N. Reed. A specification of a telephone exchange in timed CSP. Technical Report TR–19–90, Programming Research Group, Oxford University, 1990.

65. R. L. C. Koymans. *Specifying Message Passing and Time-Critical Systems with Temporal Logic.* PhD thesis, Eindhoven University of Technology, 1989.

66. R. Langerak. A testing theory for LOTOS using deadlock detection. In *Tenth International Symposium on Protocol Specification, Testing, and Verification.* Elsevier, 1990.

67. K. G. Larsen, P. Pettersson, and Wang Yi. UPPAAL in a nutshell. *Journal of Software Tools for Technology Transfer,* 1(1/2):134–152, 1997.

68. K. G. Larsen and Wang Yi. Time abstracted bisimulation: implicit specifications and decidability. In *Proceedings of the Ninth International Conference on theMathematical Foundations of Programming Semantics.* Springer, LNCS 802, 1993.

69. L. Léonard. *An Extended LOTOS for the Design of Time-Sensitive Systems.* PhD thesis, University of Liège, 1997.

70. L. Léonard and G. Leduc. An introduction to ET-LOTOS for the description of time-sensitive systems. *Computer Networks and ISDN Systems,* 29:271–292, 1997.

71. N. G. Leveson and J. L. Stolzy. Safety analysis using petri nets. *IEEE Transactions on Software Engineering,* SE-13(3):386–397, 1987.

72. Liang Chen. *Timed Processes: Models, Axioms and Decidability.* PhD thesis, University of Edinburgh, 1992.

73. G. Lowe. *Probabilities and Priorities in Timed CSP.* D. Phil thesis, Oxford University, 1993.

74. N. Lynch and F. Vaandrager. Forward and backward simulations – Part II: Timing based systems. *Information and Computation,* 128(1):1–25, 1996.

75. P. Merlin and D. J. Farber. Recovery of communications protocols – implications of a theoretical study. *IEEE Transactions on Communication,* COM-24:1036–1043, 1976.

76. R. Milner. *A Calculus of Communicating Systems.* Springer, LNCS 92, 1980.

77. R. Milner. *Communication and Concurrency.* Prentice-Hall, 1989.

78. R. Milner, J. Parrow, and D. J. Walker. A calculus of mobile processes, I and II. *Information and Computation,* 100:1–77, 1992.

79. M. W. Mislove, A. W. Roscoe, and S. A. Schneider. Fixed points without completeness. *Theoretical Computer Science,* 138(2):273–314, 1995.

80. F. Moller and C. Tofts. A temporal calculus of communicating systems. In *CONCUR '90*. Springer, LNCS 458, 1990.

81. A. Mukkaram. *A Refusal Testing Model for CSP*. D. Phil thesis, Oxford University, 1993.

82. X. Nicollin and J. Sifakis. An overview and synthesis on timed process algebras. In de Bakker et al. [27].

83. X. Nicollin and J. Sifakis. The algebra of timed processes ATP: Theory and application. *Information and Computation*, 114(1):131–178, 1994.

84. X. Nicollin, J. Sifakis, and S. Yovine. From ATP to timed graphs and hybrid systems. In de Bakker et al. [27].

85. Y. Ortega-Mallén and D. de Frutos. Timed observations: a semantic model for real-time concurrency. In *IFIP-TC2 — Working Conference on Programming Concepts and Methods*. North-Holland, 1990.

86. J. S. Ostroff. *Temporal Logic for Real-Time Systems*. Wiley, 1989.

87. J. Ouaknine. *Connections Between CSP and Timed CSP*. Transfer dissertation, Oxford University, 1997.

88. J. Ouaknine. A framework for model-checking timed CSP. Technical Report, Oxford University, 1999.

89. D. Park. On the semantics of fair parallelism. In *Abstract Software Specifications*. Springer, LNCS 86, 1980.

90. I. Phillips. Refusal testing. *Theoretical Computer Science*, 50(3):241–284, 1987.

91. G. D. Plotkin. A structural approach to operational semantics. Technical Report DAIMI FN-19, Aarhus University, 1981.

92. K. V. S. Prasad. A calculus of broadcasting systems. *Science of Computer Programming*, 25(2–3):251–283, 1995.

93. J. Quemada, D. de Frutos, and A. Azcorra. TIC: a timed calculus. *Formal Aspects of Computing*, 5:224–252, 1993.

94. J. Quemada and A. Férnandez. Introduction of quantitative relative time into LOTOS. In *Seventh International Symposium on Protocol Specification, Testing, and Verification*. Elsevier, 1987.

95. G. M. Reed. *A Uniform Mathematical Theory for Real-Time Distributed Computing*. D. Phil thesis, Oxford University, 1988.

96. G. M. Reed. A hierarchy of models for real-time distributed computing. In *Proceedings of the Fifth International Conference on the Mathematical Foundations of Programming Semantics*. Springer, LNCS 442, 1990.

97. G. M. Reed and A. W. Roscoe. A timed model for communicating sequential processes. In *13th ICALP*. Springer, LNCS 226, 1986.

98. G. M. Reed and A. W. Roscoe. Metric spaces as models for real-time concurrency. In *Proceedings of the Third International Conference on the Mathematical Foundations of Programming Semantics*. Springer, LNCS 298, 1987.

99. G. M. Reed and A. W. Roscoe. A study of nondeterminism in real-time concurrency. In *Proceedings of the Second UK–Japan CS Workshop*. Springer, LNCS 491, 1991.

100. A. W. Roscoe. *A Mathematical Theory of Communicating Processes*. D. Phil thesis, Oxford University, 1982.

101. A. W. Roscoe. Unbounded nondeterminism in CSP. *Journal of Logic and Computation*, 3(2):131–172, 1993. Also in 'Two papers on CSP', Oxford University Technical Report PRG-67, 1988.

102. A. W. Roscoe. Model-checking CSP. In A. W. Roscoe, (ed.), *A Classical Mind: Essays in Honour of C. A. R. Hoare*. Prentice-Hall, 1994.

103. A. W. Roscoe. *The Theory and Practice of Concurrency*. Prentice-Hall, 1997.

104. A. W. Roscoe, P. H. B. Gardiner, M. H. Goldsmith, J. R. Hulance, D. M. Jackson, and J. B. Scattergood. Hierarchical compression for model-checking CSP or how to check 10^{20} dining philosophers for deadlock. In *1st TACAS*. Springer, LNCS 1019, 1995.

105. B. Scattergood. The description of a laboratory robot in timed CSP. Master's thesis, Oxford University, 1990.

106. F. B. Schneider, B. Bloom, and K. Marzullo. Putting time into proof outlines. In de Bakker et al. [27].

107. S. A. Schneider. *Correctness and Communication in Real-Time Systems*. D. Phil thesis, Oxford University, 1989.

108. S. A. Schneider. Unbounded non-determinism in timed CSP. ESPRIT SPEC project deliverable, 1991.

109. S. A. Schneider. An operational semantics for timed CSP. In *Workshop on Concurrency*, 1992. PMG-63, Chalmers University.

110. S. A. Schneider. An operational semantics for timed CSP. *Information and Computation*, 116(2):193–213, 1995.

111. S A Schneider. Timewise refinement for communicating processes. *Science of Computer Programming*, 28(1):43–90, 1997. Also in 'Proceedings of the Ninth International Conference on theMathematical Foundations of Programming Semantics', Springer, LNCS 802.

112. A. Segall. Distributed network protocols. *IEEE Transactions on Information Theory*, IT-29(1):23–35, 1983.

113. R. Stamper. The specification of AGV control software in Timed CSP. Master's thesis, Oxford University, 1990.

114. S. Superville. Specifying complex systems with timed CSP: a decomposition and specification of a telephone exchange system which has a central controller. Master's thesis, Oxford University, 1991.

115. W. A. Sutherland. *Introduction to Metric and Topological Spaces*. Oxford University Press, 1975.

116. H. Tej and B. Wolff. A corrected failure-divergence model for CSP in Isabelle/HOL. In *Formal Methods Europe '97*. Springer, 1997.

117. F. Vaandrager. Verification of a distributed summation algorithm. In *CONCUR '95*. Springer, LNCS 962, 1995.

118. A. Valmari. The weakest deadlock-preserving congruence. *Information Processing Letters*, 53:341–346, 1995.

119. B. Victor and F. Moller. The mobility workbench—a tool for the π-calculus. In *Computer Aided Verification*. Springer, LNCS 818, 1994.

120. A. R. Wallace. A TCSP case study of a flexible manufacturing system. Master's thesis, Oxford University, 1991.

121. W. L. Yeung, S. A. Schneider, and F. Tam. Design and verification of distributed recovery blocks with CSP. Technical Report CSD-TR-98-08, Royal Holloway, University of London, 1998.

122. Wang Yi. *A Calculus of Real Time Systems*. PhD thesis, Chalmers University of Technology, 1991.

123. Wang Yi. CCS + time = an interleaving model for real-time systems. In *ICALP '91*. Springer, LNCS 510, 1991.

124. Zhou Chauchen, A. P. Ravn, and C. A. R. Hoare. A calculus of durations. *Information Processing Letters*, 40(5):269–276, 1991.

125. J. J. Zic. *CSP + T: a Formalism for Describing Real-Time Systems*. PhD thesis, University of Sydney, 1991.

126. A. Zwarico, I. Lee, and R. Gerber. A complete axiomatization of real-time processes. Technical Report MS-CIS-88-88, University of Pennsylvania, 1987.

Notation

Sets

$a \in S$	a is a member of the set S
$\{\}$	the empty set
$\{a_1, \dots, a_n\}$	the set of the elements listed
$\{a \mid P(a)\}$	set comprehension: the set of elements which meet predicate P
$S \cup T$, $\bigcup_{i \in I} S_i$	set union
$S \cap T$, $\bigcap_{i \in I} S_i$	set intersection
$S \setminus T$	set subtraction
$\mathbb{P} \, S$	power set of S
$\mathbb{F} \, S$	finite power set: the finite subsets of S
$\mathbb{N}$	natural numbers
$\mathbb{R}$	real numbers
$\mathbb{R}^+$	non-negative real numbers
$\lceil r \rceil$	r rounded up to the integer immediately above
$\lfloor r \rfloor$	r rounded down to the integer immediately below
I	interval of the real numbers
$[b, e)$	the half-open interval from b to e (including b and excluding e)
$[b, e]$	the closed interval from b to e
(b, e)	the open interval from b to e
$(b, e]$	the half-closed interval from b to e

Logic

$\neg P$	negation: not P
$P_1 \wedge P_2$	conjunction: P_1 and P_2
$P_1 \vee P_2$	disjunction: P_1 or P_2
$P_1 \Rightarrow P_2$	implication: P_1 implies P_2
$\forall x \bullet S$	for all x, S holds
$\forall x : T \bullet S$	for all x of type T, S holds
$\exists x \bullet S$	there is some x for which S holds
$\exists x : T \bullet S$	there is some x of type T for which S holds

Event notation

Σ	(sigma) the universal set of events
$\Sigma^{\checkmark}$	$\Sigma \cup \{\checkmark\}$
$\Sigma^{\checkmark, \tau}$	$\Sigma \cup \{\checkmark, \tau\}$
$\checkmark$	(tick) the termination event; not in Σ
τ	(tau) the internal event; not in $\Sigma^{\checkmark}$
a	external event from $\Sigma^{\checkmark}$
μ	external or internal event from $\Sigma^{\checkmark, \tau}$
$c.v$	communication event with channel c and value v
$\mathsf{channel}(c.v)$	the channel c of the compound event $c.v$
$\mathsf{value}(c.v)$	the value v in the compound event $c.v$
A	set of events $A \subseteq \Sigma^{\checkmark}$
$A^{\checkmark}$	$A \cup \{\checkmark\}$

CSP semantics

$P_1 = P_2$	P_1 and P_2 have the same behaviours
$P_1 \sqsubseteq P_2$	P_1 is refined by P_2
$P_U \sqsubseteq_T Q$	P is timewise refined by Q
$P \textbf{ sat } S$	all the observations of process P meet specification S
$P \textsf{ ref } X$	P refuses X
$P \uparrow$	P is divergent
$P \downarrow$	P is stable
$P_1 \xrightarrow{\mu} P_2 \ (\downarrow \mu)$	P_1 can perform a μ transition to P_2
$P_1 \xRightarrow{tr} P_2$	P_1 can perform the sequence tr and become P_2
$Q_1 \overset{d}{\rightsquigarrow} Q_2 \ (\wr d)$	Q_1 can perform a d evolution to Q_2

Sequences and traces

seq	a sequence of elements
$\langle\rangle$	the empty sequence
$\langle a_1, \ldots, a_n \rangle$	the sequence of elements listed
$\langle a \mid a \leftarrow seq, P(a) \rangle$	sequence comprehension
$seq_1 \frown seq_2$	concatenation: seq_1 followed by seq_2
$head(seq)$	first element of the sequence
$tail(seq)$	sequence seq without the first element
$foot(seq)$	last element of seq
$init(seq)$	seq without the last element
$\#seq$	length of the sequence
$\sigma(seq)$	the set of events appearing in the sequence
a **in** seq	a appears in the sequence seq
$seq_1 \leqslant seq_2$	sequence seq_1 is a prefix of seq_2
$seq_1 \preccurlyeq seq_2$	subsequence (not necessarily contiguous)
$seq@i$	the ith element of the sequence (counting from 0)
$seq \upharpoonright A$	the subsequence of elements of seq in A
$seq \setminus A$	the sequence of elements of seq not in A
$seq \downarrow A$	the number of occurrences of elements of A
$f(seq)$	f applying f to each element of seq in turn
channels(tr)	the set of channels used in tr
seq interleaves seq_1, seq_2	seq is an interleaving of the sequences seq_1 and seq_2
seq synch$_A$ seq_1, seq_2	seq synchronizes seq_1 and seq_2 on events in $A^{\checkmark}$
$flatten(sseq)$	the elements of $sseq$ concatenated together
$term(seq)$	seq contains a $\checkmark$
$TRACE$	the set of all finite traces
$ITRACE$	the set of infinite traces
tr	a finite trace
u	an infinite trace

Timed traces

TT	the set of timed traces
s	a timed trace
$s \upharpoonright A$	s restricted to A: $\langle (t, a) \mid (t, a) \leftarrow s, a \in A \rangle$
$s \downarrow A$	number of A's in s: $\#(s \upharpoonright A)$
$s \setminus A$	s without the elements of A: $s \upharpoonright (\Sigma \setminus A)$
$strip(s)$	s with the times removed: $\langle a \mid (t, a) \leftarrow s \rangle$
$s + t$	s delayed by t: $\langle (t' + t, a) \mid (t', a) \leftarrow s \rangle$
$s - t$	s brought earlier by t: $\langle (t' - t, a) \mid (t', a) \leftarrow s, t' \geqslant t \rangle$
$begin(s)$	the time of the first event in s (and ∞ for the empty trace)
$first(s)$	the first event to appear in s
$end(s)$	the time of the last event in the finite trace s (and 0 for the empty trace)
$last(s)$	the last event to appear in the finite trace s
$s \uparrow I$	s during I: $\langle (t, a) \mid (t, a) \leftarrow s, t \in I \rangle$
$s \parallel t$	s strictly before t: $s \uparrow [0, t)$
$s \upharpoonright t$	s before t: $s \uparrow [0, t]$
$s \uparrow t$	s after t: $s \uparrow [t, \infty)$
$s \parallel t$	s strictly after t: $s \uparrow (t, \infty)$
$s \upharpoonright A$	s projected onto A: $\langle (t', a) \mid (t', a) \leftarrow s, a \in A \rangle$

Timed refusals

$RSET$	the set of possible refusal sets: sets of timed events
$\aleph$	(aleph) a timed refusal
$\aleph \uparrow I$	$\aleph$ during I: $\{(t, a) \in \aleph \mid t \in I\}$
$\aleph \uparrow t$	$\aleph$ at t: $\{(t', a) \in \aleph \mid t' = t\}$
$\aleph \parallel t$	$\aleph$ before t: $\aleph \uparrow [0, t)$
$\aleph \uparrow t$	$\aleph$ after t: $\aleph \uparrow [t, \infty)$
$\aleph + t$	$\aleph$ translated through t: $\{(t' + t, a) \mid (t', a) \in \aleph)\}$
$\aleph - t$	$\aleph$ translated backwards through t: $\{(t' - t, a) \mid (t', a) \in \aleph, t' \geqslant t\}$
$\aleph \upharpoonright A$	$\aleph$ restricted to A: $\{(t, a) \in \aleph \mid a \in A\}$
$\aleph \setminus A$	$\aleph$ with A events removed: $\aleph \upharpoonright (\Sigma^{\vee} \setminus A)$
$\sigma(\aleph)$	the set of events appearing in $\aleph$
$begin(\aleph)$	the time of the first event in $\aleph$ (and ∞ for the empty refusal)
$end(\aleph)$	the least upper bound of times mentioned in $\aleph$

CSP processes

P	untimed CSP process
Q	timed CSP process
$STOP$	deadlock
$a \rightarrow P$	prefix
$a : A \rightarrow P(a)$	prefix choice (guarded choice)
$a_1 \rightarrow P_1 \mid a_2 \rightarrow P_2$	guarded choice
$c!v \rightarrow P$	output
$c?v \rightarrow P(v)$	input
$SKIP$	successful termination
DIV	divergence
$CHAOS$	the most nondeterministic divergence-free process
RUN	the process that will deterministically perform any event
N	process variable
$N = P$	recursive definition
$P_1 \square P_2, \quad \square_{i \in I} P_i$	external choice
$P_1 \sqcap P_2, \quad \sqcap_{i \in I} P_1$	internal choice
$P_1 \;_A\|_B P_2, \quad \|_{i \in I}^{A_i} P_i$	alphabetized parallel
$P_1 \;\|\|\; P_2, \quad \|\|\|_{i \in I} P_i$	interleaved parallel
$P_1 \underset{A}{\|} P_2$	interface parallel
$P \setminus A$	hiding
$f(P)$	renaming
$l : P$	labelling
$f^{-1}(P)$	backward renaming
$P_1 \gg P_2$	chaining
$P_1 ; P_2$	sequential composition
$P_1 \triangle P_2$	interrupt
$P_1 \triangle_e P_2$	interrupt on e
$a \overset{d}{\rightarrow} Q$	timed prefix
$Q_1 \overset{d}{\triangleright} Q_2$	timeout
$WAIT\, d; \; Q$	delay
$Q_1 \triangle_d Q_2$	timed interrupt

Index

Index of processes